# More praise for *Johann Sebastian Bach*

"This detailed, solidly grounded yet imaginative portrait of one of Europe's most influential, inventive musicians is worthy of its subject. Wolff . . . skillfully synthesizes what is unquestionably documented (regrettably little!) and confidently speculates on what can be surmised about Bach. . . . His engaging style makes the reader care about the context of Bach's life."

—*Library Journal*, starred review

"Full of stunning insights and connections."                    —*Choice*

"[A] sober, patient, and potent biography."

—Edward Rothstein, *New York Times Book Review*

"[Wolff] brings greater precision to the factual account than has hitherto been achieved by any biographer, and he trains the light of the latest scholarship on his subject with remarkable confidence and ease."

—*Los Angeles Times Book Review*

"A remarkable portrait of the man many consider history's greatest musician."

—*Seattle Times*

"[This book] is accessible to scholars and performers certainly but also to Bach lovers who may not possess a specialized musical vocabulary. It is, in short, a wonderful book. . . . I doubt that any other work will challenge its completeness and authority for years to come."

—Anthony Newman, *Wall Street Journal*

"With Christoph Wolff's major contributive work we have probably reached the last word in Bach scholarship for some time. It will become the definitive Bach biography."                    —*Tampa* (Florida) *Tribune and Times*

"Certainly the last word in current Bach scholarship."     —*Publishers Weekly*

"Unpretentiously written and eminently readable. . . . Equally suitable for the knowledgeable amateur and the academic."          —*Suddeutsche Zeitung*

"A book to be read by the patient and the hurried alike."

—*Frankfurter Rundschau*

## ALSO BY CHRISTOPH WOLFF

BOOKS

*Der Stile antico in der Musik Johann Sebastian Bachs*

*Bach-Studien: Gesammelte Reden und Aufsätze von Friedrich Smend* (ed.)

*The String Quartets of Haydn, Mozart, and Beethoven: Studies of the Autograph Manuscripts* (ed.)

*The New Grove Bach Family*

*Bach-Bibliographie: Nachdruck der Verzeichnisse des Schrifttums über Johann Sebastian Bach* (ed.)

*Orgel, Orgelmusik, und Orgelspiel: Festschrift Michael Schneider zum 75. Geburtstag* (ed.)

*Bach Compendium: analytisch-bibliographisches Repertorium der Werke Johann Sebastian Bachs* (co-ed.)

*A Life for New Music: Selected Papers of Paul Fromm* (ed.)

*Johann Sebastian Bachs Spätwerk und dessen Umfeld: Perspektiven und Probleme* (ed.)

*Johann Sebastian Bach und der süddeutsche Raum: Aspekte der Wirkungsgeschichte Bachs* (co-ed.)

*Bach: Essays on His Life and Music*

*Mozart's Requiem: Historical and Analytical Studies, Documents, Score*

*The World of the Bach Cantatas* (ed.)

*The New Bach Reader: A Life of Johann Sebastian Bach in Letters and Documents* (co-ed.)

*Driven into Paradise: The Musical Migration from Nazi Germany to the United States* (co-ed.)

*Über Leben, Kunst und Kunstwerke: Aspekte musikalischer Biographie* (ed.)

*Die Gegenwart der musikalischen Vergangenheit: Meisterwerke in der Dirigentenwerkstatt* (ed.)

*Music of My Future: The Schoenberg Quartets and Trio* (co-ed.)


EDITIONS OF WORKS BY BACH

*The Art of Fugue,* BWV 1080; Fourteen Canons, BWV 1087; Cantatas BWV 22, 23, 127, 159, and 182; *Clavier-Übung,* Parts I–IV; Concerto for Two Violins, BWV 1043; *Goldberg Variations,* BWV 988; Kyrie, BWV 233a; Mass in B minor, BWV 232; *A Musical Offering,* BWV 1079; *Organ Chorales from the Neumeister Collection; Works for Two Harpsichords*


EDITIONS OF WORKS BY MOZART

Horn Concerto, K. 370b + 371; Piano Concertos (complete); Rondos for Piano and Orchestra, K. 382, 386; *Grande sestetto concertante* (arrangement of K. 364); *Die neugeborne Ros' entzückt,* K. Anh. 11a


OTHER EDITIONS

*Anguish of Hell and Peace of Soul: A Collection of Sixteen Motets on Psalm 116;* Johann Michael Bach, The Complete Organ Chorales; Dieterich Buxtehude, The Keyboard Works; Antonio Caldara, Magnificat; Johann Gottlieb Goldberg, 24 Polonaises in All Keys; Paul Hindemith, *Cardillac,* Op. 39

Johann Sebastian Bach
in a painting by Elias Gottlob Haußmann
(1748; replica by the artist of his 1746 portrait version)

# JOHANN SEBASTIAN BACH

## The Learned Musician

CHRISTOPH WOLFF

W·W·NORTON & COMPANY

*New York · London*

First published as a Norton paperback 2001

For information about permission to reproduce selections from this book, write to
Permissions, W. W. Norton & Company, Inc., 500 Fifth Avenue, New York, NY 10110

The text of this book is composed in Garamond 3
with the display set in Garamond 3 Italic with Swash Caps
Composition by Allentown Digital Services Division of RR Donnelley & Sons Company
Manufacturing by the Haddon Craftsmen, Inc.
Book design by Jacques Chazaud

Library of Congress Cataloging-in-Publication Data

Wolff, Christoph
Johann Sebastian Bach: the learned musician/Christoph Wolff.
p. cm.
Includes bibliographical references and index.

ISBN 0-393-04825-X

1. Bach, Johann Sebastian, 1685–1750.   2. Composers—Germany—Biography.   I. Title.
ML410.B1  W793  2000
780'.92—dc21
[B]                              99-054364

ISBN 0-393-32256-4 pbk.

W. W. Norton & Company, Inc., 500 Fifth Avenue, New York, N.Y. 10110
www.wwnorton.com

W. W. Norton & Company Ltd., Castle House, 75/76 Wells Street, London W1T 3QT

11 12 13 14 15 16 17 18 19 20

*For Barbara,*
*Katharina, Dorothea, and Stephanie*

# Contents

# GENERAL ABBREVIATIONS

*Note:* For bibliographic abbreviations, see pp. 545–46.

| | | | |
|---|---|---|---|
| A | alto (voice) | rec | recorder(s) |
| B | bass (voice) | *rip* | *ripieno, ripieni* |
| bc | basso continuo | rthl., rtl. | reichst(h)aler |
| bn | bassoon(s) | S | soprano (voice) |
| cemb | cembalo | str | strings |
| cor | corno, corni | T | tenor (voice) |
| cto | continuo | ti | timpani |
| D. | Doctor | thlr. | thaler, taler |
| *div* | *divisi* | tr | trumpet(s) |
| fl | flute(s) | trb | trombone(s) |
| fg | fagotto, fagotti | trav | transverse flute(s) |
| gr. | groschen | v | violin(s) |
| instr | instrument(s) | va | viola(s) |
| M. | Magister | va d.g. | viola(s) da gamba |
| ob | oboe(s) | va d'am | viola(s) d'amore |
| ob d'am | oboe(s) d'amore | vc | violoncello(s) |
| pf. | pfennig | vne | violone, violoni |

# ACKNOWLEDGMENTS

**Frontispiece:** Courtesy of William H. Scheide, Princeton, New Jersey; **Pages 12,** 52, 368, 369: Bachhaus Eisenach; 15, 128, 416: Staatsbibliothek zu Berlin, Preußischer Kulturbesitz, Musikabteilung; 32: Evangelisch-lutherisches Pfarramt Ohrdruf; 38, 39, 452–53: Archive-Museum for Literature and Art, Kyiv; 56: Museum für das Fürstentum Lüneburg, Lüneburg; 65: Museum für Hamburgische Geschichte, Hamburg; 76: Schloßmuseum, Arnstadt; 80: Evangelisch-lutherisches Pfarramt, Arnstadt; 104, 106: Museum am Lindenbühl, Mühlhausen; 116: Stiftung Weimarer Klassik / Herzogin Anna Amalia Bibliothek, Weimar; 120, 236, 241, 320, 321, 322: Bach-Archiv Leipzig; 146, 149: Kunstsammlungen zu Weimar, Schloßmuseum, Weimar; 186, 190, 192: Bachgedenkstätte im Schloß Köthen, Köthen; 267, 268, 304: Evangelisch-lutherische Kirchengemeinde St. Thomas-Matthäi, Leipzig; 266, 403, 404, 405(both): Stadtarchiv, Leipzig; 390: Sotheby's Holdings, London; 340, 359: Stadtgeschichtliches Museum, Leipzig

# List of Illustrations

# Preface to the Updated Edition

Quite a few books on Johann Sebastian Bach have appeared over the past several decades and in particular on the occasion of the last jubilee year 2000. Virtually without exception, either they are devoted to describing the composer's life *and* works or they clearly focus on some aspects of his music. In contrast, the present book was intended as a decidedly biographical presentation, even though the biography of a musician cannot avoid discussing musical aspects and mentioning actual works. Therefore, I had to include essential musical references, but the discussion of specifically musical facts is limited to what is most necessary, and a detailed explanation of the composer's development and musical language is consciously omitted. Instead, the intention was and remains to update the current state of knowledge—what we know about Bach's life and the more immediate context of his being and his workings—which has not been done since Philipp Spitta, that is, for well over 125 years. For this purpose, as many accessible source materials as possible were taken into account and evaluated, but discussing them all, with their often varied interpretations of events, had to be passed up.

The bibliography at the end of the book makes this aim clear, even though the preface to the first edition did not say so explicitly. I have been asked repeatedly why Albert Schweitzer's Bach book of 1908, by far the most widespread and influential work ever on the composer, is not cited in the bibliography. The answer is both simple and unapologetic, because in no way does it involve neglect. Schweitzer, as a declared Wagnerian, given the impermanence of his insights for understanding Bach's expressive musical language, in fact contributed weightily, and thereby essentially dislodged Spitta. However, that certainly does not apply to the area of biography; in that regard, he not only depended on Spitta but also lagged behind him in many ways. On the whole, Spitta's biographical sketch gave authoritative direction for the twentieth century within the framework of a wonderful presentation of Bach's life and work. This orientation also pertains especially to Spitta's emphatic avoidance regarding the human side of Bach, which is difficult to approach and so is usually neglected. Therefore, this book offers an attempt, not restricted to a small part (such as chapter 11), to diminish slightly the prevailing abstract view of Bach.

Only in writing this book, and even more pointedly in the aftermath, did it become clear to me how much the late eighteenth-century tradition of understanding Bach as a musical cult figure goes back to the composer's apparent furtherance and propagation of his self-image. In the end, what we know today is that Bach was a highly self-conscious man—one who was seemingly not shy about styling himself as a kind of star in his surroundings and in the circle of his students. The question of how much the basis for the picture of musical genius—for the view of the unchanging uniqueness of his art—goes back to Bach himself I have pursued elsewhere.* Most of all, the retrospective portrayals in the Obituary, which go back to Bach's own reports, offer discernible traces in this regard (cf. the typical opinion of Reinken in his view of Bach's historic mission, pp. 212–13), as does Bach's establishment of his historical place in the framework of the family genealogy and the Old-Bach Archive (pp. 420ff.).

It speaks to the vitality of a branch of research when, in the space of roughly a decade, new knowledge has been uncovered that proves relevant to the biographical representation. Considering the ongoing systematic research in central German church, state, and communal archives that has been undertaken by the Leipzig Bach Archive since 2002, we may be sure that in the future, further pertinent materials will turn up that will require future updating. All new and genuine Bach documentary material collected through 2006–07 has now been published by the Bach Archive in volume V of the *Bach-Dokumente* series: *Dokumente zu Leben, Werk und Nachwirken Johann Sebastian Bachs, 1685–1800*, ed. Hans-Joachim Schulze (Kassel, 2007).

The publication of the present reprint of my book, in addition to allowing for the silent correction of misprints in the main text, provides the opportunity of making material corrections and adding supplementary information that seems to me especially relevant from a biographical perspective. The following paragraphs address this purpose by briefly summarizing the most important new knowledge that has been presented from 1999 through 2011 (supplied with pertinent bibliographic citations) and, where necessary, by relating them to the biographical context. To avoid costly changes, these addenda and corrigenda have not been worked into the main text. Only the

---

* "Defining Genius: Early Reflections of J. S. Bach's Self-Image," *Proceedings of the American Philosophical Society* 145 (2001): 474–81; expanded version: "Images of Bach in the Perspective of Basic Research and Interpretative Scholarship," *Journal of Musicology* 22 (2005): 503–20. See also the annotated edition of Forkel's 1802 biography, ed. Christoph Wolff, in *BD*, vol. VII (Kassel, 2008).

dates in the chronologies (pp. 143 and 525ff.) were emended and corrected, respectively.

• Author of the Newton-Bach analogy, 1750 (p. 6):

The author of the open letter of August 28, 1750, signed "A.," in which the names of Newton and Bach were first connected with each other was until now thought to be Johann Friedrich Agricola. However, the text must be ascribed to Johann Adolph Scheibe, whose name was often concealed under the pseudonym "Alfonso" and who, after the turmoil from his 1737 attack (pp. 1ff.) had died down, wrote only positively about Bach.

Kai Köpp, "Johann Adolph Scheibe als Verfasser zweier anonymer Bach-Dokumente," *BJ* (2003): 173–96.

• Musical beginnings, Buxtehude, Böhm, and Reinken (pp. 62–65, 212–15):

The most important new findings regarding Bach's youthful years result from the discovery in 2005 of Bach's earliest music manuscript. The so-called Weimar Tablature, a composite manuscript, contains among other pieces a copy of Dieterich Buxtehude's longest, technically most demanding, and compositionally most sophisticated organ chorale—the elaborate fantasy on Luther's hymn "Nun freut euch lieben Christen g'mein" BuxWV 214. The clean and error-free manuscript that originated in Ohrdruf before 1700, is notated in German tablature, and was written by the thirteen- to fourteen-year-old Johann Sebastian Bach provides the first reliable evidence for the unusually high level of proficiency and technical competence of the young student. It also demonstrates his early acquaintance with Buxtehude's organ music while studying under the tutelage of his brother Johann Christoph.

A second manuscript contains the famous and similarly extensive chorale fantasy "An Wasserflüssen Bybylon" by Johann Adam Reinken—now the earliest known source of this unusual composition. Bach's copy indicates at the end "â Dom. Georg: Böhme descriptum ao. 1700 Lunaburgi" (written out at the home of Herr Georg Böhm in the year 1700 in Lüneburg) and proves that the contact with Böhm goes back to the first year in Lüneburg, if not before, and that it was the Lüneburg organist Böhm who apparently put Bach in contact with the Hamburg master Reinken and his music. Moreover, the document clarifies Böhm's important role as mentor, and possibly also as facilitator, of Bach's stipend as choral scholar at the St. Michael's School and suggests that Lüneburg represented a decisive step in the career of the young musician.

For further details, see the extensive commentary in *Weimarer Orgeltabulatur. Die frühesten Notenabschriften Johann Sebastian Bachs sowie Abschriften seines Schülers Johann Martin Schubart mit Werken von Dietrich Buxtehude, Johann Adam Reinken und Johann*

*Pachelbel*. Facsimile and transcription, ed. Michael Maul and Peter Wollny. *Faksimile-Reihe Bachscher Werke und Schriftstücke—Neue Folge*, Bd. 4, ed. Bach-Archiv Leipzig (Kassel, 2007).

• On Johann Adam Reinken (pp. 62–65):
Newly discovered archival records regarding Reinken's year of birth prove that he was not ninety-nine when he died in 1722. The ages that Johann Mattheson gives in 1739 rest apparently on conscious exaggeration. Reinken (also spelled Reincken) was born in Deventer (Holland) in 1643. Therefore, at the time of his meeting with the Latin-school student Bach, he was not yet sixty years of age, some six years younger than Buxtehude—although from Bach's perspective he distinctly represented the older generation. At the Hamburg encounter in 1720, he was seventy-seven.

Ulf Grapenthien, "Reincken, Johann Adam," *Grove Music Online*; also his "Sweelincks Kompositionsregeln aus dem Nachlass Johann Adam Reinckens," *Hamburger Jahrbuch für Musikwissenschaft* 18 (2001): 71–110.

• On Johann Effler (p. 69):
C. P. E. Bach could not, in 1775, answer what took his father from Lüneburg to Weimar (p. 67), so Forkel's question has remained unanswered since then. My suspicion—that the Weimar court organist Johann Effler had a hand in Bach's appointment to the Weimar court during the first half of 1703—is now confirmed, on the basis of a previously unknown document. Michael Maul of the Bach-Archiv Leipzig was able to identify a note of Effler's dated March 26, 1678, in the public record office at Weimar that describes Effler's duties as organist at the Dominican church (Predigerkirche) in Erfurt as Johann Pachelbel's predecessor. The note also contains an express statement that "of the best musicians, Herr Bach . . . was taken into their ranks" and that he "handles the clavier whenever they make music."

During the period 1667–82, Johann Christian Bach was director of the Erfurt town musicians, which also employed his two younger brothers, Johann Aegidius and Johann Nicolaus (cf. p. 17). Their first cousin Johann Ambrosius Bach played in the group, too, from 1667 to 1671, as a violinist. After that, Ambrosius Bach's continued connections with Erfurt (he also married an Erfurt woman) led in 1684—a year before the birth of his son Johann Sebastian—to an offer to become director of the town music company, which he declined.

The direct musical connections that have now been identified bestow a new importance on Effler's relationship with the Bach family. They make it plain that the young Sebastian, at the latest in 1702 on his return from Lüneburg to Thüringen if not earlier, could find an influential patron in the Weimar court organist.

Possibly Effler had already played a role as a go-between in Bach's application to Sangerhausen. The contacts were not broken off during Bach's time in Arnstadt and Mühlhäusen, so that Effler in 1708, in arranging for his own successor, recommended Bach to the Duke of Weimar.

In 1704, Johann Effler worked alongside Johann Nicolaus Bach in assessing an organ of the collegiate church in Jena. Here he turned out to be an opponent of meantone temperament who, together with the oldest son of Johann Christoph Bach of Eisenach, demanded an organ tuning that, in addition to the "genus purum" of the customary keys, would enable the harmonically strengthened "genus mixtum," or "genus diatonico-chromatico-enharmonicum." Apparently, a modern temperament was preferred in the Bach family circle (see below: About the tuning of the organs in Arnstadt and Mühlhausen).

Michael Maul, "Frühe Urteile über Johann Christoph und Johann Nikolaus Bach," *BJ* (2004): 157–68.

• About the cantata "Nach dir, Herr, verlanget mich," BWV 150 (p. 99–101):
This early cantata has been variously considered of doubtful authenticity. Hans-Joachim Schulze was able to demonstrate that the work originated as one commissioned by the Mühlhausen town councillor Conrad Meckbach, whose name occurs in the cantata text in the form of an acrostic.

Hans-Joachim Schulze, "Räselhafte Auftragswerke Johann Sebastian Bachs. Anmerkungen zu einigen Kantatentexten," *BJ* (2010): 69–93.

• About the repertoire and context of the early vocal works (p. 101):
On the basis of a recent source discovery in London, the cantata fragment "Meine Seele soll Gott loben," BWV 223, ascribed to Bach since Spitta, can definitively be stricken from the Bach canon.

Remnants of the old choir library of St. Blasius's Church in Mühlhausen, together with an old inventory, have been tracked down in the Staatsbibliothek in Berlin. The works of Praetorius, Demantius, Schütz, Hammerschmidt, the elder Ahle, and Briegel contained there were available to Bach, even if we do not know whether or how he used them.

Hans-Joachim Marx, "Finderglück: Eine neue Kantate von J. S. Bach? von G. F. Händel?—Meine Seele soll Gott loben (BWV 223)," *Göttinger Händel-Beiträge* 10 (2004): 179–204; Daniel R. Melamed, "Die alte Chorbibliothek der Kirche Divi Blasii zu Mühlhausen," *BJ* (2002): 209–16.

• About the tuning of the organs in Arnstadt and Mühlhausen (p. 101):
Johann Friedrich Wender, the builder of Bach's organ in Arnstadt, was also

responsible for the successful reconstruction in 1687–91 of the organ at St. Blasius's in Mühlhausen under Johann Georg Ahle, Bach's predecessor there, who evidently used tempered tuning early on. In 1690 Ahle wrote an ode to the advantages of well-tempered tuning, developed by Andreas Werckmeister, which allowed for harmonic triads on all semitone steps of the scale. So from the summer of 1703 on, Bach continuously had at his disposal instruments that set practically no harmonic or key limitations, a fact that clearly accelerated his interest in experimenting with extreme chromatics.

> Markus Rathey, "Die Temperierung der Divi Blasii-Orgel in Mühlhausen," *BJ* (2001): 163–72.

• On Maria Barbara Bach (p. 117):
The surviving documents relating to Bach's first wife can hardly be surpassed in their limitations, recording only her baptism, marriage, and death. Nevertheless, Michael Maul of the Bach-Archiv Leipzig found a further small reference to her in the 1708 pew registry of the court church in Weimar. Under women's pews, "Fr[au]. Bachin, Hof-Organistin" is listed as having sat on the right side of the nave in row 8, seat 3, diagonally behind the wife of court capellmeister Johann Samuel Drese.

> "Lebenszeichen von Maria Barbara Bach," *Bach Magazine* 4 (2004): 31 (illustrated).

• A newly discovered vocal work from the Weimar period (pp. 129 and 133):
The original source (printed text with autograph manuscript score) of a completely unknown vocal work unexpectedly turned up at the Duchess Anna Amalia Library in Weimar. It concerns an aria for soprano, two violins, viola, and continuo composed by Bach on the occasion of the fifty-second birthday of his employer, Duke Wilhelm Ernst of Saxe-Weimar, on October 20, 1713. Bach set to music a twelve-stanza German poem by the theologian Johann Anton Mylius (1657–1724) on the duke's motto, "Omnia cum Deo, et nihil sine eo" (Everything with God, and nothing without Him). The music is composed in the form of a strophic aria with ritornello, a genre popular in late seventeenth-century Germany but not previously found among Bach's compositions. The work, written for a prominent occasion, confirms Bach's privileged position at the Weimar court even before his promotion from court organist to concertmaster in 1714.

> Michael Maul, " 'Alles mit Gott und nichts ohn' ihn'—eine neu aufgefundene Aria von Johann Sebastian Bach," *BJ* (2005): 7–34; edition within the series *Faksimile-Reihe Bachscher Werke und Schriftstücke—Neue Folge*, ed. Bach-Archiv Leipzig (Kassel, 2005). The aria will be listed in the Schmieder catalogue under BWV 1127.

- Weimar instrumental works (pp. 133ff.):

The early history of the Sonata for Organ, BWV 528, which goes back to a hypothetical trio sonata in G minor for oboe, viola da gamba, and continuo from around 1714, offers one of the few plausible traces of Bach's chamber music in Weimar.

> Pieter Dirksen, "Ein verschollenes Weimarer Kammermusikwerk Johann Sebastian Bachs? Zur Vorgeschichte der Sonate e-Moll für Orgel (BWV 528)," *BJ* (2003): 7–36.

- On the examination of the organ in Gera (p. 143):

Newly discovered documents bring about substantial revisions to Bach's commissions as organ examiner in the Thuringian city of Gera. They pertain to three (not two) organs built by Johann Georg Finke. Moreover, Bach's visit to Gera previously assigned to 1724 must now be moved to the period May 30 to June 6, 1725. Bach was accompanied by two people, presumably Anna Magdalena Bach and the barely fifteen-year-old Wilhelm Friedemann. The trip was probably connected with a visiting performance at the Osterstein Palace, the residence of Heinrich XVIII, Count of Reuss. Bach had already performed at the Reuss palace at Schleiz in 1721. He traveled from Schleiz via Gera back to Cöthen in August 1721, and on that occasion examined the organ at the palace church as well as the progress made in building the organ in the Church of the Savior; he even saw to it that the large commission for the organ in the municipal church would also go to Finke.

In 1725, Bach received a top honorarium of 30 rthl. for his certification of the two organs, in the municipal church and the Church of the Savior. On June 3, 1725, the first Sunday after Trinity, the large three-manual organ in the municipal church of St. John's in Gera was dedicated by Bach. Generous expenses for overnight lodgings and entertainment (including supplies of wine, brandy, coffee, tea, sugar, and tobacco) testify to his special VIP treatment.

In Leipzig Bach's new cantata cycle was supposed to begin on the first Sunday after Trinity in 1725, as it had the previous two years. Because of Bach's absence at the beginning of June, the irregular rhythm of the third cycle (see pp. 281ff.) was already destined from the start. Its opening cantata (BWV 39) was composed in the following year and performed on June 23, 1726.

> Michael Maul, "Johann Sebastian Bachs Besuche in der Residenzstadt Gera," *BJ* (2004): 101–20. For further updated details on Bach's organ examinations, see Christoph Wolff and Markus Zepf, *The Organs of J. S. Bach: A Handbook*, trans. Lynn Edwards Butler (Urbana, Chicago, and Springfield, 2012).

- On Augustin Reinhard Stricker (pp. 194ff.):

New research on Bach's Cöthen predecessor Augustin Reinhard Stricker provides important information about his lost German opera *Alexander und Roxane*, magnificently produced on the occasion of the wedding of King Friedrich I and Sophia Louise of Mecklenburg-Grabau in December 1708 (repeated in January 1709) at the Berlin court. Stricker, at the time chamber musician, tenor, and composer of the Prussian court capelle, sang the principal role of Neptune, god of the seas. Additionally, the cast of characters included "Dancers in the Entrée of the Amours and Plaisirs: The Prince of Cöthen, the Elder [Leopold]. The Prince of Cöthen, the Younger [August Ludwig]." Moreover, listed among the super-numeraries in Neptune's suite as well as in the ballet scenes is Margrave Christian Friedrich of Brandenburg, the king's brother and later dedicatee of Bach's Brandenburg Concertos.

Bach's later employer, at the time fourteen years of age and a pupil of the Berlin Ritterakademie, apparently received dance instruction along with his brother and participated actively in musical performances. His acquaintance with Stricker, who moved to Cöthen as capellmeister in the summer of 1714, goes back as far as the opera performances of 1708–09.

Hans-Joachim Schulze, "Von Weimar nach Köthen: Risiken und Chancen eines Amtswechsels," *Cöthener Bach Hefte* 11 (2003): 9–27.


- About Cöthen performances of cantatas BWV 21 and 199 (pp. 199, 213ff.):

Among the anonymous copyists of the original performance material of the cantata "Ich hatte viel Bekümmernis," BWV 21, Johann Jeremias Göbel has now been identified. Göbel was cantor of the Reformed (Calvinist) municipal school and therefore responsible for the music at the Reformed "Cathedral Church" (St. Jacob's Church) in Cöthen. This circumstance evinces for the first time that, on specific occasions, Bach also provided music for worship services in the main Reformed church of the principality, and not just in 1729 at the funeral of Prince Leopold. Conceivably, the occasion for the performance of BWV 21 was a Day of Repentance ceremony held in Cöthen every five years. One such service occurred during Bach's employment in Cöthen on May 1, 1721.

The discovery of the autograph violin part for the soprano solo cantata "Mein Herze schwimmt im Blut," BWV 199, rounds out our information about the Cöthen version of the work. We now know that it was performed around or after 1720 without oboe, with viola da gamba (instead of solo viola), and in the key of D minor (at low pitch, ca. Hz 392; see below: About Leipzig arrangements of Cöthen cantatas).

Michael Maul and Peter Wollny, "Quellenkundliches zu Bach-Aufführungen in Köthen, Ronneburg und Leipzig zwischen 1720 und 1760," *BJ* (2003): 97–141;

Tatjana Schabalina, "Ein weiteres Autograph Johann Sebastian Bachs in Rußland: Neues zur Entstehungsgeschichte der verschiedenen Fassungen von BWV 199," *BJ* (2004): 11–40.


* On a guest performance in Zerbst (pp. 208, 217ff.):
A recent publication turned up the text to Bach's festive birthday music for Prince Johann August of Anhalt-Zerbst on August 9, 1722, which reveals the outline of the lost secular cantata. Probably on the same day, the tenth Sunday after Trinity, a corresponding festive church cantata for the count's birthday was performed, but no traces of it have survived. Commissions for works and performances were apparently connected with a provisional joint administration of the capellmeister's office, which Bach looked after from nearby Cöthen before Johann Friedrich Fasch took over the position in September 1722. One member of the Zerbst court orchestra was Johann Caspar Wilcke, Jr., brother of Anna Magdalena Bach, who had already made frequent appearances as a singer even before her marriage to the Cöthen capellmeister.

> Barbara Reul, " 'O vergnügte Stunden / da mein Hertzog funden seinen Lebenstag': Ein unbekannter Textdruck zu einer Geburtstagskantate J. S. Bachs für den Fürsten Johann August von Anhalt-Zerbst," *BJ* (1999): 7–18; Hans-Joachim Schulze, "Johann Sebastian Bach und Zerbst 1722: Randnotizen zu einer verlorenen Gastmusik," *BJ* (2004): 209–14.


* On the 1720 trip to Hamburg (pp. 211–15):
The archival documents that deal with appointing the organist at St. Jacobi Church yield details of the procedures and prove that Bach had already come to a decision *after* his concert at St. Catharine's and *before* the audition of the other candidates. But they also point out that the expectation of a financial payment from Bach was hardly decisive for his rejectionist attitude.

> Philipp Tonner, "Bachs Bewerbung in Hamburg—eine Frage des Geldes?" *Hamburger Jahrbuch für Musikwissenschaft* 18 (2001): 207–31.


* About Leipzig arrangements of Cöthen cantatas (pp. 242ff., Tables 8.7 and 8.13):
Bach's official inauguration was originally planned for Pentecost 1723 but had to be postponed by two weeks for unknown reasons. Yet after signing his provisional contract on April 19, Bach first prepared himself for the earlier inauguration and scheduled performances of the cantata "Wer mich liebt, der wird mein Wort halten," BWV 59, for Whitsunday as well as "Erhöhtes Fleisch und Blut," BWV 173; and "Erwünschtes Freudenlicht," BWV 184, for the second and third days of Pentecost, respectively; given the time pressure, all were parodies of vocal works

from the Cöthen period. However, when the date of the inauguration was moved to the first Sunday after Trinity, Bach broke off working on BWV 59 (see pp. 242ff.). It remains to be seen whether this cantata, in its four-movement form, was performed on Whitsunday, May 16, 1723, at the "Old Service" in St. Paul's, the university church. In any case, Bach postponed the completion of the three Pentecostal cantatas to the following year, when they were performed at the Leipzig main churches (p. 273).

During his first year in Leipzig, Bach made greater use than heretofore assumed of vocal works from the Cöthen years (p. 197), in addition to cantatas from the Weimar period. We may note that the Cantata BWV 75 for the first Sunday after Trinity, still composed on Cöthen paper (p. 244); the Cantata BWV 69a for the twelfth Sunday after Trinity (p. 271); and the first town council election cantata (p. 287), whose original scores contain several movements as fair copies, reveal themselves as parodies rather than new compositions. The following movements can be traced to Cöthen models: arias no. 3 and 5 from BWV 75; the opening chorus from BWV 69a, with its typically Cöthen duet formations (based on BWV Anh. 5?); and the opening chorus and arias no. 3, 5, and 7 from BWV 119.

Detailed comparisons between the Leipzig arrangements and their Cöthen models provide conclusive evidence that the Cöthen court capelle, presumably like its Berlin predecessor ensemble and following French tradition, performed at low pitch ("Tief-Kammerton," ca. Hz 392).

Andreas Glöckner, "Vom anhalt-köthenischen Kapellmeister zum Thomaskantor: Köthener Werke in Leipziger Überlieferung," *Cöthener Bach Hefte* 11 (2003): 78–96.

• About the participants in Leipzig church music (pp. 260–63):
The normal choral complement called for by Bach in his memorandum of 1730 (one to two concertists and at least two ripienists for each vocal part of his "elite" ensemble), which has been cast into doubt by Andrew Parrott and Joshua Rifkin, is confirmed by two historical choir rosters: one from 1729 names twelve singers in the primary choir that Bach conducted, and another from 1744–45 names seventeen singers. Moreover, it has become evident that Bach's instrumentalists and singers were regularly supported by substitutes and assistants from the town musicians and by professional forces from the ranks of university students. This applies in particular to Bach's private pupils, as shown in the case of his future son-in-law, Johann Christoph Altnickol: he moved from being a paid choir singer at the Mary Magdalene Church in Breslau to Leipzig, where he attended the university and entered Bach's ensemble, taking along two fellow students.

Andrew Parrott, *The Essential Bach Choir* (Woodbridge/Suffolk, 2000). The latest exchange in a protracted discussion regarding Bach's Leipzig performing forces consists of three articles in the journal *Early Music* (*EM*): Andreas Glöckner, "On the performing forces of Johann Sebastian Bach's Leipzig church music," *EM* 38 (2010): 215–22; Andrew Parrott, "Bach's chorus: The Leipzig line. A response to Andreas Glöckner," *EM* 38 (2010): 223–36; Andreas Glöckner, "'The ripienists must also be at least eight, namely two for each part': The Leipzig line of 1730—some observations," *EM* 39 (2011): 575–86. Barbara Wiermann, "Altnickol, Faber, Fulde: Drei Breslauer Choralisten im Umfeld Johann Sebastian Bachs," *BJ* (2003): 259–66.

• New cantata text booklets and confirmed performance dates (p. 275–78):
Only six original printed text booklets of church cantatas were known until Tatjana Schabalina turned up several more such booklets in St. Petersburg, as well as an exemplar of the book with Picander's cantata cycle of 1728. Several booklets corroborate performing dates previously determined only on the basis of a philological analysis of the musical sources: (1) September 3 to 29, 1724, for BWV 33, 78, 99, 9, and 130; (2) August 27, 1725, for BWV Anh. 4; (3) June 1 to 8, 1727, for BWV 34, 173, 184, and 129; (4) Good Friday, April 24, 1734, for the performance of G. H. Stölzel's passion oratorio "Ein Lämmlein geht und trägt die Schuld" at St. Thomas's under Bach's direction.

Tatjana Schabalina, "*Texte zur Music* in Sankt Petersburg. Neue Quellen zur Leipziger Musikgeschichte sowie zur Komposition- und Aufführungstätigkeit Johann Sebastian Bachs," *BJ* (2008): 33–98, and "*Texte zur Music* in Sankt Petersburg—Weitere Funde," *BJ* (2009): 11–48. "Allein zu dir, Herr Jesu Christ," BWV 33. Facsimile of the autograph score (Scheide Library, Princeton), the original performing parts (Bach-Archiv Leipzig), and the original libretto of 1724 (Russische Nationalbibliothek, St. Petersburg). Commentary by Christoph Wolff and Peter Wollny (Leipzig, 2010).

• Bach and Stölzel (pp. 285ff.):
In addition to the Stölzel oratorio, Marc-Roderich Pfau discovered a text booklet that documents performances of Stölzel cantatas by Bach in the fall of 1735, and Andreas Glöckner argued that an entire cantata cycle by Stölzel in Bach's possession was presented in Leipzig that year. Moreover, Peter Wollny was able to demonstrate that the cantata movement "Bekennen will ich seinen Namen," BWV 200, previously considered an autograph cantata fragment by Bach, in fact constitutes Bach's arrangement of the aria "Dein Kreuz, o Bräutgam meiner Seelen" from Stölzel's passion oratorio "Ein Lämmlein geht und trägt die Schuld" (see above).

Marc-Roderich Pfau, "Ein unbekanntes Leipziger Kantatentextheft aus dem Jahr 1735—Neues zum Thema Bach und Stölzel," *BJ* (2008): 99–122; Andreas Glöckner, "Ein weiterer Kantatenjahrgang Gottfried Heinrich Stölzels in Bachs Aufführungsrepertoire?" *BJ* (2009): 95–116; Peter Wollny, *"Bekennen will ich seinen Namen*—Authentizität, Bestimmung und Kontext der Arie BWV 200. Anmerkungen zu Johann Sebastian Bachs Rezeption von Werken Gottfried Heinrich Stölzels," *BJ* (2008): 123–58.

- On Picander's cantata cycle and Bach's library—Latin Masses, French keyboard music, and an illustrated Bible (pp. 284ff., 333–35):

Peter Wollny uncovered at an archive in Mügeln (Saxony) a C. P. E. Bach composing score with a cantata from the Picander cycle, apparently performed under his father's guidance before he left Leipzig in 1734, as well as a score of an anonymous Kyrie-Gloria Mass in the hand of J. S. Bach. The previously unknown cantata "Ich bin vergnügt in meinem Stande" by C. P. E. Bach suggests that his father's church music performances in Leipzig after 1730 occasionally included works by his students and that he apparently assigned at least some cantata texts from the Picander cycle of 1728 to his students rather than composing the whole cycle himself. This may also include the fragment "Ich bin ein Pilgrim auf der Welt," BWV Anh. 190 (perhaps another composition by C. P. E. Bach).

The manuscript of the anonymous Mass in E minor, which lacks an inner folio containing the end of the "Laudamus te" and the beginning of the "Qui tollis" movements, can be dated to the late 1730s. The work, most likely of Italian origin, indicates that Bach's Leipzig repertoire of Latin church music was larger than previously known. Newly identified sources also increase the repertoire of French keyboard music in Bach's music library by including important works by François Couperin (*Second Livre des Pièces de Clavecin*, 1716–17) and Jean Philippe Rameau (*Nouvelles Suites de Pièèces de Clavecin*, ca. 1728). Moreover, the organ trio BWV 587 has been identified as derived from an early version of a sonata in Couperin's *Les nations*, which Bach most likely acquired in Weimar via Johann Georg Pisendel.

Bach's collection of Lutheran Bibles contained the famous Merian edition with some two hundred engravings (Frankfurt/Main, 1704) that turned up in private possession and is now on long-term loan at the Leipzig Bach Archive. It shows the composer's autograph initials and 1744 as the year of acquisition.

Peter Wollny, "Zwei Bach-Funde in Mügeln. C. P. E. Bach, Picander und die Leipziger Kirchenmusik in den 1730er Jahren," *BJ* (2010): 111–51; "Zur Rezeption französischer Cembalo-Musik im Hause Bach in den 1730er Jahren: Zwei neu aufgefundene Quellen," *In organo pleno: Festschrift für Jean-Claude Zehnder zum 65. Geburtstag*, ed. L. Collarile and A. Nigito (Bern, 2007), pp. 265–76; and "Fundstücke zur Lebensgeschichte Johann Sebastian Bachs

1744–1750," *BJ* (2011): 35–50; Kerstin Delang, "Couperin - Pisendel - Bach. Überlegungen zur Datierung des Trios BWV 587 anhand eines Quellenfundes in der Sächsischen Landesbibliothek - Staats- und Universitätsbibliothek Dresden," *BJ* (2007): 197–204.

- On Bach's knowledge of music literature and teaching methods (pp. 305–11, 331–35):

Surprisingly copious evidence has been found relating to the central thesis of this book, as expressed in its subtitle, "The Learned Musician." The evidence demonstrates the systematic breadth and historical depth of Bach's study of older music literature and theory as well as his pragmatic start in using this knowledge for his teaching of composition.

Already during his time in Weimar, Bach supplied himself with a volume of Masses and Mass movements by the old master of classic vocal polyphony, Giovanni Pierluigi da Palestrina. This manuscript collection, which has only recently been connected to Bach, served above all as primary study material; nevertheless, at least two of its works were later performed in Leipzig. Besides the known performance materials dating from around 1740 for a Missa *sine nomine*, an unknown Bach performance part from the same time appeared containing the Missa *Ecce sacerdos magnus*, a cantus firmus Mass directly connected with the Symbolum Nicenum of the B-Minor Mass.

An autograph manuscript in the field of theory that must be considered a unique document relating to Bach's teaching practice dates from the early to mid-1740s. Its first part contains rules, formulated by Bach, for handling syncopations in double counterpoint; its second part offers a collection of excerpts dealing with the teaching of counterpoint, fugue, and canon that Bach compiled from Latin treatises of Zarlino, Calvisius, and others, together with Latin explanations.

What Bach missed in older counterpoint teachings were the voice-leading rules for a five-part setting, especially in the framework of a modern, harmonically richer language. His absolute command of the art of multivoiced composition and his feel for pedagogically handy rules led him to construct a "Regula J. S. Bachii," which bears on the prohibition of doubling certain intervals in a five-voice setting and which can be confirmed in a previously unknown manuscript by his pupil Johann Friedrich Agricola.

The systematic way Bach approached difficult contrapuntal problems, even taking into consideration the old church modes, shows the musically challenging "mind game" dialogue of the late 1730s that he established with his eldest son, Wilhelm Friedemann. Also appearing among these important and extensive studies first discovered in 1999 is the oldest indication that Bach began work on *The Art of Fugue* before 1740.

Bach's various contributions to thorough bass practice, contrapuntal studies, and theory are now collected in the NBA Supplement (Kassel, 2011).

Christoph Wolff et al., "Zurück in Berlin: Das Notenarchiv der Sing-Akademie; Bericht über eine erste Bestandsaufnahme," *BJ* (2002): 165–80; Barbara Wiermann, "Bach und Palestrina: Neue Quellen aus Johann Sebastian Bachs Notenbibliothek," *BJ* (2002): 9–28; Walter Werbeck, "Bach und der Kontrapunkt: Neue Manuskript-Funden," *BJ* (2003): 67–96; Christoph Wolff, "Johann Sebastian Bachs Regeln für den fünfstimmigen Satz," *BJ* (2004): 87–100; Peter Wollny, "Ein Quellenfund aus Kiew: Unbekannte Kontrapunktstudien von Johann Sebastian und Wilhelm Friedemann Bach," *Bach in Leipzig—Bach und Leipzig: Konferenzbericht Leipzig 2000*, ed. U. Leisinger, *LBB* 5 (2002): 275–87.

- Chapter 9, "Musician and Scholar" (pp. 305–39):

Bibliographic reference concerning content and context of chapter 9:

*Musik, Kunst und Wissenschaft im Zeitalter J. S. Bachs*, ed. U. Leisinger and C. Wolff, *LBB* 7 (2005), includes contributions on the Latin school of Bach's time (Peter Lundgreen); on the rector of the St. Thomas School, philologist Johann Matthias Gesner (Ulrich Schindler); on the electricity experiments conducted by Bach's colleague Johann Heinrich Winckler (Myles W. Jackson); on literary theory in Bach's time (Hans Joachim Kreutzer); on music theory and the art of the possible (Thomas Christensen); on the concept of nature, style, and art in eighteenth-century aesthetics (Wilhelm Seidel); and on Bach's empiricism (Hans-Joachim Schulze).

- Latin ode, BWV Anh. 20 (p. 314):

Among the most puzzling lost works of Bach's are the Latin odes composed for a ceremony at the university in August 1723, during his first year in Leipzig. Therefore, a report about this ceremony written in Latin by an academic with an explicit appreciation of BWV Anh. 20 is all the more important. Bach is mentioned there as "summus artifex," and of the pieces, it is said that they "fit the occasion so perfectly" that "everyone admired them."

Ernst Koch, "Johann Sebastian Bachs Musik als höchste Kunst. Ein unbekannter Brief aus Leipzig vom 9. August 1723," *BJ* (2004): 215–20.

- New Bach students (pp. 327–31):

The identification by name of one of the most important Bach copyists ("Anonymous 5") leads us on the trail of a Bach pupil unknown until now. Kayser, born in 1705 in Cöthen, became a pupil of Bach's in or before 1720 and continued his instruction in Leipzig, where he simultaneously studied law and apparently was among Bach's closest assistants, perhaps serving for a time as his personal secretary. Returning to Cöthen, Kayser functioned as a court and government attorney as well as a chamber musician and court organist, and presumably also as organist of St. Agnus's Lutheran Church in Cöthen, to whose congregation he belonged (as did Bach and his family during his time there). As the possessor of important Bach sources and as teacher of Johann Christoph Oley (1738–1789) and Friedrich Wilhelm Rust (1730–1796), Kayser must be counted as the leading agent in the transmission of Bach's music in the Anhalt area; he died in 1758.

The cantor and composer Johann Friedrich Schweinitz (1708–1780) turns out to be another important Bach pupil. He later became music director at the University of Göttingen and in this capacity preceded Johann Nicolaus Forkel, Bach's first biographer.

> Andrew Talle, "Nürnberg, Darmstadt, Köthen: Neuerkenntnisse zur Bach-Überlieferung in der ersten Hälfte des 18. Jahrhunderts," *BJ* (2003): 143–72; Hans-Joachim Schulze, "Johann Friedrich Schweinitz, 'A Disciple of the Famous Herr Bach in Leipzig,'" *About Bach*, ed. Gregory B. Butler, George B. Stauffer and Mary D. Greer (Chicago, 2008), pp. 81–88.

- Repertoire of the Collegium Musicum (p. 355):

Items from the repertoire of Bach's regular Collegium Musicum concerts include compositions in a variety of vocal and instrumental genres by J. B. Bach, F. Benda, C. P. E. Bach, J. D. Heinichen, G. P. Telemann, J. G. Graun, N. A. Porpora, A. Scarlatti, and G. F. Handel—many of them previously not identified as such.

> George B. Stauffer, "Music for 'Cavaliers et Dames.' Bach and the Repertoire of his Collegium Musicum," *About Bach*, ed. Butler et al., pp. 135–56.

- Bach's music rental operation (p. 412):

Newly found documents about mailing costs for sending music to Bach's second-generation pupil Johann Wilhelm Koch, cantor in Ronneburg (Thuringia) in the years 1732–44, provide evidence—with indications like "several cantatas sent back to Mr. Bach"—for the regular renting out of Bach's cantatas, among them exacting works such as "Herr Gott, dich loben wir," BWV 16; "Schwingt freudig euch empor," BWV 36; and "In allen meinen Taten," BWV 97. Since we are not concerned here with just a single case, we can assume that St. Thomas's cantor Bach was in a way functioning as a country church music director, taking care, to a certain extent, of his wider surroundings. Therefore he carried on his music business not only in Leipzig but also in the entire region. He could hardly have limited his distribution to his own works because his challenging compositions prevented anything like the thoroughgoing distribution enjoyed a generation later by the motets and cantatas of Bach's pupil and cantor at the Holy Cross Church in Dresden, Gottfried August Homilius.

> Michael Maul and Peter Wollny, "Quellenkundliches zu Bach-Aufführungen in Köthen, Ronneburg und Leipzig zwischen 1720 und 1760," *BJ* (2003): 100–110, 120–34.

- *The Art of Fugue* and B-Minor Mass (p. 431–42):

The chapter-like systematic organization of *The Art of Fugue* is substantiated by Gregory Butler. Peter Wollny proves that Bach's second youngest son, Johann Christoph Friedrich, assisted his father in the late 1740s (he copied, for example, the "Fantasia chromatica" with its authentic title—the previously unknown source of BWV 903 was acquired in 2009 by the Leipzig Bach Archive) and that his hand shows up in additions and corrections of the autograph score of the B-Minor Mass, his father's last vocal work. Michael Maul considers the possibility that Bach prepared his Mass for a performance on St. Cecilia's Day at St. Stephen's Cathedral in Vienna on commission by Adam Count Questenberg. My own book on the Mass discusses the work in the context of an increased number of performances of Latin church music in Leipzig during the last two decades of Bach's life.

> Gregory G. Butler, "Scribes, Engravers, and Notational Styles. The Final Disposition of Bach's Art of Fugue," *About Bach*, ed. Butler et al., pp. 111–23; Peter Wollny, "Beobachtungen am Autograph der h-Moll-Messe," *BJ* (2009): 135–52; and "Fundstücke zur Lebensgeschichte Johann Sebastian Bachs 1744–1750," *BJ* (2011): 35–50; Michael Maul, *"Die große catholische Messe*. Bach, Graf Questenberg und die 'musicalische Congregation' in Wien," *BJ* (2009): 153–76; Christoph Wolff, *Johann Sebastian Bach: Messe in h-Moll* (Kassel, 2009).

- On Bach's last months and final illness (pp. 448ff.):

The last known written musical entries by the composer occur, as Peter Wollny has shown, in the original performing parts of C. P. E. Bach's Magnificat Wq 215, which was presented in Leipzig on either February 2 or March 25, 1750. The nature of the entries indicates his participation in the careful preparation of the performance, whether or not it took place under his own direction. Archival documents uncovered by Andreas Glöckner attest that Bach, despite the two eye operations he underwent at the end of March and the beginning of April, apparently remained officially in charge of church performances until the middle of May 1750. His substitute, the prefect Johann Adam Franck, was appointed only from May 17 (Whitsunday) and functioned in this capacity until Gottlob Harrer, Bach's successor, took over on St. Michael's Day, September 29, 1750.

The record of Bach pathology offers no new information but strengthens the suppositions that Bach's vision problems and a possible stroke suffered in 1749 were brought on by mellitic diabetes and that the "harmful medicaments and other things" (quoted in the Obituary), which cannot be further specified but were administered during his post-operative treatment, led to a fatal infection.

Peter Wollny, "Fundstücke zur Lebensgeschichte Johann Sebastian Bachs 1744–1750," *BJ* (2011): 35–50; Andreas Glöckner, "Johann Sebastian Bach und die Universität Leipzig—Neue Quellen (Teil I)," *BJ* (2009): 159–201; Bernhard Ludewig, *Johann Sebastian Bach in Spiegel der Medizin* (Grimma, 2000).

- Anna Magdalena Bach as widow (pp. 454–55):

New documents verify that Bach's widow received, aside from the pension distributed by the town charity office, regular donations from the university and from various other sources. With this income, she had relatively good financial security until her death in January 1760. Her unmarried daughters, who had shared a dwelling with her beginning in February 1751—and also, from 1759, with her daughter Elisabeth Altnickol, who in the meantime had been widowed—received modest contributions from, among others, the university, although not until after their mother's death. Mother and daughters probably sought to better their livelihoods through their own activities, such as sewing. In any case, Elisabeth Altnickol is specifically referred to in 1771 as "seamstress."

Maria Hübner, "Zur finanziellen Situation der Witwe Anna Magdalena Bach und ihrer Töchter," *BJ* (2002): 245–55; *Anna Magdalena Bach: Ein Leben in Dokumenten und Bildern*, ed. M. Hübner (Leipzig, 2004).

\*

I am most grateful to my publisher for making this updated edition possible.

October 2012
C. W.

# Preface

Less than a decade ago, I began the preface to my *Bach: Essays on His Life and Works* by stating that "this volume may well be understood as a book about a book the author doesn't feel quite ready to write." As far as I am concerned, things have not really changed since then. Moreover, I believe that it would be unrealistic today for anyone to attempt a comprehensive book-length study of Johann Sebastian Bach's life *and* works in the tradition of Philipp Spitta's two-volume *Johann Sebastian Bach* of 1873–80, written, astonishingly, at a time when only a small number of biographical documents had been found and published and the Bach-Gesellschaft's edition of the complete works was barely half finished. Spitta's magisterial work has challenged all subsequent generations of music historians, not so much to rewrite a full account of Bach's life and works as to update and adjust the image of Bach in order to bring it in line—as objectively as possible and as subjectively as legitimate—with the current state of scholarship. It is the second that has prompted this biographical portrait, forged on the eve of the 250th anniversary of Bach's death.

Today we have easy access both to the collected documentary materials on Bach's life and to his complete musical works and their sources. But rather than facilitating the task of a life-and-works study, the availability of the *Bach-Dokumente* and the *Neue Bach-Ausgabe* and the volume of materials they contain make it a much more challenging if not impossible scholarly enterprise. At the same time, we have become increasingly aware of sources and documents irretrievably lost as well as materials yet to be found and examined. As for the latter, while I was putting the finishing touches on the manuscript for *The New Bach Reader*, a former student of mine came across two previously unknown and highly informative Bach letters; and as this book went to press, I had the good fortune of finding the long-lost music library of the Berlin Sing-Akademie in Kyiv, Ukraine, containing key musical materials of the Bach family (primarily older and younger family members and less significantly affecting Johann Sebastian, but this book has still

benefited—if only minimally). Both of these discoveries clearly indicate that the
search for sources, so essential in Bach scholarship, will remain very much a work
in progress. So unlike Spitta, I have accepted the more modest task of writing a
biography or, more accurately, a biographical essay.

As one may expect, the subject of a biographical study determines the nature
and method of the exercise; two points must be stressed in this connection. First,
from all we know about Bach's life, it lacks exciting dimensions and does not lend
itself to a narrative that focuses on and is woven around a chronological list of
dates and events. Moreover, Bach's biography suffers from a serious lack of information on details, many of them crucial. Carl Philipp Emanuel Bach was clearly
aware of this problem when he wrote to Johann Nicolaus Forkel, his father's first
biographer, in 1775: "Since he never wrote down anything about his life, the
gaps are unavoidable." Indeed, it would not be difficult to devote entire chapters
to what is *not* known about Bach's life. Thus, conjectures and assumptions are
unavoidable, and this book necessarily calls for numerous occurrences of "probably," "perhaps," "maybe," and the like. Yet, as I try to demonstrate in these
pages, it is not impossible to reveal, even in the case of Bach, the essence of a life.

Second, Bach's music, though no substitute for biographical information (or
its lack), is a much stronger and more important presence—at least for us today—
than the composer's life story. While it would defeat the purpose of a musical
biography if the music were marginalized, the focus must nevertheless be on
musical issues of a more general nature and on music as part of the composer's
intellectual profile. A discourse on Bach's development as a composer, integrated
with a more detailed discussion of individual works, would be the subject of a
separate study that I hope to undertake later in order to complement the present
book.

The subtitle of this biographical portrait was not freely invented. The attribute
"learned" appears in the letter of dismissal written in April 1723 by Prince Leopold of Anhalt-Cöthen—someone who definitely knew whom he was describing.
More than a mere formula, the word provided this essay with a strong focus on the
atmosphere of learning and the spirit of discovery that determined much of Bach's
musical orientation and philosophy, distinguishes it so significantly from that
of other major musicians, and helps reveal his aesthetic goals. But well beyond
quoting, and elaborating on, Prince Leopold, this book is generally indebted to a
close reading of the primary documents, which I had the privilege of reviewing in
great detail in conjunction with the updated, enlarged, and revised edition of the
Bach letters and documents, now collected in *The New Bach Reader*. My decision
to quote historical documents whenever possible is based on my view that these
sources bring freshness and immediacy into the discussion of history and that even
though they may speak for themselves, they benefit from being contextualized
while offering instant correctives to erroneous interpretations.

A careful reading of the available primary sources, both musical and non-musical, is largely responsible for the contours and contents of this study and for the interpretive aspects that cannot and should not be avoided. Thus, when I stress, for instance, the importance, extent, and early maturity of Bach's compositional output before 1705, the emphasis is based not only on the relevant source materials but on my reading of them. The same is true of my conclusions about the course of Bach's life during the year 1702, his reasons for moving from Mühlhausen to Weimar, the chronological and conceptual connections between the title page of *The Well-Tempered Clavier* and his applications for the St. Thomas cantorate, and similar matters. Details of this kind, taken together, may add links and facets to a biographical narrative, which in the case of Bach resembles a highly fragmented mosaic. All the more important, then, is every attempt to walk the bridge between two poles, the down-to-earth backdrop of Bach's life and the intellectual framework of his artistry.

In more than one way, this book owes its existence to a long-established and close friendship that has led to a number of collaborative projects. When Michael Ochs, former Richard F. French Music Librarian at Harvard, moved his scene of operation to New York, he thought of twisting my arm but found much less resistance than any other publisher's emissary would have faced in persuading me to write a biographical portrait of Bach. What made the project work so smoothly from the very beginning was not only our familiarity with each other's work and work habits but, from my point of view, his remarkable understanding of the subject matter, his constructive criticism, and his considerate advice. An author cannot wish for a more competent and thoughtful editor, and I wish to thank him for seeing this project through from start to finish. With special thanks, I acknowledge the vigilant copyediting of Susan Gaustad at W. W. Norton. I also take this opportunity to express deep gratitude to my friends and colleagues Hans-Joachim Schulze, Ulrich Leisinger, and Peter Wollny (all of the Bach-Archiv Leipzig) for reading the manuscript, discussing certain points, offering many a helpful hint, and identifying errors here and there. Ruth Libbey has once again been an indispensable assistant, for which I am most grateful. John McMorrough of the Harvard Graduate School of Design kindly provided his expertise on artists' renditions of the historical choir and organ lofts at St. Thomas's of Leipzig. No one, however, has contributed to this book as much, both directly and indirectly, as my wife Barbara, with whom I have discussed, performed, studied, and listened to Bach's music for nearly forty years—my indebtedness and gratitude indeed go back that far, lovingly and completely.

C. W.

# Johann Sebastian Bach

# Prologue
## Bach and the Notion of "Musical Science"

*"What Newton was as philosopher,*
*Sebastian Bach was as musician"*
C. F. Daniel Schubart, 1784–85

Some two months after his fifty-second birthday, Johann Sebastian Bach opened a copy of a new, fashionable, and deliberately progressive music periodical and found himself the subject of a fierce attack. "Mr.——," he read, "is the most eminent of the music makers *(Musicanten)* in ——." So began an unsigned, controversial piece of music journalism (in the form of a letter) published in 1737. Bach, like any informed reader of the time, could easily fill in the blanks—"Bach" and "Leipzig"—especially after reading what followed. And while the sentence hardly strikes us today as inflammatory, the article's author and editor of the periodical, a twenty-nine-year-old upstart named Johann Adolph Scheibe, knew that the terms "eminent" and "music maker" contradicted one another. Indeed, combining them so ambivalently was a deliberate effort at damning with faint praise. A little further into the fictitious letter, and in a similarly oblique, even ironically devout, manner, Scheibe refers to "this great man" who "would be the admiration of whole nations," but only "if he had more amenity, if he did not take away the natural element in his pieces by giving them a turgid and confused style, and if he did not darken their beauty by an excess of art."[1]

Of the numerous critical points in this vitriolic yet ultimately inconsequential piece of early music criticism, what offended Bach the most was being referred to as a *Musicant*—a mere practitioner. But Bach also had his defenders. In an elaborate response published the following year,[2] Johann Abraham Birnbaum, lecturer in rhetoric at Leipzig University, immediately took issue with the utterly inappropriate label *Musicant* as applied to Bach (who was apparently enraged by Scheibe's assault):

The man in question is the *Royal Polish and Electoral Saxon Court Composer and Capellmeister, Mr. Johann Sebastian Bach* in Leipzig. . . . The Hon. Court Composer is called the most eminent of the *Musicanten* in Leipzig. This expression smacks too strongly of the mean and low, and does not fit the titles "extraordinary artist," "great man," "the admiration of whole nations," which are applied to the Hon. Court Composer in what follows. The term *Musicanten* is generally used for those whose principal achievement is a form of mere musical practice. They are employed for the purpose . . . of bringing pieces written by others into sound by means of musical instruments. As a matter of fact, not even all the men of this sort, but only the humblest and meanest of them, usually bear this name, so there is hardly any difference between *Musicanten* and beer fiddlers. If one of those musical practitioners is an extraordinary artist on an instrument, he is called not a *Musicant* but a virtuoso. And least of all does this disdainful name apply to great composers and those who have to conduct choruses. Now, let the reasonable reader himself decide whether the praise that is due the Hon. Court Composer can be fully expressed by calling him the most eminent of the *Musicanten*. This is in my opinion the same as wishing to pay a special tribute to a thoroughly learned man by calling him the best member of the last class of schoolboys. The Hon. Court Composer is a great composer, a master of music, a virtuoso on the organ and the clavier without an equal, but in no sense a *Musicant*.[3]

The controversy caught the fancy of Johann Mattheson of Hamburg, the most productive and influential writer then on the German musical scene, who weighs in on the disputed terminology in a 1740 collection of musical biographies: he readily admits that the term *Musicant,* "so much contested and resisted by some people," is usually applied to singers and instrumentalists, but he attributes its low regard to arrogance, for "some despise the beautiful name of cantor and organist," and "some even don't want to be called capellmeister, but only chamber or court compositeur."[4] Mattheson was deliberately tweaking Bach—who had by then acquired all of these titles—perhaps to express his frustration over Bach's persistent refusal to submit any autobiographical material for his long-planned biographical anthology, though he had been requested to do so for more than twenty years.[5] In fact, for private purposes Bach had actually put down a bare outline of his professional career for a family Genealogy he was compiling around 1735:

No. 24. Joh. Sebastian Bach, youngest son of Joh. Ambrosius Bach, was born in Eisenach in the year 1685 on March 21. Became
    (1) Court Musician, in Weimar, to Duke Johann Ernst, Anno 1703;
    (2) Organist at the New Church in Arnstadt, 1704 [actually 1703];
    (3) Organist at the Church of St. Blasius in Mühlhausen, Anno 1707;
    (4) Chamber and Court Organist in Weimar, Anno 1708;
    (5) Concertmaster as well, at the same Court, Anno 1714;
    (6) Capellmeister and Director of the Chamber Music at the Court of the Serene Prince of Anhalt Cöthen, Anno 1717;
    (7) Was called hence, Anno 1723, to become Music Director and Cantor at the St.

Thomas School, in Leipzig; where, in accordance with God's Holy Will, he still lives and at the same time holds the honorary position of Capellmeister of Weissenfels and Cöthen.[6]

At no time had Bach shown any interest in writing a more elaborate autobiographical statement, and he hardly needed to remind himself that his life was not exactly filled with exciting events. (For a chronology of Bach's life, see Appendix 1.) Still, his plan for a concise Genealogy would have made him ponder what it meant to have been born into a tradition that claimed not only a past but also, as he could see in his own children, a future. "Love and aptitude for music" (in the words of the Obituary),[7] the single dominating force in the life of several generations of Bachs, had pointed the way for him as well, from his first modest job as "court musician" to positions ranging from organist to capellmeister and cantor. Curiously, Bach refrained from calling himself a composer (while specifically applying the term to his uncles) but assumed, with good reason, that titles such as "capellmeister" and "music director" themselves implied the function of composer. Moreover, he knew that the most prestigious title, "Electoral Saxon and Royal Polish Court *Compositeur,*" was yet to come, though not for three long years after he had applied for it.[8] That title, which would unambiguously refer to his compositional activities, was finally awarded by the Dresden court in 1736, just after he had finished compiling the Genealogy (Carl Philipp Emanuel Bach later emended his father's entry accordingly). Birnbaum, in his published defense, replaces the image of Bach the music maker with that of Bach the virtuoso, and—by consistently referring to his subject as "the Hon. Court Composer"—emphasizes the importance of Bach the composer.

In amassing material for the Genealogy, Bach gathered manuscript scores of works by those older family members who were composers, because he realized that only their music, not their performing activities, would document and preserve the clan's musical legacy. (The collection, known as the Old-Bach Archive, would later be preserved by his son Carl Philipp Emanuel.) In this way, he could confirm his admiration for his father's cousin Johann Christoph Bach, whom he regarded as a "profound composer," and his father-in-law Johann Michael Bach, an "able composer";[9] he could perform their music and then reflect on his own contributions to musical composition—contributions of a nature, quality, and extent that were unprecedented in the family.

Not coincidentally, Bach found himself at work in 1733 on a special project that would occupy him for some time to come. On July 27 of that year, he dedicated to the electoral court in Dresden the *Missa* in B minor—the Kyrie and Gloria of what would become the *B-minor Mass:* "To your Royal

Highness I submit in deepest devotion the present small work of that science which I have attained in *musique*."[10] Stripping the phrase of the conventional formalities and courtly protocol, the statement reveals what this work was to represent: his achievements in the science of music. He was not a *Musicant* but someone who held the directorship of music in Leipzig's two principal churches; he considered himself a musical scholar producing works of musical science.

Characterizing Bach's compositional art in any general way proves an elusive task, but a strikingly passionate attempt was made by his son Carl Philipp Emanuel and Bach's student Johann Friedrich Agricola in their Obituary of "The World-Famous Organist, Mr. Johann Sebastian Bach": "If ever a composer showed polyphony in its greatest strength, it was certainly our late lamented Bach. If ever a musician employed the most hidden secrets of harmony with the most skilled artistry, it was certainly our Bach. No one ever showed so many ingenious and unusual ideas as he in elaborate pieces such as ordinarily seem dry exercises in craftsmanship."[11]

More often than not, superlatives such as these provoke skepticism, but this statement—though penned under the immediate burden of loss and the pressure of time—presents a remarkably apt summation of Bach's most important musical accomplishments. It emphasizes that his music truly demonstrates the power of polyphony, an intrinsic harmonic structure, and an imaginative and original approach in the design of complex works. No specific compositions are mentioned, such particulars being deemed unnecessary by the Obituary authors. And indeed, any of the works, whether the *B-minor Mass* or the *St. Matthew Passion, The Well-Tempered Clavier* or the *Orgel-Büchlein*, the *Brandenburg Concertos* or the sonatas and partitas for unaccompanied violin, corroborate and deepen the judgment rendered above.

In the closing section of the Obituary, Carl Philipp Emanuel Bach and Agricola enumerate further talents of Bach's: his ability to recognize without an instant's hesitation the intricate developmental potential of a musical subject, his inclination toward a serious style without rejecting the comic, his facility in reading large scores, his fine musical ear, and his skill in conducting. The confident declaration that "Bach was the greatest organist and clavier player that we have ever had" is followed by observations regarding his art of improvisation and his use of "strange, new, expressive, and beautiful ideas," his "most perfect accuracy in performance," his invention of a new fingering system, his intimate knowledge of organ construction, his facility in tuning the harpsichord, and the fact that "he knew of no tonalities that, because of impure intonation, one must avoid," a noteworthy comment in those days when few keyboard performers dared to wander beyond keys with three sharps or flats.

The Obituary also associates Bach's music with "polyphony in its greatest strength," with employing "the most hidden secrets of harmony with the most skilled artistry," and with "ingenious and unusual ideas" pervading "elaborate pieces." This extremely flattering language must be understood against the background of criticism to which Bach was subjected, most directly in Scheibe's infamous attack: that he lacked "amenity," that his style was "turgid and confused" rather than natural, and that he darkened the beauty of his works by applying "an excess of art."

Birnbaum, in his function as Bach's mouthpiece articulating the composer's views on art and nature, elegantly counters Scheibe's broadside:

The essential aims of true art are to imitate nature, and, where necessary, to aid it. If art imitates nature, then indisputably the natural element must everywhere shine through in works of art. Accordingly it is impossible that art should take away the natural element from those things in which it imitates nature—including music. If art aids nature, then its aim is to preserve it, and to improve its condition; certainly not to destroy it. Many things are delivered to us by nature in the most misshapen states, which, however, acquire the most beautiful appearance when they have been formed by art. Thus art lends nature a beauty it lacks, and increases the beauty it possesses. Now, the greater the art is—that is, the more industriously and painstakingly it works at the improvement of nature—the more brilliantly shines the beauty thus brought into being. Accordingly it is impossible that the greatest art should darken the beauty of a thing.[12]

Birnbaum's argument draws in part on *Gradus ad Parnassum* (Steps to Parnassus), a 1725 counterpoint treatise whose author, Johann Joseph Fux, refers to "art which imitates and perfects nature, but never destroys it."[13] Bach owned a copy of this important Latin treatise[14] and may well have directed Birnbaum to emphasize the ancient Aristotelian principle "art imitates nature," a dictum that lay at the heart of what Bach considered musical science. For Bach, art lay between the reality of the world—nature—and God, who ordered this reality.[15] Indeed, Leipzig philosophers subscribed to that relationship, especially when defining beauty and nature. "What is art? An imitation of nature," writes Bach's student Lorenz Christoph Mizler in the same year and place as Birnbaum's defense of Bach.[16] It follows, then, that musical structure—*harmonia,* in the terminology of Bach's time—ultimately refers to the order of nature and to its divine cause. Or, put more lyrically, "Music is a mixed mathematical science that concerns the origins, attributes, and distinctions of sound, out of which a cultivated and lovely melody and harmony are made, so that God is honored and praised but mankind is moved to devotion, virtue, joy, and sorrow."[17]

Strict rules and regulations, however they might be modified by rhetorical devices or by the new doctrine of affects, had largely kept musical composition in check, although Scheibe and other advocates of progressive concepts were charting a course toward a new aesthetic of art that would hold beauty and sensation as paramount. But the environment in which Bach worked and lived was not conducive to such ideas, nor did he seem to take much interest in them. On the other hand, he was surely influenced by the climate of inquiry and search for truth that now defined philosophy as "a science of all things that teaches us how and why they are or can be."[18] No less affected by "the dream of intellectual unity"[19] than the leading thinkers of his generation, Bach pursued his own empirical line of inquiry by exploring "the most hidden secrets of harmony with the most skilled artistry": by expanding—in scope, scale, and detail—the known limits of musical performance and composition.

Bach's intricate musical art figured in a public literary dispute between Agricola and Filippo Finazzi, an opera singer in Hamburg, that recalls the Scheibe-Birnbaum controversy. In August 1750, just days after Bach's death, Agricola wrote:

He [Finazzi] denies his [Bach's] music the effect of pleasure for the listener who would not savor such difficult harmony. Yet, assuming the harmonies [that is, musical structures] of this great man were so complex that they would not always achieve the intended result, they nevertheless serve for the connoisseur's genuine delight. Not all learned people are able to understand a Newton, but those who have progressed far enough in profound science so they can understand him will find the greater gratification and real benefit in reading his work.[20]

Here, for the first time, a parallel is drawn between Bach and Isaac Newton—not by constructing analogies between Bach's music and Newtonian science, but by explaining that Bach's music is best appreciated by real connoisseurs, just as Newton's writings are best understood by readers with a deep knowledge of science. Newton, a generation older than Bach, had earned a legendary reputation across Europe by the early eighteenth century, and by 1750 he represented the undisputed paradigm of the scientist as genius.[21] "The immortal Newton,"[22] as Mizler called him, was especially revered in Leipzig, whose university had in Bach's time become the center of Newtonianism in Germany.[23]

Isaac Newton, it is still fair to say today, played the most critical role in the foundation of modern science. In addition to his most spectacular accomplishments—inventing calculus, discovering the laws of motion and the principles of optics, and explaining the concept of universal gravitation—his fundamental contributions covered an astounding range of fields. He studied space, time, heat, and the chemistry and theory of matter; he formulated the basic concepts of mass and dynamics; he invented the gravitational theory of tides; and he helped design such scientific instruments as the reflecting telescope.[24] Toward the end of his career, he turned to alchemy, history, chronology, biblical exegesis, and theological issues. Newton's theoretical and experimental works exemplified a new kind of scientific method, characterized by a kind of "contrapuntal alternation between mathematical constructs and comparisons with the real world" (in the words of a modern scholar).[25] And a traditional element, typical of a pre-Enlightenment outlook, was Newton's firm belief that his discoveries "pointed to the operations of God." Unlike later science, which focused solely on understanding nature, the Newtonian search for truth always encompassed both natural and divine principles. Trying to grasp the relationship between God and nature led Newton to explore the boundaries between them, where he ultimately saw the fusion of natural and divine principles.[26]

Newton's groundbreaking work, highly respected by his contemporaries,[27] represents the pinnacle of the seventeenth-century Scientific Revolution. Bach, on the other hand, created no revolution, but then, the stakes were completely different. In the search for scientific truth, the principle of universal gravity, for example, would have been discovered eventually, if not by Newton then by someone else. By contrast, the search for "artistic truth" cannot be guided by classical logic leading to a true or false result; the element of individuality plays too decisive a role in all artistic endeavors. Yet Bach's music—his search for truth—was affected more, both subconsciously and consciously, than that of any other contemporary musician by the spreading culture of Newtonianism and by the spirit of discovery that followed the Scientific Revolution, which no bright and keen intellect could escape. And under the umbrella of seventeenth-century Lutheran theology, Bach's musical discoveries—like Newton's scientific advances, which Bach almost certainly did not know—took him to areas of the creative mind undreamed of before and ultimately pointed to the operations of God.

If the natural philosophy of Bach's time defined itself as "a science of all things that teaches us how and why they are or can be," Bach's musical philosophy might well be understood analogously: as the science of musical phenomena that teaches us how and why they are or can be, and also how they relate to nature—God's creation and Newton's world system.[28] The sheer scope and breadth of Newton's intellectual endeavors, too, find their analogy in the enormous and unparalleled range of interests and enterprises that characterize Bach: the complete, the learned, the perfect musician.

For Bach, schooled in seventeenth-century thought, the concept that music formed a branch of the liberal arts *quadrivium* was still as valid as it had been for Johannes Kepler, who promoted the view that music mirrored the harmony of the universe.[29] Music, then, with its traditional mathematical underpinning, provided an especially rich field of operation for a composer who was increasingly infected with scientific curiosity, totally uninterested in "dry exercises in [musical] craftsmanship," but thoroughly committed to advancing "true music," which Bach defined as music that pursued as its "ultimate end or final goal . . . the honor of God and the recreation of the soul."[30]

A list of Bach's major achievements in musical science testifies to his emphatic and consistent application of the principle of counterpoint, that is, the dynamic discourse of melodically and rhythmically distinct voices resulting in his unique compositional style. Such a list would include the following areas of compositional art, which reflect a process of musical research that uncovers "the most hidden secrets of polyphony," the application of "ingenious and unusual ideas," and the employment of "the most skilled artistry" (the works cited below are merely representative):

- fugue and canon (*The Art of Fugue*);
- major-minor tonality (*The Well-Tempered Clavier*);
- harmonic expansion (the *Chromatic Fantasy and Fugue*);
- extended polyphony (the unaccompanied violin, cello, and flute pieces);
- instrumentation (the *Brandenburg Concertos*);
- instrumental and vocal genres (Bach employed virtually all contemporary models and types—from aria, *cantate burlesque,* and canzona to oratorio, scherzo, and sinfonia);
- small-scale form (the *Orgel-Büchlein*) and large-scale form (the *St. Matthew Passion*);
- style and compositional technique, from retrospective to modern (the *B-minor Mass*);
- musical affect and meaning (the church cantatas).

Further essential features of Bach's musicianship comprise his keyboard virtuosity and his development of new manual and pedal techniques, taking into account the ergonomics of posture that carried over to other instrumental and vocal performance; his intense involvement in musical instrument technology, especially in organ building and design (which required considerable experience in mathematics, physics, acoustics, architecture, and mechanical engineering), organ and clavier serving as indispensable pieces of equipment in Bach's experimental musical laboratory; and his distinctive contributions to understanding the relationships between music, language, rhetoric, poetics, and theology. Finally, of especial importance was Bach's remarkable ability to synthesize the various components of his musical science in light of his strong sense for unified structures.

Although Bach realized the significance of theoretical discourse and must have encouraged his students to contribute to it, he himself did not.[31] He focused instead on "practical elaborations" for the instruction and delight of "those who have a concept of what is possible in art and who desire original thought and its special, unusual elaboration"—as Carl Philipp Emanuel Bach wrote after his father's death.[32] Bach was one of the most active, dedicated, and prolific teachers the world has seen. As a result, many students of his worked to disseminate his music and teachings through their own writings. In fact, soon after 1750, German music theory reoriented itself almost solely because of the prevailing influence of the "Bach School," and European music theory followed half a century later. If Bach ever came close to creating a "revolution," it was in his teaching of composition by fully integrating the principles of thorough bass, harmony, and counterpoint, elements that had previously been treated separately. This method was illustrated by two works that were circulated widely from the moment of Bach's death, first in manuscript and later in printed form: *The Well-Tempered Clavier,* which defined the principles of free and strict composition, and the collection of 370-plus four-part chorales that charted the course for tonal harmony.[33]

The Scheibe-Birnbaum controversy had turned out to be a tempest in a teapot. The impact of Bach's music and teachings was such that when the focus of the music world had clearly shifted to the Vienna of Haydn and Mozart, the musician and critic Christian Friedrich Daniel Schubart could already refer to Bach as "a genius of the highest order" and, as Agricola had done years earlier, rank him on a par with the great scientist-genius: "What Newton was as a philosopher, Bach was as a musician." In other words, as Newton brought about fundamental changes and established new principles in the world of science, Bach did the same in the world of music, both in composition and in performance.

At the turn of the nineteenth century, Schubart's appraisal was not only echoed but reinforced in the leading music periodical of the day, to which Beethoven and others subscribed: "The name of Johann Sebastian Bach radiates supremely and sublimely above those of all German composers in the first half of the past century. He embraced with Newton's spirit everything that has hitherto been thought about harmony [composition] and that has been presented as examples thereof, and he penetrated its depths so completely and felicitously that he must be justly regarded as the lawmaker of genuine harmony, which is valid up to the present day."[34]

By 1800, the continuing, indeed permanent relevance of the new foundations that Bach the lawmaker of genuine composition had laid was clearly recognized; these provided the basis for the Romantic concept of "pure music," defined as "a beautiful play with tones . . . governed by an aesthetic idea."[35] In 1799, the same periodical had published a diagram in the form of a "sun of composers." There, at the center, appears the name of Johann Sebastian Bach, surrounded in various layers by the names of other composers, the first layer comprising George Frideric Handel, Carl Heinrich Graun, and Franz Joseph

Haydn (see illustration). And Haydn, whose reputation by that time as Europe's premier composer was beyond question, is said to have been "not unfavorably impressed by it, nor minded the proximity to Handel and Graun, nor considered it at all wrong that Joh. Seb. Bach was the center of the sun and hence the man from whom all true musical wisdom proceeded."[36]

"Sun of Composers," designed by Augustus Frederick Christopher Kollmann, in an engraving in *Allgemeine musikalische Zeitung,* vol. 1, 1799.

Who is this "man from whom all true musical wisdom proceeded"? In the absence of a true classical model such as we have in literature, art, and architecture going back to antiquity, Bach's musical science (its beauty and expression included) offers a stable frame of reference even today that neither a Palestrina nor a Monteverdi, a Handel, a Beethoven, nor any other composer can provide. His is the kind of musical wisdom that is experienced alike by the keyboard beginner playing the two-part *Inventions* and the virtuoso tackling the unaccompanied cello suites, by the beginning harmony student and the mature composer, by the inexperienced listener and the sophisticated concertgoer. Throughout his life, Bach constantly strove to perfect himself in his quest for true musical wisdom. According to his Obituary, he, along with all members of the Bach family, was deemed "to have received a love and aptitude for music as a gift of nature."[37] But he himself reportedly said that "what I have achieved by industry and practice, anyone else with tolerable natural gift and ability can also achieve."[38] This statement would place him, once again, in the vicinity of a Newton: in *A Dissertation upon Genius* of 1755, William Sharpe attempts to show that "the several instances of distinction, and degrees of superiority in human genius are not, fundamentally, the result of nature, but the effect of acquisition."[39] When and how Johann Sebastian Bach acquired what, cannot be easily determined. At any rate, because Bach's timeless and global impact is not revealed in the narrow confines of his life story, all the more does understanding the musical science that underlies his works allow us some insight into his intellectual biography.

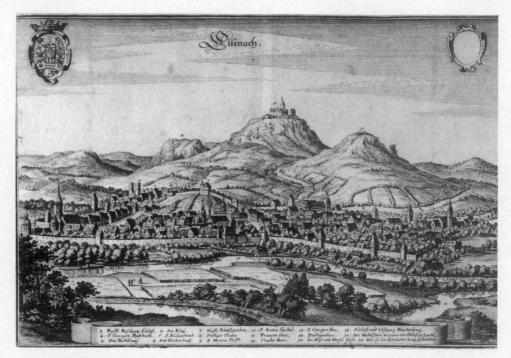

View of Eisenach in an engraving from Matthäus Merian's *Topographia* (1650).

# 1

## Springs of Musical Talent and Lifelong Influences

### EISENACH, 1685–1695

AMBROSIUS BACH AND HIS FAMILY

By an auspicious coincidence, Sebastian Nagel, town piper of Gotha and friend of Johann Ambrosius Bach, happened to be in Eisenach on the third weekend in March 1685. Whatever brought him to the town at this time, he most likely joined his fellow town piper Bach for a performance, probably one in need of reinforcement by outside musicians. They were used to helping each other out—it made sense for the musicians from the two towns, eighteen miles apart and seats of neighboring ducal courts, to team up for special occasions. Nagel and Bach, each in his capacities as town piper, director of town music, and member of the ducal capelle, the court's performing ensemble, were in charge of such events.

Thus it was that on the day following Oculi Sunday, four weeks before Easter, Sebastian Nagel and his colleague Ambrosius Bach, together with the ducal forester Johann Georg Koch, arrayed themselves around the ancient baptismal font inside St. George's, Eisenach's main church. Magister Johann Christoph Zerbst functioned as the officiating minister at the baptism of the child born to Ambrosius and Maria Elisabeth Bach on the previous Saturday, March 21. Nagel was given the honor of holding the baby over the baptismal font because he was the one of the two godfathers from whom the boy was to receive his middle name—Sebastian.[1]

The short ceremony took place on a historic site at the foot of the Wartburg, the medieval hilltop castle overlooking Eisenach. The Wartburg had formed the setting in 1207 for the famous Tourney of Song, a historic highpoint of German minstrelsy, and three centuries later provided refuge to Martin Luther while he translated the Greek New Testament into German. The venerable St. George's Church, an ancient structure whose origins date back to 1182, had witnessed the wedding in 1221 of Landgrave Louis IV of Thuringia and Elizabeth, daughter of Hungarian King Andrew II (later canonized as Saint Elizabeth, she led a simple life and personally tended the sick and the poor). The church had been substantially rebuilt in 1515, and Luther had preached there in the spring of 1521 on his way both to and from the Diet in Worms. No stranger to Eisenach, the city of his mother's birth, Luther spent the years 1498 to 1501 at the Eisenach Latin school, the same school that the child being baptized was later to attend.

Perhaps the older among the little boy's siblings observed the short christening ceremony. His mother, however, was excluded, for according to the strict customs prescribed by the Hebrew Bible and upheld by Lutherans of the time, she was not permitted to enter church until she had undergone a religious purification rite six weeks after childbirth. She may have participated in choosing the child's godfathers and thereby also in selecting his name. But both parents must have known that no other member of the extended Thuringian family of musicians bore the name Sebastian. Had they been interested in a name more readily found among family members, Johann Georg Koch, the ducal forester, could have served in Nagel's place: after all, "Georg" was the name of Ambrosius's elder brother, cantor in Schweinfurt on the Main. Nevertheless, Ambrosius—perhaps proud of the singularity within the family of his own name—not only favored the unique "Sebastian," he also chose a fellow musician as name-lending godfather.

It may not be mere coincidence that a generation later Johann Sebastian and Maria Barbara Bach selected similarly uncommon names for their two elder sons, Wilhelm Friedemann and Carl Philipp Emanuel. The name Johann Sebastian, however, would recur in the family only twice. In 1713, Ambrosius Bach's eldest son, Johann Christoph, named one of his children after his then already famous brother in Weimar, who acted as godfather at the baptism; but the baby died before he was two months old.[2] Then in 1748, Carl Philipp Emanuel Bach named his lastborn after his father, who at the time felt unfit to travel from Leipzig to Berlin for the baptism. Johann Sebastian Bach, Jr., not a musician but a gifted draftsman and painter of landscapes whose artistry was greatly admired by his contemporaries, died in 1778 in Rome at the age of twenty-nine.[3] Thus, without any action on his part, the Eisenach Johann Sebastian acquired an unmistakable and unambiguous name identification.

If anything can be said for certain about what the parents of the first Johann Sebastian in the Bach family expected of their son, it is that he would become a musician. In the Thuringian towns of the region stretching from Erfurt to Eisenach, the family name Bach had become nearly synonymous with "musician." Indeed, when a vacancy occurred in 1693 at the Arnstadt court capelle,

the count urgently called for "a Bach."[4] Although Johann Sebastian's extraordinarily individual musical personality and his future singular stature could
have been neither expected nor predicted, the fear expressed later by his step-
mother that the springs of musical talent in the family might run dry was un-
warranted. It was simply assumed that the background, working conditions,
and living circumstances of a family of professional musicians would exert an
inescapable and deep influence on all of its newborn members.

Before coming to Eisenach in 1671 as director of town music, Johann Ambrosius Bach had been town piper in Arnstadt and then, from April 1667, a
violinist in the town music company (an ensemble of professional musicians
employed by the town council) of his native Erfurt. With its eighteen thousand inhabitants, Erfurt was by far Thuringia's largest city and the region's
historical, cultural, educational, and commercial center. Politically part of
the electoral archbishopric of Mainz, Erfurt also represented a bi-confessional
entity (about 20 percent Roman Catholic) within the traditional Lutheran
heartland. (For a map showing places of Bach's activities, see Appendix 2.)

In the sixteenth century, the ancient region of Thuringia, ruled by the
Ernestine branch of the Saxon house of Wettin, split into several duchies (Saxe-

Johann Ambrosius Bach in a painting, probably by Johann David Herlicius
(c. 1685), showing Bach as a well-to-do citizen and home owner, dressed in a
fashionable Japanese kimono (see also the portrait of J. A. Reinken, p. 65).

Altenburg, Saxe-Eisenach, Saxe-Gotha, etc.), while the Albertine (electoral) section of Saxony with its capital Dresden remained intact as a political-geographical unit. Situated within the Ernestine duchies—in addition to the enclave of Erfurt and the free imperial city of Mühlhausen, two metropolitan areas—were several independent principalities ruled primarily by the counts of Schwarzburg (Arnstadt, Rudolstadt, and Sondershausen), Hohenlohe-Gleichen (Ohrdruf), and Reuss (Gera, Greiz). One of the most densely populated areas in Europe, dotted with countless small towns in a politically fractured landscape, Thuringia developed into an economically and culturally vigorous region soon after the catastrophic Thirty Years' War ended in 1648. Some of the most important intersections of east-west and north-south continental trade routes made the area particularly susceptible to foreign influences—in art and architecture, most notably from Italian and French traditions. Here, as almost nowhere else to such an extent, the manifold European trends met and merged, generating a unique climate that also paved the way for the early eighteenth-century concept of a mixed style in music.

Ambrosius was born in Erfurt on February 22, 1645, son of Christoph Bach (no. 5 in Table 1.1) and Maria Magdalena, née Grabler. Christoph Bach served from 1642 to 1654 as town musician in Erfurt and thereafter as town and court musician in Arnstadt, eleven miles away. Ambrosius and his twin brother, Christoph *(12)*, received their musical training in Arnstadt, first with their father and after his death in 1661 with their father's younger brother Heinrich *(6)*. After spending the customary five years as apprentice and two years as journeyman in Arnstadt, Ambrosius was appointed to a post in the Erfurt town music company vacated by his cousin Johann Christian *(7)*, who in 1667 was promoted to the band's directorship. In Erfurt, Ambrosius was also given the opportunity to work with another member of the town music company, his father's older brother Johann *(4)*, organist at the Prediger Church and the first distinguished musician and composer in the family. This made Ambrosius the only one among nine grandsons of Hans Bach *(2)* to learn from and work with all three sons of the family's first professional musician.

On April 8, 1668, a year after joining the Erfurt town music company, Ambrosius Bach married Maria Elisabeth Lämmerhirt, the twenty-four-year-old daughter of the late Valentin Lämmerhirt, an affluent furrier and a longtime and influential town council member in Erfurt. Elisabeth's much older stepsister Hedwig had already provided a family link: in 1638, she had married Johann Bach *(4)* and borne three musical sons, Christian *(7)*, Aegidius *(8)*, and Nicolaus *(9)*. A generation later, Johann Sebastian Bach's older sister Marie Salome would marry the Erfurt master furrier and business partner of the Lämmerhirts, Johann Andreas Wiegand, thereby affirming relations between the

Bach family and the Erfurt bourgeoisie—connections that secured a Bach dominance in the Erfurt musical scene for nearly a century.[5] The stage set by the Johann Bach / Valentin Lämmerhirt connection with the town council led to a complete reorganization of the Erfurt town music company in the 1660s: Johann Bach not only employed all three of his own sons, he also arranged for the appointments of his brother's twins, Christoph and Ambrosius. Christoph came first in 1666, and Ambrosius followed a few months later, receiving his appointment on April 12, 1667, just one day after his cousin Johann Christian (7) became director of the town music company.

Connections played a role in Ambrosius Bach's next appointment as well. The town piper of Eisenach, Christoph Schmidt, died in 1670, creating a vacancy there. His daughter Margaretha was married to Johann Christian Bach (7) of Erfurt, Ambrosius's cousin, who had apprenticed with Schmidt in Eise-

TABLE 1.1. The "Wechmar Bach" Pedigree

2.[a] Johannes [Hans] Bach (d. 1626)
Town musician
Gotha, Wechmar

| 4. Johann (1604–1673) | 5. Christoph (1613–1661) | 6. Heinrich (1615–1692) |
|---|---|---|
| Town musician, organist, composer Suhl, Schweinfurt, Erfurt | Town musician Weimar, Erfurt, Arnstadt | Town musician, organist, composer Schweinfurt, Erfurt, Arnstadt |
| 7. Johann Christian (1640–1682) Town musician (dir.) Erfurt, Eisenach, Erfurt | 10. Georg Christoph (1642–1697) Cantor, composer Themar, Schweinfurt | 13. Johann Christoph (1642–1703) Organist, court musician, composer; Arnstadt, Eisenach |
| 8. Johann Aegidius (1645–1716) Town musician (dir.), organist; Erfurt | 11. Johann Ambrosius (1645–1695) Town musician (dir.), court musician; Erfurt, Eisenach | 14. Johann Michael (1648–1694) Organist, composer Arnstadt, Gehren |
| 9. Johann Nicolaus (1653–1682) Town musician Erfurt | 12. Johann Christoph (1645–1693) Town and court musician Erfurt, Arnstadt | 15. Johann Günther (1653–1683) Organist, instrument maker Arnstadt |

[a]Refers to the numbering system in J. S. Bach's Genealogy (NBR, no. 303).

nach. Moreover, Christian Bach's brother Johann Aegidius *(8)* was married to
another Schmidt daughter. On top of that, another of Ambrosius's cousins, Johann Christoph *(13),* had served since 1665 as town organist and later also as
a member of the court capelle in Eisenach. In short, the connections could
hardly have been better, and after a pro forma audition in Eisenach on October 12, 1671, Ambrosius Bach was hired on the spot. An honorarium and expenses, as well as two days' meals and beer, were provided "for the new town
piper and the musicians he had with him."[6] Ambrosius had auditioned with
four consorts, and it seems that he brought along to his new job four assistants—three apprentices and one journeyman was a typical complement. His
appointment to the directorship of the Eisenach town music company attests
to the talents of the twenty-six-year-old musician, as does his initial salary:
whereas his predecessor Schmidt had for decades been paid a salary of 27
florins 7 groschen 8 pfennigs, and a housing supplement of 8 florins, Ambrosius's starting salary jumped to 40 florins 4 groschen 8 pfennigs, and a
housing supplement of 10 florins. (For a table of money and living costs in
Bach's time, see Appendix 3.) He also earned a considerable supplementary income—more than twice his salary—from various sources, including the court
capelle.

From the very beginning, Ambrosius Bach's musical services to the town
and the court were highly appreciated, as they continued to be throughout
his tenure. In fact, no Eisenach musician in the entire seventeenth century received as much praise as Ambrosius did. References to his extraordinary kind
of music making appear early on. One document, which exempts him from
the local brewery tax, not only points to his Christian virtues and moral conduct but praises "his particular professional qualifications, in that he can
come up with vocal and instrumental music for worship service and for honorable assemblies with persons of higher and lower ranks in such a way that
we cannot remember having ever experienced anything like it in this place."[7]
Similarly, a town chronicler's report displays unparalleled enthusiasm: "In
1672 at Easter the new town piper made music with organ, violins, voices,
trumpets and military drums, as had never before been done by any cantor
or town musician as long as Eisenach stood."[8] The event referred to here, a
festive Easter service at St. George's, actually marked the auspicious beginning of a new era in Eisenach's history. That spring, Duke Johann Georg I of
Saxe-Eisenach moved his residence permanently from Marksuhl in the countryside to Eisenach, reestablishing the old town as the capital of an independent principality.

In October 1671, Ambrosius and Elisabeth Bach moved from Erfurt (where
they had an apartment in Johann Bach's house, "The Silver Pocket," at Junker-

sand 1) to Eisenach with their four-month-old son, Johann Christoph. He was their second child; Johann Rudolf, the firstborn, had died before he was half a year old. Six children were born later in Eisenach: Johann Balthasar, Johannes Jonas, Maria Salome, Johanna Juditha, Johann Jacob, and Johann Sebastian (see Table 1.2).[9] Since Johannes Jonas died at the age of ten in 1685—just about two months after Johann Sebastian's birth—and Johanna Juditha one year later at age six, Sebastian grew up with four siblings. But he rarely saw the oldest of them, Christoph, who left Eisenach in 1686 when he was fifteen in order to study with Johann Pachelbel in Erfurt. Moreover, Balthasar, who in 1688 became an apprentice to his father, died at the age of eighteen. When the six-year-old Sebastian attended his brother's burial in 1691, it was his first conscious encounter with a death within his close circle, a situation he would eventually be exposed to much sooner, more often, and more seriously than many. In fact, from age six, Sebastian lived with his parents, one sister, Salome, and one brother, Jacob, in a family of sadly diminished and still diminishing size. He would survive all of his siblings by a considerable margin: his oldest brother died in 1721 as organist and schoolteacher in Ohrdruf, his brother Jacob a year later as court musician in Stockholm, and his sister Salome Wiegand in 1728 in Erfurt.

In the absence of public social and welfare programs, family and self-reliance played a major role in managing all kinds of hardships, and through several generations the extended Bach family was exemplary in this respect. When Ambrosius moved from Erfurt to Eisenach, he took along his youngest sister, Dorothea Maria, then nineteen and in need of intensive care because she was seriously handicapped, both physically and mentally.[10] The family was also joined by Eva Barbara Lämmerhirt, Elisabeth Bach's widowed mother, who left her Erfurt home perhaps in order to provide a helping hand to her daughter and her growing family, but perhaps also because she needed help herself. She died

## TABLE 1.2. Maria Elisabeth and Johann Ambrosius Bach's Children

| | |
|---|---|
| 1. Johann Rudolf | baptized Erfurt, January 19, 1670; died Erfurt, July 17, 1670 (age 6 months) |
| 2. Johann Christoph | bapt. Erfurt, June 18, 1671; d. Ohrdruf, February 22, 1721 (age 49) |
| 3. Johann Balthasar | bapt. Eisenach, March 6, 1673; d. Eisenach, April 5, 1691 (age 18) |
| 4. Johannes Jonas | bapt. Eisenach, February 2, 1675; d. Eisenach, May 22, 1685 (age 10) |
| 5. Marie Salome | bapt. Eisenach, May 27, 1677; d. Erfurt, December 27, 1727 (age 50) |
| 6. Johanna Juditha | bapt. Eisenach, January 28, 1680; d. Eisenach, May 3, 1686 (age 6) |
| 7. Johann Jacob | bapt. Eisenach, February 11, 1682; d. Stockholm, April 16, 1722 (age 40) |
| 8. Johann Sebastian | born Eisenach, March 21, 1685; d. Leipzig, July 28, 1750 (age 65) |

just one year after the move, in 1673, and Dorothea Maria did not live much longer either; she was buried in 1679. Three years later, two of Ambrosius's cousins, Christian (7) and Nicolaus (9), fell victim to the plague that swept through Erfurt in 1682–83 and diminished the city's population by almost half; their colleague and friend Johann Pachelbel lost his wife and baby son as well. To escape the plague, Christian's son Johann Jacob (b. 1668) moved to Eisenach and became an apprentice and then journeyman to Ambrosius. He remained with his uncle for almost ten years, but died of an unknown cause in 1692—for young Sebastian, the second death at home within a year.[11] From July 1683, Ambrosius and Elisabeth Bach also took care of the orphaned one-year-old Johann Nicolaus, who was born shortly after his father, Nicolaus (9), had died of the plague in July 1682. When the boy's mother died almost exactly a year later, it fell to Elisabeth to provide a home for her stepsister's grandson. Johann Nicolaus later went to school together with his younger cousin Sebastian and left Eisenach for Erfurt only after Elisabeth Bach's death in 1694.[12]

The Eisenach Bachs' house was always full, populated not only with children and relatives, but also with the apprentices. This meant that the house ordinarily had to accommodate three additional people between fifteen and twenty years of age, assuming that the fourth of the town piper's consorts was a journeyman who secured his own accommodation. Clearly, the need for adequate living quarters for the director of the town band cannot be underestimated. At first, Ambrosius rented an apartment in the house of the ducal head forester, Balthasar Schneider, near the Frauenplan (site of today's Ritterstrasse 11). After Ambrosius and his family acquired citizenship in Eisenach in 1674, they purchased a home. (This house, however, in which Sebastian was born, no longer stands.)[13] Situated at the Fleischgasse (the site of today's Lutherstrasse 35) in the center of town, the house was registered in Ambrosius Bach's name from 1675 to 1695. Among his later neighbors on the same street were his cousin Johann Christoph Bach (13) and the cantor Andreas Christian Dedekind. When Ambrosius purchased the house, he probably used funds left by his mother-in-law, Eva Barbara Lämmerhirt. Since the Lämmerhirts ran a successful fur business in Erfurt (from which Johann Sebastian later received a generous inheritance), town councillor Valentin Lämmerhirt's widow had not been left without means; before joining her daughter's household in Eisenach, she had sold her Erfurt house to Johann Bach for 120 florins.[14] In general, there was no serious financial trouble in Ambrosius Bach's household—quite the opposite of the rather desperate economic situation in which, for example, his Eisenach cousin and companion, the town organist Johann Christoph (13), constantly found himself.[15]

In early 1684, Ambrosius was offered the directorship of the town music company in Erfurt, a post that had been vacant since the death of Johann Christian Bach *(7)* in 1682 and that had remained unfilled while the plague was still raging. His native Erfurt, three times the size of Eisenach, made Ambrosius an attractive offer that compared favorably with his present situation. He wrote to the Eisenach town council describing the financial burden of providing for a family with six children and of employing three journeymen and an unspecified number of apprentices, the abatement of additional income resulting from frequent public mourning periods, and the constant quarrels with the "beer fiddlers" (freelance musicians), who were interfering with his business—in short, he explained that conditions in Erfurt would permit a more cost-efficient and pleasant life.[16] Though neither the Eisenach town council nor the ducal court consented to his request for dismissal, they did agree to pay him an indemnity of 1 florin during public mourning periods. Johann Sebastian would have been born in Erfurt had his parents left Eisenach then, but as it was, he grew up in the town below the Wartburg, in an environment that significantly shaped his talents, character, and outlook.

## In the Ambience of Home, Town, Court, School, and Church

Johann Sebastian Bach's baptism in 1685 took place in the immediate vicinity, within a diameter of no more than an eighth of a mile, of the four institutions that formed the foundation of seventeenth-century musical culture in Germany: town, court, school, and church. All four would not only play an essential role in Bach's later career, they also influenced the boy's formative years from the very beginning: the town hall with its music ensemble, the civic organization chiefly responsible for official and public musical events; the ducal castle with its court capelle, the center of aristocratic musical patronage; St. George's Latin School with its *Chorus musicus,* the primary domicile of high-level musical education; and St. George's Church with its organ and choir loft, the principal home of sacred music.[17] Church, castle, and town hall faced the market square in the city's busy center, and the little boy Sebastian must often have gone from one establishment to another, first at his father's side, watching him perform his duties, later fulfilling minor chores (perhaps as assistant stage manager, page turner, or the like), and eventually as a student at the Latin school and as a choirboy. It all began at home, of course, and was brought back there as well—the house of a town piper, though not an institution as such, nevertheless served as a central establishment of professional music making. Sebastian could not have realized that everything he experienced amounted to a concrete preview of his later activities, but he must have understood and probably never questioned that this was, indeed, his world and always would be. Throughout his life, he remained truthful to his Eisenach background and loyal to his Eisenach citizenship, the only one he ever carried. Later, and surely with pride, he often added his place of origin to his name: "Johann Sebastian Bach *Isenacus*" or *"Isenacensis,"* or in the abbreviated form "ISBI."

Eisenach, a town of some six thousand when Bach was born, lay well positioned on the so-called Hohe or Ober-Straße—at the time a major east-west trade and post route in Germany—between Leipzig and Frankfort-on-the-Main or, viewed on a larger scale, between Warsaw and eastern Europe on the one hand and the Rhineland, northern France, and the Netherlands on the other. Like almost everywhere else in central Germany, Eisenach had been hard hit by the Thirty Years' War, and by the time Ambrosius Bach arrived, the town had barely recovered from its turmoils. Hence the year 1672, when the city became the capital of an independent principality, marked an important turning point that basically coincided with the beginning of Ambrosius's tenure of office. The new political status of the town, whose population by 1710 would grow to around nine thousand, had a direct impact on its economy and culture and, by implication, on the musical scene at large, with the latter serving primarily but not exclusively the purposes of the court. For example, the mere fact that the dukes moved their official residence to the city made the principal church of the town the court church, a situation that affected in particular the feast days of the liturgical year. (For the Lutheran Church calendar, see Appendix 4.)

The town piper's house on the Fleischgasse also served as a base for Ambrosius's professional activities. As a result, Sebastian absorbed from the very beginning an atmosphere dominated by music and musicians, involving the entire family and almost all who lived with them. Ambrosius typically employed four assistants, of which two or three were apprentices; they were entitled to room and board in the town piper's house in exchange for services. An apprentice learned to play all types of musical instruments and generally stayed with his master for five to six years, by which time he reached the status of journeyman. After traveling and working with different masters or staying on with the original master and gaining more experience, a journeyman could then apply to fill vacant posts in the town music company. These salaried positions were usually available in two categories, art fiddlers and the higher-ranked town pipers; in Thuringia, the head town piper was usually called *Hausmann,* a traditional term deriving from his original function as the tower guard, who was also responsible for winding the public clocks.

When Sebastian was three years old, his second-oldest brother, fifteen-year-old Balthasar, having reached a certain level of musical proficiency, began to apprentice with his father. Sebastian could thus observe both his father and his big brother at work. The numerous musical activities of family members and apprentices that penetrated domestic life at the town piper's house consisted not merely of teaching, practicing, rehearsing, and performing, but also of collecting and copying music, repairing and maintaining musical instruments, and other endeavors related to an extended music-business establishment. There is no question that in an age when child labor was a mere matter of course, the sons of Ambrosius Bach became involved in their father's activities from early on, whether carrying music or instruments, cleaning brass, or restringing fiddles. They would also have assisted in performances by playing various instruments according to the level of proficiency they had acquired, versatility counting among the most fundamental and useful musical virtues.

Ambrosius's duties as director of the Eisenach town music company included, according to his contract,[18] two primary obligations. The first was performing twice daily, at 10 A.M. and 5 P.M., with a band of five at the town hall. This *Abblasen* (literally "blowing off") of so-called tower pieces, mostly for shawm or sackbut ensembles (usually sonatas, intradas, dances, and chorales), normally took place on the balcony of the town hall and rang out over the entire marketplace. The second duty was performing at worship services in St. George's Church on all Sundays and feast days, before and after the sermon and also at the afternoon Vespers, as directed by the cantor. All additional activities were undertaken for separate fees, resulting in supplementary income that typically exceeded Ambrosius's annual salary by a considerable margin. They included playing at such civic events as town council elections and receptions for out-of-town dignitaries, and at weddings, funerals, and other private occasions.

Eisenach citizens needing musical services were required to hire the members of the town music company. Beer fiddlers could serve only if the town musicians were unavailable or needed reinforcement; in such cases, the guild regulations specified that the town musicians were to collect the regular fee, while the beer fiddlers would receive just a gratuity. These regulations naturally led to constant quarreling over the exclusive, jealously guarded rights of the town musicians; they were often violated as well by townsfolk seeking specially discounted services at weddings, and Ambrosius complained more than once about pointed disagreements and unpleasant relationships with the beer fiddlers.

Shortly after taking up his post in October 1671 as *Hausmann* in Eisenach, Ambrosius became an affiliated member of the ducal court capelle, an ensemble of modest size established under dukes Johann Georg I (r. 1672–86) and

Johann Georg II (r. 1686–98) of Saxe-Eisenach.[19] When in 1672 Johann Georg I moved to Eisenach, the violinist Daniel Eberlin and four trumpeters came along from Marksuhl, the previous ducal residence, and formed the nucleus of a new court capelle; they were joined by the violinist and dance master Jean Parison and the lutenist Louis Parisel. Eberlin, who dedicated to the duke his principal published instrumental opus, a set of trio sonatas,[20] received an official appointment as court capellmeister (leader of the court musicians) and master of the pages in 1685, a position he occupied for seven years. (His future son-in-law, Georg Philipp Telemann, served as court capellmeister from 1708 to 1712.) In addition to the few full-time members, the capelle drew on part-time musicians, who functioned as lackeys and filled court service positions of various kinds. They were also regularly joined by the town musician Ambrosius Bach and his cousin the town organist Christoph Bach *(13),* who both held court appointments. According to his contract, Ambrosius was required "always to perform with his people [the town music company] in the court capelle."[21]

For special events, the court recruited additional musical personnel from neighboring town and court ensembles at Cassel, Gotha, or Arnstadt. In 1690, a band of woodwind players was added as a fashionable musical innovation, providing the capelle with a regular complement of oboes, recorders, bassoons, and drums. Also, for a period of one year beginning in May 1677, the twenty-four-year-old Johann Pachelbel served the Eisenach capelle before he went on to Erfurt as organist of the Predigerkirche, where he succeeded Johann Bach *(4).* Pachelbel's short stay clearly left a mark on Ambrosius Bach's family, suggesting a close, cordial, and lasting friendship. In 1680, Pachelbel became godfather to Ambrosius's daughter Johanna Juditha (though he was unable to travel from Erfurt for the baptism) and in 1686 teacher and mentor of Ambrosius's son Johann Christoph, at whose Ohrdruf wedding in 1694 Pachelbel performed along with his friends among the extended Bach family (see Chapter 2).

In addition to the town hall and castle, the third building located on Eisenach's large main square that made up Ambrosius Bach's base of operations was the imposing twelfth-century St. George's Church, which served both the townspeople and the ducal court. The nave of the church, with its three galleries on the south and north sides, was designed to hold more than two thousand worshippers. Here, in the western choir and organ gallery, Ambrosius regularly played with his consorts on all Sundays and feast days and for special services such as funerals and weddings. As well as accompanying the choir, they performed with vocal soloists in all sorts of concerted pieces.

The choir consisted of students from the Latin school's *Chorus musicus* (or *Chorus symphoniacus* or *Cantorey*), who were selected on the basis of their musical experience and were granted stipends as choral scholars. The cantor (choral director) also served as teacher of the fourth class *(quarta)*. At the beginning of Ambrosius's Eisenach tenure, Johann Andreas Schmidt served as cantor; he was succeeded in 1690 by Andreas Christian Dedekind, who had previously served as cantor in Arnstadt, where he became a good friend of the Bach family. The school's chorus musicus supplied the church with polyphonic music for regular services throughout the ecclesiastical year and for special services. It also performed for secular occasions such as town council elections, civic ceremonies (for example, at the town hall's *Ratskeller* for the New Year's Day celebration), staged comedies, and certain courtly events such as birthdays in the ducal family. By tradition, several times a year and especially around New Year's Day, the chorus musicus divided into smaller groups, so-called *Currenden,* that sang in the streets of Eisenach and outlying villages to collect money for the teachers and needy students. Martin Luther had once been among such *Currende* singers.

According to the Weimar Church Order of 1664 (which also applied to Eisenach), there were four designated places for polyphony in the liturgy of the main Sunday worship service: after the readings of the Epistle and the Gospel, after the sermon, and during Communion. The standard repertoire included motets and other unaccompanied *(a cappella)* music, as available in the so-called Eisenach *Cantional.*[22] This book, compiled around 1535 and used throughout the seventeenth century, contained compositions by Johann Walter, Ludwig Senfl, Josquin Desprez, Jacob Obrecht, Thomas Stoltzer, and others. More recent music was also performed: works by Michael Praetorius, Johann Hermann Schein, Heinrich Schütz, and Andreas Hammerschmidt; motet collections (for four to eight voices) by Abraham Schadaeus, Melchior Franck, Samuel Scheidt, and Ambrosius Profe;[23] and compositions of Eisenach's own Johann Christoph Bach *(13).* Vocal concertos or concertato motets invariably required the participation of the town musicians and on rarer occasions also the *capellisten* of the court, who were joined with the chorus musicus; the combined forces were usually led by the cantor, but on certain occasions (Easter 1672, for example) by the *Hausmann.*

Ambrosius Bach's sons, who all attended St. George's Latin School, were presumably members of the chorus musicus, so they would regularly have participated in vocal-instrumental performances with their father. Eight-year-old Sebastian's name shows up on a list of students in the fifth class *(quinta)* of the Latin school in the old Dominican monastery. The school offered six classes, and students generally remained in one class for two years. Although very few students actually made it through all classes, graduation from the first (*prima*, or highest) qualified them for entrance at a university. The school's excellent leadership and high reputation attracted students from a wide region. For the years 1656–97, Heinrich Borstelmann served as rector.[24] Conrector from 1675 was M. Christian Zeidler, previously a professor of Greek and Latin in Coburg; from 1693, he first substituted for the ailing Borstelmann and then held the rectorship from 1697 to 1707. Entrusted with supervising the school from 1691 to 1719 was the theologian M. Johann Christoph Zerbst, general superintendent of churches for the duchy and the clergyman who had baptized Sebastian. He himself had once been a student at the school, a member and prefect of its chorus musicus, and assistant to organist Johann Christoph Bach *(13)*—clearly someone who fit quite well into the scheme of relationships maintained by the extended Bach family.

In Eisenach, as in most regions and cities of Lutheran Germany at the time, school attendance was mandatory for all boys and girls from age five to twelve. Legislation enacted by Duke Johann Georg I in 1678 because of frequent violations specified that it was a punishable offense for parents within and outside the city walls not to send their children to school. They could, however, choose freely among the eight German schools and the Latin school, although the latter admitted boys only, aged seven to twenty-four. The German schools were mostly small neighborhood establishments, often run by a single schoolmaster, and all followed a prescribed curriculum that focused on religion, grammar, and arithmetic. While they did not ordinarily keep enrollment records, one of the German schools happened to be located in the Fleischgasse,[25] so most likely Sebastian attended there from age five to seven before joining the fifth class *(quinta)* of the Latin school.[26]

That Sebastian could enter the Latin school's *quinta* directly indicates that at the age of eight he not only was able to read and write but had also mastered the subject matters covered in the *sexta*. Both the German and Latin schools were dominated by religious instruction, with Bible, hymnal, and catechism as the most important texts. Following the Thirty Years' War, schools in Thuringia and beyond were profoundly influenced by the educational reforms of Jan Amos Comenius, bishop of the Moravian Brethren, and Andreas Reyher, rector of the gymnasium in Gotha, who modernized and restructured the century-old school plans. Without straying from the theological focus, Comenius and Reyher systematized the areas of knowledge and stressed, in addition to the study of languages, grammar, and logic, the importance of contact with objects in the environment, with "real things." As they did not consider religion and science to be incompatible, belief in God as creator and the perfection of God's creation remained as central as ever. Their books and

pedagogy (Q: "Why do you go to school?" A: "So that I may grow up right-
eous and learned") would exert a strong influence on Sebastian's schooling in
Eisenach, Ohrdruf, and Lüneburg, from the elementary level through the
*prima.*[27]

Having entered the *quinta* at a younger age than any of his brothers had, Sebastian graduated from the class in 1694 as the fourteenth of seventy-four students of the school. The teacher of the *quinta* was Johann Christoph Juncker,
and the subject matter to be covered included Luther's *Catechism,* the psalms,
and writing, reading, and grammatical exercises in German and Latin. From
the fourth class onward, the main language of instruction was Latin; here, Sebastian fell back to twenty-third place (still two places ahead of his brother
Jacob) among the students in the class. But in that year, the ten-year-old lost
both parents within the space of nine months, and it is remarkable that he did
not fall behind any further. Fortunately, his teacher was the cantor Andreas
Christian Dedekind. The boys knew him well as a close friend of the family,
and he was able to give Sebastian and Jacob much-needed support during this
particularly difficult year.

Sebastian missed forty-eight full days in the school year 1692–93, twenty-
nine and a half the next year, and fifty-one and a half the next.[28] Not surprisingly, his academic performance was the best for the year in which he was
absent the least. We can only speculate why he missed school: he may have
been ill (his brother Jacob was absent less frequently during the same time),
or he and Jacob may have been needed to assist in their father's business or take
part in other family-related matters.

It was the custom of the extended Bach family to gather together once a
year. As Bach's first biographer, Johann Nicolaus Forkel, reported,

The different members of this family had a very great attachment to each other. As it
was impossible for them all to live in one place, they resolved at least to see each other
once a year and fixed a certain day upon which they had all to appear at an appointed
place. Even after the family had become much more numerous . . . they continued their
annual meetings, which generally took place in Erfurt, Eisenach, or Arnstadt. Their
amusements, during the time of their meeting, were entirely musical. As the company
wholly consisted of cantors, organists, and town musicians, who had all to do with the
Church, and as it was besides a general custom at the time to begin everything with
Religion, the first thing they did, when they were assembled, was to sing a chorale.
From this pious commencement they proceeded to drolleries which often made a very
great contrast with it. For now they sang popular songs, the contents of which were
partly comic and partly naughty, all together and extempore, but in such a manner that
the several parts thus extemporized made a kind of harmony together, the words,
however, in every part being different. They called this kind of extempory harmony

a *Quodlibet,* and not only laughed heartily at it themselves, but excited an equally hearty and irresistible laughter in everybody that heard them.[29]

Since there were no vacation periods except for harvest time in the fall, these yearly meetings by necessity had to cut into the school schedule. They could take place only on regular weekdays, because on Sundays and religious holidays the musicians all had their church obligations to meet. Therefore, travel to a family gathering in Arnstadt or Erfurt from Eisenach would easily have cost the schoolchildren two or three days of school.

The annual tradition of family reunions may well have been confined to the generation of Hans Bach's *(2)* sons and grandsons active in the geographic triangle Erfurt-Arnstadt-Eisenach. But the actual source for Forkel's illuminating report can only be what Sebastian Bach himself later told one of his sons. It is more than likely that young Sebastian started accompanying his parents to these family gatherings at an early age, and that they had more or less ended when he reached mature adulthood. At any rate, his own and his siblings' integration into the large family of professional musicians developed as a matter of course, probably in the same way that the young children learned to handle the tools and materials of the family trade. Considering their school commitments, the children would have had sufficient time to begin a disciplined study of the string and wind instruments that a town piper was expected to master. The weekly school schedule was arranged so that there were two "half day" teaching periods, the first session from 6 to 9 A.M. (in the summer, 7–10 in winter), Monday through Saturday, and the second session from 1 to 3 P.M., with no afternoon sessions on Wednesday or Saturday. For the select chorus musicus, the cantor assembled the students on Monday, Tuesday, Thursday, and Friday for an additional hour, 12–1.

The musically inclined Sebastian also took the opportunity to spend time with his father's cousin Christoph Bach *(13),* town organist and court harpsichordist in Eisenach. Sebastian would later refer to him in the family Genealogy as "the profound composer," and Carl Philipp Emanuel Bach would add "the great and expressive composer." None of the older family members ever received comparable epithets, let alone a whole paragraph at the beginning of Sebastian Bach's Obituary, where Christoph's music is described as

strong in the invention of beautiful ideas as well as in the expression of the meaning of the words. His writing was, so far as the taste of his day permitted, *galant* and singing as well as remarkably polyphonous. To the first point, a motet written seventy-odd years ago, in which, apart from other fine ideas, he had the courage to use the augmented sixth, may bear witness; and the second point is borne out just as remarkably by a church piece composed by him for 22 obbligato voices without the slightest violence to the purest harmony, as by the fact that both on the organ and on the clavier he never played in fewer than five real parts.[30]

That the Eisenach Christoph is so clearly singled out points to the kind of role model he must have represented for Sebastian, who not only remembered what may have seemed to a child like sheer magic ("he never played in fewer than five real parts"), but who also later described Christoph's music as beautiful, expressive, progressive, and well crafted. The work "for 22 obbligato voices" is the vocal concerto "Es erhub sich ein Streit," a piece for St. Michael's Day that Sebastian later performed in Leipzig. Scored for a double choir of 5 voices each, 4 trumpets, timpani, 3 violins, 3 violas, and continuo (violoncello, violone, and organ), the work is exemplary in its design and its musical interpretation of the text (Michael and his angels fight against the dragon; Revelation 12:7–12). The instrumental introduction (Sinfonia) for strings sounds like the sweetest, most beautifully melodious angels' consort, while at the same time providing the necessary background against which the musical portrayal of a fateful battle unfolds. The opening words ("And there was war") are sung in successive vocal entrances whose martial character is underscored by simple rhythmic and intervallic patterns typical of a military band of field trumpeters and drummers. But the instruments are only gradually introduced—the timpani begin and the trumpets follow—building up the angels' fight with the dragon to an enormous climax at the words "and prevailed not," when the music reaches its first effective cadence.

According to the Obituary, this vocal concerto, which required the combined forces of the Latin school's chorus musicus, the town music company, and the court capelle, originated before 1680. If Sebastian did not actually participate in a performance in Eisenach, there would have been numerous opportunities for him to hear and perform other music of his renowned relative. Because Ambrosius was not a composer, as far as we know, Johann Christoph Bach's possibly latent influence takes on seminal importance. In the 1690s, he was the only figure of stature in Eisenach who could be identified with the creation of exciting new music, and he was also not afraid of daring something unusual ("he had the courage to use the augmented sixth"). Christoph seems to have fascinated the young boy through his compositions and, in particular, through his activities as organist.

Christoph Bach's significance as a keyboard virtuoso can hardly be judged on the basis of his surviving works for organ and harpsichord, which do not measure up in either quantity or quality to his vocal oeuvre.[31] In fact, his particular strength may well have been improvisation, and he may not have been interested in committing the results of his extemporaneous performances to paper. Again, Sebastian's father is not known to have been an expert keyboard player (although he certainly possessed at least basic skills), and so Ambrosius's cousin Christoph must have provided a most natural source of inspiration for the art of organ and harpsichord playing. Sebastian's good relations with some of Christoph's sons even after their father's death in 1703 speak for the closeness of his relationship with their father; for example, Sebastian's Eisenach classmate Johann Friedrich, Christoph's third son, would succeed him in 1708 in Mühlhausen.

The town organist was responsible for the service music at three of Eisenach's churches, St. George's, St. Nicholas's, and St. Anne's, and also for the maintenance of the churches' instruments. Both tasks kept him and his assistants busy, especially since the large organ at St. George's was in a notoriously bad state of repair. The other two churches owned relatively new instruments, St. Nicholas's dating from 1625 and St. Anne's from 1665. The organ at St. George's, by comparison, dated from 1576 and was enlarged and renovated three times before Johann Christoph Bach's arrival in 1665. Further repairs were carried out then, but by 1678 deficiencies had cropped up again. In 1691, Christoph submitted plans for an entirely new instrument, but only in 1697 was a contract signed with organ builder Georg Christoph Sterzing of Ohrdruf, at the price of two thousand florins. Final design plans for an organ of unprecedented size (fifty-eight stops on four manuals and pedal) were prepared by Bach in 1698, and what amounted to the largest organ project ever undertaken in Thuringia began to be realized soon thereafter. The work had to proceed in stages, and Bach was pleased to report in 1701 that "the new organ more and more reaches the state of completion." Sadly, he himself was never able to play the finished instrument, which was not dedicated until 1707, four years after his death.[32]

All during the 1690s, Sterzing and Christoph Bach were more or less constantly busy fixing the old instrument with its three manuals (*Oberwerk, Rückpositiv, Brustwerk*) and pedal. This activity took place at a time when the boy Sebastian could well have been around to crawl behind the organ's facade and observe what was happening inside; here he would have seen metal and wooden pipes, wind chests, trackers, bellows, and other components of a large-scale mechanical instrument whose complexity was unsurpassed by any other machine in the seventeenth century. Where else but here were the seeds sown for a lifelong fascination with organ design and technology? Moreover, Sterzing, who kept his workshop in Ohrdruf until 1697, remained accessible to Sebastian when he, too, lived there from 1695. A little over twenty years after Sebastian had left the Eisenach Latin school, in 1716, Sterzing and Johann Georg Schröter completed a new organ for the Augustinerkirche in Erfurt, and one of the two examiners brought in to test the instrument on behalf of the church consistory was the most respected organ expert in Thuringia at the time, the concertmaster and court organist to the duke of Saxe-Weimar, Johann Sebastian Bach.

Street map of Ohrdruf in a drawing (c. 1710) showing the vicinity of St. Michael's, with Lang Gasse (where Johann Christoph Bach lived), Schul Gasse (location of the Lyceum), the Ohra River, and Ehrenstein Castle (lower right corner).

# 2

## Laying the Foundations

### OHRDRUF, 1695–1700

#### IN THE CARE OF HIS OLDER BROTHER

Johann Sebastian turned nine in March 1694, and shortly thereafter began in the *quarta* of the Latin school. But just about three weeks after Easter (which fell on April 11), his mother died at the age of fifty. We do not know the cause of her death, or whether it was preceded by illness. The plain entry in the death register ("May 3, 1694. Buried, Johann Ambrosius Bach's wife—without fee"),[1] the sole reference to the end of Elisabeth Bach's life, does not even remotely hint at the gravity of the emotional responses or the wider implications of this catastrophic event for either Ambrosius Bach's family in general or its youngest member in particular. Ambrosius himself, forty-nine years old, bereaved of his wife of twenty-six years and left with three young children, surely found himself in desperate straits. Just one year earlier he had lost his twin brother, Christoph *(12)*, court and town musician in Arnstadt. Carl Philipp Emanuel Bach's annotation in the family Genealogy, based on what he must have heard from his father, gives a touching account of the close relationship between the twins:

These twins are perhaps the only ones of their kind ever known. They loved each other extremely. They looked so much alike that even their wives could not tell them apart. They were an object of wonder on the part of great gentlemen and everyone who saw them. Their speech, their way of thinking—everything was the same. In music, too, they were not to be told apart: they played alike and thought out their performances in the same way. If one fell ill the other did, too. In short, the one died soon after the other.[2]

Ambrosius may well have believed that after the deaths of his brother and especially his wife, his own end would not be far away. Nevertheless, as other sorely afflicted members of the family had done before, he found a pragmatic way out of his misery. He remembered Barbara Margaretha, the thirty-five-year-old widow of his first cousin Johann Günther Bach *(15)* of Arnstadt and daughter of the Arnstadt burgomaster (mayor) Caspar Keul. Left pregnant with their daughter, Catharina Margaretha, Margaretha Bach had remarried in 1684. With her second husband, Jacobus Bartholomaei, deacon at the New Church in Arnstadt and her senior by almost thirty years, she had another daughter, Christina Maria, in September 1685. But Bartholomaei died only three years later, and Margaretha, widowed again, was now left with two young daughters.[3] Ambrosius Bach, always keeping close ties with his many Arnstadt relatives, proposed and was accepted. The wedding ceremony was performed in Eisenach on November 27, 1694, though not in the church but at the home of the widower,[4] then a common practice for remarriages. Johann Sebastian would follow the same tradition when he remarried in Cöthen.

The family of Ambrosius Bach now included Margaretha's two daughters, ages twelve and ten. In the meantime, Elisabeth Bach's twelve-year-old step-grandson, Johann Nicolaus Bach, who had lived with Ambrosius's family for many years and spent four years in the *sexta,*[5] left Eisenach in 1694, probably soon after Elisabeth's death.[6] The timing of Ambrosius's second marriage was such that he and his new wife with their two sets of children—Marie Salome, Johann Jacob, Johann Sebastian, Catharina Margaretha, and Christina Maria—could look forward to a Christmas season that would help draw the reconstituted family more closely together. Yet there was hardly any time to establish a normal life, as Ambrosius soon fell seriously ill and died on February 20, 1695—just two days before his fiftieth birthday and "twelve weeks and one day," as Margaretha put it, into their marriage. We learn from the widow's petition for a bounty that there were hefty expenses for medicine and drugs, suggesting that Ambrosius may have suffered from a protracted illness. He was buried four days after his death.[7]

We can imagine how this sudden turn of events must have devastated Margaretha, who at age thirty-six had now lost three husbands within thirteen years, and the children, especially the two nine-year-olds, Sebastian and Christina Maria. There was little time for despair, however; among other things, the widow was responsible for keeping the town music company going for the next six months (the period in which a new director would be chosen); during this time, she received Ambrosius's full salary, out of which she had to pay his two journeymen and two apprentices. She also received collegial help: her petition for a bounty, for example, was written on behalf of "the sorrowing widow and the poor fatherless orphans" by Andreas Christian Dedekind, cantor of St. George's School.[8] The petition reveals that Ambrosius's employees, two journeymen and two apprentices "who could already pass for journeymen," were able to fulfill the scheduled obligations for the town and church music. It also shows that the widow worried about the waning of musical talent in the Bach family, six of the nine grandsons of Hans Bach (see Table 1.1) having died between 1682 and 1695. Count Anton Günther of Schwarzburg-Arnstadt had supposedly asked the widow of Ambrosius's twin, Christoph, "whether there was not another Bach available who would like to apply for [Johann Christoph's] post, for he should and must have a Bach again." Margaretha's comment in her petition sounds utterly hopeless: "But this was not to be, for the dear God has caused the springs of musical talent in the Bach family to run dry within the last few years." Understandably, her own experience during the previous twelve years made the future look bleak and made her completely blind to the younger generation, among them the greatest talent ever produced by this extraordinary family—her stepson Sebastian.

Within the span of a few months, Ambrosius Bach's family broke apart, but the broader and well-tested family support structures immediately went into effect. Ambrosius's considerations for needy members of his extended family were now reciprocated, to the benefit of his own surviving dependents. After selling the Eisenach house, Margaretha Bach seems to have moved with her two daughters back to her parental family in Arnstadt, where we lose their tracks. Marie Salome, eighteen years of age, left to join her mother's relatives, the Lämmerhirts in Erfurt. And her two little brothers, Jacob and Sebastian, were welcomed into the household of their oldest brother, Johann Christoph, newly established organist at St. Michael's in Ohrdruf. (For Sebastian, no alternative refuge existed, as his godfather Sebastian Nagel had died in 1687.) The estate of Ambrosius Bach was presumably distributed to his surviving children, who were principal heirs. The sale of the Eisenach house would have generated cash that all of them could use, the younger ones in particular for educational purposes. There was furniture to be disposed of, household goods, books, music, and especially musical instruments. Considering the usual extent of a town piper's standard equipment, each of the three sons must have inherited a basic stock of string, wind, and keyboard instruments.

Ambrosius's eldest son Christoph had studied for three years (1686–89) with Johann Pachelbel in Erfurt and, while only seventeen and still a student, had briefly held the post of organist at St. Thomas's in Erfurt (1688–89).[9] There, according to an autobiographical note, he found "both the remuneration and the structure of the organ—the latter being my principal concern—to be poor."[10] He then left Erfurt for Arnstadt, where he had been called to assist his ailing uncle Heinrich (6), Ambrosius's last surviving brother, in his various duties as organist of three churches, Our Lady's Church and at the so-called Upper Church, which primarily served the court. Heinrich Bach, in Arnstadt since 1641, had been in poor health since the early 1680s; he was first assisted by his youngest son, Johann Günther *(15)*, and then after Günther's death by his son-in-law, Christoph Herthum, who in 1671 became Christoph's godfather. So close connections were there, but Christoph could provide temporary help to his uncle for only a year—in 1690, he accepted the position as organist at St. Michael's, the principal church in nearby Ohrdruf.

Ohrdruf, a small town at the foot of the Thuringian Forest, twenty-five miles southeast of Eisenach, was the site of an ancient settlement. In 727, a group of Scottish-Irish missionary monks under Boniface had established a small Benedictine monastery with a chapel, St. Michael's, by the Ohra River. This structure, the oldest house of God in all of Thuringia, became the foundation on which a larger church was built in the early 1400s, a century before Ohrdruf accepted the Lutheran Reformation in 1525. Little is left of the historic church; on November 27, 1753, a devastating fire swept through the town, and St. Michael's fell victim to the flames. In the late seventeenth century, Ohrdruf had about 2,500 inhabitants and, with its Ehrenstein Castle (see illustration, p. 32)—a four-winged, sixteenth-century structure near St. Michael's in the center of town—served as the secondary residence of the counts of Hohenlohe-Gleichen (whose main landed property lay around Öhringen in southern Germany). Wechmar, the place Veit Bach (white-bread baker from Hungary and progenitor of the family of musicians) once settled and the hometown of his son, Hans Bach *(2)*, seven miles northeast of Ohrdruf, belonged to the same county, an enclave engulfed by the duchy of Saxe-Gotha. So by moving in 1690 to Ohrdruf, Christoph Bach in a sense returned to his family's place of origin, although until then no musician from the Bach family had ever served in the town. Only the wife of Ambrosius Bach's twin brother, Christoph had come from there, and Heinrich Bach's *(6)* daughter Anna Elisabeth was married to the Ohrdruf cantor Johann Heinrich Kühn.

The organist post at St. Michael's was a respectable one, for the church, which contained two organs, was both the town's and the county's main house of worship. The incumbent was obligated to play at the Siechhofskirche, the hospital chapel, too, and most likely at the chapel of Ehrenstein Castle whenever members of the ruling family were in town and private services were held for them. Johann Christoph's initial annual salary amounted to forty-five florins, plus in-kind compensation (grain and wood). In 1696, his salary was increased to seventy florins, and further in-kind payments were added in light of his having declined an attractive offer from Gotha to succeed his former teacher Pachelbel as town organist. The larger of the two Ohrdruf organs (with twenty-one stops on *Oberwerk, Rückpositiv,* and pedal), built only in 1675 and expanded in 1688,[11] was relatively new and must have appeared quite alluring to the eighteen-year-old organist upon his appointment. However, the instrument, built by Heinrich Brunner of Sandersleben, was incomplete and suffered from serious defects, and the necessary repairs were delayed for years, despite the Ohrdruf town council's threat to seize the organ builder's assets. Pachelbel, visiting from Gotha, provided a detailed report on the organ's unsatisfactory state of repair in February 1693. Three years later, the organ builder Christian Rothe of Salzungen wrote an expert evaluation, but it took another ten years to finish the repairs. (An apprentice to Rothe at the time, Heinrich Nicolaus Trebs, would later become a close colleague of Bach in Weimar.) In sum, St. Michael's instruments required considerable attention by the organist to be kept in playing condition. That this should be the case precisely during Sebastian's Ohrdruf years was important, for the boy, who clearly had a knack for musical instruments and their technology, was given an ideal opportunity to gain firsthand experience in organ building.

On October 23, 1694, Johann Christoph had married Johanna Dorothea Vonhoff, daughter of an Ohrdruf town councillor. The Eisenach cantor Andreas Christian Dedekind reported that he, along with Pachelbel, Ambrosius Bach, and Ambrosius's cousin Johann Veit Hoffmann, performed at a wedding in Ohrdruf in the fall of 1694—surely Christoph's, and the only occasion for the young Sebastian to have seen his elder brother's master teacher. The musical program at the ceremony conceivably included the Eisenach Johann Christoph Bach's *(13)* wedding piece "Meine Freundin, du bist schön," a dramatized compilation of texts from the Song of Songs, scored for 4 soloists, chorus, solo violin, 3 violas, and continuo. The only surviving manuscript of the piece happens to be in the hand of Ambrosius Bach, the groom's father and an accomplished violinist (see illustration, p. 38). On July 21, 1695, the first child, Tobias Friedrich, was born to the Ohrdruf organist and his wife; the second, Christina Sophia, followed in 1697. Altogether the couple had six sons and three daughters, the youngest of whom, Johann Sebastian, died as a child. Several of the sons later found employment as musicians in Ohrdruf—two of them, Johann Bernhard and Johann Heinrich, after having studied for several years with their uncle Sebastian in Weimar and in Leipzig.

When the household of Christoph and Dorothea Bach absorbed Jacob and Sebastian in 1695, their family was still small; but considering the modest income of the Ohrdruf organist, the obligation to house, feed, and teach the thirteen- and nine-year-old brothers must have caused considerable hardship. In fact, Sebastian's school record reveals that Christoph was not able to provide unassisted support, and Sebastian's Ohrdruf sojourn depended largely on the availability of free board. The same must have applied to Jacob, although he did not stay in Ohrdruf for more than a year; by July 1696, at only fourteen years of age, he returned to Eisenach as an apprentice to Johann Heinrich Halle, his father's successor as director of the town music company.

The brothers Jacob and Sebastian enrolled in the Ohrdruf *Lyceum Illustre Gleichense*, probably in late July 1695, after the Lyceum's annual final exami-

Johann Christoph Bach, wedding concerto (dialogue) "Meine Freundin, du bist schön," from the Old-Bach Archive. Title page written by Johann Sebastian Bach (c. 1740) and solo violin part (opposite) in the hand of Johann Ambrosius Bach (before 1695).

nations. This distinguished institution, which attracted students from afar, was founded around 1560 by Georg II, count of Gleichen. Sebastian, who had graduated from the *quarta* of the Eisenach St. George's School, entered the *tertia* and finished his first year, in July 1696, as no. 4, outranking many older classmates. When he graduated from the *tertia* the following year, the youth— at age twelve the youngest student in his class—had reached no. 1. The two years in the *secunda* confirm his extraordinary academic standing, ranking fifth in July 1698 and second in July 1699, when he was promoted to the *prima* at age fourteen, a full four years below the average age of that class. Sebastian had progressed from the *quinta* through the *secunda* within eight years, an educa-

tional accomplishment unprecedented in his family: neither his father nor grandfather had ever received this kind of schooling, and all three of his brothers left Latin school after completing only the *tertia,* at age fourteen or fifteen.

For most of Sebastian's Ohrdruf school years, the Lyceum was headed by a young rector, M. Johann Christoph Kiesewetter, who was appointed in June 1696 and whose energy and foresight put the school back on track after it had suffered some organizational and disciplinary problems near the end of his predecessor's tenure. Most of the disturbances were attributed to a single individual, the cantor Johann Heinrich Arnold—in Kiesewetter's words, "pest of the school, scandal of the church, and carcinome of the city." Arnold was fired and replaced in January 1698 by Elias Herda, who had previously taught in Gotha. That Herda's audition committee included Johann Christoph Bach indicates the status he had reached in just a few years' time. He also selected the vocal piece to be conducted by Herda and afterward informed the Ohrdruf superintendent, Melchior Kromayer: "We will hardly get a better one."[12]

For most of his time in Ohrdruf, Sebastian was a choral scholar under cantor Herda. The chorus musicus generated a steady income stream for its members, primarily through *Currende* singing in the streets, three times a year. In 1697, for example, a total of 242 talers 4 groschen 10 pfennigs was distributed primarily among the twenty to twenty-five choristers. Fees varied by class and function. A prefect, or assistant conductor, could earn about 20 talers per annum, an altogether respectable sum in comparison, for instance, with Christoph Bach's initial annual salary as organist (45 florins = 39 talers 9 groschen). Sebastian's earnings as a choral scholar in Ohrdruf would have been below that of a prefect, but he may well have been paid as a vocal soloist *(concertist)*. This way Sebastian could contribute to the household expenses—clearly a must. He also critically depended on the so-called *hospitia* or *hospitia liberalia,* instituted by patrician or affluent families for gifted and needy Latin school students who would receive free board and a stipend for tutoring their sons.[13] As a matter of fact, his departure from Ohrdruf in the spring of 1700 was prompted by the unexpected loss of such *hospitia.*

During his two years in the *tertia* of the Lyceum, Sebastian was taught by cantor Arnold, who apparently was a gifted scholar despite his moral shortcomings. The subject matter in the *tertia* included Latin exercises based on Reyher's *Dialogi seu Colloquia puerilia* (Gotha, 1653) and beginning Greek reading exercises; in the *secunda,* Leonhard Hutter's *Compendium locorum theologicorum* (Wittenberg, 1610; with numerous later editions), a systematic summary of Christian doctrine derived from the Bible and early Lutheran theological writings, as well as the biographies of Roman leaders by Roman historian Cornelius Nepos and letters by Cicero. The plan for the *prima* prescribed the historical writings of Roman author Curtius Rufus; *Idea historiae universalis* (Lüneburg, 1672), an influential book on world history and geography by the seventeenth-century scholar Johannes Buno; and the Latin comedies of Terence. Arithmetic was taught in all classes. Conrector Johann Jeremias Böttiger instructed the *secunda,* and the students of the *prima* worked with the rector, a distinguished scholar and pedagogue.

Rector Kiesewetter may have had connections with the Bach family in Arnstadt, having attended the gymnasium there and later having been elected pastor at the New Church in Arnstadt, a post he turned down in favor of the rectorship in nearby Ohrdruf. In 1712, Kiesewetter was appointed rector of the prestigious gymnasium in Weimar, where he would renew acquaintance with Bach. He had followed his former student's career from Ohrdruf, at one point noting in the school register that Bach had been "appointed organist at St. Sophia's [New] Church in Arnstadt, thereafter in Mühlhausen."[14]

Sebastian did not quite complete the first year of the *prima* at the Lyceum. About four months before the annual examinations in July, he and his schoolmate Georg Erdmann left Ohrdruf to complete their education at St. Michael's School in Lüneburg, far away from their Thuringian homeland. According to the exit note in the school register, Sebastian "set out for Lüneburg on March 15, 1700, in the absence of *hospitia.*" The young Lyceum cantor Elias Herda had been a choral scholar at St. Michael's in Lüneburg from 1689 to 1695, and apparently maintained good connections to his former school. He must have heard of vacancies at St. Michael's and suggested his students Bach and Erdmann for positions as choral scholars that would furnish them with the stipends necessary to complete their schooling. Rector Kiesewetter would certainly have provided academic recommendations, especially for Bach, who clearly outranked Erdmann. At this important juncture, Christoph more than likely may have preferred that the fourteen-year-old consider doing what he and their other two brothers had done at that age—enter professional life as musicians. Balthasar had been apprenticed to his father in Eisenach, and Jacob went to apprentice with his father's successor there; Christoph himself, as he wrote in an autobiographical note of December 1700, "attended school until my 15th year, [after which] my father, seeing that I was more inclined toward music than toward studies, sent me to Erfurt, to Mr. Johann Pachelbel, then organist at the Predigerkirche, in order to master the keyboard, and I remained under his guidance for three years."[15]

Quite conceivably Christoph, in recognizing Sebastian's great musical gifts and remarkable keyboard skills, urged him to study with his own teacher and old family friend, Pachelbel, now organist at St. Sebaldus Church in the free imperial city of Nuremberg, some 160 miles southeast of Ohrdruf. At the same time, he must have realized that his little brother, unlike himself, was clearly inclined toward academic studies. And so he may not have wanted to discourage him from following a path that was anything but well trodden for Ambrosius Bach's sons; that is, from completing the upper classes of the gymnasium and earning the qualification for university study.[16] Regardless of how the dynamics among Herda, Kiesewetter, Christoph, and Sebastian actually

played out, Sebastian's move to faraway Lüneburg was surely of his own free
will. In making for himself a decision with such incalculable consequences, the
boy demonstrated an astonishing degree of independence and confidence, for
he was the only one of Ambrosius's children and among the first of Hans
Bach's (2) great-grandchildren to break out of the family's ancestral territory
between Erfurt, Eisenach, and Schweinfurt. Yet the pursuit of academic goals
could hardly have been the sole driving force for this adventurous undertaking, and among other possible motivating factors, two stand out: a desire for
emancipation and autonomy (a strongly independent mind remained a salient
feature of his character), and an apparently boundless curiosity about the grand
organs of northern Germany (presaging a lifelong dedication to the organ,
organ music, and organ playing).

## SEBASTIAN'S MUSICAL BEGINNINGS

The decision to complete academic studies and pass up a musical apprenticeship indicates the priorities Sebastian set for himself. Although he would
hardly have given serious thought to a nonmusical profession, his excellent performance as a Latin school student would have led his teachers to encourage
him to strive for higher goals than becoming a town piper or organist. The
school post of cantor ordinarily required university study, and Bach may well
have contemplated this option, and perhaps even a theological career. There
were certainly enough models of musical "academics" whose educational background provided them with a broader set of opportunities, not to mention a
deeper understanding of music. In the Bach family circle alone, Johann Pachelbel had greatly benefited from gymnasium and university studies, as had Georg
Böhm. The latter, from the village Hohenkirchen near Ohrdruf, had attended
both the gymnasium in Gotha and Jena University together with Johann
Bernhard Vonhoff. Vonhoff, later town councillor in Ohrdruf, happened to be
the father-in-law of Johann Christoph, Sebastian's brother, so it is conceivable
that this connection also played a role in Sebastian's move to Lüneburg, where
Böhm was organist at St. John's.

When Sebastian set out for St. Michael's School in Lüneburg, his musical
preparation was exceptional, comprehensive, and in every respect well rounded.
He had received or simply picked up in Eisenach basic training on the standard town piper instruments, in particular the violin, his father's primary instrument. Sebastian would later play violin and viola regularly, and most likely
cello. He must have been taught the violin by his father—the violinist and
court capellmeister Daniel Eberlin having left Eisenach in 1692—and the

Stainer violin listed among the instruments in Bach's estate was perhaps an inheritance from Ambrosius.[17] At any rate, Sebastian would have taken at least a violin along to Lüneburg, as he could easily anticipate all kinds of opportunities for its use. Whatever other instruments he might have inherited from his father's collection he would probably have left in Ohrdruf in the custody of his brother, along with any other household goods from the parental home.

The mere fact that Sebastian was offered a post as choral scholar at St. Michael's indicates a solid choral background. Moreover, the reference in Carl Philipp Emanuel Bach's Obituary to "his uncommonly fine soprano voice" not only identifies the vocal range and his place in the Eisenach and Ohrdruf school choirs, it also suggests that the combination of long experience—possibly extending over eight years, from 1692 to 1700—and a beautiful voice secured for him, at least for most of the Ohrdruf years, the assignment of solo parts in the chorus musicus. Over the years, Sebastian became versed in both the *choraliter* and *figuraliter* styles—that is, liturgical plainsong and polyphonic music. Since the rich trove of Lutheran hymns, sung with or without organ accompaniment or set polyphonically, played such a crucial role in the musical and educational practice of the Lutheran German lands, Sebastian early on became intimately familiar with this vast and varied collection of tunes and sacred poetry. He grew up with the Eisenach hymnal of 1673 *(Neues vollständiges Eisenachisches Gesangbuch),* which contained, in its thousand-plus pages, no fewer than 612 hymns. The polyphonic choral literature in use then generally focused on a published repertoire of Latin and German motets from the sixteenth and seventeenth centuries, while the concerted repertoire (arias, concertos, motets, and cantatas) requiring the participation of obbligato instruments would have been drawn primarily from manuscript sources. The choral libraries of Eisenach and Ohrdruf most likely contained works by the prolific Gotha court capellmeister Wolfgang Carl Briegel, and surely by the Eisenach cantor Dedekind as well as members of the Bach family, especially Johann *(4),* Heinrich *(6),* Christoph *(13)* and Michael *(14).*[18]

The most decisive role in Sebastian's musical upbringing must be assigned to his elder brother Christoph. Not only did he provide a home for his youngest brother, he furthered Sebastian's professional musical development during the most formative years of his life. In fact, in the Obituary, Christoph is the only teacher mentioned. Characteristically, however, Carl Philipp Emanuel Bach assigns the active role in the relationship to Sebastian himself: "under his brother's guidance he laid the foundations for his playing of the clavier."[19] In other words, his brother only guided. Cousin Johann Gottfried Walther presents in his 1732 *Musicalisches Lexicon* a more objective statement when he writes that Sebastian "learned the first *principia* on the clavier from his eldest brother, Mr. Johann Christoph Bach."[20] Christoph may not have been the first to recognize the extraordinary keyboard talents of Sebastian, who must already have shown a special ability during his Eisenach years, particularly under the influence of his uncle Christoph, the town organist. But the elder brother's tutelage apparently helped the young Sebastian really concentrate on the keyboard.

"The foundations for his playing of the clavier" and "the first *principia* on the clavier" imply first and foremost the acquisition of a solid keyboard technique, involving the standard keyboard instruments—notably harpsichord and organ—and (on the organ) applying both hands and feet; second, experience with the major keyboard genres and styles, improvisatory (prelude, toccata, etc.) or strict (fugue, ricercar, etc.), freely invented or based on a given subject or choral tune; and third, familiarity with the different approaches of individual composers. Christoph, therefore, would have structured the teaching of his ten-year-old brother along the lines that Sebastian himself later used to teach his oldest son, when he was nine. The *Clavier-Büchlein vor Wilhelm Friedemann Bach,* begun in 1720, contains on the first pages some basic information about clefs, scales, and symbols for ornaments as well as a fingering exercise in C major; following are some short pieces in different but easy keys—a praeambulum, a chorale setting, a prelude, another chorale, two allemandes (very early compositions by Friedemann), and so forth; appearing later are early versions of preludes from *The Well-Tempered Clavier,* including some in difficult keys, and early versions of the two-part *Inventions* and three-part *Sinfonias* as exercises in imitative style—mostly compositions by Bach himself; still later come works by other composers.

Brother Christoph, who probably composed very little, may have used as instructional material what he had worked on with his own teacher Pachelbel. Fortunately, we can examine an actual instructional notebook of one of Christoph's fellow students. Johann Valentin Eckelt took up lessons with Pachelbel when he was, like Christoph, fifteen years old;[21] he studied with him from 1688 to 1690, the year Pachelbel left Erfurt for Stuttgart. His notebook, written in German keyboard tablature (a combination of letters for pitches and symbols for rhythmic values), represents the last phase of his lessons with Pachelbel and indicates the diversified repertoire selected for study. In the first part of the notebook, we find material provided by the teacher: a series of preludes, fugues, fantasias, capriccios, dance suites, and chorale elaborations, mainly by Pachelbel but interspersed with some by Johann Jacob Froberger, Johann Caspar Kerll, Johann Krieger, Guillaume Gabriel Nivers, Christian Friedrich Witt, and others. Pachelbel clearly offered a broad range of compositional types.

Noteworthy is a remark Eckelt made in referring to a number of pieces he copied at the end of his study period, just before Pachelbel's departure: "those I have purchased from him in addition to the chorales."[22] Pachelbel apparently sold his student some of his own music: three fugues, a toccata, and a ciaccona (with his teacher's permission, Eckelt copied them into his notebook) plus a selection of chorale elaborations (contained in another manuscript that is no longer extant). The music represented a valuable commodity that Pachelbel was interested in protecting—a point that sheds some light on an episode dating to Sebastian's early teens in Ohrdruf, as reported in the Obituary:

The love of our little Johann Sebastian for music was uncommonly great even at this tender age. In a short time he had fully mastered all the pieces his brother had voluntarily given him to learn. But his brother possessed a book of clavier pieces by the most famous masters of the day—Froberger, Kerl, Pachelbel—and this, despite all his pleading and for who knows what reason, was denied him. His zeal to improve himself thereupon gave him the idea of practicing the following innocent deceit. This book was kept in a cabinet whose doors consisted only of grillwork. Now, with his little hands he could reach through the grillwork and roll the book up (for it had only a paper cover); accordingly, he would fetch the book out at night, when everyone had gone to bed and, since he was not even possessed of a light, copy it by moonlight. In six months' time he had these musical spoils in his own hands. Secretly and with extraordinary eagerness he was trying to put it to use, when his brother, to his great dismay, found out about it, and without mercy took away from him the copy he had made with such pains. We may gain a good idea of our little Johann Sebastian's sorrow over this loss by imagining a miser whose ship, sailing for Peru, has foundered with its cargo of a hundred thousand thaler. He did not recover the book until after the death of this brother.[23]

Christoph's volume presumably contained the same kind of material that he, Eckelt, and other Pachelbel students had acquired from their teacher. In a way, then, Christoph was right to be enraged about the unauthorized copying and the potential loss of value that his collection suffered thereby. He would surely have allowed his brother to learn and perform these pieces, but considering their trade value and what he might have paid for them, he did not want them to be copied without permission. In any case, the incident does not evidence jealousy or any other kind of long-term discord between the two brothers; on the contrary, the connections between Sebastian and his brother remained close, right up to Christoph's death in 1721.

The source of the "moonlight manuscript" story can only be Sebastian himself, and he must have told it to his children in more or less the form reported in the Obituary. The metaphorical reference to the shipwreck on the way to

Peru may relate incidentally to Sebastian's study at that time of history and geography at the Ohrdruf Lyceum. There he would have learned that the Spanish vice-royalty of Peru, which until the eighteenth century included most of the South American subcontinent, was the major supplier to Europe of gold and silver. A hundred thousand talers, gold and silver, stood for the immense value these keyboard masterworks had for Sebastian, who apparently could not conquer new repertoire fast enough. Unfortunately, neither Sebastian's copy nor Christoph's volume has survived. It seems likely, however, that Christoph returned the copy to Sebastian when the latter left for Lüneburg. (The Obituary actually misreports Christoph's death as having occurred in 1700, prompting Sebastian's departure for Lüneburg.)

All we know about the "moonlight manuscript" are the names of the composers represented there (Froberger, Kerll, Pachelbel). The Eckelt Tablature gives us a better idea of the music Sebastian had available for study. But even more important are two large-scale manuscript anthologies, the so-called Andreas Bach Book and the Möller Manuscript,[24] which were compiled by Christoph shortly after 1700—undoubtedly relics of a more extensive library of keyboard music.[25] These collections indicate what a broad range of keyboard literature Sebastian had access to: from north, central, and south Germany, Italy, and France, represented by prominent composers such as Georg Böhm, Dieterich Buxtehude, Johann Adam Reinken, Johann Kuhnau, Johann Caspar Ferdinand Fischer, Nicolas-Antoine Lebègue, Jean-Baptiste Lully, Marin Marais, Tomaso Albinoni, and Agostino Steffani. Although this repertoire was copied by Christoph after his younger brother had left his home, the two anthologies help define the catholic orientation and high-quality choices of the Ohrdruf organist, who would later be called *optimus artifex* (very best artist).[26] Christoph, who bore the primary responsibility for exposing Sebastian to what was current in keyboard literature, was able to gather a technically demanding, musically attractive, and stylistically diversified body of materials, and knew how to choose from it. Only a little later, from neighboring Arnstadt, Sebastian himself contributed compositions and materials from his own collection to his brother's albums. The Andreas Bach Book and the Möller Manuscript today represent the most important extant German manuscript collections of keyboard music from around 1700. They are also among the most prominent sources that illuminate the extraordinarily rich and varied musical culture sustained institutionally by the towns, churches, and courts in seventeenth- and early eighteenth-century Germany, especially Thuringia.

Manuscript and printed collections originating in south and north Germany and especially those from Italy, France, and England differ fundamentally from Christoph's albums. They feature largely homogeneous, often parochial pieces, without regard for a broader, let alone "international," spectrum. The Andreas

Bach Book and the Möller Manuscript, on the other hand, present a highly sophisticated, multifaceted, and unbiased keyboard repertoire that offers welcome insight into the musical environment of the young Sebastian. Indeed, the two manuscript sources reveal the composers, genres, and styles that formed his musical background. At the same time, they preserve his immediate response to the challenges of seventeenth-century masters in a number of his own compositions (from his Lüneburg and Arnstadt years), which demonstrate the ability to consolidate influences as well as the foundations of a highly individualized musical language.

The two Ohrdruf albums belong to the most important sources for Sebastian's early organ and harpsichord works, though all these works date from after 1700. While they complement the few surviving autograph manuscripts of his early compositions, also from the first decade of the eighteenth century, the two albums offer no clues about the actual beginnings of Sebastian's compositional activities. Rather, they provide resounding testimony that by 1705, at about age twenty, his works already reflect an unusual degree of experience and sophistication, raising the question about what preceded them.

The earliest composition we have by one of Sebastian's own children can be found among the latest entries, from around 1745, in the second *Clavier-Büchlein vor Anna Magdalena Bach:* a clumsy compositional exercise in the form of an untitled rondo (BWV Anh. 131) by Anna Magdalena's youngest son, ten-year-old Johann Christian. Nevertheless, the piece demonstrates how early musical children with a certain professional background may have started to compose—only the child prodigy Mozart, whose compositions written at age five are preserved in versions heavily edited by his father, provides a more exceptional case. Another ten-year-old, whose father was not a musician but a medical practitioner, is said to have produced astonishing early masterworks: Sebastian's exact contemporary George Frideric Handel. No autograph of those works has survived, but a remark on an early copy of Handel's six Trio Sonatas for two oboes and continuo, HWV 380–385, reads: "The first Compositions of Mr. Handel made in 3 Parts, when a School Boy, about Ten Years of Age, before he had any Instructions and then playd on the Hautboye, besides the Harpsichord."[27] Both the dating and authenticity of these works have been doubted by one Handel scholar or another, yet before 1695, under the tutelage of his teacher Friedrich Wilhelm Zachow in Halle, Handel was not only taught to play keyboard instruments (from his eleventh year on, he occasionally substituted for his teacher on the organ) but was gradually introduced to composition as well. According to John Mainwaring's 1760 *Memoirs of the Life of the Late George Frederic Handel,* Zachow showed his young student "the different writing manner of the various nations" from his rich collection of German and Italian music, and "he made him copy rare things so that he would not only play them, but also learn how to compose in a similar manner."[28] We know from Handel's notebook of 1698, which contained works by Zachow, Froberger, Kerll, Krieger, and other keyboard masters (but has, unfortunately, been lost since the mid-nineteenth century), that he received training similar to Sebastian's at the same time, except that Handel's came from a more senior and experienced instructor.

One of the principal Baroque methods of teaching students the fundamentals of languages as well as of music consisted in memorizing and emulating so-called *exempla classica,* models by eminent masters. In that sense, performance and composition were closely interrelated, and by copying down exemplary works of different kinds, Handel, Bach, and their contemporaries learned the principles of harmony and counterpoint, melody and voice leading, meter and rhythm. Johann Christoph, having left Pachelbel's school only recently, would have transmitted to his brother the particulars of what he had learned there. How strong an influence Pachelbel had on Christoph is most strikingly reflected in Christoph's music handwriting, which closely resembles that of his teacher. Thus it would be no surprise if Sebastian's primary models in beginning composition were the same as his brother's.

No autograph manuscripts or other actual documentation of Bach's earliest compositional exercises (pre-1700) have survived, for two main reasons. First, Bach would have had no wish to recommend his earliest works as models to his own students, let alone to preserve them for archival purposes. He may actually have done with them what his son Carl Philipp Emanuel reported in 1786 about his own youthful compositions: "The most comical thing of all is the gracious precaution of the [English] King, whereby Handel's youthful works are being preserved to the utmost. I do not compare myself at all with Handel, but I recently burned a ream and more of old works of mine and am glad that they are no more."[29] Second, Bach's earliest works were presumably not written in staff notation but in German tabulature, the prevailing notational style in central and north Germany before 1700. Later on, Bach made only occasional use of this manner of notation, primarily as a space-saving device or for purposes of proofreading and correcting. Since tabulature notation went out of fashion in the early eighteenth century, tablature manuscripts were rarely preserved.

There does exist, however, a body of music unequivocally attributed to Johann Sebastian Bach that appears in reliable manuscript sources and that is believed—mainly for reasons of compositional technique and style, but also on philological grounds—to reach back into the Ohrdruf years. The most prominent of these works is found in the so-called Neumeister Collection of chorale preludes, for organ. These thirty-eight pieces, some two dozen of which date from before 1700, are preserved in a late eighteenth-century manuscript whose notation demonstrates not only that it was copied from a lost, much older manuscript, but that most pieces in this older manuscript must have been transcribed from tablature notation. The Neumeister Collection features the utilitarian and popular type of "varied and figurate chorales" for regular church services. The prevailing style model happens to be that of Johann Pachelbel as well as Johann Christoph *(13)* and Johann Michael Bach *(14)* and is thus a clear reflection of Sebastian's musical upbringing.

One of the chorales, "Christe, der du bist Tag und Licht," BWV 1096, consists, characteristically, of two sections: measures 1–25 represent a composition by Pachelbel in the form of a concentrated, closely knit fugal elaboration of the first line of the chorale; measures 26–29 of the original Pachelbel setting are replaced by a newly composed transition that leads into a 31-measure nonfugal but polyphonic ("figurate") elaboration of all four chorale lines. Sebastian apparently extended the Pachelbel piece into a 56–measure work by adding his own stylistically matching conclusion. Another chorale, "Ach Herr, mich armen Sünder," BWV 742, closely follows the Pachelbel model "Wir glauben all an einen Gott."[30] Both pieces are three-part settings, with the chorale melody presented in highly embellished fashion in the upper voice and sharply contrasting with the homogeneous accompaniment of the two lower voices. Both also specifically require the use of two manuals *(Rückpositiv* and *Oberwerk)* with contrasting registration—the type of organ Pachelbel had in the Erfurt Prediger Church and Bach played at St. Michael's in Ohrdruf (the Arnstadt organ did not have a *Rückpositiv*).

The organ chorales of the Neumeister Collection that are based on Pachelbel examples (mainly four-part compositions, most of them with *ad libitum* pedal, some with pedal *cantus firmi*) never slavishly imitate their model. What makes them stand out is their deliberate tendency to expand on the model, to go beyond its scope—often cautiously, sometimes daringly—with new forms (migrating chorale tune in the compact "Jesu, meine Freude," BWV 1105), consistent motivic construction ("Als Jesus Christus in der Nacht," BWV 1108), and chromatically enriched harmonic design ("Herzliebster Jesu," BWV 1093). Also noteworthy is the unconventional variety of final cadences: every piece ends in a different way.

Considering the makeup of what is presumably the earliest layer of the Neumeister Collection, these works may date from the later Ohrdruf years, but they hardly represent Bach's very first compositional exercises. Closer to those may be three short chorale fughettas, transmitted in sources even later than the Neumeister Collection: "Herr Jesu Christ, dich zu uns wend," BWV 749, "Herr Jesu Christ, meins Lebens Licht," BWV 750, and "Nun ruhen alle

Wälder," BWV 756. These modest and perfectly fine settings, which extend over nineteen to twenty-four measures, show close adherence to their models (*Choräle zum Praeambuliren,*[31] a collection prepared for publication by Johann Christoph Bach [*13*], and some works of Pachelbel), carefully observing the contrapuntal rules but lacking the spark of originality—all marks of genuine school exercises.

Forkel reports that when Bach was later "asked how he had contrived to master the art to such a high degree, he generally answered: 'I was obliged to be industrious; whoever is equally industrious will succeed equally well.' He seemed not to lay any stress on his greater natural talents."[32] Without a doubt, Sebastian was brought up from his earliest childhood days to observe the virtues of perseverance and constant hard work. Extreme industriousness is, however, but one side. The musical experiences that shaped Sebastian through his formative years are almost unparalleled in their quality, variety, and extent. Besides being born into a family of musicians that included great-grandfather, grandfather, father, three brothers, and numerous uncles and cousins, and being in the constant company of journeymen, apprentices, and colleagues around his parents' and uncles' houses, the thoroughly professional surroundings in which he grew up exposed him to all major facets of musical culture: instrumental and vocal, ensemble and solo, sacred and secular, performed at home or in town, court, or school. Sebastian had to understand this multifaceted setting as unified—from the more workmanlike making and maintenance of instruments, preparation of performing materials, and commissioning and contracting of deals all the way up to the artistic aspects of performance and the creation of new music, represented most significantly in the person of his uncle Christoph, "the profound composer." There is hardly a question about the overall quality of the music Sebastian grew up with, a situation comparable to the educational background of his own sons Wilhelm Friedemann and Carl Philipp Emanuel. To the question of why they excelled among his pupils, Bach provided the appropriate answer: "Because they had, from their earliest youth, opportunity in their father's house to hear good music, and no other. They were therefore accustomed early, and even before they had received any instruction, to what was most excellent in the art."[33]

The "hands on" approach Sebastian naturally absorbed became increasingly complemented by academic scholarship, especially theological and linguistic subjects that opened his mind to philosophical issues as well as logic, grammar, and style. This intellectual dimension, which may have received its major impetus at the Ohrdruf Lyceum, set him apart from the previous family tradition as much as it predestined him for the eventual crowning of it. Sebastian's increasingly inquisitive disposition led him to explore and conquer the available repertoire in all its breadth and depth; it made him eager to learn about the highly advanced mechanical engineering and technology of organ building; and it drove him to discover, in his early compositional activities, how to venture beyond his models and reach for new horizons.

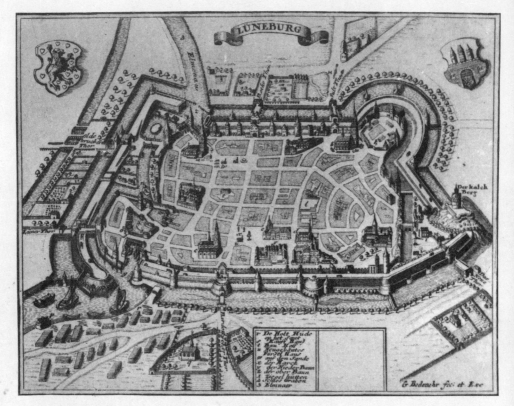

Street map of Lüneburg in an engraving from Merian's *Topographia* (1654), showing St. Michael's church and school complex (no. 3, lower right), the ducal palace (no. 6, lower center), and St. John's (no. 1, upper left).

# 3

## *Bypassing a Musical Apprenticeship*

### FROM LÜNEBURG TO WEIMAR, 1700–1703

CHORAL SCHOLAR AT ST. MICHAEL'S IN LÜNEBURG

Shortly before his fifteenth birthday, on March 15, 1700, Johann Sebastian set out for Lüneburg, well over two hundred miles to the north of Ohrdruf. Not only was he embarking on a long trip for such a young lad, he was also leaving the narrower territory that for generations had served as home for the Bach family of musicians. Considering the many connections readily available to him, he could easily have secured a musical apprenticeship in the "Bach territory" bounded by Eisenach, Erfurt, and Schweinfurt. An apprenticeship would have taken care of his financial needs, but accepting one would have meant ending his formal education, and he clearly wanted to find a way to complete Latin school. So Sebastian made a courageous decision that would also further his professional interests: to widen his experience as a senior choral scholar by taking on assignments as vocal soloist *(concertist)* and to broaden his future options by completing his academic training at an illustrious institution. He would learn to become independent as he had to adjust to an unfamiliar setting in a town four times the size of Ohrdruf and almost twice the size of Eisenach. He would also be in the immediate vicinity of Hamburg, then the largest city in Germany, not only a metropolis much grander than any place he had ever seen, but also one that could claim a great musical tradition and a legendary reputation, especially among organists and organ music devotees. The fabulous large instruments in Hamburg and other north German Hanseatic cities were unmatched anywhere and would have been a major draw for any ambitious young organist. For Bach, they were surely the most exciting prospect of what otherwise must have loomed as a frightening trip into uncertainty.

There is no doubt that both Bach and Georg Erdmann were eagerly awaited in Lüneburg by cantor August Braun, and that the Ohrdruf cantor Elias Herda,

a Thuringian from Erdmann's birthplace Leina, near Gotha, and himself a recent graduate of St. Michael's School, had paved the way for his students.[1]
Herda must have learned around Christmas 1699 that cantor Braun was in
need of experienced singers, for whom scholarships would be available; he also
knew that Thuringian boys were traditionally welcome in Lüneburg because
of their solid training in music fundamentals.[2] So Herda suggested Erdmann
and Bach when he learned that both were losing free board and stipends. Erdmann left the Ohrdruf Lyceum in January, but Bach managed to stay in school
until their joint departure for Lüneburg in March, probably through support
received from his elder brother. During that time, Bach and Erdmann had to
arrange for passports and other necessary travel documents, obtained from
St. Michael's School. Actually, the time difference between Erdmann's and
Bach's dismissal from the Lyceum must be reduced by eleven days: Protestant
Germany, lagging behind the rest of western Europe, finally adopted the Gregorian calendar in 1700, and therefore a leap occurred from February 18 to
March 1.

The two boys traveled together,[3] and Bach would later expressly refer to
Erdmann as his "schoolmate and travel companion."[4] The perils and impon-
derables of such a long-distance trip made it a virtual necessity that the
eighteen-year-old Erdmann would escort the much younger Bach. The students would have had to travel at least part of the way on foot, carrying their
belongings with them. The most direct postal route would have led them
through Gotha, Sondershausen, Nordhausen, and Brunswick, where Johann
Stephan Bach served as cantor at St. Blasius's Cathedral. Johann Stephan, a distant relative of Sebastian's and twenty years his senior,[5] might have provided
the boys with overnight shelter. By whatever means of transportation, the two
arrived in Lüneburg well before the end of March, as they were already singing
in the choir of St. Michael's School on April 3, the Saturday before Palm Sunday.[6] This arrival date must have been carefully planned, for it coincided with
the start of the most active musical period of the entire ecclesiastical year:
Good Friday, the three-day church festival at Easter, and the Sundays and feast
days through Whitsunday, another three-day festival seven weeks later.

Bach and Erdmann began their active duty as choral scholars at St. Michael's
on Palm Sunday weekend with the Saturday afternoon Vespers service, then
took part in the 6:00 A.M. Sunday Matins service, followed by the 7:15 A.M.
main service.[7] The following week included rehearsals for the music to be performed on Good Friday and Easter, the Good Friday Vespers most likely featuring the performance of a Passion story setting. The St. Michael's choral
library held recent vocal-instrumental settings by Joachim Gerstenbüttel (Telemann's predecessor in Hamburg) and Augustin Pfleger (court capellmeister at
Gottorf), though we don't know which Passions were selected for 1700 and

subsequent years. Bach and Erdmann were accepted into the so-called Matins choir, a select ensemble of fifteen musically experienced, resident scholarship students who formed the core group of the school choir and whose assignment included the daily Matins service. Supplemented by nonresident students, the Matins choir formed the nucleus of the chorus musicus, the vocal-instrumental ensemble whose twenty-five or so members performed at the regular Saturday Vespers and the Sunday main services, and, in particular, in the more elaborate musical programs at the afternoon Vespers services of special Sundays and feast days.[8] The special Vespers were the principal occasions for which concerted music was performed (between the sermon and the organ postlude), while the musical repertory of the other services consisted mainly of chant, hymns, and polyphonic motets. Additionally, the chorus musicus also undertook the regular *Currende* singing throughout the year at street corners around town and performed at weddings, funerals, and other events that provided welcome opportunities for supplementary income.

"Bach, because of his uncommonly fine soprano voice, was well received." These words from the Obituary suggest that he was not just accepted as a regular chorister but was valued for his ability to handle solo soprano parts. For April and May 1700, their first two months in the choir, Bach and Erdmann each received 12 groschen, the third-highest monthly fee among the singers, yet still half the pay of 1 taler the *concertists* received. Since subsequent school records and choir lists have not survived, we cannot ascertain what Bach's actual musical functions were nor what he earned later on.

Bach had now entered an academic and musical environment of considerable distinction. St. Michael's School at Lüneburg, an early capital of the Guelphs, was established in the fourteenth century and originally formed part of the medieval Benedictine monastery of St. Michael's, which dated back to 955. When the ancient monastery fell victim to the Reformation and was dissolved in the sixteenth century, the school took over most of its physical space. St. Michael's School and the Johanneum, the Latin school attached to St. John's Church, served as the major educational institutions not only for the rapidly growing city of Lüneburg—a salt-trade center, member of the Hansa, and the most important commercial town between Hamburg and Hanover—but also for the entire northern region of the duchy of Brunswick-Lüneburg. The highly selective St. Michael's School changed greatly in 1656 when, by ducal decree, a residential academy for fifteen to twenty young noblemen, with a separate, well-paid faculty, was added. Students at this *Ritter-Academie* were taught the regular academic subjects of theology, philosophy, classics, ethics, politics, history, mathematics, physics, and French, to which were added riding, fencing, and dancing—a program in keeping with the civil, military, and social obligations of the aristocracy. In contrast, the older St. Michael's maintained

Interior eastward view of St. Michael's Church at Lüneburg in a painting by Joachim Burmester (c. 1700).

the more traditional curricular structure of a Latin school; its distinguished faculty, led by the erudite M. Johannes Buno, its rector for forty-three years (1653–96) and the author of books on history and geography, helped maintain the highest standards of education in the liberal arts. The school served commoners—mostly nonresident students from the city and the fifteen resident choral scholars from the immediately outlying region, but some, like Bach and

Erdmann, from farther away. Official communications between St. Michael's School and the *Ritter-Academie* were limited, but the residential scholars at St. Michael's were housed in a dormitory adjacent to the young aristocrats, creating many points of contact. Moreover, the Matins choir members engaged in joint choral activities with the *Ritter-Academie* students for Matins and Vespers services. These connections provided frequent opportunities for the choral scholars to be hired as valets or as participants in musical entertainments. As a side benefit, the exposure to French language, etiquette, and style—deliberately cultivated by the *Ritter-Academie*'s training program for diplomatic service—would have been welcomed by the choral scholars as a free complement to whatever financial rewards they received.

To the young Bach, Lüneburg, with its ten thousand inhabitants, must have seemed very large. The city continued as the secondary residence of the dukes of Brunswick-Lüneburg after the two ducal houses merged in 1569, and its main market square boasted a new ducal castle, built in 1695–98 by Duke Georg Wilhelm, who reigned for forty years from his principal seat in Celle. The castle later served as a dower house for the widowed duchess, Eléonore Desmier d'Olbreuse, a Huguenot who was the main promoter of the prevailing French taste at the Brunswick-Lüneburg court.

Even though he had completed half the first year of the *prima* at the Ohrdruf Lyceum, whose academic year began in the fall, Bach most likely started over again in the *prima* at St. Michael's, where the academic year began at Easter. But while the school transfer may have resulted in some loss of time, he definitely benefited from the new and probably more demanding requirements at St. Michael's, whose excellent reputation extended well beyond the duchy. The school's rector, M. Johannes Büsche, served as Bach's principal teacher in religion, logic, rhetoric, and Latin. According to a syllabus for 1695, rector Büsche used an imposing group of textbooks for his *prima* classes: Leonhard Hutter's *Compendium locorum theologicorum* (Wittenberg, 1610), a reference work on Lutheran theology whose didactic questions and answers Bach had already begun to memorize at the Ohrdruf Lyceum; Christoph Reyher's *Systema logicum* (Gotha, 1691), whose first volume (*Prolegomena logica de natura logicae*) focuses on the definitions of fundamental terms; and Heinrich Tolle's *Rhetorica Gottingensis* (Göttingen, 1680), a concise summary of Aristotelian rhetoric. In Latin literature classes, Büsche's students read Virgil's *Bucolica* and *Aeneid*, book IV, and Cicero's *De Catilina*.

During their two years in the *prima,* students received further instruction in Latin and Greek from the conrector M. Eberhard Joachim Elfeld, son-in-law of the previous cantor at St. Michael's, Friedrich Emanuel Praetorius, and in arithmetic from the current cantor, August Braun. With Elfeld, they studied the monograph on Alexander the Great by Quintus Curtius Rufus, Cicero's *De officiis,* selections from Cicero's *Epistolae,* and Horace's *Carmina.* Elfeld was also responsible for the instruction of Greek, where the New Testament served as the main textbook; other readings included philosophical and poetic texts by Kebes of Thebes *(Cebetis Tabula),* Phocylides, Isocrates, and Theognis. *Prima* students took individual tutorials with rector Büsche and conrector Elfeld in history and geography, in which they were probably guided by the influential writings of Buno, the previous rector, and in genealogy, heraldry, German poetry, mathematics, and physics.

The demanding scholastic requirements strongly emphasized linguistics, theology, and classical literature, without neglecting the more modern academic subjects of history, geography, and physics. The curriculum was designed to prepare students for graduate study at a university in the liberal arts, theology, jurisprudence, or medicine. So by the end of his schooling, Bach was fluent in Latin and well in command of a broad spectrum of subjects. The later career of Bach's friend Erdmann, who went on to study law and eventually ended up in the Russian diplomatic service, was likely determined by his contacts with young *Ritter-Academie* noblemen and their educators. Bach profited no less from this experience in his future dealings with the aristocracy. Lüneburg must also have been where he acquired his basic knowledge of French,[9] the official language at the *Ritter-Academie,* and where he taught himself Italian, an essential language for an educated musician.

As a choral scholar, Bach was involved in the varied musical activities at St. Michael's. These not only took up a considerable amount of time, they also provided welcome further experience and opportunities. As Elias Herda had in Ohrdruf, August Braun provided the young Bach with a role model as a cantor that must have left a deep impression and filled him with respect for and interest in the office. Cantor Braun did not particularly distinguish himself as a composer (only one incomplete mourning aria of his twenty-four inventoried works has survived),[10] although he was able to make use of St. Michael's remarkable music collection, which ranked with that of St. Thomas's in Leipzig as among the oldest, largest, and richest choir libraries in Germany.[11] When the cantorate passed from Friedrich Emanuel Praetorius to Braun in 1695, an inventory recorded 1,102 items that represent a carefully chosen cross section of seventeenth-century music from Germany and Italy, primarily settings of German and Latin texts. The holdings include collections and individual compositions by many leading composers of the time and of bygone days, among them Heinrich Schütz (30 works), Johann Rosenmüller (96), Wolfgang Carl Briegel (26), Sebastian Knüpfer (27), Joachim Gerstenbüttel (41), Claudio Monteverdi, Giacomo Carissimi, Gasparo Casati (17), and Marco Giuseppe Peranda (18). Clear emphasis lay on composers of the most recent generation, some of them—in particular, Gerstenbüttel of Hamburg—still active. *A cappella* motets were balanced by vocal concertos with instrumental accompaniment, including pieces scored for large vocal-instrumental ensembles, among them a thirty-one-part Sanctus by Samuel Capricornus and a twenty-six-part concerto, "Lobe den Herrn, meine Seele," by the current Leipzig Thomascantor Johann Schelle. It seems unrealistic, however, to imagine the fifteen- or sixteen-year-old Bach roaming around the library and browsing through materials—most of it in partbooks, not scores—for study purposes; his primary musical experience was shaped by actually performing a diversified repertoire of older and newer works for a variety of liturgical, nonliturgical, and secular functions.

The music that was performed during Bach's Lüneburg years tended to favor composers active in the later seventeenth century, such as the Dresden capellmeister Peranda, the Leipzig Thomascantor Schelle, and the Hamburg Johanneum cantor Gerstenbüttel. Bach most often took part in performances in the traditional genres of motet and concerto—both *a cappella* and with participating instruments—and his experience did not remain confined to soprano parts. The Obituary reports that fairly soon after his arrival at St. Michael's, "as he was singing in the choir, and without his knowledge or will, there was once heard, with the soprano tones that he had to execute, the lower octave of the same. He kept this quite new species of voice for eight days, during which he could neither speak nor sing except in octaves. Thereupon he lost his soprano tones and with them his fine voice."[12]

Despite this curious mutation and loss of his "fine voice," Bach the choral scholar remained a member of the select Matins choir, though no longer as a soprano. A shortage of bass singers made him particularly welcome in that section.[13] "He had a good penetrating voice of wide range and a good manner of singing," as Carl Philipp Emanuel later testified.[14] Considering the *a cappella* singing duties of the Matins choir and his status as a scholarship recipient, Bach had few opportunities to take on other assignments.[15] Yet his exceptional talents as an instrumentalist, especially as an organist, were doubtless employed in many performances given by the larger vocal-instrumental ensemble, the chorus musicus, and in assisting with service playing or substituting for the official organist.

Forkel relates that Bach's "inclination to play on the clavier and organ was as ardent at this time as in his more early years and impelled him to try to do, to see, and to hear everything which, according to the ideas he then entertained, could contribute to his improvement."[16] He had at his disposal the school's keyboard instruments and the organ at St. Michael's Church, which was, up to that time, by far the largest instrument he had played.[17] Harpsichords (including, if one was available, a pedal harpsichord) offered the advantage that he could play them without additional assistance, while for private practice at the organ he always needed to engage a bellows operator at a fee, however modest. Furthermore, the St. Michael's organ with its three manuals (*Oberwerk, Rückpositiv, Brustwerk*) and pedal constantly required fixing, so that playing it offered no undiluted pleasure, though it gave him a chance to learn more about the ways of the organ. Another opportunity to further his craft materialized during the summer of 1701, when the experienced and widely traveled organ builder Johann Balthasar Held, who had worked with Buxtehude and others, lodged at St. Michael's while overhauling the school's positive organ and enlarging it by one stop.[18]

## BÖHM, REINKEN, AND THE CELLE COURT CAPELLE

Bach's great interest in the organ and his well-developed skills would have made him useful to the local organists: Friedrich Christoph Morhardt at St. Michael's; Johann Jacob Löwe von Eisenach at St. Nicholas's and St. Mary's; Johann Georg Flor at St. Lamberti;[19] and Georg Böhm at St. John's, Lüneburg's largest church at the main market square. It is likely that Bach became acquainted with all four of them, if only to gain access to their instruments. Morhardt is not known for any particular musical qualities, but he could have made works by his father, Peter, the distinguished previous organist at St. Michael's, available to the curious youth. Löwe, an octogenarian, may have welcomed Bach as an occasional assistant or substitute who, in turn, could benefit from the experiences and tales of a seasoned composer well beyond his prime. And Bach's knowledge of keyboard works by Christian Flor, Johann Georg's father, could have been prompted by contacts with the son. On the other hand, Bach's well-documented personal bonds with Georg Böhm were forged on a higher level. The two apparently maintained lifelong contacts: the 1727 publication announcement, for example, of two installments of Bach's *Clavier-Übung* (containing the partitas BWV 826–827) refers to "Mr. Böhm, organist at St. John's in Lüneburg" along with the author himself and professional colleagues in Dresden, Halle, Brunswick, Nuremberg, and Augsburg as distributors of the publications.[20]

When Carl Philipp Emanuel Bach replied to a list of biographical questions put to him by Forkel in 1775, he mentioned Georg Böhm among the most influential musicians for the young Bach.[21] But curiously, he crossed out "his teacher Böhm," and wrote instead the more neutral "Lüneburg organist Böhm." The original designation can hardly be interpreted as a slip of the pen; rather, it is an intuitive acknowledgment of a special relationship that Bach's son must have been aware of. After all, Carl was thirteen years old at the time of the *Clavier-Übung* announcement and may well have heard his father talk about Böhm and what he had learned from him. On the other hand, in his discussion of Bach's education and achievements, Carl tended to extol his father as a self-taught genius. From the outset, he believed, it was Bach's "love and aptitude for music as a gift of Nature" that urged him to move beyond the limits set by others.[22] Even Bach's older brother in Ohrdruf would have noticed the youngster progressing at a stunningly remarkable pace.

When the fifteen-year-old Bach arrived in Lüneburg, not only was he the same age at which his brother Christoph had left Eisenach to study with Johann Pachelbel, he had also reached the typical age for musicians to start an apprenticeship. Although Böhm did not have the kind of studio that Pachelbel oversaw in Erfurt, nor was he the primary reason for Bach's move, his presence in Lüneburg must have been an added attraction—in all likelihood something Bach counted on. A fellow Thuringian, Böhm had at least a tenuous connection with the Bach family.[23] Like Bach, he had completed Latin school, and had even studied briefly at Jena University. The St. Michael's choral scholar Bach would have found in him an understanding and supportive mentor, above and beyond his status as an experienced organist and composer—clearly the most accomplished keyboard virtuoso Bach had encountered so far.

Bach did not, as far as we know, receive formal lessons from Böhm, but Bach's family background and academic outlook, his solid training as a musician, chorister, and instrumentalist, and especially his rapid progress as an organist qualified him as an unusually gifted and promising junior fellow who could profit enormously from Böhm's considerable experience. The organ at St. John's, though in bad repair like the other Lüneburg church organs, was a distinguished instrument. Originally, its lack of an independent pedal made it less suitable for the typical north German organ literature, which reflected the interplay of the various organ sections—*Hauptwerk, Brustwerk, Rückpositiv,* and pedal—that constituted the magnificent large-scale instruments of the Hanseatic cities. Therefore, Böhm's own contributions to the north German organ style most likely postdate the renovation and enlargement undertaken in 1712–14 by Matthias Dropa, who added two pedal towers and so furnished the instrument with the proper *gravitas* and the capability of featuring an independent and well-rounded pedal section.

The range of compositions by Böhm to which Bach was exposed in Lüneburg is best represented by the pieces Bach appears to have made available after his return to Thuringia for his brother's keyboard anthologies, the Möller Manuscript and Andreas Bach Book. In these volumes, harpsichord suites of dances prevail among the Böhm works;[24] also included are two preludes and fugues and the chorale partita "Jesu, du bist allzu schöne"—*manualiter* organ works. In the same collections, we find two keyboard suites by Böhm's Lüneburg predecessor, Christian Flor, as well as a series of pieces by French composers, notably suites from *Pièces de clavessin* (Paris, 1677) by Nicolas-Antoine Lebègue, ornament tables by Lebègue, and suites by Charles Dieupart (Amsterdam, 1701–2). This context suggests, first of all, that Böhm played a major role in shaping Bach's background by introducing him to the genre of stylized dance in general, and to French music and performance practices in particular; and second, that he also provided Bach with compositional models—preludes and fugues of his own and of other northern composers as well as chorale variations, a genre in which he excelled. Bach's own compositional activities in all these areas appear to have begun in Lüneburg and are clearly indebted to Böhm. Traces of his influence appear in his harpsichord Overture (Suite) in F major, BWV 820; the Partita in F major, BWV 833; the Suite in A major, BWV 832; and the Prelude (and Fugue) in A major, BWV 896—all entered later, perhaps with revisions, in his brother's anthologies. The origins of Bach's chorale partitas, notably of "Christ, der du bist der helle Tag," BWV 766, "O Gott, du frommer Gott," BWV 767, and "Ach, was soll ich Sünder machen," BWV 770, belong here as well; the decided sparsity of chorale-based works in the two Ohrdruf anthologies strongly indicates that a corresponding collection of organ chorales once existed.

Böhm maintained close connections with the nearby city of Hamburg. He knew, for example, the theologian and poet Heinrich Elmenhorst, pastor at St. Catharine's Church there, to whose collection of *Geistreiche Lieder* (Lüneburg, 1700), one hundred sacred solo songs with basso continuo, he contributed fully twenty-three settings. Unlike the other orthodox Lutheran clergy in Hamburg, Elmenhorst had been a staunch defender of opera, which early on had evoked violent protest from the pulpits of conservative preachers. He even went so far as to write several opera librettos—for Johann Theile (*Orontes*, 1678), Johann Wolfgang Franck (*Michal und David*, 1679), and Johann Philipp Förtsch (*Polyeuct*, 1688), prominent figures in Hamburg opera after the establishment in 1678 of an opera house at the Goose Market. In the mid-1690s, Böhm seems to have held a seasonal appointment as a harpsichordist in the Hamburg opera orchestra.[25] This position would have brought him in contact not only with Elmenhorst but also with St. Catharine's organist, Johann Adam Reinken, a longtime member of the Hamburg opera's board of directors.

No one was better positioned than Georg Böhm to introduce the young Bach to Reinken, then in his late seventies. Dean of Hamburg's musicians, student of the Sweelinck pupil Heinrich Scheidemann, illustrious virtuoso, celebrated organist in charge of one of the largest and finest seventeenth-century instruments, and eminent composer with a strong theoretical bent, Reinken must have appeared a fascinating figure to the teenager, who made repeated trips from Lüneburg to Hamburg to hear Reinken play.[26] An anecdote that surely originates with Bach himself suggests the importance of the Reinken connection:

Since he made several trips to hear this master, it happened one day, since he stayed longer in Hamburg than the state of his purse permitted, that on his way home to Lüneburg he had only a couple of shillings in his pocket. He had not got halfway home yet when he developed a keen appetite, and accordingly went into an inn, where the savory odors from the kitchen only made the state in which he found himself ten times more painful. In the midst of his sad meditations on this subject, he heard the grinding noise of a window opening and saw a pair of herring heads thrown out onto the rubbish pile. Since he was a true Thuringian, the sight of these heads made his mouth begin to water, and he lost not a second in taking possession of them. And lo and behold! he had hardly started to tear them apart when he found a Danish ducat hidden in each head. This find enabled him not only to add a portion of roast meat to his meal but also at the first opportunity to make another pilgrimage, in greater comfort, to Mr. Reinken in Hamburg.[27]

The anonymous benefactor who played the friendly prank on Bach was probably someone who knew and admired him, perhaps a young nobleman from the *Ritter-Academie*. As the story makes clear, it cost the poor scholarship student money and considerable effort to make each thirty-mile trip to and from Hamburg, especially since it would not make sense to stay for just a day or two. Apparently, he also persuaded his cousin and schoolmate from the Ohrdruf Lyceum, Johann Ernst Bach,[28] to explore the Hamburg scene. Ernst, after graduating from the Lyceum in April 1701, "visited Hamburg for half a year at great expense, in order to improve his understanding of the organ."[29] Lüneburg offered Sebastian better possibilities for subsistence—with a long-range contact with Hamburg thrown into the bargain—than the more financially taxing route taken by his cousin. But it is conceivable that Sebastian roomed with his cousin in Hamburg, at least during the second half of 1701.

The organ of St. Catharine's was the most famous and most beautiful large instrument in north Germany, with fifty-eight stops on four manuals and pedal.[30] Bach never forgot the impression Reinken's organ made on him. His student Johann Friedrich Agricola later reminisced that Bach "could not praise the beauty and variety of these reeds highly enough. It is known, too, that the famous former organist of this church, Mr. Johann Adam Reinken, always kept them in the best tune." Bach also "gave assurance that the 32-foot *Principal* and the pedal *Posaune . . .* spoke evenly and quite audibly right down to the lowest C. But he also used to say that this *Principal* was the only one as good as that, of such size, that he had heard."[31] Without question, Bach's theoretical and practical standards for organs were shaped decisively by Reinken's instrument.

One can hardly imagine a greater asymmetry than that between Reinken and Bach—between the wealthy Hamburgian and the poor Thuringian, the almost-octogenarian and the teenager. But they must have discovered a mutual affinity that encouraged Bach to visit the elderly musician time and again, and that also led to a reencounter between the two when Reinken was ninety-seven. Reinken represented a versatile and colorful musical personality, a musician with high intellectual ambitions and an avid collector of older practical and theoretical musical literature, such as the keyboard works of Frescobaldi and the harmony treatise of Zarlino—someone who, to the young Bach, truly personified history.

Reinken's musical influence on Bach manifested itself in several ways. The old master offered direct access to the main repertoire of north German organ literature, its principles, its relationship to a specific type of instrument, and its manner of performance. Included in this repertoire was the large and encompassing oeuvre of Dieterich Buxtehude, organist in Lübeck. The close personal connections between the famous organist and Reinken allowed Bach, in Lüneburg and Hamburg, more exposure to Buxtehude than he could have gained through his Ohrdruf brother and the Pachelbel school.[32] Also, Bach may well have met Buxtehude at Reinken's house; his later trip to Lübeck (see Chapter 4) may even have resulted from an invitation issued earlier, when he could not afford to undertake such travel.

The number of Reinken's known keyboard compositions is small—nine, to be exact—but five of them are found in the two Ohrdruf anthologies of Bach's brother: two suites, a ballet, the Toccata in G major, and the Partita "Schweiget mir vom Weiber nehmen." What's missing is Reinken's impressive large-scale Chorale Fantasia "An Wasserflüssen Babylon," one of the key works of the north German organ style and a piece Bach knew well. It served not only as a model for his "Wie schön leuchtet der Morgenstern," BWV 739, a chorale setting on a smaller yet technically no less ambitious scale, but also as a reference for his elaborate homage to Reinken, the organ Chorale "An Wasserflüssen Babylon," BWV 653. Of particular importance for Bach's development as a composer were his keyboard Fugues BWV 954, 965/2, and 966/2 based on material from Reinken's trio-sonata collection, *Hortus musicus* (Hamburg, 1687).[33] These fugues number among the earliest specimens in which Bach deals with tightly constructed thematic-motivic elaboration and with the principle of double counterpoint—that is, the combination of two musical voices in which either one can function as an upper or a lower voice. Reinken's Italianate trio-sonata fugues provided Bach with the challenge of transcribing, modifying, and developing these models of permutation technique into genuine keyboard fugues.[34] These pieces, along with similar Italian models by such composers as Arcangelo Corelli, Tomaso Albinoni, and Giovanni Legrenzi, trained the

Group portrait including Johann Adam Reinken (dressed in a Japanese kimono and seated at the harpsichord) and Dieterich Buxtehude (leaning over a sheet of music showing a canon dedicated "In hon[orem]: Dit: Buxtehude et Joh: Adam Reink: fratres) in a painting by Jan Voorhout (1674).

young Bach in consistent and logical part writing, the design of closed and rounded movements, the differentiation between thematic expositions and related yet nonthematic episodes, and the integrated use and expansion of sequential patterns.

The Obituary makes no mention of the Hamburg opera or its conductor, Reinhard Keiser,[35] suggesting that Bach at the time had no particular interest in opera. But it does mention that in Lüneburg Bach "had the opportunity to go and listen to a then famous band kept by the Duke of Celle, consisting for the most part of Frenchmen; thus he acquired a thorough grounding in the French taste, which, in those regions, was at the time something quite new."[36] This formative experience occurred, however, not at Celle, which lay twice as far from Lüneburg as Hamburg, but at the newly built Lüneburg castle, the secondary residence of Duke Georg Wilhelm.[37] As it happens, the dancing master of the Ritter-Academie, Thomas de la Selle, served in the ducal court capelle;[38] so it seems likely that the noblemen of the academy regularly attended courtly events at the ducal castle in Lüneburg. Selle or one of the academy students could have provided Bach and other St. Michael's students with access to the restricted castle. Thus was Bach brought into first-hand contact with genuine French musical style and manners of performance. The experience ideally complemented his study of French keyboard suites, overtures, and ballets. Moreover, Bach's musical talents probably appealed to the aristocratic students at the *Ritter-Academie,* where French taste prevailed and where he could provide musical entertainment for a fee to supplement his stipend.

## THE INTERIM: THURINGIAN OPPORTUNITIES

After graduating from St. Michael's School in Lüneburg in the spring of 1702 (the Easter date that year was April 16),[39] Bach was no longer entitled to receive free room and board or any monetary support. He now had to find a way of keeping expenses to a minimum and of making a living by accepting temporary chores and part-time engagements, all in preparation for seeking a regular position. Increased living costs in a city of Lüneburg's size and the limitations imposed on freelance activities make it unlikely that he would have stayed there any longer than he had to.[40] He knew he would be much better off returning to his native Thuringia, where he could find shelter and a viable support system provided by the extended Bach family of professional musicians. In that setting, his qualifications as a well-trained musician and versatile instrumentalist, as well as his exceptional keyboard skills, virtually assured him of procuring temporary musical assignments and, more important, gave him the perfect venue from which to monitor opportunities for regular employment.

The two most convenient and suitable places for this kind of sojourn would have been the homes of his older siblings: Marie Salome, who was married to the well-to-do Erfurt furrier Johann Andreas Wiegand, and Johann Christoph in Ohrdruf.[41] Ohrdruf is plausible for several reasons. First, he had lived with his brother before and may even have left behind some of his belongings, such as a harpsichord, other instruments, books, or items he had inherited from his parents' household in Eisenach. Second, his Ohrdruf brother's situation had improved remarkably upon the death, only a few months after Sebastian left town, of the *quinta* teacher at the Lyceum, whose position Christoph then took over.[42] His overall economic circumstances—he owned a house and a small farm—were such that after turning down an offer to succeed Pachelbel in Gotha, he apparently never again thought of leaving Ohrdruf for greener pastures. Sebastian might have offered some welcome assistance for a few months in 1702, as a farmhand if not organist.

In the Genealogy, Bach lists as his first professional job "Court Musician, in Weimar, to Duke Johann Ernst, Anno 1703,"[43] making no mention of any activities between his graduation from St. Michael's in Lüneburg and his entry into this Weimar post in January 1703. Bach may never have related any particulars about this period, for Carl Philipp Emanuel reported to Forkel, *"Nescio* [I do not know] what took him from Lüneburg to Weimar."[44] Carl may not have known that in 1702 his father applied for an organist post at the St. Jacobi Church in the Thuringian town of Sangerhausen, yet not with the desired success. We know this from Bach's correspondence many years later with the merchant Johann Friedrich Klemm, an influential town councillor who became burgomaster of Sangerhausen. Bach was seeking Klemm's support in securing the same organist post for his third-born son, Johann Gottfried Bernhard, which Bernhard then indeed obtained. In a letter of November 18, 1736, Bach entertains the hope that the Sangerhausen town council "is now in a better position, by choosing one of my children, to keep the promise made to my humble self almost 30 years ago, in conferring the post of organist then vacant, since at that time a candidate was sent to you by the highest authority of the land, as a result of which—although at that time, under the régime of the late Burgomaster Vollrath, all the votes were cast for my humble self—I was nevertheless, for the aforementioned *raison,* not able to have the good fortune of emerging with success."[45]

Here is what we know about the 1702 organist vacancy. Gottfried Christoph Gräffenhayn, principal organist at St. Jacobi, Sangerhausen's largest church, and town judge in Sangerhausen, was buried on July 9, 1702. In November of that year, Johann Augustin Kobelius was appointed principal organist of St. Jacobi,[46] as well as its subsidiary St. Ulrich's. In this position, he supervised an assistant organist whose responsibility was limited to accompanying congregational hymns for minor services. Although the official search process had originally led the town council formally to elect the seventeen-year-old Johann Sebastian Bach, the twenty-eight-year-old Kobelius was appointed through the intervention of Duke Johann Georg of Saxe-Weissenfels, whose realm at the time included Sangerhausen (which also served as a secondary ducal residence). The new appointee had been trained under the Weissenfels court capellmeister Johann Philipp Krieger, received further credentials in Italy, served until 1702 as a member of the Weissenfels court capelle, and was deemed to be "an excellent composer, for which reason he was also entrusted with the *Directorium Chori musici"* soon after his appointment.[47]

Bach could hardly feel insulted by losing out to an experienced, older, and well-connected musician. Nevertheless, he must have been as deeply disappointed by the turn of events as the town council was embarrassed by the despotic affront to its authority and jurisdiction. After all, the council had taken a considerable risk by unanimously choosing a seventeen-year-old to succeed the seasoned town judge and organist Gräffenhayn—an extraordinary testimonial to the achievements with which Bach impressed town councillors and church officials alike. Among these officials was merchant, postmaster, and church treasurer Johann Jacob Klemm, with whom Bach maintained friendly relations that lasted beyond Klemm's death to the son, Johann Friedrich, the correspondent of 1736.[48]

Apart from Bach's enduring connections with the Klemm family, the striking evidence of the young musician's demonstrated skills must not be underestimated. Whatever audition Bach had to pass, he must have exhibited professionalism of the highest caliber in his performance, improvisation, composition, and knowledge of organ technology. He must also have been judged qualified to supervise an assistant organist and to take over, sooner or later, the direction of the chorus musicus, the vocal-instrumental ensemble of the church.

In considering where Bach learned about the vacancy, who furnished him with recommendations, and when his audition and election took place, we should remember the Bach family network, which undoubtedly played a crucial role in paving the way for one of its most promising offspring. Kobelius's appointment sometime in November 1702 suggests that Bach's successful audition took place in September or, more likely, in October, two or three months after Gräffenhayn's death. In any case, after learning in November that he would not receive the Sangerhausen appointment, Bach had little time to entertain regrets. An opportunity as court musician opened up in Weimar (the same city, incidentally, where his grandfather Christoph Bach (5) had served some sixty years earlier), and in January 1703, he joined the capelle of Duke Johann Ernst of Saxe-Weimar. Although Bach would later describe his position as that of *Hoff Musicus* (court musician),[49] the ducal treasury register lists him as "Lackey Baach,"[50] indicating that he was hired as a minor court servant. That members of the capelle (except for a few principals) had to perform nonmusical chores and valet services as well may have contributed to Bach's leaving the Weimar court service after only six months. Then again, he may have been hired as temporary additional help or a substitute in the first place, without any promise of longer-term employment.

In Weimar, Bach received a quarterly salary of 6 florins 16 groschen and, presumably, free room and board—decent compensation, yet little more than half of what he would later earn as organist in Arnstadt.[51] His functions as a member of the court capelle were left unspecified in the appointment documents, and no wonder, considering his lackey status. Since 1683, the Weimar court music had been led by the capellmeister Johann Samuel Drese, a capable but frequently ailing composer. Bach found himself in rarefied company when he took part in performances of both secular and sacred music at the court. Among the most notable members of the ducal capelle were Georg Christoph Strattner, the vice-capellmeister as well as a singer and composer, and Johann Paul von Westhoff, a leading German violinist who was the first to publish unaccompanied works for his instrument. Bach may also have provided some special services for his immediate employer Duke Johann Ernst,[52] the younger brother of the reigning Duke Wilhelm Ernst and the person officially in charge of the capelle. Since the smaller court ensembles in central Germany structurally resembled the town music companies, their members were generally required to play several instruments expertly, and Bach would have been expected to display his considerable versatility as an instrumentalist.[53] At the same time, his musical activities in Weimar most likely focused on the playing of keyboard instruments, as his particular proficiency in this domain would have been a main attraction for the court.

The actual Weimar court organist at the time was Johann Effler, the same musician Bach would eventually succeed. Considering that Effler retired prematurely in 1708 because his health no longer permitted him to fulfill his duties, he could very well have needed help in 1702. In any case, his prominent link to the Bach family extended back over thirty years.[54] Effler's distinguished career began as organist in Gehren near Arnstadt, where he was succeeded in 1673 by Johann Michael Bach (14; see Table 1.1), who would later become Sebastian's father-in-law. Effler left Gehren to take up the organist post at the Prediger Church in Erfurt previously occupied by Johann Bach (4). There he became affiliated with the town music company under the direction of Johann Christian Bach (7), and when he finally moved to Weimar as court organist in 1678, Johann Pachelbel took Effler's place in Erfurt. The myriad of connections, which are anything but coincidental,[55] offer further confirmation of a well-functioning professional and family network that helped launch young Sebastian's musical career.

How much Bach actually benefited from his family's support system is more strikingly evident in the events leading up to his appointment in Arnstadt. Ever since the brothers Christoph (5) and Heinrich Bach (6) were active there in the early 1640s, the town had served as the major hub in the life and musical activities of the family's Wechmar line. Sebastian's father Ambrosius had worked there before he joined the Erfurt town band in 1667, and his twin brother Christoph (12) spent virtually his entire career as Arnstadt court and town musician; Ambrosius's second wife, Barbara Margaretha, née Keul, was an Arnstadt burgomaster's daughter; Sebastian's brother Christoph (22) had substituted for their old and ailing uncle Heinrich Bach (6) before moving in 1690 to Ohrdruf; and Christoph's godfather was the Arnstadt court organist Christoph Herthum, husband of Maria Catharina, one of Heinrich Bach's daughters. So for Sebastian, Arnstadt represented territory that was thoroughly familiar, although a political connection proved to be even more important.

In October 1699, the consistory as governing body of the church of the count of Schwarzburg-Arnstadt commissioned a new organ for the rebuilt St.

Boniface's or New Church, from the renowned organ builder Johann Friedrich Wender of Mühlhausen.[56] After some delays, the construction took place in 1701–3, and as soon as enough stops were ready for accompanying congregational hymns, Andreas Börner was hired as organist. But Börner had to return the keys to the organ loft after every service to the Arnstadt burgomaster Martin Feldhaus, who personally supervised the work of the organ builder. Feldhaus was the brother-in-law of the two organist brothers Christoph *(13)* and Michael Bach *(14)* and was obviously most interested in getting the finest instrument he could for the 800 florins made available for the project. When the organ was finished in the summer of 1703, Feldhaus arranged for its examination. As a local expert, the town and court organist Christoph Herthum, a signatory (and probably coauthor) of the 1699 organ contract,[57] would have been called upon, but for outside expertise the burgomaster invited none other than Johann Sebastian Bach to come from Weimar. Although there were more senior and experienced Bach family members available for this purpose, Feldhaus chose the eighteen-year-old Bach to conduct the official organ examination, in all likelihood his first ever; even at this early stage in his career, Bach was reputed to possess such a phenomenal understanding of organ technology that other family members could be passed over for this task without offending anyone. At the same time, it would have taken the authority of someone of Burgomaster Feldhaus's stature to persuade not only the organ builder but also the consistory, the church superintendent, and the count of Schwarzburg-Arnstadt to accept the judgment of an eighteen-year-old.

Bach's profound knowledge of organ building, which eventually made him one of the most sought-after experts in central Germany, was grounded in many years of hands-on experience, going back to the organ crawls, tunings, and repairs he made in his childhood days. The particular repair needs of the instruments at St. George's in Eisenach and St. Michael's in Ohrdruf afforded an excellent set of practical lessons that were supplemented by his more mature experiences in Lüneburg and Hamburg and that were further informed by the shop talk that invariably took place among organ builders and organists. Also, by the time Bach was asked to inspect the new Arnstadt organ, he probably had studied and tried out more instruments, including those of the northern Hanseatic cities, than any of his Thuringian relatives. Most important, he had acquired a solid scientific foundation in the art of organ building by studying Andreas Werckmeister's manual, *Erweiterte und verbesserte Orgelprobe* (Quedlinburg, 1698).[58] The earliest extant evidence of Bach's organ expertise, his Mühlhausen organ renovation proposal of 1708,[59] demonstrates that in his principles, methods, and terminology he relied heavily on Werckmeister's influential treatise.[60]

The written report of the Arnstadt organ examination has not survived, but the payment record for the examination, entered by Feldhaus into the journal of the Arnstadt consistory, details the financial arrangements: "July 13, 1703. Upon the command of the Consistory of the Count here, Mr. Johann Sebastian Bach, Court Organist to the Prince of Saxe-Weimar, was called hither to inspect the new organ in the New Church, and the costs come to the following amounts: 2 thlr. 16gr. to Georg Christoph Weller for the hire of the horses and messenger's pay, 4 thlr. to Mr. Bach as compensation, and 1 fl. for the time that he was here, for food and lodging, making a total of 8 fl. 13 gr."[61]

It is apparent from these figures that Bach was treated as a professional in every respect (and even referred to by a title he did not hold). His travel to and from Arnstadt was arranged by private coach, he received a decent per diem (nearly a sixth of his quarterly salary at the Weimar court), and he was paid a reasonable honorarium for the examination. But he not only tested the organ, he also played the dedication recital, for which he received an additional fee of 3 florins 13 groschen "for having to try the new organ and play it the first time."[62]

The recital and examination must have occurred before July 13. According to the 1699 contract with the organ builder, the original completion had been set for St. John's Day 1701, a feast day on which the principal organists of some Thuringian churches were required to present, after the main service, a recital in order to showcase the continuing progress in their mastery of the instrument. (Such a performance was specified, for example, in Johann Pachelbel's 1678 contract at the Prediger Church in Erfurt.)[63] The actual demonstration of the new Arnstadt instrument, then, was most likely St. John's Day 1703, June 24. Both the organ examination and the inaugural recital, with all the protection and pitfalls of a "home game," proved to be nothing less than a public recognition that a new star had risen in the old established family of musicians, an altogether critical event that set Bach's career on a firm course.

## EARLY MUSICAL ACHIEVEMENTS

Bach's dedication recital in Arnstadt may even have represented a formal or disguised audition for the post of organist at the New Church. But both the Sangerhausen test of 1702 and the Arnstadt recital of 1703 raise the question of how and by what evidence the remarkable musical achievements of the ambitious Sebastian at this early juncture can be properly evaluated. The Sangerhausen and Arnstadt authorities accepted him as a finished musician, on a par with older professionals. In terms of keyboard-playing skills, Bach surpassed his competitors, and at age seventeen and eighteen he also matched and possibly exceeded the virtuosic capacities of senior masters like Reinken, Buxtehude, Pachelbel, and Böhm. While Bach would certainly not have equaled them in compositional experience and polish, in his own works he clearly accepted the challenge of their mastery and tried to measure up to or even outdo the models they established. We can conclude, then, that Bach's level of accomplishment around 1702–3 must be considered much higher than the dearth of autograph sources prior to 1714 had led us to believe.[64]

The Toccata in D minor, BWV 565, seems a particularly characteristic example of the bold, virtuosic approach of the young Bach, still not quite sure how to manage certain aspects of form and fugal counterpoint. Although the piece is transmitted only in much later copies,[65] it bears the hallmark of a youthful and unrestrained piece that fits the manner of what Bach later used to dub, according to Forkel, "Clavier hussars" (see Chapter 6). The opening passagework features persistent octave doubling, for which there is no parallel elsewhere in Bach's organ music. However, if we consider that Bach's Arnstadt organ had no *manualiter* sixteen-foot stops available, the octave doubling reflects an ingenious solution for making up that deficiency and for creating the effect of an *organo pleno* sound that typically requires a sixteen-foot basis (Exx. 3.1, 3.3, 3.4). And if the rampant figurative materials that shape the entire first section sound as though the composer got carried away, we should note that the figuration patterns remain remarkably well focused; in fact, they can be reduced to a single governing idea, the head motive that opens the work (Ex. 3.2a) and, with its inversion (b), forms the basis for a series of running variations. The intention to achieve structural unity—despite a strong improvisatory impulse—also reaches into the fugue, whose theme (Ex. 3.7) is directly derived from the head motive in both regular and inverted versions; the fugue theme also refers to a central passage from the opening section (Ex. 3.5), which, if notated differently (Ex. 3.6), reveals the relationship even more clearly. Seen in this light, the D-minor Toccata, ostensibly fashioned as a show piece, appears, below its flamboyant surface, much more disciplined and controlled. In many ways, it heralds the brilliant future of Bach's organistic art.

It is reasonable to assume that whatever repertoire Bach presented at his Sangerhausen and Arnstadt appearances, the focus of both must have been on his professional command of organ performance and organ composition. Mastery and self-reliance were called for—not the traits of an apprentice, however polished. Bach would have prepared himself thoroughly for these public performances, and although improvisation was always called for, he would certainly have written out core parts of the program with which he wanted to impress his audience in general and the jury in particular.

In his technical keyboard skills, Bach had progressed significantly beyond the state he had reached in Ohrdruf under the guidance of his older brother.

By the age of fifteen, he could play difficult pieces by Johann Jacob Froberger, Johann Caspar Kerll, and Johann Pachelbel contained in the infamous lost manuscript once copied by moonlight, and the presumably corresponding repertoire of preludes, toccatas, fantasias, canzonas, capriccios, and fugues by Froberger and Pachelbel in the Eckelt Tablature of 1692 (see Chapter 2). What the Lüneburg years added were major technical and stylistic dimensions to his performing experience, such as greater manual virtuosity and a more developed pedal technique, as well as north German and French keyboard repertoires; we find evidence for the latter in the Möller Manuscript and Andreas Bach Book (see Chapter 2). Both anthologies contain music materials that would not have been accessible to Christoph Bach—nor are they traceable elsewhere in Thuringia or central Germany—before Sebastian's return from Lüneburg.

Considering the high probability that Bach traveled to Ohrdruf after Easter 1702 and that he spent the balance of the year there, the compilation of the two Ohrdruf anthologies appears in a new light. While earlier it was assumed that Sebastian made the new repertoire available to his Ohrdruf brother only after settling in Arnstadt in 1703, it now seems more plausible that on returning to Ohrdruf in 1702 and repossessing the "moonlight manuscript" once confiscated by Christoph, Sebastian paid off with interest the debt he owed his older brother for copying from his treasured collection without permission. Christoph now acquired numerous organ and harpsichord pieces by, among others, the northerners Reinken, Böhm, Buxtehude, and Nicolaus Bruhns and the French Lebègue, Lully, Louis Marchand, and Marais. There is no question that entries in the Ohrdruf anthologies extended over several years and that Sebastian, from nearby Arnstadt, continued to make material available to his brother, but the transfer most plausibly began in the spring of 1702 rather than the fall of 1703.

The contents of the two anthologies reflect to a considerable extent the repertoire that Bach was able to collect, perform, and study in Lüneburg. However, the technical demands and styles of these pieces not only provide information about Bach's skills at the keyboard, they serve at the same time as guideposts to his own development as a composer—the processes of copying and playing, studying and composing, always went hand in hand. As the two anthologies also demonstrate, Sebastian furnished his brother with quite a few compositions of his own. These works form clusters of genres and styles that can be lined up chronologically with distinct stages of Bach's compositional development, beginning with somewhat experimental pieces that probably originated from the late 1690s, before Lüneburg (such as the Fantasia in C, BWV 570—a quasi-exercise, modeled after Pachelbel, in maintaining the simple rhythmic-melodic motif ♩♫ ), and concluding with more mature and genuinely sophisticated works likely dating from the later Arnstadt years (such as the Passacaglia in C minor, BWV 582—synthesizing and surpassing Buxtehudian and French models) and beyond.

Works that may be assigned to the transitional years 1702–3 are marked by a strong north German influence and are characterized by an original take on traditional compositional approaches. At the same time, these pieces exhibit a youthful exuberance that here and there borders on exaggeration. Among the organ works with these characteristics is the chorale "Wie schön leuchtet der Morgenstern," BWV 739 (the same piece is also transmitted in a fair copy, among the earliest extant Bach autographs). Another example is the Prelude in C major, BWV 531, which opens with a brilliant pedal solo and fugue yet narrow harmonic design. The Prelude in G minor, BWV 535a, entered by Bach into the Möller Manuscript, begins with a concise virtuosic *manualiter* opening that leads into a well-focused, ambitious synthesis of north German figurative and harmonic gestures, on the one hand, and the central German type of prelude with fugue, on the other. Finally, the Prelude in D minor, BWV 549a, features an unprecedented eight-measure solo pedal opening of considerable complexity, followed by a rhetorico-dramatic section full of harmonic surprises, an elaborate fugue, and a finale section of virtuosic figurative material. Works such as these four would have made up an ideal recital program designed to demonstrate mastery of the instrument, introduce original thoughts, and impress an audience. Whatever the pieces were that Bach actually prepared for the Sangerhausen and Arnstadt recitals, they date to the period immediately following his graduation from St. Michael's in Lüneburg, a time free of specific obligations and opportune for concentrated creative and technical work.

Among the works that figure most prominently in the chronology of Bach's early compositions is the *Capriccio on the Departure of the Beloved Brother (Capriccio sopra la lontananza de il fratro dilettissimo)* in B-flat major, BWV 992, which has traditionally been connected with the departure of Johann Jacob from Thuringia for Poland, where in 1704, according to the Genealogy, "he entered the service of the Royal Swedish Army" of King Charles XII, "as oboist *in the Guards.*"[66] However, this conclusion, resulting in a widespread but inauthentic adjustment to the title (—*del suo fratello,* to make it conform to the Italian term for full brother), is at best questionable. The individual musical movements describe, in an expressive and illuminating manner, a farewell scene with the "fratro dilettissimo," from the "coaxing by his friends to dissuade him from his journey" and a "picturing of various calamities that might overtake him in foreign parts" to a concluding fugue "all' imitazione di Posta," with a countersubject imitating a post horn. But not only does the piece fail to display any martial characteristics (such as "alla battaglia"), which occur frequently in seventeenth-century instrumental pieces, the picturesque departure of a recruit by postal coach is simply too fanciful. The Latin "frater" more likely pertains to a different kind of fraternal relationship, such as the one revealed by Bach's manner of addressing his former schoolmate Georg Erdmann, after a hiatus of more than two decades: "Noble and most honored Sir and (if still permissible) esteemed Mr. Brother."[67] Indeed, Erdmann is a most plausible dedicatee of the piece, whose chronological place, on musical grounds, fits much better before 1704 and whose origin may actually go back to Lüneburg, where it could have been written for some kind of graduation party among friends. The immediate post-Lüneburg career of Erdmann, who later entered the diplomatic service, remains unknown, but he may have left St. Michael's School as an adjutant to one of the academy noblemen.

The dating to 1702 of the Capriccio BWV 992 clarifies at the same time the origin and function of a sister piece, the Capriccio in E major *(Capriccio in honorem Joh: Christoph Bachii)*, BWV 993. The more condensed, musically more abstract, and somewhat more sophisticated E-major piece may be best understood as a tribute to the Ohrdruf brother on the occasion of Sebastian's return to Thuringia. It certainly would have been a proper expression of devotion and gratitude to his foster brother and first keyboard teacher, and also would have made manifest Sebastian's progress since leaving Christoph's tutelage.[68] The charmingly pretentious concoction of Latin and Italian, not only in the titles of the two capriccios but also in the various subheadings and author indications of other pieces from about the same period (for instance, BWV 535a: *Praeludium. cum Fuga. ex Gb. Pedaliter. per Joan. Sebast: Bachium*; BWV 549a: *Praeludium ô Fantasia. Pedaliter. ex Db. di Giovanne Seb. Bach*), point to a self-conscious search for artistic identity on the part of the young and ambitious keyboard virtuoso, who probably never saw himself as an apprentice and now tried to place himself in the company of other masters.

Panorama of Arnstadt in an engraving by Pius Rösel von Rosenhoff (c. 1700), after a painting by Meister Wolf (c. 1570, before the town fire that destoyed St. Boniface's Church), showing the town hall and main market square (at center); St. Boniface's (no. 36, immediately below the square), which was later rebuilt with no tower as the New Church; Neideck Castle (lower right); Upper (*Barfüsser*) Church (center left); Lower (Our Lady's) Church (upper left).

# 4

## *Building a Reputation*

### ORGANIST IN ARNSTADT AND MÜHLHAUSEN, 1703–1708

AT THE NEW CHURCH IN ARNSTADT

Bach's later years at the Weimar ducal court "fired him with the desire to try every possible artistry in his treatment of the organ."[1] Experimentation, however, was already deeply rooted in Bach's mental attitude. As the driving force in his youthful and enthusiastic musical endeavors, his daring won him considerable recognition and an outstanding reputation at an early age and led to his first professional position. There can be no doubt that the lackey Bach gladly exchanged his Weimar livery uniform for the civilian clothes of a town organist.

Bach's appointment to the newly created position of organist at the New Church in Arnstadt could only have resulted from his having made a superb impression on the town and church authorities when he tried out the Wender organ. Actually, he may have been offered the job before he returned to Weimar on or shortly after July 13, 1703: his certificate of appointment was dated August 9, and Bach accepted it "by handshake" five days later.[2] It has been suggested that the position was held open for him from the start of the organ construction,[3] but although the Bach family was well-known in Arnstadt, the organist Sebastian was not—at least not until his return from Lüneburg. Moreover, if a job had been waiting for him, why would he seek appointments in Sangerhausen and Weimar? And finally, Andreas Börner, who played for the services at the New Church before Bach's arrival, may have had prior claims on the post: after all, he was the son-in-law of the court organist Christoph Herthum, who in turn was related by marriage to the Bach family. For a variety of reasons, then, Sebastian could not have been a serious candidate before he had demonstrated his superior qualifications in public.

Arnstadt, the oldest city in Thuringia, was granted a city charter in 1266, five and a half centuries after its earliest documented existence, in 704, and it served in the seventeenth and eighteenth centuries as the capital of a small principality governed by the counts of Schwarzburg.[4] Scenically located at the edge of the mountainous Thuringian Forest, it embraced three churches within its walls. The Lower, or Our Lady's, Church, a Gothic basilica with a three-tiered nave, built in the late thirteenth century, was the oldest, largest, and architecturally most distinguished of the three.[5] The fourteenth-century Upper, or Barfüsser, Church, where the superintendent and head of the consistory preached, served as the town's principal church. St. Boniface's Church, a medieval edifice in the center of town, had fallen victim in 1581 to a ferocious fire. The modest and plain building erected between 1676 and 1683 on the site of the ruin—with crucial financial support provided by Countess Sophia of Schwarzburg and hence also referred to as Sophienkirche—was commonly called the New Church. Situated on the market square and adjacent to the town hall, the New Church with its wooden double galleries could accommodate over a third of Arnstadt's population of 3,800. The other two churches, especially the Lower Church, could hold far fewer.

With the completion of the organ for the New Church in 1703, the Arnstadt organist duties had to be reorganized. Previously, one town organist took charge of both Upper and Lower Churches, and a deputy organist provided the necessary assistance, mainly in the Lower Church. Christoph Herthum had been the town and court organist since the death in 1692 of Heinrich Bach (6), his predecessor and father-in-law, although his main job was kitchen manager at the court. As Herthum also functioned as organist of the court chapel at Neideck Castle, a position held earlier by both of Heinrich Bach's sons—first Johann Christoph (13) and then Johann Michael (14)—he could not take on additional obligations at the New Church. So Herthum continued as town and court organist, responsible for the Upper Church and the court chapel, and Andreas Börner was officially given the post at the Lower Church, with additional functions as a regular assistant to his father-in-law at the Upper Church and the court chapel. Börner received his certificate of appointment from the consistory of the count of Schwarzburg on August 14, 1703, the same day as Bach, whose duties lay exclusively in the New Church.

The organization of the Arnstadt church services (see Table 4.1) resulted in rather unequal workloads for the organists, not entirely reflected in their salaries. Herthum earned 57 florins as town organist and an additional 20 as court organist; Börner, who made 20 florins, had to play for a total of ten services each week;[6] and because of overlapping services, both needed their pupils' assistance in order to manage their assignments. Bach, however, received 50 florins for only four services per week in one and the same place—an extraordinarily favorable treatment (indicating the high esteem in which he was held from the outset), especially in light of the mere 30 florins Börner had received as interim organist[7] and the 40 florins paid in 1708 to Bach's successor at the New Church, his cousin Johann Ernst Bach.

Bach's contract required him to be "industrious and reliable in the office, vocation, and practice of art and science" assigned to him,

not to mix into other affairs and functions; to appear promptly on Sundays, feast days, and other days of public divine service in the said New Church at the organ entrusted to you; to play the latter as is fitting; to keep a watchful eye over it and take faithful care of it; to report in time if any part of it becomes weak and to give notice that the necessary repairs should be made; not to let anyone have access to it without the foreknowledge of the Superintendent; and in general to see that damage is avoided and everything is kept in good order and condition.[8]

His annual salary came in four installments, on the traditional Thursday paydays for each quarter: preceding Reminiscere Sunday in March, preceding Trinity Sunday in June, following the Day of the Holy Cross (September 14), and following St. Lucy's Day (December 13). He received an additional sum of 30 talers (= 34 florins 6 groschen) for board and lodging.[9] Compared with the 27 florins 9 groschen he would have earned annually as lackey and court musician in Weimar, his annual salary had now nearly doubled and his total cash compensation tripled.[10] Weddings and other special services would be paid extra, and he had opportunities for further earnings at performances with the court capelle under the direction of Paul Gleitsmann, who would audition Bach's successor and most likely played a role in Bach's appointment as well.[11]

The organ and choir loft in the New Church was built as a third gallery at the west end of the nave, with the organ displayed high and wide against the wall, filling the entire space under the barrel vault.[12] The church's interior might be regarded as an ideal organ recital hall, with both the instrument itself and the organist at the console—not hidden by a *Rückpositiv*—in full view, especially from the two double galleries alongside the nave. Thus, the New Church organist and his brand-new instrument commanded the kind of at-

## TABLE 4.1. Worship Services at the Arnstadt Churches

|  | Sun | Mon | Tue | Wed | Thu | Fri | Sat |
|---|---|---|---|---|---|---|---|
| Lower Church | 6 A.M. ES | — | — | — | — | — | 12 P.M. VS |
| Upper Church | 8 A.M. MS | 7 A.M. PS | 7 A.M. PS | — | — | 7 A.M. ES | 1 P.M. VS |
| New Church | 8 A.M. MS | 7 A.M. PS | — | 2 P.M. VS | 7 A.M. ES | — | — |
| Court Chapel | 8 A.M. MS[a] | 7 A.M. PS | — | — | — | 7 A.M. ES | — |

ES = early service, MS = main service, PS = prayer service, VS = Vesper service, with Confession.
[a]Services not held every Sunday.

tention that no other Arnstadt church could offer. Moreover, Bach's light official schedule combined with the general availability of the church for practicing provided a unique opportunity for his further musical development and
artistic growth. For the first time in his life, he had free reign over a fine instrument with no technical defects, a luxury most organists of the time could
only dream of.

Interior westward view of the New Church, now the Bachkirche, at Arnstadt in a
modern photograph showing the choir and organ loft (third gallery), the Wender
organ of 1703 (after its 1999 restoration), and two small galleries for instrumentalists
(cut into the barrel vault, upper left and right of the choir loft).

While not large, the Wender organ, with twenty-one stops on two manuals (*Oberwerk* and *Brustpositiv*) and pedal,[13] was a good-sized and resourceful instrument. The manuals extended over four octaves (CD to c‴, forty-eight keys) and the pedal over two (CD to d′, twenty-five keys), and, apart from the missing C-sharp, they did not feature an incomplete bottom octave ("short octave": no chromatic keys from C to A), an old-fashioned standard of German manual keyboards. Moreover, while the unequal mean-tone scale with its nearly pure fifths prevailed in older instruments and restricted playing to the "simple" keys with no more than two sharps or flats, Wender apparently adopted Andreas Werckmeister's new "well-tempered" tuning system, a close approximation of equal temperament (based on the principle of dividing the octave into twelve equal semitones), which allowed the organist to play in any key without spoiling its distinctive characteristics.[14] But like other seventeenth-century church organs in central and northern Germany, the organ would have been tuned at "choir pitch," which lay at least a whole tone above the then-current, modern chamber pitch (a′ = 415), and thus at least a half tone above modern pitch.[15] Werckmeister's innovative tuning system, which would later lend its name to Bach's famous collection of preludes and fugues, was hailed by many musicians, most notably by Buxtehude, who wrote a poetic preface to one of Werckmeister's books.[16] Although only few authentic parts of the original Arnstadt organ have survived, Bach certainly had at his disposal an instrument that conformed to the most modern standards of the time. He was also provided with a salaried bellows operator, Michael Ernst Frobenius, who was remunerated for the divine services as well as for tunings and repairs,[17] and who would have been paid by Bach himself for any additional assistance.

In his role as organist of the New Church, Bach reported to the superintendent of churches and member of the consistory of the count of Schwarzburg, M. Johann Gottfried Olearius, a learned man from a distinguished family of Lutheran theologians and scholars. (Bach owned a five-volume biblical commentary by the superintendent's younger brother, Johann Olearius, a professor at Leipzig University.)[18] The very Reverend Olearius, in charge of the Arnstadt clergy since 1688, had surrounded himself with a highly capable group of ministers and deacons whose homilies and preachings collectively furthered Bach's theological edification; the young organist most often heard M. Justus Christian Uthe, the main preacher of the New Church. Olearius also paid considerable attention to the quality of church music in his purview, since he had himself directed the music at Our Lady's Church in Halle, where he served earlier as deacon. Moreover, in 1692, he had delivered and subsequently published an inspiring funeral sermon for his organist at the Upper Church, Heinrich Bach,[19] whose substitute in 1689–90, Sebastian's elder brother Christoph, was also known to him. Sebastian's appointment would not have been possible without the superintendent's active support.

The primary duty of the organist of the New Church was to lead and accompany the congregational singing of hymns and to play an appropriate chorale prelude introducing each tune. He also had to play preludes and postludes at the beginning and end of the service as well as music, preferably chorale-based, during Communion. The liturgical structure of the main service for all Arnstadt churches related closely to the standard Lutheran format (see Table 4.2) and followed the *Agenda Schwartzburgica* of 1675, the ceremonial formulary for the Schwarzburg counties.[20]

In 1705, Arnstadt received a new version of its own hymnbook, *Neuverbessertes Arnstädtisches Gesangbuch* (without melodies), edited by M. Johann Christoph Olearius, the superintendent's son. Its core contents resembled other circulating Lutheran hymnals, which rarely varied from the "classic" sixteenth- and seventeenth-century hymn repertoire dating from Martin Luther and other Reformation theologian-poets through Paul Gerhardt and his generation. The liturgically prescribed hymns (as in Table 4.2) were always taken from the earliest Reformation hymns.

The *Figuralstück,* a polyphonic piece with or without instrumental accompaniment, was featured in the main and Vespers services at the Upper Church, the city's principal church, attended by the more privileged citizens and court

## TABLE 4.2. Order of the Divine Service at Arnstadt

| Congregation and Organ | Choir | Preacher and Ministrants[a] |
|---|---|---|
| Prelude | | |
| Antiphon "Komm, Heiliger Geist, erfüll die Herzen" | Kyrie and Gloria *choraliter* | |
| Hymn "Allein Gott in der Höh sei Ehr" | | Epistle lesson |
| Hymn chosen by the preacher | | Gospel lesson |
| Hymn "Wir glauben all an einen Gott" | or Credo *choraliter* | |
| | *Figuralstück* (polyphonic music; primarily at the Upper Church) | |
| Hymn *de tempore* (seasonal hymn) | | Sermon |
| | | Communion |
| | Sanctus *choraliter* | |
| | Agnus Dei *choraliter* | |
| (Music during Communion: congregational hymns, organ music) | | Administration of the Sacrament |
| Blessing | | |
| Postlude | | |

[a]Connecting versicles, canticles, collects, and other prayers are not specified; for the main service on high feast days, most German versicles, canticles, and collects were supplemented by Latin ones.

officials. Here was where the superintendent preached, and also where the princely family members worshipped when they went into town, which they frequently did, especially on feast days. On those latter occasions, court capellmeister Gleitsmann had charge of the church music and usually presented a work of his own composition.[21] The Upper Church was also home base for the Arnstadt Lyceum's chorus musicus, directed by the cantor, Ernst Dietrich Heindorff, a respected musician and close friend of the Bach family. Heindorff provided choristers for liturgical functions at the other churches as well, in particular the New Church, which kept its own substantial choir library. This collection contained the traditional sixteenth-century motet repertoire of Heinrich Isaac, Josquin, Jacob Obrecht, Pierre de la Rue, Ludwig Senfl, and others, but also more recent literature, such as Andreas Hammerschmidt's *Musicalische Gespräche über die Evangelia* of 1655, motets for four to seven voices and basso continuo for occasions falling throughout the church year. An even newer anthology, Nicolaus Niedt's *Sonn- und Fest-Tags-Lust* of 1698, comprised seventy-three small cantatas covering every Sunday and feast day across the year. Since Niedt was court organist and chancery clerk at Schwarzburg-Sondershausen, this last big publication of seventeenth-century German church music probably received much use at Schwarzburg-Arnstadt as well.

When Andreas Börner served as interim organist at the New Church, he was also put in charge of its student choir, a responsibility he may have initially retained after Bach became organist in August 1703. Bach, in any case, was not charged with directing the student choir, and during 1705–6 Johann Andreas Rambach, an older student from the Lyceum, was paid to be choral prefect (assistant director) for services at the New Church. Bach's contract lacks any specific details regarding his functions as organist beyond the expectation that he "appear promptly . . . for the divine services" and that he show himself "industrious and reliable in the office," and makes no reference whatsoever to any collaboration with the student choir, let alone participation in concerted music presented by the choir.

Two to three years into Bach's tenure of office, however, the issue of his contractual obligations became the subject of two disputes between Bach and the consistory, both related to disciplinary problems. In the first, Bach appeared before the consistory on August 4, 1705,[22] to complain about a student by the name of Geyersbach. One night, on his way home from the castle and crossing the market square, Bach passed by six students sitting on the *Langenstein* (Long Stone), when one of them, Geyersbach, suddenly

went after him with a stick, calling him to account: Why had he made abusive remarks about him? He [Bach] answered that he had made no abusive remarks about him, and that no one could prove it, for he had gone his way very quietly. Geyersbach retorted that while he [Bach] might not have maligned him, he had maligned his bassoon at some time, and whoever insulted his belongings insulted him as well; he had carried on like a dirty dog's etc., etc. And he [Geyersbach] had at once struck out at him. Since he had not been prepared for this, he had been about to draw his dagger, but Geyersbach had fallen into his arms, and the two of them tumbled about until the rest of the students who had been sitting with him . . . had separated them so that he [Bach] could continue his way home. . . . Since he did not deserve such treatment and thus was not safe on the street, he humbly requested that said Geyersbach be duly punished, and that he [Bach] be given appropriate satisfaction and accorded respect by the others, so that henceforth they would let him pass without abuse or attack.

After hearing Bach's cousin Barbara Catharina, who had accompanied him from the castle and who therefore could serve as a witness, the consistory concluded that Geyersbach "initiated the incident, since he not only addressed Bach first but also was the first to strike out." On the other hand, it developed that Bach had indeed called Geyersbach a *Zippel Fagottist* (greenhorn bassoonist), and members of the consistory admonished him that "he might very well have refrained from calling Geyersbach a *Zippel Fagottist;* such gives lead in the end to unpleasantness of this kind, especially since he [Bach] had a reputation for not getting along with the students and of claiming that he was engaged only for simple chorale music, and not for concerted pieces, which was wrong, for he must help out in all music making." Bach answered that "he would not refuse, if only there were a *Director Musices* [music director]," whereupon he was told that "men must live among *imperfecta;* he must get along with the students, and they must not make one another's lives miserable."

At the time of the incident, Bach was twenty years old, while Geyersbach and his companion, Johann Friedrich Schüttwürfel (also mentioned in the proceedings), were both twenty-three.[23] Thus, the young organist had to deal with students who were, in some cases, older than himself. The six sitting on the Long Stone had, as amateur musicians, just finished performing a serenade at a christening when Bach passed by—"tobacco pipe in his mouth" according to Geyersbach, "no tobacco pipe in his mouth" according to Barbara Catharina Bach. With or without pipe, Bach's demeanor vis-à-vis the students must have been perceived as arrogant, and the market square brawl only magnifies the troublesome relationship that was bound to emerge between two unequal parties, both serving the New Church: on the one hand, a group of Lyceum students well above age twenty who were able to form a vocal-instrumental ensemble of sorts, and on the other, an ambitious, highly gifted, and, his youth notwithstanding, eminent professional musician who not only had graduated at age seventeen, but had done so from a more prestigious Latin school. No wonder Bach sought to keep the school choir at a distance and tried to fall back on a contract that did not specifically require him to work with the students— even though the church authorities had clearly expected him to lead the choir as Börner, the interim organist, twelve years Bach's senior, had done.

Bach's reluctance if not refusal to work with the student choir came up again, this time in connection with a complaint about his prolonged absence from Arnstadt in the winter of 1705–6 when he visited with Buxtehude in Lübeck.[24] This time, the superintendent himself conducted the consistory's interrogation, which focused initially on the length of the leave of absence that had been approved. Bach "had asked for only four weeks, but had stayed about four times as long." Bach replied that he had "hoped the organ playing had been so well taken care of by the one he had engaged for the purpose that no complaint could be entered on that account." He had, in fact, hired his cousin Johann Ernst Bach as a temporary substitute—the same cousin who would later succeed him in Arnstadt—thereby mitigating to some extent the consistory's accusation. This reasoning, however, only goaded the consistory into bringing up two further matters.

First, they reproved Bach "for having hitherto made many curious *variationes* in the chorale, and mingled many strange tones in it, and for the fact that the Congregation has been confused by it." This charge represented an attack on Bach's manner of preluding for the congregational hymns and not, as the broader context of the exchange demonstrates (first he was playing "too long," then "too short"), on his accompaniment of congregational singing.[25] Typical chorale intonations of the time followed the models established by Johann Christoph and Johann Michael Bach and Johann Pachelbel, in which the hymn tune was introduced line by line for longer pieces and the initial line only for shorter ones, without modifying the chorale's melodic contours or harmonic implications. Bach departed significantly from this pattern in his large-scale chorale preludes, which are often modeled on the fantasia-like north German chorale elaborations, here dissolving a plain chorale melody into complex embellishments, there modifying its intervallic structure, here leaving behind the chorale's home key, and there introducing other features that the consistory members perceived as "curious variations" and "strange tones." Yet the temporal reference "hitherto" can hardly refer to an abrupt change in Bach's playing style after his prolonged absence, for only two or three Sundays had passed since his return from Lübeck. The accusation rather expresses an irritation that had preceded the trip, suggesting that Bach was playing large-scale chorale preludes in the mold of his early setting of "Wie schön leuchtet der Morgenstern," BWV 739.

Second, the consistory returned to the old issue—

that hitherto no concerted music had been performed, for which he was responsible, because he did not wish to get along with the students; accordingly, he was to declare whether he was willing to play polyphonic as well as monophonic music [*figural(iter) alß choral(iter)*] with the students. For a capellmeister could not be engaged just for this sake. If he did not wish to do so, he should but state that fact *categorice* so that other arrangements could be made and someone engaged who would.

At the same session of the consistory, the student Rambach who served as choir prefect was "similarly reproved for the *disordres* that have hitherto taken place in the New Church between the students and the organist." But Rambach, who was also "reproved for going into the wine cellar . . . during the sermon," put the blame on the organist by reporting that Bach "had previously played rather too long, but after his attention had been called to it by the Superintendent, he had at once fallen into the other extreme and made it too short," which probably caused laughter among the students and hence contributed to the "disorders." At any rate, the lack of collaboration between the organist and the choir, who had to occupy the same church gallery, became a disturbing matter that was not resolved by the consistory's admonitions issued on February 21, 1706.

Less than nine months later, the consistory proceedings returned to the unhappy subject: "It is pointed out to the organist Bach that he is to declare whether he is willing to make music with the students as he has already been instructed to do, or not; for if he considers it no disgrace to be connected with the Church and to accept his salary, he must also not be ashamed to make music with the students assigned to do so, until other instructions are given. For it is the intention that the latter shall practice, in order one day to be the better fitted for music."[26] This time the wording sounded like an order, understandable from the consistory's perspective given its firm resolve to establish a well-balanced structure at the New Church for performing the kind of sacred music in which vocal and instrumental elements complemented and supported one another. Bach replied that he would "declare himself in writing concerning this matter." Whether or not he ever submitted such a written statement (no such document is known), it is clear that after more than three years Bach did not see a realistic basis for a fruitful collaboration with the student choir, even knowing full well that such an arrangement would present new and enriching opportunities. For him, it could not have been the principle as such, but frustrating external conditions that discouraged him from seeking common ground for choir and organ, voices and instruments.

The consistory's assertion that "hitherto no concerted music had been performed . . . because he did not wish to get along with the students" cannot be entirely accurate. After all, the affair that provoked Bach to call Geyersbach a *Zippel Fagottist* suggests that they were engaged in making concerted music together, which involved the participation of a bassoon. Incidentally, the old German *fagott* is not the same instrument as the *basson* of the late seventeenth-century French orchestra, and although contemporary terminology is not always consistent, it seems plausible that Geyersbach played a dulcian; that is, a prototype of the bassoon, in one piece and tuned to the higher *Chorton* pitch (rather than the French type with joints, in the lower chamber pitch), the kind of instrument that—as the German name *Chorist-Fagott* suggests—played a dominant role as a continuo instrument in late seventeenth-century German church music. What is presumably Bach's earliest surviving cantata, "Nach dir, Herr, verlanget mich" BWV 150, requires a *Fagotto* in Chorton pitch and assigns it a demanding role in the fifth movement, "Aria Alto, Tenore et Basso con Fagotto"—a part probably beyond the capability of the said *Zippel Fagottist*. This cantata, for which no autograph source survives, may well belong to the second half of Bach's Arnstadt period and may have been destined for the New Church or more likely for elsewhere, such as the chapel at Neideck Castle. What little concerted music was performed by the school choir at the New Church with Bach participating as organist was probably not composed by him.

The infamous Geyersbach incident began with Bach walking home from Neideck Castle, built between 1553 and 1560, which served as the stately residence of Imperial Count Anton Günther II of Schwarzburg. Beginning in 1683, Count Anton Günther ruled both the Schwarzburg-Arnstadt and Schwarzburg-Sondershausen counties and in 1697 was promoted to princely rank by Emperor Leopold I.[27] The count was married to Auguste Dorothea, daughter of Duke Anton Ulrich of Brunswick-Wolfenbüttel, whose love for theater and music, added to the splendor of his court, provided her with magnificent surroundings during her formative years. In many ways, Wolfenbüttel served as a model for Count Anton Günther. The staff of his administration in Arnstadt numbered around 120, as well as many notable scholars and artists, among them the famous numismatists Wilhelm Ernst Tentzel, Andreas Morelli, and Christian Schlegel, but also some more obscure scientists engaged as "gold makers." In matters of culture, the count maintained good relations with Bayreuth, Brunswick, Celle, Dresden, Gotha, Halle, Cassel, Cöthen, Leipzig, Magdeburg, Munich, Nürnberg, Prague, and Weimar; moreover, he established an art collection and a court theater, and showed a keen interest in music. It was this nobleman who, after the untimely death of the Arnstadt court and town musician Johann Christoph Bach, inquired of the widow "whether there was not another Bach available . . . for he should and must have a Bach again."[28] And as head of the consistory, he was also Johann Sebastian's nominal superior: Bach's salary orders, for example, were issued in his name, and he was known for his involvement in virtually all realms of public life at Arnstadt.[29] Why should Bach have come (with sword, suggesting formal dress or uniform) from the castle that evening—and, according to Barbara Catharina's testimony, specifically from the apartment of the court organist Herthum[30]—if not from some kind of official musical engagement?

Count Anton Günther maintained a court capelle of some twenty musicians, most of them typically functioning in dual roles as musician and servant or court and town musician. After the death in 1701 of the longtime court capellmeister Adam Drese, who had once worked with Heinrich Schütz in Dresden, Paul Gleitsmann, a violinist, lutenist, and viola da gamba player and a veteran member of the capelle, took over its direction.[31] While Bach did not hold a court appointment and the Geyersbach story provides at best only indirect evidence of court connections, it would have been only natural for a musician of his background, special talents, and reputation to be drawn occasionally into the court music scene. Musical life at the Arnstadt court after 1700 is poorly documented, but we do know that in 1705 the court theater saw performances of two burlesque operettas: in February, *Das Carneval als ein Verräter des Eckels vor der Heiligen Fastenzeit* (The Carnival as a Tattler on the Loathing of the Holy Lenten Period), and in May, *Die Klugheit der Obrigkeit in Anordnung des Bierbrauens* (The Wisdom of the Government in Regulating Beer Brewing).[32] Arnstadtians were able to attend the shows through ticket sales.[33]

The court music scene with its secular and sacred dimensions would have provided numerous opportunities for Bach the keyboardist and versatile instrumentalist. And by continuing his brief Weimar court experience of 1703, the Arnstadt court would have exposed him to musical genres and repertoires that were otherwise not readily accessible to him. The earliest specimen of an Italian chamber cantata in Bach's hand, "Amante moribondo" by the Venetian composer Antonio Biffi, may well originate from there. The court would also have given Bach the opportunity to meet and perform with out-of-town musicians and might provide some kind of clue to "the unfamiliar maiden" (*frembde Jungfer*) whom, according to the consistory minutes, Bach "invited into the choir loft and let . . . make music there."[34] Female singers were traditionally barred from performing at churches with Latin school choirs, although in many smaller churches in towns and villages throughout Thuringia women participated in choirs as helpers, so-called *Adjuvanten*. In any event, the incident with the *frembde Jungfer* must have involved an out-of-town singer and not, as often assumed, Bach's distant cousin Maria Barbara, whom he married the following year.[35] Maria Barbara had been living in Arnstadt for several years, so she could scarcely have been described as "unfamiliar."

The consistory's complaint—especially petty since Bach seems to have consulted in the matter with the pastor of the New Church, Magister Uthe—may have merely annoyed him, but taken together with the forceful admonition made at the same hearing about his lack of relations with the student choir clearly indicated that he had little or no room for maneuvering. The congregation of the New Church was entitled to enjoy modern-style church music, and the consistory legitimately expected both the organist and the student choir to play a mutually constructive role in establishing a viable and attractive musical program. But Bach saw no way toward a realistic compromise. His standards and ambitions were much too remote from that of the basically leaderless choir. Bach realized that orderly progress could not be achieved with the help of a mere student prefect; a person of authority, with proper disciplinary oversight, was needed. He also realistically understood that he himself, on the basis of his youth alone, would not be in a position to claim the necessary authority, and for this reason requested a *director musices* from outside. He also avoided saying anything negative about the student choir; in fact, he expressed his willingness to participate if only under the proper leadership. In other words, he was not pointing out any lack of musical competence on the part of the choir, but a lack of discipline, which not only affected the choral situation but apparently had wider ramifications. Indeed, during Bach's time in Arnstadt, municipal and church authorities recorded many complaints about the excessive behavior of undisciplined Lyceum students.[36] So after three years, he saw little future for himself at the New Church.

As for Arnstadt itself, as much as he appreciated that his grandfather's town was the nerve center of the Bach family and provided plenty of advantages and connections, Sebastian must have felt keenly that its narrow confines and its close-knit family environment severely hampered his privacy and freedom of movement. Eying a position in the free imperial city of Mühlhausen, he showed a readiness to move again out of the traditional family realm—he had savored his time in Lüneburg, hundreds of miles away from home. He apparently deemed such a step essential to starting a family of his own and solidifying the family bonds in a different way. For he had become close to Maria Barbara, daughter of his father's cousin Michael Bach, the late organist and town scribe of Gehren, and the two of them wanted to marry. After Johann Sebastian had secured the new position, they indeed arranged for a wedding at the village church of Dornheim, three miles from Arnstadt, on October 17, 1707.

Almost to the day three years earlier, Maria Barbara had suffered the loss of her mother, Catharina Bach, widow of the Gehren organist, Michael. Maria Barbara and her older sisters, Friedelena Margaretha and Barbara Catharina—all well beyond school age—moved to Arnstadt, where they joined the households of their mother's sisters. Maria Barbara, who had turned twenty the day after her mother's burial, moved in with her godfather, burgomaster Feldhaus, and his wife Margarethe, her mother's twin sister and daughter of Johann Wedemann, town scribe in Arnstadt until his death in 1684. The sisters Elisabeth and Catharina Wedemann had married brothers, Christoph (13) and Michael (14), sons of the town and court organist Heinrich Bach (6) (see Table 4.3).

By the time of the move, in late 1704, the well-to-do Feldhaus had enough space for his orphaned nieces in the two houses he owned, one called Steinhaus (Stone House) and the other Güldene Krone (Golden Crown). He may even have provided space for Johann Sebastian: after Bach's departure for Mühlhausen,

TABLE 4.3. Daughters of the Arnstadt Town Scribe Johann
Wedemann (1611–1684) and Their Marriages

| Maria Elisabeth | November 26, 1667 | ∞Johann Christoph Bach, organist in Eisenach |
|---|---|---|
| Catharina | January 10, 1675 | ∞Johann Michael Bach, organist in Gehren |
| Margarethe[a] | February 18, 1679 | ∞Martin Feldhaus,[a] merchant and burgomaster in Arnstadt |
| Susanna Barbara | 1680 | ∞Johann Gottfried Bellstedt, assistant town scribe in Arnstadt |
| Regina | June 5, 1708 | ∞Johann Lorenz Stauber, parson in Dornheim |

[a]Godparents of Maria Barbara, Johann Sebastian Bach's future wife.[37]

Feldhaus collected the sum of 30 talers, the amount that the New Church organist received as an annual salary supplement for room and board, suggesting that the burgomaster had provided "food, bed, and room" for Bach.[38] Furthermore, Barbara Catharina Bach's testimony in the Geyersbach affair that she and her cousin Sebastian had come from organist Christoph Herthum's apartment in Neideck Castle suggests that they were crossing the market square on the way to their common home. Altogether, the three Michael Bach daughters not only added to the dense concentration of Bach family members in Arnstadt, they also reconnected Sebastian with the Bach-Wedemann branch of the family. For in Eisenach, he had grown up with the children his uncle Christoph Bach had with Elisabeth Wedemann, with most of whom he maintained a lifelong contact. Now his own future wife was a Wedemann descendant as well, and the Bach-Wedemann family network would continue to benefit him.

The fourth Wedemann daughter, Susanna Barbara, had married the Arnstadt town scribe, Johann Gottfried Bellstedt (assistant scribe prior to Wedemann's death), whose brother Johann Hermann held the same position in Mühlhausen and would eventually work out a contract with the new organist. Before being "entrusted with this commission,"[39] Hermann Bellstedt would have been the person to notify the Arnstadt clan that Mühlhausen was seeking an organist, knowing as he did that the organist of the New Church in Arnstadt was actively job hunting. Finally, Regina, the youngest of the Wedemann daughters, can be linked to the wedding of Johann Sebastian and Maria Barbara Bach in Dornheim through the widowed parson Johann Lorenz Stauber, who united the couple at St. Bartholomaeus's Church there in October 1707. Less than eight months later, Regina Wedemann and Parson Stauber followed suit, taking their own marriage vows.

The Dornheim wedding, which took place almost four months after Bach had relocated to Mühlhausen, closed a chapter of his life that had been so crucial for the young musician's development and emancipation. But he had clearly outgrown Arnstadt, the quintessential Bach-family town, and leaving would allow him to shake off some of the family chains. The choice of holding the wedding ceremony in Dornheim rather than in Arnstadt might, at first glance, suggest that Bach's problems with the Arnstadt consistory were persisting, but in fact Dornheim fell under its jurisdiction as well. Moreover, in consideration of Bach's years of service to the New Church, the usual fees for the wedding ceremony there were remitted.[40] The reason for Bach's choice, then, must have been entirely personal, for at Dornheim the officiating minister was a close family friend. Sadly, no information at all is available about the wedding festivities or the music made on this well-chosen day—October 17, a Monday. The bridegroom and guests from farther away were able to set out for the trip to Dornheim immediately after the morning services the day before.

The wedding would have been a major family event, comparable to if not surpassing the celebration in 1694 when Bach's older brother was married in Ohrdruf and his father, Ambrosius, as well as Johann Pachelbel performed. This time, only one member of the parental generation (that is, of all the grandchildren of Hans Bach) was still living: Johann Aegidius Bach *(8)*, director of the Erfurt town music company.[41] Christoph Herthum could have joined him as another representative of that generation of musicians. But Maria Barbara's and Johann Sebastian's siblings and cousins, their spouses, and some of their children could easily have formed a most respectable ensemble including among the professionals Johann Christoph Bach *(17)* of Gehren, Johann Bernhard Bach *(18)* of Eisenach, Johann Christoph Bach *(19)* of Erfurt, Johann Valentin Bach *(21)* of Schweinfurt, Johann Christoph Bach *(22)* of Ohrdruf, Johann Ernst Bach *(25)* of Arnstadt, and Johann Nicolaus Bach *(27)* of Jena, the latter a first cousin of Maria Barbara's. The event would have provided a chance to return to a famous wedding piece written by the late brother of Maria Barbara's father, Johann Christoph Bach *(13)* of Eisenach. An original set of parts for this dramatic secular work, "Meine Freundin, du bist schön," existed in Johann Sebastian's library, with a title wrapper in his own later hand (see illustration, page 38). There are also two wedding pieces by Bach that may have been written around the time of his own wedding: the cantata "Der Herr denket an uns," BWV 196, a setting of Psalm 115:12–15, with a scoring (four-part vocal ensemble, strings, and continuo) suitable for the small Dornheim church, a fifteenth-century structure with a history dating back to the twelfth century;[42] and the Quodlibet BWV 524 (scored for four voices and continuo), with a parodistic text and a plethora of coarse allusions, including references to Bach's circle of family and friends.[43] Both compositions seem to originate from 1707–8 (with the autograph of BWV 524 securely datable to Bach's Mühlhausen period), but we have no concrete evidence to connect either one with this wedding—nor, for that matter, with the slightly later Stauber-Wedemann wedding, surely another music-making opportunity for the members of the Bach family.

## "First Fruits" and the Buxtehude Experience

As annoying, embarrassing, and disruptive as the various run-ins with the consistory may have been for Bach, their overall significance was marginal. It is only because the pertinent documents transmit most of the scant biographical information we have for the Arnstadt period that their content dominates our thinking. They especially distract from the fact that for nearly four years, from August 1703 through May 1707, the young musician experienced circumstances that bordered on the ideal. In an economically secure and socially agreeable situation, Bach enjoyed an extremely light workload as organist of the New Church, leaving him time for practicing, studying, and composing. He likely occupied a comfortable room or apartment in one of the two Arnstadt houses belonging to Burgomaster Feldhaus, where he surely kept a harpsichord and perhaps other keyboard instruments. But first and foremost, he had at his disposal a brand-new organ, the perfect training equipment for refining his technical keyboard skills and for formulating his own musical ideas, testing them both in the privacy of his practice hours at the church and in front of a large audience during the divine services.

The overall musical scene in Arnstadt was active but conventional, certainly not vigorous, and perhaps on the dull side. That would have been Bach's own perception, for neither the court nor the town offered any musical figures who were able to generate excitement, let alone provide him stimulation or challenges. He soon discovered that his was the best show in town, also the one with the largest audience—around 1,500 worshippers attending the New Church every Sunday. And he clearly worked hard at his craft, even though most Arnstadters, who took the solid music making of anyone named Bach for granted, did not realize what kind of genius resided in their town.

So between the ages of eighteen and twenty-two—today's college years—Bach worked not quite in seclusion, but in circumstances that required him to satisfy entirely on his own his strong yearning to advance. He made the best out of the situation by focusing on intensive self-study, building on the broad foundations laid in Ohrdruf and Lüneburg. In Arnstadt, the Obituary relates, "he really showed the first fruits of his application to the art of organ playing and to composition, which he had learned chiefly by observing the works of the most famous and proficient composers of his day and by the fruits of his own reflection upon them."[44] Having received a solid Latin school grounding, he well understood the role of *exempla classica* for the advancement of learning and so turned to the best models, which he found in "the works of Bruhns, Reinken, Buxtehude, and several good French organists." As these preferences show, the Lüneburg-Hamburg experiences left their particular mark, but other German and Italian composers played a significant role as well. After all, from his Eisenach days he had grown up with German and Italian repertoires, whereas north German and French music represented more of a recent discovery. Carl Philipp Emanuel Bach offers a corrective when he specifies in a letter to Forkel that "besides Froberger, Kerll, and Pachelbel" (the focus of the Ohrdruf repertoire), his father "heard and studied the works of [Girolamo] Frescobaldi, the Baden Capellmeister [Caspar Ferdinand] Fischer, [Nicolaus Adam] Strunck,"[45] followed by the list from the Obituary and the added name of Georg Böhm. Even this expanded list must be considered representative at best, for we know from other evidence that at this early point he was also familiar with works of Johann Kuhnau, Giovanni Legrenzi, Arcangelo Corelli, and many others.[46]

Bach's inquisitiveness led him to quickly scrutinize and absorb these masters' different compositional approaches and their enormous stylistic breadth. Of particular interest to him were the various ways they elaborated a musical subject in fugal form. Unlike the free textures of preludes or dance movements, the rigorous polyphonic structure of a fugue required a firm command of the principles and rules of counterpoint. From the beginning, Bach savored the challenge of formulating a musical thought that would not just provide the raw material for a musical structure but that would define the shape of its individual voices, their interaction, the progress of the piece, and finally the character of the whole. "Through his own study and reflection alone he became even in his youth a pure and strong fugue writer," reports Carl Philipp Emanuel, noting that "the above named favorites—the list beginning with Froberger—were all strong fugue writers."[47]

Bach's deep immersion in the contrapuntal intricacies of composition and his analysis of many different fugal examples spurred him to form a musical logic that became an unmistakable hallmark of his style. One of his study methods consisted of taking a given model and turning it into a new work, not by arranging it but by appropriating the thematic material, subjects, and countersubjects and rewriting the score to create a different piece—a new solution to what he took to be a musical question. And in the process of recomposing, he discovered new thematic connections or contrapuntal combinations as well as new harmonic, melodic, and rhythmic features. Among such works are not only the harpsichord fugues based on Reinken's *Hortus musicus* (BWV

954, 965/2, and 966/2), but also the organ fugues BWV 574b after Legrenzi, BWV 579 after Corelli's Opus 3 of 1689, and the harpsichord fugues BWV 946, 950, and 951 after Albinoni's Opus 1 of 1694. In all these fugues, Bach explores the possibilities of double counterpoint, in which the upper and lower voices are freely switched. He was drawn to the Italian works because they, in particular, featured attractive themes in cantabile style that typical north German fugues rarely offered.

The absence of a reliable chronology for Bach's early works prevents us from determining with any precision what constituted the basket of first fruits that Bach filled between 1703 and 1707. But we can say with certainty that in his thirteen hundred days at Arnstadt, Bach worked exceedingly hard to advance his performing skills (particularly the art of improvisation, an essential element of any organist's background) and to further his compositional technique. The fluent elegance of the notation in the few surviving Arnstadt samples of Bach's music[48] hand presents ample evidence that they resulted from extensive composing on paper. Autograph manuscripts from before 1706–7 exist for only five works: the Fantasia in C minor, BWV Anh. 205; the Prelude in C minor, BWV 921; the Prelude in G minor, BWV 535a; and the chorale settings "Wie schön leuchtet der Morgenstern," BWV 739 and 764. All of them are fair copies and not composing scores, meaning that the works as such predate their autograph sources. Moreover, these manuscripts are indicative of the great care and pride with which the young composer notated and preserved his creations.

Bach's achievements before he became organist in Arnstadt have traditionally been underestimated,[49] and that applies to his Arnstadt, Mühlhausen, and early Weimar years as well. A complicating factor in defining the Arnstadt repertoire of keyboard works is that Bach made later use of some of the compositions, for both performance and teaching, which resulted in often substantial, sometimes multiple revisions. Nevertheless, we can say that the Arnstadt repertoire comprises organ chorales of various types (chorale partitas, larger and smaller chorale preludes, chorale harmonizations); fantasias, preludes, and toccatas (without fugues, with integrated fugues, and with separate fugues), as well as single fugues for organ and harpsichord; and suites, partitas, sonatas, and variations for harpsichord. In all likelihood, some of the earliest settings from the later *Orgel-Büchlein* (such as "Herr Christ, der einge Gottessohn," BWV 601, and "Ich ruf zu dir, Herr Jesu Christ," BWV 639) originate from Arnstadt;[50] probably also the Passacaglia in C minor, BWV 582, in many ways an homage to Buxtehude and Reinken. Buxtehude's ostinato works provided the immediate model for Bach, and Reinken introduced him to the permutation fugue, in which each voice enters with the same series of subject and countersubjects. The young organist and composer accepted the challenge and met it, as in so many other cases, by not merely transcending the prototypes but actually redefining the genre.

It probably took less than two years (plus the unpleasant Geyersbach affair) for Bach to realize the serious drawbacks of staying in Arnstadt. The musical scores he studied must by then have looked more attractive to him than the musical life in this Thuringian town and its vicinity. So he decided to take a month's leave in order to realize a dream. If there was ever a musician Bach was dying to meet, it was Dieterich Buxtehude—not a far-fetched desire and one he apparently shared with others: for in 1703, George Frideric Handel and Johann Mattheson had paid a short visit to Buxtehude in Lübeck, from which they returned to Hamburg with powerful impressions.[51] For them and for Bach, Buxtehude, then in his mid-sixties, signified a kind of father figure who anticipated the ideal of the autonomous composer, a category unheard of at the time. The bourgeois, liberal, and commercial atmosphere of the free imperial city of Lübeck provided Buxtehude with considerable flexibility in developing and realizing his various projects. Although he held the distinguished position of organist at St. Mary's, his overall activities were characterized by a display of artistic initiative combined with unusual managerial independence. Courtly service would not have permitted such free conduct. Buxtehude was able to develop his career as a virtuoso, to travel, and to surround himself with pupils. He regularly played public organ recitals in Lübeck, performing compositions of his own that set new standards of form, size, texture, and character. He seized numerous opportunities for composing vocal works and, acting as his own impresario, organized and financed performances of evening concerts (Abend-Musiken) at his church. For these concerts, he leaned on both Hamburg opera conventions and the Carissimi oratorio tradition to create, around 1678, the prototype of the large-scale, multisectional German oratorio, whose librettos he regularly published. He also published two collections of sonatas, Opus 1 in 1694 and Opus 2 in 1696. In short, he conducted his office of organist in the style of a municipal capellmeister, thereby serving as a clear role model, most notably for Georg Philipp Telemann when he took a post in Hamburg and Bach when he moved to Leipzig.

Moreover, Buxtehude exemplified the ideal type of the universal musician, balancing theory and practice. Scholarly theoretical erudition counted among the prerequisites for a high musical office, and Buxtehude easily filled the bill. His theoretical background, which reflected the Italian tradition of Gioseffo Zarlino, was supplied most likely through Matthias Weckmann and Reinken. However, Buxtehude placed more emphasis on musical practice: rather than writing treatises, he demonstrated his contrapuntal sophistication in diverse practical applications, thus again showing the way for the Bach of The Well-Tempered Clavier and The Art of Fugue—that is, Bach the musical scholar.

Buxtehude also involved himself in organology (the study of musical instruments). A widely recognized organ expert, he held close ties with his colleague the organist Andreas Werckmeister, the premier German musical scientist and speculative theorist at the end of the seventeenth century, and became the strongest public advocate of Werckmeister's new system of temperament. Finally, his compositional orientation included a broad spectrum of styles and genres, incorporating retrospective as well as modern tendencies, Dutch and Hanseatic traditions (through Jan Pieters Sweelinck, Heinrich Scheidemann, and Reinken), English elements (in his writing for viola da gamba), French manners (in choral movements emulating Jean-Baptiste Lully), and Italian traditions (Frescobaldi, Legrenzi, and Giacomo Carissimi). Nearly all new genres of the seventeenth century may be found in his music: concerto, motet, chorale, aria, and recitative in the vocal realm; toccata, prelude, fugue, ciaconna, canzona, suite, sonata, dance, and variation in the instrumental.

From Bach's vantage point in 1705, there was simply no other musician who could offer him so much, "so he undertook a journey, on foot, to Lübeck, in order to listen to the famous organist of St. Mary's Church there, Dieterich Buxtehude. He tarried there, not without profit, for almost a quarter of a year, and then returned to Arnstadt." This rather plain report from the Obituary does not remotely hint at the trouble Bach created for himself by his unauthorized extended stay.[52] He apparently received permission to be absent for only four weeks, from mid- or late November, so that he could be present in Lübeck for the performances on December 2 and 3 of Buxtehude's newest oratorios, *Castrum doloris* (commemorating the death of Emperor Leopold I) and *Templum honoris* (paying tribute to the new emperor, Joseph I). Bach must have learned about this forthcoming major musical event in advance, for there is no question that it largely determined the original timing of his Lübeck trip. It need hardly be added that he was expected back in Arnstadt for the busy Christmas season.

Traveling the more than 250 miles from Arnstadt to Lübeck on foot would have taken at least ten days each way. Even if he managed an occasional free or cheap ride for some part of the trip, it would still have been a long journey. Nevertheless, his lengthy sojourn in Lübeck was motivated entirely by artistic objectives. On being questioned by the superintendent after his return, Bach articulated his initial aim: "to comprehend one thing and another about his art." As neutral as this wording sounds, with its lack of emphasis on specific musical purposes (in particular keyboard and vocal music), it suggests that the main attraction lay in Buxtehude's indisputable authority as an extraordinary artist and role model, not just as a distinguished organist or composer of oratorios.

Even before Bach's visit, he possessed a basic familiarity with the master's organ works, which were available before 1700 in Thuringia (especially in the Pachelbel circle), and which would have been readily accessible to him in Lüneburg and Hamburg. Still, Buxtehude's general stature as an organist, his innovative approach to virtuosic and large-scale works in the *stylus fantasticus,* his development of a pedal technique as both a performing and compositional device, and the extent and probably well-guarded distribution of his major organ works would have been of major interest to Bach. He would have snatched any opportunity to expand the Buxtehude repertoire already in his possession: it cannot be mere coincidence that the most important and comprehensive transmission of Buxtehude's organ works in the eighteenth century eventually took place through the efforts of the circle surrounding Johann Sebastian Bach. In Lübeck, the Arnstadt visitor would also have wanted to demonstrate to the master his own organistic accomplishments in the hope of receiving acknowledgment and encouragement. For that reason, he would probably have brought large rather than little pieces of his own to show Buxtehude, compositions that ventured to measure up to their model. It thus seems plausible that Bach's multisectional organ works in the direct Buxtehude mold, with their bold but inhibited gestures—such as the Prelude and Fugue in E major, BWV 566— mostly anticipate or coincide with the Lübeck visit rather than postdate it.

Later works, reflecting the Buxtehude experience as a matter of the past, reflect a deeper and perhaps more emancipated understanding of the Lübeck master's art. The Passacaglia in C minor, BWV 582, fits in here as a work of remarkable sophistication whose twenty variations over its sweeping eight-measure ground (Ex. 4.1), culminating in a fugal elaboration, exhibit—especially in comparison with a work such as the Toccata BWV 565—absolute control over compositional principles, musical form, figurative material, fugal devices, and harmonic strategies. As indebted as it is to the musical architecture of Buxtehude's ostinato works (all of which are found in the Andreas Bach Book), notably to his Passacaglia in D minor, BuxWV 161, Bach reaches far beyond his models. Of particular significance is the imaginative fugal treatment of the thematic material. For the fugue, the passacaglia theme is divided exactly into two halves: the first part takes the same shape in which it originally occurs in the "Christe" movement *(trio en passaccaille)* of the organ Mass from André Raison's *Livre d'Orgue* of 1688 (Ex. 4.2a); the second part is transformed into an emphatically pulsating countersubject (b). A second, freely developed countersubject (c) enters immediately after themes (a) and (b) and combines with them in perfect congruence. All three subjects articulate their own distinct rhythmic beats in quarter, eighth, and sixteenth-note values. Proceeding from the outset in multiple counterpoint, theme (a), from its second entry on, is always heard simultaneously with its two countersubjects, in changing combinations:

| Measure | 169 | 174 | 181 | 186 | 192 |
|---|---|---|---|---|---|
| Soprano | | a | b | c | x |
| Alto | a | b | c | x | a |
| Tenor | b | c | x | a | b |
| Bass | | | a | b | c |
| Harmonic plan | C minor | G minor | C minor | G minor | C minor |

x = free counterpoint

The extremely regular scheme creates a perfect permutation fugue exposition "à la Reinken," yet here, too, Bach transcends his model.

The two oratorios Buxtehude presented in December 1705 exposed Bach to a vocal genre, style, and manner of performance he had never heard before. Bach's Lübeck visit lasted about sixteen weeks, from mid-October at the earliest to early February at the latest—he was back in Arnstadt taking communion on Sunday, February 7[53]—and conceivably, he was not merely a member of the oratorio audience but a participant in the large ensemble Buxtehude assembled for the two major works. After all, Bach had to finance his trip, and had to pay his Arnstadt substitute, cousin Johann Ernst Bach, so that offering his services as violinist or keyboard player would have been a logical course of action for the young, ambitious professional. Unfortunately, the music of neither *Castrum doloris,* BuxWV 134, nor *Templum honoris,* BuxWV 135, has survived (as is deplorably the case with all of Buxtehude's oratorios); their printed librettos, however, supply a number of crucial details that allow us to infer some of the more important musical features and to form a general impression of what Bach may have experienced.

The two librettos indicate that the performances were occasions of grandiose spectacle at St. Mary's Church, which had been decorated and illuminated for both events, dedicated by the free imperial city to the imperial house in Vienna. The musical presentations included both large organs and featured several instrumental and vocal choirs positioned in different galleries; and the end, at least, of *Castrum doloris* had the entire congregation join in as well. The texts of the two oratorios represent a curious mixture of sacred and secular elements chosen to suit the politically oriented occasion. Their dialogue format calls for two soloists as allegorical figures, Fame *(Gerücht)* and Prudence *(Klugheit),* and two choirs. The musical forms include double-chorus movements with *da capo* rounding off, recitatives, and strophic arias with instrumental ritornellos. The instrumental requirements as outlined in the librettos are particularly striking and were apparently without precedent or parallel. The intradas require two bands of trumpets and timpani, a ritornello "two choirs of horns and oboes," a sinfonia "twenty-five violins in unison," and a passacaglia "various instruments."

The young Bach had no opportunity to compose pieces in an oratorio-like format, but elements of Buxtehude-style compositional design and instrumental splendor are reflected in Bach's first Mühlhausen town council election cantata, "Gott ist mein König," BWV 71 (1708), written one year after the Lübeck master's death. Four more modestly scored cantatas, the Psalm cantata "Nach dir, Herr, verlanget mich," BWV 150, the funeral music "Gottes Zeit ist die allerbeste Zeit," BWV 106, the wedding piece "Der Herr denket an uns," BWV 196, and the Easter cantata "Christ lag in Todes Banden," BWV 4, are similarly indebted to the tradition of the late seventeenth century in general and to Buxtehude in particular. Their strong and unique affiliation with vocal-instrumental works of the late seventeenth century point to an origin around or before 1707–8, that is, to the late Arnstadt years.

Although Bach had no obligations to provide vocal music at the New Church and records actually stress his refusal to collaborate with the chorus musicus, he may well have begun to perform with that vocal-instrumental group after the consistory's final admonition in November 1706.[54] But a more likely scenario suggests itself: that the authorities were upset with Bach because he did occasionally perform concerted music but was unwilling "to make music [*musiciren*] with the students" from the Latin school and, worse, used an ad hoc ensemble, perhaps one that included the band of the town musician Weise or members of the court capelle. The reproof that in the fall of 1706 he "invited into the choir loft" a young female singer "and let her make music [*musiciren*] there" leads us to wonder what she was doing there if not singing a solo part, most likely in a cantata performance, for the term *musiciren* referred to performing a concerted ensemble piece that only later came to be called "cantata."

At Lutheran churches in cities and towns with Latin schools, musical services were ordinarily divided so that the cantor, generally in charge of vocal music at both church and school, selected and conducted the main polyphonic piece that followed the gospel lesson on Sundays and holidays. Organists with ambitions of presenting vocal-instrumental ensemble works (the repertoire generally in the cantor's domain) were therefore usually limited to weddings, funerals, and other special occasions. The situation at the New Church in Arnstadt fits well into this picture. The person officially responsible for vocal music was the choir prefect appointed by cantor Heindorff, who tended to his own duties at the Upper Church. However, subjecting his works to the questionable leadership of a prefect in a regular Sunday service would have been unacceptable to Bach. So it is no surprise that, with the sole exception of BWV

4 (most likely written for the Mühlhausen audition on Easter Sunday 1707), none of Bach's extant cantatas written before 1714 bear a designation for a specific Sunday or holiday; they fall instead into the typical category of "organists' music" (as opposed to "cantors' music") and, if they were based on a text for multiple purposes such as that of BWV 150 (Psalm 25), offered various possibilities for performances.

Stylistically, these works display considerable mastery, indeed a deliberate attempt at enhancing the scope and makeup of the highly flexible genre labeled "church piece," or early Lutheran cantata. A biblical text was normally set in the manner of a concertato motet, with particular attention lavished on musically suggestive individual words; hymns and hymn melodies were treated in a variety of homophonic and polyphonic ways; and free lyrics were presented as tuneful arias, derived from strophic song. The early cantatas of Bach (see Table 4.4) lack recitatives, although he had encountered them in Buxtehude's oratorios, if not before. Unlike Bach's other cantatas, BWV 4 is based exclusively on the seven stanzas of a single text, Martin Luther's Easter hymn "Christ lag in Todes Banden." A cantata usually opened with an instrumental sinfonia or sonata (sonatina). Though the instrumental forces in Bach's earliest works remain modest, he makes extremely effective use of instrumental combinations, such as the soft quartet of two recorders and two gambas in the mourning cantata BWV 106, or the independent use of violoncello in BWV 150 and fagotto in BWV 196. The overall degree of mastery by which these early pieces compare favorably with the best church compositions from the first decade of the eighteenth century, whether by Johann Philipp Krieger, Johann Kuhnau, Friedrich Wilhelm Zachow, or others, proves that the young Bach did not confine himself to playing organ and clavier but, animated by his Buxtehude visit, devoted considerable time and effort to vocal composition. The very few such early works that exist, each a masterpiece in its own right, must constitute a remnant only—partly a careful selection, partly a random bit—from a larger body of similar compositions.

"Nach dir, Herr, verlanget mich," BWV 150, Bach's earliest surviving cantata, surprises us in many ways. First, it offers refined and complex chromaticism in the opening chorus ("For thee, Lord, is my desire"). Then it presents one of Buxtehude's favorite devices—a passacaglia for chorus and orchestra, "Meine Tage in den Leiden / endet Gott dennoch in Freuden" (All my days, which pass in sadness, / God will end, at last, in gladness), which Brahms chose as the bass theme for the Finale of his Fourth Symphony; the French-style triple meter adds, however, a new facet distinct from Buxtehude. Finally, the cantata features a vocal tercet, "Zedern müssen von den Winden / oft viel Ungemach

## Table 4.4. Bach's Earliest Cantatas

| | |
|---|---|
| BWV 4 | Christ lag in Todes Banden, for SATB, 2v, va, bc: Sinfonia—**versus 1** (SATB)—v.2 (SA)—v.3 (T)—v.4 (SATB)—v.5 (B)—v.6 (ST)—v.7 (SATB) |
| BWV 106 | Gottes Zeit ist die allerbeste Zeit *(Actus tragicus)*, for SATB, 2rec, 2va da gamba, bc: Sonatina—*chorus*—*arioso* (T)—*aria* (B)—*chorus* + c.f.—*aria* (A)—*arioso* (B)+ c.f. (A)—**chorale** |
| BWV 150 | Nach dir, Herr, verlanget mich, for SATB, 2v, fg, bc: Sinfonia—*chorus*— aria (S)—*chorus*—aria (ATB)—*chorus*—chorus |
| BWV 196 | Der Herr denket an uns, for SATB, 2v, va, vc, bc: Sinfonia—*chorus*—*aria* (S)—*aria* (TB)—*chorus* |
| BWV 223 | Meine Seele soll Gott loben (fragment), for S[AT]B, instr: [Sinfonia—chorus]—aria (SB)— . . . —[*chorus*] |

*Italics* = biblical text; **bold** = hymn text; c.f. = cantus firmus (hymn tune)

empfinden" (Cedars must, from blowing zephyrs, / often suffer strains and stresses), for alto, tenor, bass, and a differentiated continuo (cello embellishing the bassoon/organ part), followed by a chorus with an elaborate accompaniment performed by the entire instrumental ensemble. Especially impressive is the beginning of the middle chorus, "Leite mich in deiner Wahrheit" (Lead me in thy truth), whose structure—derived from the keywords "lead" and "truth"— is based on a strict ascending scale that penetrates all participating voices, first vocal then instrumental, and brings form and content into absolute congruence (Ex. 4.3).

The advanced temperament in which Bach's organ was tuned allowed him to chart a daring harmonic course and to explore advanced chord progressions for which there were no precedents whatsoever. A characteristic example is found at the end of "Allein Gott in der Höh sei Ehr," BWV 715, one of several early chorale harmonizations, in which Bach exploits for a plain G-major tune all twelve notes of the chromatic scale (Ex. 4.4)—within the space of two measures. Such experiments won for him remarkable command over a widened tonal spectrum, so that in movements 2 and 6 of the cantata BWV 150 he was able to employ virtually the entire chromatic-enharmonic scale, including pitches as far off the beaten path as B-sharp. Similarly, the bold harmonic design of the *Actus tragicus,* BWV 106, ranges through the flat keys, movement by movement: E-flat major / C minor / F minor / B-flat minor / A-flat major / E-flat major. In both instances, Bach explored a tonal range and applied a harmonic language that had no parallel among his predecessors or contemporaries; they are impressive evidence of how little the modest means and restrained conditions under which the earliest cantatas were created kept the composer from venturing well beyond established musical conventions.

## At the Blasius Church in Mühlhausen

Word of the death in early December 1706 of Johann Georg Ahle, the well-known organist at St. Blasius's Church in the free imperial city of Mühlhausen, must have reached Bach in Arnstadt fairly soon. After all, the Mühlhausen town scribe was Johann Hermann Bellstedt, whose brother was not only the town scribe in Arnstadt but was also related by marriage to the Bach family (see Table 4.3). The news may also have been passed on to Bach by the Mühlhausen organ builder Johann Friedrich Wender, who had built Bach's organ at the New Church. For Johann Gottfried Walther, a distant cousin of Bach's, claimed that Wender proposed that he (Walther) apply for the Mühlhausen post.[55] Walther submitted his application along with "two church pieces of my own work," that is, two cantatas he had composed. His public audition was scheduled for Sexagesimae Sunday (February 27, 1707), but he withdrew from his candidacy because, as he later put it, "some (perhaps self-interested) acquaintances viewed such a plan as unsuitable."

Who were these acquaintances? Did Bach have anything to do with Walther's withdrawal? Unlikely, considering that Bach was more than just an acquaintance—his mother and Walther's, both Lämmerhirts from Erfurt, were cousins—and he and Walther subsequently developed a cordial and long-standing friendship. In any case, Walther's account of the events, though written more than thirty years later, illuminates how the search for a new organist at St. Blasius's proceeded, including the requirement that the candidates submit two vocal compositions. The position had, for more than a half century, been in the "possession" of father and son Ahle, both natives of Mühlhausen and both later elected members of its city council. Johann Rudolf, noted composer and theorist and eventually first burgomaster of the city as well, held the post beginning in 1654; Johann Georg, also an active composer and even more illustrious as poet laureate,[56] succeeded him in 1673. Both Ahles had left a long list of vocal compositions, many of them published,[57] and because the ceremonial music for the annual town council election service at St. Mary's Church was traditionally assigned to the St. Blasius organist, it is understandable that the Mühlhausen authorities were seeking a musician with proven abilities in vocal music.

The council records that document the Mühlhausen organist search mention no name other than Bach's, suggesting that he was the only candidate seriously considered. On May 24, 1707, at a meeting of St. Blasius's Parish Convent—a body comprising the members of the city council who resided in the parish—the influential senior consul and previous burgomaster, Dr. Conrad Meckbach, asked without any preliminaries "whether consideration should not first be given to the man named Pach [*sic*] from Arnstadt, who had recently done his trial playing at Easter."[58] Without any further deliberation, the parish convent quickly commissioned the town scribe Bellstedt to work out an agreement with Bach.

The Arnstadt organist had held his public audition for the Mühlhausen post on Easter Sunday, April 24, about a month before the meeting and almost two months after Walther's canceled date. There is reason to believe that Bach performed the Easter cantata "Christ lag in Todes Banden," BWV 4, a setting of all seven stanzas of the Easter hymn in as many movements, preceded by an instrumental sinfonia (see Table 4.4). And although no pre-Leipzig sources survive for the cantata,[59] for stylistic reasons it belongs unquestionably to the pre-Weimar repertoire. We don't know whether Bach submitted a score of BWV 4 along with some other piece as part of his application, or whether he sent in two altogether different works and composed the Easter cantata *ad hoc* for the audition, after he had learned of its date. There is in any case no question about the attraction the vocal dimension of the Mühlhausen post held for Bach, nor about his solid preparation as a composer of vocal works before the Mühlhausen audition, nor, for that matter, of the outstanding impression he made with his abilities in the vocal realm. As he would hardly have risked presenting a half-baked product, any of the works listed in Table 4.4 could have qualified as a viable submission to the search committee. At the same time, their generally mature quality implies not only that examples may once have existed of a lesser-developed technique, but also that Bach must have devoted considerable time and effort in Arnstadt toward gaining compositional experience in vocal music.

Bach needed permission to be absent for the Mühlhausen audition, and the Arnstadt church authorities could not have been much pleased to see a substitute take the appointed organist's place once again on major holidays, as one had in the 1705–6 Christmas season. But they also must have understood that he was on the lookout for a new position and may even have offered him encouragement. When they learned of his successful audition, they could not have been surprised when Bach, after a second short trip in mid-June to Mühlhausen to negotiate his new appointment, indicated his intention to resign his post at the New Church. That decision was made official on June 29, when Bach appeared before the Arnstadt consistory with a formal request for his dismissal and to return the keys of the organ.[60] By that date, both cousin Johann Ernst Bach, Sebastian's loyal Arnstadt substitute, and Andreas Börner, organist of the Lower Church, had already submitted their applications for the desirable organist post at the New Church.[61] But although Bach started in Mühlhausen on July 1,[62] the Arnstadt consistory took an agonizingly long time in deciding on a successor to this musician whose exceptional talents outweighed his occasional refusal to collaborate with an undisciplined student choir. Perhaps Count Anton Günther II himself, to whose personal attention Andreas Börner had sent his own application, was dissatisfied with the talent search under way; perhaps the extended Bach clan had to sort out things between two family members—one a Bach (and so far unemployed), the other related by marriage (with a current job in Arnstadt). Whatever the case, it took nearly a year, until the following May 14, before Ernst Bach was finally appointed—at a substantial reduction in salary compared with his predecessor's.[63]

Mühlhausen represented a step up for Bach, in both its location and its importance. The city was, after Erfurt, Thuringia's second largest, an entity of considerable historical and political importance, and the closest equivalent in central Germany to the free imperial cities of Hamburg and Lübeck. Independent of princely rule since the early thirteenth century, the city council reported directly to the emperor in Vienna. Like Erfurt's, Mühlhausen's skyline was dominated by its many church spires. No fewer than thirteen churches could be found within its walls, with St. Mary's and St. Blasius's the largest and most important. After adopting the Lutheran Reformation in 1557—quite a bit later than the surrounding principalities—Mülhausen had established a peculiar balance of power between its church and civic governments. The superintendent, as head of the church government, had his base at St. Blasius's, while the city council, as the civic government, considered St. Mary's its principal house of worship. In October-November 1627, for instance, amid the vi-

View of Mühlhausen in an engraving after Merian by Johann Friedrich Leopold (1720), showing St. Mary's Church in the upper town (no. 4) and St. Blasius's Church in the lower town (no. 6).

olent turbulence of the Thirty Years' War, the electoral assembly chaired by Emperor Ferdinand II met in Mühlhausen, and the ceremonial opening service was held at St. Mary's, with the electoral Saxon *Ober-Capellmeister* Heinrich Schütz conducting his grand polychoral concerto "Da pacem, Domine," SWV 465, written for this very occasion.

Except for such major state events, however, the musical center lay at St. Blasius's, where the organist and composer Joachim a Burck, who served there from 1566 to 1610 as the first Lutheran musician, established a distinguished tradition of church music. Remnants at the St. Blasius archive of a once-rich choir library still provide vivid testimony of that heritage.[64] Moreover, since Joachim a Burck's time, the St. Blasius organist also functioned as municipal music director, even though he did not carry that title. It became even clearer during the long tenure of the two Ahles that official musical events connected to the city council were invariably delegated to them. Bach savored his new responsibilities and opportunities, which far exceeded those of his junior position in Arnstadt. At St. Blasius's, the city's senior minister, Superintendent Johann Adolph Frohne, officiated, and Bach held the senior musical post. By appointing him, the Mühlhausen authorities demonstrated great confidence in the ability of this twenty-two-year-old to provide musical leadership. He was also expected to collaborate with the town musicians as well as with the chorus musicus and the (vocal-instrumental) chorus symphoniacus of the Mühlhausen gymnasium, the Latin school that served the two main churches. In the interest of orderly arrangements, the gymnasium assigned two of its teachers to the two churches as cantors. In Bach's time, Johann Bernhard Stier served as *quartus* and cantor at St. Blasius's, while Johann Heinrich Melchior Scheiner worked as cantor with the organist Johann Gottfried Hetzehenn at St. Mary's.[65]

Much as in Arnstadt, Bach's Mühlhausen contract did not specify the organist's involvement with vocal music in general or the choral and instrumental ensembles in particular. It merely required that, besides loyally serving the city's authorities and working for its best interests, he "show himself willing in the execution of the duties required of him and be available at all times, particularly attend to his service faithfully and industriously on Sundays, Feast Days, and other Holy Days, keep the organ entrusted to him in at least good condition, call the attention of . . . the appointed supervisors to any defects found in it, and industriously watch over its repairs and music."[66] The phrase "duties required of him," however, suggests that these were verbally outlined to Bach and that he had agreed to them at the meeting of the parish convent, where he had appeared in person on June 14, 1707.[67] At the same meeting, he was also asked "what he would ask for the position," and the details had apparently been worked out before the meeting with the town scribe Bellstedt.

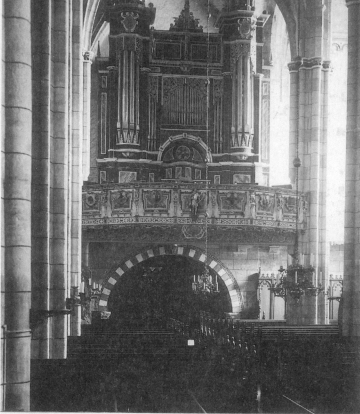

Interior westward view of St. Blasius's Church at Mühlhausen in a photograph (c. 1880) showing the choir and organ loft dating to the late nineteenth century; the gallery and main organ case from Bach's time are partially preserved.

Bach did not bargain but asked basically for what he had received in Arnstadt, 85 florins in cash—20 florins more than Ahle was paid. Additionally, Bach received considerable allowances (fifty-four bushels of grain, two cords of firewood, and six times threescore kindling—all delivered to his door) that were not available to him in Arnstadt. However, as there was nothing similar to the Feldhaus home in Mühlhausen, he would now have to take care of his own household. Since he also requested "the assistance of a wagon to move his effects," he must by then have accumulated enough furniture, musical instruments, books, scores, clothing, and other household goods to fill such a wagon.

Moreover, Maria Barbara Bach, his young wife to be, would join him soon. Although the wedding date may not yet have been set, Bach had no reason to withhold his marriage plans—which the town scribe Bellstedt, related by marriage to Maria Barbara's family, would probably have known anyway. By a happy coincidence, Bach inherited 50 florins from the estate of his Erfurt uncle Tobias Lämmerhirt, his mother's brother, who died on August 10, 1707—a sum that would help him considerably to establish his own household or to acquire, if needed, a larger and better harpsichord for his studio.

Because Bach's contract with the St. Blasius Parish Convent concerning his overall duties and earnings was vague on specifics, it fails to mention that he also held a subcontract, as his predecessors had, with St. Mary and Magdalen's Church of the Augustinian Convent, the so-called Brückenhof Church.[68] This smaller church, attached to the St. Mary and Magdalen's School for girls (founded at the old St. Augustine's nunnery in 1565, in anticipation of the Lutheran Reformation's acceptance), contained a new one-manual organ, built for 228 florins by Johann Friedrich Wender in 1701–2, at the same time the organ at the New Church in Arnstadt was under construction.[69] Traditionally, the organists of St. Blasius's and St. Mary's Churches alternated playing the weekly services for the girls' school, each receiving annually 4 florins 16 groschen, plus four bushels of wheat and sixteen "malters" of rye. Bach participated in this rotation from the very beginning, as his first payment is recorded for the Holy Cross quarter (July-September) of 1707.

Similar alternating arrangements for the two principal town organists existed with three other churches—St. Kilian's, All Saints, and Holy Cross—again with additional remuneration. Although payment records have not survived, a more detailed contract set up for Bach's second successor, Christoph Bieler, provides the necessary information and also tells us about the organist's duties at St. Blasius's. According to this 1730 document, the organist was expected "to play *figural*[*iter*] and *choral*[*iter*]"—that is, to perform preludes, fugues, and chorale elaborations as well as accompany congregational hymns—"on all Sundays and feast days and extraordinary holidays [Marian feasts and those commemorating the apostles] at the Matins, morning, and afternoon services of St. Blasius's, and at the so-called week churches [where no Sunday services were held] of St. Mary-Magdalen's, St. Kilian's, All Saints, and Holy Cross in alternation with the organist at *B*[*eatae*] *Mar*[*iae*] *Virg*[*inis*]."[70] Not specifically mentioned are two services at St. Blasius's on Tuesdays and Fridays, nor is it noted that Matins services were not held on most Sundays and feast days. In a normal week, then, Bach was responsible for altogether six services—two more than in Arnstadt, though for some additional pay. Furthermore, since Mühlhausen provided many more opportunities for weddings, funerals, and other special services at extra pay, his total income was considerably greater than it had been before.[71]

Bach's increased workload may have been partially offset with the help of assistants. The first documented pupil "who learned the playing of the clavier from Mr. Johann Sebastian Bach, and stayed with him the whole time from 1707 until 1717," was Johann Martin Schubart,[72] although the much younger Johann Caspar Vogler is reported to have received Bach's instruction in Arnstadt as a ten-year-old.[73] Both gifted youngsters certainly worked with Bach in Mühlhausen, inaugurating a steady stream of private students that ended only with his death. Schubart later succeeded Bach in Weimar, and after Schubart's early death in 1721, Vogler became his successor. Typically among professional musicians, pupils who achieved a certain proficiency could serve as apprentices and associates, roles that Schubart may have filled to ease his teacher's burdens.

The structure of the divine service in Mühlhausen did not differ much from that in Arnstadt. The service followed either the Schwarzburg Agenda of 1675, prescribed for the three Schwarzburg counties of Rudolstadt, Arnstadt, and Sondershausen but widely adopted throughout Thuringia, or the electoral-Saxon *Agenda, Das ist, Kirchen-Ordnung* (Leipzig, 1691).[74] The electoral-Saxon formulary differed from the Schwarzburg (Table 4.2) in only minor musical aspects:

- the Kyrie and Gloria were preceded by a polyphonic Introit motet for the specific Sunday or feast day (choir);
- the Sanctus was performed polyphonically, on high feast days only (choir);
- one of two Communion hymns, "Jesus Christus unser Heiland" or "Gott sei gelobet und gebenedeiet," was sung (congregation and organ).

The local hymnbook in use was the *Vermehrtes Gesang-Buch* of 1686, containing texts without melodies, and edited by Superintendent Frohne's father, Johann Bernhard Frohne, reissued in 1697 and 1703 and revised by Johann Adolph Frohne himself in 1713.

Both principal churches of the city, St. Blasius's in the lower part *(Unterstadt)* and St. Mary's in the upper part *(Oberstadt),* were originally built in the thirteenth century. The first reference to St. Blasius's stems from 1227, and the oldest bell in one of the two massive church towers bears a casting mark of 1281. In 1560–63, after the late-Gothic hall church had been enlarged, Jost Pape of Göttingen built an organ on a separate gallery at the west end of the central aisle, the instrument Joachim a Burck first played. After extensive but apparently ineffective repairs executed in 1676 by Jost Schäfer of Langensalza, the organ was substantially rebuilt and enlarged in 1687–91 by Mühlhausen's own Johann Friedrich Wender, according to plans drawn up by Johann Georg Ahle. This fairly large instrument, with thirty stops on two manuals *(Oberwerk* and

*Rückpositiv)* and pedal, was the organ Bach played the most in Mühlhausen, and it served him well. That he found small defects here and there should not surprise, considering that major parts were by then almost 150 years old. However, that Bach could persuade the parish convent to undertake a large-scale renovation and further expansion of the organ less than twenty years after the previous major overhaul speaks for the respect and admiration the young organist had won during little more than half a year in the job. On February 21, 1708, consul Conrad Meckbach, who had also been a council member when the rebuilding under Johann Georg Ahle was undertaken, submitted for discussion Bach's new plans for the organ. The following day, organ builder Wender was queried about Bach's design and estimated a cost of 250 talers for materials and labor. After further discussion and negotiations, all within only two days, a sum of 230 talers was approved for the ambitious project.[75]

Bach's "Project for New Repairs to the Organ" demonstrates thorough technological expertise and great musical imagination.[76] He deals with problems of the wind chests and stresses the importance of stable and stronger wind pressure, especially for a new thirty-two-foot pedal sub-bass stop that he proposed in order to give the organ "the most solid foundation" and for the larger pipes he requested for the sixteen-foot pedal *Posaune.* A thirty-two-foot stop must have been a particular dream of his ever since he encountered such a stop as part of Reinken's organ in Hamburg (in 1768, Johann Friedrich Agricola quotes Bach as giving "assurance that the 32-foot *Principal* and the pedal *Posaune* in the organ of St. Catharine's in Hamburg spoke evenly and quite audibly right down to the lowest C").[77] Bach suggests replacing a few old stops with new ones that would offer a more varied sound, in particular "a *Fagotto* of 16-foot tone . . . which is useful for all kinds of new *inventiones* and sounds very fine in concerted music." Special effects would be created by a new set of chimes *(Glockenspiel)* in the pedal that, according to Bach, was "desired by the parishioners." The most important matter, however, was the addition of an entire third manual *(Brustpositiv)* with seven carefully chosen metal and wood stops of different pitches, shapes, scales, and sound qualities— giving the whole organ more character, timbre, and flexibility for both solo and accompanying purposes.

The approval of these renovations apparently occurred at a most opportune moment for Bach, when major church and city officials were very proud of their new organist. Less than three weeks earlier, on February 4, 1708, he had presented his first large-scale vocal-instrumental composition at the annual inauguration of the city council, honoring the newly elected burgomasters, Adolf Strecker and Georg Adam Steinbach, and the forty-eight council members (elected for life). The ceremonial service took place at St. Mary's, but according to established tradition, the town council election music, known as the "little council piece," was always repeated at St. Blasius's on the following Sunday in the Vespers service.[78] Since in 1708 February 4 fell on a Saturday, the two performances of the state music, whose text also included a reference to Emperor Joseph I, took place on successive days. On February 11, Bach collected the honorarium of 3 talers that his predecessor Ahle had also received annually for the same purpose.[79] However, the expenses for the customary publication of the text booklet and the music—10 talers for the printer and 8 groschen for the bookbinder—were much higher than in previous years.[80] Bach had composed a work of unusual proportions and complexity that made the performances of earlier council pieces pale by comparison, as most everyone would have immediately noticed. Ahle's council pieces generally consisted of strophic arias with instrumental accompaniment. No longer a little piece, Bach's "Gott ist mein König," BWV 71, was a full-fledged multimovement cantata, a "Congratulatory Church Motet" according to its original title.[81]

The large St. Mary's Church with its several galleries and lofts had long invited polychoral music. But never before had the four-hundred-year-old church witnessed a performance with as spectacular and diversified a vocal-instrumental ensemble as it did that February in 1708, under the skilled direction of its new organist. Bach had taken a newer kind of compositional structure as his model: Buxtehude's famous Lübeck *Abend-Musiken,* which were known to have featured polychoral design. The autograph score of BWV 71 clearly lays out its polychoral plan, involving altogether seven different performing units:

| | |
|---|---|
| Instrumental choir I: | Trumpet I–III, timpani |
| Instrumental choir II: | Violin I–II, viola, violone |
| Instrumental choir III: | Oboe I–II, bassoon |
| Instrumental choir IV: | Recorder I–II, violoncello |
| Vocal choir I: | SATB solo |
| Vocal choir II: | SATB ripieno *(ad libitum)* |
| Organ: | Basso per Organo |

The tutti ensemble, combining all the units, is heard only in the first and last movements (Table 4.5). The inner movements, meanwhile, display a variety of vocal-instrumental combinations that closely match the expressive needs of the text—juxtaposing in movements 4–5, for example, the trumpet choir in "Durch mächtige Kraft erhältst du unsere Grenzen" (Through mighty power You preserve our borders) with the two contrasting woodwind choirs in "Tag und Nacht ist dein" (Day and night are Yours). Bach's refined treatment of the vocal-instrumental scoring demonstrates his ability to deal with highly differentiated patterns of sound, a skill that his experience with the organ would have taught him. But just as impressive is his sophisticated application of dif-

**TABLE 4.5. "Gott ist mein König," BWV 71: Structural Layout**

| Movement | Key | Scoring |
|---|---|---|
| 1. [Chorus:] Gott ist mein König | C major | SATB I (solo) + instr II; SATB II (rip) + instr I–IV |
| 2. Aria: Ich bin nun achtzig Jahr | E minor | T and S (solo) + organ (with chorale solo part) |
| 3. Fugue: Dein Alter sei wie deine Jugend | A minor | SATB I (solo) + organ |
| 4. Arioso: Tag und Nacht | F major | B (solo) + instr III–IV, organ |
| 5. Aria: Durch mächtige Kraft | C major | A (solo) + instr I, organ |
| 6. [Chorus:] Du wollest dem Feinde | C minor | SATB II (rip) + instr II–IV, organ |
| 7. Arioso: Das neue Regiment | C major | SATB I (solo) + div instr; SATB II (rip) + instr I–IV |

ferent compositional designs in the seven movements—for example, the integrated aria and chorale elaboration in movement 2, fugal setting in 3, chaconne in 4, and a French-style choral song (with a liturgical litany ending) in 6; his construction of the overall tonal scheme, entailing both sharp and flat keys; and finally, his wide-ranging rhythmic patterns in duple and triple meters, with further "affective" designations ("animoso" and "un poco allegro" in movement 1, "andante" in 2, "lente" in 3, "vivace" in 5, "affetuoso e larghetto" in 6, and "allegro," "andante," and "vivace" in 7).

The cantata BWV 71 put Bach on the map, so to speak: it was published well ahead of works by his contemporaries Telemann and Handel, both of whom went on to outstrip him by far in general popularity (and not one of Bach's post-Mühlhausen vocal works found its way into print during his lifetime). The "council piece" impressed the Mühlhausen authorities so deeply that even after he had moved away, they invited Bach to provide the cantatas for the two subsequent years, 1709 and 1710, and brought him back from Weimar to perform them.[82] Although the text and music for these later pieces are lost despite their having been printed, as BWV 71 had been, two other vocal works can be firmly dated to the Mühlhausen period: the cantata "Aus der Tiefen rufe ich zu dir," BWV 131, and the incompletely transmitted *Wedding Quodlibet* BWV 524, both of which survive in autograph sources. Perhaps the motet "Ich lasse dich nicht," BWV Anh. 159, belongs to this group as well; it comes down to us in a fair copy of 1712–13, but its unusual French rondeau structure, thematically based on Lully,[83] and its general relationship with BWV 71/6 suggest an earlier origin. That the score of BWV 131 bears the notation "set to music at the request of Herrn D. Georg: Christ: Eilmar" indicates a special relationship that Bach had developed with the archdeacon of St.

Mary's in Mühlhausen, whom he later invited to stand as godfather to his first child.[84] The phrase may also imply that pastor Eilmar provided the text for this cantata. And it is conceivable that Eilmar, probably against Superintendent Frohne, supported Bach in establishing what he called "a well-regulated church music," meaning regular performances at Mühlhausen's main churches of modern-style concerted vocal music—that is, cantatas. With the examples of BWV 71 and 131, Bach had certainly proven to the people of the imperial city that he was able and eager to direct them toward new musical horizons.

Considering all the perquisites of a respected and powerful musical office, including a large renovated organ and opportunities for vocal composition, we may wonder why Bach left his Mühlhausen post rather abruptly, after barely twelve months on the job. In all likelihood, he was lured away by a combination of significantly better pay and greatly improved professional conditions. There are no signs that he was trolling for employment elsewhere, and the turn of events may have surprised Bach himself as much as they startled his friends and supporters in the imperial city. In any case, sometime around the middle of June 1708, Bach traveled to Weimar, apparently at the invitation of the court. The timing of the trip may bear directly on a massive 400-florin, year-long organ renovation at the castle church, finished on June 16, by the organ builder Johann Conrad Weisshaupt of Seebergen near Gotha.[85] We know from the Obituary that Bach "undertook a journey to Weymar, had the opportunity to be heard by the reigning Duke, and was offered the post of Chamber and Court Organist in Weymar, of which post he immediately took possession."[86] What follows is a plausible sequence of events.

The old and ailing Weimar court organist Johann Effler had supervised the expensive renovation of his organ at the castle church. But when it came time to demonstrate to the duke the results of the project, he did not feel equal to the task of playing the inaugural recital; instead, he invited Bach to come from Mühlhausen to perform and also to have him take part in a critical examination of the organ builder's completed work. After all, Bach's reputation as a virtuoso organist and trustworthy organ expert could hardly have escaped Effler's attention, for in 1703 Bach had traveled from Weimar to Arnstadt for exactly the same reason. The young Bach's rapidly increasing reputation must also have reached Effler's ears. Thus, Bach played the organ, as the Obituary reports, to the delight and amazement of Duke Wilhelm Ernst; Effler asked to retire for reasons of health (only a year later, he is called "an old sick servant");[87] Bach was offered and accepted the position on the spot for a salary of 150 florins plus benefits; and Effler was granted retirement at his full salary of 130 florins. The arrangements in Weimar were completed by June 20,[88] allowing Bach to submit his letter of resignation from the Mühlhausen position right after he returned there, on June 25.

What persuaded Bach to accept such a sudden, unexpected offer at the risk of snubbing his Mühlhausen patrons and supporters? Two reasons come to mind. First, what must have seemed to him an extravagant salary that was three times what he had earned in Arnstadt and 75 percent more than he was making in Mühlhausen—a significant factor, especially considering the future of his young family (Maria Barbara was pregnant with their first child). Bach was honest enough to admit right at the top of his Mühlhausen resignation letter that the Weimar offer would permit him "to enjoy a better living," and by his repetition at the end, "the possibility of a more adequate living," he confirms the importance of the salary increase. Second, it must have meant nearly as much to him that in his new position as "chamber musician and court organist," he would be able to perform almost exclusively with professional musicians—a consideration that ties in clearly with his "goal of a well-regulated church music," as his letter of resignation has it. His brief earlier sojourn at the Weimar court in 1703 might, in fact, have spoiled him forever for a return to working day-in and day-out with an unholy mix of school choirs, nonprofessional helpers, student instrumentalists, and town musicians.

Such uninspiring tasks could explain the "hindrance" and "vexation" that Bach only hinted at in his tactful request for dismissal, dated June 25, 1708 (a highly revealing letter and the first major document in Bach's hand that survives). However, his plan for "a well-regulated church music," which he did not outline beyond referring to "the church music that is growing up in almost every township, and often better than the harmony that is fashioned here," would surely have run into all sorts of organizational, programmatic, and financial problems, some of which would have put the two leading Mühlhausen clergymen, Superintendent Frohne at St. Blasius's and Archdeacon Eilmar at St. Mary's, at loggerheads. Their personalities clashed frequently, and their many generational, administrative, and theological differences are well documented. Bach's close association with Eilmar may well have soured his relationship with Frohne, his immediate superior.

The traditional view, however, that the active Pietist Frohne may have distrusted his organist because he couldn't stand the orthodox Eilmar and that frustrations over this feud drove Bach away from Mühlhausen, does not hold up.[89] We know that even before Bach arrived on the scene, Eilmar had made some bold and unauthorized decisions about "how the divine service should be held and what, apart from the regular order, should be read, explained, and sung," for which Frohne later scolded him in one of his many militant theological pamphlets.[90] But such conflicts had nothing to do with Pietist versus orthodox points of view. The Pietist movement within the Lutheran Church of the seventeenth and early eighteenth centuries, which emphasized devotional godliness, the renunciation of worldly pleasures, and the spirit of Christian living beyond the letter of doctrine, deeply influenced the church in virtually all Lutheran lands and congregations. A large number of the cantata texts later set by Bach reflect the absorption of Pietist language and ideas and, in fact, the cross-influence of Pietist and orthodox tendencies. But as far as we can tell, Bach never let himself be drawn into the aggressive conflict between *Kirchen-* and *Seelen-Music*—traditional church music on the one hand and music for the soul on the other—which had a stifling effect on both sacred and secular musical life elsewhere in Germany.[91]

One other passage in Bach's resignation letter sheds light on his overall musical plans. In conjunction with his stated "ultimate goal, namely a well-regulated church music, to the Glory of God and in comformance with your [the parishioners'] wishes," he mentions that he had "acquired from far and wide, not without cost, a good store of the choicest church compositions." This reference to Bach's working apparatus gives us another indication of his self-directed manner of learning, which, while sparing no expense, enabled the young composer to examine a broad range of music "from far and wide" in representative examples. It also helped him gain insight into different styles, techniques, and genres by the time-tested method of surveying, copying, and emulating *exempla classica*. Bach had started to build his personal library of sacred music for study, reference, and performance purposes long before Mühlhausen. He may also have inherited materials from his own father and from Maria Barbara's father, which could well have marked one of the beginnings of what Carl Philipp Emanuel Bach later referred to as the Old-Bach Archive. Unfortunately, no real traces are left of this "good store" in its pre-Weimar state,[92] but the stylistic orientation of Bach's earliest cantatas suggests primary models that were not found among prevailing seventeenth-century pieces but rather among those in vogue around 1700 and later, with something like "late Buxtehude"—among German examples—forming a point of departure.

One day after he received Bach's letter of resignation, an obviously startled Conrad Meckbach, the same senior consul and former burgomaster who a year earlier had proposed Bach's appointment, officially presented the letter to the parish convent with the words that "the organist Pach had received a call to Weimar and had accepted the same, and accordingly made written request for his dismissal." Meckbach then submitted, with expression of regrets, that "since he could not be made to stay, consent must doubtless be given, but in notifying him it should be suggested that he help bring to completion the project [of rebuilding the organ] that had been undertaken."[93] In order to atone for the unintended commotion he had created, Bach apparently offered his help to the parish convent in finding a suitable successor. A scant two weeks later, Johann Friedrich Bach, third son of the late Eisenach organist Johann

Christoph Bach *(13)*, was presented to the parish convent and was subsequently appointed to the post vacated by his cousin—but at a salary that had dropped back to what Johann Georg Ahle had earned.[94]

Johann Sebastian Bach and the Mühlhausen authorities parted on good terms, and both he and Maria Barbara left behind a number of people with whom they had become close. Their firstborn son, Wilhelm Friedemann, was named after the Mühlhausen lawyer Paul Friedemann Meckbach, son of Conrad and apparently a friend of Sebastian's. Friedemann, together with Anna Dorothea Hagedorn, daughter of pastor Eilmar and probably Barbara's friend, served as Wilhelm Friedemann's godparents, and both attended his baptism in Weimar on November 11, 1710.[95] Bach would certainly have tended the ambitious organ-rebuilding project at St. Blasius's that he had designed, and he could easily have done so during his trips back to Mühlhausen to conduct the council pieces he wrote for 1709 and 1710. Many years later, old connections with Mühlhausen were renewed when Sebastian and Barbara's third son, Johann Gottfried Bernhard, was appointed organist at St. Mary's in 1735, succeeding his father's former colleague, Johann Gottfried Hetzehenn. When Bach accompanied his son to his audition, the parish convent held a special dinner in honor of "Herr Capell-Meister Bach of Leipzig," who examined the newly built organ at St. Mary's "without charge . . . communicated his opinion, and informed them about what was still missing."[96] Bach was fondly remembered, and his early reputation had by now been replaced by celebrity status.

Ducal palace (the Wilhelmsburg) at Weimar in a watercolor (c. 1760); the palace church is located under the elevated roof at the rear (east) flank of the building complex.

# 5

## Exploring
## "Every Possible Artistry"
### COURT ORGANIST AND *CAMMER MUSICUS*
### IN WEIMAR, 1708–1714

THE FIRST SIX YEARS AT THE DUCAL COURT

Considering the unanticipated and hectic decisions made within just a couple of weeks during June 1708, Bach acted most responsibly by seeing to a smooth and orderly transition. He appears not to have left Mühlhausen before his successor, who was chosen on July 4, could take over; but by July 14, he and Maria Barbara had relocated to Weimar. That day, "the newly arrived Court Organist from Mühlhausen" received a gift of 10 florins—equivalent to nearly a full month's salary.[1] In Weimar, the Bachs moved into an apartment at the house of Adam Immanuel Weldig,[2] master of the pages, falsettist in the court capelle, and, incidentally, an alumnus of the Leipzig St. Thomas School. This *Freyhaus* (free house), one of several dwellings across town reserved for court employees, was located directly on the market square in the center of town, a five-minute walk from the Wilhelmsburg, the ducal palace that served as the principal place of work for both Weldig and Bach. Weldig, however, sold his house in August 1713, having left Weimar at the beginning of that year to accept a similar position at the Weissenfels court. Bach may well have remained at the house and perhaps even expanded his living quarters.

At the time of the move, Maria Barbara was four months pregnant with their first child, daughter Catharina Dorothea. She would be born at their new home and baptized on December 29, 1708, at St. Peter and Paul's Church in the market square, the town's main house of worship. From a March 1709 census listing the occupants of Bach's apartment, we learn that Maria Barbara's much older, unmarried sister Friedelena Margaretha Bach joined them in Weimar, probably around the birth of their first child (she would remain in the Bach household until her death in 1729), in part to help her sister and brother-in-law with their growing family: also born in Weimar were Wilhelm Friedemann, 1710; the twins Maria Sophia and Johann Christoph, who died soon after birth, 1713; Carl Philipp Emanuel, 1714; and Johann Gottfried Bernhard, 1715.

Bach returned to a familiar territory, which he would have remembered well from the six months he had spent there only five years earlier. But he now held the respected position of court organist and chamber musician, so very little would actually have reminded him of his days as lackey. And with an initial salary of 150 florins plus incidentals (eighteen bushels of wheat, twelve bushels of barley, four cords of firewood, and thirty pails of tax-free beer),[3] he could indeed look forward to "a better living," as his Mühlhausen resignation letter reads. Although much smaller than Mühlhausen, this capital of the duchy of Saxe-Weimar had a population of about five thousand in the early eighteenth century, almost a third of whom were directly or indirectly employed by the court. More than fifty thousand people lived in the duchy as a whole, which for generations was ruled by a less than happy pattern of co-reigning dukes from the Ernestine-Saxon dynasty.

In 1683, Dukes Wilhelm Ernst and Johann Ernst III took over joint rulership after the death of their father, Duke Johann Ernst II. The older of the two brothers, Duke Wilhelm Ernst, resided at the Wilhelmsburg, a massive structure built by Duke Wilhelm IV in 1650–54 after the end of the Thirty Years' War (except for its tower, the castle would be completely laid to ruin by a devastating fire in 1774). Forty-six years old when Bach arrived in Weimar, Wilhelm Ernst was throughout his life the dominant of the co-regents. After an unhappy and childless marriage during which he lived separated from his wife, he influenced Weimar's courtly and civic life enormously, in both secular and religious affairs. On his birthday in 1696, the first opera performance was given at Wilhelmsburg Palace, though this court opera continued for only four years.[4] The duke's antiquarian and bibliophilic interests led him to establish, in 1702, a coin cabinet and a large court library under the directorship of Salomo Franck, who in the previous year had come to Weimar as secretary of the consistory (he had written an opera libretto in 1697, and would later provide cantata texts for Bach). Under the duke's guidance, the Weimar Latin School was upgraded to the level of gymnasium, offering a broader and more scholarly education. Magister Johann Christoph Kiesewetter of Ohrdruf, under whom Bach had attended the Lyceum there, was appointed rector of the gymnasium in 1712 and, in turn, hired the young Magister Johann Matthias Gesner (later Bach's rector at the St. Thomas School in Leipzig) as conrector in 1715. The gymnasium's cantor and teacher of the *quarta* had been, since 1697, Georg Theodor Reineccius, an active composer who collaborated with the town organist Johann Gottfried Walther at St. Peter and Paul's and who was responsible for providing choristers for the palace church (in 1713, Reineccius became godfather to Bach's daughter Maria Sophia, suggesting a close personal relationship).[5] Also under Wilhelm Ernst, Weimar's St. Jacob's Church, which had been destroyed earlier, was rebuilt. Bach and other members of the court capelle joined in the festive inaugural procession and then performed a Mass and a cantata at the dedication service on November 6, 1713.[6]

Duke Johann Ernst III, who occupied the more modest Red Palace nearby, and who had employed Bach in 1703, died in 1707. He had been primarily responsible for reassembling the court capelle from 1683 onward, after his father had dissolved it some twenty years earlier: he began by hiring Johann Samuel Drese as capellmeister and Johann Effler as court organist. Johann Ernst's oldest son, Ernst August, acceded to the position of co-regent in 1709—Bach's second year at Weimar—when he reached the age of majority. But from the very beginning, his uncle Wilhelm Ernst, accustomed to his statutory seniority from the days of joint rule with his younger brother, claimed absolute predominance, especially in the duchy's domestic policy. The relationship between the co-reigning dukes suffered quietly under the weight of their incompatible personalities: Wilhelm Ernst, twenty-six years older, was rigidly conservative and zealously religious, while Ernst August displayed a more enlightened attitude, though he was no less stubborn. During their long joint rule of nineteen years, both uncle and nephew had a share in provoking power struggles that at times reached preposterous proportions, as, for example, when Duke Wilhelm Ernst in one of his arbitrary despotic acts had Duke Ernst August's councilors arrested. But matters deteriorated even further after 1728, when Ernst August assumed undivided rule as absolute monarch.[7]

Bach could hardly have anticipated the roiling political climate at the Weimar court and probably assumed, naively, that in his role as a ranking court musician he would not be directly affected by disputes within the ducal family. Yet over the years, the controversial question of who had control over joint servants directly affected the members of the court capelle. Bach could not have known, for example, that in 1707, before his time, Duke Wilhelm Ernst had decreed that members of the court capelle were allowed to make music at the Red Palace only with his special permission. Wilhelm Ernst, who in June 1708 had particularly admired Bach's playing and engaged him virtually on the spot, continued to hold Bach in highest esteem. Indeed, on June 3, 1711, he ordered a substantial salary increase, from 150 to 200 florins, in response to Bach's "humble request because the salary and allowance of his predecessor [Effler had died the previous April] . . . will cease completely and revert to . . . the princely treasury." He also provided Bach with additional

Duke Ernst August of Saxe-Weimar
in an engraving by Johann Christoph Sysang (1742).

allowances.[8] Whether Bach produced an attractive outside offer or simply
made the case on the basis of his performance in Weimar, it is altogether remarkable that having been appointed at a salary substantially higher than his
predecessor's and equal to the vice-capellmeister's, Bach was now, only three
years later, put on the same pay scale as the capellmeister, Johann Samuel
Drese, whose annual salary of 200 florins remained unchanged for his entire
thirty-three-year term of office.

Despite the undeniable support he received from the Wilhelmsburg, Bach must have developed closer personal ties to the Red Palace. The young Duke Ernst August, who played both violin and trumpet and who was known for his active acquisition of musical instruments and performing materials for his large music library,[9] paid Bach in 1711–12 for giving keyboard lessons to his page Adam von Jagemann (who also received dance instruction from Bach's colleague and landlord Weldig).[10] The duke's twelve-year-old half-brother, Prince Johann Ernst, was taught the violin as a small child and, from 1707 on, studied keyboard and composition with Johann Gottfried Walther, the Weimar town organist and distant relative of Bach's (in 1708, Walther wrote an instruction manual, *Praecepta der musicalischen Composition,* for the prince and presented it to him as a nameday gift). Bach later transcribed four of the prince's compositions, for organ and harpsichord (BWV 592, 595, 982, and 987).[11] Carl Philipp Emanuel Bach reported to Forkel that along with Prince Leopold of Cöthen and Duke Christian of Weissenfels, "Duke Ernst August in Weimar . . . particularly loved him, and rewarded him appropriately."[12] Whether or not the warmer relationship with Ernst August ultimately had a negative impact on Wilhelm Ernst's attitude toward Bach, a sizable salary supplement for his final Weimar years was covered by the younger duke's treasury.[13]

Bach's double function as court organist and chamber musician reflects his versatility and expertise as a performer, but increasingly as a composer, too. As a member of the court capelle, he belonged to the group of "joint servants" and was therefore employed by both dukes and paid by the joint treasury. In 1708–9, Bach's first year, the capelle consisted of twelve mostly full-time members[14](see Table 5.1).

## TABLE 5.1. The Weimar Court Capelle, 1708–9

| | |
|---|---|
| Johann Samuel Drese | capellmeister |
| Johann Wilhelm Drese | vice-capellmeister |
| Johann Sebastian Bach | court organist and chamber musician |
| Michael Wüstenhöfer | discantist |
| Georg H. Romstedt | discantist |
| Adam Immanuel Weldig | falsettist and master of the pages |
| Johann Döbernitz | tenor and court cantor |
| Andreas Aiblinger | tenor and secretary |
| Christoph Alt | bass |
| Johann Andreas Ehrbach | violinist |
| Andreas Eck | violinist and chamber valet |
| Johann Georg Hoffmann | violinist |

This list does not include trumpeters and timpanists, who were typically counted separately in princely households and were carried by the military budget. Personal servants were not listed either, as, for example, Prince Johann Ernst's chamber valet and violin teacher, Gregor Christoph Eylenstein.[15] The list also omits the part-time musicians who occupied lackey or other courtly functions but were essential for providing musical balances when called for; nor does it include the Weimar town musicians and town organist, who often joined the court ensemble in varying roles, or the cantor and members of the chorus musicus from the Weimar gymnasium. Capellmeister Drese, then director of the Weimar court music for twenty-five years, must have been supportive of Bach's appointment. Bach, in turn, will have remembered him as well as his colleagues Alt, Ehrbach, Döbernitz, Hoffmann,[16] and Weldig, all members of the capelle back in 1703. The younger Drese, son of the capellmeister, had been away in 1702–3 studying in Venice and perhaps elsewhere in Italy at the expense of the Weimar court;[17] he was appointed to his present post after the death in 1704 of the former vice-capellmeister Georg Christoph Strattner.

Bach's principal assignment was that of court organist. In that capacity he served at the palace church at the northern end of the Wilhelmsburg's east wing, the center of Duke Wilhelm Ernst's religious and ceremonial activities. Fully integrated into the architectural design of the Wilhelmsburg, the unusually shaped church was dedicated in 1658. Built on a footprint of about 100 by 40 feet, it rose to a total height of about 90 feet from the floor to the tip of the crowning cupola.[18] The tall structure of the sanctuary, with two sets of galleries surrounding the relatively narrow rectangular hall, extended upward over three floors (see illustration, p. 146). Cut into the flat ceiling of the sanctuary (about 65 feet above the floor level) was a wide rectangular aperture—about 13 by 10 feet and surrounded by a balustrade—that opened into the music gallery, a spacious domed compartment called the *Capelle.* As was customary for music galleries, the balustrade would have been designed to serve as an elongated music stand so that singers and players could be placed—depending on the size of the ensemble—around two, three, or four flanks of the aperture. The painted cupola extending about 15 feet above the gallery level projected an open heaven and clouds with figures of angels and putti. Appropriately named *Weg zur Himmelsburg* (Road to Heaven's Castle)—for short, *Himmelsburg*—by its theologically minded planners, the pious Duke Wilhelm IV and his architect Johann Moritz Richter, the church represented the image of its true religious function: a way station between the Wilhelmsburg and heaven, between the earthly ducal residence and God's castle. The limited seating capacity of the church presented no major problem since services were attended only by the ducal families, sitting in their princely boxes, and by members of the princely household, other gentry, court officials, and select employees seated in the pews of the narrow nave and in the surrounding double galleries. For the worshippers, music from the *Capelle* above the ceiling, enhanced by the "echo tower" effect of its dazzling acoustics, would have been perceived as sounds descending from heaven—corresponding to the ancient imagery of an angels' concert.

Historical accounts describe the *Himmelsburg* as "adorned with a marvelous organ." Considering the unique architectural circumstances, its place in the *Capelle,* just behind the balustrade of the shorter east side of the rectangular ceiling opening, provided for maximum exposure and projection. We do not know what the organ actually looked and sounded like during Bach's time because the information we have about the instrument, which is no longer extant, either predates or postdates his Weimar years. A publication of 1737 specifies twenty-four stops on two manuals and pedal,[19] reflecting changes that date from a rebuilding of 1719–20. The original organ (seen in the illustration, p. 146) was built in several sections from 1658 on by one of the most famous German organ builders, Ludwig Compenius of Erfurt.[20] However, that instrument had been thoroughly overhauled and enlarged by the organ builder Johann Conrad Weishaupt immediately before Bach's arrival in Weimar; the most significant changes included new wind chests, new pedal stops (including a 32-foot subbass), and a rebuilding of the *Seitenwerk* (side organ, lower manual) into an *Unterwerk* (lower organ). Further design changes were made during Bach's nine years there, but generally the organ seems to have been in excellent technical condition throughout his tenure, for the court registers contain no entries pertaining to even minor repairs.

In Weimar, Bach developed a close personal relationship with the resident organ builder, Heinrich Nicolaus Trebs, who provided maintenance service for the organ at the court church. Trebs signed a contract on June 29, 1712, for a complete overhaul and manufacture of several new stops, in exchange for a payment of 200 florins.[21] Of the plans, drawn up by Bach, we know only that they called for a glockenspiel stop, which had also been a part of Bach's 1708 rebuilding project for the Mühlhausen organ. By October 1712, Trebs had already obtained twenty-nine chimes from a Nuremberg maker, and twelve additional ones arrived the following spring.[22] The organ project was coordinated with a redesign and expansion of the entire *Capelle*. In late June 1712, the organ's wind chests were dismantled, so that the instrument was rendered unplayable. Beginning December 21, eleven carpenters and two day laborers worked day and night installing the bellows chamber so that the organ could be played on Christmas eve.[23] But work on the instrument was by no means finished then. Bach's student Kräuter, hoping to remain longer with Bach, wrote to his Augsburg sponsors in April 1713 that "by Whitsuntide the palace organ here will be in as good a condition as possible; hence I could familiarize myself more completely with the structure of an organ, in order to be able to judge if this or that would be useful for an organ, if all repair work were executed well and not superficially, and at the same time how much, approximately, one or two ranks of pipes would cost, all of which I consider rather worthwhile."[24] Still, the project was not entirely completed even by Whitsuntide 1713. The importance of keeping the organ playable throughout much of the construction explains why Trebs took such a long time to finish it. Only on May 19 of the next year, 1714, was a bellows operator finally paid for fourteen days of "labor for the tuning of the organ," indicating that the finishing touches were being applied.[25] All this means that Bach's organistic activities at the court church were curtailed for a long period, from Christmas 1712 through May 1714, and that for half a year he could not play the organ at all.

Far fewer services were held each week at the court church than at any regular town church—in general, one Sunday and one weekday service—with Johann Georg Lairitz, the duchy's general superintendent, serving as the main preacher. According to the new Weimar formulary of 1707, *Agende, oder kurtzer Auszug aus der Kirchen-Ordnung,* the order of divine service complied with standard Lutheran practices in all major respects (see Table 4.2), but showed the following small variants: the service opened with a congregational hymn in line with the liturgical season; then a polyphonic Kyrie was performed by the choir, followed by the Gloria intonation by the pastor from the altar and the congregational Gloria hymn "Allein Gott in der Höh sei Ehr." A single Kyrie by Bach has come down to us, albeit in posthumous sources. But since the work in question—Kyrie "Christe, du Lamm Gottes," BWV 233a, for five voices and continuo, later integrated into the Mass in F major, BWV 233—not only fits stylistically among Bach's early choral fugues but also employs the Weimar melodic version of the Litany, it may confidently be placed in the early Weimar period. The existence of this Kyrie suggests that the court organist Bach played at least a modest role in the realm of vocal music, too. In his Mühlhausen resignation letter, Bach had made such a strong case for his "ultimate goal of a well-regulated church music" and expressed such a keen interest in getting more involved in vocal music that his voluntary withdrawal from it would indeed be hard to imagine. Nevertheless, as in Arnstadt and Mühlhausen, his official activities continued to focus primarily on organ music.

It would be misleading to describe Bach's musical functions at Weimar as exclusively liturgical. Of course, playing at the divine services was of central importance, but this task was essentially limited to accompanying hymns and providing introductory chorale preludes and a postlude. The remarks in the

Obituary that "the pleasure His Grace [Duke Ernst August] took in his [Bach's] playing fired him with the desire to try every possible artistry in his treatment of the organ" and that in Weimar "he wrote most of his organ works" suggest activities of a much broader scope, perhaps frequent organ recitals or performances at the end of the church services, at the request of Duke Ernst August or for the pleasure of both ducal families, guests and foreign dignitaries, and other interested parties. Similarly, when the occasion arose, Bach may also have presented solo performances on the harpsichord. Taking pride in a keyboard virtuoso of Bach's stature would have been only in keeping with the princely habit of regularly showcasing the trophies of their "talent hunters," thereby also justifying financial rewards over and above the pay scale called for by the musician's actual rank. Such courtly entertainment would then have permitted Bach to impress and captivate his audience by performing works that would ordinarily be unsuitable for worship services, because of either their disproportionate length (large-scale preludes, toccatas, and fugues) or their unconventional design (Italian concerto and other transcriptions).

Bach's "desire to try every possible artistry," a major impetus for his creative endeavors as organist in Arnstadt and Mühlhausen as well, could never have found this kind of focused support and promotion in a position under regular church and civic governance. Thus, it stands to reason that, as noted earlier, Weimar was where most of his organ works originated. This Obituary statement clearly refers to written compositions, and considering that a large portion of a capable organist's work consisted of improvised music, the organ compositions that have come down to us represent only a fraction of the music that originated from Bach's creative mind. Nevertheless, his decision to fix so many organ works—some if not most of them based on improvisations—in written form indicates that Bach considered these pieces worthy of elaboration and preservation, that the musical ideas embedded in them stimulated and challenged his compositional instincts, that the functions for which they were written required a certain degree of preparation and exercise, and finally, that these compositions would serve his increasing teaching activities. After all, Bach's Mühlhausen pupils Schubart and Vogler moved with him to Weimar, where they were joined over time by more than ten other students, among them the first complement of Bach family members: Johann Lorenz, eldest son of cousin Johann Valentin Bach of Schweinfurt, arrived in the fall of 1713 and remained for five years; Johann Bernhard, his Ohrdruf brother's second son, came to Weimar as a fifteen-year-old in late 1714 or early 1715 and stayed on until 1719, through Bach's early Cöthen years;[26] and his own son Wilhelm Friedemann surely began to receive his father's instruction well before his seventh birthday, in 1717.

Roughly half of Bach's extant organ works point either to Weimar origin or to Weimar revisions of, or amendments to, earlier works; evidence is provided both by autograph manuscripts and, in particular, by copies (or sources related to copies) made by Bach's student Johann Tobias Krebs and colleague Johann Gottfried Walther. None of these sources, however, permit us to differentiate clearly between chronological stages. Even the few samples available of Bach's music hand that are datable to the period 1708–14 feature insufficient changes in his penmanship. One of the few indirect chronological clues for Bach's keyboard works from the Weimar period relates to an important historical fact. In the spring of 1713, Prince Johann Ernst, Duke Ernst August's half-brother and a musician of professional caliber, returned from his grand tour to the Low Countries and brought back with him copies of recent music, published and in manuscript, that he had acquired in Amsterdam. Indeed, additional music shelves had to be installed in the library of the Red Palace to hold this bounty.[27] In Amsterdam, Johann Ernst may also have met the blind organist Jan Jacob de Graaf, who was known for his playing of the latest fashionable Italian ensemble concertos in keyboard transcriptions and presumably supplied the indirect model for similar transcriptions by the young prince's teachers, Walther and Bach.

Bach's organ and harpsichord transcriptions (BWV 592–596 and 972–987) from Antonio Vivaldi's *L'Estro armonico,* Op. 3 (1711), and of concertos by Alessandro and Benedetto Marcello, Giuseppe Torelli, and others, as well as compositions by the prince himself, signal the adoption in 1713–14 of the most modern Italian concerto type—not coincidentally, right after the prince's return. Compositions by Bach that are directly indebted to the Vivaldi-style ritornello concerto include the Toccata in F major for organ, BWV 540 (its canonic beginning modeled after Vivaldi's Double Violin Concerto in D minor, transcribed in BWV 596), and the opening prelude of the English Suite in G minor, BWV 808. Works such as the "Dorian" Toccata for organ, BWV 538, the Toccata in C major, BWV 564, and the Prelude in G major, BWV 541, reflect compositional principles of an older Italian concerto type, suggesting an earlier origin. That older style is represented by Tomaso Albinoni's Concertos Op. 2 (1700), with which Bach was familiar. (Also, a fragmentary continuo part for one of Albinoni's concertos, BWV Anh. I 23, written in Bach's hand around 1710 or earlier, was probably prepared for a performance with the court capelle.)

All these keyboard works demonstrate a remarkable ability to expand on their models or to synthesize different models. Bach's orientation was neither exclusively Italianate nor exclusively modernist. In the very early Weimar years, for instance, he copied Nicolas de Grigny's *Premier Livre d'Orgue* (1700);[28] also, a work such as the *Pièce d'Orgue* in G major, BWV 572, exemplifies a sovereign exercise in French style. Similarly, Bach's (lost) copy of Frescobaldi's *Fiori musicali* (1635), which bore the date 1714, is evidence of his continuing interest in the great keyboard masters of the more distant past. Taken together, Bach's Weimar keyboard music shows little uniformity, less dependence on specific stylistic models than his earlier works, and a greater tendency toward a more efficient and more individualized application of different compositional principles and techniques.

One particular seminal project not only spans the entire Weimar period, from 1708 to 1717, but also extends beyond it in both directions: the *Orgel-Büchlein* (Little Organ Book). Near the beginning of his tenure as court organist, Bach apparently intended to compile a large collection of short organ chorales that would enhance the core melodies of the Lutheran hymnbook. To this end, he prepared a bound volume (its title was added only after 1720)[29] with room for 164 settings of as many chorale melodies, all of whose headings he entered at the outset. Altogether they constitute virtually the entire "classic" Lutheran hymn repertory up to about 1675. Bach was focusing here on the melodies of his childhood days, with no attention paid to the more recent chorale melodies. The collection does not follow any specific hymnal, although the structure and sequence of the liturgical rubrics are fairly standardized in the Lutheran tradition. Most every hymnbook begins with the seasonal chorales for the ecclesiastical year (the first invariably being "Nun komm der Heiden Heiland," Martin Luther's poetic translation of the Ambrosian "Veni redemptor gentium") and continues with the topically organized hymns for all seasons (see Table 5.2, left-hand column). Of the two hymnals in use at Weimar during Bach's years there—*Auserlesenes Weimarisches Gesangbuch* of 1681 (second edition 1713) and *Schuldiges Lob Gottes, oder: Geistreiches Gesang-Buch* of 1713—the second comes closest to the *Orgel-Büchlein* in its order and contents. Bach, however, could have worked basically from memory and ordered the collection according to his own plan.

Each of the *Orgel-Büchlein*'s ninety pages in oblong-quarto format, about 6 by 7.5 inches, was ruled with six staves, and, depending on the length of the cantus firmus (the plain chorale melody), the composition had to fit on exactly one or two pages (see illustration, p. 128). This type of miniature organ chorale harks back to the style of the chorale partita, whose individual movements are closely defined in character and in motivic design. Bach also integrates into this new collection a number of preexisting settings, perhaps with minor refinements, for quite a number of the entries represent fair copies without any trace of compositional activity. He probably selected them from a portfolio of chorales that he had begun to compile much earlier and from which other, later collections might have benefited as well. The typical *Orgel-Büchlein* chorale combines tight motivic construction and refined contrapuntal devices (including strict canon) with bold expressive language and subtle musico-theological interpretation; in each, manual and pedal lines converge elegantly into a paradigmatic organ score.

The opening setting, "Nun komm der Heiden Heiland," BWV 599, a compelling chorale harmonization in broken manner (*style brisé*), with a regular, emphatic, and affective distribution of dissonant notes, is followed by a tightly constructed elaboration of "Gott durch deine Güte," BWV 600, where the soprano and tenor parts engage in strict canonic imitation (half-note motion) while the alto and bass parts present contrapuntal lines in, respectively, quarter- and eighth-note motion. The extraordinary variety of compositional approaches systematically explored in the *Orgel-Büchlein* includes many instances in which motivic inventions function as interpretive devices. For example, in "Durch Adams Fall ist ganz verderbt," BWV 637, descending chromatic phrases in the middle voices combine with falling leaps by diminished and augmented intervals in the bass to signify Adam's fall into sin, the doctrinal topic of this Lutheran teaching hymn of 1524.

Bach worked on the ambitious *Orgel-Büchlein* project over many years,[30]

"Gott durch deine Güte," BWV 600, from the *Orgel-Büchlein*, autograph score.

with the obvious intention of eventually filling the entire book in much the same way as he filled the opening sections from Advent to Easter. However, the project remained incomplete as new compositional undertakings took precedence and Bach lost interest in this type of organ chorale setting. The title supplied after 1720 specifically addresses what by then had become the pedagogical—and now primary—function of the collection, "in which a beginner at the organ is given instruction in developing a chorale in many diverse ways, and at the same time in acquiring facility in the study of the pedal." Bach kept the material for teaching purposes, adding only one complete setting after 1726, starting a second one, and revising a few older ones. But ultimately, almost three-quarters of the album leaves remained unfilled, with titles followed only by empty staves[31] (see Table 5.2).

From the beginning, Bach's Weimar appointment as court organist included as well the title "chamber musician"[32]—a designation not borne by Johann Effler, his predecessor as court organist, nor by any other member of the court capelle at the time. Although we have no appointment letter defining the specific functions of either title, we can be sure that they do not reflect a clear division of responsibilities, such as church versus chamber, sacred versus secular music, organ versus harpsichord, or keyboard versus violin. The same applies to the "concertmaster" title Bach later acquired. All members of the court capelle had to participate in both church and chamber music. The additional designation was apparently intended to elevate the court organist above the members of the court capelle to a rank just below that of vice-capellmeister and, at the same time, to broaden the scope of his activities, as the higher salary also indicated. Since Bach, after his Mühlhausen experience, would have wanted to bear responsibility for vocal-instrumental ensemble music, as chamber musician he possessed the right and obligation to play a leadership role (though subordinate to the capellmeister and vice-capellmeister) in performing with and composing for the court capelle for both sacred and secular occasions.

Vocal works that clearly belong to the Weimar period before 1714 include the sacred solo cantatas "Widerstehe doch der Sünde," BWV 54, and "Mein Herze schwimmt im Blut," BWV 199, both on texts by the Darmstadt court poet Georg Christian Lehms that were published in 1711.[33] The texts articulate general theological themes (resistance to sin and reconciliation with God, respectively), making them suitable as generic church music beyond any specific liturgical occasion within the ecclesiastical year. Both pieces, but especially BWV 199, demand a high level of vocal technique and required professional singers, who were available at the Weimar court. BWV 199, an extended eight-movement cantata scored for soprano (*Chorton* range: b–g″), oboe, strings, and continuo, may have been sung by the falsettist Weldig,

## TABLE 5.2. *Orgel-Büchlein:* Plan and Realization

| Rubric | No.[a] | BWV | Title [Gaps] | Score Status | Period[b] |
|---|---|---|---|---|---|
| **I. Chorales for the ecclesiastical year (de tempore)** | | | | | |
| Advent | 1 | 599 | Nun komm der Heiden Heiland | composing | II |
| | 2 | 600 | Gott, durch deine Güte, or: Gottes Sohn ist kommen | composing | II |
| | 3 | 601 | Herr Christ, der einge Gottessohn, or: Herr Gott, nun sei gepreiset | fair copy | I |
| | 4 | 602 | Lob sei dem allmächtigen Gott | composing | II |
| Christmas | 5 | 603 | Puer natus in Bethlehem | composing | I |
| | 6 | | [1 chorale bypassed] | | |
| | 7 | 604 | Gelobet seist du, Jesu Christ | composing | I |
| | 8 | 605 | Der Tag, der ist so freudenreich | fair copy | I |
| | 9 | 606 | Vom Himmel hoch, da komm ich her | fair copy | I |
| | 10 | 607 | Vom Himmel kam der Engel Schar | composing | II |
| | 11 | 608 | In dulci jubilo | composing | I |
| | 12 | 609 | Lobt Gott, ihr Christen, allzugleich | composing | I |
| | 13 | 610 | Jesu, meine Freude | fair copy | II |
| | 14 | 611 | Christum wir sollen loben schon | fair copy | III |
| | 15 | 612 | Wir Christenleut | fair copy | II |
| New Year's Day | 16 | 613 | Helft mir Gotts Güte preisen | fair copy | IV |
| | 17 | 614 | Das alte Jahr vergangen ist | fair copy | II |
| | 18 | 615 | In dir ist Freude | fair copy | III |
| Purification | 19 | 616 | Mit Fried und Freud ich fahr dahin | fair copy | III |
| | 20 | 617 | Herr Gott, nun schleuß den Himmel auf | fair copy | III |
| Passion | 21 | 618 | O Lamm Gottes, unschuldig | composing | III |

|  |  |  |  |  |  |
|---|---|---|---|---|---|
|  | 22 | 619 | Christe, du Lamm Gottes | fair copy | III |
|  | 23 | 620(a) | Christus, der uns selig macht | fair copy | III; rev. IV |
|  | 24 | 621 | Da Jesus an dem Kreuze stund | fair copy | I |
|  | 25 | 622 | O Mensch, bewein dein Sünde groß | composing | I |
|  | 26 | 623 | Wir danken dir, Herr Jesu Christ | fair copy | III |
|  | 27 | 624 | Hilf Gott, daß mir's gelinge | fair copy | III |
|  | 28 |  | [1 chorale bypassed] |  |  |
|  | 29 | Anh.200 | O Traurigkeit, o Herzeleid (fragment) | composing | IV |
|  | 30–33 |  | [4 chorales bypassed] |  |  |
| Easter | 34 | 625 | Christ lag in Todesbanden | fair copy | II |
|  | 35 | 626 | Jesus Christus, unser Heiland, der den Tod | fair copy | II |
|  | 36 | 627 | Christ ist erstanden | composing | II |
|  | 37 | 628 | Erstanden ist der heilge Christ | composing | II |
|  | 38 | 629 | Erschienen ist der herrliche Tag | composing | II |
|  | 39 | 630(a) | Heut triumphieret Gottes Sohn | fair copy | I |
| Ascension | 40–41 |  |  |  |  |
| Pentecost | 42–43 |  | [4 chorales bypassed] |  |  |
|  | 44 | 631(a) | Komm, Gott Schöpfer, Heiliger Geist | composing | II; rev. IV |
|  | 45–48 |  | [5 chorales bypassed] |  |  |
|  | 49 | 632 | Herr Jesu Christ, dich zu uns wend | fair copy | I |
|  | 50 | 634 | Liebster Jesu, wir sind hier | fair copy | III |
|  | 51 | 633 | Liebster Jesu, wir sind hier (distinctius) | fair copy | III |
| Trinity | 52–54 |  |  |  |  |
| St. John's | 55 |  |  |  |  |
| Visitation | 56 |  | [9 chorales bypassed] |  |  |
| St. Michael's | 57–58 |  |  |  |  |
| Apostle days | 59–60 |  |  |  |  |

**II. Chorales for all times**

| | | | | | |
|---|---|---|---|---|---|
| Catechism | 61 | 635 | Dies sind die heilgen zehn Gebot | fair copy | I |
| | 62–64 | | {3 chorales bypassed} | | |
| | 65 | 636 | Vater unser im Himmelreich | fair copy | I |
| | 66–75 | | {10 chorales bypassed} | | |
| | 76 | 637 | Durch Adams Fall ist ganz verderbt | composing | I |
| | 77 | 638(a) | Es ist das Heil uns kommen her | fair copy | I |
| | 78–84 | | | | |
| Thanksgiving | 85–86 | | {13 chorales bypassed} | | |
| Christian life | 87–90 | | | | |
| | 91 | 639 | Ich ruf zu dir, Herr Jesu Christ | fair copy | II |
| | 92–96 | | | | |
| Cross, | 97 | | {6 chorales bypassed} | | |
| Persecution | 98 | 640 | In dich hab ich gehoffet, Herr | fair copy | II |
| Temptation | 99 | | {1 chorale bypassed} | | |
| | 100 | 641 | Wenn wir in höchsten Nöten sein | composing | II |
| | 101–112 | | {12 chorales bypassed} | | |
| | 113 | 642 | Wer nur den lieben Gott läßt walten | fair copy | II |
| Church | 114–123 | | | | |
| War, Peace | 124–126 | | {17 chorales bypassed} | | |
| Death | 127–130 | | | | |
| | 131 | 643 | Alle Menschen müssen sterben | composing | II |
| | 132–140 | | | | |
| Last Judgment | 141–142 | | | | |
| Morning | 143–147 | | | | |
| Evening | 148–151 | | {27 chorales bypassed} | | |
| Grace | 152–155 | | | | |
| Weather | 156 | | | | |
| Appendix | 157–158 | | | | |
| | 159 | 644 | Ach, wie nichtig, ach wie flüchtig | fair copy | II |
| | 160–164 | | {5 chorales bypassed} | | |

*The consecutive numbering (1–164) pertains to the planned chorales; titles are given for the executed compositions only.

[b]I: c. 1708–12; II: c. 1712–13; III: c. 1715–17; IV: after 1726; rev.: revision.

while BWV 54, a three-movement cantata scored for alto (*Chorton* range: f–c″) and string ensemble, would have been sung by the alto of the capelle. The soprano cantata presents a set of alternating recitatives and arias (one aria combined with a chorale), highly differentiated, in which the solo voice links with a variety of instrumental accompaniments (solo oboe, solo viola, strings only, and full complement of oboe and strings). Striking features of the alto cantata include the sequence of dissonant chords that open the work and the concluding fugal movement with its chromatic subject. With pieces like BWV 54 and 199, Bach was continuing to write "organists' music" as before, with a view toward creating works without a restricted liturgical schedule and therefore more opportunities for re-performance. The cantata "Gleichwie der Regen und Schnee," BWV 18, based on a text by Erdmann Neumeister of 1711, most probably dates from before 1714 as well. Scored for four-part chorus and the uncommon, exquisite accompaniment of four violas and continuo, it has a specific place in the liturgical calendar—Sexagesimae Sunday—and may therefore be the first of the so-called *Jahrgangs-Kantaten,* or annual-cycle cantatas, that has survived.

Bach's privileged post of court organist and chamber musician appears to have entailed special, if loosely defined, responsibilities for the court capelle, allowing him opportunities to perform his own compositions as well as works by others. Regrettably, virtually all musical sources related to Bach's function as chamber musician and, later, as concertmaster in charge of instrumental music have vanished, which makes it impossible to assess Bach's activities and creative output in the instrumental sphere. The most reliable, if seriously abridged, picture of his instrumental ideas can be gathered indirectly from the instrumental movements of the Weimar cantatas. Only a single source can be traced directly to Weimar chamber music: a Fugue in G minor for violin and continuo, BWV 1026, in a copy made around 1714 by the Weimar town organist Johann Gottfried Walther. This oldest extant chamber composition by Bach is a sophisticated and highly virtuosic yet isolated single movement whose genesis and context remain obscure. Nevertheless, its lengthy double-stop passages, other virtuosic devices, and the idiomatic treatment of the violin demonstrate Bach's impressive technical accomplishments as a violinist and suggest that he continued to develop his violin technique. Moreover, it lends credence to a long-held assumption that Bach began work on the sonatas and partitas for unaccompanied violin, BWV 1001–1006, in Weimar (as evidenced by earlier versions of the pieces). These works seem conceptually indebted to Johann Paul von Westhoff's 1696 publication of solo violin partitas, the first of its kind; and since Westhoff, one of the preeminent violinists of his time, played in the Weimar court capelle until his death in 1705, Bach would have met him in 1703.

Additional evidence of Bach's involvement in instrumental chamber music may be found in the performing parts for the Concerto in G major for 2 violins and orchestra by Georg Philipp Telemann, jointly copied by Bach and the violinist Johann Georg Pisendel, a student of Vivaldi's and later concertmaster at the Dresden court. Pisendel traveled through Weimar in 1709, when from all appearances he and Bach performed this concerto with the court capelle. Telemann, then capellmeister at the neighboring court of Saxe-Eisenach, may well have participated in such a performance, or Bach and Pisendel could have played the work with the Eisenach capelle as well. At any rate, Bach had an opportunity to establish closer professional and personal contacts with Telemann during the latter's Eisenach years, and he invited Telemann in 1714 to become godfather to his second son, Carl Philipp Emanuel. Carl received his middle name from Telemann, who pursued his godchild's musical career with great interest and, toward the end of his long life, helped arrange for his godson to succeed him as music director in Hamburg in 1768.

The general instrumental and vocal repertoire performed by the Weimar court capelle remains a mystery. Apart from a mere reference to the performance of "much fine Italian and French music,"[34] we lack all specifics. Moreover, none of the works written for the capelle by the two Dreses, capellmeister and vice-capellmeister, have survived, as the court's music library went up in flames along with the entire Wilhelmsburg in 1774. Similarly, a substantial part of Bach's oeuvre written in the employ of the dukes of Saxe-Weimar would also have remained in the possession of the court when he left Weimar, and we can assume that the works that originated in Bach's Weimar period have been severely decimated, resulting in a picture that is full of gaps. All the more important are the few sources that shed light on what must have been a rich and varied musical scene at the ducal court (see also Table 6.5 and the related discussion). These include a set of parts for a *St. Mark Passion,* presumably by Friedrich Nicolaus Brauns, music director of the Hamburg cathedral,[35] and copied by Bach for a performance that took place at the palace church in 1711–12, if not a year earlier, presumably on Good Friday. That Bach was able to obtain this material directly or indirectly from Hamburg is evidence of his nonparochial outlook, not to mention well-functioning connections.

Relationships with neighboring courts, such as Saxe-Eisenach, where Telemann served, played an important role in Bach's life during his Weimar years. In February 1713, he received a most attractive invitation to the ducal court of Saxe-Weissenfels. For Duke Christian's thirty-first birthday on February 23, Bach was commissioned to compose the festive *Tafel-Music* for the banquet to be held at the ducal hunting lodge near Weissenfels, after completion of the chase. Since the text for this elaborate cantata, titled "Frohlockender Götter-Streit" (Jubilant Dispute of the Gods), BWV 208, was written by the Weimar court poet, Salomo Franck, the work could be considered an import from Weimar by the Weissenfels court, and in all likelihood the dukes of the related Weimar dynasty participated in the Weissenfels hunt and birthday. The musical arrangements for the festivities were probably made by Adam Immanuel Weldig (Bach's Weimar colleague and landlord), who had just moved to Weissenfels,[36] where he remained until his untimely death three years later. Bach's performance at the hunting lodge, an undoubted success, not only led to a repeat performance of the *"Hunt" Cantata* in 1716, but more important, established a long-term association with Duke Christian of Weissenfels that culminated in a titular capellmeistership bestowed on Bach in 1729. Bach's guest performance in Weissenfels did not remain unrewarded in Weimar, either, for the court had gained credit abroad by the performance of its musician. Only three days after the event, Bach received by ducal command a salary increase of 15 florins, effective immediately[37]—bringing his annual cash compensation to 215 florins, now above that of the capellmeister.

The *Hunt Cantata,* BWV 208, not only marked Bach's first documented collaboration with Salomo Franck as librettist, it is his first known secular cantata and, at the same time, his first work of truly large-scale proportions. A dramatic dialogue among four mythological figures—Diana, Pales, Endymion, and Pan (assigned to the vocal parts SSTB)—with an opulent instrumental accompaniment and a large continuo group (including 2 bassoons, a violone, and a violono grosso), the work unfolds in fifteen movements. It contains multiple examples of the three main vocal forms (recitative, aria, and chorus) handled in a host of excitingly different ways, while the forces for which they are scored are variously combined, increasing the sense of musical diversity. The accompaniments to the arias, for example, range from simple continuo writing, both with and without ensemble ritornellos, to colorful and delicately contrasting textures that feature, in turn, 2 horns, 3 oboes, 2 recorders, and solo violin. Sung by the four vocal soloists, the choruses are also textured in a wide variety of ways, from tunefully homophonic to elaborately polyphonic. This dramatic cantata has not, however, survived entirely in its original format. The autograph score, lacking the opening sinfonia, begins immediately with a short recitative. The missing instrumental introduction must have resembled, at least in scoring and key, the early (five-movement) sinfonia version BWV 1046a of the *Brandenburg Concerto* No. 1—if it was not in fact that very work.

If the cantata BWV 208 is indicative of Bach's remarkable accomplishments and reputation in the realm of courtly musical entertainment outside of

Weimar, then we can be sure that he would have reached a similarly unchallenged stature at the Weimar court by early 1713 as well and would have done, or would soon do, similar things there. We can surmise that he prepared and composed instrumental and vocal music for the Weimar court capelle more heavily than the surviving musical sources bear out. Indeed, Philipp David Kräuter expressly refers to his learning experience with Bach as including "composing concertos and overtures";[38] it is inconceivable that the teacher himself did not also compose such works. Bach's consummate skill and innovative approach in handling instrumental ensemble pieces is manifest in the great variety of instrumental movements he composed for his sacred cantatas in Weimar before and after 1714. Some of them, like the sinfonias of BWV 12 and 21, may have their actual origin in chamber works written for the court capelle.

Given the broad scope of activities and opportunities in Weimar, it is difficult to see why Bach should have found it tempting in late 1713 to seriously consider a new position, that of organist and music director at Our Lady's (or Market) Church in Halle on the Saale. Two possible reasons that could have motivated Bach to leave Weimar come to mind. The first is the new and very large organ, with sixty-five stops on three manuals and pedal, that was under contract to the organ builder Christoph Cuntzius for the spacious Our Lady's Church. (Bach, along with Johann Kuhnau and Christian Friedrich Rolle, examined the organ after its completion in 1716.)[39] The Obituary makes a relevant point in this regard: "Despite all this knowledge of the organ, he never enjoyed the good fortune, as he used to point out frequently with regret, of having a really large and really beautiful organ at his constant disposal."[40] The Halle organ would indeed have been enormously attractive to Bach, and he may have derived belated if vicarious pleasure when his son Wilhelm Friedemann, some thirty years later, took that very position. The second reason relates to political or organizational problems emerging at the Weimar court and court capelle, possibly foreshadowing those that contributed to his eventual departure for Cöthen.

## CLAVIER VIRTUOSO AND ORGAN EXPERT

In a 1752 reminiscence, the distinguished Berlin court musician Johann Joachim Quantz discusses the state of instrumental music and the development of musical taste in the late seventeenth century. He singles out "the art of organ playing, which had to a great extent been learned from the Netherlanders," and emphasizes that it "was already at this time in a high state of advancement, thanks to [Froberger, Reinken, Buxtehude, Pachelbel, Nicolaus Bruhns] and some other able men. Finally, the admirable Johann Sebastian Bach brought it to its greatest perfection in recent times."[41] In Quantz's view, the art of organ playing included both performance and composition. Himself a flute virtuoso and composer for his instrument, the interdependence for Quantz of playing technique on the one hand and compositional ideas on the other was an essential concept for any performer-composer, as it clearly was for Bach. Bach's instrumental orientation and vocal background from childhood days complemented one another, as his keyboard skills were supplemented by his string experience and augmented by a compositional focus that eventually took in the widest possible spectrum of musical instruments and human voices; all this was supported by a deep knowledge and keen awareness of technological and physiological details and balanced by intellectual discipline and temperamental sensitivity.

The foundations for Bach's systematic approach to virtually all his musical undertakings were laid well before he entered professional life. Yet the Arnstadt, Mühlhausen, and early Weimar years—with their fairly limited obligations and their considerable personal latitude and economic security—presented the enormously gifted, highly motivated musician with ideal opportunities for exploration, experimentation, and training. Nor should it be forgotten that early on he received much support from influential political figures such as Councillor Klemm of Sangerhausen, Burgomaster Feldhaus of Arnstadt, Consul Meckbach of Mühlhausen, and Duke Ernst August of Saxe-Weimar. He likewise won encouragement and esteem from eminent senior colleagues like Böhm, Reinken, Effler, and the organ builder Wender, not to mention other members of the Bach clan.

As an organist and keyboard player, Bach had studied everything he could lay his hands on, from very old repertoires—his library eventually contained three copies of Elias Nicolaus Ammerbach's *Orgel oder Instrument Tabulatur* of 1571 and a manuscript copy of Frescobaldi's *Fiori musicali*—to works of German, French, and Italian masters from the previous generation, to compositions by his own contemporaries.[42] By around 1714, Bach had explored virtually all genres of organ and clavier music, meeting a variety of musical challenges in most categories of keyboard composition common to both organ and harpsichord, but also in the more harpsichord-specific repertoire. By the time Bach turned twenty-five in 1710, he had reached the peak of his technical facility at the keyboard, which he would then, of course, strive to refine further. However, he also had to learn to acknowledge that limits did exist. In conjunction with Bach's "admirable facility in reading and executing the compositions of others (which, indeed, were all easier than his own)," Forkel relates a revealing anecdote, the source of which could only have been Bach himself, who probably taught his children a lesson about pride going before a fall:

He once said to an acquaintance, while he lived at Weimar, that he really believed he could play everything, without hesitating, at the first sight. He was, however, mistaken; and the friend [perhaps Johann Gottfried Walther] to whom he had thus expressed his opinion convinced him of it before the week was passed. He invited him one morning to breakfast and laid upon the desk of his instrument, among other pieces, one which at the first glance appeared to be very trifling. Bach came and, according to his custom, went immediately to the instrument, partly to play, partly to look over the music that lay on the desk. While he was perusing them and playing them through, his host went into the next room to prepare breakfast. In a few minutes Bach got to the piece which was destined for his conversion and began to play it. But he had not proceeded far when he came to a passage at which he stopped. He looked at it, began anew, and again stopped at the same passage. "No," he called out to his friend, who was laughing to himself in the next room, and at the same time went away from the instrument, "one cannot play everything at first sight; it is not possible."[43]

Forkel, largely on the basis of reports from the two oldest Bach sons and partly on the basis of published eyewitness accounts,[44] provides particularly useful information about Bach's keyboard technique and its physiological underpinnings. He also gives a chronological sense of how Bach's fingering system developed when he refers to the new mode of fingering—including use of the thumb—in François Couperin's *L'Art de toucher le Clavecin* of 1716 and expressly states that "Bach was at that time above 30 years old and had long made use of this manner of fingering." He then continues:

Bach was, however, acquainted with Couperin's works and esteemed them, as well as the works of several other French composers for the harpsichord of that period, because a pretty and elegant mode of playing may be learned from them. But on the other hand he considered them as too affected in their frequent use of graces, which goes so far that scarcely a note is free from embellishment. The ideas they contained were, besides, too flimsy for him.

Without drawing a parallel with the famous priority dispute between Newton and Leibniz about the invention of calculus, Forkel recognizes the revolutionary impact of the seemingly simple method of making the thumb a "principal finger,"[45] acknowledges that Couperin and Bach reached their conclusions independently of each other, stresses Bach's far more comprehensive approach, and summarizes its principal features:

According to Sebastian Bach's manner of placing the hand on the keyboard the five fingers are bent so that their points come into a straight line, and fit the keys, which lie in a plane surface under them, that no single finger has to be drawn nearer when it is wanted, but every one is ready over the key which it may have to press down. What follows from this manner of holding the hand is:

(1) That no finger must fall upon its key, or (as also often happens) be thrown on it, but only needs to be *placed* upon it with a certain consciousness of the internal power and command over the motion.

(2) The impulse thus given to the keys, or the quantity of pressure, must be maintained in equal strength, and that in such a manner that the finger be not raised perpendicularly from the key, but that it glide off the forepart of the key, by gradually drawing back the tip of the finger towards the palm of the hand.

(3) In the transition from one key to another, this gliding off causes the quantity of force of pressure with which the first tone has been kept up to be transferred with the greatest rapidity to the next finger, so that the two tones are neither disjoined from each other nor blended together. The touch is therefore, as C. Ph. Emanuel Bach says, neither too long nor too short, but just what it ought to be.

The advantages of such a position of the hand and of such a touch are very various, not only on the clavichord, but also on the pianoforte and the organ. I will here mention only the most important.

(1) The holding of the fingers bent renders all their motions easy. There can therefore be none of the scrambling, thumping, and stumbling which is so common in persons who play with their fingers stretched out, or not sufficiently bent.

(2) The drawing back of the tips of the fingers and the rapid communication, thereby effected, of the force of one finger to that following it produces the highest degree of clearness in the expression of the single tones, so that every passage performed in this manner sounds brilliant, rolling, and round, as if each tone were a pearl. It does not cost the hearer the least exertion of attention to understand a passage so performed.

(3) By the gliding of the tip of the finger upon the key with an equable pressure, sufficient time is given to the string to vibrate; the tone, therefore, is not only improved, but also prolonged, and we are thus enabled to play in a singing style and with proper connection, even on an instrument so poor in tone as the clavichord is. . . .

The natural difference between the fingers in size as well as strength frequently seduces performers, wherever it can be done, to use only the stronger fingers and neglect the weaker ones. . . . Bach was soon sensible of this; and, to obviate so great a defect, wrote for himself particular pieces, in which all the fingers of both hands must necessarily be employed in the most various positions in order to perform them properly and distinctly. By this exercise he rendered all his fingers, of both hands, equally strong and serviceable, so that he was able to execute not only chords and all running passages, but also single and double shakes in which, while some fingers perform a shake, the others, on the same hand, have to continue the melody. . . .

When Bach began to unite melody and harmony so that even his middle parts did not merely accompany, but had a melody of their own, when he extended the use of the keys, partly by deviating from the ancient modes of church music, which were then very common even in secular music, partly by mixing the diatonic and chromatic scales, and learned to tune his instrument so that it could be played upon in all the 24 keys, he was at the same time obliged to contrive another mode of fingering, better adapted to his new methods, and particularly to use the thumb in a manner different from that hitherto employed. . . .

From the easy, unconstrained motion of the fingers, from the beautiful touch, from the clearness and precision in connecting the successive tones, from the advantages of the new mode of fingering, from the equal development and practice of all the fingers of both hands, and, lastly, from the great variety of his figures of melody, which were employed in every piece in a new and uncommon manner, Sebastian Bach at length acquired such a high degree of facility and, we may almost say, unlimited power over his instrument in all the keys that difficulties almost ceased to exist for him.[46]

Forkel, who was born in 1749 and was of Mozart's generation, paid special attention to Bach's importance for the clavier—that is, harpsichord, clavichord, and fortepiano—just at a time when playing of the clavier, particularly the fortepiano, was spreading among a broad constituency of bourgeois society. And at a time when organ playing and organ music had assumed more of a peripheral role, Forkel realized the central position of the organ in Bach's life and works, especially in his formative years. Though himself not an accomplished organist, he discusses the subject matter with remarkable insight and, noting the close interrelationship of performance and composition, underscores Bach's idiomatic treatment of the instrument. Although he points out that many of the principles of Bach's clavier playing "may also be applied, in general, to his playing on the organ," he recognizes that "the style and mode of managing both instruments [that is, instrument types] are as different as their respective purposes." Apart from the technical makeup, placement, and function of the organ as a typical church instrument, he discusses the distribution of voices and the effect of "open harmony" (in which the voices are spread out from high to low) and explains: "By this means, a chorus, as it were, of four or five vocal parts, in their whole natural compass, is transferred to the organ."

The vocal spacing of lines that Forkel brings up here is intimately connected with Bach's early attempts at creating a truly idiomatic organ texture. Two kinds of deceptive cadences that are closely related yet different in terms of their successful realization provide a case in point. In the early D-minor Toccata, BWV 565, Bach seems unperturbed by the narrowly spread fermata chord (Ex. 5.1), whereas the later Passacaglia, BWV 582, shows a mature approach in well-spaced "vocal" textural design (Ex. 5.2).

Forkel continues:

In this manner, Bach always played the organ; and employed, besides, the obbligato pedal, of the true use of which few organists have any knowledge. He produced with the pedal not only the fundamental notes, or those for which common organists use the little finger of the left hand, but he played a real bass melody with his feet, which was often of such a nature that many a performer would hardly have been able to produce it with his five fingers. . . .

To all this was added the peculiar manner in which he combined the different stops of the organ with each other, or his mode of registration. It was so uncommon that many organ builders and organists were frightened when they saw him draw the stops. They believed that such a combination of stops could never sound well, but were much surprised when they afterwards perceived that the organ sounded best just so, and had now something peculiar and uncommon, which never could be produced by their mode of registration.

This peculiar manner of using the stops was the consequence of his minute knowledge of the construction of the organ and of all the single stops. He had early accustomed himself to give to each and every stop a melody suited to its qualities, and this led him to new combinations which, otherwise, would never have occurred to him. In general, his penetrating mind did not fail to notice anything which had any kind of relation to his art and could be used for the discovery of new artistic advantages. His attention to the effect of big musical compositions in places of varying character; his very practiced ear, by which he could discover the smallest error, in music of the fullest harmony and richest execution; his art of perfectly tuning an instrument, in so easy a manner—all may serve as proofs of the penetration and comprehension of this great man. . . .

His profound knowledge of harmony, his endeavor to give all the thoughts an uncommon turn and not to let them have the smallest resemblance with the musical ideas usual out of the church, his entire command over his instrument, both with hand and foot, which correspond with the richest, the most copious, and uninterrupted flow of fancy, his infallible and rapid judgment by which he knew how to choose, among the overflow of ideas which constantly poured in upon him, those only which were adapted to the present object—in a word, his great genius, which comprehended everything and united everything requisite to the perfection of one of the most inexhaustible arts, brought the art of the organ, too, to a degree of perfection which it never attained before his time and will hardly ever again attain.[47]

In the chapters on "Bach the Clavier Player" and "Bach the Organist," Forkel presents a most instructive, well-founded, and, in the last analysis, indispensable commentary on what the Obituary had previously conveyed in much less explicit terms, in the declarative sentence "Bach was the greatest organist and clavier player that we have ever had." Moreover, by declaring that "his great genius . . . comprehended everything and united everything," he draws the quintessence and proper conclusion out of a largely technical discussion that helps explain Bach's notion of musical science, a concept that also included a thorough knowledge of organ construction. According to the Obituary, Bach "not only understood the art of playing the organ, of combining the various stops of that instrument in the most skillful manner, and of displaying each stop according to its character in the greatest perfection, but he also knew the construction of organs from one end to the other. . . . No one could draw up or judge dispositions for new organs better than he."[48]

We must keep in mind that the organ represented one of the most complicated—and in the case of the Dutch and north German instrument types, also the largest—"machines" in existence from the sixteenth through the eighteenth centuries. The sound-producing miracle behind an ornamental and symmetrical facade of glistening metal pipes embodied the science of mechanical engineering, physics (acoustics), chemistry (metallurgy), and mathematics as well as architecture and the handicraft of carpentry and plumbing. It comprised a myriad of individual parts using all sorts of metal, wood, leather, ivory, cloth, and other materials. Its combination of wind chests, bellows, ranks of pipes, and keyboards was capable of producing colorful sonorities of different dynamic ranges, whose spectrum and volume depended on the size of the instrument.

Bach's hands-on experience, self-directed study, natural curiosity, and frequent contact with skillful organ builders made him an organ expert of the first rank whose indisputable competence was recognized early on and put to use by himself and others throughout his professional life. The importance of his involvement in various organ designs, rebuildings, and repairs must not be underestimated; the documented cases (Table 5.3) can only be considered representative. And what began as a virtually exclusive focus on organ building later expanded to include numerous other types of keyboard, woodwind, and string instruments in whose design, construction, and sonorities he became keenly interested (see Chapter 11).

Bach's written examination reports demonstrate an impressive thoroughness; he missed hardly any minutiae. Forkel gives us some idea of how Bach tested the instrument from its console: "The first thing he did in trying out an organ was to draw out all the stops and to play with the full organ. He used to say in jest that he must first of all know whether the instrument had good lungs. He then proceeded to examine the single parts."[49] The Mühlhausen project, for which we have Bach's first surviving report, shows the high degree of importance he attached to the configuration, character, and balance of stops within the organ. He cared in particular about the *gravitas* of the instrument, granted ideally by a new *Untersatz,* a thirty-two-foot stop, but he thought of improving it also by changing the shallots and enlarging the resonators for the existing *Posaune,* a sixteen-foot reed stop. He proposed the exchange of

## TABLE 5.3. Bach's Organ Projects and Examinations

| Date | Place, Church | Organ Builder | Organ[a] | Reference |
|---|---|---|---|---|
| 1703 | Arnstadt, New Church | J. F. Wender | new: 23 (II, P) | *NBR,* no. 15 |
| 1706 | Langewiesen (near Gehren) | J. Albrecht | new: ? | *BD* II, no. 18 |
| 1708 | Mühlhausen, St. Blasius's | J. F. Wender | rebuilt: 37 (III, P) | *NBR,* no. 31 |
| 1708/12 | Ammern (near Mühlhausen) | J. F. Wender | new: 13 (I, P) | *BJ* 1993: p. 88 |
| 1710 | Traubach (near Weimar) | H. N. Trebs | new: 11 (I, P) | *BD* II, nos. 50, 50a |
| 1712–14 | Weimar, palace church | H. N. Trebs | rebuilt: 24 (II, P) | Jauernig 1950 |
| 1716 | Halle, Our Lady's | C. Cuntzius | new: 65 (III, P) | *NBR,* no. 59 |
| 1716 | Erfurt, Augustiner Church | G. C. Stertzing, J. G. Schröter | new: 39 (III, P) | *BD* I, no. 86 |
| 1717 | Leipzig, St. Paul's | J. Scheibe | new: 53 (III, P) | *NBR,* no. 72 |
| 1723 | Störmthal (near Leipzig) | Z. Hildebrandt | new: 14 (I, P) | *BD* II, nos. 163–164 |
| 1724 | Gera, St. John's | J. G. Finke | new: 43 (III, P) | *BD* II, nos. 183, 183a |
| 1731–32 | Stöntzsch (near Pegau) | J. C. Schmieder | rebuilt: 12 (I, P) | *BD* II, no. 298 |
| 1732 | Kassel, St. Martin's | N. Becker | rebuilt: 33+ (III, P) | *BD* II, no. 316 |
| 1735 | Mühlhausen, St. Mary's | C. F. Wender | rebuilt: 43 (III, P) | *BD* II, no. 365 |
| 1737–38 | Weissensee (near Naumburg) | C. W. Schäfer | new: (II, P) | *BJ* 1999 |
| 1739 | Altenburg, palace church | T. H. G. Trost | new: 38 (II, P) | *BD* II, no. 453 |
| c.1742 | Bad Berka | H. N. Trebs | new: 28 (II, P) | *BD* II, no. 515 |
| 1743 | Leipzig, St. John's | J. Scheibe | new: 22 (II, P) | *BD* II, no. 519 |
| 1743–46 | Naumburg, St. Wenceslas's | Z. Hildebrandt | new: 53 (III, P) | *NBR,* no. 236 |
| 1746 | Zschortau (near Delitzsch) | J. Scheibe | new: 17 (I, P) | *NBR,* no. 235 |
| 1748 | Unknown | H. A. Cuntzius | new | *BJ* 1977 |

[a]Number of stops and sections (manuals, pedal).

*Gemshorn* stop for "a *Violdigamba* 8 foot, which would concord admirably with the 4-foot *Salicional*." He then differentiated between pipe materials, requested "good 14-ounce tin" for the three *Principalia* in the facade of "the new little *Brustpositiv*," and asked that the *"Stillgedackt* 8´, which accords perfectly with concerted music," be made of "good wood" because that would sound "much better than a metal *Gedackt*."[50]

In his report on the Hildebrandt organ at St. Wenceslas's in Naumburg, which he tested in 1746 together with Gottfried Silbermann, Bach writes that in a regular examination "every part specified and promised by the contract" had to be inspected, "namely keyboards, bellows, wind chests, channels, pedal and manual action, with its various parts, registers and stops pertaining thereto, both open and stopped, as well as reeds."[51] Accordingly, he notes in the same report that "each and every part has been made with care" and that "the pipes are honestly delivered in the material specified," but suggests that the organ builder "go through the entire organ once more, from stop to stop, and watch out for more complete equality both of voicing and of key and stop action." The Scheibe organ at St. Paul's Church in Leipzig showed more deficiencies; Bach suggests precautions "to forestall sudden blasts of wind"; remedies "in respect to inequality of voicing" so that the lowest pipes of several stops "shall not speak so coarsely and noisily, but rather produce and maintain a clear and firm tone"; and adjustments so that "the touch of the organ" be made "somewhat lighter" and "the keys not go down so far."[52] He could also look well beyond the customary aspects, as he does in the same 1717 report, where he finds fault with "the whole structure of the organ" and the fact "that it will be hard to get at every part," yet sympathizes with the organ builder because "he was not granted the additional space he requested in order to arrange the structure more conveniently." He also advises that the part of a window that "extends behind the organ should be shielded on the inside by a little wall, or by a heavy piece of sheet iron, to avoid further threatened damage from the weather." Bach never dealt unfairly with organ builders, whom he considered to be close colleagues. On the contrary, "his justice to the organ builders . . . went so far that, when he found the work really good and the sum agreed upon too small, so that the builder would evidently have been a loser by this work, he endeavored to induce those who had contracted for it to make a suitable addition, which he, in fact, obtained in several cases."[53]

Most important, Bach knew how to get patrons and congregations pleased and excited about their new organ by demonstrating what might be done with it, however unconventional. A posthumous report on Bach's 1739 dedication of the Trost organ at the Altenburg palace church reads:

For an organist, to yield to the singing congregation is better than to have it his way. Only a few are able to direct the congregation as the old Bach could do, who, on the great organ in Altenburg, played the Credo hymn ["Wir glauben all an einen Gott"] in D minor, but for the second stanza lifted the congregation to E-flat minor, and for the third one even up to E minor. That, however, only a Bach and an organ in Altenburg could make happen. This, all of us are not, and have not.[54]

Weimar Palace Church (the *Himmelsburg*) in a painting by Christian Richter (c. 1660).

# 6

## *Expanding Musical Horizons*

### CONCERTMASTER IN WEIMAR, 1714–1717

A CAREER CHOICE

"On Friday, March 2, 1714, His Serene Highness the Reigning Duke most graciously conferred upon the quondam Court Organist Bach, at his most humble request, the title of Concertmaster, with official rank below that of Vice-Capellmeister Drese, for which he is to be obliged to perform new works monthly. And for rehearsals of those, the musicians of the capelle are required to appear on his demand."[1] It was apparently Bach himself who requested this promotion to the newly created post of concertmaster of the Weimar court capelle. He was in a position to do so because he had been offered the post of organist and music director at Our Lady's Church in Halle. The exact spelling-out of the Weimar rank indicates that the duke was unwilling to put Bach on an equal footing with the vice-capellmeister, even though Bach's salary since the spring of 1713 had risen even above that of the capellmeister.

Bach's formal charge to perform newly composed church pieces once a month was based on a model created in 1695 for then vice-capellmeister Georg Christoph Strattner, which regulated the monthly division of labor for Sunday performances at the palace church in such a way that the capellmeister Johann Samuel Drese was responsible for three Sundays and the vice-capellmeister Strattner for one. We can assume that this schedule continued when Drese's son Johann Wilhelm attained the vice-capellmeistership after Strattner's death in 1704. With Bach now entering the scheme of alternation, it seems that he asked for an equal share with the vice-capellmeister, so that the two of them were assigned to one monthly performance each as the aging and increasingly impaired capellmeister reduced his load. Prior to this formal arrangement, Bach was probably asked to take over a Sunday performance only occasionally, when a special need arose—a situation he would have chafed at as being inadequate—so he now aimed at regularizing both his role and his schedule.

Rather than having two vice-capellmeisters with one simultaneously serving as court organist and thereby holding a more privileged position, the court administration agreed to Bach's "humble request" to reshape his original appointment and include him as concertmaster in the leadership team of the court capelle. It was an ingenious solution. Creating a new position with a respectable title was in itself a novel idea at the Weimar court, and while the duties attached to the job cut into those of the capellmeister and vice-capellmeister, their ranks at the top of the court capelle hierarchy could remain intact. But what were the specific functions of the concertmaster? Beginning in the later seventeenth century, the larger court establishments employed for their capelle a "Maitre de Concert," or "Concert-Meister," as leader of the instrumentalists—"Regente bey der Instrumental Music," as Johann Mattheson put it.[2] Musicians appointed to such a post would discharge their primary duties from the first-violin chair; they were also responsible for all technical aspects of the performances, from making up the ensemble according to the varying requirements to organizing the rehearsals, positioning the players, and conducting performances, especially those of a purely instrumental nature.

The reference to rehearsals in the concluding sentence of his appointment notification confirms that Bach was indeed put in charge of these tasks. Additional instructions from the court at the time of Bach's promotion seem to reflect certain demands he had made for improving the quality of the performances. For example, the court issued a directive that "the rehearsing of the pieces at the home [of the capellmeister] has been changed, and it is ordered that it must always take place at the *Kirchen-Capelle* [the music gallery in the palace church], and this is also to be observed by the Capellmeister." It is clear that this new regulation refers not just to performances of pieces composed by the concertmaster but to all pieces. Bach must have stood behind this major change, which reflects nothing less than an indirect reprimand of the capellmeister and, by extension, of the vice-capellmeister for maintaining too lax a regime. That Bach claimed and was given more authority is reflected in the order that "the musicians of the capelle are required to appear on his demand"—apparently in order to improve discipline and achieve better musical results. Although the wording of the promotion announcement and the changing of rehearsal venue applied specifically to church music, the consequences were surely felt throughout the activities of the court capelle. Through the duke's discreet yet forceful action, the balance of power within the capelle had definitely shifted to Bach. At the same time, the fact that the upper ranks remained unchanged likely remained a source of continuing troubles and frustrations for him.

Cross section of the *Himmelsburg* in an architectural drawing (c. 1660).

The concertmaster appointment was the result of negotiations that extended over at least three months. It all began with the attractive offer to succeed Friedrich Wilhelm Zachow, Handel's teacher, who for twenty-eight years had occupied the distinguished post once held by Samuel Scheidt at Our Lady's in Halle. After a lengthy search process, the Halle church board elected Bach as Zachow's successor on December 13, 1713; a proffer agreement was negotiated the following day and approved by the board on January 11, 1714. The contract then was sent to Bach in duplicate by special courier, with the expectation that he would immediately return one signed copy. Instead, and apparently while the courier was waiting,[3] Bach wrote back to August Becker, chairman of the church board, on January 14, informing him about a delay in his "final decision" for the following reasons:

First, that I have not yet received my definite dismissal and, second, that in one and another respect I should like to have some changes made, in respect of the salary as well as of the duties; concerning all of which I will inform you in writing in the course of this week. Meanwhile, I am returning the one copy [of the agreement], and since I have not yet received my definite dismissal, you will not take it amiss, my Most Honored Sir, that I am at the moment not yet able to engage myself elsewhere by signing my name before I am really released from service here. And as soon as we can agree upon the *station,* I shall appear at once in person and show by my signature that I am really willing to engage myself in Your Honors' service. Meanwhile, I beg you, Most Honored Sir . . . to make my excuses to [the church board] that at the present moment time has not allowed me to give any categorical decision, both because of certain obligations at Court in connection with the Prince's birthday and because the church services in themselves did not permit it; but it shall be given this week formally and without fail.[4]

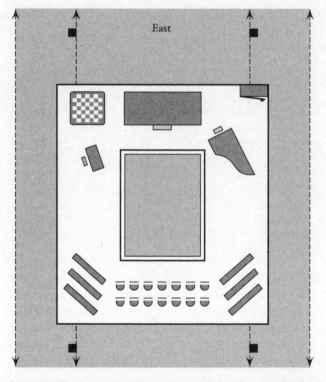

Floor plan of the *Capelle,* or music gallery, at the *Himmelsburg.* Aside from the organ, this rehearsal and performance space reportedly accommodated 1 spinet, 1 harpsichord, 14 armchairs for the principal members of the court capelle, six red-painted benches for supplementary musicians, 1 table, and 1 closet for storing instruments. The placement of the furniture in this drawing is hypothetical.

Bach was buying time, and he had good reasons for doing so. The weeks after December 14 were indeed filled with major obligations: first, the festivities on Christmas Day, marking the seventeenth birthday of Prince Johann Ernst, which because of the prince's keen musical interests may well have developed into a minor music festival; and second, the frequent church services during the Christmas season. Asking for his dismissal from court service at such a time would have been particularly awkward, so it made sense to postpone the matter until the middle of January. He is, in fact, unlikely to have formally requested his dismissal before January 14, but since his visit to Halle (lasting over two weeks) could not have been a secret at the Weimar court, he may only have hinted at his success and then received a signal that his salary might be increased. The promised letter to Halle is lost, but the minutes of the church board meeting of February 1 allude to Bach's attempt at renegotiating the agreement and mention a request for "a supplement to the salary," which was refused. Instead, Bach was given an ultimatum "to make a definite decision within two days." Again, his reply has not survived, but at a meeting of the board on March 1, it was recorded that Bach had "declared himself negatively."[5]

This decision created great disappointment in Halle and some consternation among the church board members, who sensed deceptive dealings on Bach's part. Reacting to their astonishment, Bach reminded August Becker in a sternly worded letter of March 19 that he had not, after all, applied for the post. "The Most Honored Collegium applied to me," he wrote, and only then "I presented myself." How Bach's invitation to present himself in Halle came about may be surmised, with the chief pastor of Our Lady's, D. Johann Michael Heineccius, playing a decisive role. Earlier, Heineccius supported an ambitious project of Zachow's to have a new organ built for the church; Zachow, however, did not live to see his project through. A contract with the organ builder Christoph Cuntzius of Halle was finally signed on September 30, 1712, just seven weeks after Zachow's death, calling for a very large instrument comprising sixty-five stops on three manuals and pedal and an equally enormous fee of 6,300 talers. As things stood, this project of unprecedented size and expense—for the organ builder as well as for the city of Halle—would have to be undertaken without close supervision by a competent resident organist. Clearly, a well-recognized consultant was needed, and the Weimar court organist Bach was only about sixty miles away, half a day's coach trip. Heineccius might have learned about Bach and his reputation as an organ expert from Weimar's general superintendent Lairitz, from theological colleagues, or from the organ builder Cuntzius and his network.[6] Although Bach's consultantship in Halle has not been documented,[7] his presence there for more than two weeks in late 1713 and the special treatment he was to receive there can hardly be explained otherwise; moreover, Bach later served, along with Johann Kuhnau of Leipzig and Christian Friedrich Rolle of Quedlinburg, on the committee to examine the finished organ in the spring of 1716.

Bach's trip to Halle at the invitation of the church board, sometime between November 28 and December 1, 1713, was not intended to promote him as a candidate for the Zachow post, although he must have known that the vacancy had not yet been filled. Four distinguished organists who made the final cut, Gottfried Kirchhoff of Quedlinburg, Valentin Haußmann of Schafstädt, Melchior Hoffmann of Leipzig, and Simon Conrad Lippe of Magdeburg, had already auditioned for the job before the process was interrupted: King Frederick I of Prussia died on February 25, 1713. During the subsequent state mourning period (one year), which affected Halle as part of electoral Brandenburg, public performances of concerted music were prohibited. The church board, eager to save money, saw no reason to seek a quick solution to the Zachow succession and put the matter on hold. Melchior Hoffmann, organist of the New Church in Leipzig, was commissioned to set to music a mourning text by pastor Heineccius and to present the work at the official state memorial service for the Prussian king on May 1. The choice of Hoffmann for this important and highly visible event indicates that he was then considered the leading candidate. Yet the position was still open when Bach traveled to Halle, presumably to advise on the large-scale organ project. He was put up at the city's most luxurious hotel, the Inn of the Golden Ring, located on the market square right across from Our Lady's Church. All his expenses were paid, as the innkeeper's itemized invoice to the church board shows.[8]

|  |  |  |
|---|---|---|
| Expenses Mr. Pach [*sic*] has incurred |  |  |
| For food | 2 rthl. | 16 gr. |
| For beer |  | 18 gr. |
| For brandy |  | 8 gr. |
| For heat | 1 rthl. | 4 gr. |
| For lodging and light | 2 rthl. |  |
| For tobacco |  | 4 gr. |
| Summa | 7 rthl. | 2 gr. |
| [signed:] Joh. Sebast. Bach | J. H. Eberhardt [innkeeper] | |

Bach ate and drank well—his 18 groschen would buy thirty-two quarts of beer at retail price. While there, he was apparently approached about the vacant position at Our Lady's and asked "to present himself," which he did. But as he indicated in his letter of January 14, he had planned to leave directly afterward: "I, after presenting myself, should immediately have taken my leave

if the request and courteous invitation of D. Heineccius had not compelled me
to compose and to perform the piece you know of."[9] So Bach agreed to a formal audition, and on the spot—presumably in his comfortable and well-heated
hotel room, cheered by tobacco and brandy—he composed a cantata to a text
provided by pastor Heineccius, prepared the performing materials, rehearsed
the piece, and performed it. The church board managed to circumvent the restrictions of the ongoing state mourning period either by staging a nonpublic
performance at the church or, more likely, by finding a way to lift the restrictions for a public performance on the second Sunday in Advent, December 10
of that year, or during a weekday service. Moreover, Bach was paid an honorarium of 12 talers for his audition piece,[10] a gesture entirely out of line with
established practices. In every way, Bach's treatment by the church and town
authorities proves that they attached extraordinary importance to having the
court organist, organ expert, and composer Johann Sebastian Bach in town.

The identity of the test cantata Bach wrote in Halle has, unfortunately, not
been established,[11] but it impressed the church authorities so deeply that they
chose to ignore the previous list of candidates, including Melchior Hoffmann,
and elected Bach as Zachow's successor, on December 13. The minutes of the
church board meeting record not only the majority vote but also that Bach was
asked to appear, probably on the following day, and that "the organist post was
offered to him, for which he duly thanked the *Collegium* and accepted the position."[12] On the next day, December 15, Bach returned to Weimar.

The contract that was drawn up after Bach left but predated to December
14 specified the official duties of the organist in five paragraphs:[13] (1) to play
the organ at the regular services on Sundays, Saturdays, and feast days; (2) "on
high and other feasts, as well as on every third Sunday, to present with the cantor and choir students, as well as with the town musicians and other instrumentalists, a moving and well-sounding sacred work; and on particular
occasions such as the second and third days of Christmas, Easter, and Pentecost,
to perform short concerted pieces with the cantor and the students, and also
at times with some violins and other instruments"; (3) "to communicate in
good time to the chief pastor . . . D. Heineccius, for his approval, the texts and
music chosen"; (4) "to accompany attentively the regular chorales and those
prescribed by the minister . . . slowly and without embellishment, in four and
five parts, on the Diapason, to change the other stops at each verse, also to use
the *Quintaden* and the reeds, the *Gedackt,* as well as syncopations and suspensions, in such a manner that the congregation can take the organ as the basis
of good harmony and unison tone"; and (5) to take good care of "the large and
small organs, as well as the Church regal and other instruments belonging to
the Church." Finally, the contract set the annual salary at the rate of 140 talers,
to which were added 24 talers for housing and 7 talers 12 groschen for fire-

wood. Catechism and wedding services would be paid separately at the rate of 1 taler each. However, "secondary employment during the present engagement" would not be permitted.

The contract generally reflects the long and distinguished musical tradition at Our Lady's Church, but some of its surprisingly detailed points, especially regarding the choice of cantata texts and music as well as the style of chorale accompaniment, reveal Heineccius's strong interest in musical matters. There is no evidence that Bach objected to any of these instructions. The musician and the pastor enjoyed a relationship marked by mutual respect: for his Christmas cantata BWV 63, Bach used a text by Heineccius, and the two dined together with August Becker at the dedication of the completed organ in 1716, a clear indication that Bach's rejection of the Halle offer had no lasting effect. The position, incidentally, was filled in May 1714 by Melchior Hoffmann, but his attempt at moonlighting with the Leipzig Collegium Musicum got him fired in little more than a month. On July 30, the church board appointed Gottfried Kirchhoff, who stayed at Our Lady's for more than thirty years until, in 1746, Wilhelm Friedemann Bach accepted the post that his father had "found reasons to reject" (as the Obituary put it).[14]

In his March 19 letter to August Becker, Bach makes it clear that economic reasons forced him to refuse the appointment and firmly rebuffs any accusation of having engaged in shady tactics:

It is not to be assumed that one will go to a place where one's situation is worsened; but this I could not learn accurately in a fortnight or three weeks, since I am wholly of the opinion that even after many years one cannot rightly know one's livelihood in a place where one must count incidental fees as part of one's income, let alone in a fortnight; and that is more or less the reason why I first accepted and then, on request, in turn rejected the appointment. But it is by no means to be inferred from all these circumstances that I should have played such a trick upon the Honored Church Board in order to induce my most Gracious Master to increase my salary, since the latter already shows so much graciousness toward my service and art that I do not have to journey to Halle in order to have my salary increased. Accordingly I regret that the assurance of the Honored Church Board has thus had a somewhat uncertain outcome, and add the following: Even if I had received just as good a salary in Halle as here, should I not then have been bound to prefer the prior service to the other one?[15]

An issue the letter does not raise, because it would have been of no interest to its recipient, was that of personal career choice, a choice that Bach was clearly aware of making. The prospect of having at his disposal a new and very large organ would, without any doubt, have furthered the organist and virtuoso in Bach; the Cuntzius organ under construction would have opened up unanticipated and fabulous perspectives. On the other hand, the section of the Halle agreement regarding the opportunity to compose and perform cantatas on a regular monthly schedule must have appealed to him so greatly that he used it as a bargaining point to achieve basically the same goal in Weimar. Indeed, he could envision that composing for and performing with the Weimar court capelle would be more satisfying than working with the Halle church ensembles—even though as city organist and music director in Halle, unlike the post of court organist and concertmaster in Weimar, he would not be subordinate to any other musician. The decision against Halle, then, amounted to nothing less than a profound change in his basic orientation: away from a primary focus on organ and keyboard skills and toward the broader options and deeper commitment of a composer, with an ever-expanding musical horizon.

Although we have no information about Bach's negotiations with the Weimar ducal court, we can assume that he never formally asked for dismissal, since the court was ready to adjust his salary, rank, and duties. To be sure, the court could have blocked Bach's departure regardless, but if it had, Bach would certainly have mentioned to Becker that he had not obtained permission to leave court service. For all intents and purposes, he could count on the continuing support of the court, notably from Duke Ernst August at the Red Palace. For the time being, he could be pleased with what he procured for himself: a salary increase, a title change within a newly defined rank order, and, most important, expanded responsibilities, especially the assignment "to perform new works monthly."

## Mostly Music for "The Heaven's Castle"

Unlike any other member of his extended family, Bach had from the very beginning engaged in composition, as he explored in particular—indeed in a systematic way—the various genres of keyboard music. The extent to which he devoted himself to composing a substantial repertoire of organ and harpsichord works was by no means common practice, let alone a requirement for the job of organist. Bach had also gained substantial experience in creating vocal music: the three Mühlhausen town council cantatas and the large-scale Weissenfels *Hunt Cantata* of 1713 clearly defined both his remarkable accomplishment and his promise, while establishing his reputation beyond that of organist and keyboard virtuoso. However, his deliberate career decision of early 1714 translated for the first time into a real mandate as a composer in that he assumed the principal responsibility for composing new works, specifically cantatas for the palace church according to a monthly schedule. Where the opportunity of composing vocal works had until then been most agreeable and sought-for yet random and exceptional, it now became his job, and the newly appointed concertmaster threw himself wholeheartedly into the task. Indeed, he managed to turn the novel assignment into a real program, spurred by the same kind of self-propelled energy he had previously directed toward keyboard composition.

Bach's concertmaster promotion dated from March 2, 1714, two days before Oculi Sunday, so that the fourth Sunday following his new appointment fell on March 25. It was this double feast day of Palm Sunday and Annunciation for which Bach prepared the inaugural cantata to be performed in his new capacity: "Himmelskönig, sei willkommen," BWV 182, scored for four voices (SATB), recorder, violin, two violas, violoncello, and continuo (violone and organ) (Table 6.1). The concurrence that year of Palm Sunday and the Marian feast, a rarity in the liturgical calendar, provided an incentive for the ambitious overall design of the piece. Consisting of eight movements, with ten-part scoring for the tutti movements, it permitted Bach to make a major artistic statement and, at the same time, to show the court capelle at its best.

The poetic makeup of the libretto links it to Salomo Franck, the secretary of the ducal consistory in Weimar, who was to publish two annual cycles of cantata texts, for 1715 and 1717.[16] The text draws on Psalm 40:8–9 for the recitative (no. 3) and on Paul Stockmann's 1633 Passion hymn "Jesu Leiden, Pein und Tod" for the penultimate movement (no. 7). In a typical Lutheran reinterpretation, the Marian Feast of the Annunciation is given a Christological focus: instead of honoring Mary, it venerates Christ as the true King of Heaven. Through the sacred poetry of the cantata, the piece becomes an effective and expressive musical sermon on the Palm Sunday gospel (Matthew 21: Jesus' tri-

TABLE 6.1. Cantata "Himmelskönig, sei willkommen," BWV 182

| | |
|---|---|
| 1. Sonata: | Grave. Adagio—rec, v, [rip v], 2va, bc (C [4/4]; G major) |
| 2. Chorus: | Himmelskönig, sei willkommen—SATB, instrumental tutti (C; G major) |
| 3. Recitativo: | Siehe, ich komme, im Buch ist von mir geschrieben—B, bc |
| 4. Aria: | Starkes Lieben, das dich, großer Gottessohn—B, v, 2va, bc (C; C major) |
| 5. Aria: | Leget euch dem Heiland unter—A, rec, bc (C; E minor) |
| 6. Aria: | Jesu, laß durch Wohl und Weh—T, bc (3/4; B minor) |
| 7. Chorale: | Jesu, deine Passion—SATB, instrumental tutti (¢; G major) |
| 8. Chorus: | So lasset uns gehen in Salem der Freuden—SATB, instrumental tutti (3/8; G major) |

umphal entry into Jerusalem), lauding Christ the healer of the world (no. 4), admonishing the faithful to meet him properly (no. 5), praying "Let me not abandon, Lord, the banner of thy cross" (no. 6), foreshadowing Christ's Passion and its meaning (no. 7), and culminating in the anticipation of the believers' entry into the eternal Jerusalem, "the Salem of gladness" (no. 8). The Sonata is designed in overture manner and, by featuring a concerted violin-recorder duo accompanied almost exclusively by plucked strings, creates a distinct ensemble sound that draws immediate attention to the unfolding musical score and, no less important, insures that the leading role of the new concertmaster would not be lost on the audience.

Cantata performances in the *Himmelsburg* ("Heaven's Castle"), or palace church, primarily involved the core group of the Weimar court capelle, whose personnel is described on two complementary lists (combined in Table 6.2).[17] From March 1714, the group consisted of three leaders, seven singers, and five instrumentalists. Compared with the size of the capelle in 1700, the only earlier year for which membership is documented,[18] the ensemble had grown from twelve to fifteen. The members of the capelle fell into the category of joint servants, in the employ of both dukes. However, the singer Thiele and the bassoonist Ulrich appear on the private payroll of Duke Wilhelm Ernst, as do the field musicians, who, in Weimar as elsewhere, were carried on the military budget and augmented the court capelle on demand. The singers Blühnitz and Alt (son of the vice-cantor), who appear only on the 1714 list, seem to count among the secondary members of the capelle. The exact number of secondary members, who must have included vocalists as well as instrumentalists, cannot be determined, as the individuals would have been listed without any musical designation under the broader category of lackeys, where Bach had found himself at one time. The town musicians were also drawn upon fairly regularly, and eight choristers from the gymnasium were delegated for court service.[19] Georg Theodor Reineccius, teacher of the fourth class at the gymnasium and town cantor, directed the school ensembles, while the court cantors Christoph Alt (also teacher of the fifth class at the gymnasium) and Johann Döbernitz led the choirboys delegated from the gymnasium to the court cantorei. Altogether, the resources for mounting sacred and secular musical performances at the Weimar court, by smaller and larger ensembles, were considerable and quite adaptable.

For cantata performances under Bach's direction, it is safe to say that the concertmaster led the capelle from the first violin. Carl Philipp Emanuel Bach writes that "in his youth, and until the approach of old age, he played the violin cleanly and penetratingly, and thus kept the orchestra in better order than he could have done with the harpsichord."[20] So it is particularly appropriate that in performing his first cantata under the new arrangements, Bach presented himself simultaneously as composer, concertmaster, and violin soloist. The absolute leadership role of the concertato violin in the opening movement of BWV 182 is clear from the first measure, as it is in the first aria (no. 4). Since Bach could not play violin and organ at the same time, the organ part would have been taken over by one of his best students, such as Johann Martin Schubart or Johann Caspar Vogler, who had been with him since Arnstadt and Mühlhausen, respectively.[21] Otherwise, the scoring of cantata 182 required

## Table 6.2. The Weimar Court Capelle, 1714–15 (combined list)

*Core group*

| | |
|---|---|
| Johann Samuel Drese | Capellmeister |
| Johann Wilhelm Drese | Vice-capellmeister |
| Johann Sebastian Bach | Concertmaster and court organist |
| Johann Philipp Weichardt | Discant |
| Johann Christian Gerrmann | Discant |
| Christian Gerhard Bernhardi | Alto (predecessor: Johann Jacob Graff) |
| Andreas Aiblinger | Tenor and secretary |
| Johann Döbernitz | Tenor and court cantor |
| Christoph Alt | Bass and [vice] court cantor |
| Gottfried Ephraim Thiele | Bass, master of the pages, and secretary |
| Johann Andreas Ehrbach | Chamber musician, violinist, and registrar of the art chamber |
| Johann Georg Hoffmann | Chamber musician and violinist— nonresident, lived in Jena |
| Andreas Christoph Ecke | Chamber musician and violinist |
| August Gottfried Denstedt | Chamber musician, violinist, and secretary |
| Bernhard George Ulrich | Bassoonist |

*Field musicians*

| | |
|---|---|
| Johann Christoph Heininger | Trumpeter and chamber groom |
| Johann Christian Biedermann | Trumpeter and palace ward |
| Johann Martin Fichtel | Trumpeter |
| Johann Wendelin Eichenberg | Trumpeter |
| Johann Georg Beumelburg | Trumpeter |
| Conrad Landgraf | Trumpeter |
| Andreas Nicol | Timpanist |

*Additional musicians*

| | |
|---|---|
| Gottfried Blühnitz | Alto |
| Philipp Samuel Alt | Bass |
| Lackeys | Instrumentalists and singers |
| Town musicians | Instrumentalists |
| Gymnasium choristers | Singers |

*Sources:* (a) introduction of two new court marshals and list of participants (April 6, 1714); (b) survey of ducal servants (c. 1715).[22]

a minimum of seven to eight players—concertmaster plus instrumentalists—
and a corresponding four-part vocal ensemble.[23]

Because of the unique architectural design of the *Himmelsburg*, the performance took place in the elevated gallery space designated as *Capelle* (see illustration, p. 150, and discussion, Chapter 5). From 1712 to 1714, a major
renovation of the entire performance space of the *Himmelsburg* was undertaken.
The plans called for a significant expansion of the musicians' *Capelle* that would
result in more floor space, a higher vaulted ceiling for the cupola, and better
lighting.[24] Also, the large wooden ceiling cover for the rectangular aperture was
repaired, redesigned, and repainted. It worked by means of a slide mechanism,[25] closing off the sanctuary ceiling for church services without organ or
polyphonic music and for rehearsals in the *Capelle,* which in winter was heated
separately. For regular church services, the cover was left open.[26] Thirteen new
armchairs were acquired in October 1713, and a year later the armchair for the
capellmeister was newly upholstered; these fourteen chairs accommodated the
principal members of the court capelle during the sermon and other parts of
the service. Thiele, as master of the pages ranking above the capellmeister,
would have taken his more prominent place with the court pages elsewhere in
the church, while the court cantor supervised the choirboys situated by the positive organ on the first arcade gallery behind the altar; they joined the capelle
only for the cantata performance preceding the sermon. When additional players and choristers were present on the *Capelle,* they could be seated there on "six
red-painted" benches.[27]

Most details about participating musicians cannot be determined, but the
surviving performance materials for Bach's Weimar cantatas suggest that a
great deal of variety was possible because of the considerable expert resources
available. On the whole, however, the architectural and acoustical conditions
favored a relatively small instrumental-vocal ensemble. The old capellmeister
Drese seems to have been inactive as a performing musician for most if not all
of Bach's Weimar period. His son, the vice-capellmeister, certainly conducted
the performances for which he was responsible and perhaps also took over his
father's share, but we don't know whether he played an instrument or sang
when he was not conducting. We don't know to what extent Bach could involve students of individual court musicians, including his own. And we don't
know whether the harpsichord available in the *Capelle* (like the organ, under
service contract with Trebs) was ordinarily used for cantata performances in addition to the organ. At the very least, the harpsichord must have been substituted as a continuo instrument during the construction periods that rendered
the organ unplayable. Considering the recent changes made to the organ,
which included improvements in the pedal (addition of *Untersatz* 32 foot,
larger wind chests) and the redesign of the separate barrel vault above the

organ for better sound reflection, the continuo group would presumably have carried greater weight. We know from original Weimar performing parts that even works of chamber-music-like qualities (e.g., the cantatas BWV 18 and 199) included violoncello, fagotto, and violono in addition to the organ, indicating that the bass fundament received proper emphasis.

A 1702 description of the Wilhelmsburg palace refers to the *Himmelsburg* with its *Capelle* as "a world-famous masterpiece of architecture . . . there one hears with the greatest pleasure the most delicate and most agreeable music, made by virtuoso and adroit vocal and instrumental musicians."[28] After the improvements to the church were completed in 1714, the quality of sound projected from the *Capelle* into the marble-walled church below would have been even more spectacular, augmenting the illusionary effect of music made in and coming from heaven.

In March 1714, Bach began translating his duty "to perform new works monthly" into an extraordinary artistic program closely related to his goal of "a well-regulated church music." Until then, he had been able to compose and perform cantatas only rarely and irregularly, but earlier works such as cantatas BWV 18, 54, and 199 demonstrate the direction in which the new concertmaster planned to move. The sequence of cantatas for the years 1714–17 only confirmed Bach's commitment to defining his personal cantata style broadly yet in line with the most recent practices at Protestant princely courts in Thuringia.

The "modern" German church cantata actually originated in 1700 near Weimar, at the neighboring court of Saxe-Weissenfels. The capellmeister there, Johann Philipp Krieger, set to music the *Geistliche Cantaten statt einer Kirchen-Music* (Sacred Cantatas Instead of a Church Music) by the young Lutheran theologian and poet Erdmann Neumeister. A native of the duchy, Neumeister was active at various places in central Germany before moving to the distinguished chief pastorate of the St. Jacobi Church in Hamburg. For his innovative collection of sacred poems, which were closely related to the prescribed lessons throughout the ecclesiastical year, Neumeister took as his model the libretto of the Italian secular cantata. (He also adopted the new name in place of the standard German term *Kirchen-Music,* which designated the principal musical piece following the gospel lesson.) Neumeister thus made use of the prevailing types of metric and rhymed verse found not only in cantatas but also in opera librettos: recitatives and arias, free and varied literary forms that originated in the seventeenth-century Italian madrigal. This kind of madrigalistic poetry was aimed at advancing the expressive relationship between words and music and therefore seemed eminently suitable for spiritual meditations set to music. At the same time, the poetically driven decision to accept the recitative-aria form immediately revolutionized the style of church music, which was now closely and lastingly tied to the world of opera. This connection made church music susceptible to further new developments, such as the adoption of the da-capo aria, the tripartite structure of the later seventeenth-century Venetian opera that, with its repeat of the first part of the piece (**ABA**), became the dominating aria type of the early eighteenth century.

Neumeister's pure aria-recitative poetry was soon modified to integrate two additional textual elements, biblical dicta and strophic hymns. This mixed type shows up first in an anonymous annual cycle of cantata texts published in 1704, written apparently by Duke Ludwig Ernst of Saxe-Meiningen and set to music by his court capellmeister, Johann Ludwig Bach, a distant cousin of Johann Sebastian's. This cantata form used three textual components—biblical prose, free poetry (aria, recitative), and chorale—and was emulated in 1711 by the Darmstadt court poet Georg Christian Lehms[29] and simultaneously adopted by Neumeister himself,[30] in his publication of cantata poems written for Georg Philipp Telemann, then capellmeister at the court of Saxe-Eisenach. Originating as a literary-musical genre favored by the central German Protestant courts, the modern church cantata benefited from the taste-setting influence of the aristocracy, which insured its wide distribution and acceptance well beyond the courtly realm. By the second decade of the eighteenth century, it set the standard in cities and towns throughout Lutheran Germany. Earlier, multisectional church pieces lacked any formal design, with freely combined texts—biblical, chorale, and (mainly strophic) aria—that were composed in the manner of a vocal concerto or concertato motet (consisting of chorales and chorale elaborations with arias added in). All of Bach's pre-Weimar "cantatas" adhere to that form, probably because it was not until Weimar that he was given a chance to set madrigalistic poetry to music. However, the recitatives and arias of the *Hunt Cantata*, BWV 208, his first (albeit secular) composition of a Salomo Franck text in the new genre, demonstrate how quickly and completely he mastered these unaccustomed forms.

The extant repertoire of cantatas from Bach's Weimar period, amounting merely to some twenty works, does not give us an accurate picture of his compositional output of cantatas from March 1714 through December 1717 (see Table 6.3). Even assuming that he produced only one cantata per month, as his concertmaster contract of 1714 required, he would have composed nearly twice as many works as we can now document. Moreover, the net loss of three cantatas during the three-month state mourning period for Prince Johann Ernst, during which no musical performances were permitted,[31] would have been balanced by the lost funeral piece "Was ist, das wir Leben nennen," BC B 19. Considering Bach's special relationship with the Red Palace, it is hardly plausible that another composer would have been commissioned.[32] And the funeral piece is by no means the only work for which the music has been lost. We know of four other cantatas definitely written by Bach in Weimar—one cantata (BWV 80a) from Franck's 1715 cycle and three cantatas (BWV 70a, 147a, and 186a) from the 1717 cycle—whose scores have not survived.

TABLE 6.3. Cantatas for the *Himmelsburg,* 1713–17

| BWV | Title | Liturgical Date | Scoring |
|---|---|---|---|
| Unpublished texts (1714), by various (unnamed) authors | | | |
| 182 | Himmelskönig, sei willkommen | Palm Sunday/ Annunciation | SATB; rec, v, [v rip], 2va, bc |
| 12 | Weinen, Klagen, Sorgen, Zagen | Jubilate Sunday | SATB; tr, ob, 2v, 2va, bc |
| 172 | Erschallet, ihr Lieder | Whitsunday | SATB; 3tr, ti, ob, 2v, 2va, bc |
| 21 | Ich hatte viel Bekümmernis | 3rd Sunday after Trinity*a* | SATB; 3tr, ti, ob, 2v, 2va, bc |
| 63 | Christen, ätzet diesen Tag | Christmas Day | SATB; 4tr, ti, 3ob, 2v, va, bc |
| Salomo Franck, *Evangelisches Andachts-Opffer* (Weimar, 1715) | | | |
| 132 | Bereitet die Wege | 4th Sunday in Advent | SATB; ob, 2v, va, bc |
| 152 | Tritt auf die Glaubensbahn | Sunday after Christmas | SB; rec, ob, va d'am, va d. g., bc |
| 155 | Mein Gott, wie lang, ach lange | 2nd Sunday after Epiphany | SATB; 2v, va, bc |
| 80a | Alles, was von Gott geboren | Oculi | music lost |
| 31 | Der Himmel lacht | Easter Sunday | SSATB; 3tr, ti, 3ob, taille, 2v, 2va, bc |
| 165 | O heilges Geist- und Wasserbad | Trinity Sunday | SATB; 2v, va, bc |
| 185 | Barmherziges Herze | 4th Sunday after Trinity | SATB; ob, 2v, va, bc |
| 161 | Komm, du süsse Todesstunde | 16th Sunday after Trinity | SATB; 2rec, 2v, va, bc |
| 162 | Ach! ich sehe, jetzt | 20th Sunday after Trinity | SATB; 2v, va, bc |
| 163 | Nur jedem das Seine | 23rd Sunday after Trinity | SATB; 2v, va, bc |
| Salomo Franck, *Evangelische Sonn- und Festtages-Andachten* (Weimar, 1717) | | | |
| 70a | Wachet! betet! betet! wachet! | 2nd Sunday in Advent | music lost |
| 186a | Ärgre dich, o Seele, nicht | 3rd Sunday in Advent | music lost |
| 147a | Herz und Mund und Tat und Leben | 4th Sunday in Advent | music lost |

Erdmann Neumeister, *Geistliches Singen und Spielen* (Gotha, 1711)

| 18 | Gleichwie der Regen und Schnee | Sexagesimae[b] | SATB; 4va, bc |
|----|-------------------------------|----------------|----------------|

Erdmann Neumeister, *Geistliche Poesien* (Frankfurt, 1714)

| 61 | Nun komm der Heiden Heiland | 1st Sunday in Advent | SATB; 2v, 2va, bc |
|----|------------------------------|----------------------|--------------------|

Georg Christian Lehms, *Gottgefälliges Kirchen-Opffer* (Darmstadt, 1711)

| 54 | Widerstehe doch der Sünde | Oculi Sunday[b] | A; 2v, 2va, bc |
|-----|---------------------------|-----------------|-----------------|
| 199 | Mein Herze schwimmt im Blut | 11th Sunday after Trinity[b] | S; ob, 2v, va, bc |

Unpublished funeral text, presumably by Salomo Franck (Weimar, April 2, 1716)

| deest | Was ist, das wir Leben nennen (BC B 19), parts I and II | music lost | |
|-------|---------------------------------------------------------|------------|--|

*Note:* Original Weimar parts and/or scores are extant for all works except BWV 54, 161, and those marked lost.

[a]Originally "in ogni tempo" (for any time); expanded version of an earlier composition.
[b]Originally without specific liturgical designation, i.e., for any time.

Apart from the questions surrounding the extent of Bach's cantata output, the exact chronological order of the Weimar works remains uncertain.[33] Only four cantatas bear autograph dates, for 1714 (BWV 21 and 61)[34] and 1715 (BWV 185 and 132); because of their liturgical designations, we can easily date them to June 17 and December 2, 1714, and July 14 and December 22, 1715. Despite these performance dates, however, most movements of BWV 21 relate to an earlier, undatable version of the work, as does the opening movement of BWV 61. The cantata BWV 18 and the solo cantatas BWV 54 and 199 stem in all likelihood from before the concertmaster appointment. Articulating general theological themes, they seem not to have been conceived for specific dates within the ecclesiastical year. At least for BWV 199, however, a repeat performance is ascertainable, on the eleventh Sunday after Trinity (August 12, 1714). Thus, we can ascribe seven cantata performances (the others are BWV 12, 172, 21, 61, 63, and 152) to the year 1714 following the March 25 inaugural presentation of BWV 182. Yet according to the projected schedule of one cantata every four weeks (Palm Sunday, Jubilate Sunday, Whitsunday, Third Sunday after Trinity, etc.), eleven performances should have taken place from Visitation/Palm Sunday through the Sunday after Christmas (December 30); so four works are lost for 1714. The Christmas cantata BWV 63, in all likelihood performed on Christmas Day 1714, did not fall into the regular monthly schedule, but the musically demanding Christmas season may have called for an accelerated response on Bach's part. Because of its atypically large instrumental ensemble (including 4 trumpets, timpani, and 3 oboes), it may also have been unsuitable for the more intimate performance space of the palace church. Since on high feast days the ducal family occasionally joined the town congregation for services at St. Peter and Paul's Church, both BWV 63 and the similarly opulent Easter cantata BWV 31 (uniquely requiring a five-voice choir together with a large orchestra) may well have been performed there.

Matching the projected schedule for the two subsequent years with the extant cantata repertoire yields similar results, even with the three-month state mourning period (from August 1, 1715) taken into account. The cantatas from Franck's 1715 text collection *Evangelisches Andachts-Opffer* distribute over both years, with BWV 80a, 31, 165, 185, 163, and 132 apparently belonging to 1715 and BWV 155, 161, and 162 to the following year, toward the end of which Bach turned to Franck's *Evangelische Sonn- und Festtages-Andachten,* published in 1717 (BWV 70a, 186a, and 147a). So for twenty-four minus three months, only twelve works have survived. The apparent losses cannot be attributed solely to the dispersal of Bach's estate in 1750 and its subsequent misfortunes. (Aside from Bach's missing works, we have no extant compositions at all from the pen of either one of the Dreses.) On the other hand, not a single cantata performance can be traced to 1717, Bach's final Weimar year, suggesting that traditional estimates of numerous material losses have been overstated. Bach may well have refrained from composing any cantatas at all that year, either on the order of a superior or owing to a personal decision. Indeed, events occurring in December 1716 point in that direction.

Johann Samuel Drese died on December 1. Neither the cause of the old capellmeister's death nor the length of time that he may have been completely incapacitated is known, but according to the source evidence for BWV 70a, 186a, and 147a, Bach took over all the musical responsibilities immediately following Drese's death and wrote cantatas for three consecutive Advent Sundays, December 6, 13, and 20 of 1716. The performances on the first two Sundays apparently took place, but the autograph score for the third cantata, BWV 147a, was left unfinished (and completed only later in Leipzig).[35] What motivated Bach to break off the work so abruptly? The most plausible reason may be found in an emerging if not already boiling conflict about leadership responsibilities for the court capelle between vice-capellmeister Drese and concertmaster Bach. Not that Bach expected to be chosen over the vice-capellmeister as the new head of the court capelle; on the contrary, his promotion in 1714 to concertmaster "with official rank below that of Vice-Capellmeister Drese" should have made it clear to him that Johann Wilhelm Drese was in line to succeed his father. After all, the younger Drese had been sent to Venice in 1702–3 at the expense of the Weimar court in order "to habilitate himself in music and composition," and appointed vice-capellmeister not long after his return (see Chapter 5).

But although Bach accepted the organizational arrangements of 1714 and did not expect a promotion to capellmeister while Johann Wilhelm Drese was active, he made an extraordinary contribution to the cantata repertoire for the *Himmelsburg*—extraordinary even considering the incomplete transmission of his works. Two major factors stimulated Bach's interest in the cantata genre, which went through a conceptual transformation after 1710 and which he himself had been able to explore only sporadically. The most important was the collaboration with Salomo Franck, an erudite poet of considerable accomplishments. With Franck providing the librettos for nearly all of Bach's cantatas written in Weimar from 1714 on, the composer was given the chance to work with lyrics of very high quality, in both form and content. Franck's elegant poetic language and the pure, straightforward theological message in his sacred texts provided Bach with an ideal vehicle for his own musical thoughts and, in general, for the advancement of his compositional art. The other main factor was the professional competence and versatility of the Weimar court capelle as well as the congenial and intimate space available at the palace church for the performance of sacred music.

The performance space accounts for the predominantly chamber-music-like character of the Weimar cantatas and their scoring for a smallish yet colorful ensemble. The repertoire exhibits a great diversity in the choice of instruments, the size of the ensemble notwithstanding (see Table 6.3). While he stuck to no standard scoring patterns, Bach made one fundamental change in the spring of 1715: he moved from the traditional German (and also French-style) five-part string score (with two violas), which had prevailed in his cantatas up to and including the Easter cantata BWV 31, to the Italianate four-part score (with one viola), which he now established as a new norm. Apart from this change, Bach's instrumental ensembles vary from a pure string body—to a mixed group involving one or more winds. Particularly distinctive colors are featured in BWV 152, whose delicate five-part ensemble comprises recorder, oboe, viola d'amore, viola da gamba, and basso continuo. Many cantatas begin with an elaborate Sinfonia or Sonata (BWV 12, 18, 21, 31, 152, 182), and all contain arias with ornate instrumental obbligati, sometimes of unusual makeup—BWV 163/3 (3rd movement) uses two obbligato cellos. Even where only a pure string ensemble is called for, as in BWV 161/3, the dense imitative treatment of the homogeneous score immediately draws the listener's attention.

The vocal dimension of the cantatas is equally attractive and varied, both in the choral sections and in the solo movements. The spectrum of choruses ranges from the traditional concertato motet (BWV 21/1), chorale motet (BWV 182/7), fugue (BWV 182/2), freer concerto type (BWV 31/1), and extended bipartite form (BWV 63/1 and 7) to highly innovative settings such as chorale elaboration in overture style (BWV 61/1), chaconne with motet (BWV 12/2), and choral litany in combination with a solo recitative (BWV 18/3). The recitatives and arias demand from the singers no less technical proficiency than the instrumental parts require of their players. Italianate melodic declamation and phrasing with emphatic expression (BWV 21/3: "Seufzer, Tränen, Kummer, Not") prevails from 1714 on. Expansive vocal duet structures occur in some movements (BWV 21/8 and 152/6: Christ and Soul in dialogue) and sophisticated textures in others (BWV 54/1: dissonant pulsating chords at the very beginning; 54/3: chromatic counterpoint). Four-part chorale settings are not yet the standardized feature in the Weimar cantatas that they later become in the Leipzig works; some cantatas lack chorales entirely (BWV 54, 63, 152), while others feature chorale harmonizations with an embellished instrumental discant (BWV 12/7, 172/6, 31/9). In the *Himmelsburg* cantatas, beginning in 1715 and in line with their chamber-music-like qualities, Bach conspicuously de-emphasizes the role of the chorus by confining it to plain concluding chorales (BWV 132, 155, 161–63, 165, and 185).

Taken together, the impressive series of cantatas written between 1713 and 1716 amount to a systematic exploration of nearly all compositional possibilities that could be drawn into vocal-instrumental music—in terms of genre, form, technique, scoring, and texture on the broader level, and metric-rhythmic patterns, key choices, thematic treatment, and harmonic designs on the narrower. Of particular importance to Bach was the challenge of matching his fluent and increasingly complex musical language with the structured prose and poetry of the cantata librettos at his disposal. The texts by Neumeister, Lehms, and Franck offered cantata forms based on combinations of such diverse literary sources as biblical quotations, modern poetic verses, and traditional hymns. Although three general patterns prevail (see Table 6.4), the distribution, sequence, and type of movements exhibit an overall formal flexibility.

These text forms required Bach to sharpen his sense of musical contrast and continuity in designing multimovement structures. But more important, they supplied him with a rich and diversified body of expository material for which he developed a musical language that underscored its innate meaning. With scholarly zeal, Bach immersed himself here in the compositional opportunity he had sought in early 1714 when he negotiated for the concertmaster position.

Returning to the question of the original size of Bach's Weimar cantata output, we can find a clue in the court's allocations of music paper. Three paper

**TABLE 6.4. Weimar Cantata Types**

| I. *Aria and chorale* | | II. *Aria and recitative* | | III. *Recitative, aria, biblical text, and/or chorale* | |
|---|---|---|---|---|---|
| BWV 12 | BWV 70a | BWV 54 | BWV 152 | BWV 18 | BWV 80a |
| Aria*a* | **Aria** | Aria | Aria | Recitative (biblical) | Aria, with instrumental chorale |
| Arioso | Aria | Recitative | Recitative | Recitative, with interpolated **Litany** | Recitative **Aria** |
| Aria | Aria | Aria | Aria | Aria | Recitative |
| Aria | Aria | | Recitative | **Chorale** | Aria |
| Aria | Aria | | Aria (dialogue) | | **Chorale** |
| **Chorale** | **Chorale** | | | | |

*a*Boldface indicates choral movement.

deliveries of one ream (480 sheets) each were made to Bach in October 1714, June 1715, and May 1717,[36] and he (and his copyists) could not have used this supply (amounting to 5,760 pages) for anything but the fulfillment of official musical duties. Yet Bach's surviving Weimar cantata scores and parts in their entirety, including those composed before October 1714, as well as copies of vocal works by other composers, make up barely one-fourth of a single ream. In other words, measuring Bach's vocal productivity from October 1714 through the end of 1717 by paper deliveries and disregarding the possibility that he used more than that, the survival rate of Weimar performing materials amounts to at most 15 to 20 percent—and this includes not only the materials related to the cantata repertoire, but also to the keyboard and instrumental ensemble works and to other composers' pieces copied for the Weimar court capelle (see Table 6.5).[37]

Because so relatively few of the original musical sources from Bach's Weimar period have come down to us, they do not convey a balanced picture of his activities as court organist, chamber musician, and concertmaster. And given what has survived, the disproportionate relationship between materials from the last three years in Weimar and the first six is particularly troublesome. Should Bach's creative output not have been fairly equal over the nine and a half years? Where in the realm of instrumental ensemble music and keyboard works is the rough equivalent to the cantata repertoire from 1714–16? Happily, a large number of secondary sources, notably copies made by Bach's students, supplement the hopelessly incomplete autograph materials and shed some light on the Weimar keyboard repertoire. While confirming what the

Obituary says, that "he wrote most of his organ works" there,[38] the copies do not permit a reliable survey, much less a precise chronology. Nevertheless, among the large number of separately transmitted organ chorales, most early versions of the Great Eighteen (BWV 651–668) originated after 1708, and all of them were written before 1717. Moreover, the bulk of the preludes (toccatas, fantasias) and fugues (notably BWV 538, 540, 541, 542, 545, and 564), the *Pièce d'Orgue*, BWV 572, and the concertos BWV 592–596 stem from the court organist period. As for the harpsichord repertoire, larger work groups that belong to the later Weimar years (after 1714) include at least the concerto transcriptions BWV 972–987, the so-called *English Suites* (suites *avec prélude*), the *Chromatic Fantasy*, BWV 903, and the beginnings of *The Well-Tempered Clavier*.

In addition to his palace church duties as court organist and concertmaster, Bach would have taken part throughout his Weimar tenure in the secular activities of the court capelle, certainly in his capacity as harpsichordist and violinist but surely also as composer of keyboard pieces, chamber music, and orchestral works. Whether or not Bach's apparent retreat in 1717 from cantata

TABLE 6.5. Autograph Manuscripts Outside the Cantata
            Repertoire

| BWV | | Date |
|---|---|---|
| **Works by Bach** | | |
| Anh. 159 | Motet "Ich lasse dich nicht" (partial autograph) | 1712–13 |
| 596 | Concerto in D minor, after Vivaldi | 1714–17 |
| 599–644 | *Orgel-Büchlein* | 1708–17 |
| 660a | Trio "Nun komm der Heiden Heiland" | 1714–17 |
| 1073 | Canon perpetuus à 4 | 1713 (dated) |
| **Works by other composers** | | |
| Anh. 23 | T. Albinoni, Concerto in E minor, op. II/2 | before 1710? |
| | J. Baal, *Missa* in A major | 1714–17 |
| | F. B. Conti, "Languet anima mea" | 1716 |
| | G. Frescobaldi, "Fiori musicali" [lost] | 1714 (dated) |
| | M. G. Peranda, Kyrie in C major | 1708–17 |
| | —, *Missa* à 6 | 1714–17 |
| | C. Dieupart, *Suites de claveçin* | 1709–14 |
| | N. de Grigny, *Premier Livre d'Orgue* | c. 1709–12 |
| | H. N. Brauns(?), *St. Mark Passion* | c. 1710–12 |
| Anh. 24 | J. C. Pez, *Missa* in A minor | 1714–17 |
| | J. C. Schmidt, "Auf Gott hoffe ich" | 1714–17 |
| | G. P. Telemann, Concerto in G major | c. 1709? |
| Anh. 29 | Anon., *Missa* in C minor (violoncello part only) | 1714–17 |

composition was voluntary, he may at that point have increased his output of instrumental music (although the extant sources are too spotty to allow us to draw firm conclusions). However, based on the supposition that the Sinfonia in F major, BWV 1046a, an early version of the *Brandenburg Concerto* No. 1, may have served as an instrumental introduction to the performance of the *Hunt Cantata,* BWV 208, in 1713, 1716, or both, and in light of additional considerations, we can say that most and perhaps all of the *Brandenburg Concertos* may date from the Weimar years (see Chapter 7). At any rate, their generally "conservative" style raises questions about a Cöthen origin, and the principal source for the six concertos is the 1723 presentation copy prepared for the Margrave of Brandenburg from revised versions. Moreover, their compositional concept as *Concerts avec plusieurs instruments*—that is, compositions capitalizing on the endless adaptability of the concerto principle and on the exploration of multiple and daring instrumental combinations—fits nowhere better than it does in the Weimar cantata repertoire. More than any period in Bach's creative life, the Weimar years catalyzed the formation and consolidation of his personal style—a response to the modern Italian concerto style.

## "MUSICAL THINKING": THE MAKING OF A COMPOSER

The choice Bach made at the turn of 1714 to delve further into composition and not limit himself to keyboard genres and virtuoso organ performance did not come like a bolt from the blue. The decision grew logically out of a deep-rooted drive to commit musical thoughts to paper, to think about and embark on their further elaboration, to refine the technical skills necessary for the theoretical underpinnings and compositional control of the musical substance at hand, and constantly to challenge his musical imagination.

The earliest, most thoughtful, and quite informative (if not unbiased) discussion of Bach's beginnings as a composer can be found in Forkel's 1802 biography, in which the pertinent section begins with a plain statement: "Bach's first attempts at composition were, like all first attempts, defective."[39] Like the Obituary, which emphasizes that Bach was largely self-taught as a composer, Forkel stresses that he started essentially "without a guide" to conduct him "from step to step" and, therefore, began as a "finger composer" who liked "to run or leap up and down the instrument, to take both hands as full as all the five fingers will allow, and to proceed in this wild manner till they by chance find a resting place." Perhaps the most prominent surviving example of this course, which Bach "did not follow long," is the organ Toccata in D minor, BWV 565, as refreshingly imaginative, varied, and ebullient as it is structurally undisciplined and unmastered; and we can understand only too well

why the self-critical Bach did not use this *coup de main* later on for teaching purposes (which also explains its oddly peripheral transmission).[40]

Forkel's reference to the manner of "Clavier hussars (as Bach, in his riper
years, used to call them)" appears to be based on reliable sources—reports by
the two oldest Bach sons, who may have related their father's own critical account:

He soon began to feel that the eternal running and leaping led to nothing; that there
must be order, connection, and proportion in the thoughts, and that to attain such object[ive]s, some kind of guide was necessary. Vivaldi's Concertos for the violin, which
were then just published, served him for such a guide. He so often heard them praised
as admirable compositions that he conceived the happy idea of arranging them all for
his clavier. He studied the chain of ideas, their relation to each other, the variation of
the modulations, and many other particulars.

Forkel's chronological frame is mistaken, for he puts Bach's Vivaldi transcriptions of the mid-Weimar years together with his studying, some ten years earlier, the music of Frescobaldi, Froberger, Kerll, Pachelbel, Buxtehude, and
others. However, this conflated view should not detract from the notion that
Bach's study of Vivaldi represents a critical moment, perhaps the culmination
point, in a development of self-guided learning that began with the study of
fugue and peaked in a thoroughly analytical approach to the modern Italian
concerto style of Vivaldi, the Marcellos, and their contemporaries, resulting in
the emergence of new structural designs.

According to the Obituary, Bach became a strong fugue writer at an early
age "through his own applied reflection" on models by Buxtehude, Reinken,
and others. And the evidence in both instrumental and vocal examples from
well before the Weimar period overwhelmingly supports this view. Forkel's key
insight into Bach, however, addresses a more fundamental aspect of musical
composition: he writes that Vivaldi's works "taught him how to think musically." Bach transcribed Italian concertos during the mid-Weimar years of
1713–14 (see Table 6.5), exactly when his experimental tendencies were leading him toward forming a genuinely personal style. The fact that Forkel links
only Vivaldi's name to the concerto transcriptions suggests the latter's preeminent role for Bach. Further evidence lies in the relatively large number of Vivaldi transcriptions—nine, of which five are based on Vivaldi's concerto
collection *L'Estro armonico,* Op. 3, published in 1711. It is likely, therefore, that
Bach himself passed on to his students and family the impression that his experience with Vivaldi's compositions above all "taught him how to think musically." Forkel elaborates on the idea of musical thinking by emphasizing that

"order, coherence, and proportion"—or better, order/organization, coher-
ence/connection/continuity, and proportion/relation/correlation (the original
German terms *Ordnung, Zusammenhang,* and *Verhältnis* are not easily rendered
by single words)—must be brought to bear on musical ideas. Bach, then,
recognized in Vivaldi's concertos a concrete compositional system based on
musical thinking in terms of order, coherence, and proportion—an illuminating though abstract historical definition of Vivaldi's art as exemplified in
his concertos.

What do order, organization, connection, coherence, continuity, proportion, and relation mean in the process of musical composition? Curiously,
Bach's definition of musical thinking (as transmitted through Forkel) makes
no reference to form and genre as objects of learning. Indeed, concerto transcription is only a means to the goal of learning how to think musically. Even
more surprising, the definition entirely bypasses the fundamentals of compositional technique: counterpoint, harmony, melody, meter and rhythm, thoroughbass, voice leading, instrumentation, and other elements. If Forkel
accurately articulated Bach's thinking, then Bach conceived of compositional
method primarily in abstract functional terms, as he also defined harmony—
that is, as accumulated counterpoint.[41]

This decidedly functional approach is novel both as a concept in the history
of musical composition and in Bach's own compositional experience. His earlier study of fugue, concerto, sonata, suite, motet, aria, and other genres had
moved along the traditional paths, which he successfully expanded. Vivaldi's
concertos, however, confronted him with an entirely new set of problems and
possibilities. This is not to say that to him Vivaldi was the first and only
musician to develop a new compositional concept, but (beginning with his
Op. 3) he was certainly the primary exponent as well as the intellectual and
practical architect of a new method that influenced the course of eighteenth-
century music.

Concerto composition provided an ideal vehicle for exploring and developing ways of "musical thinking," and those ways quickly penetrated other instrumental and vocal genres. The concerto as a musical genre or form was a
secondary consideration, and the same was true of counterpoint, thematic invention, and other technical aspects of composition, including even word-tone
relationships in vocal works. What Bach dubbed musical thinking was, in
fact, nothing less than the conscious application of generative and formative
procedures—the meticulous rationalization of the creative act.

The inseparable functions of order, coherence, and proportion appear in extreme clarity at the beginning of the Largo of Vivaldi's Op. 3, No. 3 (transcribed in BWV 978) (Ex. 6.1). The movement consists of an essentially

straightforward elaboration of a basic, even rudimentary musical idea: a plain D-minor triad. Bach certainly never claimed to have turned to Vivaldi for inspiration regarding the *ars inveniendi,* but he did so here for an example of how to apply a manner of musical thinking to the development of ideas of varying, even poor, substance. The principal components of this process are easily identified: (a) a triadic chord; (b) a linear melodic variant derived from (a); and (c) a coherent and harmonically mutating chordal sequence (Ex. 6.2).

The generative motivic substance (a) contains the potential for developing further motives—(b) and (c), both related and contrasting to (a)—and juxtaposing them. The ideas are hierarchically organized—(a) = tutti, (b) = solo—with an irreversible order. In the course of the movement, both the primary idea (a) and the secondary ideas (b) and (c) develop variants in order to secure continuity and change, yet throughout the movement—in a gradually unfolding scheme of order, coherence, and relation—each measure possesses an unmistakable identity. Moreover, the successive order of measures constitutes a chain of clearly structured correlations and metric periodization, with shifting proportions between chordal and figurative measures. Musical thinking in this movement means something very different from pursuing such conventional compositional techniques as, for example, harmonizing a melody or designing a fugal exposition by finding a proper imitative scheme for subject and answer. Vivaldi's novel method means defining the substance of a musical idea with the aim of elaborating on it, a process that observes the closely interrelated categories of order, connection, and proportion and thereby unifying a piece.

In principle, the design of the first (fast) movement of the same Vivaldi concerto closely resembles that of the Largo. The movement opens with a ritornello (a musical section that returns), each part of which contains motives that function as constituent members of the whole (Ex. 6.3a–d). The antecedent section (mm. 1–2), for example, presents a head motive that gives the entire piece its identity from the outset and makes the ritornello distinctly recognizable as the most crucial part of the movement's formal structure. The two opening measures establish, especially in Vivaldi's original version, a strong contrast: the first measure represents a melodic foreshadowing of the chordal sequence (tonic-dominant-tonic) that follows in the second measure (Ex. 6.3a). Bach's modified version cancels Vivaldi's sharp juxtaposition of the two measures (which, at the same time, foreshadows the application of the tutti-solo principle) and thereby loosens the prevailing asymmetric rhythmic pulse ♪ ♩ . However, by changing the bass line in measure 2, Bach gains a new contrapuntal dimension, as a result of which the opening two measures are now linked by motivic imitation and by the continuity of pulse. Both of these features underscore the identity of this head motive and also reflect genuine "musical thinking." Put another way: at the beginning, a germinal cell is formulated that offers potential for multifaceted elaboration; all subsequent elements occurring in the ritornello as well as in the episodes can be related to the harmonic, melodic, and rhythmic contents of this head motive.[42]

The ritornello itself, moreover, establishes order by setting up a fixed organizational scheme with the proper sequence of musical ideas (Ex. 6.3a–d), their systematic connection, their correlation, and finally, their logical succession. It introduces a ranking of individual sections by their striking musical character and recognizability and by their classification of harmonic functions (closed, like T-D-T, or open, like T-D). The complete ritornello, lasting just twelve measures, also propels the principle of continuity/coherence through the mutual connection of its members and motives, the continuity of texture and declamation, the regulation of periodicity and sectional interplay, and the preservation of a multilayered context. As Forkel observed, Bach "studied the chain of the ideas, their relation to each other, the variety of the modulations, and many other particulars." In short, whatever is covered under the proportion principle intimately relates to order and coherence as well. All three parameters are interdependent and interpenetrating.

The historical significance of Vivaldi's concerto-style method, reflected in the widespread influence his music enjoyed after the publication of *L'Estro armonico,* has its foundation in a fruitful dialectic of two different aesthetic premises: simplicity (implying a broad spectrum from purity, clarity, and correctness to graceful and natural elegance) and complexity (implying intellectual analysis, sophisticated elaboration, and rational control). These two poles mark the full range in the process of genuine musical thinking, which Bach nearly always tipped in the direction of complexity. Nevertheless, he adopted and transformed the process on the basis of his own experience and preferences. The chorale settings of the *Orgel-Büchlein,* for example, contributed a strong sense for motivic and contrapuntal detail to his compositional approach.

No compositional genre that Bach touched would remain unaffected by his process of "modular" construction. The second aria of the cantata "Komm, du süße Todesstunde," BWV 161 of 1715–16 presents a case in point. Its basic compositional material is a direct musical translation of the phrase "Mein Verlangen ist, den Heiland zu umfangen" (my desire is to embrace my Savior), the opening line of the poetic text that captures the spirit of the whole aria. The initial vocal entry consists of three short motives of two measures each (Ex. 6.4). Motive (a) presents the opening statement, which, with its appoggiatura on the stressed syllable "Ver-*lan*-gen" (desire), essentially defines the musical character of the aria. Motive (b) further intensifies declamation and affect, by way of a melisma in the form of a broken descending scale; and motive (c) then has the function of both concluding the phrase and presenting a meaningful and figuratively "embracing" culmination point, which underscores the key words "den Heiland zu umfangen" (to embrace the Savior). Bach uses this generative vocal material in order to construct an instrumental introduction/ritornello that elaborates on the vocal idea and, indeed, enhances it by mobilizing all possibilities of a four-part homogeneous and polyphonic string score (Ex. 6.5). The symmetries of the vocal phrase are wholly preserved, yet texturally, harmonically, and contrapuntally enriched to further bolster the close word-tone relationship of this setting. In particular, the musical imagery of "embracing" penetrates and amplifies the second half of the ritornello so that, appropriately for a vocal piece, constructive and interpretive levels are kept in perfect balance—a vivid demonstration that the principles of order, coherence, and proportion also comprise a linguistic and semantic dimension that Bach adheres to.

Bach's Weimar cantata scores, but also his *Orgel-Büchlein* chorales and other keyboard works, show conclusive evidence of an increasingly abstract approach to composition, in which the compositional process moved away from the keyboard to the writing table. Probably in the later Arnstadt years and long before 1713, when composing his trial cantata for Our Lady's in Halle at the Inn of the Golden Ring apparently presented no problem for him, the desk in his study or composing room (*Componir-Stube,* as the office of the Leipzig Thomascantor used to be called) had become his primary work space for writing music. Carl Philipp Emanuel Bach, in a letter to Forkel, mentions that "if I exclude some (but, *nota bene,* not all) of his clavier pieces, particularly those for which he took the material from improvisations on the clavier, he composed everything else without instrument, but later tried it out on one."[43] As for the instrument itself, Forkel related that Bach "considered the clavichord as the best instrument for study" and "the most convenient for the expression of his most refined thoughts," as he preferred the "variety in the gradations of tone . . . on this instrument, which is, indeed, poor in tone, but on a small scale extremely flexible."[44]

Bach's confrontation with the modern Italian concerto idiom in the years before 1714 ultimately provoked what became the strongest, most lasting, and most distinctive development toward shaping his personal style: the coupling of Italianism with complex yet elegant counterpoint, marked by animated interweavings of the inner voices as well as harmonic depth and finesse. Bach's adaptation, integration, and command of both modern and traditional compositional approaches represent a systematic attempt at shaping and perfecting his personal musical language and expanding its structural possibilities and expressive powers.

## HIGH AND LOW POINTS

Despite the fact that Bach had, in the younger Duke Ernst August, a devoted and supportive patron throughout his Weimar tenure of office, his court service as organist and concertmaster could hardly have remained unaffected by the ongoing bitter and steadily worsening feud between the two co-reigning dukes. Nevertheless, by all indications, both dukes ranked Bach as the court's top musician. There is simply no other explanation for what happened on March 20, 1715, just a year after his concertmaster appointment: "Notice [was] given to the two Capellmeisters, Drese Senior and Junior, upon the order of His Most Serene Highness the Reigning Duke, that henceforth, in the distribution of perquisites and honoraria, the Concertmaster Bach is to receive the portion of a Capellmeister."[45] The idea was to bring Bach's benefits and extra pay in line with those of the capellmeister and vice-capellmeister (the remaining in-kind differences were immaterial), increasing his total compensation beyond that of everyone else in the court capelle. His favorable treatment is particularly obvious in light of the arrangements made after his departure from Weimar in 1717, when the younger Drese was appointed capellmeister and Bach's student Schubart took over the post of court organist (see Table 6.6).

Bach's function in the court capelle, however, must not be seen as one of supplanting or displacing the capellmeister and vice-capellmeister. True, the old Drese was ailing and basically emeritus, but his son received the same kind of music paper deliveries as Bach, a clear indication that the vice-capellmeister played an active role. Since none of his compositions have survived, we cannot judge his musical standing or stylistic orientation. But his Italian training must have borne some fruits in his works and perhaps also in his programming preferences. Already before his trip to Italy, the younger Drese had received a monetary supplement of 34 florins for copying services, a sum he continued to collect through 1717.[46] The payments show that the

## TABLE 6.6. Comparison of Annual Base Salaries, 1708–18

|  | 1708 | 1711 | 1713 | 1714 | 1718 |
|---|---|---|---|---|---|
| Johann Samuel Drese, capellmeister | 200 fl. | 200 | 200 | 200 | — |
| Johann Wilhelm Drese as vice-capellmeister | 150 | 150 | 150 | 150 | |
| —as capellmeister | | | | | 200 |
| Johann Effler, court organist | 130 | — | — | — | — |
| Johann Sebastian Bach as court organist | 150 | 200 | 215 | | |
| —as court organist and concertmaster | | | | 250 | — |
| Johann Martin Schubart, court organist | — | — | — | — | 130 |

vice-capellmeister was largely responsible for the acquisition and preparation of performing materials for the court capelle.

The vice-capellmeister acted in all likelihood as a loyal "joint servant"—as a court official who served both dukes, as the members of the court capelle were required to do. Bach fell into the same category, although he enjoyed a much closer relationship with the musically inclined Duke Ernst August and his younger half-brother, Prince Johann Ernst. Musical activities at the Red Palace were apparently abundant, much to the annoyance of Duke Wilhelm Ernst, who issued several orders that forbade the members of the court capelle to engage in separate services there. Trespassing servants could be fined and subject to arrest,[47] yet there are no documentary traces of Bach having run into disciplinary problems with the older duke before his final months of service. He apparently managed to find a way out of the dilemma, perhaps by receiving some sort of limited special dispensation as private music instructor of Johann Ernst, possibly also of Ernst August. Otherwise it would be difficult to explain Bach's extra pay of 50 florins in 1716–17 from the treasury of the Red Palace.[48] He had received similar extra pay in 1709–10, and in 1714 he mentions in a letter "certain obligations at court in connection with the Prince's [Johann Ernst's] birthday," on the previous December 25, celebrated at the Red Palace.

To what extent the Red Palace maintained a musical establishment separate from the court capelle remains unclear, but there is sufficient evidence for a vigorous musical scene in which both ducal brothers participated as performers, Ernst August as violinist and trumpeter and Johann Ernst as violinist and keyboard player. Ernst August also continued to pursue his father's interests in the collection of musical instruments at the Red Palace. In May 1715, he acquired a *Lautenwerk* (gut-strung harpsichord type) from Johann Nicolaus Bach, its inventor and maker, and it is hard to imagine that Johann Sebastian did not have a leading hand in this musical business transaction with his cousin in nearby Jena. The regular members of the capelle were, as joint servants, statutorily limited to functions accommodating both ducal families, so the Red Castle had to rely on outside forces for its musical projects. Johann Gottfried Walther, the town organist, was certainly available, particularly since he had taught the young Johann Ernst the basics of composition. Moreover, as the increasingly famous court organist and concertmaster Bach attracted a growing number of capable private students—among them Johann Tobias Krebs and Johann Gotthilf Ziegler—his students also seem to have been drawn into opportunities provided at the Red Palace. Schubart, for example, was paid for copying services and was also sent on a special mission to Prince Johann Ernst in Frankfurt.[49]

On receiving the news in August 1715 of the untimely death of his eighteen-year-old brother, Duke Ernst August declared a six-month, duchy-wide mourning period through February 2, 1716. Every kind of music was banned, though church music was allowed to resume prematurely on November 10, the twenty-first Sunday after Trinity.[50] Bach, like all members of the court capelle, received 12 florins for buying mourning clothes. On April 2, two months after the mourning period was lifted, a memorial service was conducted at the *Himmelsburg,* with the performance of an elaborate funeral piece. The lengthy text for the multimovement work, "Was ist, das wir Leben nennen," BC [B19], has survived, but not the music. Two days after the performance, Duke Ernst August's treasury paid out 45 florins 15 groschen "for presented *Carmina.*" Among the four recipients were the "Consistorial Secretary Franck" and the "Concertmaster Bach"—suggesting that Salomo Franck wrote the text and Bach the music for this special occasion.[51]

Three other events of 1716 related to Red Palace affairs held particular significance for Bach. On January 24—still during the mourning period—Duke Ernst August married Princess Eleonore Wilhelmine of Anhalt-Cöthen at Nienburg Palace on the Saale River. Salomo Franck's collection of poems *Heliconische Ehren- Liebes- Und Trauer-Fackeln,* published in 1718, contains the text of the wedding cantata performed on the occasion; the music has not survived, but again, Bach remains its most likely composer. Three months later, Ernst August celebrated his twenty-eighth birthday, an event for which the treasury of the Red Palace paid for two horn players from Weissenfels, who lodged in Weimar from April 23 to 27. Bach's *Hunt Cantata,* BWV 208, commissioned for Duke Christian of Saxe-Weissenfels and first performed at Weissenfels in 1713, now received a performance in Weimar, with the original congratulatory text references to "Chri-sti-an" in Bach's autograph score replaced by the three syllables "Ernst Au-gust" (BC G3). Only a few weeks later, as the new Duchess Eleonore Wilhelmine of Saxe-Weimar celebrated her first Weimar birthday, Franck wrote another allegorical cantata text, *Amor, die Treue und die Beständigkeit,* published in the same 1718 collection. Once again the work was "musically performed,"[52] and once again the music is lost—yet here, too, the most plausible composer is Bach.

Ernst August's brother-in-law, Prince Leopold of Anhalt-Cöthen, surely attended the wedding of his sister in January and perhaps also the birthday celebrations in April and May, but there can be no doubt that on either one, two, or all three occasions he had the opportunity to hear and admire the Weimar concertmaster Bach. Even if Bach did not compose the 1716 wedding and birthday cantatas, his participation as concertmaster would have been indispensable. At any rate, it seems clear that the prince knew Bach before 1717 and that the connections were made through Duke Ernst August, probably as soon as he learned that his new brother-in-law eagerly pursued similar musical interests.[53] And when the Cöthen capellmeistership fell vacant in 1717, Leopold promptly proceeded to hire Bach.

How long had Bach actually pondered leaving Weimar? His rejection of the attractive Halle offer of 1713 indicates that he saw at least something of a future for himself at the Weimar court. But his experiences there must have grown increasingly frustrating: the reduction in format of his cantatas in 1715–16 may reflect difficulties with the performing ensemble at his disposal; his working relationship with the two Dreses as his immediate superiors may have prevented further advancement; and the hostile atmosphere between the ducal cousins may have discouraged him from developing a positive long-term outlook in Weimar. But regardless of what caused his disenchantment with Weimar, Bach had reason to believe that his reputation in the outside world was growing steadily. In 1716, for example, he was invited back to Halle, where church and town officials apparently harbored no ill feelings. He made the trip in order to examine, along with Johann Kuhnau of Leipzig and Christian Friedrich Rolle of Quedlinburg, the recently completed Cuntzius organ at Our Lady's Church. The five-day visit included a dedication recital by Bach, and ended with a celebratory dinner on Jubilate Sunday, May 3[54]—complete with fish and four kinds of meat (beef, ham, mutton, and veal), in addition to plenty of vegetables, fruit, and other delicacies. Though not listed on the menu, a good supply of beer, wine, and liquors would have complemented the meal and reminded Bach of the opulent treatment he had received in Halle a few years earlier at the Inn of the Golden Ring.

The following year, Bach was asked to present a musical Passion at the palace church in Gotha, where the capellmeister to the duke of Saxe-Gotha lay dying. On Good Friday, March 26, Bach substituted for the fatally ill Christian Friedrich Witt. He received 12 talers for this guest performance, and although "20 bound [text] booklets for the Passion to be performed this year were delivered to the princely chapel,"[55] no copies have survived, leaving us in the dark about the exact nature of the text as well as the music. However, a later reference to a Passion composed by Bach in 1717 corroborates the Gotha documents,[56] and at least some musical portions of this Gotha or Weimar Passion (BC D1) were probably absorbed into the second version of the *St. John Passion* of 1725.[57] Bach's guest performance in Gotha also raises the question of his possible candidacy for the capellmeistership at the ducal court.

But another ploy was in the works, and it would have been surprising if Bach had not learned about it sooner or later. Duke Ernst August of Saxe-Weimar came up with the idea of offering Georg Philipp Telemann a kind of "super-capellmeistership" at three Saxe-Thuringian courts: the capellmeister-ship at Saxe-Eisenach (which Telemann had held from 1708 to 1712) was still unoccupied, while Saxe-Weimar had become vacant in December 1716 and Saxe-Gotha in April 1717.[58] But Telemann eventually declined, preferring to stay as music director in Frankfurt. In the meantime, Bach had traveled to Cöthen that summer, and while there, he signed an agreement on August 5 to accept the post of capellmeister to the prince of Anhalt-Cöthen, collecting 50 talers as "most gracious recompense upon taking up the appointment."[59]

Bach himself could hardly have initiated the contact with the Cöthen court, well outside the Saxe-Thuringian realm. More likely, the whole scheme was di-rected by Duke Ernst August, who would have been eager to block Johann Wilhelm Drese's appointment as Weimar capellmeister and, at the same time, to find a suitable station for Bach elsewhere, since he realized that he would not be able to force Bach's appointment for the Weimar post against the will of his cousin, the co-reigning duke. The *General Capellmeister* solution with Telemann was arguably devised to circumvent the Drese appointment in Weimar and to make up for the loss of Bach. While that ingenious plan ulti-mately failed, having placed Bach with the duke's brother-in-law, Prince Leopold of Anhalt-Cöthen, was a good deal for both. For Prince Leopold, hir-ing Bach was a real coup, and for Bach, the newly expanded Cöthen court capelle provided a much more attractive and promising situation than Weimar, Gotha, or Eisenach had. Actually, Telemann must have understood that as well. He might also have gotten an earful about the quarreling dukes in Weimar from a reliable source—none other than his friend Bach.

The watershed year 1717 also saw the first printed reference to Bach—another sign of his growing reputation. Johann Mattheson relates in *Das be-schützte Orchestre* that he had "seen things by the famous organist of Weimar, Mr. Joh. Sebastian Bach, both for the church and for the fist [that is, vocal and key-board pieces], that are certainly such as must make one esteem the man highly."[60] At around the time when this short yet significant statement was published, Bach's fame received a further boost by one of the most notable events in his life, an aborted contest at the electoral court in Dresden with the keyboard virtuoso Louis Marchand of Paris. The captivating story of the con-test was first published during Bach's lifetime and by the end of the eighteenth century had become one of the most popular musical anecdotes circulating in Germany.[61] It was frequently embellished and cited as proof of the supremacy of German over French music or an example of German profundity versus French superficiality. The earliest literary reference to the incident was made in 1739 by Johann Abraham Birnbaum, who claimed that Bach had "fully maintained the honor of Germans, as well as his own honor." But Birnbaum was in fact making a different point: he was defending Bach's musicianship against accusations by Johann Adolph Scheibe, who ranked Handel's keyboard art over that of Bach and, in the course of the argument, declared that there was no Frenchman of particular adroitness on both clavier and organ. It is here that Birnbaum calls up his hero Bach, who is said to have held his own against "the greatest master in all France on the clavier and organ."

As Carl Philipp Emanuel Bach put it in 1788, his father was not "a challenging musical braggard" and "anything but proud of his qualities and never let anyone feel his superiority. The affair with Marchand became known mainly through others; he himself told the story but seldom, and then only when urged."[62] The event is not independently documented, so its details cannot be verified. Dresden, however, had previously been the site of another famous keyboard contest arranged in the mid-1650s by the then electoral crown prince Johann Georg II, Augustus the Strong's grandfather, for the prize of a golden chain; the contestants were Johann Jacob Froberger, organist at the Viennese imperial court, and Matthias Weckmann, court organist in Dresden.[63]

Louis Marchand is indeed known to have traveled to Dresden in 1717, but his performances there could not have taken place before October because the state mourning period after the death of the queen mother extended through St. Michael's Day, September 29. According to undated treasury records, Marchand received for his playing at the court two medals worth 100 ducats[64]—the only documentary evidence of his presence in Dresden. On the other hand, the substance of the legendary affair is transmitted consistently enough to warrant the authenticity of a story whose most comprehensive account is found in the Obituary:

The year 1717 gave our Bach, already so famous, a new opportunity to achieve still further honor. Marchand, the clavier player and organist famous in France, had come to Dresden and let himself be heard by the King with exceptional success, and was so fortunate as to be offered a highly paid post in the Royal service. The concertmaster in Dresden at the time, [Jean-Baptiste] Volumier, wrote to Bach, whose merits were not unknown to him, at Weymar, and invited him to come forthwith to Dresden, in order to engage in a musical contest for superiority with the haughty Marchand. Bach willingly accepted the invitation and journeyed to Dresden. Volumier received him with joy and arranged an opportunity for him to hear his opponent first from a place of concealment. Bach thereupon invited Marchand to a contest, in a courteous letter in which he declared himself ready to execute *ex tempore* whatever musical tasks Marchand should set him and, in turn, expressed his expectation that Marchand would show the same willingness—certainly a proof of great daring. Marchand showed himself quite ready to accept the invitation. The time and place were set, not without the foreknowledge of the King. Bach appeared at the appointed time at the scene of the contest, in the home of [Joachim Friedrich Count Flemming,] a leading minister of state, where a large company of persons of high rank and of both sexes was assembled. There was a long wait for Marchand. Finally, the host sent to Marchand's quarters to remind him, in case he should have forgotten, that it was now time for him to show himself a man. But it was learned, to the great astonishment of everyone, that Monsieur Marchand had, very early in the morning of that same day, left Dresden by a special coach. Bach, who thus remained sole master of the scene of the contest, accordingly had plentiful opportunity to exhibit the talents with which he was armed against his opponent. And this he did, to the astonishment of all present. The King had intended to present him on this occasion with 500 talers; but through the dishonesty of a certain servant, who believed that he could use this gift to better advantage, he was deprived of it, and had to take back with him, as the sole reward of his efforts, the honor he had won. . . . For the rest, our Bach willingly credited Marchand with the reputation of fine and very proper playing. Whether, however, Marchand's Musettes for Christmas Eve, the composition and playing of which is said to have contributed most to his fame in Paris, would have been able to hold the field before connoisseurs against Bach's multiple fugues: that may be decided by those who heard both men in their prime.[65]

The affair, which took place in the electoral Saxon capital, was apparently organized by Bach's counterpart at the Dresden court capelle, concertmaster Woulmyer, a Flemish violinist who generally went by the frenchified name Volumier. The latter probably invited Bach on behalf of his colleagues at the court capelle who may have been annoyed by Marchand's notorious arrogance and eccentric behavior, which was attested to even in his obituary of 1732.[66] Quite possibly, the whole plot was devised in the hope of sabotaging a court appointment for Marchand. At any rate, Bach was assigned the role of challenger in that he sent Marchand a letter, apparently "at the suggestion and command of some important personages of the court there,"[67] likely among them the influential host of the planned contest, General von Flemming. (Count Flemming, incidentally, served from 1724 to 1740 as governor of Leipzig and became one of Bach's most supportive aristocratic patrons there; Bach composed several congratulatory birthday pieces for him: the *Dramma per musica* BWV 249b of 1725 as well as the later cantatas BWV Anh. 10 and BWV 210a.)

How great a disappointment it must have been for Bach, the Dresden court musicians, and the assembled guests that the actual contest never took place should not be underestimated. Listening to the two virtuoso opponents separately could not compare to the thrilling atmosphere of a musical match in which two star performers would challenge each other "to execute *ex tempore* whatever musical tasks [they] should set [themselves]." What they might have performed can only be guessed, but they would surely have focused on their own best technical skills and stylistic specialties. Here Bach would have found himself in a far more advantageous position, for he was not only thoroughly familiar with the contemporary French keyboard repertoire and stylistic idioms, but he specifically knew works by Marchand (the Möller Manuscript, one of his Ohrdruf brother's anthologies, contained a Suite in D minor from Marchand's published *Pièces de claveçin, Livre Premier* of 1702). Bach's own keyboard suites reflected, from the very beginning, a deliberate attempt to integrate genuine French elements into this quintessential courtly-French genre. Moreover, in his consistent application of French terminology in the most mature and elaborate set of keyboard suites from the Weimar period, the so-called *English Suites* (the title of BWV 806a reads "Prelude avec les Suites | composeé | par | Giov: Bast: Bach"), Bach does more than pay mere lip service to their French stylistic orientation. At the same time, he also blends in Italian concerto elements (for instance, in the Prélude to BWV 808), satisfies his own predilection for fugal textures (especially in the concluding Gigue movements), and indulges in a variety of polyphonic writing that penetrates the structure of virtually every suite movement. It is conceivable and even likely that his Dresden performance included material from the *English Suites,* but Bach might also have included bravura pieces of the kind represented by the *Chromatic Fantasy and Fugue,* BWV 903, which require unparalleled keyboard skills.

In any keyboard technique, genre, or style, Bach would have been in familiar territory. Marchand, on the other hand, could capitalize only on a much narrower range of musical experience, if his compositional output and its homogenous French design are taken as a guide. Italian or German music would not have been easily accessible in France, and, as Marchand's works demonstrate, his travels did not bring about any compositional transformation or any stylistic adjustment resulting from foreign influence. At the same time, Marchand would hardly have confined himself to the lightweight kind of music contained in the *Nouvelle suitte d'airs pour deux tambourins, musettes ou vielles par Mr Marchand,* pieces composed by another member of the extended Marchand family of musicians though mistakenly attributed in the Obituary to Louis.[68] Bach was definitely ready to meet a different and more challenging Marchand, the one he knew from the *Pièces de claveçin* and the one he credited "with the reputation of fine and very proper playing."

No sources focusing on the Bach-Marchand affair provide any information on what other contacts Bach may have made during his brief visit to the Saxon capital at a time of significant change for its flourishing music scene.[69] The electoral prince Friedrich August had returned in late September 1717 from a year's sojourn in Venice and brought back with him a complete Italian opera troupe, headed by Antonio Lotti, the newly appointed Dresden court capellmeister, and his deputy, Johann David Heinichen—the only German musician engaged by the electoral prince in Venice. Provisionally established in the fancy-dress hall, the new opera venture was opened on October 25, 1717, with Lotti's *Giove in Argo,* a pastoral melodrama in three acts. Bach would have taken note of the production preparations, though he probably did not meet Lotti or we would have heard about it from Carl Philipp Emanuel or from other sources.[70] He did see not only concertmaster Woulmyer, but most likely also the violinist Johann Georg Pisendel (who had previously visited with him in Weimar) and probably also Heinichen, an alumnus of the St. Thomas School in Leipzig, with whom he maintained good relations until Heinichen's untimely death in 1729.

We can assume that most members of the Dresden capelle attended Bach's performance at the mansion of Count Flemming. More important, however, Bach was able to get a feel for the vibrant, rich, abundant musical life at the electoral Saxon and royal Polish court of Dresden, a European cultural center on a scale far beyond anything he had known before. In Dresden, unparalleled sums of money were spent for art and entertainment: the personnel budget alone of the Italian opera company amounted to 45,033 talers, the French ballet cost 17,700 talers, and the stage sets, decorations, and costumes for the opera *Giove in Argo* 8,578 talers. The salaries for musicians were similarly off chart (and not just reflecting the higher cost of living in the Saxon capital): capellmeister Lotti, along with his wife, the singer Santa Stella, earned 10,500 talers; vice-capellmeister Heinichen made 1,200 talers and concertmaster Woulmyer the same—exactly three times as much as the future Cöthen capellmeister. Of course, Bach would hardly have known of these figures, but his brief first brush with the Dresden court gave him a good idea of conditions in a world-class musical center.

On his return to Weimar, Bach's disappointment over the noncontest with Marchand must have been severely compounded by the loss of the prize he had won, supposedly by a nasty act of embezzlement whose particulars remain obscure. After all, 500 talers represented a large sum of money for Bach, substantially more than twice his current annual salary in Weimar and even 100 talers above his future salary as Cöthen capellmeister. Add to this his frustrations over the capellmeister-less situation at the Weimar court and his own "lame duck" status as concertmaster, and we can imagine his impatience as he anticipated the promising appointment as princely Cöthen capellmeister. Soon after his return from Dresden, he made some demand—for an earlier dismissal, perhaps, or something else related to his imminent departure—that embroiled him in a situation where he lost his temper. Whether he managed to enrage Duke Wilhelm Ernst directly or only a high official in the Wilhelmsburg, nothing apparently could save him from serious trouble; an intervention of his protector, Duke Ernst August, could even have made matters worse. As a result of the incident, "on November 6, the *quondam* concertmaster and organist Bach was confined to the County Judge's place of detention for too stubbornly forcing the issue of his dismissal and finally on December 2 was freed from arrest with notice of his unfavorable discharge."[71]

The wording "*quondam* [erstwhile] concertmaster" suggests that Bach had already quit his Weimar court service by early November, but that his dishonorable release was not yet formally granted until a month later. Apparently for no other reason than a show of anger,[72] the Cöthen capellmeister-designate was kept in jail for nearly four weeks, a period that marked the absolute low point in Bach's professional life. Understandably, the episode is not reported in the Obituary nor in any other early biographical source,[73] although a useful hint is provided by Ernst Ludwig Gerber (whose father, Heinrich Nicolaus Gerber, studied with Bach in Leipzig during the 1720s) when he relates that Bach wrote his *Well-Tempered Clavier,* Part I, "in a place where ennui, boredom, and the absence of any kind of musical instrument forced him to resort to this pastime."[74] Though we cannot take this to mean that the work was begun and completed during Bach's imprisonment, a substantial portion of the twenty-four preludes and fugues may well have originated in this unhappy venue.

After his release from prison on December 2, Bach could not leave Weimar in a great hurry, for he needed to move a family of six. Whether he himself made a quick trip to Cöthen in order to be present, in his capacity as capellmeister, at the festivities on the occasion of Prince Leopold's birthday on December 10 is questionable. But if so, he would have had to combine this trip with a sojourn in nearby Leipzig, where by special invitation of the rector of the university, he spent December 16–18 examining the new large organ made by Johann Scheibe for St. Paul's (University) Church.[75]

Bach's departure dealt the Weimar court capelle a near-fatal blow that permanently dampened the quality of musical life at the ducal court there. While the death of the old capellmeister Drese, almost exactly a year earlier, did not call for swift action because his absence made no noticeable difference, the loss of Bach left an acute gap. A genuine crisis was at hand, as both Wilhelm Ernst and Ernst August must have recognized. As the members of the capelle fell into the category of joint servants, the decision made after Bach's departure by the co-reigning dukes required a compromise: Johann Wilhelm Drese (presumably Duke Wilhelm Ernst's candidate) was promoted from vice-capellmeister to capellmeister, and Bach's longtime student and assistant Johann Martin Schubart (apparently Duke Ernst August's candidate) was appointed chamber musician and court organist, both on January 5, 1718. The posts of vice-capellmeister and concertmaster remained vacant, but the copyist's fee was now reassigned from Drese to the capellist August Gottfried Denstedt (see Table 6.2), and to avoid a net loss for the capelle, the lutenist Gottlieb

Michael Kühnel was hired as an additional court musician.[76] However, the salaries of the leadership group of the court capelle were basically what they had been ten years earlier (see Table 6.6). During the intervening years, virtually all incremental funds for the court capelle were spent on Johann Sebastian Bach, as both dukes clearly understood that investing in him would bring them more than their money's worth.

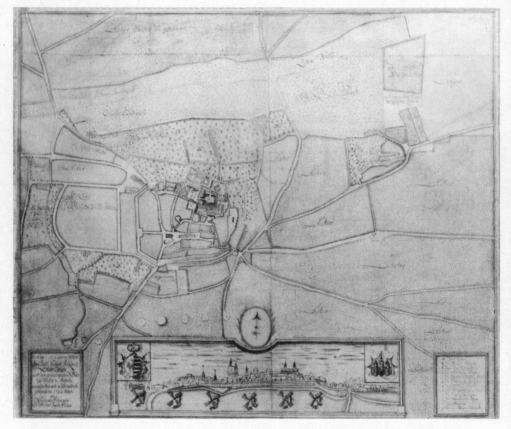

Street map of Cöthen, with town view, in an ink and wash drawing by Nicolaus
Hitzinger (c. 1730).

# 7

## Pursuing "the Musical Contest for Superiority"

### CAPELLMEISTER IN CÖTHEN, 1717–1723

It seems a curious coincidence that Bach, right before settling in Cöthen, spent a few days in Leipzig, where he would eventually move—from Cöthen. As noted earlier, he had been invited by the rector of Leipzig University to examine the recently completed organ at St. Paul's Church (simultaneously the main lecture hall of the university), and his short stay allowed him some time to form at least a superficial impression of Leipzig and perhaps to meet with the old and distinguished cantor at St. Thomas's, Johann Kuhnau. Bach knew Kuhnau as leader of the team that had examined the organ at Our Lady's Church in Halle in 1716 and therefore would certainly have valued his opinion of the new fifty-three-stop Scheibe organ at the University Church. Most of Bach's time, however, was devoted to examining the organ itself, about which he wrote a lengthy report on December 17, the Friday before the fourth Sunday in Advent.[1] Although he had found fault with a few details— notably uneven wind pressure, inequality of voicing, and heavy action—he generally praised the organ builder's work and suggested that Scheibe "be held harmless for the parts he has constructed." Upon submitting his report on December 18, the day of his departure from Leipzig, Bach collected a fee of 20 talers from the rector, Professor Rechenberg—five times as much as he had received some fourteen years earlier for his first organ examination at Arn- stadt. Then a mere lackey, he now signed the organ report and the receipt of his fee as "Capellmeister to the Prince of Anhalt-Cöthen." But there was yet another and more significant difference. In 1703, the eighteen-year-old Bach was looking forward to a career as organist; in 1717, he had effectively brought that career to an end, at least in a formal sense, for he would never again hold a post as organist. The chapter as court organist in Weimar was closed, and he had now, at age thirty-two, reached the peak of the conventional musical hierarchy. He was headed for Cöthen to take his place as princely capellmeister.

From Leipzig to Cöthen—the contrast could hardly have been sharper: here a bustling, wealthy metropolis with over thirty thousand inhabitants, a commercial town and seat of the most prestigious German university, there a modest and rather dull residential town of about one-tenth the size (the entire, predominantly agrarian, principality of Anhalt-Cöthen had a population of only ten thousand); here several big Lutheran churches with an active musical life (in one of which Bach had just examined a large, brand-new organ), there, in Calvinist surroundings, a single Lutheran town church with a poorly maintained organ and no musical life to speak of; here a cultural and musical tradition that extended over several centuries, with a notable number of celebrities, especially among the cantors at St. Thomas's, there a tiny, courtly musical establishment, recently installed, that had been abandoned by its capellmeister before it could even begin to flourish. Would Bach, coming from Leipzig and having recently glimpsed unparalleled courtly splendor in Dresden, have had no qualms about going as capellmeister to Cöthen?

But Bach knew that he had no choice and that there was little if any room for doubts. Eager to get away from Weimar, he was looking forward to a unique opportunity: he could expect to work for a patron whose musical background and interests were as strong as he could wish for and whose personal support was unquestionable; he would be one of the best-compensated court officials in the principality,[2] evidence of the prestige that came with the position and of the high priority assigned to it by the reigning prince; and he would be in charge of an elite professional ensemble whose core group of musicians had recently been recruited from Berlin and whose overall caliber by far exceeded that of the Weimar ensemble. Indeed, Bach would find conditions that would encourage him to pursue further "the musical contest for superiority"—a course so forcefully confirmed by his recent experience at the Dresden court. That the actual competition with the French virtuoso Marchand did not materialize would only have intensified his eagerness and impatience to meet his equal and, just as important, to find a match in musical personnel for the proper realization of his musical ideas. In this regard, the Cöthen court capelle would serve him well.

Bach picked up his first pay on December 29, 1717;[3] the wording in the princely account records—"the newly arrived Capellmeister"—suggests that he had arrived just in time for the celebration of New Year's Day, traditionally one of the major musical events at the Cöthen court. Contrary to a long-held view, he did not move to Cöthen right after his release from detention and dishonorable discharge from the Weimar court on December 2, or there would have been an earlier payment record—for example, on a date close to Prince

Leopold's birthday on December 10. It is unlikely, then, that Bach was present for the birthday festivities that year even though technically his appointment dated back to August 7, when he signed his Cöthen contract and accepted a gift of 50 talers. And in fact, the December 29 payment was back pay: his basic annual salary of 400 talers prorated for the five months from August through December.[4] This means that Bach, who collected his Weimar salary through the third quarter of 1717, was paid twice in August and September. For the fourth (St. Lucia) quarter, he received no pay from the Weimar court, either as additional punishment in conjunction with his arrest, for unauthorized absences from the castle church or from Weimar itself (his trip to Dresden in the fall?), or for both reasons. The last quarter payment went instead to Bach's student and successor Johann Martin Schubart, who probably stood in for him whenever needed.

Relocating his family and personal effects to Cöthen, some seventy miles northeast of Weimar, was a much bigger undertaking than his move nine and a half years earlier from Mühlhausen to Weimar. The family had grown to six, with the oldest daughter, Catharina Dorothea, now nine years old and the three boys, Wilhelm Friedemann, Carl Philipp Emanuel, and Johann Gottfried Bernhard, seven, three, and two, respectively; Maria Barbara's sister Friedelena came along, too. For the first three and a half years, the Bach family rented a spacious apartment in a house close to the main gate of the princely palace (most likely at what is today's parsonage, Stiftstrasse 12) belonging to Elisabeth Regina Schultze, widow of Oberamtmann Johann Michael Schultze. (In the 1690s, before the Agnus Church was built, the house had accommodated the worship services of the small Lutheran congregation in Calvinist Cöthen.) When that house was purchased in 1721 for the Lutheran parson, Bach probably moved to another (unknown) place, likely again no more than a short walk away from the palace.[5]

First documented in 1115, Cöthen had served since 1603 as the residence for the rulers of the small principality of Anhalt-Cöthen. The larger region of Anhalt, a level area situated between the foot of the lower Harz Mountains and the river Elbe, was once ruled by the Ascanians, one of the most ancient houses of Germany, and was later divided into several principalities held by various branches of the family. The division of 1603 created the almost equally small principalities of Anhalt-Dessau, Anhalt-Bernburg, Anhalt-Cöthen, Anhalt-Plötzgau, and Anhalt-Zerbst, which were surrounded for the most part by Saxon and Prussian territories. The town of Cöthen was dominated by its princely palace and gardens, designed by the architect brothers Bernhard and Peter Niuron of Lugano and built in stages between 1597 and 1640. Two prominent staircase towers framed the central structure of the palace. Its southern wing, the *Ludwigsbau,* was named for Prince Ludwig of Anhalt-Cöthen, who had laid the foundation for Cöthen's cultural claim to fame in 1617 by establishing the *Fruchtbringende Gesellschaft,* or Fruit-Bearing Society, a literary organization modeled after the Florentine *Accademia della Crusca* whose aim was maintaining the purity of the German language. Under Ludwig's second successor and nephew, Prince Emanuel Leberecht (r. 1691–1704), the cultivation of music found its modest but solid beginnings, even though its further development stagnated for almost ten years after his death until Prince Leopold, his son, completed the father's vision of a prospering court music.[6]

As hereditary prince, the ten-year-old Leopold succeeded his father immediately, but as a minor, he was placed under the guardianship of his mother, Princess Gisela Agnes, who assumed rule. Small size and relative insignificance prevented the principality from pursuing any real foreign policy. Moreover, although Prince Emanuel Leberecht's will entrusted his wife with the regency, he had resolved that the Prussian king serve as superior guardian.[7] This move made internal and local politics loom all the larger; and indeed, during the eleven years of the princess mother's government, religious and social affairs stood very much at the center. In 1596, the still undivided duchy of Anhalt had adopted Calvinism as its state religion, in accordance with the principle *cuius regio, eius religio* (literally, "whose territory, his reli-

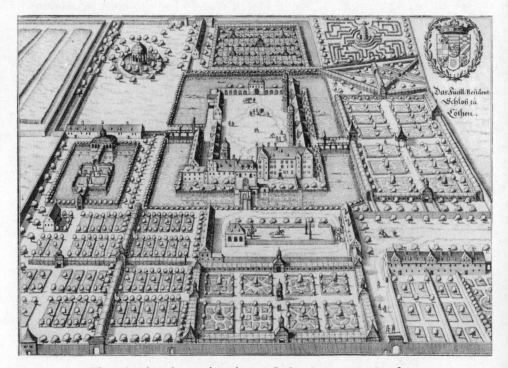

The princely palace and gardens at Cöthen in an engraving from
Matthäus Merian's *Topographia* (1650).

gion"), an agreement reached under the 1555 Peace of Augsburg by which
the ruler's religion was automatically declared the official faith of the region.
Of Lutheran descent and landed gentry, Gisela Agnes (née von Rath), however, fiercely observed her own religious beliefs, staunchly championed the
principality's Lutheran minority, and showed little interest in dynastic concerns and commitments. After her marriage in 1692 with Prince Emanuel
Leberecht, fundamentally a misalliance of birth and religion, she had built—
with the express support of her Calvinist husband, who favored the free and
public exercise of religious observances—a new church for the Lutherans that
was dedicated in 1699 and unsubtly named St. Agnus's Church. Later, as
reigning princess mother, she built a school for her fellow Lutherans (which
Bach's children attended) and established a foundation for Lutheran girls and
women of gentle birth. Fond of an unpretentious life-style, she chose after her
husband's death to reside with her children in a modest house across the
street from St. Agnus's Church. While she ruled with considerable wisdom,
political prudence, and a strong sense of equity and social justice, she also
kept a firm grip on everything that would benefit the largely underprivileged
Lutherans. Her persistence in championing the cause of her co-religionists
eventually created numerous bitter conflicts with her son after he acceded to
power, as Leopold strongly upheld the "reformed" Calvinist tradition of his
dynasty.

For most of his mother's interregnum, Leopold stayed away from Cöthen.
From 1707 to 1710, he attended the *Ritteracademie* in Berlin, one of the preeminent schools for young princes in Germany, to round off his formal education. Following a custom in the higher echelons of the aristocracy, he then set
out on a grand tour, escorted by his steward and private tutor, Christoph Jost
von Zanthier, who led the princely entourage of seven that included a page who
kept the prince's diary.[8] In October 1710, Leopold, then almost sixteen, traveled to The Hague and Amsterdam in the Netherlands, then to England,
crossed parts of Germany and France, and ended up in Italy. After a visit to
Venice and a three-month stay in Rome during the spring of 1712, he returned
home in April of the following year by way of Florence, Venice, Vienna,
Prague, Dresden, and Leipzig.[9] Along the way, he enjoyed opera, especially in
The Hague and in Venice, and acquired a considerable amount of published
music.[10] Recurring expenses for harpsichord rentals and repairs as well as for
strings attest to considerable musical activity,[11] but Leopold also showed a
keen interest in art, architecture, and books. For seven months, including a
major stretch of his Italian journey, the prince was accompanied by Johann
David Heinichen, who worked in Italy for six years before taking up the post
of electoral Saxon capellmeister in Dresden at the beginning of 1717. They met
in Rome, where Leopold wanted "to accept him as his composer and to take
him along on his further travels," according to Johann Adam Hiller, a musi-

cian writing in 1769, who added: "This Prince Leopold was a great connoisseur and champion of music; he himself played the violin not badly and sang a good bass."[12] An inventory of instruments in the prince's private possession, compiled before they were auctioned off after his death, indicates that he also played the harpsichord and the viola da gamba.[13] Hiller's general assessment of Leopold's musical interest and competence matches that of Bach, who refers to Leopold in a 1730 letter as one "who both loved and knew music."[14] After the prince's formal accession to power on May 14, 1716, he was able to devote full attention to his favorite pastime.

The Cöthen court capelle had its very rudimentary beginnings in 1691, then comprising a mere three trumpets and timpani. Prince Emanuel Leberecht enlarged the ensemble in 1702 to six members and restructured it so that only one trumpeter remained. Christoph Krull, one of the new court musicians, was asked to serve as music instructor for Leopold. Five years later and perhaps at the instigation of her son, the reigning princess mother, not particularly disposed toward the court music, reluctantly appointed three Cöthen town pipers to serve simultaneously as court musicians, two of whom—Wilhelm Andreas Harbordt and Johann Freitag, Sr.—were still active when Bach arrived (see Table 7.1). Bach fired Harbordt after less than a month, but in general, the better Cöthen town musicians continued to complement the court capelle. The woodwind player Johann Gottlieb Würdig even made it to the higher rank of chamber musician.

Prince Leopold of Anhalt-Cöthen
in an engraving by Martin Bernigeroth (c. 1715)

## TABLE 7.1. The Cöthen Court Capelle, 1717–23[17]

| | | |
|---|---|---|
| Bach, Johann Sebastian | Capellmeister | August 1, 1717, to April 30, 1723 (titular to March 31, 1729) |
| *Members by the end of 1717* | *Title or function* | *Principal instruments (if known) and remarks* |
| Spieß, Joseph[a] | *Premier Cammer Musicus* | violin |
| Abel, Christian Ferdinand | Chamber musician | violin, viola da gamba |
| Lienicke, Carl Bernhard[a] | Chamber musician | violoncello |
| Rose, Johann Ludwig[a] | Chamber musician | oboe; also (until June 1722) fencing teacher |
| Marcus, Martin Friedrich[a] | Chamber musician | violin; left in June 1722 |
| Torlé, Johann Christoph[a] | Chamber musician | bassoon |
| Würdig, Johann Gottlieb | Chamber and town musician | flute (recorder), until June 1722; concurrently and beyond 1722, director of town pipers |
| Freitag, Johann Heinrich | Chamber musician | flute (recorder); died on August 1, 1720 |
| Harbordt, Wilhelm Andreas | Court and town musician | died August 1719 |
| Freitag, Immanuel Heinrich Gottlieb | Court musician; then chamber musician | June 1720 to April 1721 on leave to Berlin; promoted on return |
| Freitag, Johann, Sr. | Court and town musician | |
| Weber, Adam | Court and town musician | |
| Göbel, Johann Bernhard | Copyist | left in June 1718 |
| Krahl, Johann Christoph | Court trumpeter | also chamber groom |
| Schreiber, Johann Ludwig | Court trumpeter | died March 28, 1723 |
| Unger, Anton | Court timpanist | also innkeeper in town; died December 1719 |
| *Members appointed 1718 and later* | | |
| Gottschalck, Emanuel Leberecht | Copyist | from April 1719; previously organist at St. Agnus Church; succeeded J. B. Bach; also served as Prince Leopold's chamber valet |
| Rolle, Christian Ernst | Court musician | from June, 1722; replaced Marcus; also organist at St. Agnus Church |
| Vetter, Carl Friedrich | Court musician | tenor; June 1718 to |

|  |  | August 1720 |
|---|---|---|
| Fischer, Johann Valentin | Court musician | June 1718 to June 1720 |
| Monjou, Jean François | Court musician | from June 1719; also master of pages |
| Volland, Johann | Court timpanist | from early 1720; replaced Unger, without fixed salary; also innkeeper |
| Wilcke (Bach), Anna Magdalena | Chamber musician | soprano; June (?) 1721 through April 1723 |
| *Associates* |  |  |
| Bach, Johann Bernhard | Copyist | July 1718 through March 1719; temporarily replaced Göbel |
| Colm, Johann | Copyist (?) | June 1719 to June 1721 |
| Two Monjou daughters | Singers | June 1720 to June 1721 |
| Kelterbrunnen, Johann-David | Dancing master | from June 1722 |

*Previously (until 1713) member of the Berlin court capelle of King Friedrich I of Prussia.

In 1713, a unique opportunity arose for the court to hire at one stroke a substantial contingent of excellent musicians. This came about when Friedrich Wilhelm I of Prussia, the "Soldier King," rose to power in not-too-distant Berlin and dissolved his father's cherished court capelle. The young Prince Leopold, not yet of age and still on his grand tour, learned about the new Prussian king's act of cultural barbarism, through indirect channels or perhaps through relationships formed at the *Ritteracademie* in Berlin. In any case, he managed to persuade his mother to hire a core group of the Berlin virtuosos for the Cöthen capelle. Indeed, she proceeded so swiftly that around the beginning of 1713, six distinguished musicians moved from Berlin to the small residential town of the Anhalt-Cöthen principality, some hundred miles away: the capellmeister Augustin Reinhard Stricker and his wife, singer and lutenist Catharina Elisabeth Stricker; oboist Johann Ludwig Rose; violinists Joseph Spieß and Martin Friedrich Marcus; and bassoonist Johann Christoph Torlé. The cellist Carl Bernhard Lienicke rejoined his former colleagues in 1716, shortly after Leopold's accession to power, when the violinist and gambist Christian Ferdinand Abel was appointed as well (along with his brother Johann Christoph, a landscape gardener). Stricker now led a first-rate ensemble that, together with the *ripienists*—most of them recruited from among the local town musicians—formed a capelle of respectable size and even compared favorably, in both size and quality, with the musical establishments of much larger courts.

What made Augustin Reinhard Stricker, in his early forties, consider leaving such a favorable station after just three and a half years? One possibility is that Leopold simply dismissed him when the opportunity arose to hire Bach. Another relates to a move in 1716 by the electoral palatinate court to Neuburg on the Danube, Heidelberg, and Mannheim, where the versatile and productive musician Gottfried Finger was in the service of the new elector, Count Palatine Carl Philipp. Ten years earlier, Finger, Stricker, and Jean Baptiste Volumier had collaborated in composing the music for *Der Sieg der Schönheit über die Helden,* an opera performed in December 1706 at the marriage ceremonies of the future Prussian king, crown prince Friedrich Wilhelm. Stricker, primarily a singer (tenor) and composer, and his wife Catharina may have been lured away by Finger in the hope of reentering the world of opera, which had no place in Calvinist Cöthen. Indeed, Finger and Stricker collaborated again on stage works for Neuburg, *Crudeltà consuma amore* in 1717 and *L'amicizia in terzo* in 1718—the latter piece including as well contributions by Johann David Heinichen, who had given Prince Leopold music lessons in Rome.[15] Hence, a scheme hatched by Leopold and the increasingly influential Heinichen to accommodate Stricker's operatic aspirations and at the same time ease him out of Cöthen to make room for Bach seems quite plausible. Strangely, all traces of Stricker are lost soon after 1718, when he is last mentioned as electoral palatinate chamber composer.

At the end of 1717, when Bach took up Stricker's responsibilities in Cöthen, the court capelle numbered sixteen members (not including the capellmeister) and consisted almost exclusively of instrumentalists (Table 7.1). In both size and structure, then, the ensemble differed fundamentally from the Weimar capelle (Table 6.2), reflecting its very different functions. While performances of music at the palace church services, for example, played a major role in Weimar, sacred music was clearly of secondary importance at the reformed Cöthen court. Therefore, the Cöthen capelle never included a full complement of singers (soprano, alto, tenor, and bass), nor did it have any standing arrangements with a chorus musicus from the Latin school. Bach must have been particularly pleased to work with the core group of eight chamber musicians, well trained and distinguished virtuosi; five of them were former leading members of the Prussian court capelle, but the other three, Abel, Freitag, and Würdig, as well as the trumpeters and timpanist, would hardly have been inferior. Bach, as the ninth instrumental virtuoso, rounded out the group of soloists, which was complemented by at least five *ripienists* (including the copyist). Considering the small size of the town and the regularity of their professional collaboration, these musicians were bound to form a closely knit community. Bach apparently developed particularly warm and lasting personal relationships with some of his colleagues. So he became godfather in 1720 to

Sophia Charlotta, daughter of the gambist Christian Ferdinand Abel (whose most famous son, Carl Friedrich, would become an associate of Johann Christian Bach in London and co-established the Bach-Abel concert series in 1765),[16] and served as godfather in 1728—five years after he had left Cöthen—to Leopold, son of the violinist Joseph Spieß.

The membership of the capelle fluctuated quite a bit during Bach's tenure, but the musicians who died or quit were replaced, leaving the overall size of the group stable. The net loss of one musician over Bach's entire Cöthen period is insignificant, especially if we consider that qualified musicians could always be found among the court personnel, from the town, and from the so-called *Expectanten,* that is, people who served in the expectation of future possible employment.

One of the first decisions Bach had made as the newly appointed concertmaster in Weimar was to relocate the rehearsals of the capelle from capellmeister Drese's apartment to the castle church, in order to exercise greater control over the ensemble. For essentially the same reasons, he held the Cöthen capelle rehearsals at his own house—convenient for the musicians, since they all lived in town—and collected from the court an annual rent subsidy of 12 talers for this purpose throughout his tenure as capellmeister. In a report of 1722, the cantor of Cöthen's St. Jacobi Church extolled Bach's regular rehearsal practice: "The princely capelle in this town, which week in week out holds its *Exercitium musicum,* makes an example that even the most famous virtuosi rehearse and exercise their things together beforehand."[18] This regular rehearsal schedule suggests a weekly or even more frequent program of courtly performances. In keeping with practices at other courts, musical soirées and other forms of musical entertainment must have been an integral part of courtly life at Cöthen, even though we lack specific information and, even more regrettably, most of the actual music made on those occasions. The repertoire would have consisted primarily of instrumental music for larger and smaller ensembles, concertos and sonatas in particular, as well as solo pieces such as keyboard and lute suites.[19] Nevertheless, we can be sure that at least Bach's instrumental compositions whose extant primary sources can be securely dated to the Cöthen years, such as the *Brandenburg Concertos,* the *French Suites, The Well-Tempered Clavier,* the Sonatas and Partitas for solo violin, and the Suites for solo cello (even if some of them may be of earlier origin), were performed at various courtly functions.

The only specific information we have on regular performances at the Cöthen court, however, pertains to two annual events in close proximity: Prince Leopold's birthday on December 10 and New Year's Day. Both occasions were filled with a great deal of music making that included vocal soloists, and the published texts of some congratulatory pieces survive. The librettist hired by the court for these events was Christian Friedrich Hunold (alias Menantes), at the time one of Germany's most acclaimed poets, who taught poetry and rhetoric at Halle University. Hunold had made a name for himself by writing librettos for the Hamburg and Brunswick operas, set by Reinhard Keiser and Caspar Schürmann; he also wrote the text for Keiser's 1705 Passion oratorio "Der blutige und sterbende Jesus." Hunold provided texts for three congratulatory cantatas presented on Leopold's birthdays in 1718, 1719, and 1720—the term *Serenata* in the titles suggesting evening performances—for a sacred cantata performed on Leopold's birthday in 1718, and for a secular cantata performed at the New Year's Day celebration in 1720 (see Table 7.2). Bach's music has survived for only two of the works, BWV 134a and 173a (we have the autograph score for both, also the original performing parts for BWV 134a). For all the other texts, the musical sources are either incomplete (BWV 66a, 184a, and 194a) or entirely lost, although the compositions reappeared in later reworkings as sacred cantatas. This picture extends, unfortunately, to works on texts by authors, mostly anonymous, other than Hunold (who died in 1721).

## TABLE 7.2. Vocal Works Composed for Cöthen

| BWV | Cantata | Function |
|---|---|---|
| Anh. 5 | Lobet den Herren, alle seine Heerscharen | Leopold's birthday, 1718 (church music) |
| 66a | *Serenata,* Der Himmel dacht auf Anhalts Ruhm und Glück | Leopold's birthday, 1718 |
| 134a | *Serenata,* Die Zeit, die Tag und Jahre macht | New Year's Day, 1719 |
| Anh. 6 | Dich loben die lieblichen Strahlen der Sonne | New Year's Day, 1720 |
| Anh. 7 | Pastoral dialogue, Heut ist gewiß ein guter Tag | Leopold's birthday, 1720 |
| 184a | Fragment: [text unknown] | ? (New Year's Day, 1721, or Leopold's birthday, 1720) |
| Anh. 197 | Ihr wallenden Wolken | ? (New Year's Day) |
| 173a | *Serenata,* Durchlauchtster Leopold | Leopold's birthday, 1722 |
| Anh. 8 | *Musicalisches Drama* [text unknown] | New Year's Day, 1723 |
| 194a | Fragment: Text unknown | ? (before November 1723) |
| 203 | Cantata, Amore, traditore | ? (before 1723) |
| 36a | Steigt freudig in die Luft | Princess's birthday, November 30, 1726 |
| 244a | Funeral music | Leopold's funeral, 1729 |

Even if we limit the estimate of Bach's vocal output in Cöthen to the two most prominent and regularly recurring performing dates from January 1718 to through January 1723, the survival rate is devastating. Only nine of the twenty-two works we can reasonably expect Bach to have composed for these occasions left any record of their existence, and actual musical sources, direct or indirect, have come down to us in just five cases (Table 7.3). If we expand the limits and include the five years from 1723 in which Bach had moved to Leipzig but continued to serve the Cöthen court as titular capellmeister, the situation looks even more deplorable. Three reasons help to explain these losses. First, some of the manuscript scores and parts may have been kept in the library of the Cöthen court capelle, which disappeared without a trace. Second, Bach must have retained a substantial portion of these materials himself, since he made later use of them in reworking secular cantatas for the sacred repertoire, though he may have discarded pages he no longer needed. Third, Bach's heirs probably deemed manuscripts containing the mainly secular occasional works to be useless as performance materials and of less interest than those of the sacred cantatas, with the result that they were left to the vagaries of time and circumstance.

We have at best a sketchy musical impression of the vocal repertoire Bach created in Cöthen, but a number of characteristic features stand out. The vocal parts of all secular works are limited to solo singers, often only two. Many of the works, often designed as allegorical dialogues (for example, between Fame and the Fortune of Anhalt in BWV 66a, between Divine Providence and Time in BWV 134a), feature elaborate duets and solos that put considerable technical demands on the court singers, whose professional artistry is often challenged. The orchestral parts, however, are no less demanding, though in contrast to the Weimar repertoire the scoring is more standardized, with four-part string texture as the norm and, in accordance with availability, a more limited use of winds. Moreover, the rhythmic-metric designs of arias and cho-

## TABLE 7.3. Principal Musical Events at the Cöthen Court, 1717–28

|                          | 1718   | 1719 | 1720   | 1721 | 1722  | 1723 | 1724–28 |
|--------------------------|--------|------|--------|------|-------|------|---------|
| New Year's Day           |        |      |        |      |       |      |         |
| —sacred cantata:         | ?      | ?    | ?      | ?    | ?     | ?    | ?       |
| —secular cantata:        | ?      | 134a | Anh. 6 | 184a | G52?  | 194a | ?       |
| Leopold's birthday       |        |      |        |      |       |      |         |
| —sacred cantata:         | Anh. 5 | ?    | ?      | ?    | ?     | ?    | ?       |
| —secular cantata:        | 66a    | ?    | Anh. 7 | ?    | 173a  | ?    | ?       |

ruses show, in line with the prevailingly secular function of these works, a multiplicity of dance types: for example, BWV 66a/1 includes a Gigue-Passepied; BWV 66a/3 a Pastorale; BWV 173a/6–7 a Bourrée; BWV 184a/4 a Polonaise; 184a/6 a Gavotte; BWV 173a/4 a movement "Al Tempo di Menuetto." The movements also show a corresponding decrease in the use of imitative textures.

The only documented performance of a church cantata within the reformed service at the Cöthen palace church is that of "Lobet den Herrn, alle seine Heerscharen," BWV Anh. 5. The Calvinist liturgy left little if any room for concerted church music, so it required some special occasion for a cantata to find its way into the service. An early reprint of Hunold's text indicates that the actual performance of BWV Anh. 5 took place on December 10, 1718, and that the work consisted of an opening chorus (Psalm 103:21) followed by three pairs of recitatives and arias.[20] Performances of similar works may have occurred on the prince's birthdays in other years and, if only rarely, on some other occasions. As Lutherans, Bach and his family did not normally attend the reformed service at the palace church, but the baptism of their son Leopold Augustus was held there on November 17, 1718,[21] because the godfather, after whom the baby was named, was Prince Leopold himself—evidence of a personal side to the relationship between the reigning prince and his capellmeister. The child, the only one born to the Bachs in Cöthen, died before his first birthday and was buried on September 28.[22]

Johann Sebastian and Maria Barbara Bach, like the families of other Lutheran members of the court capelle (such as the Abels), ordinarily attended the St. Agnus Church in town, where they rented their own pews.[23] Indeed, Bach's attendance is documented by the entries of his and other family members' names in the register of communicants.[24] The church's organ was built by Johann Heinrich Müller of Aken in 1708. Princess Gisela Agnes had provided 1,000 talers for the new instrument with twenty-eight stops on two manuals (*Hauptwerk* and *Rückpositiv*) and pedal, the best and largest available in Cöthen during Bach's tenure.[25] If Bach wanted to play the organ, or if he needed an instrument for teaching purposes, this was it. Very occasionally, he may also have played this organ at a service, but Christian Ernst Rolle, who—surely on Bach's recommendation—joined the court capelle, was the regular organist at St. Agnus's. The cantor there was Johann Caspar Schulze, who asked Bach to serve as godfather to his daughter Sophia Dorothea in 1722.[26] Bach and members of the court capelle may have performed a cantata now and then at the Lutheran service, though only indirect testimony for Cöthen performances is provided by the sources of a few cantatas (BWV 132, 172, and 199). For example, manuscript evidence shows that the Weimar cantata "Mein Herze schwimmt im Blut," BWV 199, was performed around 1720 in a modified version, that is, in the key of D minor and with a viola da gamba replacing the obbligato viola in movements 6 and 8. Where the performance of this intimate soprano solo cantata took place is not known—it might have been the Cöthen palace church, the St. Agnus Church, or even a location outside of Cöthen. But since Bach, the gambist Abel, and Bach's second wife, the princely court singer Anna Magdalena Bach, were all members of the Lutheran congregation, a performance at St. Agnus's cannot be ruled out.

The loss of original sources, especially of performing materials, and the absence of information about Bach's regular musical activities at the Cöthen court apart from birthday and New Year's festivities extend to the instrumental repertoire as well. However, there exists virtually no tangible evidence that any of the known concertos, orchestral suites, or sonatas by Bach were actually performed, let alone composed, in Cöthen, with the sole exception of an original set of parts dating from about 1720 for the *Brandenburg Concerto* No. 5, BWV 1050. At the same time, it is inconceivable that capellmeister Bach did not compose most of the standard repertoire that the Cöthen capelle needed for its regular performances, the rest consisting of a broad selection of works by other composers. The capelle kept one salaried copyist and even paid an additional copyist repeatedly from 1719 to 1721, indicating that the preparation of new performing materials required more than one. Moreover, expenses for the music library regularly included bookbinding costs. Curiously, no expenses for the purchase of manuscript or printed music are recorded before 1723, which likely means that most or all of the music was produced by Bach and the other composer-performers of the capelle, such as Joseph Spieß.[27] But the bookbinding costs were considerable; in 1719–20, for example, they amounted to 30 talers, a sum sufficient to bind scores and parts for some fifty ensemble and orchestra works of medium size, or roughly one new work per week.[28] Though this amount represents only a ballpark figure, it looks entirely reasonable—not just for a single year but for the entire period of Bach's capellmeistership—and would anticipate the cantata production schedule Bach later followed in Leipzig. In over five years, from the beginning of 1718 to May 1723, that would have amounted to well over 350 compositions, mainly chamber and orchestral music, but also serenades and other vocal works. And even if only two-thirds of this repertoire stemmed from the capellmeister's pen, the assumed losses would exceed 200 pieces.

More specific information is provided by the printing-cost entries in the court account books. For both the prince's birthday and New Year's Day throughout Bach's tenure, the records identify expenses paid to the printer Löffler in Cöthen. The first entry in 1720 reads, "for printing two New Year *Carmina* for the princely capelle," evidence that indeed two pieces, presumably one sacred and one secular, were performed. And the fact that the sum paid, 2 talers, is consistently the same implies that two compositions were called for each time (see Table 7.3).[29] The honorarium for the text was usually paid to the capellmeister, who was charged "to solicit the New Year's poem," that is, to make the necessary arrangements with the poet.[30] As a result, Bach had free rein to choose the poet and some say in the text's subject matter.

Further testimony to the affluent musical life at the princely court is furnished by payments for guest musicians—the most significant expense category next to the regular salaries budgeted for the court capelle. Among the instrumentalists and singers from outside who joined the capelle for various performances were a discantist (male soprano or falsettist) from Rudolstadt in October 1719; the discantist Preese from Halle, concertmaster Lienicke from Merseburg (a relative of the Cöthen capellist), and concertmaster Vogler from Leipzig in December 1718 and April 1719; the famous bass Riemschneider for several weeks in 1718–19; a singer from Weissenfels and a foreign musician who played a "bandoloisches instrument," a variant of the guitar-like Spanish bandurria, in July 1719; a discantist and a lutenist from Düsseldorf in August 1719; a "musician" in October 1719; two horn players in September 1721 and June 1722; and two Berlin musicians in September 1721.[31] These guest appearances had at least a twofold purpose: on the one hand, they gave Bach the opportunity of presenting an artist of exceptional talent, perhaps one with a rare instrument, and on the other, they allowed the possibility of hiring soloists for special performances or simply of recruiting additional musicians for larger projects. Horn players, for instance, were ordinarily not available to Bach, so if he wanted to perform a work such as the *Brandenburg Concerto* No. 1, he would have had to turn to guest musicians. Still, for the most part, Bach used singers rather than instrumentalists from outside.

Unlike in Weimar, a vocal ensemble was never an integral part of the core group in the Cöthen capelle, yet singers, especially discantists, were needed not just for the birthday and New Year's festivities but throughout the year, if only irregularly. Among the pieces that would fit the category of general musical entertainment is Bach's cantata "Amore traditore," BWV 203, for solo bass and concertato harpsichord. The form of this three-movement piece (aria-recitative-aria) closely resembles a prototype cultivated by Bach's predecessor, Reinhard Stricker.[32] BWV 203, however, replaces the obbligato violin or oboe, typical of the Stricker cantatas, with a brilliant harpsichord solo part, making the work an extraordinary showpiece for two virtuosos. Bach may have written this cantata to take advantage of an unusual situation that occurred at the end of his first year in Cöthen, when the celebrated bass Johann Gottfried (Giovanni Goffredo) Riemschneider—a "virtuoso singer"[33] who would later be engaged by Handel for the Italian opera in London[34]—arrived for an extended stay at the princely court. At the same time, if BWV 203 was indeed composed for Riemschneider, would Bach not have written more than one work for such a unique talent? This is but another hint at the incalculable riches we are missing from Bach's musical oeuvre.

The dearth of information on details of musical life at the princely court combined with the losses of repertoire, in particular of Bach's own compositions for the Cöthen capelle, does not obscure the fact that Bach found himself in a musically ideal situation. First, he was working with a capelle whose professional core group comprised some of the finest musicians he could wish for. Second, the demands of the office left him considerable time to pursue his own interests. But most important of all, he found himself under the patronage of a supportive and understanding prince whose notions of courtly splendor sought to balance modest understatement with luxurious excess. In a 1730 letter to his Lüneburg classmate Georg Erdmann, Bach seems to wax nostalgic about his time as Cöthen capellmeister: "There I had a gracious Prince, who both loved and knew music, and in his service I intended to spend the rest of my life."[35] Even if the last phrase is not to be taken literally—for one can hardly imagine Bach not feeling the overall limitations and constraints of the Cöthen scene—it emphasizes his overall satisfaction. On the other hand, the letter goes on to point at a turn of events that soon contributed to Bach's seeking a new venue. "It must happen," he wrote, "that the said *Serenissimus* should marry a Princess of Bernburg, and that then the impression should arise that the musical interests of the said Prince had become somewhat lukewarm, especially as the new Princess seemed to be an *amusa*." On December 11, a day after his birthday in 1721, Leopold was married to the nineteen-year-old Friederica Henrietta, princess of Anhalt-Bernburg—another event for which Bach would have been commissioned to write the ceremonial music, but no trace of which has survived. Sometime after the wedding date, Bach noticed a change in the court's attitude toward musical affairs, which he attributed to a negative influence of the unmusical princess on his patron.

It is hard to measure objectively if this attempt at accounting for something that Bach could otherwise not explain has any legitimacy. Besides, the princess died before Bach left Cöthen. (Her death on April 4, 1723, would also have called for a work by the court capellmeister, but no such funeral piece has turned up.) Clearly measurable, on the other hand, is a drop in the court's budget for musical activities (see Table 7.4).[36] After a noticeable increase in expenditures for the first two fiscal years (July to June) after Bach's appointment, appropriations decreased for 1720–21, remained flat for another year, and decreased again for 1722–23, Bach's last year in office. The development is anything but dramatic, as the average music allotment amounted to only 4 percent

## TABLE 7.4. Music Budget of the Cöthen Court, 1717–23

| Fiscal Year | Expenses | Variance | Remarks |
|---|---|---|---|
| 1717–18 | 2,033[a] | | Includes 23 talers for departed capellmeister Stricker. |
| 1718–19 | 2,248 | +10.6% | Includes 2 new hires (Vetter, Fischer), guest musicians, and bookbinding costs; 138 talers for a new harpsichord and 40 talers for 2 "Innsbruck" violins; 12 talers for renting rehearsal space in Bach's house (constant through 1722–23); funds for harpsichord strings and repairs. |
| 1719–20 | 2,270 | +1% | Includes 67 talers for guest performers and 14 talers 5 groschen for bookbinding (the highest cost level for both items during Bach's tenure). |
| 1720–21 | 2,130 | –6% | Includes 11 talers for bookbinding; no guest musicians in 1720. |
| 1721–22 | 2,130 | +/–0% | Includes 6 guest musicians, 1 new hire (A. M. Bach, from May 1722). |
| 1722–23 | 1,936 | –9% | Includes savings of 2 monthly salaries for Bach and his wife (May–June, 1723, c. 116 talers); with their full salaries, the annual expenses of 2,052 talers would have reflected a reduction of 3.6%. |

[a]Expenses in talers. Global budget of the princely chamber, 1716–26: average total annual income—58,179 talers; average total annual expense—54,884 talers.

of the entire court budget.[37] Incidentally, music represented the last expense category within title 1, the princely family's personal expenses and the largest item of the court budget. Titles 2–13 consisted of expenses (listed here in order of size)[38] for general costs (title 13); building maintenance and construction (4); the palace kitchen (5); court and country administration (2); the palace wine cellar (6); the palace gardens (3); the princely stables (7); messenger and mail service (9); the printing office (10); debt service (11); personal asset and property service (12); and charity (13)—embarrassingly, the prince's lowest priority.

Although the court consistently ran a small surplus (see Table 7.4), there was virtually no financial leeway, especially since after the small principality's redistricting in 1715 the income from two of the four districts was transferred to the prince's mother upon her retirement from her regency.[39] Moreover, after the prince's marriage in 1721, the princess received an annual allowance of 2,500 talers, a sum within title 1 that exceeded the entire music budget. At about the same time and also within title 1, Leopold established a palace guards regiment of fifty-seven soldiers whose budget reached 2,688 talers by

1723–24. Typically, the palace guard served no apparent purpose, and only whimsical, absolutist demeanor could have been responsible for such a (hardly affordable) pseudo-military extravaganza. In early 1723, when Princess Frieder-ica Henrietta asked her brother, Prince Victor Friedrich of Anhalt-Bernburg, for a cash payment of 1,000 talers, he suspected "a minor emergency" because "he had heard from a Cöthen individual that the prince [Leopold] wanted to borrow 2,000 talers, but nobody was willing to lend him any money."[40]

The change in the overall financial situation could hardly have escaped capellmeister Bach. Although from a global perspective the music budget showed little variance, the results in absolute terms were more than alarming. The membership of the capelle decreased—mainly by deaths and attrition—from seventeen salaried musicians in 1717–18 to fourteen in 1722–23. After Bach's new hires, Vetter and Fischer, left in 1720, no proper replacements were made (see Table 7.1). Two years later, in June 1722, the court flutist and director of the town pipers, Johann Gottlieb Würdig, also left the capelle—probably not voluntarily, for it looks as though Bach had to fire him. Würdig's salary had previously been reduced three times for disciplinary reasons, once be-cause he chose not to show up for the New Year's music in 1719 and twice for irregular rehearsal attendance. Again, Bach was apparently prevented from re-placing Würdig. Instead, Johann David Kelterbrunnen, not a musician, was hired by the court as dancing master. There being no evidence of Bach's advo-cacy for such a position, might this have been a sign (or interpreted by Bach as such) of the influence of the *amusa* princess? At the beginning of his capellmeistership, Bach was able to add members to the capelle and, by 1718–19, to achieve a net gain, yet now he had to preside over net losses. The period of modest growth for the Cöthen capelle was indeed short, and even though the budget for the court music showed no real downturn until 1721–22, Bach must have seen the handwriting on the wall, or else he would not have considered, in late 1720, the organist post at Hamburg's St. Jacobi Church as a possible alternative. A period of genuine financial and personnel retrenchment at the court began in 1721, coinciding, in Bach's perception, with the end of his patron's bachelorhood.

There is another way of looking at the financial picture of the Cöthen court music, from a perspective that was certainly not Bach's. At the beginning of his tenure, Bach's salary of 400 talers represented almost exactly one-fifth of the music budget, while the salary of the next-highest paid musician, Joseph Spieß, amounted to one-tenth of the budget (the chamber musicians' salaries were all around 150 talers, and the other capelle members earned a mere frac-tion of that, down to an annual pay of 32 talers). Considering that the per-sonnel costs represented the bulk of the musical expenses and that toward the end of his residential period as Cöthen capellmeister the combined salaries for

Bach and his wife (700 talers) made up as much as a third of the entire budget, we must ask whether Bach may have miscalculated the financial flexibility of his revered patron. The princely singer Anna Magdalena Bach was not only the first full-time female member of the capelle, she was also the highest paid court musician after the capellmeister, earning twice as much as the chamber musicians. Her salary of 300 talers would easily have funded two or three highly qualified instrumentalists, and had Bach chosen to follow that course, he would have maintained the original personnel strength of the capelle. Perhaps he gambled that Anna Magdalena's appointment would not adversely affect the personnel budget. He certainly would not have realized that this appointment exhausted Leopold's financial latitude within the narrow margins he had for indulging in personal inclinations (of which music was but one),[41] as well as displays of Baroque courtly splendor. Leopold also faced family pressures and intrigues, involving particularly the princess mother Gisela Agnes (who survived Leopold by more than eleven years) and, increasingly, his younger brother and successor, Prince August Ludwig.[42]

It fits well into the picture of an economizing Prince Leopold that he declined to appoint a new capellmeister after Bach departed for Leipzig in May 1723; nor was the court singer Anna Magdalena Bach replaced. Instead, engagements of outside musicians increased significantly, reaching a level higher than ever before: eleven guest performances in 1724 and nine in 1725. The court capelle was now led by Bach's longtime deputy, Joseph Spieß, who kept the title *Premier Cammer Musicus* but was not promoted to concertmaster. In a formal sense, Bach remained the actual princely Cöthen capellmeister and officially continued to bear the title—more than a mere token of the high esteem in which he was held by Prince Leopold. Indeed, the prestige and reputation of the sovereign of a minor principality might well have profited from the fact that the new cantor and music director at St. Thomas's simultaneously carried the title of princely Anhalt-Cöthen capellmeister in the city of Leipzig. The warm personal relationship between Bach and his assiduously musical patron appears not to have changed, nor was the capellmeistership just a title. Not only was Bach prominently represented among the later guest performers, he continued to write works for Cöthen; on a more personal level, he dedicated a copy of his first printed keyboard work, the Partita in B-flat major from the *Clavier-Übung,* BWV 825, to the princely family at the birth on September 12, 1726, of the firstborn to Prince Leopold and his second wife, Charlotte Friederica Wilhelmine of Nassau-Siegen, and included a poem in honor of Emanuel Ludwig, the princely baby.[43]

Bach first returned to Cöthen in July 1724 for a performance that also involved Anna Magdalena for which the two together received 60 talers; also engaged for the guest performance was the organist Johann Schneider of Saalfeld and the tenor Carl Friedrich Vetter, once a member of the Cöthen capelle.[44] The next documented visit, again with Anna Magdalena, relates to the birthdays in December 1725 of Princess Charlotte and Prince Leopold, at which "the Leipzig Cantor Bach and his wife . . . gave a number of performances."[45] In all likelihood, the capellmeister returned to his former place of work at least once a year, but the only other known visit took place in January 1728, apparently in conjunction with the New Year's Day festivities. It was probably the last time Prince Leopold heard Bach perform, for he died on November 19 of that year, a few weeks before his thirty-fourth birthday.

Nearly five years after having left the Cöthen court service, Bach paid his beloved former patron final honors when he composed and performed—with Anna Magdalena, son Wilhelm Friedemann, and musicians from Halle, Leipzig, Merseburg, Zerbst, Dessau, and Güsten—the music for the state funeral that took place four months after the prince's death, on Wednesday and Thursday, March 23–24, 1729. The two compositions have not survived, but the court records specify that the first piece (BC B21)—described as lasting "a considerable time"—was performed at the 10 P.M. service on Wednesday in the illuminated reformed town church and cathedral St. Jacobi, whose walls were veiled in black.[46] The music began on the arrival in the church of the funeral procession, following the horse-drawn hearse with the princely casket, but nothing is known about its genre, scoring, or character. After the performance, the short service continued with a prayer, the congregational hymn "Nun lasset uns den Leib begrab'n," the entombment in the family crypt, and the benediction, followed by another hymn, "Herzlich lieb hab ich dich, o Herr."

The libretto for the second and apparently larger work, "Klagt, Kinder, klagt es aller Welt," BWV 244a (BC B22), performed the following morning at the memorial service in the same church, was written by Bach's Leipzig poet Christian Friedrich Henrici, alias Picander. It describes an elaborate work of twenty-four movements divided into four sections, to be integrated into the lengthy memorial service, at the center of which stood a sermon on Psalm 68:21, "Wir haben einen Gott, der da hilft, und einen Herrn, der vom Tod errettet" (We have one God of salvation and one Lord, who rescues us from death), a verse Bach also set as the opening to section II of his funeral music. The lost music borrowed two movements from the 1727 *Tombeau*, BWV 198, for Christiane Eberhardine, saxon electoress and queen of Poland, as well as seven arias and two choruses from the *St. Matthew Passion*, BWV 244, of the same year. Although we have no information on the changes incorporated by Bach in reworking the borrowed music, the parody models provide a reliable sense of the work's general scale and character. And that Bach turned to the greatest work he had composed till then, the *St. Matthew Passion,* shows his desire to pay homage to his revered prince with the best music of which he was capable.

## TRAVELS AND TRIALS

Cöthen's location within the mostly rural territory of the small principality and a good distance away from any city of size would certainly have created a sense of isolation and narrowness for anyone. Even for Bach, who by 1717 had had only short brushes with larger cities such as Halle, Leipzig, Dresden, Hamburg, and Lübeck, Cöthen was much smaller and more remote than either Arnstadt, Mühlhausen, or Weimar. However, as the principal mail-coach line from Hamburg to Leipzig via Magdeburg led through the little princely residential town, often mockingly dubbed "Cow Cöthen," residents could see an inviting and convenient prospect for escape. Bach must have welcomed the opportunity to travel more than ever before; in any case, he took more trips while in Cöthen than he did in any other five-year period of his life. His professional travels, both in the service of the court and on his own, contributed to his musical, social, and cultural experience while they also expanded his political and geographic horizons (see Table 7.5). A survey of his travels readily illustrates that Bach's life, lived within narrow geographic confines, was very different from that of the cosmopolitan Handel, for example, his compatriot of the same age. Yet the strictures did not foster an attitude of provincialism on Bach's part, especially when it came to the requirements of his "trade," musical performance and musical science. On the contrary, just as he was ready to face any challenge by Louis Marchand, he was even more curious and eager to meet George Frideric Handel.

Bach first attempted to meet Handel in June 1719 by making a trip to nearby Halle, Handel's hometown. We know about this trip only through what Forkel called a "very just and equitable estimate of Bach's and Handel's respective merits," published anonymously in 1788. That author, who could hardly have been anyone other than Carl Philipp Emanuel Bach, takes issue with a question asked after Bach's death by Friedrich Wilhelm Marpurg, with reference to Louis Marchand's "defeat" by Bach:

"Did not the great Handel avoid every occasion of coming together with the late Bach, that phoenix of composition and improvisation, or of having anything to do with him?" etc. And the commentary is: Handel came three times from England to Halle:

the first time about 1719, the second time in the thirties, and the third time in 1752 or 1753. On the first occasion, Bach was Capellmeister in Cöthen, twenty short miles from Halle. He learned of Handel's presence in the latter place and immediately set out by stage coach and rode to Halle. The very day he arrived, Handel left. On the second occasion, Bach unfortunately had a fever. Since he was therefore unable to travel to Halle himself, he at once sent his eldest son, Wilhelm Friedemann, to extend a most courteous invitation to Handel. Friedemann visited Handel, and received the answer

### TABLE 7.5. Bach's Professional Travels, 1703–50[a]

| | |
|---|---|
| Altenburg | 1739 (organ examination) |
| Arnstadt | 1703 (organ examination) |
| Berlin | 1719 (harpsichord purchase); 1741, 1747 (guest performances at court: keyboard) |
| Carlsbad | 1718, 1720 (with Prince Leopold and members of the Cöthen court capelle) |
| Cassel | 1732 (organ examination, accompanied by Anna Magdalena) |
| Cöthen | 1724, 1725 (guest performances, with Anna Magdalena); 1728 (guest performance); 1729 (guest performance at Prince Leopold's funeral, with Anna Magdalena and Wilhelm Friedemann) |
| Dresden | 1717 (contest with Marchand); 1725, 1731 (organ recitals at St. Sophia's); 1733 (dedication, *Missa* BWV 232); 1736 (organ recital at Our Lady's), 1738, 1741 (purpose unknown) |
| Erfurt | 1716 (organ examination) |
| Gera | 1724 (organ examination) |
| Gotha | 1717 (guest performance: Passion) |
| Halle | 1713 (audition); 1716 (organ examination); 1719 (failed attempt at meeting Handel) |
| Hamburg | 1720 (audition) |
| Langewiesen | 1706 (organ examination) |
| Leipzig | 1717 (organ examination, St. Paul's Church); 1723 (audition) |
| Lübeck | 1704–5 (Buxtehude's *Abendmusic,* etc.) |
| Mühlhausen | 1707 (audition); 1709, 1710 (guest performances: town council election cantata); 1735 (organ examination) |
| Naumburg | 1746 (organ examination, St. Wenceslaus's) |
| Potsdam | 1747 (guest performance at court: keyboard) |
| Sangerhausen | 1702 (audition) |
| Schleiz | 1721 (guest performance at court) |
| Traubach | 1712 (organ examination) |
| Weimar | 1708 (organ recital, palace church) |
| Weissenfels | 1713 (guest performance at court: BWV 208); 1725 (guest performance: BWV 249a); 1729 (guest performance); 1739 (purpose unknown, with Anna Magdalena) |
| Zerbst | 1722 (guest performance at court) |
| Destination unknown: | 1729 (absent from Leipzig for 3 weeks, before March 20); 1736 (absent for 2 weeks, after July 17) |

[a]Documented voyages only, exclusive of family trips and short trips within the immediate vicinity of Leipzig.

that he could not come to Leipzig, and regretted it very much. (J. S. B. was at that time already in Leipzig, which is also only twenty miles from Halle.) On the third occasion, J. S. was already dead. So Handel, it seems, was not as curious as J. S. B., who once in his youth walked at least 250 miles to hear the famous organist in Lübeck, Buxtehude. All the more did it pain J. S. B. not to have known Handel, that really great man whom he particularly respected.[47]

While there is no evidence whatsoever that Handel deliberately avoided Bach, the assumption that one was "not as curious" as the other is probably correct.

Earlier in 1719, Bach had been in Berlin to acquire a new harpsichord for the Cöthen princely court that had been ordered from Michael Mietke, court instrument maker in Berlin, who was famous for building fine, elegantly decorated harpsichords. Possibly Bach had previously visited Berlin in order to commission the instrument, but on March 1 the court treasury advanced him 130 talers "for the harpsichord built in Berlin and travel expenses."[48] We can deduce that the harpsichord arrived in Cöthen on or shortly before March 14, because that day the chamber valet and copyist of the capelle, Gottschalck, was reimbursed for 8 talers cartage "for the Berlin *Claveçyn*" (which no longer exists, but was still listed in an 1784 capelle inventory as "the grand harpsichord with 2 manuals, by Michael Mietke in Berlin, 1719; defect"). The dates suggest that Bach stayed in Berlin for a week to ten days, a period that afforded him the opportunity to make various contacts and also to perform at the Prussian court. Appropriate connections could easily have been made for him by those of his Cöthen colleagues who, six years ago, had left the court capelle of King Friedrich I of Prussia. Here he most likely met Margrave Christian Ludwig of Brandenburg, brother of the deceased king and youngest son of the "grand elector," Friedrich Wilhelm of Prussia. The margrave maintained his own small capelle in Berlin, whose members likely remained in touch with their former colleagues now in Cöthen.[49] And it was Margrave Christian Ludwig for whom, two years later, Bach assembled *Six Concerts avec plusieurs Instruments,* the *Brandenburg Concertos.* As a matter of fact, Bach reveals unmistakably in his 1721 preface of the dedication score that he had indeed played for the margrave two years earlier:

As I had a couple of years ago the pleasure of appearing before Your Royal Highness, by virtue of Your Highness's commands, and as I noticed then that Your Highness took some pleasure in the small talents that Heaven has given me for Music, and as in taking leave of Your Royal Highness, Your Highness deigned to honor me with the command to send Your Highness some pieces of my composition: I have then in accordance with Your Highness's most gracious orders taken the liberty of rendering my most humble duty to Your Royal Highness with the present concertos, which I have adapted to several instruments.[50]

Just as Bach successfully managed to combine both princely and personal business in Berlin, the trip's main purpose—purchasing a new state-of-the-art harpsichord for the Cöthen court—also greatly benefited him both officially and personally: as princely capellmeister on the one hand and as keyboard virtuoso on the other. This kind of dual support and patronage from the court was, after all, also in the best interest of the prince. An extraordinary musician in his service would only shed glory on the princely court, and even if Bach traveled by himself and performed at other courts, he would do so as the capellmeister of the prince of Anhalt-Cöthen.

There were two special occasions on which the prince found himself in a position to showcase Bach and the elite ensemble abroad, both times at Carlsbad (today's Karlovy Vary) in northwestern Bohemia, some 130 miles south of Cöthen. Of feeble health since age twenty-one, Prince Leopold followed the advice of his physician, Dr. Gottfried Weber,[51] to take the waters at this fashionable spa. Its saliferous medicinal springs were said to have been discovered in the fourteenth century by Emperor Carl IV, who had then chartered the town. However, its development and promotion as an elegant health and vacation resort emerged only in 1711, when the newly crowned Emperor Carl VI and his family began their regular summer visits from Vienna to the "imperial spa" at the Bohemian shoulder of the Ore Mountains. Carlsbad then quickly attracted the upper echelons of the European aristocracy, many of whom stayed there for a major part of the summer season.[52] Prince Leopold visited only twice, in 1718 and 1720, but remained each time for over a month.

On both his trips, from mid-May to mid-June in 1718 and from late May to early July in 1720, the prince took along his capellmeister and several musicians of the court capelle. The first time, Bach was joined by Joseph Spieß and five other musicians; servants were paid "to help carry the princely *ClaviCymbel* to Carlsbad."[53] We lack specific details on the size of Leopold's musical entourage on the second visit, but we can be sure that on both sojourns rather than having his musicians entertain him in solitude, he chose rather to feature the virtuosos of his capelle, in particular his capellmeister-composer-keyboard artist, before a distinguished audience at the numerous parties arranged for the noble socialites. Besides drinking the waters, the guests spent their leisure time hunting, dining, and enjoying the shows presented by the theatrical and musical groups or individual performers brought along by their noble owner-sponsors.[54] Among the early habitual visitors were two exceedingly wealthy and influential Bohemian-Moravian arts patrons, Franz Anton Count Sporck of Prague and Adam Count Questenberg of Jaroměřice. They and their equal and would-be counterparts helped institute a seasonal atmosphere in which the villas, watering places, hotels, casinos, and pavilions of Carlsbad formed an exquisite backdrop to what may have been the earliest regular summer festival of the performing arts. Here the Cöthen court capelle under Bach made its debut in 1718, most likely presenting instrumental ensemble works for up to seven players (even eight, if Prince Leopold participated) and keyboard solo pieces. Here also, Bach and his colleagues could establish personal and professional contacts, and it seems likely that Bach's later connections with the counts Sporck and Questenberg date back to Carlsbad.

The second Carlsbad trip coincided with what was doubtless the most tragic event in Bach's entire life, the sudden and startling loss of Maria Barbara, his wife of twelve and a half years and mother of their four children, Catharina Dorothea, Wilhelm Friedemann, Carl Philipp Emanuel, and Johann Gottfried Bernhard, ranging in age from eleven to five. Twins born in 1713 had died shortly after birth, and Leopold Augustus,[55] their Cöthen-born son, died very early, too (see Table 11.1). The reference in Bach's Obituary to Maria Barbara's death at age thirty-six, though brief and to the point, reflects nevertheless the childhood memory of its co-author—surely an unforgettably traumatic experience for the six-year-old Carl Philipp Emanuel: "After thirteen years of blissful married life with his first wife, the misfortune overtook him, in the year 1720, upon his return to Cöthen from a journey with his Prince to Carlsbad, of finding her dead and buried, although he had left her hale and hearty on his departure. The news that she had been ill and died reached him only when he entered his own house."[56]

Several days at least had elapsed between Maria Barbara's death and Bach's arrival in Cöthen. Who would have greeted him first with the shocking news? Whether it was one of the children or Friedelena, their mother's older sister, who had lived in the household for more than a decade, the family's grief was immeasurable and enduring. No causes for Maria Barbara's death are known, and only the burial is documented. The stony entry in the deaths register under July 7, 1720, reads: "The wife of Mr. Johann Sebastian Bach, Capellmeister to His Highness the Prince, was buried," and notes that the full choir of the Latin school sang at the funeral and not, as usual, a partial choir.[57] This gesture, together with a generous reduction in the fee charged by the school, beautifully demonstrates the special respect accorded to this daughter of a well-known composer, wife of a now-famous composer, and mother of their fellow student Wilhelm Friedemann.

Only four months after his wife's death, Bach set out on another long-distance trip, this time by himself. His destination was Hamburg, where the post of organist of St. Jacobi's Church had fallen vacant with the death on September 12 of Heinrich Friese, organist and clerk of the church, and successor to the renowned Matthias Weckmann. There can be no question that the thirty-five-year-old widower was unsettled by the devastating tragedy that had afflicted him and his family, but at the same time he might also have wanted to take a fresh look at options that presented themselves elsewhere. He would certainly have been attracted by the church's famous instrument—a four-manual organ with sixty stops built in the years 1688–93 by Arp Schnitger, the most celebrated north German organ builder—and by the seductive prospects of the Hamburg musical scene, which had so fascinated him as a teenager. Back then, the penniless St. Michael's School choral scholar had had to walk or hitchhike the thirty miles from Lüneburg to Hamburg. Now a renowned capellmeister, he traveled the more than two-hundred-mile distance by mail coach ("first class," so to speak) to what was then Germany's largest metropolis, where one or more concerts were prearranged. Prince Leopold would hardly have objected to anything that prominently featured his capellmeister—who else could put his tiny principality on the map? The vacancy at St. Jacobi, very likely the center of a grand scheme designed by unknown but influential wire pullers to lure Bach to Hamburg, was for him perhaps no more than an excuse to escape temporarily from the provincial climate of Cöthen and breathe new air. Bach would certainly have known about St. Jacobi, but was he also told about another vacancy expected to occur in the not-too-distant future? There may well have been forces at work trying to build up Bach as a future candidate for the cantorate at the Hamburg Johanneum and the musical directorship of the five principal churches. That position was still held by the failing seventy-year-old Joachim Gerstenbüttel, who in fact died in April 1721. Then again, one might reasonably wonder whether Bach's November 1720 visit was a corollary to a contrasting (or corresponding) scheme, masterminded by the same or a different group of strategists, who arranged for Georg Philipp Telemann to present his opera *Socrates* in Hamburg only two months later, in January, and finally landed him Gerstenbüttel's job in July 1721.[58] Might there have been a plan to attract both Telemann and Bach to Hamburg?

There are no documents that explain the circumstances surrounding Bach's trip to Hamburg. Most illuminating, however, is the relevant passage in the Obituary, taking up more than twice the space than the entire period of his Cöthen capellmeistership:

During this time, about the year 1722 [*sic*], he made a journey to Hamburg and was heard for more than two hours on the fine organ of St. Catharine's before the Magistrate and many other distinguished persons of the city, to their general astonishment. The aged organist of this church, Johann Adam Reinken, who at that time was nearly a hundred years old, listened to him with particular pleasure. Bach, at the request of those present, performed extempore the chorale "An Wasserflüssen Babylon" at great length (for almost half an hour) and in different ways, just as the better organists of Hamburg in the past had been used to do at the Saturday vespers. Particularly on this, Reinken made Bach the following compliment: "I thought that this art was dead, but I see that in you it still lives." This verdict of Reinken's was the more unexpected since he himself had set the same chorale, many years before, in the manner described above; and this fact, as also that otherwise he had always been somewhat inclined to be envious, was not unknown to our Bach. Reinken thereupon pressed him to visit him and showed him much courtesy.[59]

This report, first of all, stresses Bach's continuing preeminence as an organ virtuoso who had not lost any of his remarkable capacity since giving up his post at Weimar. The reaction of the venerable ninety-seven-year-old Reinken to Bach's organ playing can hardly be overrated. Bach was regarded as the only organist of rank in his generation who not only preserved the traditions of the seventeenth century but developed them further. For Bach, therefore, Reinken's pronouncement must have been more than a simple compliment, because he would have sensed its historical significance. Indeed, he probably shaped its precise formulation, since he was undoubtedly the primary transmitter of the Reinken quote and hence responsible for its inclusion in the annals of music history.[60] Moreover, that Bach performed "before the magistrate and many other distinguished persons of the city, to their general astonishment," indicates that the event was prearranged, advertised, and apparently attended by such prominent people as Erdmann Neumeister, the cantata librettist and senior minister of St. Jacobi, and Johann Mattheson, music director of the Hamburg cathedral.

No specific date is documented, but Bach's organ recital probably followed the Vespers service at St. Catharine's on Saturday, November 16, during which he may have presented his dialogue cantata "Ich hatte viel Bekümmernis in meinem Herzen," BWV 21, an earlier work whose text ("I had much distress in my heart, but your consolation restores my soul") and music at this particular point in Bach's life would have revealed a deeply personal dimension.[61] The original sources of this Weimar cantata reveal definite traces of a performance during the Cöthen years (in the version BC A99b). A detailed reference to this work, with critical remarks on its text declamation, shows up in Mattheson's *Critica Musica* of 1725,[62] the more remarkably since Mattheson would hardly have had any other chance of getting to know this cantata than at Hamburg in 1720. Similarly, Mattheson cites theme and countersubject of Bach's G-minor Fugue in his *Grosse General-Bass-Schule* of 1731.[63] His statement "I knew well where this theme originated and who worked it out artfully on paper," probably refers to the same event, suggesting that the Fantasy and Fugue in G minor, BWV 542, formed part of Bach's organ recital program, not as an improvised piece but—appropriate for a work of such complexity—one that was artfully written out. Likewise, Bach's chorale improvisations may have involved some premeditation and may indeed have drawn on two versions of his large-scale four- and five-part elaborations of the hymn "An Wasserflüssen Babylon," BWV 653a–b, one of which features prominent use of double pedal.

Even though all these details regarding Bach's performances at St. Catharine's remain conjectural, they support the notion of how carefully Bach prepared his Hamburg appearance. And if the dialogue cantata BWV 21 was no longer truly representative of his more recent achievements, it was, with its eleven movements, his most extended work in the cantata genre. BWV 542, too, even though its fugue was composed before 1720, shows thoroughly innovative approaches that are immediately recognizable: a fantasy of exceptional rhetorical power and unparalleled harmonic scope, with towering chromatic chords over descending pedal scales that create the illusion of endless space;[64] an exemplary fugue on a symmetrically constructed theme (in itself a transformation of a Dutch folk tune, probably a special homage to Reinken's Dutch connections);[65] and a texture of exciting flexibility, with an uncompromising obbligato pedal part.

The event at St. Catharine's, the church of the Hamburg magistrate, could never have been arranged without the patriarchal Reinken having a hand in it. It may even be that this nonagenarian, who over two generations had played a key role in Hamburg's musical life, was the driving force behind Bach's appearance in Hamburg, together with his son-in-law Andreas Kniller, organist at St. Peter's and, like Reinken, a member of the search committee for the St. Jacobi post. But the Jacobi affair was essentially reduced to a side show because the standard rules of competition would not permit preferential treatment of any single candidate; and Bach was indeed a candidate for the position—how serious a candidate we will probably never know. While there is no evidence that he truly intended to leave the Cöthen capellmeistership after only three years (even with his less idealized view of the post), and while he himself hardly took the initiative to apply for the Hamburg organist post, he was certainly willing to explore the situation. So at a meeting on November 21,[66] the trustees of St. Jacobi named Bach as one of eight candidates,[67] determined the selection process, set the date and modalities for the competition, and declared that "all the competent [candidates] should be admitted to trial, if they requested to be." The audition took place after the Thursday evening prayer service on November 28, but only four competitors participated. The church minutes specify that two withdrew, another did not show up, and "Mr. Bach had to return to his prince on November 23." The formal election was supposed to be held on December 12, but since the four professional judges were not satisfied with the results of the audition,[68] the trustee Johann Luttas asked for a postponement of the decision "until he should receive a letter from Mr. Johann Sebastian Bach, Capellmeister at Cöthen"—an unmistakable indication that Bach, even though he had left the city, was considered the top candidate.

At least Luttas and pastor Neumeister had heard Bach perform at St. Catharine's and strongly supported his candidacy. At the next meeting, on December 19, Luttas had Bach's letter in hand, which he then "read aloud in full." Here, Bach apparently asked that his name be removed from consideration, "whereupon it was resolved in God's Name to proceed to the choice, and thus Johann Joachim Heitmann was chosen by a majority vote, *viva voce,* as organist and clerk of the St. Jacobi Church."

The newly elected organist demonstrated his gratitude by the payment of 4,000 marks, in deference to a deplorable custom regarding the sale of municipal and church offices that had prevailed for some time in Hamburg.[69] Johann Mattheson did not mince words when he wrote in *Der musicalische Patriot* of 1728:

I remember, and a whole large congregation will probably also remember, that a few years ago a certain great virtuoso, whose merits have since brought him a handsome Cantorate, presented himself as candidate for the post of organist in a town of no small size, exhibited his playing on the most various and greatest organs, and aroused universal admiration for his ability; but there presented himself at the same time, among other unskilled journeymen, the son of a well-to-do artisan, who was better at preluding with his talers than with his fingers, and he obtained the post, as may be easily conjectured, despite the fact that almost everyone was angry about it.[70]

Since Bach's letter to Johann Luttas has not survived, it is impossible to tell what prompted his premature departure and whether he withdrew when he learned that a substantial bribe was expected if he won the appointment; other personal reasons and Prince Leopold's objections may also have played a role. Nevertheless, the circumstances surrounding the appointment apparently generated not just chagrin in Hamburg society but real anger. Indeed, they provoked Erdmann Neumeister to a public condemnation in his Christmas sermon shortly after the new organist was appointed, as Mattheson relates:

The eloquent chief preacher, who had not concurred in the Simoniacal deliberations, expounded in the most splendid fashion the gospel of the music of the angels at the birth of Christ, in which connection the recent incident of the rejected artist gave him quite naturally the opportunity to reveal his thoughts, and to close his sermon with something like the following pronouncement: he was firmly convinced that even if one of the angels of Bethlehem should come down from Heaven, one who played divinely and wished to become organist of St. Jacobi, but had no money, he might just as well fly away again.

The Hamburg affair seems to have had no repercussions whatsoever at the Cöthen court or in the court capelle. Bach received permission the following year to make a major new appointment to the capelle, perhaps because of the acclaim he met with on his trip. And the summer of 1721 saw a young soprano singer by the name of Anna Magdalena Wilcke appear on the Cöthen scene, not just as an ordinary court musician but carrying the higher rank of a chamber musician. We don't know how Bach knew her, where he heard her for the first time, nor where and when he hired her. His professional connections were manifold and widespread, so it would not have taken much effort to find a capable vocalist for the Cöthen court. But this appointment had, perhaps even from the beginning, deeply personal implications. Anna Magdalena is mentioned for the first time in the register of communicants at the St. Agnus Church for June 15, 1721 (the first Sunday after Trinity), where she is listed as "14. Mar. Magd. Wilken." Some three months later, her name appears in the September 25 baptismal register of a baby born to the palace cellarman, Christian Hahn; she is listed as godmother in two different entries, as "Miss Magdalena Wilckens, princely singer here" and "Magdalena Wülckin, chamber musician."[71]

Curiously, Bach's name appears in the same documents on the same dates. The June communion register lists him as "65. Herr Capellmeister Bach." Before this, Bach's name is found in the register four times, from October 1718 to August 1720. In other words, he received communion only once or twice a year, so the joint occurrence of the names Wilcke and Bach may not be coincidental, even though their names appear far apart (spouses are usually listed consecutively). In the September baptismal register, however, Bach is also designated a godparent, and his name is followed immediately by that of Magdalena Wilcke. Their joint appearance here may be more meaningful, because of a prevailing custom that couples engaged to be married serve together as godparents. As engagements were never officially recorded, we cannot be sure that that was the case here. Of course, neither document offers the remotest hint as to when and how Bach got to know the singer, but certain clues lend credence to a plausible explanation.

Bach is known to have taken only one professional trip during 1721,[72] in conjunction with an early August guest performance in Schleiz at the court of Heinrich XI Count von Reuss, for whose great-grandfather Heinrich Schütz had composed his *Musicalische Exequien.*[73] Traveling from Cöthen to Reuss County in southeast Thuringia would have taken Bach through Weissenfels, which lies about halfway between the two and where he had well-established connections dating back to his first guest performance there in 1713; a Weissenfels stopover would have provided an opportunity to touch base with former colleagues in the court capelle of the duke of Saxe-Weissenfels. From about 1718, this ensemble included the trumpeter Johann Caspar Wilcke, who had previously served as "court and field trumpeter" to the duke of Saxe-

Zeitz. Wilcke's son Johann Caspar, Jr., was at the time trumpeter at the court of Anhalt-Zerbst, a principality bordering on Anhalt-Cöthen. Wilcke also had four daughters: Anna Katharina, married to the Weissenfels court groom and trumpeter Georg Christian Meissner; Johanna Christina, married to Johann Andreas Krebs, trumpeter colleague of the younger Wilcke in the Zerbst court capelle; Dorothea Erdmuthe, married to Christian August Nicolai, a fellow trumpeter of the older Wilcke in the Weissenfels capelle; and the unmarried Anna Magdalena. Christina and Magdalena had received thorough training as singers, most likely by the famous *cantatrice* Pauline Kellner, who was engaged at the Weissenfels court from 1716.[74] The two sisters may have functioned at the court as "singing maids," comparable to the two Monjou daughters in Cöthen (see Table 7.1).[75] The first documented public performance that included Magdalena Wilcke occurred in 1720 or 1721. Without a specific date, the court account books at Zerbst record a payment of "6 talers for the trumpeter Wilke of Weissenfels who has performed here, and 12 talers for his daughter who performed with the capelle a few times";[76] one notes that the nineteen-year-old singer earned twice as much as her father (but possibly for several performances).

If, in passing through Weissenfels on his August trip to Schleiz, Bach indeed visited the Wilcke family, it could not have been a first encounter with Magdalena because she had been in Cöthen in June. Was she there, then, for an audition, and was Bach now offering her a job? Had she already been given the position in June, and was Bach now visiting with the parents in order to ask for their daughter's hand? Quite possibly, Magdalena joined the Cöthen capelle around or before June 15, 1721, in the high-ranking post of chamber musician. In this case, Bach must have been assured of her extraordinary qualifications, either from an audition at some point in the spring or from a performance on some earlier occasion (the latter may have happened at the neighboring court of Anhalt-Zerbst).[77] Considering the close connections between the various central German principalities, the audition may have been held in any of several places. Moreover, considering the complex interrelationships among the musicians and their families, it would have been unusual for Bach not to have encountered at some time the extended Wilcke family of musicians.[78]

When Magdalena Wilcke celebrated her twentieth birthday in Cöthen on September 22, 1721, having reached top rank and pay in a princely capelle with her first professional appointment (above that of her father and brother),[79] she could rightfully anticipate a most promising career as a singer. And she definitely planned to continue her professional life when the capellmeister asked her to marry him. Bach himself supported her intention, and thus she remained fully active in the capelle until their move to Leipzig. The Bach household had continued to run smoothly, managed by Johann Sebastian's sister-in-law Friedelena Bach, with the help of a maid named Anna Elisabeth.[80] Still, when on December 3, 1721—nearly one and a half years after Maria Barbara Bach's death—the widowed Johann Sebastian Bach and Anna Magdalena Wilcke "were married at home, by command of the Prince,"[81] it certainly brought a dramatic and generally uplifting change for Bach and his four children. And they seem to have celebrated the happy event in opulent style. Around the time of the wedding, Bach contracted a major shipment of Rhine wine, at a discount granted him by the Cöthen *Ratskeller:* four pails and eight quarts (one pail = sixty-four quarts) for 84 talers 16 groschen (more than a fifth of his annual salary).[82] In all likelihood, the wedding was attended by many members of the Bach and Wilcke families and by friends and colleagues at the Cöthen court, as the date selected for the ceremony, the Wednesday after the first Sunday in Advent, insured that weekend church obligations would not prevent any of the guests, most of them musicians, from attending.

Probably not long after the wedding but sometime in 1722, Anna Magdalena started an album in which Johann Sebastian entered compositions for her to play in order to improve and cultivate her keyboard skills or that he would play to entertain her. She herself wrote the title page, *Clavier-Büchlein vor Anna Magdalena Bachin, Anno 1722,* and a few headings, but the musical entries are written exclusively in Johann Sebastian's hand. They include, at the beginning, composing scores of five short yet highly refined harpsichord suites, BWV 812–816—first versions of pieces that would eventually become the set of the six so-called *French Suites.* Besides these suites of stylish dances, representing the most fashionable genre of galant keyboard music, the album also includes a chorale prelude on "Jesu, meine Zuversicht," BWV 728, and an easy-to-play (unfinished) *Fantasia pro Organo* in C major, BWV 573, indicating that Bach wanted his wife to feel at home on his own instrument as well. Unfortunately, as the album has survived in a dreadfully mutilated state, with only twenty-five leaves remaining out of about seventy to seventy-five, the precious document provides information that is more suggestive than exhaustive about the couple's intimate and serious musical companionship.

By around the time of their first anniversary and two years after the Hamburg trip, Bach made a serious bid for the position of cantor at St. Thomas's and music director in Leipzig, which had fallen vacant with the death on June 5, 1722, of Johann Kuhnau. What motivated him? He had apparently grown frustrated with the Cöthen situation and did not see much of a future there—despite the fact that his good relations with Prince Leopold had not changed and that he had, as he later put it, "intended to spend the rest of my life" at the court. The capelle budget suffered a cut in 1722 that signaled trouble; to make things worse, the violinist Martin Friedrich Marcus had to be dismissed and was not replaced. Some long-standing internal quarrels within the princely family flashed up noticeably in August 1722 over issues of power sharing and feudal pensions that undermined Prince Leopold's authority and resulted in severe losses of income for his court.[83] Leopold's continuing health problems posed an additional risk for Bach. Moreover, the smoldering religious feud between two Protestant constituencies—the Lutheran minority championed by the princess mother versus the Calvinist majority supported by the reigning prince and his retinue—was now directly affecting Bach's family. For example, the fact that he and Anna Magdalena had been married at home, following the custom for second marriages, meant that Bach—a Lutheran marrying a Lutheran—was exempted from paying the fee of 10 talers to the Lutheran St. Agnus Church. But since the exemption had been made "by command of the prince," thus establishing an unwelcome precedent, it resulted in an official, annoying complaint.[84] A more serious situation arose out of some setbacks to the Lutheran school that Bach's children attended. A memorandum to the princess mother dated 1722 addresses the lack of space and shortage of teachers, citing an extreme example of 117 children being lumped into one class. In addition, the theological, educational, and moral qualifications of the school's inspector, St. Agnus pastor Paulus Berger, were earnestly in question.[85] All this commotion in the court and school formed the immediate background for Bach's intentions "to seek his fortune elsewhere," a phrase he also used in his 1730 letter to Georg Erdmann.[86]

News about Leipzig, about forty miles away, was not hard to come by in Cöthen. On August 11, 1722, without much delay, the Leipzig town council had elected Georg Philipp Telemann to the cantorate. Having begun his musical career in 1701 in Leipzig, where, as a law student at the university, he founded a Collegium Musicum and also served briefly as organist and music director of the New Church before he departed for Sorau in 1704,[87] Telemann was well remembered in the city. He also fulfilled the ambitious expectations of the council in that he was a famous musician who, both as music director in Frankfurt and then as cantor and music director in Hamburg, had held comparable municipal positions. In many ways, Telemann was a natural choice, but after weighing his options seriously for three months, he declined the appointment in November 1722. The Hamburg city council had improved his financial situation so that the Leipzig post no longer seemed as attractive, even though the musical and academic establishment at St. Thomas's was better than that at the Johanneum. Also, Hamburg let him simultaneously take over the directorship of the opera at the Goose Market and the leadership of the Collegium Musicum, an offer that ultimately must have tipped the balance. Since Telemann auditioned for the St. Thomas post in August, he would have passed two times through Cöthen on his way to and from Leipzig. It is quite possible that he interrupted his trip at least once, probably on his return to Hamburg, to see his friend Bach and his eight-year-old godchild Carl Philipp Emanuel. Thus Bach may have learned about Telemann's negotiations and, later, even about the turn of his plans before anyone in Leipzig knew. Was it perhaps Telemann himself who encouraged Bach to throw his hat into the ring when the competition was reopened?

The Leipzig authorities were now back where they had started, and the inner city council—the executive body of the larger, three-tiered council—began, at a meeting on November 23, 1722, to reevaluate the remaining five of the original set of candidates from which they had chosen Telemann: Johann Friedrich Fasch, capellmeister to the court of Anhalt-Zerbst; Georg Lembke, cantor in Laucha; Christian Friedrich Rolle, cantor at St. John's in Magdeburg; Georg Balthasar Schott, organist and music director at the New Church in Leipzig; and Johann Martin Steindorff, cantor at the cathedral of St. Mary in Zwickau.[88] Also, two new names had come up in the meantime: Andreas Christoph Duve, cantor at St. Mary's in Brunswick, and Georg Friedrich Kauff-mann, organist and music director in Merseburg. But the councillors were unable to agree on a rank list of these seven, and they also disagreed about the selection criteria. Two factions with conflicting views had formed, one primarily interested in an academically trained, solid teacher, the other chiefly in a musical luminary who would help upgrade the city's rather dull musical scene and make it more comparable to places like Frankfurt and Hamburg, not to mention their electoral Saxon capital of Dresden, on which the more ambitious of the Leipzig councillors kept a permanent eye.

By the time of the next meeting on December 21, another two names had sprung up: Christoph Graupner, capellmeister to the court of Hesse-Darmstadt, and Johann Sebastian Bach. According to the council minutes, Burgomaster Gottfried Lange presented

> those who were to be subjected to examination for the cantorate . . . namely, Capellmeister Graupner in Darmstadt and Bach in Cöthen; Fasch, on the other hand, declared that he could not teach, along with his other duties, and the candidate from Merseburg requested again that he be admitted to examination.
>
> *Resolved:* Rolle, Kauffmann, and also Schott should be admitted to examination, especially with regard to the teaching.[89]

The stage was now set for the second round, and the group headed by the influential Burgomaster Lange, who also chaired the board of the St. Thomas Church and who had previously been a law professor at Leipzig University and a government official in Dresden, prevailed. Two court capellmeisters, Graupner and Bach, turned out to be the favorites; the third capellmeister, Fasch, was dropped from consideration because he "could not teach." Graupner was ranked ahead of Bach, for two reasons. First, like Telemann, he was a familiar figure in Leipzig; an alumnus of the St. Thomas School, he had also been a private pupil of former cantors Schelle and Kuhnau. Second, from 1704 to 1706, he had studied law at Leipzig University. In fact, the only major candidate without a university education was Bach (all his predecessors in the St. Thomas cantorate since the sixteenth century and all his successors until well into the nineteenth century were university trained)—evidence that the Leipzig authorities had no doubts about Bach's academic qualifications and chose in his case to ignore all conventions. Besides, Bach was by no means unknown in Leipzig. In 1717, he had examined the new organ at St. Paul's Church upon the invitation of the university; and Burgomeister Lange, at a later point in the proceedings of the city council, pointedly remarked that "Bach excels at the keyboard."[90] Lange, who had been a ministerial assistant to Count Flemming in Dresden at the time of the Marchand affair, may have been one among "the large company of persons of high rank" who heard Bach play at the count's mansion.

The clear preference given to the two candidates of capellmeister rank is also reflected in the fact that each was asked to present two cantatas, one before and one after the sermon, at his audition, set for the second Sunday after Epiphany (January 17, 1723, Graupner) and Estomihi Sunday (February 7, Bach). The other candidates had to content themselves with one cantata performance each.[91] Graupner, however, received special recognition in that he was invited to present, outside of the officially scheduled cantorate trials, a Magnificat for the 1722 Christmas Vespers at St. Thomas's and St. Nicholas's Churches. Two days before his audition, on January 15, the city council discussed the cantor's appointment again and basically agreed, in advance of the formal trial performance, to offer Graupner the job, with the warning from Burgomaster Lange that "precaution should be taken to see that he could obtain dismissal from his court."[92] Meanwhile, in Cöthen, Bach prepared for *his* audition by setting to music two texts that were sent to him from Leipzig, "Jesus nahm zu sich die Zwölfe" (in a six-movement structure) and "Du wahrer Gott und Davids Sohn" (in three movements), cantata poetry that closely resembles the verses found in Graupner's audition pieces, "Lobet den Herrn, alle Heiden" (seven movements) and "Aus der Tiefen rufen wir" (three movements). The poet is not known, but the most probable candidate seems to have been Burgomaster Lange, who not only had a track record as a poet and opera librettist[93] but also showed a keen personal interest in shaping the Kuhnau succession in what he thought would be the right way. Would that turn out to be the right way for Bach as well? Perhaps composing texts of the kind he had not set since Weimar helped Bach overcome doubts he harbored about making the right move: "At first, indeed, it did not seem at all proper for me to change my position of Capellmeister for that of Cantor. Wherefore, then, I postponed my decision for a quarter of a year; but this post was described to me in such favorable terms that finally (particularly since my sons seemed inclined toward [university] studies) I cast my lot, in the name of the Lord, and made the journey to Leipzig, took my examination, and then made the change of position."[94]

When Bach arrived in Leipzig for his examination and audition, he brought along with him the finished cantata scores and most of the performing parts. On February 8, the Monday after the cantorate trial, he was reimbursed 20 talers for his expenses, the same amount allowed Telemann, though Bach had a much shorter distance to travel, suggesting that he stayed in Leipzig for more than a week. (Telemann spent exactly two weeks there when he auditioned the previous year.) Bach and the Leipzig authorities needed time for all kinds of discussions relating to the position, but of utmost importance for Bach were the preparations for performing the two cantatas, "Jesus nahm zu sich die Zwölfe," BWV 22 (for SATB, oboe, strings, and continuo), and "Du wahrer Gott und Davids Sohn," BWV 23 (for SATB, 2 oboi d'amore, strings, and continuo). These were ambitious compositions: BWV 23, with its expansive duet solos, clearly follows the model of the Cöthen congratulatory cantatas, while BWV 22 more readily foreshadows the cantata type that would prevail in the first months of Bach's tenure as the new cantor. From the original sources of the two works, we can deduce that the performing materials brought along from Cöthen needed to be completed. We can see as well that Bach decided to extend BWV 23 by one movement, the elaborate chorale setting "Christe, du Lamm Gottes," BWV 23/4, adding to the orchestra a cornetto and three trombones to double the choir parts and giving the work, with the text and melody of the German Agnus Dei, a more liturgical character. This movement was not a newly composed piece but was taken from a finished work, most likely the Weimar (or Gotha) Passion of 1717, BC D1, which Bach brought along to Leipzig in his baggage—perhaps to be able to show an example of a large-scale composition, perhaps to offer it for performance in case such a work was needed for the upcoming Good Friday Vespers. The need apparently did not arise, but in the added finale to BWV 23 the people in Leipzig were given a taste of what such a work might be like. Although hardly anyone would have known then how promising it really was, newpapers in Leipzig and elsewhere reported on the audition for the cantorate by the "the Hon. Capellmeister of Cöthen, Mr. Bach . . . the music of the same having been amply praised on that occasion by all knowledgeable persons."[95] Oddly, and perhaps significantly, none of the other auditions left a trail in the newspapers.

Despite the favorable impression left in Leipzig, Bach returned to Cöthen without the promise of a job; Graupner had been chosen before Bach had even arrived on the scene. But Lange's fears came true: Landgrave Ernst Ludwig of

Hesse-Darmstadt did not grant his capellmeister the requested dismissal, and Graupner was forced to decline the Leipzig offer, as he informed the Leipzig authorities on March 22. On April 9, almost two weeks after Easter, the city council returned to the matter of the cantorate, but unfortunately the minutes of this important meeting have survived only incompletely. We can see, though, that the faction preferring a teacher-cantor took the lead: after

the man who had been favored[Graupner] . . . the others in view were the Capellmeister at Cöthen, Bach; Kauffmann in Merseburg; and Schott here, but none of the three would be able to teach [academic subjects] also, and in Telemann's case consideration had already been given to a division [of the duties].

*Appeals Councillor Platz:* The latter suggestion he considered for several reasons somewhat questionable; since the best could not be obtained, a mediocre one would have to be accepted; many good things had once been said about a man in Pirna.[96]

Here the minutes break off, with the sixty-five-year-old Abraham Christoph Platz recalling what he had heard about someone whose name he could not remember: Christian Heckel, cantor in Pirna, who seemed competent in teaching both music and academic subjects (Latin grammar and Luther's Catechism were traditionally the cantor's domain). Platz urged the council to turn away from the best musicians (like Telemann, Graupner, Bach, Kauffmann, and Schott) and instead look for the best teachers, even if their musical qualifications were only "mediocre." Though the rest of the arguments pro and con remain unknown, Lange and his followers somehow persuaded the council to reach a compromise with respect to the teaching function and to make Bach an offer. Having learned a lesson about unpredictable sovereign rulers, the council invited Bach back to Leipzig and asked him to sign a preliminary pledge that he would

not only within three or, at the most, four weeks from this date make myself free of the engagement given me at the Court of the Prince of Anhalt-Cöthen, but also, when I actually enter upon the duties of the said post of Cantor, conduct myself according to the School Regulations now in effect or to be put into effect; and especially I will instruct the boys admitted into the School not only in the regular classes established for that purpose but also, without special compensation, in private singing lessons. I will also faithfully attend to whatever else is incumbent upon me, and furthermore, but not without the previous knowledge and consent of a Noble and Wise Council, in case someone should be needed to assist me in the instruction in the Latin language, will faithfully and without ado compensate the said person out of my own pocket.[97]

On April 19, when Bach put his signature under this pledge, he already knew that his patron had generously granted him the dismissal: a letter, signed by Prince Leopold on April 13, was in the mail. It refers to the service of "the Respectable and Learned Johann Sebastian Bach, since August 5, 1717, as Capellmeister and Director of Our Chamber Music," and states "that we have at all times been well content with his discharge of his duties, but the said Bach, wishing now to seek his fortune elsewhere, has accordingly most humbly petitioned Us to grant him a most gracious dismissal, now therefore We have been pleased graciously to grant him the same and to give him highest recommendation for service elsewhere."[98]

On April 22, shortly after the arrival of the prince's letter, the entire city council, this time in a joint assembly of all three councils, moved to proceed with Bach's election. First, Burgomaster Lange summarized the long process by recounting how Telemann "had not kept his promise" and by clarifying that Graupner had privately (but never formally) been offered the job, but that "he could not obtain his dismissal." He then turned to the new candidate: "Bach was Capellmeister in Cöthen and excelled on the clavier. Besides music he had the teaching equipment; and the Cantor must give instruction in the *Colloquia Corderi* [a textbook of piety, letters, and behavior] and in grammar, which he was willing to do. He had formally undertaken to give not only public but also private instruction. If Bach were chosen, Telemann, in view of his conduct, might be forgotten."[99]

Councillor Platz spoke next, emphasizing that Bach "must accommodate himself to the instruction of the youth. Bach was fitted for this and willing to do it, and accordingly he cast his vote for him." Since the two antagonists had now reached agreement, the entire council voted unanimously for Bach. The burgomaster concluded the meeting, but not without mentioning another crucial point that spoke in favor of Bach. He noted that "it was necessary to be sure to get a famous man, in order to inspire the [university] students." Because the church music in Leipzig traditionally depended on qualified student performers, whom Johann Kuhnau had had trouble attracting, Lange was confident that the new appointment would change that situation for the better and that things generally "would turn out well." And he must then have appreciated the letter that Christoph Graupner, after learning the outcome, wrote on May 4, assuring the city council that Bach is "a musician just as strong on the organ as he is expert in church works and capelle pieces," and one who "will honestly and properly perform the functions entrusted to him."[100]

Not all the technical details of the appointment were settled when Bach returned to Cöthen to inform his patron of his official election to the distinguished post at St. Thomas's and to prepare himself and his family for a major, almost instant change in their lives. About two and a half months earlier, on his way home after the Leipzig audition, the outcome had been uncertain. He may then have thought back to Hamburg in 1720, Halle in 1713, and even

Sangerhausen in 1702 and realized that he had never lost an audition, however complicated the subsequent deliberations had become. And complicated they became once again, but the outcome was finally clear and right. What may have gone through his mind is hinted at in his 1730 letter to Erdmann: "it pleased God that I should be called hither to be Director Musices and Cantor at the St. Thomas School."[101]


## A Canon of Principles, and Pushing the Limits

In the fall of 1722, when Bach submitted his application for the Kuhnau succession, he must have realized that he would need to present his credentials as a competent instructor of music. A simple declaration of willingness and readiness to teach would not suffice, and evidence of pertinent experience would be due at the interviews conducted, at the time of the public audition, by the rector of the St. Thomas School, M. Johann Heinrich Ernesti, and possibly by members of the inner council. There was certainly no need to prove himself as a musician outside the audition, but he held no university degree, nor had he ever studied at a university. His academic background was shaped by the excellent schools he had attended; he had received top grades and, after all, graduated from the acclaimed St. Michael's School in Lüneburg, an institution of supra-regional reputation—although by now, his education lay twenty years back. In the meantime, while he had never engaged in any school or classroom teaching, he had nonetheless developed considerable experience in the private instruction of individual students. Having attracted private pupils early on and having maintained an active and growing teaching studio ever since, he knew well that he was a passionate and successful teacher. But how could he demonstrate this to his examiners?

In reviewing his studio practices, Bach probably realized that he could, in fact, produce tangible evidence of having developed innovative and unparalleled instructional materials. Always, his teaching of keyboard instruments went well beyond the drill of mere technical skills and included an introduction to basic musical systems, especially to the principles of musical composition. With particular care, he had prepared the instruction of his ten-year-old firstborn with the *Clavier-Büchlein vor Wilhelm Friedemann Bach* (1720). He began with a quick review of the tone system (clefs, pitches, and registers of voices), ornaments, and fingering, spending no more than three pages on these preliminary matters. He then turned to little preludes, chorale elaborations, dance settings, a group of more substantial preludes in different keys (including such remote and difficult keys as C-sharp minor and E-flat minor), a simple fugue, fifteen praeambula in strict two-part counterpoint (all in different keys, in ascending and descending order), followed by fifteen strict three-part fantasias (organized in the same manner), and suites by Telemann, Johann Christoph Richter, and Gottfried Heinrich Stölzel—all interspersed with the young student's own exercises in composition. The various compositional models, examples of which are found in this Little Clavier Book, he had either already collected elsewhere more systematically (for example, the short chorale preludes of the Weimar *Orgel-Büchlein*) or would soon undertake to compile (as in *The Well-Tempered Clavier,* a collection of preludes and fugues written over the years that included some of the preludes from the Friedemann Bach Book and the *Aufrichtige Anleitung* [Upright Instruction],[102] a revised version of the praeambula and fantasias from the Friedemann Bach Book).

The manuscript sources themselves provide no conclusive information on how far *The Well-Tempered Clavier* or the *Aufrichtige Anleitung* had progressed by the time Bach began preparing himself as a candidate for St. Thomas's. Both autograph scores are fair copies and dated 1722 and 1723, respectively. The context clearly suggests, however, that the two manuscripts were completed in the fall and winter of 1722–23 and that their corresponding title pages, including that added to the *Orgel-Büchlein,* were conceived in conjunction with Bach's application to the cantorate. All three elaborate titles emphasize the pedagogical intent and method of the materials contained in the volumes and introduce Bach as the author of exemplary and serviceable textbooks.

(1) "**The Well-Tempered Clavier,** or preludes and fugues through all the tones and semitones, both as regards the *tertia major* or *Ut Re Mi* and as concerns the *tertia minor* or *Re Mi Fa.* For the use and profit of the musical youth desirous of learning as well as for the pastime of those already skilled in this study" [a volume of 90 pages in folio format, dated 1722].

(2) "**Aufrichtige Anleitung,** wherein the lovers of the clavier, and especially those desirous of learning, are shown a clear way not only (1) to learn to play clearly in two voices but also, after further progress, (2) to deal correctly and well with three obbligato parts; furthermore, at the same time not only to have good *inventiones* but to develop the same well and, above all, to arrive at a singing style in playing and at the same time to acquire a strong foretaste of composition" [a volume of 62 pages in quarto format, dated 1723].

(3) "**Orgel-Büchlein,** in which a beginner at the organ is given instruction in developing a chorale in many divers ways, and at the same time in acquiring facility in the study of the pedal since in the chorales contained therein the pedal is treated as wholly obbligato.

> In Praise of the Almighty's will
> and for my neighbor's greater skill."

[A volume of 182 pages (many unfilled) in quarto format; undated and primarily written in Weimar; the title page was added in Cöthen, ca. 1722–23.]

None of these collections was specifically composed for Leipzig, but the final preparation of the fair copies of *The Well-Tempered Clavier* and the *Aufrichtige Anleitung* and, in particular, the carefully coordinated phraseology of all three title pages would have gone a long way toward impressing the authorities in Leipzig, especially an experienced master teacher like rector Ernesti. Bach's organist, concertmaster, and capellmeister background would have sufficed to establish his credentials as music director and leader of vocal-instrumental ensembles, but private instrumental lessons and especially keyboard instruction was an integral part of the cantor's daily activity at St. Thomas's. (Indeed, most resident students of the school had a keyboard instrument in their study cubicles.)[103] Therefore, these keyboard volumes epitomizing a fundamentally pragmatic approach to musical science would not only demonstrate Bach's didactic experience but, more important, underscore his stature as musical scholar, deemed essential for a successor to the learned Johann Kuhnau and for as ambitious and demanding an academic environment as St. Thomas's.

Not without reason did Prince Leopold, in his wonderfully supportive letter of dismissal, characterize Bach as "well learned" in order to introduce him into his new Latin school ambience: the new cantor, ranking in the faculty hierarchy of the school immediately below the rector and conrector, deserved proper recognition as *musicus bene doctus* or *musicus pereruditus.* At the time, Leopold knew and understood his capellmeister better than most, and he could genuinely appreciate the kind of musical science represented in a work such as *The Well-Tempered Clavier.* The three collections offer a systematic exploration of clearly defined musical goals in the form of well-structured, sophisticated keyboard exercises and lessons addressing the various needs of "the musical youth," the "beginner at the organ," and generally "those desirous of learning." And the *Orgel-Büchlein*'s title page summarizes Bach's pedagogical credo in a homespun poetic two-liner: "in Praise of the Almighty's will / and for my neighbor's greater skill" ("Dem Höchsten Gott allein zu Ehren / dem Nechsten, draus sich zu belehren").

In the *Aufrichtige Anleitung,* Bach demonstrates, in two sets of fifteen contrapuntal pieces, how a coherent musical setting can be developed out of a single short and clearly delineated yet freely conceived idea (*inventio,* or invention), first in the form of strict two-part compositions (one voice each for the right and left hands) with emphasis on voice leading; then in the form of strict three-part compositions, with emphasis on triadic harmonies, that is, on three voices "sounding together" (*sinfonia,* from the Greek *symphonia*). At the same time, the book teaches basic keyboard technique and fingering—in the first in-

vention, for example, the basic motive demands through-

out the absolutely equal use of all five fingers of both hands—as well as a
"singing style" of performance. Additionally, Bach explores the diatonic range
of the tonal system without straying beyond the traditional framework of the
fifteen keys (not exceeding four sharps or flats) that are playable in unequal
temperament (a system of tuning in which the octave had not yet been divided
into twelve equal semitones) and that endow each key with a distinct character. In the *Aufrichtige Anleitung,* Bach decided to organize the inventions and
sinfonias systematically in an ascending key scheme; the earlier version of the
collection presented the pieces in ascending and descending order, pursuing a
different kind of structural logic—six ascending "white" keys, C to A, with
their "natural" root triads (C major, D minor, . . . to A minor) followed by nine
descending keys, B to C, with root triads requiring sharps and flats (B minor,
B-flat major, . . . to C minor; see Table 7.6).

The revised key structure of the *Aufrichtige Anleitung* conforms to the
uniformly ascending key scheme of *The Well-Tempered Clavier,* but illustrates
how to differentiate between the conventional diatonic scheme, on the one
hand, and the fully developed chromatic scheme of twenty-four keys based
on the premise of equal temperament, on the other. Bach's use of Andreas
Werckmeister's term "well-tempered" (*wohl temperirt*) indicates his preference for a slightly modified system of tuning with "all the thirds sharp,"[104]
enabling him to play in all twenty-four keys without losing the characteristic features of individual keys—a loss that occurs if the octave is divided
into absolutely equal semitones (what was to become a new standard would

## TABLE 7.6. Diatonic vs. Chromatic Keys—Unequal Temperament vs. a Well-Tempered System

*Aufrichtige Anleitung,* BWV 772–801
   Preambles and Fantasias (1720 version):
      C → d → e → F → G → a → b ← B♭ ← A ← g ← f ← E ← E♭ ← D ← c
   Inventions and Sinfonias (1723 version):
      C - c → D - d → E♭ → E → e → F - f → G - g → A - a → B♭ → b
*The Well-Tempered Clavier,* BWV 846–869
   Preludes and Fugues (1722):
      C-c → C♯-c♯ → D-d → E♭-e♭(d♯)ᵃ → E-e → F-f → F♯-f♯ → G-g → A♭-g♯♭ →
      A-a → B♭-b♭ → B-b

---

Capital letters = major mode; lowercase letters = minor mode.
→ = move to higher key, ← = move to lower key.
ᵃEnharmonic demonstration within minor mode: Prelude in e♭ (6 flats), Fugue in d♯ (6 sharps).
ᵇEnharmonic demonstration contrasting major and minor modes: A♭ (major) vs. g♯ (minor).

have been regarded then as a serious drawback). Bach's primary purpose in writing *The Well-Tempered Clavier*, then, was to demonstrate in practice the musical manageability of all twenty-four chromatic keys, a system that earlier had been considered only theoretically. Before and around 1700, the general spirit of discovery spurred by the Scientific Revolution had prompted a new spurt of mathematical and physical research, predominantly by German scholars like Werckmeister, to expand and systematize the conventional tonal system. Johann David Heinichen, a student of the Thomascantor Kuhnau, had by 1710 devised the circle of fifths, clarifying the harmonic interrelationships within a system of twenty-four modes or keys,[105] and several composers wrote small experimental pieces in remote keys. But as late as 1717, Johann Mattheson still deplored that "although all keys can now, per temperament [tuning], be arranged in such a way that they can be used very well, diatonically, chromatically, and enharmonically," a true *demonstratio* was lacking.[106] It fell to Bach, who accepted this challenge, to demonstrate the compositional practicability of the new system of twenty-four keys, and he did so on an unparalleled level of compositional refinement and technical perfection.

*The Well-Tempered Clavier* established the parameters of a twenty-four-key system, with twelve major and minor modes (since the terms "major" and "minor" were not yet in general use, Bach's title describes the modes in terms of the determining interval of a major or minor third). The "theme" of every Prelude and Fugue, therefore, is first and foremost its key, as shown in the most basic form at the beginning of the collection. The first Prelude introduces the C-major key in its most rudimentary form, the C-major triad, as a point of departure; the Fugue then completes the demonstration by introducing C major in terms of horizontal harmony, that is, by way of a linear subject that defines the key. This quasi-system of vertical and horizontal definition of the keys is pursued throughout the work. Bach also shows how to preserve the idiosyncrasies of the individual keys: in E minor, for example, he continues a tendency to stress the old Phrygian subsidiary "dominants" of the key—A minor and C major—that resulted from the need to avoid the B-major triad, which sounds extremely harsh in unequal temperament. The unique collection of twenty-four preludes and fugues also aspires to a second goal, the juxtaposition of two fundamentally different kinds of polyphonic musical settings: improvisatory and free-style scoring in the preludes versus thematically controlled and strict contrapuntal voice leading in the fugues. The preludes therefore present a wide variety of textural choices, from rudimentary chordal models (such as the *arpeggiando* and *perpetuum mobile* styles of the first two) to dance-type and imitative polyphonic settings. Fugal technique, on the other hand, is presented in various kinds of scoring, using two (1 fugue), three (11 fugues), four (10 fugues), and five voices (2 fugues). Additionally, the use of all metric categories (**c**, **¢**, 3/4, 3/8, 6/4, 6/8, 9/8, 12/8, 12/16, 24/16), different stylistic models, and a multiplicity of special compositional features contributes to the overall kaleidoscopic spectrum of the collection.

More than any other of Bach's works composed before 1722, the preludes and fugues of *The Well-Tempered Clavier* manifest his resolve to leave nothing untried, even if it meant exploring avenues where no one had gone before. In demonstrating that the tonal system could be expanded to twenty-four keys not just theoretically but practically, Bach set a milestone in the history of music whose overall implications for chromatic harmony would take another century to be fully realized. He set the stage by exploiting fully the chromatic and enharmonic potential of the keys, especially in pieces such as the fugues in C-sharp minor (BWV 849/2), E Minor (BWV 855/2), F minor (BWV 857/2), F-sharp minor (BWV 859/2), and B minor (BWV 869/2). Each individual piece, whether prelude or fugue, helped push the limits of musical composition, resulting in twenty-four diverse yet internally unified structures of musical logic. Simultaneously, standards of musical performance were brought to a new high if only in the necessary and uncompromising application of all ten fingers of the keyboard player.

In establishing a multifaceted canon of technical standards and compositional and aesthetic principles, *The Well-Tempered Clavier* is complemented, and in part preceded, by works of similarly profound ambitions. Both the *Orgel-Büchlein* and the *Aufrichtige Anleitung* explore how to invent, develop, and elaborate on a precisely delineated musical idea, one that is either derived from given material (such as the melody and affect of a hymn) or freely conceived. In a similar systematic way, both also focus on the buildup of stylistically appropriate performing skills (*cantabile,* or "singing," for example) for two hands managing a two- or three-part contrapuntal structure on the harpsichord, or for two hands and two feet negotiating the complex textures of an organ setting. But as we may ascertain by comparing the Weimar *Orgel-Büchlein* with the later collections, the refined and advanced compositional art that characterizes the Cöthen repertoire emerged gradually over the years. And although keyboard works play a decisive role in this respect—harpsichord and organ functioning as his experimental laboratory—Bach's musical efforts were from the outset much more encompassing and covered a broad range of instrumental and vocal compositions.

We can easily discern Bach's experimental forays by looking at his Cöthen repertoire: works either composed in Cöthen or written in Weimar and revised and collected in Cöthen. The serious losses of Bach's vocal output are unfortunately paralleled in the instrumental realm—with the possible exception of the keyboard works—although we cannot judge the extent since the Obituary describes that part of Bach's musical estate simply as "a mass of . . . instrumental pieces of all sorts and for all kinds of instruments."[107] Yet regardless of the fragmentary transmission, and even limiting our focus to the collections for which dated (or datable) original sources have survived, the Cöthen works as a group are strikingly consistent in their high quality and common purpose (see Table 7.7).

In the keyboard category, the *French Suites* supplement the other collections by adding a crucial genre of composition (*sans prélude,* without prelude) otherwise missing. Taken together with the *English Suites,* BWV 806–811, *avec prélude* (with prelude) and of earlier origin, they demonstrate a new level of achievement in this genre, not just by concentrating on the suite type *sans prélude* but also by presenting more compact and more sharply focused stylizations of the traditional dances. In the non-keyboard categories, Bach's compositional choices indicate clearly that here, too, he preferred to travel

## TABLE 7.7. Instrumental Collections from the Cöthen Period

| BWV | Work | Date | Remarks |
|---|---|---|---|
| | **Keyboard works** | | |
| | Clavier Book for | | |
| | Wilhelm Friedemann: | 1720ff. | autograph |
| 772–801 | 15 Praeambula and 15 Fantasias | | —predominantly |
| 924–932 | 9 Preludes | | composing scores |
| 846ff. | 11 Preludes | | |
| | Clavier Book for Anna Magdalena: | 1722ff. | autograph |
| 812–817 | 5 *French Suites (sans prélude)* | | —composing score |
| | *The Well-Tempered Clavier:* | 1722 | autograph |
| 846–869 | 24 Preludes and Fugues | | —fair copy, revised |
| | *Aufrichtige Anleitung:* | 1723 | autograph |
| 772–801 | 15 Inventions and 15 Sinfonias | | —fair copy, revised |
| | *Orgel-Büchlein:* | 1723 | autograph (Weimar |
| 599–644 | 45 organ Chorales | | origin)—title page added in Cöthen |
| | **Solo and ensemble works** | | |
| 1001–1006 | *Sei Solo. . . . Libro Primo* | 1720 | autograph |
| | 6 Partitas and Sonatas for violin solo | | —fair copy, revised |
| 1007–1012 | [*Sei Solo. . . . Libro Secondo*][108] | ? | Anna Magdalena Bach's copy, c. 1728 |
| | 6 Suites for violoncello solo | | |
| 1046–1051 | *Concerts avec plusieurs instruments* | 1721 | autograph |
| | 6 "Brandenburg Concertos" | | —fair copy, revised |

completely untrodden musical paths. Indeed, both collections of unaccompanied violin and cello pieces create the maximum effect with a minimum of instrumental "tools." Once again, Bach the quintessential instrumentalist raises and redefines the technical standards of performing by fully exploiting the idiomatic qualities of the violin and cello. Remarkably, the free improvisatory and strict imitative realizations of his sonata-style movements and his suite (partita) dances with their rhythmic and textural flair reveal no deficiencies whatsoever when compared with the keyboard works from the same period. In fact, the transcription of the four-part Fugue in G minor for solo violin (BWV 1001/2) as an organ Fugue (BWV 539/2) shows how music originally designed to be played on the four strings of a violin does not, when performed on the manuals and pedal of an organ, gain in a structural sense: the two versions are merely a translation from one instrumental idiom into another.

Bach's unaccompanied violin and cello compositions also epitomize virtuosity, and, on account of their singularity, to a degree even greater than his keyboard works of comparable technical demands. Both sets of solo pieces demonstrate Bach's command of performing techniques but also his ability to bring into play, without even an accompanying bass part, dense counterpoint and refined harmony with distinctive and well-articulated rhythmic designs, especially in the dance movements. Instrumental virtuosity is displayed on a less intense yet larger scale in the *Brandenburg Concertos,* a collection of six *Concerts avec plusieurs instruments* (concertos with several Instruments)—so called in the original score because the pieces feature the concerto genre in varying configurations of solo instruments. "Several instruments" actually understates the case, for Bach makes use, again in a systematic manner, of the widest imaginable spectrum of orchestral instruments. The modest title does not begin to suggest the degree of innovation exhibited in the daring combinations, as Bach once again enters uncharted territory. Every one of the six concertos set a precedent in its scoring, and every one was to remain without parallel.

The design of the concertos reflects the composer's own choice and shows no evidence of any external influence as, for example, a request from a commissioning patron. Moreover, contrary to conventional wisdom, the collection does not reflect specific structure of ensembles available either to the margrave of Brandenburg or to the prince of Anhalt-Cöthen. In any case, the origin of most if not all of these concertos, at least in their earliest versions, most likely predates Bach's Cöthen appointment. Their overall layout as well as voice-leading details, thematic-motivic treatment, and imitative polyphony definitely predate the standards set by *The Well-Tempered Clavier.* But there is a further consideration that argues against a Cöthen origin. Eighteenth-century protocol would have required Bach, while in the employ of Prince Leopold, to obtain formal permission for dedicating such a work to another sovereign, and it is hard to imagine that Bach could have submitted to the margrave of Brandenburg a bundle of works originally written for the prince of Anhalt-Cöthen—especially if the prince was fond of them and considered them his property. We can therefore assume that Bach carefully selected from outside the restricted Cöthen contingent the best of his concerto compositions that would properly fit into an uncommon collection. In the end, the six concertos embody a repertoire fashioned more for its instrumental diversity than for any other reason.

The selection criteria appear to follow a scheme that highlights in half a dozen examples a maximum number of different solo instruments and their combinations (see Table 7.8). All three orchestral families are included, with their main subspecies: brass instruments with trumpet and French horn (corno da caccia); woodwinds with recorder (flauto and flauto d'echo),[109] transverse flute, oboe, and bassoon; and strings with violin, piccolo violin, viola, cello, and viola da gamba. The only instrument lacking a solo function is the double bass (violone), a pivotal member of the continuo group, while another component of the continuo group, the harpsichord, is assigned a prominent, indeed exceptional, obbligato part.

Bach juxtaposes the solo groups and their *ripieno* support in the opening and finale movements—modifications are made for the middle movements—with highly imaginative choices: a rich array of brass, woodwinds, and strings in an eleven-part score in Concerto No. 1; a heterogeneous treble solo of trumpet, recorder, oboe, and violin in Concerto No. 2; and a trio of violin and 2 echo recorders, where the dominating concertato violin alternatively functions as a *bassetto* (high bass) in Concerto No. 4. Even more surprising is Bach's treatment

**TABLE 7.8.** *Concerts avec plusieurs instruments* ("Brandenburg Concertos"): Scoring

|  | Solo | Ripieno |
|---|---|---|
| Concerto 1 (F major) | *2 corni da caccia, 3 oboes, bassoon, violino piccolo* | *2 violins, viola, continuo* |
| Concerto 2 (F major) | trumpet, *recorder, oboe, violin* | 2 violins, viola, continuo |
| Concerto 3 (G major) | *3 violins, 3 violas, 3 cellos* | continuo |
| Concerto 4 (G major) | violin, *2 flauti d'echo* | *2 violins, viola, continuo* |
| Concerto 5 (D major) | *transverse flute, violin, harpsichord* | violin, viola, continuo |
| Concerto 6 (B-flat major) | *2 violas,* 2 violas da gamba, *cello* | *continuo* |

*Italics* indicate scoring of middle movements.

of all-string ensembles: in Concerto No. 3 a ninefold solo group of three stratified trios of 3 violins, 3 violas, and 3 cellos, and in Concerto No. 6 a six-part score with two contrasting but low-register trio formations, 2 violas and cello (the "modern" four-stringers) on the one side and 2 violas da gamba and violone (the "old-fashioned" six-stringers) on the other. Another special case is presented by Concerto No. 5, which in its middle movement features transverse flute, violin, and harpsichord, the most fashionable chamber trio of the time, but which in its outer movements turns that trio into a concertino with a commanding harpsichord part—the first time in the history of the concerto that a solo keyboard instrument is so boldly integrated. Adding his quasi-signature as a composer–harpsichord virtuoso, Bach included in the dedication score for the margrave an elaborate sixty-four-measure harpsichord cadenza that would find its equivalent only later in the written-out piano concerto cadenzas of Mozart and Beethoven.

It has been suggested with good reason that Concerto No. 5, in an earlier version, was written for Bach's 1717 expected meeting with Louis Marchand and that Bach was joined for the performance by his colleagues from the Dresden court capelle, violinist Jean-Baptiste Woulmyer and flutist Pierre-Gabriel Buffardin.[110] This credible hypothesis may well recall Bach's encounter with Marchand as depicted in the Obituary as an engagement "in a musical contest for superiority." The extravagantly virtuosic harpsichord part of Concerto No. 5 indeed turns this concerto into a showpiece highlighting the brilliant technique of its performer. However, all the *Brandenburg Concertos* celebrate performing virtuosity, and beyond that, all of them collectively testify to the compositional virtuosity—the facility, finesse, mastery, and genius—of their creator.

This balance of performing and compositional virtuosity both marks and circumscribes the canon of principles that Bach established in the remote and isolated environs of the Cöthen court, with the encouragement of an understanding patron. Composing desk and practice studio were never far apart in Bach's creative life, but the Cöthen atmosphere particularly nourished his pursuit of an art that amounted to nothing less than a personal branch of musical science. The basic nature of musical competition changed as he set himself on a course distinct from that of peers like Telemann and Handel—but without ever losing interest in what they were doing. While Telemann's concertos and Handel's keyboard suites contributed significantly to the instrumental repertoire, they generally remained within the conventional framework. Wherever possible, Bach chose to expand that framework. But to him, striving for "musical superiority" meant much more than pushing the limits of performing skills and compositional techniques. It meant systematizing the new paths he was forging through the maze of twenty-four keys, countless genres, a profusion of styles, a myriad of technical devices, melodic and rhythmic fashions, vocal and instrumental idioms. And especially, it meant integrating the canon of compositional principles he had established, most notably in the *Aufrichtige Anleitung* and *The Well-Tempered Clavier,* not merely to teach others but to challenge himself. Only in this way could Bach assure himself of never falling below the prevailing standards and forfeiting the quest for novel solutions.

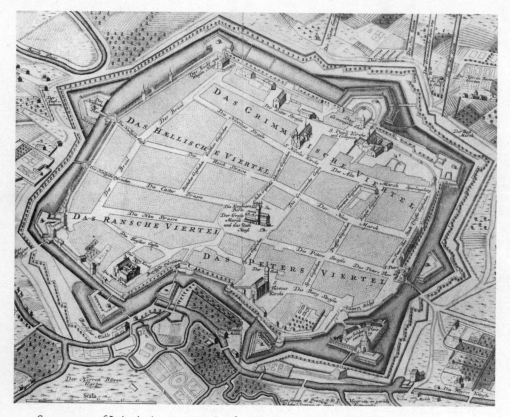

Street map of Leipzig in an engraving by Matthaeus Scutter (1723), showing the town hall (at center), St. Thomas's Church (below center), St. Nicholas's Church (above center), and St. Paul's (University) Church (to the right).

# 8

## Redefining a Venerable Office

### CANTOR AND MUSIC DIRECTOR
### IN LEIPZIG: THE 1720s

<br>

A CAPELLMEISTER AT ST. THOMAS'S

"Leipzig, May 29, 1723. This past Saturday [May 22] at noon, four wagons
loaded with household goods arrived here from Cöthen; they belonged to the
former Princely Capellmeister there, now called to Leipzig as *Cantor Figuralis*.
He himself arrived with his family on 2 carriages at 2 o'clock and moved into
the newly renovated apartment in the St. Thomas School."[1] This item, reported by a Hamburg newspaper, was not just local news. Apparently the
same people—probably Leipzig city officials—who in February had informed
the press about Bach's well-received audition wanted to announce that the
princely capellmeister not only had won the appointment but also had, indeed,
arrived in the city. The move signaled what would turn out to be a twenty-
seven-year-long tenure as *Cantor et Director Musices,* Bach's official title describing his function as cantor at the St. Thomas School and music director
responsible for the four city churches. Bach would actually be the longest-
serving Thomascantor since Valentin Otto, who had held the position for forty
years (from 1564). During the almost year-long interval following Johann
Kuhnau's death, first choir prefect Johann Gabriel Roth—a capable and highly
regarded substitute who in 1726 went as cantor to Geringswalde and in 1730
as town cantor to Grimma—bore primary responsibility for meeting both the
instructional needs of the school and the musical needs of the churches,[2] but
now a new beginning was in sight. Of even greater significance than
capellmeister Bach's taking up the cantor's regular duties was the expectation
that he would play a crucial role in reshaping the city's musical life, a role that
only "a famous man," in the words of the reigning burgomaster, could fulfill.

From the beginning, the ambitions of the Leipzig city fathers—led by Dr.
Gottfried Lange, burgomaster and chairman of the board of the St. Thomas
Church—were the driving force in naming a new cantor. They regarded the ap-

pointment as a chance to bolster the attractiveness and reputation of the city, which was well-known as a center of trade and learning. Originally a Slavic settlement called Lipsk (*urbs Libzi,* place of the linden trees) and uniquely located in a fertile plain at the confluence of the Pleisse, White Elster, and Parthe Rivers, Leipzig was chartered between 1156 and 1170. It rapidly developed into a significant commercial center at the intersection of several important ancient trade routes spreading in all directions—southwest to Nuremberg, Augsburg, and Italy; west to Erfurt, Frankfurt, the Rhinelands, the Netherlands, Switzerland, France, and Spain; northwest to Magdeburg and either the Netherlands via Brunswick, the Netherlands and England via the port of Hamburg, or Scandinavia and Russia via the port of Lübeck; north-northeast to Berlin and the Baltic Sea ports of Wismar, Rostock, Stettin, and Stralsund; northeast to Frankfurt-on-the-Oder, Danzig, Königsberg, and the Baltics; southeast to Dresden and from there to either Breslau, Cracow, Lublin, and Russia or southeast to Prague, Vienna, and Hungary. From the twelfth century on, special imperial and papal privileges enabled the city to establish regular trade fairs, which by 1458 were held three times a year for a week to ten days each: the New Year's Fair beginning on January 1, the Easter or Jubilate Fair in the spring (beginning on Jubilate Sunday), and the St. Michael's Fair in the fall (beginning on the Sunday after St. Michael's Day). By around 1710, Leipzig had surpassed Frankfurt-on-the-Main as "the marketplace of Europe," the premier trade fair locale in the German lands, regularly attracting between six thousand and ten thousand exhibitors and visitors.[3]

In contrast to Hamburg and Frankfurt, its principal mercantile rivals, Leipzig was also the seat of a university. Founded in 1409, Leipzig University provided the scene for the famous religious disputation between theology professors Martin Luther, Andreas Karlstadt, and Johann Eck in 1519 and, by the beginning of the eighteenth century, had grown into one of Germany's largest and most distinguished institutions of higher learning. In many ways, the often mutually supportive forces of business and mercantile economy on the one hand and higher education and erudite scholarship on the other turned out to be a most powerful combination for Leipzig, unique in comparison with other renowned German university towns like Jena, Heidelberg, and Tübingen. An eminent professoriate, a dynamic and forward-looking academic youth, and a literate bourgeoisie advanced the development of the city as an unrivaled center of the book trade and of scientific and general publishing.[4] These activities contributed markedly to Leipzig's reputation, by the middle of the eighteenth century, as Germany's intellectual capital—a place of irresistible attraction for young people desirous of superb academic schooling and general education, as was, for example, the young Goethe.

Smaller than Hamburg and equal in size to Frankfurt, Leipzig was held back more seriously and lastingly in the aftermath of the Thirty Years' War than either of those two. But beginning around 1700, the city, with some thirty thousand inhabitants,[5] experienced a period of unprecedented growth and affluence, and by the 1730s boasted nine banks that handled monetary transactions.[6] The prosperous, proud, and influential merchant families, many of them prominently represented on the three-tiered city council, were struck by a real building fever. By 1710, the Romanus, Apel, and Hohmann families had set the standard for opulent new edifices with ornate facades. These grand bourgeois houses, which occupied entire blocks and whose large-scale dimensions often accommodated courts as well as wings for exhibition facilities and commercial use, would transform the cityscape within but one generation. Outside the city walls, elaborate parks were laid out, complete with hothouses, orangeries, lodges, and the like; two fancy parks of the Bose family were outstanding examples of French-style horticultural design. All these enterprises fundamentally changed the architectural profile of the city and its immediate surroundings. Contributing to an atmosphere of growing bourgeois cognizance of higher culture was an interest in art collecting among prosperous citizens, merchants who built large collections of paintings, drawings, engravings, and sculptures. The grandest among them, Johann Christoph Richter's art cabinet in his Thomaskirchhof mansion (with four hundred works by Titian, Raphael, Lucas van Leyden, Rubens, and others),[7] and Gottfried Winckler's collection (with paintings by Leonardo, Giorgione, Veronese, Tintoretto, Rubens, Hals, Breughel, Rembrandt, and others)[8] at the city's main market square were accessible to the public; Winckler offered free general admission on Wednesday afternoons from 2 to 4.[9] As elegant coffeehouses contributed to the quality of social life, Leipzig saw its promotion of bourgeois gallantry, its cultivation of exquisite fashions and excellent manners, and the international flavor of its bustling business traffic—mainly in conjunction with the frequent fairs—earn it the nickname "Little Paris."[10]

Throughout the first half of the eighteenth century, this vibrant period of economic expansion coupled with a reaction to the bold and ambitious moves of electoral Saxony's powerful ruler, Augustus II (the Strong), spurred a remarkable competition with other cities—notably Hamburg, Frankfurt, and increasingly the nearby capital of Dresden—that formed the immediate backdrop for Bach's appointment. It was the mission of the Lange faction of the city council to make Leipzig not merely the city of Apollo and Mercury, the Greek gods of trade and wisdom (as invoked by the libretto of the secular cantata "Apollo et Mercurius," BWV 216a, of 1728–31), but a home of the visual and performing arts as well. Consequently, Picander's libretto for BWV 36c/9

of 1725 praises Leipzig as "our Helikon," an unabashed reference to the moun-
tain seen as the mythological seat of the muses. Not everything went according to plan: the Leipzig opera had failed in 1720, and its building served as a
penitentiary facility until the second half of the eighteenth century, there
being no interest in rescuing a bankrupt operation. On the other hand, other
secular musical entertainment was generally flourishing, promoted mainly by
two local music societies, or Collegia Musica. One of the two, founded by
Georg Philipp Telemann in 1701, operated successfully on a professional level
and, on Bach's arrival and for some time to come, continued under the able
leadership of Georg Balthasar Schott, organist and music director at the New
Church. Beginning in 1723, the regular weekly performances of this Collegium Musicum were staged at the premises of the entrepreneurial *cafétier*
Gottfried Zimmermann, with outdoor performances during the summer. The
other and apparently older Collegium,[11] directed from 1723 by Johann Gottlieb Görner, organist at St. Nicholas's and St. Paul's, performed at Enoch
Richter's coffeehouse.

Still, the most prominent musical activities took place every Sunday and
feast day at the services in the two principal churches, St. Thomas's and St.
Nicholas's, under the direction of the St. Thomas School cantor. At his disposal
for this purpose were the school's first cantorei and the city's small troupe of
salaried musicians, town pipers and art fiddlers; for more ambitious programming of sacred music, collaboration with members of the Collegia Musica was
deemed essential. Kuhnau, the solid cantor, had largely lost touch with the
Collegia, and Bach, the famous capellmeister, was expected to remedy that situation. It was for this reason that in the final selection process of the Kuhnau
succession, the town council outflanked the city clergy, which had traditionally set qualifications for the cantorate. Before they were even asked to take part
in the decision, Bach was elected to the post, was offered the job, and accepted
at the burgomaster's office on May 5.

Formalities then had to be observed. On May 7 or 8, Bach underwent a
thorough examination, conducted in Latin, to test his theological competence.
The examiner appointed by the electoral consistory in Dresden, seventy-three-
year-old D. Johann Schmid, professor of theology at Leipzig University and a
notoriously tough examiner known to flunk cantorate candidates,[12] certified in
a statement recorded in Latin and German that "Mr. Jo. Sebastian Bach replies
to the questions propounded by me in such a wise that I consider that the said
person may be admitted to the post of Cantor in the St. Thomas School."[13] The
document—co-signed by D. Salomon Deyling, who had participated in the
test as associate judge and who, since 1721, served as church superintendent
of Leipzig and simultaneously as professor of theology at the university—
was immediately sent to Dresden. The superintendent's presentation of Bach's

candidacy to the supervisory authorities concluded with a request for confirmation and ratification of the appointment.[14] The latter, dated May 13 and accompanied by a copy of the *Formula Concordiae*,[15] arrived back at the superintendent's office virtually by return mail.[16]

Deyling was miffed by what he considered the town council's breaches of protocol by consulting him only after Bach had already been offered the can-

St. Thomas Square, Leipzig, in an engraving by Johann Gottfried Krügner, Sr. (1723), showing the church, the school before its renovation and enlargement, and a group of choral scholars walking across.

torate by the burgomaster, who had also permitted Bach to make a private arrangement with Carl Friedrich Pezold, *collega tertius* and later conrector of the St. Thomas School. Under that agreement, Pezold would teach the five academic classes that ordinarily formed part of the cantor's assignment: two each in Latin etymology and Latin syntax for the *tertia,* and one in catechism for the *tertia* and *quarta.* Bach benefited here from an understanding reached previously between the burgomaster and Telemann, by which the cantor would cede 50 talers from his salary as recompense for a substitute instructor. In disapproval of the council's high-handed action, Deyling stayed away from the formal introduction ceremony of the cantor at the St. Thomas School, on Monday, June 1, 1723, and asked the inspector of the school and pastor at St. Thomas's, Christian Weiss, to serve instead as his deputy. The town council, on the other hand, countered by having councillor Gottfried Conrad Lehmann, who now chaired the board of the St. Thomas School, reproach superintendent Deyling publicly, in front of the faculty and students, for his absence—a skirmish well documented in a small flood of paperwork exchanged among Deyling, Weiss, and the town scribe on behalf of the council.[17] More than half a year later, Deyling testified to the Dresden Consistory after obtaining "further information" that the cantor's private arrangement with Pezold had worked out well and that Bach behaved responsibly in that "when the Third Colleague has had to be absent for illness, or on account of other hindrances, [he] has also visited the class and has dictated an exercise for the boys to work on."[18]

Whether or not Bach was aware of these quibbles among his superiors, he himself played no active role in the affair. Eventually, he would have his own exchanges with the town and church administrations and with yet a third bureaucracy, that of Leipzig University. Indeed, Bach's first official obligation in his new post, even before he was formally installed as cantor, related to the traditional linkage between the cantorate and the university. Like Kuhnau and his predecessors, Bach assumed responsibility for certain musical functions at the university, in particular at the so-called Old Service at St. Paul's (University) Church four times a year: on the first days of Christmas, Easter, and Pentecost and on the Reformation Festival. So he began his university duties on Whitsunday, May 16,[19] a full two weeks before his installation as cantor. It remains unclear, however, whether the composition he apparently prepared for this service, the relatively short cantata "Wer mich liebet, der wird mein Wort halten," BWV 59, was performed then. The extant original performing parts of BWV 59 date from 1724, though the autograph score was definitely written in the spring of 1723. Other criteria support the view that this cantata, with a different set of performing parts, was composed for the Pentecost service at the University Church:[20] the compact form, with the text taken from Erdmann Neumeister's *Geistliche Poesien* of 1714 (abbreviated from seven to four movements); the opening duet relating closely to the duet movements from the Cöthen cantata repertoire; the unusually modest scoring for soprano and bass solo (choir used only for the four-part chorale) and for an instrumental ensemble that includes trumpets and timpani but no other winds. Bach would have had to make the appropriate arrangements for the performance at St. Paul's with the first prefect of the St. Thomas choir, Johann Gabriel Roth, who had been in charge of the performances at St. Thomas's and St. Nicholas's during the interim period since Kuhnau's illness and death. But Bach had worked with him already the previous February, in conjunction with his audition; and now, as cantor designate, he needed to arrange a smooth transition to a new and orderly regime. The relative proximity of Cöthen facilitated matters considerably and enabled Bach to make the trip to Leipzig during the month following his election (on April 22, 1723) at least four times.

On the last of these trips, Johann Sebastian and Anna Magdalena Bach arrived on May 22, the Saturday before Trinity Sunday, with their entire family: five children (including the newborn Christiana Sophia Henrietta, Anna Magdalena's first child) and Friedelena Bach, their sister-in-law. They moved into the renovated cantor's apartment in the south wing of the St. Thomas School building on the Thomaskirchhof, the square extending from the south flank of St. Thomas's Church. The apartment, extending over three floors and apparently ready to accept the contents of the "four wagons loaded with household goods," may altogether have provided more space than the Bach family had known in Cöthen. The apartment also contained the cantor's office, the so-called composing room, which also accommodated the school's large music library (except for the materials that were kept at the churches). From there, Bach, like the rector who resided in the north wing of the school building, had direct access to the school itself, an advantage from which his children benefited as well. The two eldest sons were immediately accepted as *externi,* that is, nonresident students; twelve-year-old Friedemann entered the *tertia* and nine-year-old Carl the *quinta;* their younger brothers would eventually follow. From the outset, Bach must have realized that the broadened educational opportunities for his sons at a Latin school as distinguished as St. Thomas—a school with close links to Leipzig University—would be a major attraction of his new position.

Bach's finances did not improve as dramatically as they had with his moves from Mühlhausen to Cöthen and then to Weimar. The main difference was that his fixed annual salary, paid quarterly, amounted to little more than 100 talers, a fourth of what he had earned in Cöthen. However, he received free housing and payments for heat and light, a major advantage, and supplemental income from various special endowment funds,[21] as well as from weddings and funerals. Unlike his predecessors, he also received, by virtue of his organological expertise, annual payments for maintaining the church harpsichords.[22] In 1730, Bach estimated his annual income from the Leipzig cantorate to be about 700 talers, exactly the sum of his and his wife's combined salaries in Cöthen.[23] Anna Magdalena no longer earned a salary, nor would she ever again, but Bach knew that Leipzig would offer opportunities for considerable income over and above the figure of 700 talers. On the other hand, when he accepted the Leipzig position, he apparently was led to expect an income of at least 1,000 if not above 1,200 talers in cantorate-related income—figures that must have been mentioned in the verbal negotiations with Burgomaster Lange because that income level had also played a role in the discussions with Telemann and Graupner.[24] It seems, therefore, that over the years and certainly by 1730, Bach discovered that his actual earnings from the cantorate did not quite match "the favorable terms" as originally described to him.

While Bach may have sat in the church on Trinity Sunday 1723 listening critically to the music performed under the direction of the first prefect, Roth, he formally took up his new responsibilities during the following week in order to prepare for the coming Sunday. Then on May 30, the first Sunday after Trinity, Bach produced, for the morning service at St. Nicholas's, his first Leipzig cantata, "Die Elenden sollen essen," BWV 75, an extended work in two parts with the sermon intervening. The autograph score suggests that this cantata was composed in Cöthen, though Bach definitely wrote its sister piece, "Die Himmel erzählen die Ehre Gottes," BWV 76, after his arrival in Leipzig. The two works display a similar layout and scoring: 1 trumpet, 2 oboes, strings, and continuo; all four concertists of the choir are called upon for the arias and recitatives. Additionally, BWV 76 introduces the viola da gamba in a solo role, and both cantatas make use of alternating oboes and oboi d'amore, the latter introducing a new sonority in Leipzig churches that was probably heard for the first time in Bach's audition piece, BWV 23. Both cantatas are based on texts by an unnamed author who seems to have supplied the librettos of the audition cantatas BWV 22 and 23 as well. A good case can be made for authorship by Gottfried Lange, the poet-burgomaster who, after all, bears chief responsibility for launching the Leipzig career of Bach, the capellmeister-cantor.[25]

The musical event was duly noted in newspapers and chronicles; the official press release of June 3 reads, "This past Sunday, the Princely Capellmeister, Mr. Bach, who had been called hither from Cöthen by the Honorable and Most Wise Council of this town to fill the vacant post of Mr. Kuhnau, Directoris Chori Musici, who died here last year, presented, in entering upon his office, his music before and after the sermon."[26] And in the *Acta Lipsiensium Academica,* the university chronicler adds that Bach's music found general approval ("with good applause").[27] Curiously, the university chronicler also refers to Bach as "the new Cantor and Director of the Collegium Musicum," surely a misrepresentation of Bach's official title of *Cantor et Director Musices,* or *Director Chori Musici.* Yet, particularly in view of the closeness of the chronicler to the affairs of the university-related Collegium, the reference may imply that the new cantor, for his first Leipzig performance, had been able to mobilize members of the Collegia Musica. That they would rejoin the music making in the city's two main churches under the cantor's direction had been a high hope of the town fathers.

On the Monday following his first performance, Bach was formally introduced at the St. Thomas School by the chair of the school board, councillor Lehmann, in the presence of the faculty and students. According to a report written by the chief town clerk, Lehmann and Bach "were received downstairs by the Rector, Magister Ernesti, and led into the upper auditorium. . . . The students performed a piece outside the door, and at its conclusion all filed into the auditorium." Councillor Lehmann then proceeded with the official presentation in which Bach

was admonished faithfully and industriously to discharge the duties of his office, show the authorities his respect and willingness, cultivate good relations and friendship with his colleagues, conscientiously instruct the youth in the fear of God and other useful studies, and thus keep the School in good repute. The resident students and the others who attend the School were likewise admonished to give obedience and show respect to the new Cantor, and the speech was concluded with a good wish for the welfare of the School.

The cantor was expected to respond, but on the instruction of superintendent Deyling, pastor Christian Weiss quickly rose to make the presentation and carry out the official installation on behalf of the consistory, an act branded by Lehmann as "an innovation which must be brought to the attention of a Noble Council." After extending his congratulations to the new cantor, Lehmann put this to the assembly "at once," having perceived Weiss's action as an encroachment by the church on the civic authorities, already a sore point between the church consistory and the city council. But before the unexpected interruption led to a sidebar dispute between Lehmann and Weiss,

the new Cantor expressed his most obliged thanks to a Noble and Wise Council, in that the same had been most graciously pleased to think of him in conferring this office, with the promise that he would serve the same with all fidelity and zeal, would show due respect to his superiors, and in general to conduct himself that his greatest devotion should always be observed. Whereupon the other instructor of the School congratulated him, and the occasion was concluded with another musical piece.[28]

St. Thomas's was established in 1212 by Margrave Dietrich of Meissen as an Augustinian prebend with a convent and hospital. Leipzig, a town without a prince or a bishop in residence, already had an older church of Romanesque origin, St. Nicholas's, which as *templum oppidanum* (city temple) continued to serve through the subsequent centuries as the city's main parish church. In 1240, Dominican monks built another church, St. Paul's, which in the fifteenth century became the university's church and simultaneously functioned as its main auditorium. By the time St. Paul's was erected, the Augustinian prebendaries at St. Thomas's had founded a school for the poor that selected the most gifted among needy students, primarily from the vicinity of Leipzig but also from farther away. A singing school from the start, the *Schola Thomana* required the students to earn their stipends by singing at the church services. The school's first cantor of note was Georg Rhau, who early on joined the Reformation, performed his twelve-voiced *Missa de Sancto Spiritu* in June 1519 at St. Thomas's (marking the opening of the theological dispute between Luther, Karlstadt, and Eck), and was dismissed by the school in 1520 because he had converted. Rhau subsequently started a successful music editing and publishing business in Wittenberg that later had an immense influence on the dissemination of Protestant musical repertoires throughout the German lands, though it took nearly twenty more years until the Reformation won out and the city officially accepted the Lutheran faith—an occasion marked in 1539 by a sermon delivered by Luther himself on Whitsunday at St. Thomas's. When the Augustinian prebend was dissolved four years later, the St. Thomas School became a civic institution but continued its social mission, musical tradition, and academic distinction as the area's most selective Latin school.

In the middle of the sixteenth century, the choral scholars numbered only twenty-two, but with the school under the jurisdiction of the city council, wealthy citizens began to make charitable gifts and bequests on behalf of needy and gifted boys. The endowment that provided the operational means for the school grew steadily and supported, by the time of Kuhnau and Bach, fifty-five resident students *(alumni)* in the four upper classes, *prima* to *quarta*. In addition, the school accepted about twice that number of qualified nonresident students *(externi)*, who lived with their families in Leipzig. The *alumni*, however, in exchange for room and board, were obliged to sing at the regular worship services in four of the city's churches on all Sundays and feast days; they earned supplementary stipends by singing at funerals and weddings, also by *Currende* singing around New Year's Day and on other occasions, in the streets of the town and at the houses of affluent citizens. The regular musical functions of the choral scholars made it essential that the cantor play a decisive role in the rigorous admissions process: for the limited number of *alumni* positions, rector and conrector tested the applicants' academic qualifications, while the cantor examined their musical background and potential.[29]

This committee of three proposed its rank list to the chairman of the board of the St. Thomas School, usually one of the three Leipzig burgomasters. In only a single instance during Bach's tenure of office has the admissions documentation survived,[30] from which we learn that nine spaces for *alumni* became available in the spring of 1729. Bach tested the twenty-four applicants (who came from as far away as Aurich in east Friesland and whose ages ranged from thirteen to nineteen) and determined that fourteen of them could "be used in music," meaning in polyphonic music rather than merely in the singing of hymns. Five of those fourteen with additional qualifications, such as "has a good voice and fine proficiency," were admitted in May (Meißner, Krebs, Kittler, Hillmeyer, and Neucke), along with one after a reexamination (Wünzer: "has a somewhat weak voice, and little proficiency as yet, but he should [if private practice is diligently maintained] become usable in time"), and three who, according to Bach, had "no musical accomplishments" (Dieze, Ludewig, and Zeymer). Ludewig and Zeymer, however, were listed in 1730 among the motet singers,[31] indicating that Bach's training did indeed make a difference. The remaining five among the musically capable applicants (Landvoigt, Köpping, Krause, Pezold, and Scharff) were either admitted as *externi* or deferred as *alumni* and admitted later.

The cantor ranked third among the senior St. Thomas faculty of four, whose other members consisted, in 1723, of M. Johann Heinrich Ernesti, then a septuagenarian who held the position of rector simultaneously with that of professor of poetics at the university; the conrector, L(icentiate). Christian Ludovici, who also held a professorship at the university and in 1724 transferred there altogether; and the *tertius*, M. Carl Friedrich Pezold, a classics scholar who had agreed to take over Bach's academic teaching obligations (in 1731, he was promoted to conrector). After the death of rector Ernesti in 1729, M. Johann Matthias Gesner was appointed to that post, but he remained in it only briefly—much to the disappointment of Bach, who knew him from Weimar and who found in him a most supportive superior; in 1734, Gesner accepted an appointment as founding dean of Göttingen University (to be established in 1737) and was succeeded as rector by M. Johann August Ernesti (a distant relative of the other Ernesti), who also taught simultaneously at the school and the university. The rector and principal instructor of the *prima* carried a weekly teaching load of fifteen hours, while the conrector and *tertius* as instructors of the *secunda* and *tertia* classes taught for seventeen hours. The cantor traditionally taught twelve classroom hours in addition to his regular musical and administrative duties; having no class specifically his own, the cantor worked with the four upper classes, *prima* down to *quarta.*

In the sequence of eminent Protestant cantors serving the Thomana since the mid-sixteenth century, Bach was the tenth (see Table 8.1). He was, however, the first one to focus exclusively on the musical education of the upper classes. By special arrangement with the *tertius,* his teaching load was reduced to seven classes. This reduction did not, however, result in a net decrease of Bach's actual teaching functions, because he invested more than any of his predecessors in private vocal and instrumental instruction as well as in rehearsal time—a necessity considering the dramatic increase in the musical demands on his students as compared, for example, with what Kuhnau had required of them. Classes at the St. Thomas School were held weekdays from 7 to 10 A.M. and from 12 to 3 P.M.; the remaining unscheduled time was reserved for individual study, in the cubicles for the *alumni* and at home for the *externi.* The cantor taught his "musical exercises with all classes" on Monday, Tuesday, and Wednesday at 9 and 12 and on Friday at 12, seven hours per week, at the school's auditorium; he had no scheduled classes on Thursday or Saturday. The classes were compulsory for all resident and nonresident students, altogether some 150 youngsters, so Bach was assisted by the four choral prefects appointed by him from among the senior and musically expert students. We may assume that Bach himself worked mostly with smaller groups of the more advanced students, whom he then coached, perhaps with students in the audience observing, and that he performed regularly, giving explanations and demonstrations of musical concepts. All his teachings were imbued with the educational goals stated in the school's regulations for its preceptors, namely to instruct their students "in the knowledge and fear of God" and "in the vivid knowledge of divine essence and will," the very same goals with which Bach himself had been raised.[32]

## TABLE 8.1. Protestant Cantors at the St. Thomas School, to 1800

| 1519–1520 | Georg Rhau | 1657–1676 | Sebastian Knüpfer |
| 1540–1549 | Ulrich Lang | 1677–1701 | Johann Schelle |
| 1549–1551 | Wolfgang Figulus | 1701–1722 | Johann Kuhnau |
| 1553–1594 | Valentin Otto | 1723–1750 | Johann Sebastian Bach |
| 1594–1615 | Seth Calvisius | 1750–1755 | Johann Gottlob Harrer |
| 1616–1630 | Johann Hermann Schein | 1756–1789 | Johann Friedrich Doles |
| 1631–1657 | Tobias Michael | 1789–1800 | Johann Adam Hiller |

For the music instruction in the upper classes and for his private lessons, Bach apparently used no textbooks (at Latin schools, musical notation was taught to the younger students before they reached the *quarta*). Instead, he formulated his own rules and principles for theoretical subjects (an example is his *Vorschriften und Grundsätze zum vierstimmigen Spielen des General-Baß oder Accompagnement,* Precepts and Principles for Playing the Thoroughbass or Accompanying in Four Parts)[33] and focused chiefly on practical examples from the vocal and instrumental repertoire. Since his successors in the St. Thomas cantorate, notably his student Johann Friedrich Doles, made frequent use of the Bach motets for regular choral exercises, it seems likely that Bach himself established this practice. A work such as the eight-voice motet of 1726–27, "Singet dem Herrn ein neues Lied," BWV 225, may in fact have been composed just for this purpose—no other being known. As a choral etude for double choir, to be sung alternatively with or without instrumental support, it would have given Bach the possibility of training his students in the vocal techniques and genres (movements 1 and 3a: eight-part concerto; 2: four-part aria and four-part chorale juxtaposed; 3b: four-part fugue) that he needed for his demanding cantata repertoire. The motet's biblical texts, from Psalm 98:1–3, "Singet dem Herrn ein neues Lied" (Sing unto the Lord a new song) and Psalm 150:2 and 6, "Lobet den Herrn in seinen Taten / Alles was Odem hat, lobe den Herrn. Halleluja" (Praise the Lord for His mighty acts / Let everything that has breath praise the Lord), as well as the chorale stanza "Wie sich ein Vater erbarmet" (As a father has mercy / for all his young small children / the Lord will also forgive us / when we as children purely fear Him), would have been particularly appropriate for teaching how such a piece of music fit into the daily lives and duties of the choral scholars. Similarly suitable for pedagogical purposes and regular repeated performances would have been the five-part chorale motet "Jesu, meine Freude," BWV 227, in which Johann Franck's 1653 hymn is connected with the central doctrinal New Testament passage Romans 8:1, 2, 9–11, "Es ist nun nichts Verdammliches an denen, die in Christo Jesu sind" (There is therefore no condemnation for them who are in Christ Jesus, who walk not after the flesh, but after the Spirit). This diversified structure of five-, four-, and three-part movements, with shifting configurations of voices and a highly interpretive word-tone relationship throughout, wisely and sensibly combines choral exercise with theological education.

It is clear that the traditional sixteenth-century motets from the standard collections (such as Erhard Bodenschatz's *Florilegium Portense* of 1618), which were still regularly performed at the beginning of services during Bach's time, would have been insufficient to prepare the choral scholars for the challenges

they had to meet in Bach's cantatas. It was therefore necessary for Bach to prepare the pupils by way of demanding and interesting pieces that would keep
them on their toes. There had been regular complaints during Kuhnau's time
about disorder and a lack of discipline among the choral scholars, and both
Kuhnau and rector Ernesti were blamed. But no complaints about disciplinary
problems are recorded for Bach's classes or performances (although he was reproached in 1729 for negligence in the arrangements regarding academic
classes and for canceling singing classes).[34] A stiff schedule of fines discouraged
students from disturbing performances: for a noticeable (musical) mistake, 1
groschen had to be paid, and for an intentional and mischievous mistake, 3
groschen (1 groschen would buy two quarts of beer). This money was subtracted from the students' extra income from funerals and other services and
was used by the cantor for the acquisition of music and the maintenance of instruments.[35] In general, the school regulations reminded everyone that "our ancestors have determined that music should be practiced at the St. Thomas
School, and that the *alumni* should provide it for all the city's churches. Therefore, they should be mindful of their duty and office by exercising this art as
much as possible, and consider that they perform a good deed which the heav-
enly host pursues with the greatest pleasure."[36]

Under his contract, Bach was required to instruct "not only in vocal but also
in instrumental music."[37] While most of his instrumental lessons took place
in private or small groups, the classroom exercises may also have involved instrumental performances and coaching. The large amount of instrumental
music by Bach that was copied in the 1750s by Christian Friedrich Penzel,
then one of the school's prefects, suggests that Bach's own ensemble compositions—chamber works for one instrument and harpsichord but also concertos
and overtures—may also have played a role in his musical exercises at the
school, especially for the training of his best players, whether or not they were
needed for the cantata performances. The auditorium was equipped with a
small organ and a harpsichord (in his office, on the same floor level, the cantor kept instruments that could be added as needed) and also served as rehearsal
space for the church performances. And as noted earlier, each *alumni* cubicle either contained or provided easy access to a keyboard instrument, so that students could prepare for lessons and learn their cantata parts. Lessons and
rehearsals had to take place during the daily periods for individual study, outside the scheduled classroom hours. The school's regular teaching schedule
was maintained rigidly on all workdays throughout the year, with the exception of the religious holidays and the three periods of the fairs, which usually
involved additional musical commitments.

The cantor was in charge of the music in four churches: St. Nicholas's and

St. Thomas's, the city's two main parish churches; the New Church, which was the old Franciscan Barfüsser Church, rebuilt in 1699 (renamed St. Matthew's in 1876 and destroyed in World War II); and the smaller St. Peter's Church, built in 1505 and enlarged 1710–12 (torn down in 1886). The fifty-five *alumni,* that is, the resident choral scholars from the upper four classes, were thus divided into four *cantoreien,* with distinct assignments requiring different musical accomplishments (see Table 8.2). Choir I, consisting of the most select singers from the upper classes under the direction of the cantor, provided the cantatas and, in general, the concerted music at the two main churches in an alternating schedule (for details, see the following section, "Mostly Cantatas"). This choir was joined by the town music company for cantata performances conducted by the cantor; it also sang the Introit motet under the direction of the first prefect, a member of this choir. Choir I together with the town musicians also performed four times a year at the Old Service in St. Paul's, where the regular services on high feast days and during the fair periods featured concerted music performed under the direction of its music director by university students who had formed a Collegium Musicum. Choir II served the two main churches and performed in alternation with choir I, under the direction of the second prefect; choir II ordinarily performed only motets, without an instrumental ensemble. Choir III, conducted by the third prefect, served the New Church and sang motets and chorales; concerted music was presented there on high feast days and during the fairs by another Collegium Musicum under the direction of its organist and music director—a tradition established in 1704 by Georg Philipp Telemann. Choir IV, led by the fourth prefect, was responsible merely for hymn singing at St. Peter's.

It was within this fairly tight organizational framework that Bach began, from the moment of his arrival in Leipzig, to take charge of the cantorate in true capellmeisterly fashion. The repertoire of music he created for Leipzig demanded the performing standards he had grown used to in Weimar and Cöthen and was unwilling to relinquish. At the same time, his works offered a richness of ideas, forms, and sonorities that went well beyond established conventions. Focusing initially on a bold program of church music that was unprecedented for Leipzig (or anywhere else, for that matter), he engaged, over his twenty-seven-year tenure, generations of St. Thomas School students, the town music company, and a host of supplementary musicians for a total of some 1,500 performances of cantatas, passions, oratorios, and similar works, playing to a captive audience of more than two thousand each time.[38]

By the end of the 1720s and after six years in office, Bach the capellmeister-cantor had managed to place himself in a commanding position vis-à-vis Leipzig's music organizations, sacred and secular. When a major reshuffling of

## TABLE 8.2. Organization of Leipzig Church Music, 1723–50

| St. Thomas's | St. Nicholas's | New Church | St. Paul's[a] |
|---|---|---|---|
| *Cantor and Music Director*—Johann Sebastian Bach | *Music Director*—Johann Sebastian Bach  *Cantor*[c]—Johann Hieronymus Homilius | *Organist and Music Director*—Georg Balthasar Schott (to March 1729) | *Music Director* (Old Service)[b]—Johann Sebastian Bach |
| *Organist*—Christian Gräbner (to fall 1729)  Johann Gottlieb Görner (from fall 1729) | *Organist*—Johann Gottlieb Görner (to fall 1729)  Johann Schneider (from August 1730) | Carl Gotthelf Gerlach (from May 1729) | *Music Director* (regular service)— Johann Gottlieb Görner  *Organist*—Johann Christoph Thiele |

### Vocal and Instrumental Ensembles

*Concerted music* (cantatas)

| St. Thomas's | St. Nicholas's | New Church | St. Paul's |
|---|---|---|---|
| Choir I and town music company[d] (+instrumentalists)[e] | | Collegium Musicum I (on high feasts and during the fair) | Choir I and town music company (Old Service);[b] Collegium Musicum II (on other feasts and during the fair) |

*Motets*

| St. Thomas's | St. Nicholas's | New Church | St. Paul's |
|---|---|---|---|
| Choir I (1st prefect) | Choir II (2nd prefect) | Choir III (3rd prefect) | St. Peter's Church |

*Chorales*

| St. Thomas's | St. Nicholas's | New Church | St. Paul's |
|---|---|---|---|
| Choir I | Choir II | Choir III | Choir IV (4th prefect) |

*Liturgical chant*

| St. Thomas's | St. Nicholas's | New Church | St. Paul's |
|---|---|---|---|
| Altar singers[f] | Altar singers | | |

[a]St. Paul's schedule differed from that of St. Thomas's, enabling organist and music director to serve both.

[b]Held four times per year: first day of Christmas, Easter, and Pentecost; Reformation Festival.

[c]The cantorei of the Latin school at St. Nicholas's provided music outside the main services.

[d]Choir I (with town music) under Bach's direction and choir II alternated between the two churches. The St. Thomas choirs I–IV and the town music company performed on all Sundays and feast days.

[e]Regular supplement: town music apprentices, St. Thomas School students, and Collegium Musicum members.

[f]Singers from the lower classes of the St. Thomas School.

important positions took place in 1729 on Georg Balthasar Schott's acceptance of a cantorate in Gera and the death of Christian Gräbner, the St. Thomas organist, Bach claimed for himself the directorship of Leipzig's first and best Collegium Musicum. He also helped reorganize the organists' scene by moving the able Johann Gottlieb Görner from St. Paul's to St. Thomas's and by appointing two capable young musicians, his own students Carl Gotthelf Gerlach and Johann Schneider, as organists at the New Church and St. Nicholas's; all three would remain in their posts for the rest of their careers. Such powerful stature in the city (and consequently within the St. Thomas School as well) bolstered by a steadily growing supra-regional reputation and by princely, ducal, and electoral-royal honorary titles at the courts of Cöthen, Weissenfels, and Dresden, respectively, made Bach practically invulnerable, and probably to some extent ungovernable. It seems to have been the latter quality—not the unique musical achievements of unquestionable value to Leipzig—that prompted Burgomaster Stieglitz, in the city council's talks about the succession after Bach's death, to declare that "the School needed a Cantor and not a Capellmeister."[39] And indeed, never again would the Thomana have a capellmeister.

## MOSTLY CANTATAS

When Bach took over the St. Thomas cantorate in the spring of 1723, he moved from courtly to municipal service, from unpredictable despotic rule and princely caprices (benevolent or not) to a more slowly operating civic bureaucracy and collegial administration. More important to him than such external conditions, however, was the opportunity finally to realize his artistic aspirations: "the ultimate goal of a regulated church music," which he had described in 1708 to the Mühlhausen town council and which he had tried to pursue, on a more restricted level, at the Weimar court. Fifteen years later, he was now back in a similar situation—as the leading musician of a municipality—but with far greater authority, experience, and means to prevail. An additional source of encouragement must have been the reputation of the venerable office at St. Thomas's as the leading cantorate in Protestant Germany, esteemed for its uninterrupted sequence of distinguished incumbents such as Calvisius, Schein, Michael, Knüpfer, Schelle, and Kuhnau and their exemplary creative work.

Even before he officially assumed his Leipzig office, Bach must have decided to supply the two main churches with works of his own composition. Once in Leipzig, unlike any of his predecessors, all of whom were also active composers, he embarked on a program to provide a piece of concerted music—a cantata—for every Sunday and feast day of the ecclesiastical year, except for the Lenten weeks preceding Christmas and Easter, when concerted music was traditionally suspended. Such a repertoire required no fewer than sixty cantatas annually, an enormously challenging task (especially during the first several years) demanding extraordinary concentration and discipline. Only gradually could Bach build up a repertoire of sacred music that would eventually enable him to draw on a rich cache of materials for years to come.

In order for the St. Thomas School to serve the two main churches equally well, a scheme of alternation had been devised early in the seventeenth century, so Bach's cantata performances alternated in a steady rhythm between St. Thomas's and St. Nicholas's. For the high feasts of the ecclesiastical year, the morning performance in one church was repeated at the afternoon service in the other, so that the congregations of both parishes would benefit. The headings in the printed booklet for the *Christmas Oratorio*, BWV 248, for example, indicate how the arrangement worked in 1734–35:[40]

| | |
|---|---|
| Part I (Christmas Day): | Mornings at St. Nicholas's and afternoons at St. Thomas's |
| Part II (2nd day of Christmas): | Mornings at St. Thomas's and afternoons at St. Nicholas's |
| Part III (3rd day of Christmas): | At St. Nicholas's |
| Part IV (New Year's Day): | Mornings at St. Thomas's and afternoons at St. Nicholas's |
| Part V (Sunday after New Year's Day): | At St. Nicholas's |
| Part VI (Epiphany): | Mornings at St. Thomas's and afternoons at St. Nicholas's |

The prescribed pauses occasioned by the two Lenten periods came in handy, enabling Bach and his musicians to prepare for the demanding performance schedule from Christmas to Epiphany and for the outstanding musical event of the year, the Passion performance on Good Friday, followed by the three-day Easter holiday. According to Leipzig tradition, the ecclesiastical year comprised regular Sundays and various kinds of feast days: the high feasts of Christmas, Easter, and Pentecost (three days each, with the first two formally celebrated as high feasts), Ascension, the Marian feasts, St. John's and St. Michael's Days, and the Reformation Festival (see liturgical calendar in Appendix 4). The two Lenten periods extended from the first Sunday in Advent to Christmas and from Invocavit Sunday to Easter; regular Sundays were those from the first after Epiphany to Estomihi, from Quasimodogeniti to Exaudi, and from the first after Trinity to the twenty-seventh. Not celebrated as an ecclesiastical feast, the Monday after St. Bartholomew's Day (August 24) was observed with a ceremonial service at St. Nicholas's marking the annual election of the city council.

The cantata performance filled the niche as the principal music piece in the liturgy of the Mass, or main service, formerly occupied by the Gospel motet, which in the Lutheran tradition since the Reformation had functioned to enhance the reading of the Gospel. This motet, which immediately followed the Gospel lesson prescribed for the day according to the ancient proper of the Mass, generally highlighted one or more central verses from the Bible. In the later seventeenth century, the Gospel motet was replaced by a concertato motet with aria and chorale supplements and after 1700 by the cantata, at which time the multisectional cantata poetry moved from merely highlighting a passage from the biblical lesson to interpreting it as well. The theologian-poet Erdmann Neumeister initiated the development that resulted in the cantata's function as a musical sermon. Therefore, all of Bach's Leipzig cantata texts follow a standard pattern firmly grounded in the bifocal homiletic structure of a Lutheran sermon: *explicatio* and *applicatio,* biblical exegesis and theological instruction succeeded by practical and moral advice. The libretto ordinarily opens with a biblical dictum, usually a passage from the prescribed Gospel lesson that serves as a point of departure (opening chorus). It is followed by scriptural, doctrinal, and contextual explanations (a recitative-aria pair), leading to considerations of the consequences to be drawn from the lesson and the admonition to conduct a true Christian life (another recitative-aria pair). The text concludes with a congregational prayer in the form of a hymn stanza (chorale).

In his autograph score of "Nun komm der Heiden Heiland," BWV 61, a Weimar cantata re-performed in Leipzig on the first Sunday in Advent—the traditional beginning of the ecclesiastical year—Bach wrote down the order of the service with the somewhat unusual particulars for this Sunday (concerted Kyrie without Gloria, omission of the Latin Credo, addition of the Litany):[41]

---

*Order of the Divine Service in Leipzig*
*on the First Sunday in Advent: Morning*

(1) Preluding
(2) Motet
(3) Preluding on the Kyrie, which is performed throughout in concerted manner
(4) Intoning before the altar
(5) Reading of the Epistle
(6) Singing of the Litany
(7) Preluding on [and singing of] the Chorale
(8) Reading of the Gospel [*crossed out:* and intoning of the Creed]
(9) Preluding on [and performance of] the principal music [*Haupt-Music*]
(10) Singing of the Creed [Luther's Credo hymn]

(11) The Sermon

(12) After the Sermon, as usual, singing of several verses of a hymn

(13) Words of Institution [of the Sacrament]

(14) Preluding on [and performance of] the music [i.e., another concerted piece]. After the same, alternate preluding and singing of chorales until the end of the Communion, and so on.

Bach's notes provide welcome information on the function of the organ, which is generally not specified in the liturgical formularies. The organ introduced, by preluding, the singing of congregational hymns,[42] but also played a prelude before the cantata in the key of its first movement, during which the instruments were tuned.[43] At the same time, Bach's list for this particular Sunday omits important details about the structure of the principal morning service in the Leipzig main churches (see Table 8.3); for example, no mention is made of the fact that major parts of the service, especially on high feasts (including Salutations, Collects, and Benedictions), were still conducted in Latin.[44] The order of the services throughout the church year was officially prescribed in two important, complementary formularies: *Vollständiges Kirchen-Buch* of 1710 and AGENDA, *Das ist, Kirchen-Ordnung of 1712.* They were supplemented by two practical handbooks for the use of parishioners, *Leipziger Kirchen-Andachten* of 1697 and *Leipziger Kirchen-Staat* of 1710, and also by two major hymnals: the choral hymnal edited by Gottfried Vopelius, *Neu Leipziger Gesangbuch . . . Mit 4. 5. bis 6. Stimmen* of 1682 and the standard congregational hymnal, *Das Privilegirte Ordentliche und Vermehrte Dreßdnische Gesang-Buch* of 1725, containing words only but supplied with elaborate indices, lessons throughout the year, the Psalter, and other appendices.

## TABLE 8.3. Order of the Mass *(Amt)* at Leipzig's Main Churches

| Occasion[a] | Congregation and Organ | Choir | Preacher and Ministrants[b] |
|---|---|---|---|
| F | | Hymnus (*figuraliter,* or polyphonic) | |
| FR | Prelude [*1*][c] | | |
| FR | | Introit motet [2] | |
| L | | Canticle (*choraliter,* or chant) | |
| FR | Prelude [3] | Kyrie (*figuraliter*) [3] | |
| L | | Kyrie (*choraliter*) | |
| FRL | | | Gloria (Latin intonation) [4] |
| FR | | Gloria: Et in terra pax (*figuraliter*) | |
| L | | Gloria: Et in terra pax (*choraliter*) [4] | |

| | | | |
|---|---|---|---|
| FRL | | | Salutation, Collect<br>Epistle [5] |
| L | Litany [6] | | |
| FR | Prelude [7] | | |
| FRL | Hymn (de tempore) [7] | | |
| FRL | | | Gospel [8] |
| FRL | | | Credo (Latin intonation) |
| FR | Prelude [9] | Cantata I, 7:30 A.M. [9] | |
| L | | Credo: Patrem<br>omnipotentem (choraliter) | |
| FR | Prelude [10] | | |
| FRL | Hymn: Wir<br>glauben all an<br>einen Gott [10] | | |
| FRL | | | Announcement of sermon |
| FR | Prelude | | |
| FRL | Hymn | | |
| FRL | | | Text of the sermon |
| FRL | | | The Lord's Prayer |
| FRL | | | Sermon, 8 A.M.<br>(1 hour) [11] |
| FRL | | | Prayers, announcements<br>Benediction |
| FR | Prelude [12] | | |
| FRL | Hymn [12] | | |
| F | | | Praefatio (Latin<br>intonation) |
| F | | Sanctus<sup>d</sup> (figuraliter) | |
| RL | | | Communion admonition |
| FRL | | | Words of Institution<br>of the Sacrament [13],<br>Communion |
| FR | Prelude [14] | Cantata II<sup>e</sup> (under<br>Communion) [14] | Administration of<br>the sacrament |
| FR | Prelude [14] | | |
| FRL | Hymns<br>(under<br>Communion) [14] | | |
| FRL | | | Versicle, Collect,<br>Benediction |
| FR | Prelude | | |
| FRL | Hymn | | |
| F | | Hymnus (figuraliter) | |

<sup>a</sup>F = festal seasons, R = regular Sundays, L = Lent. The service began at 7 A.M. and lasted for
    about three hours.
<sup>b</sup>With the exception of the pulpit parts, chanted in recitation tone.
<sup>c</sup>Figures in brackets refer to the "Order of the Divine Service . . ." (Bach's note) above.
<sup>d</sup>Without Osanna, Benedictus, and Agnus Dei.
<sup>e</sup>Second part of cantata I, separate second cantata, or concerted piece of a different kind.

All hymns for the services—including those sung before and after the sermons—were traditionally selected by the cantor from the repertoire of the Dresden *Gesangbuch,* of which a revised and expanded version was published in 1725. It was Leipzig tradition since the Reformation that the morning sermon interpreted the Gospel and the afternoon sermon the Epistle, so that appropriate hymns could be chosen.[45] In the late 1720s, however, a brief conflict flared up between Bach and Gottlieb Gaudlitz, then subdeacon at St. Nicholas's, over the selection of hymns for the Vespers service (see Table 8.4). Gaudlitz claimed the right to choose the hymns before and after the sermon and also to select a new hymn not included in the Dresden *Gesangbuch.* Bach apparently resisted what he considered an improper appropriation, so Gaudlitz filed a complaint with the consistory, which in September 1728 issued written support for the subdeacon.[46] Bach then protested to his own superiors, the city council, in the hope that this group, which often found itself at odds with the consistory anyway, would affirm

The customs hitherto followed at the public divine service, and not to make any innovations. . . . Among these customs and practices was the ordering of the hymns before and after the sermons, which was always left solely to me and my predecessors in the Cantorate to determine, in accordance with the gospels and the Dresden *Gesangbuch* based on the same, as seemed appropriate to the season and the circumstances. . . . Magister Gottlieb Gaudlitz has taken it upon himself to attempt an innovation and has sought, in place of the hymns chosen in accordance with the established use, to introduce others. . . . It may be added that when, in addition to the concerted music, very long hymns are sung, the divine service is held up, and all sorts of disorder would have to be reckoned with; not to mention the fact that not a single one of the clergymen except Magister Gaudlitz, the Subdeacon, wishes to introduce this innovation.[47]

The subject of introducing new hymns came up again in a 1730 memorandum from the city council to superintendent Salomon Deyling, in which he was advised "that in the churches of this town . . . new hymns hitherto not customary, shall not be used in public divine services." This unequivocal statement suggests that the cantor's position had prevailed, at least regarding the introduction of new hymns. Bach's general preferences for the traditional repertoire, with emphasis on the hymns written by Martin Luther and Reformation and post-Reformation poets, remains evident throughout his vocal works and organ chorales.

Although the cantor's responsibility extended to all musical parts of the service, Bach's major effort and greatest personal interest centered on the performance of the *Haupt-Music,* that is, the cantata. Before composing the cantata, he had to select its text and prepare it for publication in the form of booklets that the congregation could read before or during the performance. These booklets, in conveniently small octavo format, contained the cantata texts for several Sundays in a row, usually six. Besides the libretto of the *Christmas Oratorio,* five such booklets have survived: (1) from the second Sunday after Epiphany to Annunciation, 1724; (2) from Easter Sunday to Misericordias Domini, 1724; (3) from the third to the sixth Sunday after Trinity,

TABLE 8.4. Order of the Vespers Service at the Leipzig Main Churches

| Occasion[a] | Congregation and Organ | Choir | Preacher and Ministrants |
|---|---|---|---|
| FR | Prelude | | |
| F | | Hymnus *(figuraliter)* | |
| RL | | Motet *(figuraliter)* | |
| F | | Cantata (repeated from morning service) | |
| FR | Prelude | | |
| FRL | Hymn *(de tempore)* | | |
| | | | Psalm |
| | | | The Lord's Prayer |
| FR | Prelude | | |
| FRL | Hymn | | |
| FRL | | | Announcement of sermon |
| FRL | Hymn | | |
| FRL | | | Sermon |
| L | | | Catechism (Advent season) |
| | | | Passion harmony (Passion season) |
| FRL | | | Prayers, Collect, Benediction |
| FR | Prelude | | |
| F | | Magnificat (Latin, *figuraliter*) | |
| RL | German Magnificat hymn | | |
| FRL | | | Responsory, Collect, Benediction |
| FRL | Hymn: Nun danket alle Gott | | |

[a]F = festal seasons, R = regular Sunday, L = Lent. The service began at 1:30 P.M.

1725; (4) from Easter Sunday to Misericordias Domini, 1731; and (5) from Whitsunday to Trinity, 1731.[48] That twelve such booklets were needed per year gives us an inkling of the advance planning necessary for carrying out Bach's musical program. Moreover, the booklets were apparently printed at the cantor's expense and then, with the help of students or his own children, distributed to subscribers and other interested and more affluent citizens. The sales helped not only to recover the printing costs but also to secure some significant extra income that was then used to pay for additional musicians (particularly instrumentalists) and other performance-related expenses.[49]

Otherwise, the only regular stipend available to hire extra musicians, amounting to about 12 talers per annum, was provided by the city council for one or two students from the university to assist in Bach's church performances; it was used especially to fill a need for bass singers in 1726–27, 1729, and 1745.[50] But most of the vocal concertists were found among the *alumni* assigned to the first choir, an elite group consisting of the best twelve to sixteen singers. Their entry ages as resident choral scholars varied, but they usually began as thirteen- or fourteen-year-old sopranos,[51] invariably with prior singing experience in other Latin school choirs, and they stayed for a maximum of eight years, usually two years per class. Because in the eighteenth century the change of voice occurred later than it does today,[52] many of the boys could sing soprano for several more years. On entry, Bach judged his best singers to have a "good voice," "fine voice," "strong voice," or "good strong voice," and whoever had "a fine proficiency" or "hit the notes very prettily" was thus deemed secure in matters of intonation and sight reading, experienced in performance practices, and adept in proper musical expression.

The size of his vocal ensemble is defined by Bach in an important memorandum to the city council dated August 23, 1730 ("Short but Most Necessary Draft for a Well-Appointed Church Music"),[53] which states that the fifty-five *alumni* of the school

are divided into 4 choirs, for the 4 churches in which they must partly perform concerted music with instruments, partly sing motets, and partly sing chorales. In the three churches, namely St. Thomas's, St. Nicholas's, and the New Church, the pupils must all be musical. St. Peter's receives the residue, namely those who do not understand music and can only just barely sing a chorale.

Every musical choir should contain at least 3 sopranos, 3 altos, 3 tenors, and as many basses, so that even if one happens to fall ill (as very often happens, particularly at this time of the year, as the prescriptions by the school physician for the apothecary must show), at least a double-chorus motet may be sung. (N.B. Though it would be still better if the group were such that one could have 4 subjects on each voice and thus could provide every choir with 16 persons.)

Earlier in the same document, Bach specifies that

in order that the choruses of church pieces may be performed as is fitting, the vocalists must in turn be divided into 2 sorts, namely concertists and ripienists. The concertists are ordinarily 4 in number; sometimes also 5, 6, 7, even 8; that is, if one wishes to perform music for two choirs. The ripienists, too, must be at least 8, namely two for each part.

The instrumental ensemble available to Bach consisted of a core group of eight—that is, the salaried members of the town music company (four town pipers, three art fiddlers, and one associate)—which had remained stable in size for several generations and as such was entirely insufficient for the performance of cantatas (see Table 8.5).[54] The number, however, is misleading, for in order to take advantage of their privileges of performing (outside their church and municipal obligations) for a fee at private civic functions, most town musicians maintained their own sub-band of family members, pupils, and associates.[55] Although the regular income of the town musicians was not that high in absolute terms, they were the best-paid musicians in the city, with many opportunities for additional income beyond their fixed salary; as a result, every vacancy gave rise to a generous supply of applicants. Auditions were held and judged by Bach in his capacity as their immediate supervisor and on behalf of the city council, his voice also counting at promotions from art fiddler to town piper. Various testimonials written by Bach demonstrate the seriousness with which he was involved in the affairs of the town musicians. For example, when the aging town piper Gentzmer needed an official adjunct in 1745, Bach examined Carl Friedrich Pfaffe, who for three years had served as an associate, and testified that he "has taken his trial examination in the presence of the other Town Musicians; whereupon it was found that he performed quite well and to the applause of all those present on all the instruments that are customarily employed by the Town Pipers—namely Violin, *Haubois, Flute Travers., Trompette, Waldhorn,* and the remaining bass instruments—and he was found quite suited to the post of assistant that he seeks."[56]

The astonishing range of skills that were expected of town musicians, especially at the rank of town piper, bespeaks the high degree of flexibility Bach enjoyed in making instrumental assignments. And the stability of the core group meant that Bach could shape his ensemble and its playing style very much to his liking. He actually experienced no change in personnel until

1730, when Christian Ernst Meyer accepted the post of tower watchman at St. Thomas's (though he may still have been available to perform church music); the first major disruption occurred only when Bach's virtuoso trumpeter, Gottfried Reiche, died in 1734. In general, Bach's opportunities to appoint musicians of his choice to the ensemble were limited. Nevertheless, the overall resourcefulness of the company with its full complement of adjuncts and apprentices must have been considerable, judging by the combined inventories of instruments in the estates of the town pipers Rother, Gleditsch, and Oschatz: 2 trumpets, 2 timpani, 3 horns, 2 cornettos, 2 recorders, 4 oboes, 1 transverse flute, 1 piccolo flute, 6 violins, 2 violoncellos, and 1 violone (never mind that both St. Thomas's and St. Nicholas's each possessed its own set of church instruments).[57]

**TABLE 8.5. The Leipzig Town Music Company, 1723–50**

| | | Instrument[a] | Successors |
|---|---|---|---|
| *Town Pipers* | | | |
| (1) Gottfried Reiche[b] | 1706–34 | *trumpet 1* | Ulrich Heinrich Ruhe, from 1734 |
| (2) Christian Rother[b] | 1708–37 | *violin 1* | Johann Friedrich Kirchhoff, from 1737 |
| (3) Johann Cornelius Gentzmer[b] | 1712–51 | *trumpet 2* | |
| (4) Johann Caspar Gleditsch[b] | 1719–47 | *oboe 1* | Johann Christian Oschatz, from 1747 |
| *Art Fiddlers* | | | |
| (5) Heinrich Christian Beyer | 1706–48 | *violin 2* | Andreas Christoph Jonne, from 1748 |
| (6) Johann Gottfried Kornagel | 1719–54 | *oboe 1* | |
| (7) Christian Ernst Meyer | 1707–30 | — | Johann Friedrich Caroli, 1730–38 |
| | | | Johann Christian Oschatz, 1738–47 |
| | | | Carl Friedrich Pfaffe, from 1748 |
| *Associate* | | | |
| (8) Candidate for permanent position | | *bassoon* | |

[a]Principal instrument (from Bach's memorandum of August 23, 1730).
[b]Previously art fiddler.

Bach himself, having grown up in a town piper's household, would have been intensely aware of the potential and pitfalls to be encountered in a town music ensemble, and kept a wary eye on its quality and reliability. His Leipzig troupe, with a regular head count of about ten to fifteen, included adjuncts and apprentices who normally served as tutti players. More often than not, therefore, he would have needed to add expert instrumentalists to play solo parts and to serve as principals. These had to be recruited from among his own private pupils (both Thomana students and outsiders) and from the student body at the university, where he could always find able musicians who would perform for a regular fee or even for free—either in the hope of being paid for a future engagement or to earn a reduction in Bach's fee for their lessons, or simply because they wanted to take part. A list of documented participants from 1723 to 1730 alone speaks for itself, as many of them would later pursue musical careers: Johann Christian Weyrauch, Georg Gottfried Wagner, Johann Friedrich Caroli, Friedrich Gottlieb Wild, Johann Christoph Samuel Lipsius, Ephraim Jacob Otto, Bernhard Friedrich Völkner, Christoph Gottlob Wecker, Carl Gotthelf Gerlach, Johann Friedrich Wachsmann, and Johann Christoph Hoffmann.[58] Bach's testimonial for Wild, written in 1727, reports that

during the four years that he has lived here at the University, [he] has always shown himself to be diligent and hardworking, in such a manner that he not only has helped to adorn our church music with his well-learned accomplishments on the *Flaute traversiere* and *Clavecin* but also has taken special instruction from me in the clavier, thorough bass, and the fundamental rules of composition based thereon, so that he may on any occasion be heard with particular approval by musicians of attainment.[59]

Two years later, he wrote about Wecker "that his knowledge *in Musicis* has made him a welcome guest everywhere, particularly since he has a good command of various instruments and no less can well afford to make himself heard *vocaliter,* and equally he has been able to give creditable assistance in my church and other music."[60]

Bach's performances not only needed a sufficient number of performers, they also required that the musicians be extremely well trained, because he expected of them much more than they were used to providing. He expressly characterized this challenge when he wrote in 1736 that "the concerted pieces that are performed by the First Choir, which are mostly of my own composition, are incomparably harder and more intricate."[61] In addition to the technical demands, there was the problem posed by sheer quantity—having to deal week after week with one difficult piece after another, a relentless challenge no previous cantor had put before his musicians. Nevertheless, Bach carefully designed his performance schedule in such a way that he achieved a reasonable balance of what he could demand from himself and from others.

A brief consideration of the packed performance calendar for Bach's first Christmas season in Leipzig reveals, on the one hand, his interest in presenting an extraordinary citywide musical program, and on the other, his awareness of what was doable and what was not (see Table 8.6). To begin with, he started on the first Sunday in Advent and on Christmas Day with repeat performances of Weimar cantatas (including BWV 63), so that he had more time before Christmas to compose new works, among them the Magnificat in E-flat major, BWV 243a, his first large-scale vocal work for Leipzig, and the cantatas BWV 40, 64, 190, 153, 65, and 154—all to be prepared and then performed within a span of two weeks. The lavish and differentiated scoring for the works on the high feast days is immediately apparent: BWV 63 is Bach's biggest Weimar score, the Magnificat is his heretofore biggest Leipzig score and the only five-voiced concerted piece before the *Mass in B minor,* and the cantatas BWV 40, 190, and 65 are carefully scaled. At the same time, he designed the cantatas for the lesser feasts in such a way as not to strain the choir unduly. For example, the difficult opening chorus of the cantata BWV 64 for the third day of Christmas has instruments (cornetto and trombones) supporting the choristers by doubling their parts, an expedient that would compensate for the lack of rehearsal time. Similarly, the cantata BWV 153 for the Sunday after New Year's Day and BWV 154 for the Sunday after Epiphany require the choir to sing only simple four-part chorales.

The performances took place in the west end (rear) choir lofts of St. Thomas's and St. Nicholas's, both spacious, three-aisled, late-Gothic-hall churches whose interior design, however, was so drastically changed in the later eighteenth and nineteenth centuries that the original architectural features of the organ and choir lofts are no longer visible. At St. Nicholas's, the choir loft on the west wall of the church opened toward the center aisle, with the organ loft situated next to it, opening toward the south aisle; a connecting gallery bridged the gap between the two and provided space primarily for the instrumentalists (see illustration, p. 268). At St. Thomas's, the organ and choir lofts on the west wall formed more of a unified structure that opened toward the center aisle (see illustrations, pp. 266–67). The organ in the last bay of the center aisle was positioned above and behind the choir loft, which filled the penultimate bay, level with the first (stone) gallery that extended over both south and north flanks of the church and afforded space for visitors. The second (wooden) gallery above the first, on both south and north flanks, augmented the space for visitors but did not run across the west wall. Instead, two separate "town piper galleries"—on the level of the organ loft and above the choir loft—bridged the space between the third-to-last and second-to-last col-

## TABLE 8.6. Performance Schedule, Christmas 1723–24

*First Sunday in Advent, November 28*

| | | |
|---|---|---|
| 7:00 A.M. Mass, *N:* | Nun komm der Heiden Heiland, BWV 61; | |
| | *scoring:* S*AT*B*, str, bc | —old work |
| 1:30 P.M. Vespers, *T:* | Nun komm der Heiden Heiland, BWV 61 | —repeat |
| | | performance |

*Christmas Day, December 25*

| | | |
|---|---|---|
| 7:00 A.M. Mass, *T:* | Christen, ätzet diesen Tag, BWV 63: | |
| | S*A*T*B*, 4tr/ti, 3ob, str, bc | —old |
| | Sanctus D major, BWV 238: SATB, str, bc | —new |
| 9:00 A.M. Service, *P:* | Christen, ätzet diesen Tag, BWV 63 | —repeat |
| 1:30 P.M. Vespers, *N:* | Christen, ätzet diesen Tag, BWV 63 | —repeat |
| | Magnificat E-flat major, BWV 243a: | |
| | S*S*A*T*B*, 3tr/ti, 2rec, 2ob, str, bc | —new |

*Second day of Christmas, December 26*

| | | |
|---|---|---|
| 7:00 A.M. Mass, *N:* | Darzu ist erschienen der Sohn Gottes, | |
| | BWV 40: SA*T*B*, 2cr, 2ob, str, bc | —new |
| | Sanctus D major, BWV 238 | —repeat |
| 1:30 P.M. Vespers, *T:* | Darzu ist erschienen der Sohn Gottes, | |
| | BWV 40 | —repeat |
| | Magnificat E-flat major, BWV 243a | —repeat |

*Third day of Christmas, December 27*

| | | |
|---|---|---|
| 7:00 A.M. Mass, *T:* | Sehet, welch eine Liebe, BWV 64: | |
| | S*A*TB*(+ cto/3trb), 1ob d'am, str, bc | —new |

*New Year's Day, January 1*

| | | |
|---|---|---|
| 7:00 A.M. Mass, *N:* | Singet dem Herrn ein neues Lied, | |
| | BWV 190: SA*T*B*, 3tr/ti, 3ob, str, bc | —new |
| 1:30 P.M. Vespers, *T:* | Singet dem Herrn ein neues Lied, | |
| | BWV 190 | —repeat |

*Sunday after New Year's Day, January 2*

| | | |
|---|---|---|
| 7:00 A.M. Mass, *T:* | Schau, lieber Gott, wie meine Feind, | |
| | BWV 153: SA*T*B*, str, bc | —new |

*Epiphany, January 6*

| | | |
|---|---|---|
| 7:00 A.M. Mass, *N:* | Sie werden aus Saba alle Kommen, BWV 65: | |
| | SA*T*B*, cr, 2rec, 2ob da caccia, str, bc | —new |
| 1:30 P.M. Vespers, *T:* | Sie werden aus Saba alle kommen, | |
| | BWV 65 | —repeat |

*First Sunday after Epiphany, January 9*

| | | |
|---|---|---|
| 7:00 A.M. Mass, *T:* | Mein liebster Jesus ist verloren, | |
| | BWV 154: SA*T*B*, 2ob d'am, str, bc | —new |

*N* = St. Nicholas's; *T* = St. Thomas's; *P* = St Paul's (University) Church.[62]
*Soloist.

umn pairs, providing a continuous instrumental gallery surrounding the choir loft on three sides.[63] In other words, singers in the choir loft facing the altar had the organ behind them (one level up) and the instrument galleries to the left and right (one level up as well). The two town piper galleries, built in

Interior eastward view of St. Thomas's Church, Leipzig, in a computer-generated image based on a nineteenth-century watercolor by Hubert Katz, showing the "swallow's nest" organ and the choir loft, located opposite the main choir and organ lofts, as they would have appeared during Bach's time.

Interior westward view of St. Thomas's Church, Leipzig, in a computer-generated image based on a modern photograph, showing the main choir and organ lofts as they would have appeared during Bach's time; the separate galleries were for instrumentalists (to the left and right above the choir and level with the organ loft, with the strings ordinarily placed on the left side and the winds on the right), with the violone, trumpets, and timpani on either side of the organ *Rückpositiv*.

Interior westward view of St. Nicholas's Church at Leipzig in a watercolor by Carl Benjamin Schwarz (c. 1785), showing the organ and choir lofts after the 1784 renovation of the church interior.

1632, provided stands for ten players on either side: for the art fiddlers (string players) on the south and the town pipers (wind players) on the north; continuo players, trumpeters, and drummer would be positioned to the left and right of the organ's *Rückpositiv*. The galleries were enlarged in May 1739 at the expense of Burgomaster Jacob Born and certainly in consultation with Bach, but the extent of the expansion is not known.[64] It must be assumed however, that the galleries now provided space for substantially more instrumentalists than the original twenty. Before this expansion, additional players were either squeezed into the available gallery space or joined the singers in the choir loft one level below, probably behind them. The singers apparently placed their music stands close to the railing of the loft so that their voices would project directly into the nave of the church.

On the first Sunday after Trinity 1723, Bach began his first annual cycle of cantatas. Of the "five full annual cycles [*Jahrgänge*] of church pieces, for all the Sundays and holidays" mentioned in the summary worklist of the Obituary, only the first three have been transmitted in recognizable and relatively intact form. About two-fifths of the cantata repertoire must be considered lost, so

very little can be said about the character of the fourth and fifth cycles.[65] This
in turn makes it difficult to draw firm conclusions about the evolution of the
cantata in Bach's hand throughout the 1720s, by far his most productive period of cantata composition. What clearly emerges, however, are two aims: first,
to provide himself and his office during the first several years of his tenure with
a working repertoire of substantial size that he would be able to draw on later;
to set certain goals for the individual cycles that would enable him to explore
the flexible cantata typology as widely as possible, to leave his own distinct
mark, and—as in other areas of compositional activity—to push the genre beyond its current limits.

Bach's decision to use mainly his own works for the required church performances was a programmatic one and directly related to his intention to
thoroughly modernize Leipzig church music. It must be considered symptomatic in this respect that, in contrast to earlier and later practices, Kuhnau's
musical estate was not acquired by the St. Thomas School. Whether or not
Bach himself advised against it, he was expected to change things. This in turn
let him fulfill an apparently long-held desire to focus on the kind of vocal-
instrumental writing that met his own musical ends, even though the enterprise would burden him enormously for some time to come. Bach realized, of
course, that he was putting himself in an unaccustomed position. Never before
had he had to produce music on a comparable scale, so it is all the more understandable that he would make use of older pieces that would, with or without surgery, fit into the project. As a result, an important characteristic of the
first cantata cycle of 1723–24 is the integration of the bulk of his Weimar cantata repertoire as well as the adaptation of Cöthen cantatas. However, a look at
the entire cycle (Table 8.7) also reveals that Bach did not cut corners. On the
contrary, his ambitions during the first year were so far-reaching that he
planned on providing for many Sundays either two-part cantatas or two different but complementary works for performance before and after the hour-
long sermon, as evidenced by fourteen such compositions: BWV 75, 76, 21,
24+185, 147, 186, 179+199, 70, 181+18, 31+4, 172+59, 194+165, 22+23,
and BWV deest + 182. If he did in fact follow through on his plan for the entire year, several dozen other cantatas from the first cycle have been lost.

The concept of a so-called double cycle was actually realized in the 1720 libretto collection *Gott-geheiligtes Singen und Spielen* by Johann Oswald Knauer,
whose texts Bach used for BWV 64, 69a, and 77. Bach's text selection for the
first year indicates a rather eclectic and pragmatic approach, dictated by such
considerations as the integration of existing works and the ready availability
of suitable texts. Besides Knauer, only Erdmann Neumeister (for BWV 24) can
be identified among the authors; the majority of the librettists remain un-

known. Nevertheless, we can trace the emergence of three favorite text forms, although they may not be related to three different authors: (1) biblical dictum (from the Gospel lesson)–recitative–aria–recitative–aria–chorale in BWV 136, 105, 46, 179, 69a, 77, 25, 109, 89, and 104 for the eighth to the fourteenth, the twenty-first, and twenty-second Sundays after Trinity and for Misericordias Domini; (2) biblical dictum–recitative–chorale–aria–recitative–aria–chorale in BWV 48, 40, 64, 153, 65, and 67 for the nineteenth Sunday after Trinity, four Christmas season feasts, and Quasimodogeniti; and (3) biblical dictum–aria–chorale–recitative–aria–chorale in BWV 83, 144, 66, 104, 166, 166, 86, 37, and 44 for Purification, Septuagesimae, Easter Monday, and Misericordias Domini to Exaudi.

## TABLE 8.7. First Annual Cantata Cycle (*Jahrgang* I)— Performance Schedule, 1723–24

| BWV | | Cantata | Liturgical Date | Performance[a] |
|---|---|---|---|---|
| *Cantatas on texts of various poets:* | | | | |
| 75 | | Die Elenden sollen essen (2 parts) | 1st Sunday after Trinity | 5/30/1723 |
| 76 | | Die Himmel erzählen die Ehre Gottes (2 parts) | 2nd Sunday after Trinity | 6/6/1723 (*a,s*) |
| 21 | * | Ich hatte viel Bekümmernis (2 parts) | 3rd Sunday after Trinity | 6/13/1723 |
| 24 | | Ein ungefärbt Gemüte | 4th Sunday after Trinity | 6/20/1723 |
| 185 | * | Barmherziges Herze der ewigen Liebe | 4th Sunday after Trinity | |
| 167 | | Ihr Menschen, rühmet Gottes Liebe | St. John's Day | 6/24/1723 |
| 147 | † | Herz und Mund und Tat und Leben (2 parts) | Visitation | 7/2/1723 |
| 186 | * | Ärgre dich, o Seele, nicht (2 parts) | 7th Sunday after Trinity | 7/11/1723 (*a,s*) |
| 136 | | Erforsche mich, Gott, und erfahre mein Herz | 8th Sunday after Trinity | 7/18/1723 |
| 105 | | Herr, gehe nicht ins Gericht mit deinem Knecht | 9th Sunday after Trinity | 7/25/1723 |
| 46 | | Schauet doch und | | |

| | | | |
|---|---|---|---|
| | sehet, ob irgendein Schmerz sei | 10<sup>th</sup> Sunday after Trinity | 8/1/1723 |
| 179 | Siehe zu, daß deine Gottesfurcht nicht Heuchelei sei | 11<sup>th</sup> Sunday after Trinity | 8/8/1723 |
| 199 * | Mein Herze schwimmt im Blut | 11<sup>th</sup> Sunday after Trinity | |
| 69a | Lobe den Herrn, meine Seele | 12<sup>th</sup> Sunday after Trinity | 8/15/1723 |
| 77 | Du sollt Gott, deinen Herren, lieben | 13<sup>th</sup> Sunday after Trinity | 8/22/1723 |
| 25 | Es ist nichts Gesundes an meinem Leibe | 14<sup>th</sup> Sunday after Trinity | 8/29/1723 |
| 138 | Warum betrübst du dich, mein Herz | 15<sup>th</sup> Sunday after Trinity | 9/5/1723 |
| 95 | Christus, der ist mein Leben | 16<sup>th</sup> Sunday after Trinity | 9/12/1723 |
| 148 | Bringet dem Herrn Ehre seines Namens | 17<sup>th</sup> Sunday after Trinity | 9/19/1723(?) |
| 48 | Ich elender Mensch, wer wird mich erlösen | 19<sup>th</sup> Sunday after Trinity | 10/3/1723 |
| 162 * | Ach! ich sehe, itzt, da ich zur Hochzeit gehe | 20<sup>th</sup> Sunday after Trinity | 10/10/1723 |
| 109 | Ich glaube, lieber Herr, hilf meinem Unglauben | 21<sup>st</sup> Sunday after Trinity | 10/17/1723 |
| 89 | Was soll ich aus dir machen, Ephraim? | 22<sup>nd</sup> Sunday after Trinity | 10/24/1723 |
| 163 * | Nur jedem das Seine | 23<sup>rd</sup> Sunday after Trinity | 10/31/1723 |
| 60 | O Ewigkeit, du Donnerwort, I | 24<sup>th</sup> Sunday after Trinity | 11/7/1723 |
| 90 | Es reißet euch ein schrecklich Ende | 25<sup>th</sup> Sunday after Trinity | 11/14/1723 |
| 70 † | Wachet! betet! betet! wachet! (2 parts) | 26<sup>th</sup> Sunday after Trinity | 11/21/1723 |

*Start of ecclesiastical year*

| | | | |
|---|---|---|---|
| 61 * | Nun komm der Heiden Heiland, I | 1<sup>st</sup> Sunday in Advent | 11/28/1723 |
| 63 * | Christen, ätzet diesen Tag | 1<sup>st</sup> day of Christmas | 12/25/1723 |
| [243a | Magnificat in E-flat major | 1<sup>st</sup> day of Christmas (Vespers)] | |
| 40 | Darzu ist erschienen | | |

| | | | | |
|---|---|---|---|---|
| | der Sohn Gottes | 2nd day of Christmas | 12/26/1723 | |
| 64 | Sehet, welch eine Liebe hat uns der Vater erzeiget | 3rd day of Christmas | 12/27/1723 | |
| 190 | Singet dem Herrn ein neues Lied (incomplete) | New Year's Day | 1/1/1724 | |
| 153 | Schau, lieber Gott, wie meine Feind | Sunday after New Year's Day | 1/2/1724 | |
| 65 | Sie werden aus Saba alle kommen | Epiphany | 1/6/1724 | |
| 154 | Mein liebster Jesus ist verloren | 1st Sunday after Epiphany | 1/9/1724 (a,s) | |
| 155 | * | Mein Gott, wie lang, ach lange | 2nd Sunday after Epiphany | 1/16/1724 (a,t) |
| 73 | Herr, wie du willt, so schicks mit mir | 3rd Sunday after Epiphany | 1/23/1724 (a,t) | |
| 81 | Jesus schläft, was soll ich hoffen? | 4th Sunday after Epiphany | 1/30/1724 (a,t) | |
| 83 | Erfreute Zeit im neuen Bunde | Purification | 2/2/1724 (a,t) | |
| 144 | Nimm, was dein ist, und gehe hin | Septuagesimae | 2/6/1724 (a,t) | |
| 181 | Leichtgesinnte Flattergeister | Sexagesimae | 2/13/1724 (a,t) | |
| 18 | * | Gleichwie der Regen und Schnee | Sexagesimae | |
| 22 | * | Jesus nahm zu sich die Zwölfe | Estomihi | 2/20/1724 (a,t) |
| 23 | * | Du wahrer Gott und Davids Sohn | Estomihi | |
| — | | [Siehe eine Jungfrau ist schwanger] | Annunciation | 3/25/1724 (a,t) |
| 182 | * | Himmelskönig, sei willkommen | Annunciation | |
| [245 | | St. John Passion, 1st version | Good Friday (Vespers) | 4/7/1724] |
| 31 | * | Der Himmel lacht | Easter Sunday | 4/9/1724 (a,t) |
| 4 | * | Christ lag in Todes Banden (later moved to cycle II) | Easter Sunday | |
| 66 | ‡ | Erfreut euch, ihr Herzen | 2nd day of Easter | 4/10/1724 (a,t) |
| 134 | ‡ | Ein Herz, das seinen Jesum lebend weiß | 3rd day of Easter | 4/11/1724 (a,t) |
| 67 | | Halt im Gedächtnis | | |

|  |  | Jesum Christ | Quasimodogeniti | 4/16/1724 (*a,t*) |
|---|---|---|---|---|
| 104 |  | Du Hirte Israel, höre | Misericordias Domini | 4/23/1724 (*a,t*) |
| 12 | * | Weinen, Klagen, Sorgen, Zagen | Jubilate | 4/30/1724 |
| 166 |  | Wo gehest du hin? | Cantate | 5/7/1724 |
| 86 |  | Wahrlich, wahrlich, ich sage euch | Rogate | 5/14/1724 |
| 37 |  | Wer da gläubet und getauft wird | Ascension Day | 5/18/1724 |
| 44 |  | Sie werden euch in den Bann tun (I) | Exaudi | 5/21/1724 |
| 172 | * | Erschallet, ihr Lieder | Whitsunday | 5/28/1724 |
| 59 | * | Wer mich liebet, der wird mein Wort halten (I) | Whitsunday | |
| 173 | ‡ | Erhöhtes Fleisch und Blut | 2nd day of Pentecost | 5/29/1724 |
| 184 | ‡ | Erwünschtes Freudenlicht | 3rd day of Pentecost | 5/30/1724 |
| 194 | * | Höchsterwünschtes Freudenfest | Trinity Sunday | 6/4/1724 |
| 165 | * | O heilges Geist- und Wasserbad | Trinity Sunday | |

*a* indicates date taken from autograph score (*s*) or original text booklet (*t*).
\* Re-performance of pre-Leipzig work, in some cases with minor changes.
† New version of pre-Leipzig work.
‡ Parody.
Brackets indicate works that were written by another composer or that are not extant.

Despite their heterogeneous nature, the cantatas from the first cycle establish some characteristic features that remain constant for the entire Leipzig cantata repertoire, such as the grand style choral opening (only rarely do solo pieces appear right at the start) and the closing four-part chorales that are simple but expressive. The newly composed choral and instrumental ensembles are larger than those of the Weimar cantatas, as are those of Weimar cantatas re-performed in Leipzig (for example, two recorders are added to BWV 18 and the string complement is enlarged in BWV 182). The instrumentation is more refined yet also more standardized (all the cantatas call for a full four-part string ensemble usually with fixed wind groups, such as three trumpets and timpani or double oboes and recorders). While the overall scoring patterns may seem less capricious and colorful than in the Weimar cantatas (compare Table 6.3), Bach's unbowed spirit of discovery continued to spur his exploration of new instrumental sonorities and combinations. From the start, he regularly made use of the new lower-register oboe types not available to him before, in particular the oboe d'amore and oboe da caccia, and from the spring of 1724 he began using the transverse flute. Instrumental virtuosity is heightened, and the technical demands on the vocal ensemble and soloists are no less striking.

Bach's compositional goals remained unchanged: not one to write aria after aria, chorus after chorus, and cantata after cantata, he expanded the cantata genre by broadening the scope of the conventional types of choruses, arias, recitatives, and chorales. The development of his opening cantata choruses—a major focus in the first cantata cycle—is breathtaking. In these expansive movements, the orchestral and choral sections become fully integrated (as opposed to the traditional separation of instrumental introduction and choral complex), and in addition, the entire vocal-instrumental apparatus engages in an intensive, multilayered musical interpretation of the text. In the impressive initial series of newly composed cantatas, BWV 75, 76, 24, 167, 136, 105, and 46, the last two mark a new plateau of artistic accomplishment in the church cantata genre, both in the intricacy of their compositional design and in the vigorous musical expression and striking rhetorical power of their opening choruses: "Herr, gehe nicht ins Gericht mit deinem Knecht" (Lord, enter not into judgment with thy servant), BWV 105/1, for four-part choir and a compact ensemble of horn, 2 oboes, doubling strings, and continuo—an eight-part score extending over 128 measures; and "Schauet doch und sehet, ob irgendein Schmerz sei" (Behold, and see if there be any sorrow), BWV 46/1, for four-part choir and trumpet, 2 recorders, 2 oboi da caccia, strings, and continuo—a thirteen-part score 142 measures long. By comparison, Bach's largest pre-Leipzig cantata chorus, "Ich hatte viel Bekümmernis," BWV 21/2, is a nine-part score of 58 measures, with a 20-measure instrumental sinfonia. Bach incorporated the music of BWV 46/1 ten years later into the Gloria section of the *B-minor Mass,* a clear testimony of the value he attached to the quality of this movement.

The development of interpretive imagery in Bach's musical language also took a new turn in the first months at Leipzig. For example, an aria like "Wie zittern und wanken / der Sünder Gedanken, / indem sie sich untereinander verklagen" (How tremble and waver / the sinners' thoughts / in that they accuse one another), of cantata BWV 105, translates the poetic text precisely into a fitting musical idea (see Ex. 8.1). First of all, the rhyme structure of the initial lines of the poem (wanken / Gedanken) determines Bach's symmetric phrasing of the corresponding vocal declamation. Then, the texture of the setting is fashioned to represent the image of "trembling *and* wavering" simultaneously by a two-layered score: the motive of wavering thoughts in the floundering and halting melodic gestures that alternate between soprano and oboe in an overlapping manner, and the trembling thoughts in a string accompaniment based on a tremolo figure that proceeds, for purposes of intensification, at two different speeds. The word-generated texture thus created in this passage provides a strong unifying device that helps structure the instrumental ritornello and the movement as a whole, so that other, similarly word-generated musical ideas, like the long melisma on "verklagen" from the next line, can blend in without compromising their identity (Ex. 8.2). Incidentally, the melodic-rhythmic shape of that melisma shows the demanding vocal technique Bach now required of his singers—a tribute to the effectiveness of his vocal lessons over a span of barely two months.

Considering the many adjustments and complications he faced during his first year in office, it is remarkable that Bach, despite some unavoidable (though not haphazard) scrambling for suitable cantata texts, was able to create an annual cycle that established new compositional standards not just for himself but for the cantata genre itself. At the same time, the first *Jahrgang* in toto possessed neither literary conformity nor overall musical consistency. For his second annual cycle of 1724–25, however, Bach could, with his increased preparation time, turn to the proven concept of a cantata cycle based on a uniform libretto type. While entire cycles had been set by a number of his colleagues, most notably Georg Philipp Telemann (beginning with his Eisenach cycle of 1711) but also Gottfried Heinrich Stölzel in Gotha and Johann Friedrich Fasch in Zerbst, Bach himself had never been in a position to compose a full *Jahrgang*—his Weimar settings of Salomo Franck's *Evangelisches Andachts-Opffer* of 1715 had to pursue a monthly rather than weekly schedule. But on the first Sunday after Trinity 1724, Bach could begin with a most promising cantata project of great homogeneity, whose scope he was able to define himself (Table 8.8). Every cantata was to be based on a seasonal church hymn of the ecclesiastical year; the first and last stanza of the hymn were to serve as the opening and final movements of the cantata, and the internal hymn stanzas were to be variously paraphrased, condensed, and reconfigured to accommodate the metric structure of the madrigal verses for recitatives and arias.[66]

## TABLE 8.8. Second Annual Cycle (*Jahrgang* II)— Performance Schedule, 1724–25

| BWV | Cantata | Liturgical Date | Performance |
|---|---|---|---|
| *Chorale cantatas:* | | | |
| 20 | O Ewigkeit, du Donnerwort, II (2 parts) | 1ˢᵗ Sunday after Trinity | 6/11/1724 |
| 2 | Ach Gott, vom Himmel sieh darein | 2ⁿᵈ Sunday after Trinity | 6/18/1724 |
| 7 | Christ unser Herr zum Jordan kam | St. John's Day | 6/24/1724 |

| | | | |
|---|---|---|---|
| 135 | Ach Herr, mich armen Sünder | 3rd Sunday after Trinity | 6/25/1724 |
| 10 | Meine Seel erhebt den Herren | Visitation | 7/2/1724 |
| 93 | Wer nur den lieben Gott läßt walten | 5th Sunday after Trinity | 7/9/1724 |
| 107 | Was willst du dich betrüben | 7th Sunday after Trinity | 7/23/1724 |
| 178 | Wo Gott der Herr nicht bei uns hält | 8th Sunday after Trinity | 7/30/1724 |
| 94 | Was frag ich nach der Welt | 9th Sunday after Trinity | 8/6/1724 |
| 101 | Nimm von uns, Herr, du treuer Gott | 10th Sunday after Trinity | 8/13/1724 |
| 113 | Herr Jesu Christ, du höchstes Gut | 11th Sunday after Trinity | 8/20/1724 |
| 33 | Allein zu dir, Herr Jesu Christ | 13th Sunday after Trinity | 9/3/1724 |
| 78 | Jesu, der du meine Seele | 14th Sunday after Trinity | 9/10/1724 |
| 99 | Was Gott tut, das ist wohlgetan, I | 15th Sunday after Trinity | 9/17/1724 |
| 8 | Liebster Gott, wenn werd ich sterben? | 16th Sunday after Trinity | 9/24/1724 |
| 130 | Herr Gott, dich loben alle wir | St. Michael's Day | 9/29/1724 |
| 114 | Ach lieben Christen, seid getrost | 17th Sunday after Trinity | 10/1/1724 |
| 96 | Herr Christ, der einge Gottessohn | 18th Sunday after Trinity | 10/8/1724 |
| 5 | Wo soll ich fliehen hin | 19th Sunday after Trinity | 10/15/1724 |
| 180 | Schmücke dich, o liebe Seele | 20th Sunday after Trinity | 10/22/1724 |
| 38 | Aus tiefer Not schrei ich zu dir | 21st Sunday after Trinity | 10/29/1724 |
| 115 | Mache dich, mein Geist, bereit | 22nd Sunday after Trinity | 11/5/1724 |
| 139 | Wohl dem, der sich auf seinen Gott | 23rd Sunday after Trinity | 11/12/1724 |
| 26 | Ach wie flüchtig, ach wie nichtig | 24th Sunday after Trinity | 11/19/1724 |
| 116 | Du Friedefürst, Herr Jesu Christ | 25th Sunday after Trinity | 11/26/1724 |

*Start of ecclesiastical year*

| | | | |
|---|---|---|---|
| 62 | Nun komm der Heiden Heiland, II | 1st Sunday in Advent | 12/3/1724 |
| 91 | Gelobet seist du, Jesu Christ | Christmas Day | 12/25/1724 |

| 121 | Christum wir sollen loben schon | 2nd day of Christmas | 12/26/1724 |
|---|---|---|---|
| 133 | Ich freue mich in dir | 3rd day of Christmas | 12/27/1724 |
| 122 | Das neugeborne Kindelein | Sunday after Christmas | 12/31/1724 |
| 41 | Jesu, nun sei gepreiset | New Year's Day | 1/1/1725 |
| 123 | Liebster Immanuel, Herzog der Frommen | Epiphany | 1/6/1725 |
| 124 | Meinen Jesum laß ich nicht | 1st Sunday after Epiphany | 1/7/1725 |
| 3 | Ach Gott, wie manches Herzeleid, I | 2nd Sunday after Epiphany | 1/14/1725 |
| 111 | Was mein Gott will, das g'scheh allzeit | 3rd Sunday after Epiphany | 1/21/1725 |
| 92 | Ich hab in Gottes Herz und Sinn | Septuagesimae | 1/28/1725 |
| 125 | Mit Fried und Freud ich fahr dahin | Purification | 2/2/1725 |
| 126 | Erhalt uns, Herr, bei deinem Wort | Sexagesimae | 2/4/1725 |
| 127 | Herr Jesu Christ, wahr' Mensch und Gott | Estomihi | 2/11/1725 |
| 1 | Wie schön leuchtet der Morgenstern | Annunciation | 3/25/1725 |
| [245 | St. John Passion (2nd version) | Good Friday (Vespers) | 3/30/1725] |

*(End of chorale cantata cycle; for later additions, see Table 8.9.)*

### Cantatas on texts of unknown origin:

| 249 ‡ | Kommt, gehet und eilet | Easter Sunday | 4/1/1725 |
|---|---|---|---|
| 4 * | Christ lag in Todes Banden | Easter Sunday | |
| 6 | Bleib bei uns, denn es will Abend werden | 2nd day of Easter | 4/2/1725 |
| 42 | Am Abend aber desselbigen Sabbats | Quasimodogeniti | 4/8/1725 |
| 85 | Ich bin ein guter Hirt | Misericordias Domini | 4/15/1725 |

### Cantatas on texts by Mariane von Ziegler:

| 103 | Ihr werdet weinen und heulen | Jubilate | 4/22/1725 |
|---|---|---|---|
| 108 | Es ist euch gut, daß ich hingehe | Cantate | 4/29/1725 |
| 87 | Bisher habt ihr nichts gebeten in meinem Namen | Rogate | 5/6/1725 |
| 128 | Auf Christi Himmelfahrt allein | Ascension Day | 5/10/1725 |

| 183 | Sie werden euch in den Bann tun, II | Exaudi | 5/13/1725 |
|---|---|---|---|
| 74 | Wer mich liebet, der wird mein Wort halten, II | Whitsunday | 5/20/1725 |
| 68 | Also hat Gott die Welt geliebt | 2nd day of Pentecost | 5/21/1725 |
| 175 | Er rufet seinen Schafen mit Namen | 3rd day of Pentecost | 5/22/1725 |
| 176 | Es ist ein trotzig und verzagt Ding | Trinity Sunday | 5/27/1725 |

\* Re-performance.
‡ Parody.
Brackets indicate works that were written by another composer or that are not extant.

It is hard to imagine that this fascinating, unprecedented project of chorale cantatas was initiated by anyone but Bach himself, and it is most likely that he also had a hand in the choice of hymns if only because of the direct musical implications for the chorale melodies.[67] The way in which the project proceeded and eventually ended strongly suggests that Bach's anonymous librettist was a close collaborator who resided in Leipzig. According to the most likely among various hypotheses, the author of the chorale cantata texts was Andreas Stübel, conrector emeritus of the St. Thomas School, a man of solid theological background (if somewhat nonconformist views) and ample poetic experience.[68] Stübel's death on January 27, 1725, after only three days of illness and after he had received from the printer texts for the booklet of cantatas to be performed from Septuagesimae Sunday (January 28) to Annunciation (March 25) 1725, would explain the abrupt ending of the chorale cantata cycle with "Wie schön leuchtet der Morgenstern," BWV 1, on the feast of Annunciation in that year. Not anticipating any such fateful turn, Bach had started the *Jahrgang* with energy and imagination, and the period from before June 11, 1724, to March 25, 1725, ended up as his most productive cantata year ever: forty cantatas were newly composed in almost as many weeks. On average, that comes to more than one cantata per week, and considering that certain celebrations—St. John's, St. Michael's, and the Marian feasts—and the great cluster of holidays at Christmastide required the performance of two or three pieces within a week, Bach's artistic productivity borders on the incredible.

That Bach went about his grand project systematically becomes immediately evident from the musical planning of the opening movements, especially at the beginning of the chorale cantata *Jahrgang* (II). Thus, the first cantata of the cycle, BWV 20, is designed in the manner of a French overture—an emphatic and most felicitous prelude to the cantata sequence in its entirety. After opening the cycle with a piece of such a modern sort, the second work, BWV 2, stresses the weight of tradition. Its Reformation-period chorale tune (in the Phrygian mode) is treated in a retrospective motet style, a dense five-part setting of imitative polyphony with a cantus firmus in long notes in the alto voice and without the accompaniment of obbligato instruments. In the cantatas for the following weeks, Bach explores further applications of cantus firmus technique, beginning with the opening movements of BWV 7 and 135, in which the chorale melodies appear in the tenor and bass voices, respectively, and of BWV 10, which presents the melody in both soprano and alto. Subsequent cantatas offer a broad array of cantus firmus treatments that develop thematic-motivic elements derived from chorales. Bach allows these musical materials to determine the vocal and instrumental profile of the chorale-based settings, giving each its own character and distinctive format.[69] According to the prevailing pattern, the final movements of the chorale cantatas present straight-forward four-part chorale harmonizations in Bach's usual unadorned style. But there are surprises in store. In cantata BWV 38, for example, Bach harmonizes the very first tone of the hymn "Aus tiefer Not" with a daring dissonance, a third-inversion dominant-seventh chord. Moreover, in the same work, as in some other chorale cantatas, he subjects the internal movements to cantus firmus treatment, by either using embellished portions of the chorale melody for the development of an aria theme (BWV 38/3), building a free recitative over a strict cantus firmus bass line (BWV 38/4), or constructing a vocal tercet in fugato manner (BWV 38/5), all movements again based on materials drawn from the cantata's chorale.

In the spring of 1725, when the delivery of chorale cantata texts came to a sudden halt, Bach had to come up with an emergency solution for the rest of the year. On Easter Sunday, he re-performed an old work, "Christ lag in Todes Banden," BWV 4, which fit in well despite its traditional outlook; consisting of unaltered chorale stanzas only, it represented the *per omnes versus* (pure hymn text) type of chorale cantata. Works of mixed origin and structure followed until Bach turned, for the remaining weeks until Trinity Sunday, to nine cantata texts by the young Leipzig poet Christiane Mariane von Ziegler,[70] daughter of the former burgomaster Franz Conrad Romanus. However, he chose to make some substantial changes to her words, and although she published her cantata texts later in the form of a complete annual cycle,[71] Bach did not return to her sacred poetry.

The Thomascantor must surely have regretted his inability to complete the chorale cantata cycle in 1725, because he tried sporadically to fill in some gaps, perhaps with the intention of rounding off or even finishing the *Jahrgang* (Table 8.9). Texts for all Sundays and feast days from the first Sunday after Trin-

**TABLE 8.9.** Chorale Cantatas (later additions)

| BWV | Cantata | Liturgical Date | Performance |
|---|---|---|---|
| 177 | § Ich ruf zu dir, Herr Jesu Christ | 4<sup>th</sup> Sunday after Trinity | 7/6/1732 (s) |
| 9 | Es ist das Heil uns kommen her | 6<sup>th</sup> Sunday after Trinity | 1732–35 |
| 137 | § Lobe den Herren, den mächtigen König der Ehren | 12<sup>th</sup> Sunday after Trinity | 8/19/1725 |
| 80b | Ein feste Burg ist unser Gott (new version) | Reformation Festival | 1728–31 |
| 80 | Ein feste Burg ist unser Gott (1<sup>st</sup> movement new) | Reformation Festival | 1740 |
| 140 | Wachet auf, ruft uns die Stimme | 27<sup>th</sup> Sunday after Trinity | 11/25/1731 |
| 14 | Wär Gott nicht mit uns diese Zeit | 4<sup>th</sup> Sunday after Epiphany | 1/30/1735 (s) |
| 112 | § Der Herr ist mein getreuer Hirt | Misericordias Domini | 4/8/1731 |
| 129 | § Gelobet sei der Herr (see Table 8.10) | Trinity | 1732 |
| 117 | § Sei Lob und Ehr dem höchsten Gut | unknown | 1728–31 |
| 192 | § Nun danket alle Gott | unknown | 1730 |
| 100 | § Was Gott tut, das ist wohlgetan, III | unknown | 1732–34 |
| 97 | § In allen meinen Taten | unknown | 1734 (s) |

(s) indicates date taken from autograph score.
§Based on pure hymn texts, without paraphrased stanzas.

ity up to and including Annunciation were apparently completed by the original librettist of the chorale cantata cycle, so Bach could later set a few texts that he had not needed in 1724–25, such as BWV 14 and 140 (there was neither a fourth Sunday after Epiphany nor a twenty-seventh Sunday after Trinity), or did not compose then, such as BWV 9 (Bach was out of town on the sixth Sunday after Trinity).[72] However, having lost his librettist, Bach tried to finish the incomplete cycle also with cantatas based on unparaphrased hymns, that is, chorale cantatas of the *per omnes versus* variety—represented in the 1724–25 cycle solely by BWV 107. He began filling in gaps as early as in the summer of 1725 (BWV 137), added BWV 129 in 1726, and thereafter several others, among them such magnificent works as BWV 112 and 177. The chorale cantata cycle was, nonetheless, never brought to completion, at least not according to the surviving sources. Transmission patterns indicate, how-

ever, that in Bach's library the nonchorale cantatas that filled the liturgical calendar from Easter to Trinity Sunday in 1725 were integrated within the third
cycle,[73] apparently in order to maintain the conceptual homogeneity of the
chorale cantata repertoire.

With the inception of the third annual cycle, the nearly uninterrupted cantata production of the previous year came to an end and, in all likelihood, was
never resumed with that degree of intensity. The third *Jahrgang* (Table 8.10)
covered a time span of about two years. As documented by a text booklet for
the third to sixth Sundays after Trinity 1725,[74] there are some definite gaps for
which compositions by Bach must once have existed. On the other hand, for
a major stretch in 1726 Bach performed no fewer than eighteen cantatas from
the pen of his cousin Johann Ludwig Bach, capellmeister at the ducal court of
Saxe-Meiningen, and on Good Friday of that year, a Passion by Friedrich Nicolaus Bruhns. Altogether, from mid-1725 to early 1727, Bach seems to have
composed cantatas only at irregular intervals. Whatever the reason for this
change of pace, it allowed him time to prepare his largest composition ever, the
*St. Matthew Passion,* for performance on Good Friday 1727.

### TABLE 8.10. Third Annual Cantata Cycle (*Jahrgang* III)— Performance Schedule, 1725–27

| BWV | Cantata | Liturgical Date | Performance |
|---|---|---|---|
| *Cantatas on texts by various poets:* | | | |
| *1725–26* | | | |
| 168 | Tue Rechnung! Donnerwort | 9th Sunday after Trinity | 7/29/1725 |
| 137 | Lobe den Herren, den mächtigen König[a] | 12th Sunday after Trinity | 8/19/1725(?) |
| 164 | Ihr, die ihr euch von Christo nennet | 13th Sunday after Trinity | 8/26/1725 |
| 79 | Gott der Herr ist Sonn und Schild | Reformation Festival | 10/31/1725 |
| 110 | Unser Mund sei voll Lachens | Christmas Day | 12/25/1725 |
| 57 | Selig ist der Mann | 2nd day of Christmas | 12/26/1725 |
| 151 | Süßer Trost, mein Jesus kömmt | 3rd day of Christmas | 12/27/1725 |
| 28 | Gottlob, nun geht das Jahr zu Ende | Sunday after Christmas | 12/30/1725 |
| 16 | Herr Gott, dich loben wir | New Year's Day | 1/1/1726 |
| 32 | Liebster Jesu, mein Verlangen | 1st Sunday after Epiphany | 1/13/1726 |
| 13 | Meine Seufzer, meine Tränen | 2nd Sunday after Epiphany | 1/20/1726 |
| 72 | Alles nur nach Gottes Willen | 3rd Sunday after Epiphany | 1/27/1726 |

|  | [18 cantatas by Johann<br>Ludwig Bach | between Purification and<br>13ᵗʰ Sunday after Trinity | 2/2/1726]<br>9/15/1726] |
|---|---|---|---|
|  | [*St. Mark Passion* by<br>F. Nicolaus Brauns (?) | Good Friday (Vespers) | 4/19/1726] |
| 146 | Wir müssen durch<br>viel Trübsal | Jubilate | 5/12/1726(?) |
| 43 | Gott fähret auf mit<br>Jauchzen (2 parts) | Ascension Day | 5/30/1726 |
| 129 | Gelobet sei der Herr,<br>mein Gott*ᵇ* | Trinity | 6/16/1726 |

## 1726–27

|  |  |  |  |
|---|---|---|---|
| 39 | Brich dem Hungrigen<br>dein Brot (2 parts) | 1ˢᵗ Sunday after Trinity | 6/23/1726 |
| 88 | Siehe, ich will viel Fischer<br>aussenden (2 parts) | 5ᵗʰ Sunday after Trinity | 7/21/1726 |
| 170 | Vergnügte Ruh,<br>beliebte Seelenlust | 6ᵗʰ Sunday after Trinity | 7/28/1726 |
| 187 | Es wartet alles auf<br>dich (2 parts) | 7ᵗʰ Sunday after Trinity | 8/4/1726 |
| 45 | Es ist dir gesagt, Mensch,<br>was gut ist (2 parts) | 8ᵗʰ Sunday after Trinity | 8/11/1726 |
| 102 | Herr, deine Augen sehen<br>nach dem Glauben (2 parts) | 10ᵗʰ Sunday after Trinity | 8/25/1726 |
| 35 | Geist und Seele wird<br>verwirret (2 parts) | 12ᵗʰ Sunday after Trinity | 9/8/1726 |
| 17 | Wer Dank opfert, der<br>preiset mich (2 parts) | 14ᵗʰ Sunday after Trinity | 9/22/1726 |
| 19 | Es erhub sich ein Streit | St. Michael's Day | 9/29/1726 |
| 27 | Wer weiß, wie nahe mir<br>mein Ende | 16ᵗʰ Sunday after Trinity | 10/6/1726 |
| 47 | Wer sich selbst erhöhet | 17ᵗʰ Sunday after Trinity | 10/13/1726 |
| 169 | Gott soll allein mein<br>Herze haben | 18ᵗʰ Sunday after Trinity | 10/20/1726 |
| 56 | Ich will den Kreuzstab<br>gerne tragen | 19ᵗʰ Sunday after Trinity | 10/27/1726 |
| 129 | Gelobet sei der Herr,<br>mein Gott*ᵇ* | Reformation Festival | 10/31/1726 (?) |
| 49 | Ich geh und suche<br>mit Verlangen | 20ᵗʰ Sunday after Trinity | 11/3/1726 |
| 98 | Was Gott tut, das ist<br>wohlgetan, II | 21ˢᵗ Sunday after Trinity | 11/10/1726 |
| 55 | Ich armer Mensch,<br>ich Sündenknecht | 22ⁿᵈ Sunday after Trinity | 11/17/1726 |
| 52 | Falsche Welt, dir trau<br>ich nicht | 23ʳᵈ Sunday after Trinity | 11/24/1726 |

| 36 | Schwingt freudig euch | | |
| | empor (earlier version) | 1ˢᵗ Sunday in Advent | 1726–30 |
| 58 | Ach Gott, wie manches | | |
| | Herzeleid (II) | Sunday after | |
| | | New Year's Day | 1/5/1727 |
| 82 | Ich habe genung | Purification | 2/2/1727 |
| 84 | Ich bin vergnügt mit | | |
| | meinem Glücke*ᶜ* | Septuagesimae | 2/9/1727(?) |
| [244 | *St. Matthew Passion,* | | |
| | 1ˢᵗ version | Good Friday (Vespers) | 4/11/1727] |

*Note:* Table does not include re-performances of earlier cantatas.
Brackets indicate works that were written by another composer or that are no longer extant.
*ᵃ*Later integrated into cycle II.
*ᵇ*Added later (~1732) to cycle II, with Trinity Sunday as destination (Table 8.9).
*ᶜ*Later added to cycle IV.

Like those of the first *Jahrgang,* the cantatas of the third present no unifying concept, as Bach reverted to texts of varying and usually older origin. Above all, he favored sacred poetry by Georg Christian Lehms from 1711 (BWV 110, 57, 151, 16, 32, 13, 170, 35), then texts by Salomo Franck from 1715 (BWV 72) and Erdmann Neumeister from 1714 (BWV 28). Finally Bach also turned to a 1704 collection attributed to Duke Ernst Ludwig of Saxe-Meiningen (BWV 43, 39, 88, 187, 45, 102, 17) that was also set by Johann Ludwig Bach and that often presents two contrasting biblical dicta, one from the Old Testament (an introductory movement) and one from the New (a middle movement). However, apart from an uninterrupted sequence of Lehms cantatas beginning on Christmas Day 1726, no clear compositional pattern emerges. Notable is the relatively frequent occurrence of solo (BWV 52, 84, 35, etc.) and dialogue (BWV 58, 32, 49, etc.) cantatas, but of particular significance in the third cycle—as also in the fourth—is Bach's use of preexisting concerto movements as opening instrumental sinfonias (BWV 156, 174, and 120a); the opening chorus of BWV 110 is a reworking of a concerto movement. From the summer of 1726 on, obbligato organ parts in BWV 146, 35, 169, and 49, later also in BWV 188 and 29, introduce a completely new dimension into Bach's Leipzig church music. Perhaps his eldest son, Friedemann, was drafted to take the solo parts, but the often incomplete notation of the organ parts suggests that the composer himself took his place at the organ bench, leaving the conducting to the first choir prefect. This innovative integration of solo organ into his cantatas, which incidentally allowed for an impressive display of the church instrument, was yet another brilliant idea of the capellmeister-cantor, whose third cantata cycle bears his unmistakable mark as an instrumentalist and organ virtuoso.

Following the third cycle came a fourth that must, with the exception of a few remnants, be considered lost (Table 8.11). Conceptually resembling the second, this fourth *Jahrgang* returns to the plan of a uniform series of librettos. Their fertile and versatile author, Picander—*nom de poésie* of Christian Friedrich Henrici—would become over the years Bach's most important Leipzig producer of texts. The collaboration between Bach and Picander, who held the public office of post commissioner in Leipzig and later served as country and city tax commissioner, seems to have begun in early 1725 with a congratulatory secular cantata for the court of Weissenfels, BWV 249a, that was subsequently transformed into an Easter cantata (see Table 8.8) and later became the *Easter Oratorio,* BWV 249. A year after the first performance of the *St. Matthew Passion,* Picander's finest piece of sacred poetry, he published a complete cycle of *Cantaten auf die Sonn- und Fest-Tage durch das gantze Jahr.* In

## TABLE 8.11. Fourth Annual Cantata Cycle ("Picander *Jahrgang*")

| BWV | Cantata | Liturgical Date | Performance |
|---|---|---|---|
| *Cantatas on texts by Christian Friedrich Henrici (Picander), published 1728:* | | | |
| 197a | Ehre sei Gott in der Höhe (incomplete) | Christmas Day | 12/25/1728(?) |
| 171 | Gott, wie dein Name, so ist auch dein Ruhm | New Year's Day | 1/1/1729(?) |
| 156 | Ich steh mit einem Fuß im Grabe | 3rd Sunday after Epiphany | 1/23/1729(?) |
| 84 | Ich bin vergnügt mit meinem Glücke | Septuagesimae | 2/9/1727 |
| 159 | Sehet, wir gehn hinauf gen Jerusalem | Estomihi | 2/27/1729(?) |
| [244 | *St. Matthew Passion,* 1st version/2nd performance | Good Friday (Vespers) | 4/15/1729] |
| Anh. 190 | Ich bin ein Pilgrim auf der Welt (fragment) | 2nd day of Easter | 4/18/1729(?) |
| 145 | Ich lebe, mein Herze, zu deinem Ergötzen | 3rd day of Easter | 4/19/1729(?) |
| 174 | Ich liebe den Höchsten von ganzem Gemüte | 2nd day of Pentecost | 6/6/1729[a] |
| 149 | Man singet mit Freuden vom Sieg | St. Michael's Day | 9/29/1728–29 |
| 188 | Ich habe meine Zuversicht | 21st Sunday after Trinity | 10/17/1728(?) or 11/6/1729 |
| *(Outside the 1728 publication:)* | | | |
| 157 | Ich lasse dich nicht, du segnest mich denn | Purification | after 1727 |

[a]Original performing parts dated.

the preface, dated June 24, 1728, Picander writes, "Actuated by the requests of many good friends, and by much devotion on my own part, I resolved to compose the present cantatas. I undertook the design the more readily, because I flatter myself that the lack of poetic charm may be compensated for by the loveliness of the music of our incomparable Capellmeister Bach, and that these songs may be sung in the main churches of our pious Leipzig."[75]

Even if this statement was only wishful thinking on the author's part, Bach definitely completed nine cantatas on Picander's texts (Table 8.11) and may have composed others whose sources have not survived. Indeed, traces of lost materials may be found in the two printed editions of Bach's four-part chorales published in 1765/69 and 1783–87.[76] Among the chief features of the Picander cantatas is the interpolation of chorale and free poetry in arias and choruses, giving the composer opportunities for various sorts of combinatorial techniques (as in BWV 156/2, 159/2, and nos. 1 and 19 of the *St. Matthew Passion*).

## TABLE 8.12. Cantatas and Related Works Outside the Annual Cycles

| BWV | Cantata | Liturgical Date | First Performance |
|---|---|---|---|
| 36 | Schwingt freudig euch empor (2 parts) (new version) | 1st Sunday in Advent | 12/2/1731 |
| 248 ‡ | *Christmas Oratorio,* Parts I–VI | Christmas Day to Epiphany | 12/25/1734– 1/6/1735[a] |
| 249 | *Easter Oratorio* (new version) | Easter Sunday | ~1738 |
| 158 | Der Friede sei mit dir | 3rd day of Easter | 1724–1735 |
| 11 ‡ | *Ascension Oratorio* | Ascension Day | 5/19/1735 |
| 34 ‡ | O ewiges Feuer, o Ursprung der Liebe | Whitsunday | 1746–47 |
| 30 ‡ | Freue dich, erlöste Schar (2 parts) | St. John's Day | 1738 |
| 51 | Jauchzet Gott in allen Landen | 15th Sunday after Trinity | 9/17/1730(?) |
| 50 | Nun ist das Heil und die Kraft (single movement) | St. Michael's Day | uncertain |
| 200 | Bekennen will ich seinen Namen (single movement) | unknown | 1742 |
| 248a | Text unknown (music surviving in BWV 248/VI) | unknown | 1734 |
| 1045 | Sinfonia (cantata lost) | unknown | 1743–46 |

‡ Parody.
[a]Original score dated.

As for the Obituary's reference to a total of five complete annual cantata cycles, the fifth is hardly recognizable among the extant sources, let alone reconstructible (Table 8.12). This *Jahrgang* would not, in all likelihood, have had the kind of consistency displayed by the second and Picander cycles. And if the first *Jahrgang* (1723–24) had indeed been planned and largely completed as a double cycle, the fifth could be found there, that is, in the "other half" of the first. But while there are some modest signs of Bach's continuing though reduced production of church cantatas and related works, among them the two oratorios for Christmas and Ascension Day, BWV 248 and 11, as well as the cantata fragments BWV 200, 248a, and 1045, the list of extant works provides little evidence for postulating a late—post-1730—cantata cycle. As far as we can see, the cantatas written after 1729 contribute nothing essentially new to Bach's output in this genre. However, we can note his increased receptiveness toward new stylistic trends, especially in arias of the later cantatas (BWV 200, 248a, and 30); particularly noteworthy are revisions of existing works for re-performances, as Bach drew on the rich repertoire that he had created in his productive cantata years of the 1720s.

Complementing the extensive body of the *Jahrgang* cantatas are occasional works and cantatas for certain regular functions (Table 8.13), but even though some were written for special events such as an organ dedication or the 1730 jubilee of the Augsburg Confession, they do not in principle differ from the cantatas for the Sundays and feast days of the ecclesiastical year. The town council election pieces constitute a particularly important group, however, because they fall into the category of official state music for which the cantor and music director at St. Thomas's bore the responsibility. They were performed at the service that took place annually on the Monday after St. Bartholomew's Day (August 24) at St. Nicholas's, after the formal election of the new city council and the rotation of the burgomaster seats. Like the sermon, the cantata was separately commissioned, with both the preacher and the cantor receiving extra fees. "Have ordered from Mr. Superintendent, D. Deyling, the sermon for the inauguration of the new Council, on this coming Monday, likewise the doorkeeper ordered the music from Herr Cantor," notes the town scribe on August 22, 1729.[77] The commissioned piece was due within exactly one week, but because the performance of the council piece always fell on a Monday, Bach had to prepare two different cantatas for the subsequent Sunday and Monday. And as the city council election service was a major communal-political event, Bach would have taken special care with a performance that invariably required a large ensemble and festive scoring with trumpets and timpani.

The autograph score of BWV 119 specifies a continuo group of "Violoncelli, Bassoni e Violoni all'unisono col Organo," such plural listing indicating the

## TABLE 8.13. Cantatas for Special Occasions

| BWV | Cantata | Purpose | Date |
|---|---|---|---|
| 119 | Preise, Jerusalem, den Herrn | Election of city council | 8/30/1723[a] |
| Anh. 4 | Wünschet Jerusalem Glück (lost) | " | 1726 or 1728 |
| 193 | Ihr Tore (Pforten) zu Zion | " | 8/25/1727 |
| 120 ‡ | Gott, man lobet dich in der Stille | " | 1742 |
| Anh. 3 | Gott, gib dein Gerichte dem Könige (lost) | " | 8/25/1730 |
| 29 | Wir danken dir, Gott, wir danken dir | " | 8/27/1731 |
| Anh. 193 | Herrscher des Himmels, König der Ehren (fragment) | " | 8/29/1740 |
| 69 | Lobe den Herrn, meine Seele (II) | " | 8/26/1748 |
| Anh. 14 | Sein Segen fließt daher wie ein Strom (lost) | Wedding Mass | 2/12/1725 |
| 34a | O ewiges Feuer, o Ursprung der Liebe (2 parts) | " | probably 1726 |
| 197 | Gott ist unsre Zuversicht (2 parts) | " | 1736–37 |
| 195 | Dem Gerechten muß das Licht (2 parts) | " | 1742 |
| 120a ‡ | Herr Gott, Beherrscher aller Dinge (2 parts, incomplete) | " | probably 1729 |
| 157 | Ich lasse dich nicht, du segnest mich denn | Funeral service | 2/6/1727 |
| 194 ‡ | Höchsterwünschtes Freudenfest (2 parts) | Organ dedication | 11/2/1723[a] |
| 190a | Singet dem Herrn ein neues Lied (lost) | Bicentennial of the Augsburg Confession | 6/25/1730 |
| 120b | Gott, man lobet dich in der Stille | | 6/26/1730 |
| Anh. 4 | Wünschet Jerusalem Glück | " | 6/27/1730 |
| Anh. 15 | Siehe, der Hüter Israel (lost) | Special homage | unknown (Leipzig period) |

‡ Parody.
[a] Original score dated.

size of the orchestra and underscoring the ceremonial nature of the music to be performed, which always included a processional march to accompany the exit of the town council from the church at the end of the service. Bach's score of BWV 120 makes reference to such an "Intrada con Trombe e Tamburi," which has not come down to us. What has survived, however, are reports in the Leipzig papers of the so-called council sermon on August 31, 1739, on which occasion "the Royal and Electoral Court Composer and Capellmeister, Mr. Joh. Seb. Bach, performed a music that was as artful as it was pleasant; its text was: CHORUS. Wir dancken dir, Gott, wir dancken dir."[78] This performance of cantata BWV 29 began with an elaborate concerto movement for organ solo and orchestra, a sophisticated arrangement of the first movement of the Partita in E major for unaccompanied violin, BWV 1006, that most likely featured the composer as soloist. The terms "artful" and "pleasant," however banal they may strike us today, are highly favorable judgments that far exceed what newspapers of the time generally wrote about a musical performance.

## THE "GREAT PASSION" AND ITS CONTEXT

On Good Friday 1727, close to the end of his fourth year in Leipzig, Bach presented at St. Thomas's a work of extraordinary musical dimensions, the *Passion According to St. Matthew,* BWV 244. When Anna Magdalena Bach later identified an apparently disjoined continuo part as belonging "zur groß Bassion" (to the great Passion),[79] everyone in the Bach family circle knew what she meant, for not only did the "great Passion" overshadow all Bach's other settings of the biblical Passion story, but its outsized formal dimensions and performance requirements, its compositional sophistication and technical mastery, and its powerful and poignant expressive qualities left behind all that had been customary or even conceivable in sacred music of the time. The *St. Matthew Passion,* which formed the pinnacle of the vocal works composed by Bach for the Leipzig churches, reached its lofty heights on the shoulders of his earlier works. To be sure, the large-scale Passion music benefited from the extraordinary experience Bach had gained in four years that burst with unceasing cantata composition and performance. However, two works in particular played an especially important role in the conceptualization and grandiose design of the "great Passion": the Magnificat of Christmas 1723 and the *St. John Passion* from the spring of 1724.

The Magnificat, BWV 243a, the first larger-scale composition for the Leipzig main churches, was performed at a small festival of sacred music during Bach's first Christmas season in his new city. Of the various works performed then (see Table 8.6), Bach's only setting of the Canticle of the Virgin

(Luke 1:46–55) represented the fullest and most elaborate compositional effort of his then-young career. Having begun his duties after the high feasts of Easter and Pentecost had already passed, Christmas 1723 offered the first opportunity for an exhilarating musical statement. At Vespers services in Leipzig, "the Magnificat was sung in German on regular Sundays but performed in concerted form and in Latin on high feasts."[80] Following a local Christmas tradition that had originated in the late Middle Ages and had also been observed by his predecessors,[81] Bach expanded the setting of the Magnificat by interpolating four German and Latin songs of praise, so-called *Laudes:* "Vom Himmel hoch, da komm ich her," "Freut euch und jubiliert," "Gloria in excelsis Deo," and "Virga Jesse floruit." At St. Thomas's, these inserted movements were performed from the east organ loft, the swallow's nest opposite the main musicians' gallery at the west end of the church. But even at St. Nicholas's, where the performing conditions did not permit this kind of stereophony, the double-choir structure of such an expanded Magnificat could not but produce a splendid and festive effect (see Table 8.14). Apart from its unusual five-part choral setting and rich instrumental scoring, the piece's symmetric frame and the different polyphonic textures and expressive gestures of the individual movements were distinctive innovations. Bach's close reading of the concluding Lesser Doxology, with the phrase "sicut erat in principio" (as it was in the

## TABLE 8.14. Magnificat in E-flat major, BWV 243a

| Vocal-Instrumental Ensemble I: | Vocal-Instrumental Ensemble II: |
|---|---|
| *Magnificat* | *Laudes* |
| 1.   Magnificat: SSATB, 3tr/ti, 2rec, 2ob, str, bc | |
| 2.   Et exultavit: S II, str, bc | |
| | A. Vom Himmel hoch: SSATB, bc |
| 3.   Quia respexit: S I, ob, bc | |
| 4.   Omnes generationes: SSATB, 2ob, str, bc | |
| 5.   Quia fecit: B, bc | |
| | B. Freut euch und jubilieret: SSAT, bc |
| 6.   Et misericordia: AT, str, bc | |
| 7.   Fecit potentiam: tutti | |
| | C. Gloria in excelsis Deo: SSATB, str, bc |
| 8.   Deposuit potentes: T, str, bc | |
| 9.   Esurientes: A, 2rec, bc | |
| | D. Virga Jesse floruit: SB, bc |
| 10.   Suscepit Israel: SSA, tr, str, bc | |
| 11.   Sicut locutus est: SSATB, bc | |
| 12.   Gloria Patri: tutti | |

beginning), resulted in a finale that presents a literal repeat of the opening movement, not as an abstract architectural device but as an effort to translate this portion of the text meaningfully into music.

A decade later, between 1732 and 1735, Bach substantially revised the Magnificat. For the new version, BWV 243, he deleted the interpolated Christmas movements, thereby neutralizing its liturgical destination, transposed the piece from E-flat to D major, one of the standard "trumpet keys," and modified the instrumentation by replacing recorders with the more modern transverse flutes and, for movement 10, the solo trumpet with two oboes in unison. These largely pragmatic decisions, which converted the Magnificat into a Vespers repertoire piece, indicate that Bach was striving to convert his Magnificat into a liturgical work that would be suitable for any festive occasion.[82]

If Christmas 1723 plunged Bach into a whirlwind of musical activities, the subsequent Good Friday, April 7, 1724, provided an opportunity of a very different kind. After a *tempus clausum* longer than that of Advent—six weeks of Lent during which no concerted music was permitted except on the Marian feast of Annunciation, March 25—the morning service on Good Friday at the Leipzig main churches followed a long-standing tradition: singing the *St. John Passion* in the four-part polyphonic setting by Martin Luther's musical adviser, the Wittenberg cantor Johann Walter, as reprinted in the 1682 choir songbook by Gottfried Vopelius.[83] Protestant churches in other cities, especially court churches, had long before introduced more modern versions of the musical Passion, and by around 1700 they also incorporated contemplative and other pieces as well as arias and recitatives, with instrumental accompaniments. Leipzig's New Church, since Telemann's years a hotbed of innovation in matters of sacred music, saw the performance of a Passion oratorio at the Good Friday morning service in 1717,[84] so that Johann Kuhnau felt under pressure to compete. But the Leipzig consistory resisted until 1721, when councillor Gottfried Lange, noting that people were flocking to the Good Friday service at the New Church and that cantor Kuhnau "very much liked to perform the Passion historia in figural style,"[85] was able to persuade the consistory to give in. Although they granted no changes for the morning service, they allowed the Vespers liturgy to be revised in order to accommodate a musical Passion in place of the traditional practice, under which the congregation sang rhymed Passion paraphrases in the form of the twenty-three-stanza hymn by Sebald Heyden "O Mensch bewein dein Sünde groß" of 1525 or the twenty-four stanzas of Paul Stockmann's "Jesu, Leiden, Pein und Tod" of 1633. And as the St. Thomas sexton, Johann Christoph Rost, duly noted, "on Good Friday of the year 1721, in the vesper service, the Passion was performed for the first time in concerted style."[86]

The composition then presented was Kuhnau's *St. Mark Passion,* which has survived only in incomplete form.[87] But even from the fragment, we can see that Kuhnau established a model that remained valid for Bach insofar as it focused on the unaltered biblical narrative distributed among soloists (evangelist and various *soliloquentes,* or solo speakers: Jesus, Peter, Pilate, etc.) and choir (various *turbae,* or crowds: High Priests, Roman Soldiers, Jews, etc.), interrupted here and there by hymn strophes and contemplative lyrics—so-called madrigal pieces set to freely composed verse, mainly in the form of arias. The whole structure was divided into two parts, one to be performed before and one after the Vespers sermon. Sexton Rost was describing what had become a musical service, with the preached sermon at the center extended and enveloped by the musical sermon of the dominant musical Passion. The first part was sandwiched between two congregational hymns, "Da Jesus an dem Kreuze stund" of 1640 and "O Lamm Gottes unschuldig" of 1545, and the second part was always followed by the sixteenth-century motet "Ecce quomodo moritur justus" (Isaiah 57:1–2) by Jacob Handl.

While the 1721 Good Friday Vespers service featuring Kuhnau's *St. Mark Passion* took place at St. Thomas's, the Passion performance of 1722 was held at St. Nicholas's and that of 1723 under the direction of the first prefect, Johann Gabriel Roth, back at St. Thomas's, since the venue alternated yearly between the two churches. Evidently, no one thought to inform Bach, who innocently scheduled his *St. John Passion* for April 7, 1724, at St. Thomas's. This plan came to the attention of the city council, "since the title of the music sent around this year revealed that it was to take place again in St. Thomas's." The upshot was that just four days before the performance, Bach was instructed to change the location to St. Nicholas's. According to the council proceedings, he quickly agreed to comply, "but pointed out that the booklet was already printed, that there was no room available, and that the harpsichord needed some repair, all of which, however, could be attended to at little cost; but he requested at any rate that a little additional room be provided in the choir loft, so that he could place the persons needed for the music, and that the harpsichord be repaired."[88] At the council's expense, a flyer announcing the new location was printed and the necessary arrangements regarding harpsichord and performance space were made. For the *St. John Passion,* Bach needed to accommodate a vocal-instrumental ensemble that was larger than what he had used at St. Nicholas's before, even larger than that for the cantata BWV 63 or the Magnificat (Table 8.6). Indeed, since on Good Friday the motet singers were not needed at St. Thomas's, Bach must have intended to combine the first and second choirs, a circumstance he would later use to advantage for the double-choir scoring in the *St. Matthew Passion.* Moreover, additional forces on the instrumental side were also required, not merely to enlarge the string section and to provide dual continuo accompaniment (organ plus harpsichord), but to permit sonorities of special effect (transverse flutes,[89] viole d'amore, viola da gamba, and lute) as demanded by the pathos and expression in the biblical narrative in general and the lyrical reflections upon it in particular.

Because of the Leipzig consistory's apparent requirement of adhering to the biblical Passion text, Bach could not use an existing Passion oratorio text such as a famous 1712 libretto by the Hamburg consul Barthold Heinrich Brockes, *Der für die Sünde der Welt Gemarterte und Sterbende Jesus,* in which biblical narrative is supplanted by rhymed paraphrases and which Reinhard Keiser, Telemann, Handel, Johann Mattheson, Gottfried Heinrich Stölzel, Johann Friedrich Fasch, and many other composers set to music. So Bach or a collaborator had to assemble the appropriate texts to complement the biblical narrative. The result was a compilation of individual poems excerpted from publications by Brockes, Christian Weise, and Christian Heinrich Postel (see Table 8.15) that recalls the heterogeneity of texts in the first annual cantata cycle. Bach did, however, take the gospel of St. John as a point of departure and structured the entire work around the design of the biblical narrative. The musical disposition of the Passion clearly suggests that Bach based his composition on a close reading of the biblical dialogue and its literary structure, especially in the tribunal scene in part II, central to the Passion story in the book of John. A likely starting point for Bach's compositional plan was the existence of repeated text passages in the Gospel account, such as the words "Jesum von Nazareth" and "Kreuzige ihn." Also the concentration of different crowd responses (*turba* choruses) in the central scene of part II must have suggested to him the possibility of providing a strong, unifying, and well-focused musical architecture by establishing a system of musical correlations.

In its harmonic design and compositional plan, Bach's musical setting of the biblical narrative from John 18:1 to 19:42 gives the impression of a through-composed score independent of the chorales and contemplative arias yet mindful of them. Bach's blueprint is especially apparent in the coherent way that the dramatic and ardent dialogue of the tribunal scene in part II unfolds from movement 16 to 18, 21, 23, 25, and 27. While the interjected chorales and arias function as pillars of harmonic stability, they also enhance the intensity and depth of expression reflected in the rapid sequence of sharp and flat keys—nos. 19 (three flats) →22 (four sharps) →24 (two flats) →28 (three sharps) →35 (four flats)—and the correspondingly contrasting colors of vocal-instrumental sonority.

The Passion performance of 1724 provided Bach with the first opportunity to put his own stamp on the Good Friday Vespers service, which had only recently become the musical highpoint of the year (the sermon, for all its length,

**TABLE 8.15. Libretto Design of the *St. John Passion*, BWV 245 (first version, 1724)**

| Gospel | Chorales | Free Poetry (choruses and arias) |
|---|---|---|
| ***Part I: Before the sermon*** | | |
| | | 1. Herr, unser Herrscher (author unknown) |
| 2. John 18:1–8 | 3. O große Lieb | |
| 4. John 18:9–11 | 5. Dein Will gescheh | |
| 6. John 18:12–14 | | 7. Von den Stricken (Barthold Heinrich Brockes) |
| 8. John 18:15a | | 9. Ich folge dir gleichfalls (author unknown) |
| 10. John 18:15b–23 | 11. Wer hat dich so geschlagen | |
| 12. John 18:24–27, Matthew 26:75 | | 13. Ach, mein Sinn (Christian Weise) |
| | 14. Petrus, der nicht denkt zurück | |
| ***Part II: After the sermon*** | | |
| | 15. Christus, der uns selig macht | |
| 16. John 18:28–36 | 17. Ach großer König | |
| 18. John 18:37–19:1 | | 19–20. Betrachte/Erwäge (Brockes) |
| 21. John 19:2–12a | 22. Durch dein Gefängnis (Christian Heinrich Postel) | |
| 23. John 19:12b–17 | | 24. Eilt, ihr angefochtnen Seelen (Brockes) |
| 25. John 19:18–22 | 26. In meines Herzens Grunde | |
| 27. John 19:23–27a | 28. Er nahm alles wohl in acht | |
| 29. John 19:27b–30a | | 30. Es ist vollbracht (Postel) |
| 31. John 19:30b | | 32. Mein teurer Heiland (Brockes) |
| 33. Matthew 27:51–52 | | 34–35. Mein Herz (Brockes) / Zerfließe (unknown) |
| 36. John 19:31–37 | 37. O hilf, Christe, Gottes Sohn | |
| 38. John 19:38–42 | | 39. Ruht wohl (unknown) |
| | 40. Ach Herr, laß dein lieb Engelein | |

*Second version (1725)*, substituted (II) and added (+) movements: 1II. O Mensch, bewein (chorale chorus); 11+. Himmel, reiße (aria with chorale); 13II. Zerschmettert mich (aria); 19II(20). Ach windet euch nicht so (aria); 40II. Christe, du Lamm Gottes (chorale chorus).

could be thought of as a mere interruption of an essentially musical service). He was able to define the event and to shape both its perception by the worshippers and their expectations for subsequent years. Never before had Bach been in a position to engage in such a showcase performance, one that needed to be exceptionally well prepared and that greatly advanced his experience with large-scale compositions. In its textual components and organization, he adhered to Kuhnau's model—presumably a requirement of the Leipzig clergy—but he chose dimensions that exceeded any of his two-part cantatas, the Magnificat, or the lost Weimar Passion of 1717. Lacking a homogenous libretto, he designed the work along the lines of the seventeenth-century Passion *historia,* with the biblical text, punctuated by hymn stanzas, functioning as the structural backbone. This approach also allowed for substantial changes that Bach later made to the work, replacing some of the poetical movements in order to modify its external gestalt, musical content, and theological character.

Such changes are particularly evident in the second version of the *St. John Passion,* performed a year later, on Good Friday 1725. Bach replaced the opening and concluding movements with two chorale elaborations, "O Mensch, bewein dein Sünde groß" and "Christe, du Lamm Gottes." Also, one of three aria substitutions featured a chorale, "Jesu deine Passion," which along with "O Mensch, bewein" was especially well chosen.[90] Bach clearly intended these true classics from the rhymed Passion repertoire to help adapt the *St. John Passion* to the ongoing cycle of that year's chorale cantatas. By using these two complex chorale settings to frame the entire work, he demonstrated the impact and significance of a musical architecture—not merely to present a novel formal accent but to forge a genuine new identity for the piece. A third revision of the *St. John Passion* may have been prompted by Bach's having composed his *St. Matthew Passion,* as he now dropped the only two passages that were drawn from the Gospel of St. Matthew (Peter's lament and the earthquake scene). There is also a fourth version—dating to 1749, the year before Bach's death—that undoes most of the structural changes made since the first but requires larger forces than before. Judging by the surviving set of original performing parts, the orchestra consisted of an expanded body of strings (with additional stands for violins, violas, and violoncellos) and a continuo group bolstered by a contrabassoon, to provide an especially weighty foundation.

In addition to these four discernible versions of the *St. John Passion* that emerged in its twenty-five-year history, Bach began, around 1739, a thorough revision of the work, which by then had already undergone two massive transmutations. This revision, intended to preserve the work in an autograph fair copy and to restore the basic structure of the original version, also entailed a careful stylistic overhaul of the entire score. For whatever reason, Bach broke off after twenty pages, in the middle of the tenth movement. Because that revision remained unfinished, an aura of incompleteness surrounds the *St. John Passion*.[91] Conceivably, Bach stopped his work because of an unpleasant affair that took place in the spring of 1739, recorded by the town scribe on March 17, ten days before Good Friday:

Upon a Noble and Most Wise Council's order I have gone to Mr. Bach here and have pointed out to the same that the music he intends to perform on the coming Good Friday is to be omitted until regular permission for the same is received. Whereupon he answered: it had always been done so; he did not care, for he got nothing out of it anyway, and it was only a burden; he would notify the Superintendent that it had been forbidden him; if an objection were made on account of the text, [he remarked that] it had already been performed several times.[92]

The incident, emanating from the civic rather than church authorities, clearly involved an issue of administrative supervision. We do not know whether Bach's angry reaction resulted in the cancellation of a performance of his own composition and the last-minute substitution of another work (possibly Telemann's Brockes Passion, which Bach must have performed at around that time), as a calendar of Passion performances during Bach's Leipzig period cannot be reconstructed without omissions and conjectures (see Table 8.16).[93]

## TABLE 8.16. Calendar of Passion Performances in Leipzig, 1723–50

| | | | | | |
|---|---|---|---|---|---|
| 1724 | N | *St. John*, BWV 245—version I | 1739 | N | ? Brockes Passion (Telemann) |
| 1725 | T | *St. John*, BWV 245—version II | 1742 | T | ? *St. Matthew*, BWV 244—version II |
| 1726 | N | *St. Mark* (Brauns) | 1745 | | *St. Luke* (anonymous) |
| 1727 | T | *St. Matthew*, BWV 244—version I | 1747[a] | | Brockes Passion (Handel) |
| 1728 | N | ? *St. John*, BWV 245—version III | 1748[a] | | Passion pasticcio (Keiser, Handel) |
| 1729 | T | *St. Matthew*, BWV 244—version I | 1749 | N | *St. John*, BWV 245—version IV |
| 1730 | N | *St. Luke* (anonymous) | before 1750[a] | | Passion oratorio (C. H. Graun) |
| 1731 | T | *St. Mark*, BWV 247 | before 1750[a] | | Passion pasticcio (Graun-Telemann-Bach-Kuhnau-Altnickol) |
| 1732 | N | ? *St. John*, BWV 245—version III | | | |
| 1736 | T | *St. Matthew*, BWV 244—version II | | | |

N = St. Nicholas's; T = St. Thomas's.
[a]Possibly concert hall performances.

The complex genesis and transformations of Bach's first Leipzig Passion—one is tempted to speak of *St. John "Passions"*—demonstrate a degree of continuing freshness, originality, and experimental radiance that makes the work stand out in many ways, notwithstanding that in terms of sheer compositional sophistication and artistic maturity, it serves as a forerunner of two later works, the *Passions According to St. Matthew* and *St. Mark*. Of the five Passions mentioned in the Obituary,[94] only two survive, *St. John* and *St. Matthew;* for *St. Mark,* we possess only Picander's libretto of 1731. Nevertheless, we know some of its musical content, scoring, and instrumentation because the piece derives from earlier works by way of parody, most notably from the *Funeral Ode,* BWV 198, of 1727 (there is reason to believe that the libretto itself was created with the reuse of extant material in mind). The reference in the Obituary to five Passions may include the lost work presented in 1717 at Gotha (BC D1) and, erroneously, an anonymous *St. Luke Passion* that Bach copied out and performed with a few additions of his own.

Of the three Leipzig Passions, the *St. John* in all of its versions lacks textual unity—the madrigal lyrics were compiled from various poetic sources—and the remarkable adaptability of the work cannot entirely conceal this inherent aesthetic problem. No doubt conscious of the difficulty, Bach began looking for a different kind of text, but not quite the oratorio type created by Barthold Heinrich Brockes in which the biblical narrative was replaced with rhymed paraphrases. Bach's unsuccessful search for a suitable text may well have hindered him from composing a new work for two successive Good Fridays and made him turn instead to modifying his *St. John Passion* for 1725 and selecting the *St. Mark Passion* by Friedrich Nicolaus Brauns for 1726. He had performed Brauns's work in Weimar, and he now adjusted it to fit Leipzig liturgical practice and musical conditions (BC D 5). When in 1725 Picander (Christian Friedrich Henrici) published an oratorio text of the Brockes type, *Erbauliche Gedancken auf den Grünen Donnerstag und Charfreytag über den leidenden* JESUM *in einem* ORATORIO *entworffen* (Devotional Thoughts for Holy Thursday and Good Friday about the Suffering Jesus, Fashioned into an Oratorio). Bach surely paid attention to this libretto, which was dedicated to (and perhaps commissioned by) Franz Anton Count von Sporck of Bohemia. It could easily have been this sample from Picander's adept and agile poetic pen that brought the two Leipzig artists together.[95] Whether Bach eventually commissioned Picander or Picander approached Bach, a close collaboration is beyond doubt, both on the conceptual level and in matters of detail. The Brockes model loomed large (and Picander emulated its allegorical dialogue between the Daughters of Zion and the Faithful) and the poetic language of Salomo Franck also proved inspiring, but it became of utmost importance for the Gospel text to be preserved intact and for the lyrics to reflect the appropriate theological scope. Bach may in fact have alerted Picander to pertinent sources, such as the Passion homilies of Heinrich Müller, a seventeenth-century Lutheran theologian whose works could be found among the literature in Bach's library.[96] Some structural features seem to have been specifically requested by the composer. For example, the allegorical dialogue is arranged so that the Daughters of Zion and the Faithful do not just appear successively but simultaneously, as in aria no. 20, where the soloist from choir I sings "Ich will bei meinem Jesu wachen" (I will wake with my Jesus) while choir II responds "So schlafen unsre Sünden ein" (Thus will our sins go to sleep)—this kind of conjunction being essential for the double-choir design to work.[97] Likewise, the combination of free lyrics with hymn strophes (most prominently featured in the opening chorus) may have been suggested by Bach, reflecting as it did his keen interest in multilayered polyphonic structures that include a cantus firmus.

What emerged was a libretto that used the same textual components as the *St. John* but avoided the pitfalls of heterogeneous lyrics. And with its more abundant and complex madrigal-style poetry, Picander's *St. Matthew Passion* libretto indeed constituted, from a literary point of view, a unified Passion oratorio. While the libretto for the later *St. Mark Passion,* again by Picander, borrowed from preexisting material, which presented certain impediments, the *St. Matthew Passion* libretto enabled Bach to conceive a wholly original work and to compose it in a single sweep. There was neither room nor need for the kind of radical alterations that the *St. John Passion* underwent, even though Bach nearly always found occasion to change and improve. In the case of the *St. Matthew Passion,* a significant revision occurred only once after its first performance at St. Thomas's on April 11, 1727, and this for the purpose of enhancing the work's monumental character by extending its musical dimensions and by expanding and refocusing its performing forces, while leaving the overall design and libretto intact. It was in 1736, when the work was performed for the third time, that Bach replaced the simple chorale "Jesum lass ich nicht von mir," BWV 244b, which originally concluded part I, with the massive chorale setting "O Mensch, bewein dein Sünde groß," appropriated from the second version of the *St. John Passion.* Additionally, he created a more decisive division of the entire ensemble into two vocal-instrumental bodies by assigning separate continuo groups to choirs I and II, instead of letting one common continuo section provide the fundament for both choirs. Finally, in addition to the regular spaces for choir and instruments, Bach used the swallow's nest organ and choir loft in the performance. He assigned the cantus firmus lines of the two choruses that framed part I (nos. 1 and 29) to a third choir made up of sopranos with organ support,[98] a decision that mobilized virtually all available musical resources at St. Thomas's and must surely have resulted in a spectacular effect. And if sexton Rost, in his list of Passion performances, specified merely "1736. St. Thomas's, with both organs,"[99] his remark shows that this unusual feature by no means went unnoticed.

The definitive character of Bach's 1736 revision of the *St. Matthew Passion* and concomitant performance decisions is expressed by the calligraphic autograph fair copy that he set out to prepare that year and that he later completed with great scrupulousness. There is no comparable manuscript score from Bach's hand that is so carefully laid out and written in two colors of ink, red and dark brown. Red is applied to the biblical text of the evangelist and *soliloquentes,* the chorale melody "O Lamm Gottes unschuldig" in the first movement, and a few rubrics (Gothic lettering is used throughout, except for Old Testament quotations in the Gospel, which are displayed in Latin script). It could not be more evident that in 1736 Bach considered this score as his most significant work. In fact, he treasured the manuscript so much that even when the opening pages were damaged by some mishap in later years, he carefully restored them by pasting on strips of paper and replacing lost staves.[100] But while Bach could hardly imagine that the "great Passion," more than any of his other works, would make history in the truest sense of the word, he knew full well from the earliest planning stages that this composition would be special—indeed, that nothing like it had ever been attempted before.

In many ways, the time, space, focus, and meaning of the musical Vespers service on Good Friday gave Bach a unique chance to set his imagination free, and he grasped the opportunity from the very beginning by composing the *Passion According to St. John.* Yet one discerns everywhere in the *St. Matthew Passion* his intention, already clear from the work's internal and external dimensions, of surpassing everything that had been written previously, by himself and by other composers. The score, containing sixty-eight movements, some of extraordinary length, required an eight-voice double choir and a well-equipped double orchestra.[101] And he was able to call on the rich experience he had gained through his involvement with the church cantata over a period of four years. However, Bach's ambitions went far beyond the monumental format that he deliberately chose. We can best understand his approach as an artist to the musical shaping of the Passion story by seeing how he planned it so as to bring out a wealth of interconnections, and how he employed musical forms and compositional techniques in an imaginative and totally unschematic manner in order to serve the most sacred biblical text of the Lutheran faith on the highest feast day of the Reformation church.

The primary structural backbone of the *St. John Passion* and, therefore, its compositional focus rest on the Gospel narrative. In the *St. Matthew Passion,* by contrast, it is Picander's madrigal poems, lyrical contemplations of individual scenes in the Passion story, that shape the work. None of the original text booklets from Bach's performances have survived, but the first reprint of the text in volume II of Picander's collected works, *Ernst-Schertzhaffte und Satyrische Gedichte,* published in 1729, shows how the biblical Passion narrative is framed and punctuated by seventeen poems, most of them bipartite (nos. 1, 5–6, 8, 12–13, etc., in Table 8.17). Hence the biblical material is divided, in accordance with the poet's conception and its realization by the composer, into fifteen scenes and two introductions, to which both the lyrical meditations and the pointed interspersing of hymn stanzas relate. All of the lyrics are introduced by biblical references—for example nos. 5–6, "When the woman anointed Jesus"—so that the reflective and interpretive function of every single poem and musical setting becomes immediately clear.

## TABLE 8.17. Libretto Design of the *St. Matthew Passion,* BWV 244 (first version, 1727)

| Poetry by Picander (choruses, arias) | Gospel | Chorales |
|---|---|---|
| **Part I—*Before the sermon*** | | |
| *The Daughters of Zion* [I] *and the Faithful* [II]: | | |
| 1. Kommt, ihr Töchter* (I/II) | 2. Matth 26:1–2 | 3. Herzliebster Jesu |
| *When the woman anointed Jesus:* | 4. 26:3–13 | |
| 5–6. Du lieber Heiland/Buß and Reu (I) | 7. 26:14–16 | |
| *When Judas took the 30 silver pieces:* | | |
| 8. Blute nur, du liebes Herz (II) | 9. 26:17–22 | 10. Ich bins, ich sollte büßen |
| *When Jesus kept the Passover:* | 11. 26:23–29 | |
| 12–13. Wiewohl mein Herz / Ich will dir mein Herze (I) | 14. 26:30–32 | 15. Erkenne mich, mein Hüter |
| | 16. 26:33–35 | 17. Ich will hier bei dir stehen |
| *When Jesus quailed at the Mount of Olives* (*Zion and the Faithful*): | 18. 26:36–38 | |
| 19–20. O Schmerz* / Ich will bei meinem Jesu wachen (I/II) | 21. 26:39 | |
| *After the words "O my Father . . . let this cup pass from me":* | | |
| 22–23. Der Heiland fällt / Gerne will ich mich bequemen (II) | 24. 26:40–42 | 25. Was mein Gott will |
| *When Jesus was captured (Zion and the Faithful):* | 26. 26:43–50 | |
| 27. So ist mein Jesus nun gefangen (I/II) | 28. 26:51–56 | 29. Jesum laß ich nicht von mir |

*Part II—After the sermon*

*The Faithful and Zion:*

| | | |
|---|---|---|
| 30. Ach, nun ist mein Jesus hin (I/II) | 31. 26:57–59 | 32. Mir hat die Welt |
| *After the words "But Jesus kept silent":* | 33. 26:60–63a | |
| 34–35. Mein Jesus schweigt / Geduld (II) | 36. 26:63b–68 | 37. Wer hat dich<br>so geschlagen |
| *When Peter wept:* | 38. 26:69–75 | |
| 39. Erbarme dich (I) | | 40. Bin ich gleich<br>von dir gewichen |
| *After the words "It is not lawful . . . because<br>it is the price of blood":* | 41. 27:1–6 | |
| 42. Gebt mir meinen Jesum wieder (II) | 43. 27:7–14 | 44. Befiel du deine<br>Wege |
| | 45. 27:15–22 | 46. Wie wunderbarlich |
| *After the words "What evil has He done?":* | 47. 27:23a | |
| 48–49. Er hat uns allen wohlgetan /<br>Aus Liebe (I) | 50. 27:23b–26 | |
| *When Jesus was scourged:* | | |
| 51–52. Erbarm es Gott / Können Tränen<br>meiner Wangen (II) | 53. 27:27–30 | 54. O Haupt voll<br>Blut und Wunden |
| *When Simon of Cyrene was compelled to<br>bear His cross:* | 55. 27:31–32 | |
| 56–57. Ja freilich will in uns /<br>Komm, süßes Kreuz (I) | 58. 27:33–44 | |
| *When Jesus was crucified (Zion and the Faithful):* | | |
| 59–60. Ach Golgatha / Sehet, Jesus hat<br>die Hand (I; I/II) | 61. 27:45–50 | 62.Wenn ich einmal<br>soll scheiden |
| *When Jesus was taken down from the cross:* | 63. 27:51–58 | |
| 64–65. Am Abend / Mache dich,<br>mein Herze, rein (I) | 66. 27:59–66 | |
| *After the words "And they sealed the stone"<br>(Zion and the Faithful):* | | |
| 67–68. Nun ist der Herr / Wir setzen uns<br>mit Tränen nieder (I/II) | | |

---

*With chorale interpolated.
ªChanged in 1736 to "O Mensch, bewein dein Sünde groß" (from *St. John Passion*, 1725 version).

It is another distinguishing mark of the *St. Matthew Passion* that Bach chose to draw deliberately on the complete repertoire of forms cultivated in the sacred and secular music of his day. Even Baroque opera, the most representative genre of the age, could not compare in its range of compositional types and forms, for opera finds no place for movements based on a cantus firmus, which belong exclusively to the domain of sacred music, or for settings in the style of a polyphonic motet (of which there are several examples among the *turba* choruses of the Passion). In any case, such a degree of polyphonic elaboration, typical of the church style in general and Bach's artistic preferences in particular, was worlds away from operatic practice. But well beyond questions of form, genre, and compositional technique, the *St. Matthew Passion* project challenged Bach's whole concept of musical science, requiring him to analyze the literary material, the symbolic and affective imagery, and the theological content as well as to consider the appropriate representation of the Passion story. He met the challenge by making optimal use of all musical means, from the widely diverse singing voices and instrumental sonorities (exclusive of brass) to the broad spectrum of melodic inventions, rhythmic patterns, harmonic structures, and key choices. And with respect to the last two in particular, the composer of *The Well-Tempered Clavier* not only had the advantage of his cutting-edge experimental background, he also sought to extend this experience to the realm of vocal-instrumental music.

By having the *St. Matthew Passion* meander through the keys while drawing on an extraordinary array of colors in the instrumental obbligato accompaniments of the arias, Bach was exploring the widest possible range of musical expression. The settings of the Picander poems function as pillars of stability, from the dual tonality and modality in the opening chorus through the full chromatic realm of keys up to four sharps and flats—the maximum range for a mixed group of instruments not regulated by equal temperament. But given those limitations, Bach does not shy away from breaking out of these restrictions when underscoring extreme affects or imagery. In the harmonically unique arioso no. 59 ("Ach Golgatha"), for example, he fully exploits all twelve chromatic pitches, moves through chords as remote and extreme as A-flat minor and F-flat minor (requiring double flats), and lets the alto voice end the piece with an unresolved tritone, D-flat to G. Likewise, in the death scene, no. 61a, after using the pitch of F-flat for the word "Finsternis" (darkness), he sets Jesus's last words, the Hebrew "Eli, Eli, lama asabthani," in B-flat minor (five flats), near the bottom end of the circle of fifths, and to complete the descent to the absolute depth of despair, he sets the subsequent translation one step beyond that, in E-flat minor (six flats). In a kind of counterpoint to this extreme venture at the brink of the key system—at once compellingly expressive and symbolic—and on a greatly spaced-out scale, Bach pursues a corresponding yet reverse tonal descent in his key choices for the "Passion chorale"—the melody of "Herzlich tut mich verlangen" in nos. 15, 17, 44, 54, and 62—whose successive key signatures (####/♭♭♭/##/♭/♮) demarcate the path of inevitability no less forcefully. One cannot but notice how much further Bach takes his sophisticated and decisively innovative compositional planning here than he does in the *St. John Passion.*

The two principal, fundamentally different textual layers that constitute the libretto of the *St. Matthew Passion*—madrigal poetry on the one hand, holy Scripture and chorales on the other—are nowhere abruptly juxtaposed. On the contrary, Picander and Bach both set a premium on seamless integration that is already manifest in the opening chorus, in which freely conceived verse and chorale text and melody perfectly blend into each other: the cantus firmus "O Lamm Gottes, unschuldig" (O innocent lamb of God) immediately responds to the dialogue "Seht ihn! Wie? Als wie ein Lamm!" (See him! How? Just as a lamb!). The opening chorus thus provides a summation of what the entire Passion oratorio aims to achieve in theological content, literary structure, and musical expression. Picander's allegorical dialogue and lament "Kommt, ihr Töchter" is set by Bach in the manner of a French tombeau, as a funeral march for the multitude of believers who ascend to Mount Zion and the holy city of Jerusalem. "The Daughters of Zion," in allegorical personification of Jerusalem, the site of Christ's suffering, call on "the Faithful," representing the contemporary believer, to join them in witnessing the Passion of Christ. In the Apocalypse of St. John, the site of Christ's Passion is counterposed to the vision of the eternal Jerusalem, whose ruler is the Lamb. Here we find the reason for the connection between the aria text "Kommt, ihr Töchter, helft mir klagen" (Come, you daughters, help me lament), set by Bach in E minor, and the chorale "O Lamm Gottes, unschuldig" set in G major: "celestial" major proclaiming Christ's innocence and "terrestrial" minor accentuating Christ's suffering are contrasted, yet integrated in one and the same musical setting.

This theologically meaningful poetic and musical dialectic is placed by Picander and Bach as a kind of vision that precedes the account of the Passion and provides an ultimate goal for the gradual unfolding of the drama. Throughout the musical score, the tension between major and minor modes is never resolved; quite the reverse, it becomes increasingly acute in the course of the Passion story, in the constant oscillation between sharp and flat keys before finally subsiding in the final chorus in C minor. The beginning of the work thus determines its ending: the dual tonality and modality of the opening chorus, E minor and G major, exposes the dramatic tension that the final chorus can only partly resolve. The true resolution will come only when the radiant major mode, enhanced by the triadic fanfares of the trumpets, resonates two days later in the Easter Sunday cantata. Through its reference to the innocent Lamb as the ruler in Zion, which is the celestial Jerusalem, *St. Matthew*'s opening chorus provides the "Passion set to music" with a mighty visionary or, theologically speaking, eschatological prologue. And when the G-major chorale sung from the swallows' nest organ loft at St. Thomas's above the so-called Triumphal Arch—that is, from the altar side—pierced the E minor and thereby forced a modal switch, the music revealed its deep symbolic dimension right from the outset. For the tremendous show of musical force (two choirs and two orchestras on the main west gallery, a distant third choir on the small east gallery) was not meant as a display of powerful and luxuriant sound. The chorale reverberating from the chancel side of the church warned the audience and alerted skeptics at the outset that what awaited them was not "theatrical" music,[102] but music that indisputably proclaimed its sacred and liturgical character.

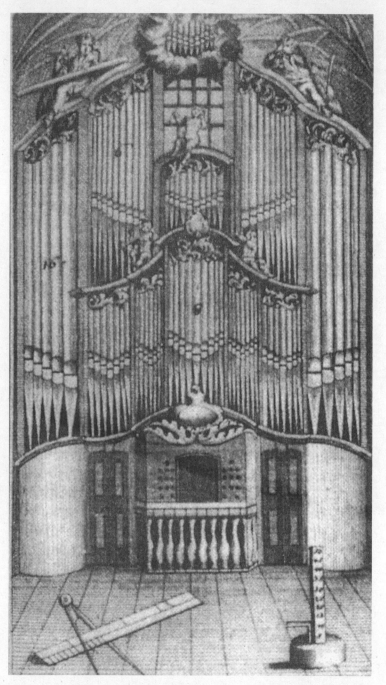

The Scheibe organ of St. Paul's (University) Church, Leipzig, in an engraving made for the instrument's dedication (1717).

# 9

## *Musician and Scholar*
### COUNTERPOINT OF PRACTICE
### AND THEORY

*Musicorum et cantorum magna est distantia*
*Isti dicunt, illi sciunt quae componit musica*
*Nam qui facit quod non sapit diffinitur bestia*

Singers and musicians, they are different as night and day.
One makes music, one is wise and knows what music can comprise.
But those who do what they know least are to be designated beast.
GUIDO OF AREZZO

### PERFORMER, COMPOSER, TEACHER, SCHOLAR

By a curious coincidence, Guido's eleventh-century didactic poem was first published in a 1774 volume of medieval musical treatises, edited by Prince Abbot Martin Gerbert of St. Blasien in the Black Forest, that also contains a passing reference to Bach as "the father of organists in Germany."[1] Had Bach been familiar with the Guidonian poem, he would in his mind have substituted *Musicant* for the Latin term *cantor* (singer), because in eighteenth-century German usage *Musicant* denoted the ordinary music maker of the street-musician and beer-fiddler variety and was the very term that provoked Bach's reaction to the 1737 attack by Johann Adolph Scheibe.[2] At the same time, Bach would not have wanted to pit the musical performer and the musical scholar against each other as mutually exclusive species. On the contrary, for himself and for his educational ideals, he cultivated the concept of the musician-scholar, or performer-composer. Indeed, he proudly claimed the designation "virtuoso" for himself, as M. Birnbaum affirmed in his defense against Scheibe's assault: "If one of those musical practitioners is an extraordinary artist on an instrument, he is called not a *Musicant* but a virtuoso."

Bach's early reputation as an instrumental virtuoso prevailed throughout his lifetime and for decades later. Prince Abbot Gerbert's reference reflects the fact that Bach's fame was based primarily on the impression he had made not only in numerous virtuosic performances, but also through the wide dissemination of his keyboard works and the dispersion of a large number of pupils. In contrast to the keyboard repertoire, Bach's vocal and instrumental compositions circulated to a significantly lesser degree outside of Weimar, Cöthen, and Leipzig. Nevertheless, in these places (most notably in Leipzig), the capellmeister Bach left a strong mark, too, as a leader of unusually demanding and complex performances. It is the technical sophistication and depth of substance reflected in the works themselves, whether for keyboard, other instruments, voices, or choir and orchestra, that is invariably stressed from early on in writings about Bach as performer. Scholarly thought and theoretical command in penetrating and shaping the musical material always played a role in Bach's compositions and always presented a challenge for the performer (not to mention the listener). And the climate of the university town of Leipzig must have had a particularly influential effect on Bach's daily work, on the development of his musical mind, on his artistic orientation, and on his aesthetic choices. If Guido's *cantor* and *musicus* were antagonistic and incompatible paradigms, Bach deliberately nourished their complementary relationship and, more than that, aimed at the complete integration of practitioner and theorist without compromising quality on either side. That the academic atmosphere of the St. Thomas School and, by extension, Leipzig University fostered such an approach sheds light on the context in which Bach's Leipzig works originated, on the people involved in their performance, and, not to be ignored, on his primary audience.

Had Bach not been so aware of his intellectual disposition, of his fascination with musical scholarship and his love for teaching—altogether genuine interests of a learned musician—he would hardly have considered the post as cantor at St. Thomas's. And what proved to be a strong secondary draw was the chance to arrange for the education of his sons Wilhelm Friedemann, Carl Philipp Emanuel, and Johann Gottfried Bernhard, all of whom attended the St. Thomas School in preparation for university studies. Indeed, all three later enjoyed the benefits of a university education not available to their father or grandfathers: Friedemann studied in Leipzig, Carl in Leipzig and Frankfurt on the Oder, and Bernhard in Jena. There had always been considerable overlap of the St. Thomas senior faculty and Leipzig University, and more often than not the school's rector and conrector simultaneously held professorships at the university. The palpable effect this connection had on the level of instruction and the atmosphere of learning at the school led a significant number of its graduates to continue their education at one or more of the four faculties of Leipzig University—theology, law, medicine, and philosophy.

The Faculty of Philosophy, formerly the Faculty of Arts, had a particularly close curricular relationship with the Schola Thomana, as the origins of both institutions were firmly rooted in the seven liberal arts as defined since medieval times: the *trivium,* consisting of grammar, logic, and rhetoric, and the *quadrivium,* comprising arithmetic, geometry, astronomy, and music. The age of humanism and the spirit of the Lutheran Reformation had brought about changes in the school's curriculum that led to a more comprehensive study of the classics, a closer study of the Scriptures, and a new respect for scientific knowledge; the educational focus, however, remained religious. The curricular reforms created strong interdisciplinary bonds among all subject areas, including music. Although choir practice, singing lessons, and musical performance clearly dominated at St. Thomas and similar Latin schools, music's relations with mathematics (as exemplified in the tuning systems, proportions of intervals, and the geometry of organ pipes) were not forgotten and offered many a link with contemporary science. Moreover, the connections with rhetoric and poetics were manifold, in both the choral and instrumental repertoire (for instance, in the prosody of a recitative and the meter and rhyme of an aria). The compositional treatment of sacred texts in motets and cantatas in particular offered numerous entry points for discourse that was both musically and theologically informed. Hence, Bach's instruction would have closely resembled that of his academic colleagues; at the same time, the pressures of a relentless performing schedule probably forced the cantor to take a pragmatic stand and stress drill and practice over intellectual dialogue.

Having no patience for theory isolated from practice, that is, detached from composition and performance, nor any inclination to get involved in literary discussion,[3] Bach never contributed to the literature of music theory. Yet he owned and studied books such as Friedrich Erhard Niedt's *Musicalische Handleitung* of 1710, Johann Joseph Fux's 1724 counterpoint treatise, *Gradus ad Parnassum,* and Johann David Heinichen's 1728 composition manual, *Der General-Baß in der Composition.* And he had a real interest in theoretical discourse on music, or it would be difficult to understand why so many of his private pupils went on to write theoretical works, including Lorenz Christoph Mizler's annotated translation of Fux's treatise, and perhaps also Friedrich Wilhelm Marpurg's *Abhandlung von der Fuge.*[4] Bach satisfied his own desire to engage in practical theory by designing writing projects that would suit his teaching aims. Those aims, however, could not be separated from his composing and performing goals, as we can see in such works as the *Orgel-Büchlein,* the *Aufrichtige Anleitung,* both parts of *The Well-Tempered Clavier,* the collection of four-part chorales, and *The Art of Fugue.* The latter—showing no stronger theoretical bent than any of the others but the only one published around Bach's time, albeit posthumously[5]—allowed its editors to engage in a retrospective review of the very qualities that meant so much to Bach and that so clearly articulated the philosophy of his approach, while the subject was fresh in their minds. In 1756, Carl Philipp Emanuel Bach described *The Art of Fugue* as "the most perfect practical fugal work,"[6] a characterization that complements Friedrich Wilhelm Marpurg's statement in the preface to the work's second edition (1752): "No one has surpassed [Bach] in thorough knowledge of the theory and practice of harmony."[7]

"Practical throughout" (that is, composition as theoretical thought translated into communicative musical language), *The Art of Fugue* "accomplishes what many skillful men have suggested in their writing." And in this first announcement of the work to be published—placed in the scholarly periodical *Critische Nachrichten aus dem Reiche der Gelehrsamkeit* (Critical News from the Land of Erudition) in 1751—the second-oldest of Bach's sons continues to emphasize his father's method of teaching: "While the rules we were given were good and abundant, the needed examples were lacking. Yet one knows how fruitless instruction is without illustration, and experience shows what unequally greater advantage one draws from practical elaborations rather than from meager theoretical direction."[8] Incidentally, no theoretical work on fugal composition existed before Marpurg's 1753 treatise, *Abhandlung von der Fuge*, which is largely based on *The Art of Fugue*, Bach's practical "treatise." There Bach systematically exemplifies the art of fugal counterpoint in exactly the same way that the *Orgel-Büchlein* exemplifies the art of elaborating a cantus firmus, the *Aufrichtige Anleitung* the art of inventing and developing musical ideas, *The Well-Tempered Clavier* the art of exploring the complete range of the tonal system, and the four-part chorales the art of writing with "the natural flow of the inner voices and the bass."[9] Moreover, and notably, none of these works focuses on a single issue; on the contrary, each of them deals with several at once. To mention only a few of them: *The Art of Fugue* demonstrates the concept of a single theme, the many possibilities for its treatment, and the technique of two-, three-, and four-part counterpoint; *The Well-Tempered Clavier* is written in free and strict styles, in the form of preludes and fugues; and the *Orgel-Büchlein* and the four-part chorales pay vital attention to the word-tone relationship. In the end, they all deal also with the challenges of performance, both in a technical sense ("acquiring facility," playing "correctly") and in the manner of presentation ("cantabile," "all parts singable throughout").[10] None of these works is primarily didactic; in fact, they all are conceived, as the title pages of the *Clavier-Übung* series invariably stipulate, "for music lovers, to refresh their spirits."

For Bach, the ultimate rationale for being a musician, that is, a performer-composer, was not to pursue some sort of mental construct but "to make a well-sounding harmony to the honor of God and the permissible delectation of the soul."[11] And whether he wrote a cantata and conducted its performance or composed and played a keyboard piece, the latent counterpoint of theory and practice and the objective of teaching through music formed a distinct back-drop for all his endeavors as a musical scholar. Carl August Thieme, Bach's student for ten years at the St. Thomas School and later the school's conrector, took the cantor's dictation and recorded his *Precepts and Principles for Playing the Thorough-Bass or Accompanying in Four Parts . . . for His Students in Music,*[12] where Bach offers a definition of thoroughbass as "the most perfect foundation of music." Bach continues, paraphrasing from Niedt's *Musicalische Handleitung,* that "the end and ultimate cause, as of all music, so of the thoroughbass, should be none else but the glory of God and the recreation of the soul/mind [*Gemüth*]. Where this is not observed, there is no real music but only a devilish blare and hubbub."[13]

At Cöthen or Weimar, Bach would have taken the same position, but in Leipzig his stature as a performer-composer assumed the additional dimension of a musical scholar, whose instruction needed to complement the newer teaching methods of logic informed by philology and science. His language, therefore, reflects a terminology different from Niedt's,[14] in that he speaks of "cause/reason" (*causa = Ursache*) and also discusses "principles" (*Grundsätze*) of the thoroughbass as a fundamental element in music, the latter term introduced by Christian Wolff in translating the Greek *axiom* and the Latin *principium.*[15] Not unlike his philosophical colleagues who explored, probed, and taught the *principia* of philosophy,[16] Bach explored, probed, and taught the principles that govern music—not only its physical, technical side but also its spiritual and emotional dimension. For in order to achieve the ultimate goal, a composer—as Bach's student Lorenz Christoph Mizler put it—must have "sufficient understanding of the tones and of human emotions."[17] On the one hand, "all effects of music are based on the various ratios of the tones," and therefore "geometry is necessarily of great benefit to music and the knowledge of the tones." On the other hand, however, a primary mistake by composers is that they "make insufficient or no effort at imitating nature," that is, the nature of humans, their thought and emotions/affects/passions. And whoever can "mix the natural tones—that is, the harmonic triad—with words according to their meaning in such a way that they resemble human emotions, is imitating nature in music."

Mizler emphasizes that *Weltweisheit* (wisdom of the world), the term of the German Enlightenment for "philosophy," is of crucial value "to gain a sufficient knowledge of human emotions." Hence, Gottfried Wilhelm Leibniz's principle of sufficient reason, that nothing can be so without there being a reason why it is so, applies to composers, who need to understand the causal interaction between the nature of music and human nature. Philosophy, understood in the broadest sense—ranging from logic, poetics, and philology to mathematics, physics, metaphysics, and theology without sharp disciplinary borders, as the careers of some of Bach's Leipzig faculty colleagues illustrate— represented the core of the liberal arts curriculum that Bach's students were exposed to, whether at St. Thomas's or the university, and that Bach had to mirror in his own teachings. He would, therefore, have found no fault with Mizler's argument that "a composer must not do anything without cause, and must have a rational intention, that is, a wish to stimulate or calm human emotions." On the contrary, that is precisely what Bach meant by thoroughbass's twofold causal interaction, first between the "consonances and dissonances" of thoroughbass and the resulting "well-sounding harmony," second between music reflecting the glory of God (who ordered everything by number, measure, and weight) and music reflecting and serving the nature of man for the renewal of spirit, mind, and soul.

There is no question that the academic climate and surroundings of the St. Thomas School and Leipzig University shaped Bach's thinking and had a profound impact on his daily work. After all, the community of students and colleagues formed the core of his audience. As a performer-composer, he had no competition in town. He moved among the distinguished scholars of the academic community: his professorial colleagues at the St. Thomas School, the erudite Lutheran clergy, and his academic friends. Their daily work and the level and content of their intellectual discourse, ranging from conservative theological and philosophical orthodoxy to progressive rationalism, influenced his own thinking. And the products of their scholarship provided the immediate context for his own musical products. While not directly comparable in terms of actual content (after all, we don't even know which books by his Leipzig colleagues Bach read), they were related in terms of their function as educational, enlightening, and uplifting contributions to the intellectual environment at large.

Bach was drawn into the narrower realm of Leipzig University for purely external reasons as well, for he remained an *Isenacus,* a burgher of Eisenach, for his entire life. He never acquired Leipzig citizenship, but benefited from the privileged status and legal protection of the "university relatives": after his death, for example, the university functioned as probate court for his estate. Yet his horizon was forged neither by the small localities in which he lived and worked, including the unassuming city of Leipzig, nor by the narrow range of his travels. As compared with the cosmopolitan orientation and experience of colleagues like Handel and Telemann, Bach's world was defined not so much by geographic boundaries as by the greater universe of scholarship, which knows no boundaries and where the very concepts employed in approaching the world are themselves a topic of intellectual inquiry. Just as Leipzig academicians ranging from conservative to progressive in this age of reason were seeking to discover the laws governing God's creation and explain the causes and principles of nature, Bach undertook his own empirical and open-ended inquiry into the secrets and principles of music in order to offer his own resounding explanations and reverberating demonstrations.

## MUSIC DIRECTOR AT THE UNIVERSITY

The long-standing arrangements between the Academia Lipsiensis (Leipzig University), one of the oldest German universities, and the cantors at St. Thomas's pertained especially to the divine service held for the academic community at St. Paul's, the University Church, four times a year (on Christmas Day, Easter Sunday, Whitsunday, and the Reformation Festival). The connection was evident as well at the so-called *Quartals-Orationes*—academic orations held each quarter—and other ceremonial academic events. Owing to the established personal union of the St. Thomas cantorate and the academic music directorate, there was no question about who would compose the ceremonial music when the university celebrated its three-hundredth anniversary in 1709. So cantor Kuhnau, who also held a law degree from the university, wrote for the occasion "Der Herr hat Zion erwehlet," a cantata performed on December 4.[18] The following summer, however, when the university increased its academic worship services at St. Paul's from four per year to weekly on Sundays throughout the year, the previous arrangements—involving the Thomascantor only on a part-time basis—had to be substantially modified. An organist had to be appointed for the New Divine Service, as the newly instituted Sunday service was called (Kuhnau himself had served as organist for the four annual academic services until this point),[19] and concerted music had to be provided for the feast days outside of what was now dubbed the Old Divine Service and for the Sundays during the trade fairs. As long as he could, Kuhnau resisted any effort to appoint a second academic music director in charge of the New Service, fearing that it would only result in a further drain on the limited personnel resources available in the city for music. The activities of the Collegium Musicum at the New Church under the direction of Telemann and his successors had taught Kuhnau an unpleasant lesson in unwelcome competition, and he worried that St. Paul's would become a home for the city's other Collegium Musicum. For a while, therefore, performances by members of the latter Collegium took place irregularly and informally, and definitely without financial support from the university. But after Kuhnau's death and during the vacancy of the cantorate, the opportunity arose for a reorganization of the church music at St. Paul's.

Johann Gottlieb Görner, a former Kuhnau student, St. Thomas School alumnus, organist at St. Nicholas's since 1721, and leader of one of the two Collegia Musica in town, had for some time conducted the concerted music at St. Paul's "out of his own free will and without asking for anything." Now on April 3, 1723, only a few weeks before Bach's election to the St. Thomas cantorate, the university agreed to Görner's request and appointed him music director for "the New Divine Service, at ordinary Sunday and feast day sermons," specifying that "the old music, however, for the quadrimester festal sermons remain with the town cantor."[20] Bach, then, took up his Leipzig office with the additional obligation of academic music director, but the Thomascantor was no longer the only one holding that title. Moreover, in the absence of any formal contract for either Bach or Görner with the university, the division of responsibilities was less clear than it should have been; not surprisingly, problems arose during Bach's first half-year in Leipzig over compensation and incidental fees connected with his university duties, that is, the cantata performances at the Old Service and the singing of motets at the quarterly academic orations. At the time of his negotiations with the city council in the spring of 1723, he was led to believe that he could expect 12 talers from the university for the Old Service alone, a situation symptomatic of the informal and disastrously inaccurate manner in which Burgomaster Lange and others made projections of the cantor's prospective annual income of 1,000 to 1,200 talers—the city fathers probably being unaware of the arrangements the university had just made with Görner. So Bach was understandably taken aback when he ended up with only half the expected amount. He suspected that the modest salary Görner received for the New Service was actually taken from what used to be paid to the cantor for the Old Service,[21] and he was probably right, even though the university council insisted that payments for the two different services were "entirely unrelated."[22]

The problems were not wholly financial, however. Bach also wanted a more clearly defined role with respect to musical functions at the university over and above those at the Old and New Services. He based his argument on the premise that before the creation of the New Service, the cantor and music director of the Old Service was in charge of all musical performances at the university. And to support this view, he called on the widows of his two predecessors, Sabina Elisabeth Kuhnau and Maria Elisabeth Schelle, as witnesses. But by the fall of 1725, with two years having gone by, the discussions going nowhere, and the university owing him a substantial amount of money, he decided to appeal directly to the highest authority, King Friedrich August I, the university's protector. Bach formally complained about the loss of honoraria for "the *Directorium* of the music at the conferring of doctoral degrees and other solemn University occasions in St. Paul's," activities that "used to belong, indisputably, at least as far as music was concerned, to the Old Divine Service." Since he was invited to play a recital on the Silbermann organ of St. Sophia's Church in Dresden on or before September 20, 1725, Bach could hand-deliver his first letter of September 14 to the court. Yet this and two subsequent letters of November 3 and December 31 did not bring about the desired result. For the king's decision, communicated to the university by a written decree dated January 21, 1726, affirmed the university's position in the matter.[23]

Because the cantor at St. Thomas's reported as a municipal officer to another jurisdiction, Bach could hardly have realized that from the university's perspective, its autonomy was at stake. When the cantorate changed hands, the university authorities seized the opportunity to keep its affairs more strictly separate, leaving Bach caught in the middle of an increasingly suspicious and rivalrous relationship between the city and the university. It may only gradually have dawned on him what it actually meant to have signed a pledge prepared for him by the city council specifying, in part, that he should "not accept or wish to accept any office in the University" without their consent. Clearly, neither the city nor the university was eager to share the cantor. Yet despite such an inauspicious beginning, Bach conscientiously attended to the Old Service, taking his ensembles four times a year across the city to St. Paul's, just a three-minute walk from St. Nicholas's and no more than seven minutes away from St. Thomas's, for a repeat performance of the cantata. He carried out this task for twenty-seven years, receiving a fixed annual fee of 13 talers 10 groschen,[24] a bit more than one-eighth of his fixed cantor's salary—not bad, really, for four cantata (repeat) performances per year, compared with the sixty due at the city's principal churches. The conducting of motets for the quarterly orations (included in that fee) he normally delegated to one of his choir prefects, so a portion of what he collected from the university he did not even have to personally "earn." He and Görner seem to have gotten along quite well, or Bach would not have supported Görner's appointment as organist at St. Thomas's in 1729 (see Table 8.2).[25] After all, the two collaborated on a weekly basis from 1723 to 1750, and upon Bach's death Görner as a family friend and "university relative" was appointed guardian for the children Johann Christoph Friedrich, Johann Christian, Johanna Carolina, and Regina Susanna Bach.[26]

As compared with the divine service at Leipzig's principal churches, the academic worship at St. Paul's, both the Old Service and the New, was centered on the sermon, with a sharply abbreviated liturgy that was largely limited to congregational hymn singing.[27] The cantata performance in the Old Service took place after the sermon, which always dealt with the Gospel lesson of the day, and a subsequent hymn. Since the academic service began at 9 A.M. and the sermon would not end until well after 10, enough time remained for Bach and his vocal-instrumental musicians to relocate, even if the main service at St.

Thomas's or St. Nicholas's lasted the full three hours from 7 to 10, as it always did on Christmas Day, Easter Sunday, Whitsunday, and the Reformation Festival. The cantata performed at St. Paul's would ordinarily be the same work that had been presented earlier that morning, as it would be too much of a strain to consider anything but a repeat performance—all the more since there would have to be a further repeat in the early afternoon, at the Vespers of the church that had not heard a cantata performance at the morning service.

St. Paul's, a thirteenth-century hall church that was considerably expanded between 1471 and 1521 by the addition of a late-Gothic chancel, had served as the university's house of God from 1409. It was fitted in 1710–12 with double galleries in order to increase its seating capacity, a direct result of the decision to establish a regular service there every Sunday. The church (which survived World War II but was demolished in 1968 in order to make room for a new building of Karl Marx University) fulfilled a secular function as well in that it operated as the university's main auditorium. Most of the larger academic ceremonies took place there, including the quarterly orations. Right at the beginning of Bach's Leipzig tenure, on August 9, 1723, a ceremonial gathering took place at the Auditorium Philosophicum of the *Fürsten Collegium* (Princes' Collegium) on the Ritterstrasse, on the occasion of the birthday of Duke Friedrich II of Saxe-Gotha, who was visiting the university. The rector and professors attended, and the oration dedicated to the guest of honor was, as the local press reported, "accompanied by an exquisite music that Mr. Johann Sebastian Bach had composed to special Latin odes, which were printed for such purpose."[28] Neither the music nor the text of these Latin odes, BWV Anh. 20, survives, but the evidence suggests that Bach tended to be called on for particularly important and ceremonial occasions, even though such assignments could provoke the question of whose area of responsibility was involved.

Indeed, the question arose in 1727 at one especially prominent event, when the university community paid homage to the deceased Saxon electoress and queen of Poland, Christiane Eberhardine. The estranged wife of Augustus the Strong, Christiane had decided to uphold her Lutheran faith after her husband converted to Roman Catholicism to make himself eligible for the Polish crown. The memorial oration planned for October 17 was organized by a student group of young noblemen, headed by Hans Carl von Kirchbach. As their ambitious plans included the performance of mourning music, Kirchbach approached the two most eminent Leipzig authors, commissioning the text from Johann Christoph Gottsched, professor of philosophy and poetics at the university and head of the Deutsche Gesellschaft, a literary society (to which Kirchbach belonged as well), and the music from Bach. As soon as Johann Gottlieb Görner got wind of this plan, he filed a complaint with the university, fearing a precedent if Kirchbach were permitted to bypass him by going directly to the Thomascantor, and he requested that Kirchbach be asked either to commission him instead of Bach or to pay him an indemnity. But Kirchbach—who, like others, may have considered Görner a "lousy composer"[29]— claimed, when he appeared on October 9 before the university administration, that he had already promised the music to Bach and paid him the honorarium, and that Bach already "had for eight days been at work composing."[30] A compromise was reached by having Kirchbach immediately ask Bach to sign a pledge, formulated by the university secretary and dated October 11, 1727. Its crucial passage reads: "Now, therefore, I recognize that this is purely a favor, and hereby agree that it is not to set any precedent. . . . likewise that I am never to make any claim to the directorship of the music in St. Paul's, much less contract with anyone for music for such solemnities or otherwise, without the consent and permission of a Worshipful University here."[31]

As could easily have been anticipated, Bach refused to sign the document because he still had his own unresolved claims against the university with regard to the division of responsibility. Yet he probably worked out a quiet understanding with Görner, who, after all, was compensated by Kirchbach with 12 talers, and the entire affair remained a one-time event. Despite a less than smooth start, Bach finished the composition of the *Tombeau de S. M. la Reine de Pologne,* BWV 198, delicately scored for four voices and "instruments douces" appropriate for a royal funeral music (2 transverse flutes, 2 oboes d'amore, 2 violas da gamba, 2 lutes, strings, and continuo), and the performance took place as scheduled—with the two parts of the work framing the oration delivered by Kirchbach himself. The Leipzig chronicler described the notable event:

In solemn procession, while the bells were rung, the Town Officials and the Rector and Professors of the University entered St. Paul's, where many others were present, namely, princely and other persons of rank, as well as not only Saxon but also foreign Ministers, Court and other Chevaliers, along with many ladies.

When, then, everyone had taken his place, there had been a prelude by the organ, and the Ode of Mourning written by Magister Johann Christoph Gottsched, member of the *Collegium Marianum,* had been distributed among those present by the Beadles, there was shortly heard the Music of Mourning, which this time Capellmeister Johann Sebastian Bach had composed in the Italian style, with *Clave di Cembalo,* which Mr. Bach himself played, organ, violas di gamba, lutes, violins, recorders, transverse flutes, &c., half being heard before and half after the oration of praise and mourning.[32]

Bach chose to disregard the poetic structure of Gottsched's rhymed *Funeral Ode* by reorganizing and subdividing the nine equally shaped stanzas asymmetrically in order to set them in the Italian manner, that is, in the form of recitatives and arias. Whether or not the poet was happy with that decision, he continued his occasional collaboration with Bach, begun in 1725 with the *Wedding Serenata,* BC G 42, by accepting another joint commission in 1738, BWV Anh. 13 (the music for neither work survives). The latter represented a commission on behalf of the university for an official reception in April 1738 for the royal family from Dresden. In anticipation of the visit, the university council, chaired by rector Christian Gottlieb Jöcher,[33] had resolved "(1) that a cantata be ordered, (2) that the same be composed by the cantor, Mr. Bach, and (3) that the latter be entrusted with the direction of the music"[34]—evidence of the unequivocal preference for Bach on the part of the academic leadership when it came to illustrious events. And they came through handsomely, with a fee of 50 talers for the cantor.

Closer to home, a more modest funeral service was held almost exactly two years later, on October 20, 1729: Johann Heinrich Ernesti, rector of the St. Thomas School, had died at age seventy-seven, and since he had also been a university professor, the service took place at St. Paul's. Bach set the music on the scriptural text that served as basis for the sermon, Romans 8:26–27 ("The Spirit helps our infirmities"), in the form of a double-choir motet with concluding chorale. For this piece, "Der Geist hilft unsrer Schwachheit auf," BWV 226, Bach would have used his two best vocal ensembles, the first and second choirs of the St. Thomas School. According to the extant performing materials, the singers in the choir loft were accompanied by the small organ[35] and reinforced by doubling instruments, choir I supported by strings and choir II by woodwinds.

Of Bach's performances at St. Paul's outside the Old Service, only these two mourning services can be documented, though there were surely others, and not solely vocal-instrumental ensemble music in conjunction with academic events. It must have interested Bach especially that St. Paul's housed a new organ, built by Johann Scheibe, with fifty-three stops on three manuals and pedal, at the time one of the largest and finest instruments anywhere in Germany.[36] At the invitation of the university rector, Bach himself had examined the instrument when it was finished in December 1717 and when Görner was organist at St. Paul's. For the first time in his life, an organ was available to Bach for which "he could not find enough praise and laud, especially for its rare stops which were newly made and could not be found in many organs."[37] And because he would collaborate with the organ builder Scheibe for twenty-five years until the latter's death in 1748 (see Table 5.2), we can be sure that Bach made use of the organ at St. Paul's whenever he needed an instrument for teaching, practicing, or public performances.

Contemporary descriptions of the service for Queen Christiane Eberhardine make specific references to an organ prelude and postlude that, given the importance of the ceremonial event, only Bach could have played. A particularly fitting piece would be the Prelude and Fugue in B minor, BWV 544, the prelude of which would have drowned out the instrumental ensemble's tuning for BWV 198, also in B minor;[38] the autograph fair copy of BWV 544 dates from 1727–31. Beyond such speculation, however, it must be emphasized that Bach's activities as an organ recitalist are generally the most inadequately recorded; reports are limited to organ examinations and dedications or to concerts played out of town (see Table 7.5). Not a single recital is documented for Leipzig, yet it would be absurd to conclude that Bach never played there in public and that his reputation as "world-famous organist"—so the heading of the Obituary—was not based on his exposure to Leipzig audiences for nearly three decades. Although no longer holding a post as organist, he remained active as an organ composer and virtuoso throughout his Leipzig years. His output of organ music, even if limited to the repertoire with original and datable sources (see Table 9.1), is distributed evenly over time, and out-of-town public recitals are documented as late as 1747 in Berlin. And works like the Prelude and Fugue in E minor, BWV 548, demonstrate Bach's remarkable ability to lift the genre of prelude and fugue to an entirely new level, well beyond the scope of *The Well-Tempered Clavier,* giving it a distinct organistic profile and virtuoso showpiece character. Moreover, BWV 548 in particular reveals the performer-composer's formidable command not only in sustaining great length (the prelude runs over 137 measures and the fugue over 231) but also in balancing improvisatory and constructive elements. Both the prelude and fugue integrate concerto-like features into their innovative large-scale designs, the prelude displaying a complex ritornello structure **ABA-B(c/b)-A-B(c/b)-A**

## TABLE 9.1. Representative Organ Works from the Leipzig Period

| BWV | Title | Date (source) |
|---|---|---|
| 525–30 | Six Sonatas | 1727–32 (autograph ms.) |
| 541 | Prelude and Fugue in G major (revised version) | c. 1733 (autograph ms.) |
| 544 | Prelude and Fugue in B minor | 1727–31 (autograph ms.) |
| 548 | Prelude and Fugue in E minor | 1727–32 (partial autograph ms.) |
| 552, etc. | *Clavier-Übung,* part III (for contents, see Table 10.7) | 1739 (original edition) |
| 562 | Fantasia and Fugue (fragment) in C minor | c. 1747–48 and earlier (autograph ms.) |
| 645–50 | Six Chorales ("Schübler") | c. 1747 (original edition) |
| 651–68 | Eighteen Chorales (revised versions) | 1739–42, 1746–47 (partial autograph ms.) |
| 769 | Canonic Variations on "Vom Himmel hoch" | c. 1747–48 (autograph ms., original edition) |

(the middle sections of **B** introduce new material [C] in alteration with modified **B** material [b]), and the fugue an unprecedented "antidevelopmental" da capo form **A-B(b/a-c/a-b/a-a-c)-A** (**B** consists of interludes [b, c] with citations and elaborations of the fugue theme [a]).[39]

The best, if not the only suitable, place for the display of Bach's organistic art would have been St. Paul's. Leipzig musicians, like actors, dancers, and performing artists of all kinds, were regularly offered rich opportunities for showcasing their talent during the three annual trade fairs, when schools were closed and the whole population became caught up in the fair bustle. In such a context, Bach the organ virtuoso would have been a major attraction, but the combination of St. Paul's grand organ—for a long time the largest instrument in all of Saxony—and the city's renowned organist would have proved even more spectacular. As for the content of a typical Bach recital in Leipzig and the show of appreciation for the master of the keyboard, it would have resembled his out-of-town programs. A characteristic example, an appearance in Dresden, is reported in newspapers of September 21, 1725:

When the Capell-Director from Leipzig, Mr. Bach, came here recently, he was very well received by the local virtuosos at the court and in the city since he is greatly admired by all of them for his musical adroitness and art. Yesterday and the day before, in the presence of the same, he performed for over an hour on the new organ in St. Sophia's Church preludes and various concertos, with intervening soft instrumental music in all keys.[40]

Here is evidence that during at least one of the two consecutive recitals on the thirty-one-stop Silbermann organ, Bach introduced a novel genre: organ concertos with accompanying string instruments, in all likelihood prototypes of works that were soon integrated into cantata sinfonias of the third *Jahrgang* and, still later, transformed into harpsichord concertos. Some of them may even have been devised as organ concertos from the outset: the original version of the concerto BWV 1053 is a prime candidate.[41] Whether or not the 1725 recitals in the Saxon capital were a preview of what was planned for the upcoming St. Michaelmas Fair in Leipzig, we can take for granted that Leipzig audiences were exposed to the same exciting organ performances and innovative repertoires as concertgoers in Dresden, only more frequently; and where else in Leipzig would Bach have played if not at St. Paul's?[42] Fittingly, the university's auditorium, the place where Bach would practice, teach, and present his improvisations and newest works, was the venue in Leipzig most closely identified with scholarship, with both the cultivation of traditional erudition and the creation of new knowledge. In the musical world, Bach was peerless, the absolutely dominant figure in Leipzig. Those with whom he had to match wits—to a considerable extent in the public arena—were the academic luminaries of the university.

## PROFESSORIAL COLLEAGUES AND UNIVERSITY STUDENTS

From his first days in Leipzig, Bach cultivated and maintained connections with the city's political, commercial, and clerical establishment as well as its intellectual elite. In particular, he could rely on support from the highest-ranking state dignitary, General Joachim Friedrich von Flemming, governor of Leipzig. Representing the Saxon electoral court and residing at the Pleissenburg, not far from the St. Thomas Church, Count Flemming had hosted Bach at his mansion in Dresden for the Marchand contest in 1717. As one of the Thomascantor's staunchest patrons, he commissioned congratulatory cantatas to be performed as serenades *(Abend-Music)* on his birthday, August 25. We know of two such works for which the music is lost, BWV 249b (1726), and BWV Anh. 10 (1731), both with lyrics by Picander; a third work, BWV 210a, with adjusted text underlay referring to Flemming, was presented between 1727 and 1732. But apart from the normal business he regularly had to conduct with town, church, and university officials, the contacts that provided Bach with the most important challenges and interactions were with the professoriate of the university.

Yet Bach was by no means integrated into the close-knit academic community. He knew well that without university study, let alone a degree, he lacked the formal qualifications required in academe. Moreover, his other connections mattered to him: the offspring of a town piper, he felt comfortable in craft circles that included organ builders, other instrument makers, and musicians in general. His court music experience and, in particular, his incontestable standing as a keyboard virtuoso made him a welcome and respected insider in all domains of professional music making. Indeed, like many of his musician colleagues, he may well have disdained the exclusive and often arrogant world of the professoriate. Nevertheless, Leipzig offered him challenges whose social aspects must have been difficult for him to accept but whose intellectual side he had no reason to avoid. Just the opposite: the increased intellectual dimension noticeable in Bach's Leipzig works reciprocates these challenges. He not only delivered what was expected of him, but more often than not he took up the gauntlet and returned it in the form of musical daring.

Bach's daily routine put him in frequent touch with representatives of the university. For example, his superior in church activities was Salomo Deyling, superintendent of the Leipzig church district, who simultaneously held the distinguished chair of *professor primarius* in the Faculty of Theology. Bach maintained a respectful distance from this eminent theologian eight years his senior, dealing with him primarily on the bureaucratic level. But there were others among the Leipzig professoriate with whom Bach had direct or indirect relations of a more fruitful kind, ranging from the collegial to the personal:[43]

### I. Thomana faculty with university appointments

- Johann Heinrich Ernesti, rector of the St. Thomas School from 1684 until his death in 1729; from 1680 assessor in the Faculty of Philosophy and from 1691 professor of poetics; published numerous works, among them books on Suetonius and on epigrams, and a *Compendium hermeneuticum.* Ernesti's wife, Regina Maria, was godmother of Gottfried Heinrich Bach (b. 1724).
- Christian Ludovici, conrector from 1697 to 1724, when he resigned from the Thomana and moved full time to the university. From 1693 assessor in the Fac-

Magister Johann Heinrich Ernesti,
rector of the St. Thomas School, 1684–1729,
in an engraving by Martin Bernigeroth (c. 1720).

ulty of Philosophy, from 1699 associate professor of oriental languages and the Talmud, and from 1700 until his death in 1732 professor of logic; served two terms, 1724–25 and 1730–31, as *rector magnificus.* Published many works, primarily on Hebrew topics, including a commentary on Rabbi Levi ben Gerson, as well as a *Compendium logicum.*

- Johann Christian Hebenstreit, conrector from 1724 to 1731. From 1715 assessor in the Faculty of Philosophy, resigned from the Thomana in 1731 to become associate professor of Hebrew and oriental languages and in 1740 professor of theology; succeeded Salomo Deyling in 1755 as *professor primarius* and served 1745–46 as university rector. Author of many philological and theological books. His wife, Christiana Dorothea, was godmother of Bach's daughter Christiana Dorothea (b. 1731).

- Johann Matthias Gesner, rector from 1730 to 1734; failed to receive a university appointment in Leipzig and therefore left for Göttingen University, where he became the first professor appointed to the new university and founding dean of the Faculty of Philosophy.[44] A prolific author on classical philology—Cicero, Horace, Pliny, Quintilianus, and others—he also published a dictionary of Latin etymology. In his 1738 edition (with commentary) of Marcus Fabius Quintilianus's first-century *Institutio oratoria,* a classic treatise of ancient rhetoric, Gesner writes the

Magister Johann Matthias Gesner,
rector of the St. Thomas School, 1730–34,
in an engraving by Christian Nicolaus Eberlein (c. 1745).

greatest homage paid to Bach in the eighteenth century, in the form of an address to Quintilianus:

You would think but slightly, my dear Fabius, of all these [the accomplishments of the citharists], if, returning from the underworld, you could see Bach (to mention him particularly, since he was not long ago my colleague at the Leipzig St. Thomas School), either playing our clavier, which is many citharas in one, with all the fingers of both hands, or running over the keys of the instrument of instruments, whose innumerable pipes are brought to life by bellows, with both hands and, at the utmost speed, with his feet, producing by himself the most various and at the same time mutually agreeable combinations of sounds in orderly procession. If you could see him, I say, doing what many of your citharists and six hundred of your tibia players together could not do, not only, like a citharist, singing with one voice and playing his own parts, by watching over everything and bringing back to the rhythm and the beat out of thirty or even forty musicians, the one with a nod, another by tapping with his foot, the third with a warning finger, giving the right note to one from the top of his voice, to another from the bottom, and to a third from the middle of it—all alone, in the midst of the greatest din made by all the participants, and, although he is executing the most difficult parts himself, noticing at once whenever and wherever a mistake occurs, holding everyone together, taking precautions everywhere, and repairing any unsteadiness, full of rhythm in every part of his body—this one man taking in all these harmonies with his keen ear and emitting with his voice alone the tone of all the

Magister Johann August Ernesti,
rector of the St. Thomas School, 1734–59,
in an engraving by Johann Friedrich Bause (1778).

voices. Favorer as I am of antiquity, the accomplishments of our Bach, and of any others who may be like him, appear to me to effect what not many Orpheuses, nor twenty Arions, could achieve.[45]

Bach, who knew Gesner from Weimar (where the classicist served from 1715 as conrector of the gymnasium and head of the ducal court library), may have been involved in bringing him to Leipzig in 1730, just after he had served for a scant year as rector of the gymnasium in Ansbach. Gesner's wife, Elisabeth Caritas, was godmother of Bach's son Johann August Abraham (b. 1733).

- Johann August Ernesti, conrector from 1731 (appointed by Gesner) and rector from 1734 to 1758; from 1742 simultaneously associate professor of ancient classical literature at the university, from 1756 professor of rhetoric, and from 1759, after resigning his Thomana post, professor of theology. One of the most widely published academic authors, he wrote works on Homer, Cicero, New Testament hermeneutics, and many other subjects. In the later 1760s, Goethe attended his lectures.[46] Godfather of Bach's sons Johann August Abraham (b. 1733) and Johann Christian (b. 1735).
- Johann Heinrich Winckler, instructor at the St. Thomas School from 1731 to 1739 (as *collega quartus,* another Gesner appointee); from 1729 (at age twenty-six) assessor in the Faculty of Philosophy, from 1739 associate professor of Greek and Latin, from 1742 professor of logic, and from 1750 professor of physics (successor to Mentz, see below); served three terms as *rector magnificus,* 1744–45, 1747, and 1749, and was in 1747 elected to membership in the Royal Society, London. After publishing in philosophy and classics (on Cicero, among others), he turned to scientific subjects and became one of the most influential eighteenth-century German scientists, with ground-breaking publications on experimental physics in general and on electricity in particular, including *Gedanken von den Eigenschaften, Würkungen und Ursachen der Electricität* of 1744;[47] his *Anfangsgründe der Physik* was translated into English (1757) and soon thereafter into French and Russian. As with Ernesti, Goethe studied with Winckler, too.[48]

  In 1732, Winckler wrote the libretto for Bach's cantata "Froher Tag, verlangte Stunden," BWV Anh.18 (music lost), performed at the dedication of the renovated and enlarged St. Thomas School. In a 1765 treatise, *Untersuchungen der Natur und Kunst,* he mentions in a discussion on acoustical phenomena a "musical connoisseur" whose ears can "differentiate between innumerable tones," and cites Gesner's comment on Bach.[49]

## II. Members of the St. Thomas clergy with university appointments

- Urban Gottfried Siber, minister at St. Thomas's from 1714 until his death in 1741; from 1714 simultaneously professor of ancient church history in the Faculty of Theology, as first incumbent of the chair, with a command of Latin, Greek, Hebrew, French, Italian, and Spanish; author of many books. He baptized three Bach children: Gottfried Heinrich (b. 1724), Johann August Abraham (b. 1733), and Johann Christian (b. 1735).

- Romanus Teller, minister at St. Thomas's and St. Peter's from 1737 to 1740; from 1738 associate professor of theology, published numerous theological books. Bach chose him as his father confessor, 1738–40.[50]

- Christian Weiss, Jr., minister at St. Nicholas's from 1731 to 1737 and from 1740 associate professor of theology at the university. Son of Pastor Christian Weiss, Sr. (Bach's father confessor, 1723–36), he was godfather of Bach's daughter Johanna Carolina (b. 1737). His sister, Dorothea Sophia Weiss, godmother of Bach's son Johann Christoph Friedrich (b. 1732), was married to Johann Erhard Kapp, professor of rhetoric at Leipzig University.

- Christoph Wolle, minister at St. Thomas's from 1739; from 1721 assessor in the Faculty of Philosophy, and from 1748 professor of theology. He was a pupil at the St. Thomas School in 1715–18 and sang under Kuhnau. A versatile linguist (he mastered Latin, Greek, Hebrew, Spanish, Italian, English, and Dutch) and much-appreciated preacher, he was more closely connected with Enlightenment philosophy than any other Leipzig theologian at the time, as reflected in his numerous books on dogmatics, ethics, and hermeneutics. Bach's father confessor, 1741–50.[51]

### III. Members of the Philosophy and Law Faculties

- Johann Jacob Mascov, from 1719 professor of constitutional law and history and member of the city council; from 1735 also head of the council library, and from 1737 city judge. Author of many historical works, mainly on the Holy Roman Empire, from the Middle Ages through the seventeenth century. One of the most illustrious and widely known members of the faculty, he attracted in particular students from aristocratic families, whom he instructed in issues of government. Like Baudis, he participated in Bach's election and remained generally supportive of Bach's decisions that required town council approval, such as appointments to the town music company.[52]

- Johann Christoph Gottsched, from 1725 assessor in the Faculty of Philosophy, from 1730 associate professor of logic, from 1734 professor of poetics, logic, and metaphysics; served four terms as rector: 1738–39, 1740–41, 1742–43, and 1748–49. He was the leading figure in the early German Enlightenment. Particularly influential were two of his early works, which saw several reprints: *Versuch einer critischen Dichtkunst* of 1730, a book on literary and linguistic theory and practice, drama, rhetoric, and poetics, and *Erste Gründe der gesamten Weltweisheit* of 1733, his chief philosophical work.

  Bach's librettist for BWV 198, Anh. 13 and Anh. 196, he wrote in 1728 that "in Saxony, Capellmeister Bach is head and shoulders above his peers" and later made other favorable references to Bach in several of his publications.[53] Gottsched, himself son of a Lutheran pastor, regularly attended services at St. Thomas's and had in common with Bach two father confessors, deacon Teller and then archdeacon Wolle.[54] Louise Adelgunde Victoria Kulmus, a harpsichordist and lutenist, wrote in 1732 to Gottsched, to whom she was engaged and who had mailed her the newly published *Clavier-Übung,* part I: "The clavier pieces by Bach that you sent and the lute works by [Johann Christian] Weihrauch are as beautiful as they are difficult. After I played them ten times, I still felt like a beginner. Of these two great masters, I appreciate anything more than their caprices; these are unfathomably difficult."[55]

- Friedrich Mentz, from 1711 assessor in the Faculty of Philosophy, from 1725 professor of logic, from 1730 professor of poetics (Johann Heinrich Ernesti's successor), and from 1739 until his death in 1749 professor of physics; served two terms as rector, 1735–36 and 1743–44. Published on Plato and other subjects.

  Mentz, a book collector, owned a sixteenth-century manuscript *album amicorum* that contained a musical entry, dated April 27, 1597, by the composer Teodoro Riccio, in the form of an enigmatic canon. Around 1740, Mentz showed the canon to Bach and apparently asked him to resolve the riddle notation. Bach wrote out the "Resolutio Canonis Ricciani"—a rare example of an augmentation canon, where the note values of the canonic part are doubled—on a separate leaf, which Mentz then added to the album.[56]

- Gottfried Leonhard Baudis, member of the Leipzig town council from 1715 to 1735 and professor of law from 1734 until his death in 1739; served as counsel to the Leipzig appellate court, from 1736–37 as rector, and published numerous philosophical, legal, and historical books. Baudis's wife, Magdalena Sibylla, was godmother of Bach's son Ernestus Andreas (b. 1727).

- Andreas Florens Rivinus, professor of law from 1725 and *rector magnificus* for two terms, 1729–30 and 1735–36; left in 1739 for Wittenberg University. Author of many books on historical and contemporary legal problems. He was godfather of Bach's son Ernestus Andreas (b. 1727). His brother, Johann Florens Rivinus, also a lawyer and judge at the Leipzig superior court, was Johann Christian Bach's godfather.

  Bach composed the cantata "Die Freude reget sich," BWV 36b, for a member of the Rivinus family, most likely for the inauguration of Andreas Florens Rivinus as rector in 1735. An earlier version of this work, "Schwingt freudig euch empor," BWV 36c, was originally commissioned as a congratulatory piece for an older professor whose identity remains unknown, and may have been re-performed on the birthday of St. Thomas rector Gesner, on April 9, 1731.

- Gottlieb Kortte (Corte), professor of law from 1726 until his death in 1731 (at age thirty-three); author of numerous legal and historical works. The cantata "Vereinigte Zwietracht der wechselnden Saiten," BWV 207, was commissioned from Bach as a congratulatory piece to be performed in conjunction with Kortte's appointment to a professorship in December 1726.

- August Friedrich Müller, professor of philosophy and law from 1731 and rector for two terms, 1733–34 and 1743–44; published numerous legal treatises. The *dramma per musica, Der zufriedengestellte Aeolus,* BWV 205, with a text by Picander, was commissioned for a performance on Müller's name day, August 3, 1725.

While there is evidence linking all of the above-named persons in some way to Bach, the information is superficial and based entirely on external data that provide no clues to the character and content of the relationships. Moreover, the professoriate represented but one constituency of the academic community, the circles of which also included Johann Abraham Birnbaum, who obtained a master's degree in 1721 at age nineteen and immediately began teaching rhetoric at the university on a part-time basis, and whose later connections with Bach are amply documented. Similarly, Bach and his wife, Anna Magdalena, frequented the house of the affluent and influential merchant Georg Heinrich Bose, a music lover and next-door neighbor on St. Thomas Square.[57] Indeed, close ties of friendship connected the Bach family with the Boses, whose son taught as professor of physics at Wittenberg University. One of their daughters married D. Friedrich Heinrich Graff, judge at the Leipzig superior court and a relative of the Rivinus family of legal scholars. Graff stood godfather to the Bach children Gottfried Heinrich (b. 1724) and Regina Susanna (b. 1742) and in 1750 assisted the family in settling the Bach estate; a copy of the *Clavier-Übung* I in Graff's possession provides evidence of his musical interests.[58] All the details of Bach's relationships with these prominent Leipzig citizens do not tell a coherent story, but they demonstrate unmistakably the extent to which Bach moved in an academic atmosphere. Whether performing in churches or other surroundings, his audience likely exerted considerable influence on the conduct of his office, the direction of his musical goals, and conceptual aspects of his composing activities.

As Thomana faculty and students attended services at the church adjacent to their school, they were joined by faculty members and students from the university, including the above-mentioned Birnbaum, Gottsched, Kapp, Ludovici, Müller, Rivinus, and Winckler, all of whom regularly worshiped at St. Thomas's. The academic and academically trained constituency of the congregation was substantial—Leipzig boasted by far the largest university in the German-speaking countries, with forty-four full professors,[59] a good number of associate professors, many assessors and part-time lecturers, and a student enrollment averaging 280 in the winter semester and 125 in the summer semester.[60] Even the city council was unusually well equipped with highly educated people; for example, of the twenty-eight councillors who elected Bach in 1723, fourteen held doctorates. Burgomasters Dr. Lange and Dr. Born worshiped at St. Thomas's, while the majority of the council attended St. Nicholas's, the traditional "council's church," whose makeup was similar—the St. Nicholas School faculty and students and a share of the university community. Although these constituencies made up little more than 10 percent of the regular Sunday churchgoers, they were joined by other segments of the city's intellectual elite: attorneys, physicians, and scholars and editors attracted by Leipzig's book-publishing industry. To all this we may add the extended community of wealthy merchant families, scattered aristocracy, and a strong contingent throughout the year of visitors from out of town.

The overwhelmingly well-educated and well-to-do congregation members, who rented seats in their preferred pews,[61] correlated with the erudite, professorial style of preaching that obtained in the city's main churches, following the level and tone set by superintendent D. Deyling, *professor primarius* of the Theological Faculty, who delivered the regular Sunday morning sermon at St. Nicholas's throughout Bach's tenure.[62] A comparison here might be as inappropriate as it is unavoidable, but the poetic, theological, and musical depth as well as the style and virtuosic execution of the "cantata sermon" from the choir loft clearly aimed at matching the forceful and virtuoso performance from the pulpit, even though the time allotted to the cantor was less than half of that taken by the preacher. Both catered to the same audience, with remarkably little regard for the simple folk and the less well educated attending the same services.[63]

While many of Bach's regular listeners would have been moved by his music and appreciated its artful design and impassioned performance, very few possessed a close understanding of its internal structure. Most of those who did and were fascinated by it, or who wanted to learn more about it, were to be found among the performers. Next to the most musically accomplished—privately instructed St. Thomas *alumni* and the top players of the town music company—Bach could rely on a solid group of musicians with professional ambitions who were studying at the university, mostly in the Faculties of Law, Philosophy, and Theology, and wanted to prepare themselves for careers as cantors, court musicians (with secondary expertise in legal or diplomatic service), and the like. They took private lessons with Bach, and many probably paid for them by participating as vocalists or instrumentalists in the regular cantata performances or assisting in other tasks. Those who paid for lessons generally showed "themselves willing to do this in the hope that one or the other would in time receive some kind of reward and perhaps be favored with a *stipendium* or *honorarium*," as Bach wrote in 1730,[64] but the expected benefits were not easy to come by, and the cantor had to fight hard for them with the city council or find supplementary sources of income—for example, through the sale of text booklets.

Nevertheless, Bach had a steady supply of gifted and versatile university students who received private lessons from him.[65] Some sixty such senior students—not including Thomana *alumni* who chose not to enter Leipzig University—can be confirmed,[66] though the actual number may be well above a hundred. By a conservative estimate, four to six professional-caliber students were working closely with Bach at any given time in Leipzig. Numerous testimonials Bach wrote for his best students demonstrate the comprehensive experience they gained under his tutelage. As a case in point, we read in a 1730 letter of reference for Johann Christian Weyrauch, candidate of laws, "that he not only masters various instruments but can also well afford to make himself heard *vocaliter,* has given many examples of his skill, and also can show on request what he has done in the art of composition."[67] A testimonial from 1748 for Johann Christoph Altnickol, candidate of theology but provided by Bach with the self-styled academic title of "candidate in music," relates that its bearer "not only did . . . act for four years diligently as assistant for our *Chorus Musicus,* but he also has shown, in addition to his vocal performance, such outstanding work on various instruments as one could desire from an accomplished musician. A number of fine church compositions of his have found no less ample approval in our town."[68]

The wealth of performance activities introduced Bach's students to many of the basics any musical leader had to master, from the right way to position ensembles in different performing spaces to the design of instruments, their technology, and their proper use. Here they benefited from Bach's own hands-on experience, as son Carl Philipp Emanuel recalled in 1775:

As a result of frequent large-scale performances of music in churches, at court, and often in the open air, in strange and inconvenient places, he learned the placing of the orchestra, without any systematic study of acoustics. He knew how to make good use of this experience, together with his native understanding of building design so far as it concerns sound; and these were supplemented in turn by his special insight into the proper design of an organ, the disposition of stops, and the placing of the same.

Bach always stressed the practical side of music, if only to confront his students with the results of their efforts, so he kept them away from purely speculative matters. Again, Carl Philipp Emanuel underscored that his father "like myself or any true musician, was no lover of dry, mathematical stuff." Even when he taught musical composition, Bach disregarded neutral writing exercises and trained his students directly on the basis of keyboard practice, introduced them to the principles of thoroughbass as the foundation of music, and had them conceptualize chorale harmonization as the interplay of polyphonic voices:

Since he himself had composed the most instructive pieces for the clavier, he brought up his pupils on them. In composition he started his pupils right in with what was practical, and omitted all the dry species of counterpoint that are given in Fux and others. His pupils had to begin their studies by learning pure four-part thoroughbass. From this he went to chorales; first he added the basses to them himself, and they had to invent the alto and tenor. Then he taught them to devise the basses themselves.[69]

Bach's students apparently copied out their teacher's own chorale settings from his cantatas and oratorios. One such compilation from the mid-1730s survives; written in the hand of Thomana *alumnus* Johann Ludwig Dietel, later cantor in Frankenhain,[70] it underscores the central pedagogical role Bach assigned to the writing of chorales—further affirmed by Bach's contribution to the Schemelli *Gesang-Buch* of 1736, BWV 439–507—and suggests that Bach may have planned to publish an edition of his chorales, as Graupner had in 1728 and Telemann in 1731.[71] At any rate, Carl Philipp Emanuel's first two-volume edition of Bach chorales of 1765/69 may have been motivated as much by his father's teaching methods as by his own plans to compile and publish models of "the art of writing" that drew "appropriate attention to the quite special arrangement of the harmony and the natural flow of the inner voices and the bass."[72]

The methodical approach of Bach's teaching was special in every respect but truly unique in the sophisticated and challenging materials he provided. His approach is brought to life in an illuminating account given in 1790 by Ernst Ludwig Gerber, author of the first comprehensive biographical dictionary in music. There he reports on the education that his own father, Heinrich Nicolaus Gerber, received when, at age twenty-two, he

went to Leipzig, partly to study law and partly to study music with the great Sebast. Bach. . . . In the first half year, as he arranged his courses, he had heard much excellent church music and many a concert under Bach's direction; but he had still lacked any opportunity that would have given him courage enough to reveal his desires to this great man; until at last he revealed his wish to a friend, named [Friedrich Gottlieb] Wild,[73] later organist in St. Petersburg, who introduced him to Bach.

Bach accepted him with particular kindness because he came from [the Thuringian county of] Schwarzburg, and always thereafter called him *Landsmann* [compatriot]. He promised to give him the instruction he desired and asked at once whether he had industriously played fugues. At the first lesson he set his *Inventions* before him. When he had studied these through to Bach's satisfaction, there followed a series of suites, then *The Well-Tempered Clavier.* The latter work Bach played altogether three times through for him with his unmatchable art, and my father counted these among his happiest hours, when Bach, under the pretext of not feeling in the mood to teach, sat himself at one of his fine instruments and thus turned these hours into minutes. The conclusion of the instruction was thoroughbass, for which Bach chose the Albinoni violin solos; and I must admit I have never heard anything better than the style in which my father executed these basses according to Bach's fashion, particularly in the singing of the voices. This accompaniment was in itself so beautiful that no principal voice could have added to the pleasure it gave me.[74]

While in Bach's tutelage, Heinrich Nicolaus Gerber copied the materials he was given to study, signed the finished volumes, and added to his name

*"L{itterarum} L{iberalium} S{tudiosus} ac M{usicae} C{ultor}"* (student of liberal letters and devotee of music). The manuscripts Gerber assembled from late 1724 to 1726 corroborate the information in the biographical report, even in terms of their chronological sequence:[75] at the beginning, we find the *Aufrichtige Anleitung* (Gerber copied all fifteen inventions and fifteen sinfonias), then eight *French* and seven *English Suites* (copied from a larger collection of suites with and without preludes)[76] and twenty-one movements from the partitas that were published in 1731 as *Clavier-Übung,* part I, and finally, *The Well-Tempered Clavier*[77] and the realization of the Albinoni figured bass (including Bach's corrections)[78]—a truly demanding course of study for only two years.

Heinrich Nicolaus Gerber, later court organist at Schwarzburg-Sondershausen, was one of a large and impressive group of composers who received their training from Bach and that included, apart from Bach's own sons, Carl Friedrich Abel, royal court musician in London; nephew Johann Ernst Bach, court capellmeister in Eisenach; Johann Friedrich Doles, Bach's second successor in Leipzig; Gottfried August Homilius, cantor at Holy Cross in Dresden; Johann Ludwig Krebs, court organist in Altenburg; Johann Christian Kittel, town organist in Erfurt; Johann Gottfried Müthel, city organist in Riga; and Johann Trier, organist of St. John's in Zittau. A substantial number of Bach students also actively engaged in literary contributions and theoretical writings on music; aside from Wilhelm Friedemann[79] and Carl Philipp Emanuel Bach, the most prominent were the following:

- Christoph Nichelmann, pupil of Bach's at the St. Thomas School and from 1739 active as a composer and harpsichordist in Berlin; published in 1755 a major treatise on the controversy over the merits of the French and Italian styles, *Die Melodie nach ihrem Wesen sowohl, als nach ihren Eigenschaften.*
- Lorenz Christoph Mizler, who wrote his thesis on musical art as a part of philosophical erudition *(Dissertatio quod musica ars sit pars eruditionis philosophicae)* at Leipzig University and taught there from 1737 to 1743. He dedicated the published thesis (1734) to Johann Mattheson, Georg Heinrich Bümler, and Johann Sebastian Bach and acknowledged in its preface, "Your instruction in *musica practica,* most celebrated Bach, have I used with great profit, and I regret that it is not possible for me to enjoy it further."[80] He edited the *Musikalische Bibliothek* (1736–54), translated and annotated Fux's *Gradus ad Parnassum* (1742), and published several musical treatises.
- Johann Friedrich Agricola, who attended Leipzig University from 1738 to 1741, studied with Bach during that period. He later became capellmeister at the Prussian court in Berlin, where he played an influential role as a composer and prolific writer on music; he also translated and annotated Pier Francesco Tosi's *Opinioni de' cantori antichi e moderni* (1723) under the title *Anleitung zur Singekunst.*

- Johann Philipp Kirnberger, whose studies in Leipzig closely overlapped with Agricola's, also ended up in Berlin, as capellmeister to Princess Amalia, sister of King Friedrich II. Of all of Bach's students, he most deliberately transmitted his teacher's concepts and methods in musical composition, particularly in his major two-volume treatise *Die Kunst des reinen Satzes in der Music* (1771), in which he focuses like Bach on both principles and practical examples. In 1784–87, he collaborated with Carl Philipp Emanuel Bach on a new, four-volume edition of the four-part chorales, *Johann Sebastian Bachs vierstimmige Choral-Gesänge.*

For Bach, a steadfast working relationship with his best students must have been particularly important, and at times even crucial, not only for what they learned from him but also for what he picked up from them: from their academic studies (for which he may occasionally have envied them) and from their musical interests and contributions, as his own changing stylistic orientation in the 1730s and 1740s definitely reflects. He may also have hoped that they would carry on his ideas—perhaps remembering the encouraging words said to him by the venerable old organist Reinken: "I thought that this art was dead, but I see that in you it still lives."[81] But if such wishful thinking ever crossed Bach's mind, it did not come true, as none of his students came remotely close to Bach's mastery in either composition or performance or in his intellectual control over and penetration of musical subject matter. They did, however, play all the more decisive a role in the preservation, dissemination, and veneration of their teacher's incomparable music. In particular, their faithful spreading of his musical methods and principles shows that Bach's inordinate investment in the teaching of his musical philosophy was by no means in vain. On the contrary, scores of students and their pupils' students helped organize and eventually consolidate Bach's lasting influence, a phenomenon that none of Bach's contemporaries sustained. Neither Handel nor Scarlatti, Rameau, nor Telemann ever engaged so fully in the kind of teaching that Bach enjoyed throughout his life. More important, none of them could, as Bach did, put their teaching on an academic stage—the secret that allowed his smallish world to burst into a limitless orb.

## MATERIALS AND METAPHYSICS

Bach used the word "apparatus" to designate his personal music library and "things" to refer to individual musical works[82]—plain terms suggesting a matter-of-factness that does not in the least signal the importance these materials actually held for him. The shelves in his study, the so-called composing room in the cantor's apartment, and the adjacent walls contained both his private library and the music collection of the St. Thomas School—altogether several hundred printed and manuscript items of sixteenth- and seventeenth-century materials.[83] Bach made no major additions to the old choral library of the St. Thomas School (of which only a few scattered remnants have survived),[84] and his decision not to include, for example, Johann Kuhnau's musical estate signified his intention not to bank on the repertoire of even the preceding generation, let alone earlier repertoires. Nevertheless, the old collection provided an opportunity to examine works by antecedents in the cantorate, such as those by Johann Hermann Schein, Sebastian Knüpfer, Johann Schelle, Heinrich Schütz, Christoph Bernhard, Johann Rosenmüller, Augustin Pfleger, Samuel Friedrich Capricornus, and other German composers; or by Giacomo Carissimi, Marco Peranda, Giovanni Battista Bassani, Giovanni Valentini, and other Italians. Bach's easy access to extremely rare manuscript and printed works by the sixteenth-century composers Thomas Crequillon and Nicolaus Rost or by such obscure minor figures as Albericus Mazak and Heinrich Fresman even suggests that Johann Gottfried Walther may have obtained the pertinent bio-bibliographic information for his *Musicalisches Lexicon* from his Leipzig cousin.[85] Except for some isolated cases, however, there is no evidence that Bach made practical use of the old choral library, which held, according to Kuhnau's testimony, some scores that were "quite torn" and "eaten away by mice." One such exception is Bach's own preparation of the performing parts, with supporting cornetto, trombones, and basso continuo, of the six-part *Missa sine nomine* from Palestrina's *Liber V. Missarum* of 1590.

Rather than capitalizing on the old library, Bach continued to build, with his own money, a personal collection of vocal and instrumental music for study and performance purposes whose origins went back to his youth. Although the true extent and actual makeup of this collection cannot be judged from the available evidence, a list of representative composers hints at the catholic scope of Bach's "apparatus":[86]

*German composers*
- older generation (b. 1620–49): Johann Christoph and Johann Michael Bach, Dieterich Buxtehude, Johann Caspar Ferdinand Fischer, Johann Jacob Froberger, Johann Caspar Kerll, Johann Adam Reinken
- middle generation (b. 1650–79): Johann Bernhard, Johann Ludwig, and Johann Nicolaus Bach, Georg Böhm, Johann Krieger, Johann Pachelbel, Johann Christoph Pez, Johann Christoph Schmidt, Johann Hugo von Wilderer
- younger generation (b. 1680–): Johann Friedrich Fasch, Carl Heinrich and Johann Gottlieb Graun, George Frideric Handel, Johann Adolph Hasse, Johann David Heinichen, Conrad Friedrich Hurlebusch, Johann Ernst of Saxe-Weimar, Johann Ludwig Krebs, Christian Petzolt, Johann Christoph Richter, Georg Andreas

Sorge, Gottfried Henrich Stölzel, Georg Philipp Telemann, Johann Gottfried Walther, Jan Dismas Zelenka

*French composers*
- older generation (b. 1620–49): Jean-Henri D'Anglebert, Jacques Boyvin, André Raison
- middle generation (b. 1650–79): François Couperin, Charles Dieupart, Pierre Du Mage, Nicolas de Grigny, Louis Marchand

*Italian composers*
- early classics: Giovanni Pierluigi da Palestrina, Girolamo Frescobaldi
- older generation (b. 1620–49): Giovanni Legrenzi, Marco Giuseppe Peranda, Giuseppe Torelli
- middle generation (b. 1650–79): Tomaso Albinoni, Giovanni Battista Bassani, Antonio Biffi, Antonio Caldara, Arcangelo Corelli, Antonio Lotti, Agostino Steffani, Antonio Vivaldi
- younger generation (b. 1680–): Francesco Conti, Francesco Durante, Pietro Antonio Locatelli, Alessandro and Benedetto Marcello, Giovanni Battista Pergolesi

In its quality, breadth, and depth, Bach's personal music library easily matched the larger collections assembled by contemporaries such as Heinrich Bokemeyer in Wolfenbüttel, Johann Mattheson in Hamburg, and Jan Dismas Zelenka in Dresden. If anything, however, Bach's collection was more diversified than most others, especially in its holdings of keyboard music and instrumental repertoires. We know, for example, that he played a key role in the transmission of Buxtehude's organ works. Moreover, his wide connections made it possible for him to obtain important new pieces of music literature, even from far away. Thus, one of the earliest traces north of the Alps of Pergolesi's *Stabat Mater* leads to Bach's library, less than ten years after the Neapolitan origin of this unpublished work. Bach's interest in the piece, to the extent that he arranged it in a German paraphrase, "Tilge, Höchster, meine Sünden," BWV 1083, demonstrates that he was as anxious to keep stylistically up-to-date as he was attracted by exemplary works of widely varying genres, styles, and techniques. Bach apparently acquired most of his music library from close friends and colleagues such as Zelenka in Dresden[87] and through the channels of the Leipzig book trade.

Bach's practical music collection was complemented by theoretical books, but the subsequent losses in this realm are so serious that we can obtain only a most superficial impression of its scope and orientation. We have direct evidence that he owned Angelo Berardi's *Documenti armonici* of 1687 (manuscript copy), the German edition of Johann Joseph Fux's *Gradus ad Parnassum* of 1742 (translated and annotated by his student Mizler), Heinichen's *Der General-Bass in der Composition* of 1728, Niedt's *Musicalische Handleitung* of 1710, Walther's *Musicalisches Lexicon* of 1732 (also its first installment of 1729), and Andreas Werckmeister's *Orgel-Probe* of 1698, but the only book that survives with an ownership mark in Bach's hand is the Latin edition of Fux's *Gradus ad Parnassum* of 1725.[88]

Similarly, of Bach's substantial theological library, only a single item has come down to us: the three-volume 1681 edition of the Lutheran Bible, with detailed commentaries by Abraham Calov. All the other books—more than fifty titles, many of them multivolume works—are known exclusively through the inventory of Bach's estate.[89] This 1750 list indicates that Bach had assembled an extensive scholarly collection of theological literature with emphasis on Lutheran classics, in particular two editions of Martin Luther's complete works (the seven-volume "Altenburg" edition of 1661–64 and the eight-volume "Jena" edition of 1555–58) and several copies of major works by the reformer (for example, his commentary on the Psalms). Of particular importance are Bible commentaries such as Johann Olearius's three-volume *Haupt Schlüßel der gantzen Heiligen Schrift* (Main Key to the Entire Holy Scripture) of 1678 and books of a homiletic character (especially sermon collections in several volumes by such leading figures as August Pfeiffer, Heinrich Müller, and Erdmann Neumeister). These works, especially those relating to the Calov Bible, which shows heavy underlining, annotations, and many other traces of regular use, shed light on Bach's reading habits and on his study of biblical exegesis in preparation for his own settings of scriptural texts and sacred poetry.

Of all the books and manuscripts owned by Bach, only his theological library is carefully recorded (with monetary valuation) in the estate inventory of 1750. Nevertheless, we must ask whether Bach's theological collection was actually larger than the list indicates and included works other than those of seventeenth-century and older authors, especially books by younger Leipzig theologians, colleagues such as Christoph Wolle, with whom he had a personal relationship. We must also ask why other categories of Bach's library are completely missing from the inventory. What happened to books on theory and on organ building, to hymnals, collections of sacred and secular poetry (Franck, Lehms, Neumeister, Picander, etc.), contemporary theological books, and other literary and scholarly volumes? The quasi-shelf-warmers seem to dominate the list—largely old-fashioned theological items left after materials more useful to the heirs had already been picked over. For example, in the category of hymnals, the inventory contains only the Wagner *Gesangbuch* of 1697, the best-organized collection of hymns (without notation of melodies) available at the time and for Bach surely a frequently consulted reference. But Bach's copy of this unwieldy eight-volume work remains untraced, whereas Michael Weisse's 1538 Bohemian Brethren hymnal with melodies did survive, though it was not included in the estate list.[90] We can only conclude that the more appealing library materials were removed and distributed before the book inventory was compiled and the theological leftovers were parceled out.

On a related subject, an auction receipt (explaining how Bach complemented his Calov Bible, acquired in 1733, with the copy of the Altenburg edition of Luther's collected works that Calov had used for his commentary) provides welcome information about Bach's acquisition and collection methods: "These *Teütsche und herrliche Schrifften des seeligen Dr. M. Lutheri* [German and Magnificent Writings of the Late Dr. Martin Luther] (which stem from the library of the eminent Wittenberg general superintendent and theologian Dr. Abraham Calov, which he supposedly used to compile his great German Bible; also, after his death, they passed into the hands of the equally eminent theologian Dr. J. F. Mayer), I have acquired at an auction for 10 rthl., anno 1742, in the month of September."[91] Although an isolated document, this receipt suggests that Bach may have gone about developing his library in a particularly systematic manner, that he was interested in the provenance of his acquisition, that he was willing to pay as much as a tenth of his fixed annual salary at a book auction, and most important, that he saw himself, if only privately, as a biblical interpreter in the succession and company of these eminent theological scholars. But for Bach, theological and musical scholarship were two sides of the same coin: the search for divine revelation, or the quest for God.

The 1739 definition of music in the *Großes Universal Lexicon,*[92] Johann Heinrich Zedler's monumental encyclopedia of knowledge, bears the unmistakable stamp of the old cosmological argument for the existence of God. Music is defined as "everything that creates harmony, that is, order. And in this sense it is used by those who assert that the whole universe is music."[93] Bach would not have disagreed with the unknown author of this article. Since seventeenth-century scientists had demonstrated that the planets and the earth were governed by the same laws, the relationship between cosmic harmonies and audible music, let alone the incomparably small world of musical composition concerned with manipulating tones, appeared even more strongly unified. So, as the universe of divine creation was felt to be ever more complex and interconnected, the idea of its unity had become, for a musician of Bach's intellectual disposition, more conclusive and compelling, and at the same time more inviting of his participation.

For Bach the performer, composer, teacher, and musical scholar, his daily work—the production and realization of music—was regulated by the very same unifying forces, as he demonstrated in one of his most simple yet meaningful compositions: the canon BWV 1072 for eight voices and two choirs, which he entitled *Trias harmonica* (the harmonic triad). The work reveals, with disarming logic and clarity, his philosophy of music as governed by the principle of counterpoint, not just in the figurative sense of achieving an absolute synthesis of theory and practice, but notably in the strictest sense of a compositional technique designed to show "polyphony in its greatest strength" and to master "the most hidden secrets of harmony," to quote from the Obituary.[94] Indeed, the little canon shows that a triad is not merely a sound made up of vertically organized intervals, but the inevitable result of accumulated contrapuntal (horizontal) lines that also govern the rhythmic structure. In other words, the canon illustrates that the vertical and horizontal organization of musical polyphony is intrinsically regulated by the rules of counterpoint, the most central principles to which the composer Bach subscribed.

The oldest source for BWV 1072 happens to be an engraved example in Friedrich Wilhelm Marpurg's *Abhandlung von der Fuge* of 1753, but comparison with similar canons suggests that Bach originally wrote it in the form of a riddle canon as an album entry for a colleague or student.[95] In enigmatic notation (Marpurg published only its resolution), the endless canon would read 𝄞 . But how could this rudimentary melody resolve in a plain triad, presumably one in C major 𝄞 ?

The riddle consists in finding the solution to the crucial instruction "for 8 voices and two choirs." If four voices present the melody in successive entries at half-note distances, that group constitutes choir I. Choir II then consolidates the triadic sound by presenting the same melody in inverted form, that is, starting with the note G, again in successive entries at half-note distances but with the first entry occurring a quarter-note beat after the first entry of choir I. This way, the two choirs represent two distinct entities that join in creating a harmonic triad—a simple exercise, yet one that has many implications (Ex. 9.1).

First, the melody of the canon is based on the *hexachordum naturale,* the natural hexachord (six-note scale) of the medieval diatonic scale, ascending from C to A. The diatonic scale permits only two other hexachords that have the same intervallic structure: the *hexachordum molle,* ascending from F to D (with a B-flat, therefore *mollis* (minor) = soft B), and the *hexachordum durum,* ascending from G to E (with a B-natural, therefore *durum* (major) = hard B). The natural hexachord is the only one that does not have to deal with the ambiguity of the note B; and whether produced by the proper numerical division of the octave, by the natural harmonic series (as created, for example, by a trumpet in C), or by just intonation, it creates the C-major triad, the acoustically purest of all triads, which represents the natural, God-given, most perfect harmonic sound.

Second, the canon melody differentiates between consonant and dissonant notes: the dissonant ones are written exclusively as passing tones, thus stressing the fundamental contrapuntal law that dissonances are permitted only on weak beats. The canon melody also features the classic contrapuntal rule of introducing smaller note values by way of an augmented (dotted) note; and the relationship of choirs I and II implies the rhythmic phenomenon of syncopation. Moreover, the short two-measure melody, if not repeated, extends exactly over the length of a *nota brevis,* or breve, which serves as the cornerstone of the medieval system of musical mensuration. Before the invention of the clock, large units of time could be measured only by the movement of the earth, creating seasons as well as day and night and the lunar calendar, while small units of time could be marked only by the beat of the human pulse. But then the system of measured music, as developed and first described in Franco of Cologne's thirteenth-century treatise *Ars cantus mensurabilis,* offered a way to link the beat of the human heart to the time scheme of the universe. His key unit for measuring time was the breve, called *tempus musicum*—a term, incidentally, used by Bach in another riddle canon, BWV 1078, to demarcate successive canonic entries.[96] The *Trias harmonica* canon, on the other hand, demonstrates the division of the *tempus musicum* unit by contrapuntal means, so that the pure C-major triad resounds in quarter-note beats that project, together with the transitional dissonances, a continuing chain of eighth-note beats. In other words, the counterpoint defines not just the vertical sound, but time and the horizontal rate of speed as well.

Third, the little canon not only defines time in purely musical—that is, audible—terms, it also defines space. Two-dimensional space is demarcated in a visual manner, by the notation itself, the up- and downward direction of notes. Three-dimensional space is introduced by the double-choir feature, two spatially separate entities presenting distinct material. Additionally, the canon addresses the phenomenon of progressive and regressive time in that it can be performed forward and backward. The piece ingeniously demonstrates the creation of the harmonic triad by way of four simultaneously applied contrapuntal methods—normal and inverted, and forward and retrograde motion—and added to this musical space-time capsule is the dimension of unity and infinity, for a *canon infinitus* resounds endlessly. In his modest canon, Bach subjects the concepts of space and time and their complex interrelationship (a main philosophical theme of the late seventeenth and early eighteenth centuries) to a treatment that actually captures both natural phenomena in a single musical event.

Surprisingly, the little canon turns out to offer a profound lesson in music theory, composition, philosophy, theology, and above all in the unity of knowledge. What may initially look and sound like a primitive piece of music reveals its sophisticated construction as a true mirror of the well-ordered universe, illustrating how counterpoint generates harmony and rhythm and how the abstract philosophical concepts of space and time coalesce in a concrete musical subject to create the *trias harmonica naturalis,* the C-major triad, which is the only truly perfect chordal harmony. The same triad, not coincidentally, stands at the head of *The Well-Tempered Clavier,* which introduces for the first time in history the complete spectrum of the twenty-four keys, defining tonalities well beyond the ancient hexachord system. Even more important, it is this sound that symbolized the dogma of the Holy Trinity. Like no other combination of tones, the natural triad could make audible and believable the *trias perfectionis et similitudinis* (the triad of perfection and [God-] likeness), the abstract "image of divine perfection,"[97] and, at the same time, the essential identity between the Creator and the universe.

Resembling the model of seventeenth-century scientific inquiry, Bach's musical inquiry demonstrates its results as it proceeds. His musical knowledge is invariably tied to his musical experience, as his compositions so amply manifest, whether canon, concerto, cantata, or anything else. And fully aware that Bach's music always invites one to discover "polyphony in its greatest strength" and "the most hidden secrets of harmony," Carl Philipp Emanuel Bach issued the warning that only "those who have a concept of what is possible in art and who desire original thought and its special, unusual elaboration will receive from it full satisfaction."[98] Showing what is possible in art, however, meant for Bach much more than demonstrating a mere philosophical theorem.[99] Too full-blooded a performing musician, Bach would not have been interested in pursuing an abstract goal. Yet he definitely wanted his musical science understood as a means of gaining "insight into the depths of the wisdom of the world" (according to Birnbaum's statement on Bach's behalf),[100] reflecting a metaphysical dimension in his musical thought. Considering the general intellectual climate in which Bach moved, metaphysics would not have been too obscure or remote a subject, especially as it pertained to his theological concerns and Lutheran beliefs.

In the precious few recorded statements about his own theoretical, theological, and philosophical thinking, Bach only once used the term "demonstration" *(Beweis),* so central in the philosophical-scientific methodology of his day. Some time after 1733, he annotated in his study Bible Abraham Calov's commentary on 1 Chronicles 29:21, a passage that deals with King David's exemplary role for the divine service. There he wrote to himself in the margin: "NB. A splendid demonstration that . . . music has been mandated by God's spirit." Bach would have known that the notion of music ordered or decreed by the divine spirit was not susceptible of strict empirical proof, yet even scientists of his time, including Newton and German Newtonians such as Johann Heinrich Winckler of Leipzig, believed that theological principles were capable of empirical demonstration and saw no conflict between science and Christianity. For in their view, the works of God they had studied only magnified the glory of God.[101] And the "Soli Deo Gloria" at the end of Bach's scores provides vivid testimony to his own stand in this respect. He, too, would see the directing hand of the world's Creator in the branch of science he knew best and probably better than anyone else in his day.

How deeply and to what end would musical science in the form of composition let Bach penetrate the wisdom of the world? How and where would he find traces of the invisible? As he understood the basic materials of music to be directly related to the physical design of the universe, he also grasped the metaphysical dimension of music, as we can deduce from another marginal comment in his Calov Bible. A section of 2 Chronicles 5, titled by Calov "As the glory of the Lord appeared upon the beautiful music," deals with the presence of the invisible God at the divine service in the Temple. Verse 13 ends with the words "when they lifted up their voice with the trumpets and cymbals and instruments of music, and praised the Lord . . . then the house was filled with a cloud." It is at this very point where Bach added his own comment: "NB. With devotional music, God is always present in his grace." Music prompted the appearance of the glory of God in the cloud, and the cloud demonstrated God's presence. Bach picked up the Hebrew notion of the presence of the invisible prompted by a physical phenomenon, the sound of music, but for the Lutheran theologian Bach, the metaphysical presence of God's grace replaced the visible proof of the physical cloud. Yet the presence of God's grace was to him no less manifest than the actual sound of music that would bring it about, if it were only devotional and attentive, directed toward one subject.[102]

Bach's concentrated approach to his work, to reach what was possible in art, pertained to all aspects of music, from theory to composition and from performance to physiology and the technology of instruments. In the final analysis, this approach provides the key to understanding his never-ending musical empiricism, which deliberately tied theoretical knowledge to practical experience. Most notably, Bach's compositions, as the exceedingly careful musical elaborations that they are, may epitomize nothing less than the difficult task of finding for himself an argument for the existence of God—perhaps the ultimate goal of his musical science.

Panorama of Leipzig in an engraving by Johann Georg Schreiber (1712), showing the town hall, market square (the venue for performances by Bach's Collegium Musicum and public receptions), St. Nicholas's, and St. Paul's (upper center).

# 10

## *Traversing Conventional Boundaries*

### SPECIAL ENGAGEMENTS:
### THE 1730s

AT A CROSSROADS

More than any stretch of time since Bach had moved to Leipzig, the years 1729–30 brought about a series of significant events that influenced his working conditions. March 1729 saw Bach assume the directorship of the city's most prestigious Collegium Musicum, a decision that considerably broadened the scope of his overall musical activities. Traditionally linked with the organist post at the New Church, the Collegium leadership became available when its longtime director, Georg Balthasar Schott, left his New Church post for a cantorate in Gotha. Bach seized the moment and secured the Collegium for himself, placing his protégé, Carl Gotthelf Gerlach, as organist at the New Church—a shrewd maneuver that, with its spillover effect on the organists' scene at St. Thomas's and St. Nicholas's (see Table 8.2), consolidated Bach's firm grip on Leipzig's principal musical institutions.

The new Collegium directorship complemented not only his full-time commitment to the St. Thomas cantorate but also his continuing function as nonresident court capellmeister. Although his low-profile Cöthen capellmeistership formally terminated on March 23–24, 1729, with the funeral ceremonies for Prince Leopold, Bach managed in good time to procure a similar appointment at the court of Duke Christian of Saxe-Weissenfels so that he could hold the title of court capellmeister without interruption. Connections to the Weissenfels court and its capelle extended back to 1713, but they were renewed and strengthened by Bach's marriage to Anna Magdalena, daughter of a Weissenfels court trumpeter. Then, when the Duke of Weissenfels paid a visit to the 1729 New Year's Fair in Leipzig, Bach performed for him (on January 12) the homage cantata "O angenehme Melodei," BWV 210a. Less than six weeks later, Bach spent several days in Weissenfels for guest performances at the duke's birthday festivities,[1] most likely the occasion at which he was awarded the honorary post;[2] he was now capellmeister to a ducal court that was politically more prestigious than the principality of Anhalt-Cöthen, musically more richly endowed,[3] and, at just over twenty miles from Leipzig, even closer than Cöthen.

An event in July 1729 with multiple repercussions for the Saxon-Thuringian music world, if not for Bach himself, was the death of Johann David Heinichen, court capellmeister in Dresden. Formerly choral scholar at St. Thomas's under Johann Kuhnau, a graduate of Leipzig University, and two years Bach's senior, Heinichen had headed the most important musical establishment in German lands. Only months before his death, the Leipzig newspapers had announced that his voluminous treatise *Der General-Bass in der Composition,* published the previous year, was available from Bach in Leipzig— one of the many signs of Bach's close ties with his esteemed colleague from the Dresden court capelle, an institution he now regarded with even greater envy, realizing that his lack of background in Italian opera rendered him ineligible for that capellmeistership. Yet whoever did succeed Heinichen in nearby Dresden, Bach knew that the appointment would have more than a ripple effect on the wider surroundings.

Another death, however, occurred much closer to home. Professor Johann Heinrich Ernesti passed away that October at age seventy-seven, and the resulting vacancy of the St. Thomas rectorate lasted over eleven months, ending only with the arrival of Johann Matthias Gesner. The unanimous election of the new rector by the city council on June 8, 1730, prompted councillor Höltzel to remark that he "wished that it would be better than with the cantor."[4] This grievance by a single council member remained unspecific, but it could only have referred to Bach's "capellmeisterly" conduct of the cantorate. Indeed, the accumulation of activities undertaken by the St. Thomas senior faculty beyond the school service proper, with the cantor apparently up front, motivated a clause in the contract with Gesner. Contrary to long-standing tradition, the agreement prevented him from accepting a university office—the very point that soon led to the premature departure from Leipzig of this extraordinary scholar and pedagogue and a condition that was then conspicuously not applied to his successor.[5] On the other hand, Gesner's rectorate was greeted with much enthusiasm and high expectations, as his arrival signaled a promising new beginning that was to be visibly underscored by a sweeping renovation of the St. Thomas School building in 1731–32. Bach himself, foremost among those who welcomed the new rector and may even have helped lure him to Leipzig, would benefit from the construction project like nobody else. It seems all the more puzzling, then, that despite these mostly favorable developments, Bach seemed to find himself at a crossroads, as he makes clear in a letter of October 28, 1730, to his classmate from Latin school days, Georg Erdmann:

This post was described to me in such favorable terms that finally (particularly since my sons seemed inclined toward [university] studies) I cast my lot, in the name of the Lord, and made my journey to Leipzig, took my examination, and then made the change of position. Here, by God's will, I am still in service. But since (1) I find that the post is by no means so lucrative as it was described to me; (2) I have failed to obtain many of the fees pertaining to the office; (3) the place is very expensive; and (4) the authorities are odd and little interested in music, so that I must live amid almost continual vexation, envy, and persecution; accordingly I shall be forced, with God's help, to seek my fortune elsewhere. Should Your Honor know or find a suitable post in your city for an old and faithful servant, I beg you most humbly to put in a most gracious word of recommendation for me—I shall not fail to do my best to give satisfaction and justify your most gracious intercession in my behalf. My present post amounts to about 700 talers, and when there are rather more funerals than usual, the fees rise in proportion; but when a healthy wind blows, they fall accordingly, as for example last year, when I lost fees that would ordinarily come in from funerals to an amount of more than 100 talers. In Thuringia I could get along better on 400 talers than here with twice that many, because of the excessively high cost of living.[6]

This is a set of extraordinarily honest statements made in a private letter by a frustrated man who had never failed to do his best but had waited in vain for official recognition of his accomplishments over seven years as composer and performer of an unparalleled repertoire of music for Leipzig's main churches. Bach now painfully realized that his regular income as cantor depended in part on soft money and that, for example, the "more than 100 talers" from funeral fees could not be counted on. In addition, he now understood much better the cost of living in a large commercial city ten times the size of a small princely residential town. He also saw the discrepancy between a fixed salary of 400 talers and the misleading—even outright false—promises of "favorable terms" (1,000–1,200 talers) described to him in 1723 when he applied for the cantorate. In his calculations, Bach omitted earnings from his new Collegium Musicum commitments and from other activities such as giving private instruction, performing recitals, and examining organs, but such additional income would also have counted separately from a fixed salary.

Why did Bach reveal his dissatisfaction to Erdmann? The two had last exchanged letters in 1726,[7] but it is clear from the opening of Bach's 1730 letter that he wanted to respond to a request from his old friend to provide "some news of what had happened to [him]." So writing the letter gave Bach, above all, an opportunity to let off steam. It is unlikely that he contacted Erdmann about any specific position in faraway Danzig, a city about whose musical scene he would hardly have known anything except by hearsay. The only position of some distinction was held by Maximilian Dietrich Freißlich, capellmeister at St. Mary's Church, a Thuringian by birth who was approaching the age of seventy. If Bach had heard a rumor about Freißlich's frail health (indeed, he would die on April 10, 1731), he would have been informed only incompletely, because Freißlich's stepbrother Johann Balthasar Christian, the former court capellmeister at Schwarzburg-Sondershausen (with close ties to Arnstadt), had already moved to Danzig in 1729–30 to prepare for the succession at St. Mary's.[8] Moreover, the musical conditions and the pay would definitely have been less attractive than those in Leipzig, and Danzig could not offer comparable schooling opportunities for his sons. For all these reasons, it is hard to imagine that Bach seriously speculated about St. Mary's in Danzig.

At the time he wrote to Erdmann, Bach could look forward to a collaborative relationship with a new rector and to new ventures involving the Collegium Musicum. At the same time, though, he must have felt locked into his Leipzig post and its disappointing financial setting, which paled in comparison to the prestigious, truly lucrative, and altogether attractive capellmeister opening at Dresden, previously held by a St. Thomas graduate. But Bach knew full well that the Dresden court was on the lookout for someone to reestablish its Italian opera company, which had collapsed a decade earlier in the wake of Antonio Lotti's departure (Johann Adolph Hasse would be invited in 1731, but not formally appointed until December 1, 1733). Nevertheless, Dresden played a role in Bach's thinking when he reevaluated his situation in Leipzig. He would need more than the rector's support. The immediate context for the fourth point raised in the Erdmann letter—"the authorities are odd and little interested in music"—may be garnered from the memorandum Bach had sent two months earlier, on August 23, to the Leipzig city council and to which he had not yet received a reply (which never materialized; perhaps the Erdmann letter was even prompted by a verbal notification that there would be no reply). In this memorandum, which he titled "Short but Most Necessary Draft for a Well-Appointed Church Music," Bach outlined his concept for significant improvements and demanded better pay for his instrumentalists, who, for worry about bread, "cannot think of improving." And here he drew a direct comparison with the musical conditions in the Saxon capital, clearly in the hope that the city fathers, always wary about Dresden's dominance, would feel challenged: "To illustrate this statement with an example one need only go to Dresden and see how the musicians there are paid by his Royal Majesty. It cannot fail, since the musicians there are relieved of all concern for their living, free from *chagrin* and obliged each to master but a single instrument; it must be something choice and excellent to hear."[9]

From Bach's perspective, it was indeed an odd government that expected him to bring luster to the city by mounting regular performances of the finest conceivable church music with essentially the same setting and budget that Kuhnau had had at his disposal. How could they expect him to attract and inspire the university students with stipends that "should have been increased rather than diminished"? The authorities were indeed showing little interest in music if they would not even agree with his concept, let alone meet his demands. From their own penny-pinching perspective, however, it was hard to understand why the cantor needed more money. To their ears, the performances went well, and they were surely impressed with a work of such unprecedented proportions and size of performing forces as the *St. Matthew Passion.* They thought the cantor was doing very well, raising funds for his projects by selling text booklets and by other means, and even enlarging his pool of musicians by drawing the Collegium Musicum from the New Church into the musical establishment of St. Thomas's and St. Nicholas's. If he was able to attract the best musicians in town, why spend more money? But the authorities did not understand how much Bach struggled; they did not see that he was weary of asking his musicians to play for very little or nothing, and that these musicians were forced by circumstances to accept money-making engagements for weddings and other private events rather than take the time to practice and rehearse Bach's challenging works. Most of the city fathers thus failed to understand Bach's primary concern, namely "that the state of music is quite different from what it was, since our artistry has increased very much, and [as] the taste has changed astonishingly, and accordingly the former style of music no longer seems to please our ears, considerable help is therefore all the more needed to choose and appoint such musicians as will satisfy the present musical taste, master the new kinds of music, and thus be in a position to do justice to the composer and his work." The intent of Bach's memorandum could not have been more to the point, but the council apparently lacked the political will to respond positively; and the long-standing skepticism about the ambitious capellmeister-cantor among councillors who wanted to see more of a modest schoolmaster-cantor did not help. These people would have viewed Bach's declaration pitting the "different state of music," "increased artistry," and "changed taste" against the "former style of music" primarily as self-serving. Why such opulent instrumentation, why such difficult technical demands on the musicians if a scaled-down version would do just as well? Why not hold the person creating these excessive needs responsible for meeting the demand rather than have the state pay for it? If the cantor could mount an extravaganza like the *St. Matthew Passion* in two presentations, 1727 and 1729, requiring twice as many forces as a normal cantata, his persuasive skills could have known few bounds.

But there was another obstacle that made a positive reaction from the council difficult. Only three weeks before Bach submitted his memorandum, the council had discussed his arrangements for a substitute teacher to take over the Latin classes that traditionally formed part of the cantor's teaching load. They concluded that M. Pezold (Gesner promoted him in 1731 to conrector) "attended to the functions poorly enough," and suggested that "the cantor might take care of one of the lowest classes; he did not conduct himself as he should (without the foreknowledge of the burgomaster in office [he] sent a choir student to the country; went away without obtaining leave), for which he must be reproached and admonished."[10] If Bach was unwilling to teach, the council then suggested replacing Pezold with M. Abraham Kriegel, *collega quartus* (later *tertius*), to admonish Bach. Some harsh words fell at the meeting; one of the councillors stated, "Not only did the Cantor do nothing, but he was not even willing to give an explanation of that fact; he did not hold the singing class, and there were other complaints in addition; a change would be necessary, a break would have to come some time." Another went so far as to say that "the Cantor was *incorrigible.*" On August 25, Burgomaster Born reported back to the council that he "has spoken with the Cantor, Bach, but he shows little inclination to work," that is, teach the Latin classes. So the instruction was transferred to M. Kriegel, but there was more to come. On September 23, the fees for inspecting the dormitory were supposedly distributed among the three colleagues who had shared duties during the rector vacancy: the conrector received 130 talers and the *tertius* 100, but the cantor nothing.[11] Against this background, we can understand very well the resulting posture of both parties: the council's unwillingness to act on the cantor's memorandum of August 23 and Bach's annoyance with the council, as expressed in the Erdmann letter of October 28.

Bach, however, had chosen to present his "Draft for a Well-Appointed Church Music" at a most opportune moment, at least from his point of view. Johann Matthias Gesner, rector of the gymnasium in Ansbach, formerly conrector and court librarian in Weimar, had been elected to the post of rector of St. Thomas's on June 8, 1730. The city council had deliberately chosen an outsider because an internal promotion would have created much jealousy.[12] Bach, too, in his letter to Erdmann spoke of living amid "envy," apparently resulting from his greater visibility and outside recognition. So with Gesner's arrival imminent, Bach was surely looking forward not only to renewing an old acquaintance but also to a fresh perspective for the school.[13] Rector Gesner had ambitious plans for the Thomana, as evidenced by the renovation of the school building in 1731–32 at a total cost of 17,408 talers.[14] Cantor Bach, for his part, was thinking of much more modest sums of money but probably neglecting to consider what the council must have spotted right away, namely that personnel costs over time ordinarily exceed capital investments. In his memorandum, Bach outlined the need for a standing instrumental ensemble of twenty to twenty-four players to complement the choir of twelve to sixteen singers (see Table 10.1). A later account by Gesner, which mentions "thirty or even forty

**TABLE 10.1. Bach's Standard Ensemble for a "Well-Appointed Church Music" (1730)**

| Vocalists | | Number | Instrumentalists | Number |
|---|---|---|---|---|
| *Concertists:* | Soprano | 1–2 | Violin I | 2–3 |
| | Alto | 1–2 | Violin II | 2–3 |
| | Tenor | 1–2 | Viola I | 2 |
| | Bass | 1–2 | Viola II | 2 |
| | | | Violoncello | 2 |
| | | | Violone | 1 |
| *Ripienists:* | Soprano | at least 2 | Flute (recorder or transverse) | 2 |
| | Alto | at least 2 | Oboe | 2–3 |
| | Tenor | at least 2 | Bassoon | 1–2 |
| | Bass | at least 2 | Trumpets | 3 |
| | | | Timpani | 1 |
| Total: | | 12–16 (+) | | 20–24 |

*symphoniaci"* performing under Bach's direction,[15] indicates that the standard performing group indeed consisted of that number of musicians.

We can assume that Bach coordinated his plans with the rector-designate—probably during one of Gesner's return visits from Ansbach before his move to Leipzig in September 1730—and that he consulted with Gesner before submitting his memorandum to the council, safe in the knowledge that the rector would support him. Bach's strategy was smart. He described the worst-case scenario, juxtaposing his salaried staff—the town musicians Reiche, Gentzmer, Rother, Beyer, Gleditsch, Kornagel, and the associate (Table 8.5)—with the actual needs of his instrumental ensemble, pointing out 6 vacancies (third trumpet, timpani, viola, cello, violone, and third oboe) and making the case for supplementary personnel (two first violinists, two second violinists, two violists, and two flutists), adding up to fourteen musicians.[16] Even paying these players at ordinary town musicians' rates[17] would have cost the city more than 700 talers per year and, over Bach's remaining time in Leipzig, would have required nearly the same outlay as the entire St. Thomas School renovation. Bach purposely left out the town musicians' assistants, university students, other *Adjuvanten,* and volunteers recruited from the local Collegia Musica. Naming them would have defeated the purpose of the memorandum, to make a strong case for enlarging his "salaried" ensemble, with a clear emphasis on instrumentalists; vocalists are dealt with only in an appendix because they were primarily a school matter, related to admissions policy. For political reasons, Bach provided net rather than gross quantities throughout. The "almost continual vexation" he wrote of to Erdmann included the frustrating juggling act of constantly having to fill the ranks of his ensemble with ringers, having to

keep reassigning his people according to their best capabilities, and always trying not to offend anyone by his decisions. No wonder that he yearned for truly
professional musicians, each a specialist on his instrument and "capable of performing at once and *ex tempore* all kinds of music, whether it come from Italy
or France, England or Poland, just as may be done, say, by those virtuosos for
whom the music is written and who have studied it long beforehand, indeed,
know it almost by heart, and who, it should be noted, receive good salaries besides, so that their work and industry is thus richly rewarded."[18]

Bach's strategy of making no reference to the alternative resources available
to him probably backfired. The city fathers listening to Bach's church performances didn't miss anything. They certainly had heard drums, even though
Bach claimed not to have a timpanist. And why should they care about a third
oboe, never mind the more sophisticated arguments about artistry, taste, and
style, which were definitely wasted on them. Bach probably realized that and
never returned to the subject. He had long learned how to manage his affairs
and was not trying to renegotiate his contract; he just had a temporary flash
of hope that things might be significantly improved with the arrival of a new
rector and the readiness of the council for a major capital investment in the St.
Thomas School. If he saw himself at a crossroads in 1730, he still made no serious move to get away. All things considered, there was hardly a better place
for him than Leipzig—Telemann in Hamburg had his own struggles with the
city's senate and, in terms of performing forces, much less to work with. In
Bach's Leipzig, its churches, the university, his ensembles, his private students, his instruments, and his studio combined to provide a rich spectrum of
possibilities, which he zealously pursued without fear of interference by superiors. Here the Weimar jail experience and the death of Prince Leopold of
Anhalt-Cöthen may have reminded him that civic government had its advantages and that he would encounter few problems in steering his own course—
in that sense, he was indeed incorrigible. He did not resign, but he shifted his
emphasis. After investing his primary efforts in the cantorate for six years and
creating a remarkable working repertoire of church music, he would now turn
more to other pursuits.

Regardless, however, the St. Thomas School continued to take up most of
Bach's time and commitments. On June 5, 1732, for the rededication of the
magnificently renovated school building, Bach performed the cantata "Froher
Tag, verlangte Stunden," BWV Anh. 18 (music lost), on a text written by the
*collega quartus,* M. Johann Heinrich Winckler. Six hundred copies of the libretto
were printed, indicating that the event was well attended. Unfortunately for
Bach, the Gesner regime was short-lived, lasting barely four years. According
to a later report by a former student, Gesner "visited the singing lessons (otherwise rarely attended by a rector), and listened with pleasure to the perfor-

mance of church pieces."[19] With the cantata "Wo sind meine Wunderwerke,"
BWV Anh. 210 (librettist unknown, music lost), the St. Thomas School bid
him a musical farewell. After Gesner had left for Göttingen University, his conrector, the twenty-seven-year-old Johann August Ernesti, an extraordinarily
gifted and prolific scholar, was elected to the post and formally inaugurated on
November 21, 1734. A welcoming cantata by Bach, "Thomana saß annoch be-
trübt," BWV Anh. 19 (text author Johann August Landvoigt, music lost),
sounded on this day, suggesting that a similar performance took place in 1730
when Gesner acceded to the rectorate, though no trace of any such composition remains. At the city council meeting on November 2, 1734, at which
Ernesti's election took place, councillor Stieglitz remarked that "his office as
chair of the St. Thomas School was made very difficult by the Cantor, as the
latter did not do at the School what he was obliged to do."[20] It seems that under
Gesner, Bach may have managed to reduce his school activities further and del-
egate more work to his four assistants, or prefects.

The main reason Bach had to depend on good prefects was the simultane-
ous commitments to keep four churches supplied with singers every Sunday
and feast day throughout the year, but he also used them for regular singing
lessons, instrumental lessons, and rehearsals. An incident involving the appointment of the first, or general, prefect by rector Ernesti (who was twenty-
two years Bach's junior) over the cantor's objections—among others, that "he
could not accurately give the beat in the two principal kinds of time"[21]—and
a dispute about the cantor's prerogative to appoint the choral prefects[22] resulted
in a protracted affair that began in the summer of 1736. It left a long paper
trail through February 1738, with four letters of complaint by Bach to the city
council, Ernesti's reply and rebuttal, a decree of the council, two appeals by
Bach to the consistory, and finally the king's decree.[23] The conflict destroyed
what must initially have been a good relationship between rector and cantor:
Ernesti had served in 1733 and 1735 as godfather to Bach's children.[24] It also
demonstrated that Bach stubbornly fought for his rights, eventually taking advantage of his honorary court position in Dresden to outmaneuver the rector.
The royal decree of December 17, 1737, sent to the consistory in Leipzig, provides a supportive précis of Bach's stand:

Whereas Our Court Composer, Johann Sebastian Bach, has complained to Us about the
present Rector of the St. Thomas School in Leipzig, Magister Johann August Ernesti,
that he has had the effrontery to fill the post of Prefect without his concurrence, and
with a person whose ability *in musicis* is very poor, and when, noticing the latter's
weakness and the resulting disorder in the music, he [the cantor] saw himself compelled to make a change and to choose a more accomplished person in his place, the
said Rector Ernesti not only opposed his purpose but also, to his great injury and hu-

miliation, forbade all the boys, in general assembly and on pain of whipping, to give their obedience in the arrangements the Cantor had made.[25]

The decree ends by directing the consistory to "take such measures . . . as you shall see fit." On the following February 5, the consistory requested superintendent Deyling and the council to draw up a report, which has not survived to tell us the official outcome of this drawn-out case. The wording of the royal decree, however, strongly suggests that the affair was settled in favor of the court composer, if only with some further admonitions to Bach regarding his school duties. The depth of the dispute, however, is conveyed in the summary account from Johann Heinrich Köhler's *Historia Scholarum Lipsiensium* of 1776:

With Ernesti Bach fell out completely. The occasion was the following. Ernesti removed the General Prefect [Gottfried Theodor] Krause for having chastised one of the younger students too vigorously, expelled him from the School when he fled [to avoid the public whipping to which Ernesti had sentenced him] and chose another student [Johann Gottlob Krause] in his place as General Prefect—a prerogative that really belongs to the Cantor, whom the General Prefect has to represent. Because the student chosen was of no use in the performance of the church music, Bach made a different choice. The situation between him and Ernesti developed to the point of charge and countercharge, and the two men from that time on were enemies. Bach began to hate those students who devoted themselves completely to the *humaniora* and treated music as a secondary matter, and Ernesti became a foe of music. When he came upon a student practicing on an instrument, he would exclaim "What? You want to be a beer-fiddler, too?" By virtue of the high regard in which he was held by the Burgomaster, Stieglitz, he managed to be released from the duties of the special inspection of the School [dormitories] and to have them assigned to the Fourth Colleague. Thus when it was Bach's turn to undertake the inspection, he cited the precedent of Ernesti and came neither to table nor to prayers; and this neglect of duty had the worst influence on the moral training of the students. From that time on, though there have been several incumbents of both posts, little harmony has been observed between the Rector and the Cantor.[26]

Back in the early 1730s, Bach could not have anticipated anything like the prefect dispute and its consequences, but he *was* prepared for continuing and new conflicts. By picturing himself at a crossroads as he did in the Erdmann letter of 1730, and by declaring, "I shall be forced, with God's help, to seek my fortune elsewhere," he probably gained the needed self-confidence and determination, stamina and staying power. Perhaps he was reminded of his own crossroads when, in 1733, he composed the dramatic cantata *Hercules at the Crossroads,* BWV 213. In the middle of the piece, at the crucial turning point, the allegorical figure of Virtue poses the question (in recitative style) "Whither, my Hercules, whither?" and the accompanying basso continuo features only two notes, but notes that represent the ultimate in terms of incompatible choices: the tritone C and F-sharp. Hercules here, Bach there, and vice versa. Bach the composer knew extremely well how to negotiate musical cliffs as he confidently navigated two supposedly disagreeing harmonic landscapes, an aria in B-flat major followed by one in the totally incompatible key of A major. At the same time, he knew full well that negotiating real life was more troublesome.

## DIRECTOR OF THE COLLEGIUM MUSICUM AND ROYAL COURT COMPOSER

The first reference to what became a new and major chapter in Bach's Leipzig period can be found in the postscript to a letter he wrote on March 20, 1729, to his former student Christoph Gottlob Wecker, now cantor at Schweidnitz in Silesia: "The latest is that the dear Lord has now also provided for honest Mr. Schott, and bestowed on him the post of Cantor in Gotha, wherefore he will say his farewells next week, as I am willing to take over his *Collegium.*"[27] From 1720, Georg Balthasar Schott had been organist of the New Church in Leipzig and, as the custom had been since Telemann's time, also director of the city's most prestigious Collegium Musicum. Throughout the seventeenth century, musically active university students had formed private societies that played an increasingly important role in Leipzig's public musical life, as they were often led by the city's most prominent professionals, such as Adam Krieger, Johann Rosenmüller, Sebastian Knüpfer, Johann Pezel, and Johann Kuhnau. In 1701, the young and energetic law student and first organist of the recently rebuilt New Church, Georg Philipp Telemann, founded a new Collegium that, he wrote, "often assembled up to 40 students."[28] He was succeeded by Melchior Hoffmann, who directed the organization for ten years beginning in 1705. A Leipzig chronicler reported in 1716 that Hoffmann's Collegium had numbered between fifty and sixty members, performed twice weekly, and produced many virtuosos who later gained important positions as cantors, organists, and court musicians[29]—no exaggeration, since celebrities such as the Gotha capellmeister Gottfried Heinrich Stölzel, the Dresden concertmaster Johann Georg Pisendel, and the international opera star and bass singer Johann Gottfried Riemschneider had all performed under Hoffmann. After Hoffmann's premature death in 1715, his Collegium was briefly led by Johann Gottfried Vogler, who handed it over around 1718 to Schott and took charge of a smaller Collegium, founded on Telemann's model by Johann Friedrich Fasch and directed, during Bach's time, by Johann Gottlieb Görner (Table 8.2).

The activities of the "Schottische" Collegium Musicum received a significant boost in 1723 when it began a close collaboration with Gottfried Zimmermann, proprietor and operator of the city's largest and most prominent coffeehouse. Located on Catharinenstrasse, Leipzig's most prestigious avenue off the main market square, the mansion (destroyed in World War II) contained a hall suitable for performances by large ensembles, including trumpets and timpani, and for an audience of up to 150. Zimmermann established a series of weekly two-hour concerts throughout the year, held outdoors in his coffee garden during the summer months. Although he did not sell tickets, we can assume that he attracted an audience who, before and after the concerts, would patronize his restaurant—a bourgeois emulation of the courtly practice of *musique de table.* He must have fared quite well with his concert series because he acquired several musical instruments specifically to support the Collegium, among them at least two violins, one viola, two bassoons, and two violones[30]— indicating that he was prepared to accommodate large ensembles needing a strong basso continuo group that included two bassoons and two double basses.

In late March 1729, Bach assumed the directorship of the Collegium, immediately renamed the "Bachische" Collegium Musicum. The transition was likely a smooth one, as Schott had previously collaborated with him and, from his earliest days in Leipzig, Bach had benefited from the pool of qualified Collegium musicians for performances at St. Nicholas's and St. Thomas's. Moreover, throughout the 1720s, Schott had served as Bach's main substitute whenever the latter was out of town or otherwise prevented from performing his duties[31] (a function taken over after Schott's departure by Carl Gotthelf Gerlach), another sign of the close collaborative relationship between Bach and the music directors at the New Church. Not surprisingly, the newly arrived capellmeister and famous virtuoso Bach soon participated in performances by Schott's Collegium, an organization that prided itself on being the training ground for Germany's finest church, town, and court musicians. In one case, on March 12, 1727, Bach led forty musicians in his *Abend-Music* "Entfernet euch, ihr heitern Sterne," BWV Anh. 9 (music lost), as part of the birthday celebration for King August II (Augustus the Strong), an event held in the king's presence that also included three hundred torch-carrying students.[32] The Collegium would surely have taken part in other student-sponsored performances as well, such as that of cantata BWV 193a (music lost) on the king's name day, August 3, 1727, the *Funeral Ode* BWV 198 for the queen later that year, and congratulatory pieces for university professors, including BWV 36c and 205 in 1725 and BWV 207 in 1726. Heinrich Nicolaus Gerber's report that in 1724, before he became a student of Bach's, "he had heard much excellent church music and many a concert under Bach's direction"[33] suggests that the capellmeister, as the city's most eminent musician, was invited to be the Collegium's principal guest conductor and frequent soloist from the beginning of his Leipzig tenure.[34]

There is no question that the Collegium directorship amounted to a major commitment: Bach was now responsible, in addition to his regular church music obligations, for preparing and carrying out a weekly series of performances throughout the year. The schedule of these *ordinaire Concerten,* presented in a well-coordinated way by the city's two Collegia, was made even more demanding by the additional commitments of the thrice-yearly trade fairs (Table 10.2). Lorenz Christoph Mizler's 1736 *Announcement of the Musical Concerts at Leipzig* represents but one reference to what had become a crucial cell for the development of public concert life in Germany:

Both of the public musical Concerts or Assemblies that are held here weekly are still flourishing steadily. The one is conducted by Mr. Johann Sebastian Bach, Capellmeister to the Court of Weissenfels and music director at St. Thomas's and at St. Nicholas's in this city. . . . The other is conducted by Mr. Johann Gottlieb Görner, music director at St. Paul's and organist at St. Thomas's. . . .

The participants in these musical concerts are chiefly students here, and there are always good musicians among them, so that sometimes they become, as is known, famous virtuosos. Any musician is permitted to make himself publicly heard at these musical concerts, and most often, too, there are such listeners as know how to judge the qualities of an able musician.[35]

Complementing Mizler's description, Johann Heinrich Zedler's 1739 *Grosses Universal Lexicon* defines a Collegium Musicum as "a gathering of certain musical connoisseurs who, for the benefit of their own exercise in both

## TABLE 10.2. Weekly Concert Series *(Ordinaire Concerten)* of the Leipzig Collegia Musica

*Collegium musicum (I), directed by Johann Sebastian Bach*

| Friday | 8–10 P.M. (winter) | at Zimmermann's coffeehouse, Catharinenstrasse |
| --- | --- | --- |
| Wednesday | 4–6 P.M. (summer) | at Zimmermann's coffee garden, Grimmischer Steinweg |
| Tuesday and Friday | 8–10 P.M. (fair)[a] | at Zimmermann's coffeehouse |

*Collegium musicum (II), directed by Johann Gottlieb Görner*

| Thursday | 8–10 P.M. | at Richter's coffeehouse (Schellhafer Hall), Clostergasse |
| --- | --- | --- |
| Monday and Thursday | 8–10 P.M. (fair)[a] | at Richter's coffeehouse |

[a]New Year's Fair (early January); Jubilate, or Easter, Fair (April/May); and Michaelmas Fair (September/October).

vocal and instrumental music and under the guidance of a certain director, get together on particular days and in particular locations and perform musical pieces. Such Collegia are to be found in various places. In Leipzig, the Bachian Collegium Musicum is more famous than all others."[36]

During the summer of 1737, after more than eight years as Collegium director, Bach temporarily withdrew from its leadership and handed it over to his colleague at the New Church, Carl Gotthelf Gerlach, who had previously substituted for him on occasion.[37] The reasons for this arrangement are unknown, but the demands of the weekly concert schedule may have interfered with other plans or simply been too heavy for the fifty-two-year-old Bach.[38] Nevertheless, he remained closely associated with the Collegium and even conducted one of its *extraordinaire Concerten* on April 28, 1738, with a performance of the cantata "Willkommen! Ihr herrschenden Götter der Erden," BWV Anh. 13, on a libretto provided by Johann Christoph Gottsched. It is particularly regrettable that the music for this work has not survived, because Lorenz Christoph Mizler refers to it in his refutation of Johann Adolph Scheibe's attacks on Bach's style when he writes that "anyone who heard the music that was performed by the students at the Easter Fair in Leipzig last year . . . , which was composed by Capellmeister Bach, must admit that it was written entirely in accordance with the latest taste, and was approved by everyone. So well does the Capellmeister know how to suit himself to his listeners."[39]

Gerlach's interim leadership ended on October 2, 1739, the Leipzig newspapers having announced the previous day that "the Royal-Polish and Electoral-Saxon Court Composer Bach has resumed the directorship of the Collegium Musicum."[40] Bach continued as Collegium director at least until the *cafétier* Zimmermann's death in May 1741 and possibly for several more years; Gerlach took over permanently in 1746. By then, however, the situation had changed, for in 1743 sixteen Leipzig aristocrats and merchants established the "Grand Concerts" *(Grosse Concert),* a series that by 1750 drew audiences of two to three hundred.[41] Gerlach himself was involved in this new organization, which apparently attracted the best personnel from both academic Collegia (whose activities ended in the 1750s). Considering his stature and commanding position in Leipzig, Bach was surely involved in the Grand Concerts, though more likely as a critical commentator than as a supporter or participant.[42] As an ambitious father, he would have welcomed this venue for his two youngest sons.

The "Bachische" Collegium Musicum existed for at least twelve years, from 1729 to 1741. A major focus for Bach in the 1730s, the group affected his work in at least three important ways: (1) it allowed him to perform a diversified repertoire of contemporary music that interested him; (2) it provided opportunities for composing works to be performed at the regular weekly series and at special concerts; and (3) it supported his ongoing church music projects. The Collegium also offered a rich sphere of activity for his sons and students. For example, in a testimonial of 1737 for Bernhard Dietrich Ludewig, later town organist in Schmölln, Bach writes that Ludewig "in various years frequented my Collegium Musicum with diligence, untiringly participated in the same, playing various instruments as well as making himself heard many times *vocaliter.*"[43] No particulars are known about the specific membership, which already in Hoffmann's time numbered fifty to sixty, but the Collegium must have been dominated by university students and certainly included all of Bach's private students among them. Throughout Bach's directorship, Gerlach participated as alto singer, violinist, and harpsichordist, perhaps even as a kind of assistant director.[44] Also, former students still residing in Leipzig and members of the academic community at large, such as Johann Abraham Birnbaum and Louise Adelgunde Gottsched, may have regularly participated. Town musicians may have joined the ensemble: Johann Friedrich Caroli, appointed art fiddler in 1730, matriculated at Leipzig University in 1719 and doubtless played in at least one of the academic Collegia. Johann Polykarp Büchner, bass singer at the Weissenfels court, seems to have joined the Collegium in the late 1730s—an additional example of professional musicians playing a role there.[45] Finally, the concerts often featured debuts and returns of well-known guest artists, including the Dresden capellmeister Johann Adolph Hasse, his wife, the diva Faustina Bordoni, and the lutenist-composer Silvius Leopold Weiss, among many others, who came to visit Bach in Leipzig during the 1730s.

Vocal and instrumental pieces by a great variety of composers must have been included in the weekly series of "ordinary" concerts, but it is impossible to reconstruct, even in the broadest outlines, any of the more than five hundred two-hour programs for which Bach was responsible. Pertinent performing materials from the 1730s are extremely sparse; among the traceable compositions are four orchestral overtures by Johann Bernhard Bach; the cantata "Armida abbandonata" by George Frideric Handel; the Concerto Grosso in F minor, Op. 1, No. 8, by Pietro Locatelli; three Italian cantatas ("Dal primo foco in cui penai," "Sopra un colle fiorito," and "Ecco l'infausto lido") by Nicola Porpora; and the cantata "Se amor con un contento" by Alessandro Scarlatti.[46] Additionally, "Mr. Bach de Leipzig" is found among the subscribers to Telemann's *Nouveaux Quatuors* (flute quartets), published in Paris in 1738,[47] which suggests that he wanted the pieces for the Collegium series. Although these few works and composers cannot be considered representative at all, they confirm that the repertoire was both instrumental and vocal, that Italian solo cantatas played a role, and that the newest kind of music (such as the Porpora cantatas and the Telemann quartets) was introduced.[48]

Among Bach's own works, one group of pieces particularly suitable for the Collegium series belongs in the category, popular in the early eighteenth century, of "moral" cantatas, that is, vocal compositions whose lyrical texts deal with virtues and vices (Table 10.3). The so-called *Coffee Cantata,* BWV 211, for example, humorously addresses a theme (coffee addiction) particularly fitting for the locale where it was performed, probably more than once. Repeat performances were likely for these works because they were not related to a specific occasion. Of particular interest to the intellectual audience would have been Bach's dramatic cantata "The Contest between Phoebus and Pan," BWV 201, in which the composer wittily elaborates, in the form of a singing contest, on the aesthetic criteria for high and low styles of music and presents his own preferences for the sophisticated, learned style of high art vis-à-vis the shallow manners and trivial effects of popular musical fashions. At the same time, this cantata displays the ingenuity with which Bach judiciously embraces elements of popular culture—if only in mythological and academically elevated dress—and effectively wins the laughter over to his side. The aria sung by Pan, the loser of the contest, makes use of one of the stock effects of early comic opera, the rapid repeat of a single syllable, while its pointed poetic and musical perversion, "so wa-a-a-a-ckelt das Herz" (so wobbles the heart), makes a mockery of the device. Thus, Pan receives a fool's cap and Midas, his judge, earns himself ass's ears. This cantata clearly belongs among the first pieces composed for the weekly series; it may well have served as a programmatic season opener for the summer or winter series of 1729 and was repeated in later seasons as well, the last time as late as 1749.[49]

While it is safe to assume that most if not all of Bach's keyboard pieces from at least 1729 to 1741 (especially parts I, II, and IV of the *Clavier-Übung* series and part II of *The Well-Tempered Clavier*) would have been presented at the weekly concerts, a core repertoire of Bach's chamber music had an even closer

## TABLE 10.3. Moral Cantatas for the *Ordinaire Concerten*

| BWV | Title (poet) | Date |
|---|---|---|
| 204 | Ich bin in mir vergnügt<br>"On Contentment" (Christian Friedrich Hunold) | 1726–27 |
| 201 | Geschwinde, geschwinde, ihr wirbelnden Winde<br>*Dramma per musica* "The Contest between Phoebus and<br>Pan" (Picander) | 1729 |
| 216a | Erwählte Pleißen-Stadt<br>"Apollo and Mercury" [On the City of Erudition and<br>Commerce] (Christian Gottlob Meißner) | 1729? |
| 211 | Schweigt stille, plaudert nicht<br>*Dramma per musica* "About Coffee" (Picander) | 1734 |

connection with Collegium activities (Table 10.4). This is not to say that all works for which only Leipzig materials exist were specifically written for the Collegium; some may be of pre-Leipzig origin, others may have been written for a different purpose, and still others may result from commissions by the likes of the Berlin flutist Michael Gabriel von Fredersdorf (chamberlain to King Friedrich II of Prussia), whose name can be connected with the Flute Sonata BWV 1035 and Bach's trip to Berlin in 1741. Nevertheless, the bulk

TABLE 10.4. Instrumental Music for the *Ordinaire Concerten*

| BWV | Title | Scoring | Date of Performance Materials |
|---|---|---|---|
| *Sonatas* | | | |
| 1023 | Sonata in E minor | violin, bc | after 1723 (?) |
| 1034 | Sonata in E minor | flute, bc | ~1724 (?) |
| 1014–19 | Six sonatas | harpsichord, violin | ~1725 (?) |
| 1033 | Sonata in C major | flute, bc | 1731 |
| 1021 | Sonata in G major | violin, bc | 1732–35 |
| 1038 | Sonata in G major | flute, violin, bc | 1732–35 |
| 1030, 1032 | Two sonatas | harpsichord, flute | 1736–37 |
| 1027–29 | Three sonatas | viola da gamba, harpsichord | ~1736–41 |
| 1039 | Sonata in G major | 2 flutes, bc | ~1736–41 |
| 1025 | Trio in A major | violin, harpsichord | 1739 |
| 1035 | Sonata in E major | flute, bc | ~1741? |
| 1031 | Sonata in E-flat major | harpsichord, flute | ?[a] |
| *Concertos* | | | |
| 1044 | Concerto in A minor | flute, violin, harpsichord, str, bc | 1729–41 |
| 1064 | Concerto in C major | 3 harpsichord, str, bc | 1729–41 |
| 1063 | Concerto in D minor | 3 harpsichords, str, bc | ~1730 |
| 1065 | Concerto in A minor | 4 harpsichords, str, bc | ~1730 |
| 1041 | Concerto in A minor | violin, str, bc | ~1730 |
| 1043 | Concerto in D minor | 2 violins, str, bc | ~1730–31 |
| 1061 | Concerto in C major | 2 harpsichords, str, bc | 1732–35 |
| 1052–58 | Seven concertos | harpsichord, str [1057: 2rec], bc | 1734–39 |
| 1060 | Concerto in C minor | 2 harpsichords, str, bc | ~1736 |
| 1062 | Concerto in C minor | 2 harpsichords, str, bc | ~1736 |
| *Suites* | | | |
| 1066 | Suite in C major | 2ob, bn, str, bc | ~1725 |
| 1069 | Suite in D major | 3tr/ti, 3ob, bs, str, bc | ~1725 |
| 1068 | Suite in D major | 3tr/ti, 2ob, str, bc | 1731 |
| 1067 | Suite in B minor | flute, str, bc | ~1738–39 |

*Note:* The performance materials were available for multiple purposes, including lessons and performances at the St. Thomas School.
[a] Earliest copy of score dated 1748–49.

of what has survived and an even greater lot of lost pieces would surely have
been performed at the Collegium concert series; and most of the extant pieces
actually suggest Leipzig origins.[50]

Public announcements in the Leipzig press now and then refer to particular concerts. For example, the resumption of the concert series, temporarily suspended during the state mourning period for King Augustus the Strong, is
announced for June 17, 1733, at Zimmermann's coffee garden with the following special notice: "The beginning will be made . . . with a fine concert. It
will be maintained week by week, with a new *Clavicymbel,* such as had not been
heard here before, and lovers of music as well as virtuosos are expected to be
present." Although Bach became involved with Gottfried Silbermann and his
fortepiano constructions in the mid-1730s, the subtle and elusive sound of the
first generation of fortepianos would have been unsuitable for outdoor concerts.
More likely, the instrument in question was an attractive and powerful new
harpsichord, perhaps one with which Bach introduced his new concertos for
harpsichord and orchestra to the Leipzig public. "Such as had not been heard
here before" may serve as a kind of general motto for Bach's Collegium programs, in which he tried to present the best and the newest in musical repertoire, artists, and instruments. And with the concertos for one, two, three,
and four harpsichords, he himself set new standards for the dynamic interplay
between keyboard soloist and instrumental ensemble—indeed, he established
a new genre that his sons consolidated and that by the end of the century had
become the most favored concerto type by far.

Bach's Collegium activities were not confined to the weekly "ordinary"
concerts at Zimmermann's coffeehouse. The first known event outside the series in the form of "extraordinary" concerts *(extraordinaire Concerten)* was the
performance of the cantata BWV Anh. 11 for the name day in 1732 of Augustus the Strong, presented less than half a year before the king's death (the
works previously performed in the king's honor, BWV Anh. 9 and BWV
193a, had been guest performances during Schott's Collegium directorship).
Soon after the accession to the throne of his son, King August III, Bach
started a loose sequence of special concerts dedicated almost exclusively to
the electoral-royal house in Dresden, for birthdays, name days, and political
events, sometimes in the presence of royal family members (Table 10.5). In
contrast to the weekly series, for which few details and no programs are known,
the extraordinary concerts are generally well documented, with most of the librettos, many scores, and even performing materials extant, usually with ver-
ifiable dates, often accompanied by reports in newspapers and chronicles as well
as receipts and other archival references. We know, for example, that Bach
usually collected 50 talers for composing a cantata in honor of the royal fam-

Zimmermann's coffeehouse in Leipzig, the principal performance site of Bach's Collegium Musicum, in an engraving by Johann Georg Schreiber (1712).

ily,[51] a fee equivalent to half of his fixed annual salary (and, incidentally, the same fee Mozart requested when he was commissioned to write his Requiem in 1791). This explains how attractive these special concerts, which were occasionally sponsored by Leipzig University (BWV Anh. 9, BWV 215, BWV Anh. 13), must have been for him. In a number of instances, the Breitkopf music-publishing firm's invoices to Bach (for the printing of the text both in presentation copies for the honorees and in plain booklets for the general public)[52] provide information about the attendance, based on the number of copies for sale: for indoor performances at Zimmermann's coffeehouse, 150 (BWV 205a, 214) or 200 copies (BWV 206); for outdoor performances in Zimmermann's coffee garden, also 150 (BWV 207a, 215) or 200 copies (BWV Anh. 12, BWV 213); but for outdoor performances in front of the royal residence, Apel House on the south side of the market square, and in the presence of the king, 312 (BWV Anh. 11), 600 (BWV Anh. 13), and even 700 copies (BWV 215). The sum 700 was the equivalent to over 2 percent of the city's entire population of some 30,000, but the Leipzig chronicler Riemer reported that for this prominent event "many people came in from the country to see it";[53] with nonpaying spectators added, the market square must have been crowded to capacity.

We are also informed by Riemer about the performances themselves. We learn, for example, about the gala style in which the first anniversary of the Saxon elector Friedrich August II's accession as king of Poland was celebrated on October 5, 1734, with the presentation of the cantata "Preise dein Glücke, gesegnetes Sachsen," BWV 215, in the presence of the royal couple:

About nine o'clock in the evening the students [at the University] here presented Their Majesties with a most submissive evening serenade [BWV 215] with trumpets and drums, which the Hon. Capellmeister, Johann Sebastian Bach, Cantor at St. Thomas's, had composed. For this, six hundred students carried wax tapers, and four Counts acted as marshals in presenting the [text of the] music. The procession made its way up to the King's residence [Apel House]. When the musicians had reached the *Wage* [weigh house on the north flank of the market square], the trumpets and drums went up on it, while others took their places in another choir at the *Rathaus.* When the text was presented, the four counts were permitted to kiss the Royal hands, and afterward his Royal Majesty together with his Royal Consort and the Royal Princes did not leave the windows until the music was over, and listened most graciously and liked it well.[54]

The performance of this *Cantata gratulatoria in adventum Regis,* its nine movements lasting well over thirty minutes, was preceded by a formal entrance march and accompanied by a processional piece with trumpets and drums (the music has not survived).[55] The polychoral design, with the separate positioning of the brass section (3 trumpets and timpani) from the rest of the instrumental ensemble (2 transverse flutes, 2 oboes, strings, and continuo), is further reinforced by the double choirs—Bach's only secular cantata requiring eight vocal parts (two each of SATB; concertists were in choir I). On the day after the performance, Bach's principal trumpeter and senior member of the town music company, the sixty-seven-year-old Gottfried Reiche, collapsed in front of his house on the Stadtpfeifergasse and died of a stroke. "And this supposedly came about because he suffered great strains from playing on the previous day at the royal music, and the smoke from the torches had also caused him much discomfort."[56]

Though not strictly speaking part of his Collegium activities, Bach was at times commissioned to write secular works for performances outside of Leipzig. Two such occasions, which involved members of the landed gentry, are documented and suggest that for these purposes the ensembles were recruited from the Collegium membership. On September 28, 1737, Bach performed one of his most extended secular cantatas, "Angenehmes Wiederau," BWV 30a, at the estate of Johann Christian von Hennicke in Wiederau, some twelve miles southwest of Leipzig; its twelve movements take up more than three-quarters of an hour. This homage to Hennicke, chamberlain of the Naumburg, Merseburg, and Zeitz cathedral chapters and a member of the electoral cabinet, was prompted by his acquisition of the Wiederau manor in the fall of 1737. A similar event occurred on August 30, 1742, when Bach presented his *Cantate burlesque* "Mer hahn en neue Oberkeet," BWV 212, an homage to Carl Heinrich von Dieskau at his Kleinzschocher estate near Leipzig. Dieskau, the district captain of Leipzig, also held court positions in Dresden, first as "Directeur des Plaisirs" and from 1747 as director of the royal capelle and chamber music. The text of this so-called *Peasant Cantata* is written in an Upper Saxon dialect, and the piece is emphatically burlesque in tone. The overture parodies a rustic ensemble with a three-part peasant trio of violin, viola, and double bass, its apparently unmotivated shifts suggesting a potpourri of dances. At various points in the work, moreover, Bach quotes snatches of popular tunes of the day: in movement 3, the "grandfather's dance" "With me and you into the feather bed" ("Mit mir und dir ins Federbett"); in movement 8, the *Folies d'Espagne;* and in movement 16, the drinking song "How can a thousand ducats help us" ("Was helfen uns tausend Dukaten"). This last secular cantata of Bach's may actually mark one of his final engagements with his Collegium Musicum. It also recalls Forkel's statement at the end of his biography that, "notwithstanding the main tendency of his genius to the great and sublime, he [Bach] sometimes composed and performed something gay and even jocose; his cheerfulness and joking were those of a sage."

Like his sacred cantatas, Bach's occasional secular works were often finished

**TABLE 10.5.** The *Extraordinaire Concerten* in Honor of the Electoral-Royal Family

| BWV | Title (Librettist) | Occasion |
|---|---|---|
| Anh. 9 | *Dramma per musica:* Entfernet Euch, ihr heitern Sterne[a] (Christian Friedrich Haupt) | Elector's birthday, May 12, 1727 |
| 193a | *Dramma per musica:* Ihr Häuser des Himmels, ihr scheinenden Lichter[a] (Christian Friedrich Henrici) | Elector's name day, August 3, 1727 |
| Anh. 11 | *Dramma per musica:* Es lebe der König, der Vater im Lande[a] (Henrici) | Elector's name day, August 3, 1732 |
| Anh. 12 | Cantata: Frohes Volk, vergnügte Sachsen[a] (Henrici) | Elector's name day, August 3, 1733 |
| 213 | *Dramma per musica, Hercules at the Crossroads:* Laßt uns sorgen, laßt uns wachen (Henrici) | Prince's birthday, September 5, 1733 |
| 214 | *Dramma per musica:* Tönet, ihr Pauken! Erschallet Trompeten! (unknown) | Electoress's birthday, December 8, 1733 |
| — | Serenade[b] (*BC* G 20/*BD* II, no. 346) (unknown) | King's coronation, January 17, 1734 |
| 205a | *Dramma per musica:* Blast Lärmen, ihr Feinde! (unknown; Henrici?) | King's coronation, February 19, 1734?[c] |
| 215 | *Dramma per musica:* Preise dein Glücke, gesegnetes Sachsen (Johann Christoph Clauder) | King's election day, October 5, 1734 |
| 206 | *Dramma per musica:* Schleicht, spielende Wellen (unknown) | Elector's birthday, October 7, 1736[d] |
| 207a | Cantata: Auf schmetternde Töne der muntern Trompeten (unknown) | Elector's name day, August 3, 1735? |
| Anh. 13 | Serenade: Willkommen! Ihr herrschenden Götter der Erden[a] (Johann Christoph Gottsched) | Homage for royal couple, April 28, 1738 |
| — | Serenade[b] (*BC* G 25) (unknown) | Elector's birthday, October 7, 1739 |
| 206 | *Dramma per musica:* Schleicht, spielende Wellen (*BC* G 26) (unknown) | Elector's name day, August 3, 1740[e] |
| 208a | Cantata: Was mir behagt ist nur die muntre Jagd (Franck) | Elector's name day, August 3, 1742 |

[a]Music lost.
[b]Text and music lost.
[c]Originally prepared for January 17, 1734, but replaced by another (unknown) work.
[d]Originally prepared for October 7, 1734, but replaced by BWV 215.
[e]Second performance of BWV 206, with some changes.

just before they had to be performed. According to Bach's own colophon *(Fine | D[eo] S[oli] Gl[oria]. | 1733. | den 7 Dec.)*, the score of "Tönet, ihr Pauken," BWV 214, for example, was completed on the day preceding its performance. For the composition of "Preise dein Glücke," BWV 215, only three days in all were available to Bach because the royal family had decided on very short notice to attend the 1734 Michaelmas Fair in Leipzig; he therefore used for the opening movement a reworked version of "Es lebe der König," BWV Anh. 11/1, composed two years earlier. Four homage librettos (BWV 193a, Anh. 11–12, BWV 213, BWV 30a, and BWV 212) were delivered by Picander, who made a specialty of this kind of *ad hoc* poetry, for which he and similar rhymesmiths were sneered at as "congratulators" by poets like Gottsched, who considered themselves of a higher class (although Gottsched himself provided the text for BWV Anh. 13). The favorite format of Bach and his librettists for these secular cantatas was the *dramma per musica,* a term that also designated opera. And indeed, in both textual dramaturgy and musical design, there was no difference between the genres, the main distinction being that cantatas were shorter and unstaged. And as in opera seria, the subjects and dramatis personae were ordinarily drawn from classical mythology: Apollo, Hercules, Mars, Pallas, and other familiar figures engage in the dialogues. Alternatives occur in librettos dealing with figurative myths (Mercury and Apollo representing Leipzig) or with philosophical and political topics involving allegorical figures (lust and virtue, providence and piety; or the Pleiße [Leipzig's river] along with the Elbe [Dresden's river] representing Saxony, the Weichsel River Poland, and the Danube River Hapsburg Austria).

Leipzig audiences, deprived since 1720 of their own opera house, could experience in Bach's *drammi per musica* something of what was offered by the royal opera in Dresden. At the same time, Bach's pieces were by no means poor or makeshift substitutes for real opera. His compositions demonstrate, at every step, full mastery of the dramatic genre and the proper pacing of the dialogues. After Johann Adolph Hasse's first production in 1731 of his opera *Cleofide,* Bach frequently traveled to the Dresden opera and, as Forkel reports, often "took his eldest son with him. He used to say in jest some days before his departure: 'Friedemann, shan't we go again to hear the lovely Dresden ditties?' Innocent as this joke was in itself, I am convinced that Bach would not have uttered it to anybody except this son who, at that time, already knew what is great in art and what is only beautiful and agreeable."[57] Here Forkel points to an important characteristic of Bach's secular cantata movements, choruses, arias, and recitatives alike: they are infinitely more elaborate than those ordinarily found in opera scores, yet no less moving, meaningful, or effective. Especially when it comes to creating musical imagery such as Hercules and his Echo in BWV 213/5, orchestral semantics such as the soft murmuring of playing waves in BWV 206/1, or specific word-tone relationships such as "exploding metal" in BWV 214/4, Bach proceeds with unparalleled imagination, technical sophistication, and a strong sense for immediate effects.

Unlike the librettos of the moral cantatas, virtually all the homage cantata texts address the specific occasion for which the work was written, often with references to its dedicatee. And since the occasion would not normally recur, repeat performances, with few exceptions, had to be ruled out. However, as there was no principal genre difference between secular and sacred cantatas, their ready adaptability as sacred cantatas allowed the music of many secular cantatas a permanent place, albeit with different texts. Bach made the most of this situation, apparently counting on that possibility all along. Thus, going well beyond the parody technique he had applied when adapting Cöthen works to Leipzig church cantatas, he converted the bulk of his occasional cantatas to sacred compositions, thereby further expanding and enriching the available repertoire. Works like the Kyrie and Gloria of the Mass in B minor, BWV 232$^I$; which date to 1733, and the *Christmas Oratorio,* BWV 248, of 1734–35 benefited in particular from Bach's highly discerning and methodical processes of adaptation.

By letting Bach tap directly into a large pool of musicians, his post as director of the Collegium Musicum had a stabilizing effect on the performing ensemble he needed for St. Thomas's and St. Nicholas's and to some extent helped offset the city council's unwillingness to provide more and better-paid personnel. One of the first manifestations of Bach's newly won "command" over the city's best musicians occurred on the second day of Pentecost in 1729, shortly after he had become Collegium director. At this performance, he opened the cantata BWV 174 with a festive sinfonia that was a lavishly expanded version of the first movement of the third *Brandenburg Concerto,* with a large ensemble of 2 horns, 3 oboes, 3 solo violins, 3 solo violas, 3 solo cellos, *ripieno* strings, and continuo (including bassoon and violone), the likes of which had heretofore not been heard. Although Bach may have realized that such demonstrations of his capacity to mobilize large-scale forces would eventually undermine his efforts to obtain funding for additional personnel, he was determined to make the best possible use of the sacred repertoire he had created in the 1720s. It is not possible to reconstruct the kind of musical calendar for the 1730s and 1740s that can be assembled for 1723–1725 and the later 1720s (Tables 8.7–11); nonetheless, there is plenty of evidence that Bach reperformed a large number of cantatas, even if specific dates can rarely be assigned. It remains unclear if Bach intended to keep the annual cantata cycles largely intact and to present them in order. In only a single instance do the original performance parts suggest the re-performance of a whole cycle, or at least a major segment of it: the chorale cantata *Jahrgang* seems to have been performed again sometime between 1732 and 1735, as we can deduce from the consistent performance instructions (e.g., organ "tacet" markings) for a dozen or so cantatas.[58]

Apart from additions to the chorale cantata cycle, which Bach tried to complete but never did, the new contributions to the repertoire of church cantatas are for the most part works derived from occasional secular compositions. Particularly prominent examples are cantatas BWV 30 and 36, but Bach pursued the same procedure also with some larger-scale works, beginning with the *St. Mark Passion* of 1731 (which drew heavily on the *Funeral Ode* of 1727) and ending with a group of three oratorios from 1734–35 to 1738 (Table 10.6). However, the parody process was not limited to the transformation of secular cantata movements into sacred works. The Kyrie-Gloria Masses of the 1730s, for instance, are based almost entirely on parody models from sacred cantatas.

The first and largest of the five Kyrie-Gloria Masses sets the aesthetic trend for the whole group of Latin liturgical works by presenting a highly select cross section of particularly elaborate cantata movements. This is the only such work whose genesis is known, at least in its broad outlines. On February 1, 1733, King Augustus the Strong died in Warsaw, and on the following day a state mourning period was declared for the customary duration of six months. The music-free half year provided Bach with a welcome opportunity to pursue a project that might have been on his mind for some time but could now be realized. Like his father, the new Saxon elector and Polish king, August III, demonstrated great interest in all the arts, sharing with his Viennese wife, Maria Josepha, a special fondness for Italian poetry and music (the Hapsburg archduchess had been a student of the imperial capellmeister Giuseppe Porsile). Chamber, theater, and church music were equally well cultivated at their court; the electoral couple often played an active role in determining such details as opera casts and stage sets, and their children received a thorough musical education.[59] Since her arrival in Dresden in 1719, Maria Josepha had lent the strongest support to the development of music for the court church. Thus, she personally saw to acquiring for the court church's music library the estates of court capellmeisters Johann Christoph Schmidt and Johann David Heinichen, concertmaster Jean-Baptiste Volumier, and later, court composers Jan Dismas Zelenka and Giovanni Alberto Ristori and concertmaster Johann Georg Pisendel.[60]

Bach had always maintained a close relationship with the Dresden court capelle, so he was given a prominent place in the festivities surrounding the premiere of Hasse's opera *Cleofide* on September 13, 1731: he was invited to play a recital, at three in the afternoon the next day, on the Silbermann organ at St. Sophia's Church in Dresden. The occasion inspired the lyricist Johann Gottlob Kittel (Micrander) to publish a poem in the Dresden newspaper along

## TABLE 10.6. Major Additions to the Sacred Music Repertoire in the 1730s

| BWV | Work (Scoring) | Date | Known Parody Models |
|---|---|---|---|
| Cantatas: see listings in Tables 8.9, 8.12, and 8.13 | | | |
| Oratorios | | | |
| 247 | St. Mark Passion (music lost) | 1731 | For movements 1, etc.: BWV 198/1, etc. |
| 248 | Christmas Oratorio (see Table 10.8) | 1734–35 | For 1, 8, 15, 24: BWV 214/1, 7, 5, 9; for 4, 19, 29, 36, 39, 41: BWV 213/9, 3, 11, 1, 5; for 47: BWV 215/7; for 54, 56, 57, 61–64: lost church cantata |
| 11 | Ascension Oratorio (SATB, 3tr/ti, 2trav, 2ob, str, bc) | 1735 | For 1: BWV Anh. 18/1; 4, 8: BWV Anh. 196/3, 5 |
| 244 | St. Matthew Passion (revision) | 1736 | |
| 249 | Easter Oratorio (revision of cantata BWV249) | 1738 | |
| 245 | St. John Passion (incomplete revision) | 1739 | |
| Latin works[61] | | | |
| 243 | Magnificat in D major (revision; see Table 8.14) | 1733 | |
| 232[1] | Mass in B minor (SSATB, 3tr/ti, cor da caccia, 2trav, 2ob (d'am), str, bc) | 1733 | For 7: BWV 29/1; 9: BWV 46/1 |
| 234 | Mass in A major (SATB, 2trav, str, bc ) | 1738 | For 2: BWV 67/6; 4: BWV 179/5; 5: BWV 79/2; 6: BWV 136/1 |
| 236 | Mass in G major (SATB, 2ob, str, bc) | 1738–39 | For 1: BWV 179/1; 2: BWV 79/1; 3: BWV 138/5; 5: BWV 79/5; 5: BWV 179/3; 6: BWV 17/1 |
| 235 | Mass in G minor (SATB, 2ob, str, bc) | late 1730s | For 1: BWV 102/1; 2: BWV 72/1; 3–6: BWV 187/4, 3, 5, 1 |
| 233 | Mass in F major (SATB, 2cor, 2ob, str, bc) | late 1730s | For 1: BWV 233a; 4: BWV 102/3; 5: BWV 102/5; 6: BWV 40/1 |

with a brief report of the concert given "in the presence of all the Court musicians and virtuosos in a fashion that compelled the admiration of everyone." The poem draws an analogy between Orpheus and Bach, who, "whene'er he plays, does each and all astound."[62] In the spring of 1733, Bach saw an opportune moment to achieve, with the support of his Dresden colleagues, a more formal relationship with the court by dedicating a major composition to the new elector. He wanted to stress his official function as cantor and music director in Leipzig, so the choice of work was easy to determine: since the Mass represented the only major genre in the realm of sacred music shared by Lutherans and Roman Catholics, it was the most suitable type of work that the Lutheran cantor could submit to a Catholic court, especially one in which most of the landed gentry and high society maintained their hereditary Lutheranism. And when Bach undertook to compose a large-scale solemn Mass for a five-part choir and an orchestra with trumpets and timpani, he chose the type most functional for both the Lutheran service in Leipzig and the Catholic service in Dresden, which set only the Kyrie and Gloria of the Mass ordinary. Indeed, such abbreviated Masses, the only kind performed on high feasts at the Leipzig main churches, were also the preferred type at the Dresden court church.[63]

Bach completed the *Mass in B minor,* BWV 232$^I$, by July 1733 at the latest, revising a number of movements from extant compositions for this purpose (see Table 10.6). Along with the *Mass,* he also seems to have revised his Magnificat of 1723, the work on which the five-part choral texture of the *B-minor Mass* is modeled; this new version modernized the instrumentation and eliminated the inserted Christmas *laudes* in order to make it liturgically suitable for any time of year. Although the Magnificat revision can be dated only roughly—between 1732 and 1735—it would have been logical for Bach to review this, his only large-scale piece of Latin church music, in conjunction with the Kyrie-Gloria Mass project.[64] Conceivably, the Magnificat in its new version was first performed at the Vespers service on July 2, the Marian feast of the Visitation and also the fourth Sunday after Trinity, when public performances were permitted to resume after relaxing the state mourning period.[65]

A performance of the Kyrie-Gloria Mass, BWV 232$^I$, may actually have taken place within the mourning period, when the new elector paid a visit to Leipzig on April 20–21, 1733, for a special reception by the city council. The entire population was required to line up in festive clothing at 8 A.M. on the first day of the visit, on both sides of Grimma Street, from the market square through the Grimma Gate to St. John's Church at the cemetery outside the city wall. On the second day, again at 8 A.M., a special fealty celebration took place at St. Nicholas's in the presence of King August III, with a sermon on Psalm 28:8–9 delivered by superintendent Deyling. After 10 A.M., His Royal Highness was carried in a sedan chair from the church to the bourse for a reception given there by the region's chivalry.[66] The two-hour bi-confessional service must have included music, although no particulars are known. Latin church music, however, would have been most appropriate, and a Kyrie-Gloria Mass would have been equally acceptable to Lutheran and Roman Catholic constituencies. Unfortunately, no original Leipzig performing materials exist for BWV 232[I], making it impossible to confirm a performance of this work in Leipzig on this (or any other) date.

On the other hand, the Mass was definitely performed at the Saxon capital in July 1733, as evidenced by the extant Dresden performing parts[67] and by the inscription on the title wrapper in which the set was offered to the court after the performance: "To His Royal Majesty and Electoral Highness of Saxony, demonstrated with the enclosed Mass—for 21 [voices], 3 violins, 2 sopranos, alto, tenor, bass, 3 trumpets, timpani, 1 hunting horn, 2 transverse flutes, 2 oboes, 2 bassoons, violoncello, and continuo—his most humble devotion, the author, J. S. Bach."[68] The phrasing here emulates the pattern known from the dedicatory libretto of cantata BWV 210a, performed on January 12, 1729, as an homage to the duke of Weissenfels.[69] The word "demonstrated" suggests an anticipated or past performance—in the case of the Mass, perhaps even two past performances: one back in April in Leipzig, in the presence of His Royal Highness, and one that had taken place recently in the capital, in

Wilhelm Friedemann Bach
in a watercolor, probably by his cousin
Gottlieb Friedrich Bach (c. 1733).

all likelihood not attended by the elector. Although we have no direct information about the Dresden performance, the following three facts help us deduce its date, location, and participants.

First, on June 22, 1733, Wilhelm Friedemann Bach was elected organist at St. Sophia's Church in Dresden, succeeding the deceased court organist Christian Petzold. Thus, as of July 11, the day on which Wilhelm Friedemann was given keys to the church, Bach had a real foothold in the Saxon capital. St. Sophia's must therefore be considered the most likely performance site for the Mass. Moreover, its organ, the best church instrument in Dresden, was tuned to chamber pitch (a whole tone lower than the choir pitch of the organs at St. Thomas's and St. Nicholas's in Leipzig) and matched the notation of the organ part of the Dresden set.

Second, the preparation of the Dresden performing parts included no Thomana copyists but was carried out almost exclusively by family members. The composer himself wrote most of the parts; he was assisted by his wife, Anna Magdalena, their sons Friedemann and Carl, and one unidentified hand, probably that of a private student. All four Bachs may also have participated in the performance, perhaps jointly with Dresden court musicians, whose involvement seems to be confirmed by the curious fact that the title wrapper of the set was not written out by the composer but by Gottfried Rausch of Dres-

Carl Philipp Emanuel Bach
in a watercolor, probably by his cousin
Gottlieb Friedrich Bach (c. 1733).

den, a scribe frequently engaged by the court church composer and interim head of the court musicians, Jan Dismas Zelenka. In other words, the performance took place with Zelenka's support, which in turn implied the general support of the court capelle.

Third, the set of parts for the Mass was dedicated along with a letter by Bach dated Dresden, July 27—a Monday. This suggests a performance at St. Sophia's on the previous day, the eighth Sunday after Trinity,[70] probably as a special afternoon concert comparable to the organ recitals Bach had given there before.

The letter accompanying the Mass indicates a motive for dedicating the work to the elector and prospective king:[71] Bach was applying for a court title as protection against further injuries inflicted by the Leipzig authorities. Such an appeal had to be submitted to the Dresden court personally. Even if Bach could have approached a high court official with his petition immediately after the Leipzig fealty service on April 21, he would have been taking a big risk—and given the great commotion that day and the need for a ranking intermediary, the opportunity would not likely have materialized anyway. The whole matter would have seriously backfired if the following petition had fallen into the hands of a Leipzig official:

My Most Gracious Lord, Most Serene Elector, Most Gracious Lord!
To Your Royal Highness I submit in deepest devotion the present small work of that science which I have achieved in *musique,* with the most wholly submissive prayer that Your Highness will look upon it with Most Gracious Eyes, according to Your Highness's World-Famous Clemency and not according to the poor *composition;* and thus deign to take me under Your Most Mighty Protection. For some years and up to the present moment, I have had the Directorium of the Music in the two principal churches in Leipzig, but have innocently had to suffer one injury or another, and on occasion also a diminution of the fees accruing to me in this office; but these injuries would disappear altogether if Your Royal Highness would grant me the favor of conferring upon me a title of Your Highness's Court Capelle and would let Your High Command for the issuing of such document go forth to the proper place. Such most gracious fulfillment of my most humble prayer will bind me to unending devotion, and I offer myself in most indebted obedience to show at all times, upon Your Royal Highness's Most Gracious Desire, my untiring zeal in the composition of music for the church as well as for the orchestra, and to devote my entire forces to the service of Your Highness, remaining in unceasing fidelity Your Royal Highness's most humble and most obedient servant,

Johann Sebastian Bach[72]


We do not know in what form Bach submitted the petition or the Mass to the court, but we can assume that the overall approach, from the performance of the Mass to its formal presentation, was well prepared and, in particular, that Bach had secured in advance the support of influential colleagues from the Dresden court capelle and of prominent court officials. At any rate, the petition was indeed forwarded to higher administrative levels of the court, according to a presentation entry of August 19, 1733,[73] but then it apparently got stuck—for a long time and for reasons not immediately apparent, but perhaps related to the interim situation of the court music before the arrival of the new capellmeister, Johann Adolph Hasse, in December 1733. We can assume that Bach was both puzzled and disappointed by the court's nonreaction, considering the many performances given from 1732 by Bach's Leipzig Collegium Musicum in honor of the electoral-royal family. If gestures like these failed to remind Dresden of the outstanding petition, what else would? Finally, perhaps after consulting with a confidant such as Count Hermann Carl von Keyserlingk, Russian ambassador to the Dresden court from 1733 and a patron and friend, Bach decided to renew the petition. On September 27, 1736, the Dresden cabinet minutes recorded that Bach "asks for the title of *Compositeur* of the Royal Court Capelle."[74] From then on, things moved expediently, and after more than three years since the original petition, a certificate that "conferred upon Johann Sebastian Bach, on the latter's most humble entreaty and because of this ability, the title of Compositeur to the Royal Court Capelle" (Electoral Saxon and Royal Polish Court *Compositeur*) was issued on November 19.[75] The document was initialed by the king, certified by Prime Minister Heinrich von Brühl, to be personally handed over to Bach in Dresden by von Keyserlingk.

Less than two weeks later, Bach traveled to Dresden for a recital on the brand-new organ in the newly erected Our Lady's Church to express his appreciation for the court appointment. The large three-manual instrument, built by Gottfried Silbermann, the Saxon court organ maker, had been dedicated only on November 25, 1736. Then, on the Saturday before the first Sunday in Advent, December 1, according to the Dresden newspapers,

the famous Capellmeister to the Prince of Saxe-Weissenfels and Director Musices at Leipzig, Mr. Johann Sebastian Bach, made himself heard from 2 to 4 o'clock on the new organ in the church of Our Lady, in the presence of the Russian Ambassador, von Keyserlingk, and many persons of rank, also a large attendance of other persons and artists, with particular admiration, wherefore also His Royal Majesty most graciously named the same, because of his great ability in composing, to be His Majesty's Composer."[76]

From 1738 to 1750, Bach's name regularly appeared in the listings of the Dresden court calendar in the section on the royal court and chamber music as "church composer." However, whether Bach's offer to provide "music for the church as well as for the orchestra" resulted in any official commissions remains very much in doubt. Beyond the Kyrie-Gloria Mass in B minor, BWV 232[I], the old Dresden court music library does not seem to have held much by the Leipzig composer; traceable is only the autograph of the keyboard Fantasia in C minor, BWV 906.[77] On the other hand, contacts maintained by "Capellmeister Bach and other friends of music in Leipzig with the virtuosos of the royal capelle in Dresden" were so close that they permitted a nearly daily exchange of musical news,[78] and the frequent visits to Leipzig by Dresden colleagues Hasse, Faustina Bordoni, Silvius Leopold Weiss, and others reflect a reciprocal interest in the connection. Friedemann Bach's presence in Dresden until 1746 must also have contributed to his father's maintaining closer ties with the capital and to making appearances at court as performer and composer, perhaps also jointly with his son. Such a possibility is suggested, for example, by the performing parts for Wilhelm Friedemann Bach's Concerto in F major for two harpsichords, Fk 10 (BWV Anh. 188), prepared around 1742 by Johann Sebastian. Activities like these notwithstanding, the Dresden court title seems to have had its desired effect of protecting Bach from further unpleasantness in Leipzig. It apparently helped resolve the prefect dispute with the St. Thomas rector, which had smoldered from the summer of 1736 to early 1738; since that year, no further complaints from either side are on record, suggesting either that the conflicting parties quietly resigned themselves to the inevitable fact of their working together or that Bach's court appointment indeed made him nearly invulnerable—none of his superiors or colleagues could boast a similar mark of distinction. And none of the city councillors, clergy, or St. Thomas or university faculties achieved comparable name recognition beyond the borders of Leipzig; none of their obituaries would carry the epithet "world-famous."

By the mid-1730s, Bach had been able to consolidate and anchor his position in Leipzig in both sociopolitical and musical terms. And no document affirms his musical position more tangibly than the calligraphic fair copy he prepared in 1736 of his "great Passion"—the revised and expanded version of the St. Matthew Passion—a personal statement made by the fifty-one-year-old composer that the work truly represented the pinnacle of his career and was, in general, an unequaled musical monument. But this truly unique composition was surrounded and complemented by similarly ambitious, innovative, and unmatched works within a broad spectrum of genres: sacred and secular cantatas, oratorios and Latin works, concertos and sonatas, and, especially, the most sophisticated and challenging keyboard music ever written. Bach knew better than anyone else that these works, taken together or considered individually, had raised not only the technical standards of composition and performance but the depth of musical content and the level of aesthetic claims.

## THE *CLAVIER-ÜBUNG* PROJECT

Throughout the 1730s, the Collegium Musicum stood at the center of Bach's weekly activities, a situation that not only fostered his cultivation of church music but also encouraged him to compose and perform keyboard music. The concert series likely included Bach's most recent solo keyboard works together with sonatas and concertos featuring prominent harpsichord parts, usually played by the composer himself and sometimes by his sons and students. We cannot overestimate the astonishment and awe that must have met Bach when he mounted the first performances of concertos starring the harpsichord as the single solo instrument rather than part of a concertino group (flute, violin, and harpsichord), as in the *Brandenburg Concerto* No. 5. Bach here put himself in the forefront of a new genre that, within the next half century, would transform the European landscape of public concert life and become the quintessential domain of composing virtuosos such as Mozart and Beethoven. The impact of Bach's novel approach[79] was compounded in three ways: first, he created an impressive series of harpsichord concertos (six such works have survived) that firmly established the clavier concerto as a viable genre; second, he added several concertos for two, three, and four harpsichords, strings, and continuo that helped broaden the general concept of the keyboard concerto; and third, he motivated his four sons and students like Christoph Nichelmann to contribute to the genre, further expand on it, and spread the concept by putting many of their concertos into print.

Of all Bach's keyboard activities from the 1720s and 1730s, the clavier concertos generated the most spectacular effect, by their innovative approach and compelling virtuosity. Even so, they represent only a fraction of his keyboard compositions, which, taken together, demonstrate not only how well he kept pace with such luminaries on the greater European scene as Domenico Scarlatti, François Couperin, Jean-Philippe Rameau, and George Frideric Handel, but also how decisively he kept the lead in advanced playing technique and refined compositional art. The Fantasia and Fugue in C minor, BWV 906— the Fantasia being Bach's most "Scarlattian" piece and the fragmentary Fugue one of his most daring explorations of chromatic counterpoint—present a particular case in point, and two autograph fair copies Bach made of the Fantasia in the late 1730s signal the importance he attached to it. He also decided to add a second part to the Cöthen *Well-Tempered Clavier,* in many ways his most revolutionary keyboard work so far. The composition of this sequel, which included reworkings and transpositions of some extant preludes and fugues, took place during the late 1730s. The so-called London Autograph, the most complete original source we have, belongs to the years 1738–42, but it neither constitutes the earliest trace of the work nor does it mark the endpoint of Bach's pursuit of this project. In its external dimensions, part II exceeds its forerunner of two decades earlier by about a quarter, and in its stylistic orientation, it reflects a rapprochement with the preferences and needs of a younger musical generation.

But as extensive as Bach's manuscript repertoire of new keyboard music from the 1730s may be, it was clearly overshadowed by a commanding project: the *Clavier-Übung* series (Table 10.7). By publishing, between 1731 and 1741, this comprehensive "keyboard practice" in four parts, Bach provided the most convincing evidence not only of his intent to renew an emphasis on his accustomed métier as clavier and organ virtuoso (despite the fact that he had not held a formal post as organist since 1717) but also of his desire to put a public face on his activities as a keyboard artist. The overall content of the series indicates Bach's pragmatic approach. He selected genres and compositional types with broad appeal, though he did not compromise in the degree of compositional elaboration or performing standards.

Curiously, Leipzig's lively publishing business and book trade had never paid much attention to publishing music. Even a long-established German music-publishing center like Nuremberg never really recovered from the Thirty Years' War and remained, in the early eighteenth century, technologically and commercially far behind the corresponding enterprises in Amsterdam, London, and Paris. By 1800, however, largely through the activities of the Breitkopf firm, then Hoffmeister and Kühnel (later C. F. Peters) and others, Leipzig was well on the way to becoming the unrivaled leader in music publishing. Bernhard Christoph Breitkopf, who had invested considerably in the technology of scientific publishing and whose *Biblia Hebraica* of 1725 marked, in Gottsched's words, the beginning of a "new epoch of German book printing," moved slowly into music publishing, mainly after 1756.[80] The initial steps were actually connected with Bach and modestly foreshadowed a major collaboration with his son Carl Philipp Emanuel. In 1736, Breitkopf published as his very first music item the *Musicalisches Gesangbuch,* edited by George Christian Schemelli; according to its preface, "the melodies to be found in this musical songbook have been in part quite newly composed and in part improved in the thoroughbass by the most noble Mr. Johann Sebastian Bach."[81] Bach had most texts of his secular cantatas in the later 1730s printed by Breitkopf (who specialized in movable type) and, later on, the front matter for the *Musical Offering* and *The Art of Fugue* as well, but for the *Clavier-Übung* he turned initially to the Leipzig engraving shop of Johann Gottfried Krügner and later to the Nuremberg music publisher Christoph Weigel, Jr., and his successor, Balthasar Schmid.[82]

Bach's Opus 1, a collection of six partitas, appeared in 1731 under the title *Clavier-Übung,* one that had also served his predecessor, Johann Kuhnau, for two sets of keyboard partitas published in 1689 and 1692. Although not yet designated as Opus 1, Bach's collection had previously been issued in single installments of the six partitas. The first came out in the fall of 1726, along with the following announcement: "The Capellmeister to the Prince of Anhalt-Cöthen and Director Chori Musici Lipsiensis, Herr Johann Sebastian Bach, intends to publish a collection of clavier suites of which the first Partita has already been issued, and, by and by, they will continue to come to light until the work is complete, and as such will be made known to amateurs of the clavier. Let it be known that the author is himself the publisher of his work."[83] As the publisher, Bach acted at his own financial risk, so it was prudent for him to invest in the project gradually so that expenses would largely be recovered by sales; after the first installment of 1726, the other five were issued over the next four years. For distribution, Bach recruited six colleagues in well-chosen locations who agreed, on a commission basis, to serve as sales agents in their areas: Christian Petzold of Dresden, organist at St. Sophia's and royal chamber musician; Johann Gotthilf Ziegler of Halle, organist at St. Ulrich's; Georg Böhm of Lüneburg, organist at St. John's; Georg Heinrich Ludwig Schwanenberger of Brunswick, violinist at the court capelle of Brunswick-Wolfenbüttel; Gabriel Fischer of Nuremberg, member of the town music company; and Johann Michael Roth of Augsburg, also member of the town music company. When Bach had tested the market and determined that the individual partitas sold well, he arranged to reprint all six partitas in one volume.

The numbering of the *Clavier-Übung* as Opus 1 indicates that further publications would follow. The concept of an ambitious series of sequels perhaps coalesced in light of similar undertakings by Georg Philipp Telemann, who began in 1728 to bring out a series of works under the title *Der Getreue Musik-Meister* (The True Music Master),

in which are arranged for singers as well as for instrumentalists all types of musical pieces for different voice parts and nearly all commonly used instruments and containing moral, operatic, and other arias, as well as trios, duets, solos, etc., sonatas, overtures, etc., and also fugues, counterpoints, canons, etc., hence all the most current music according to the Italian, French, English, Polish, etc., manners both serious as well as spirited, and lighthearted . . . you might conceive of performing.

Although much less comprehensive than Telemann's project (which was never fully realized), the four parts of Bach's *Clavier-Übung* emerged as a systematic and complete survey of the art of keyboard music as seen from Bach's perspective. First, he included music specifically for the most important keyboard instruments: one-manual harpsichord (part I), two-manual harpsichord (parts II and IV), and large organ as well as organ without pedals (part III). Second, the leading national styles (part II) are complemented by an enormously rich spectrum of other styles, both retrospective and modern (parts III and IV); we find religious hymns (part III) and even a burlesque quodlibet (part IV). In the end, all the standard genres, forms, and categories are represented: suite, concerto, prelude, fugue, chorale settings of all kinds, and variations. All fundamental compositional methods are to be found, from free-voiced improvisatory pieces to imitative polyphony, cantus firmus technique, and strict canon. Everything from solo works and duets to settings with five and six obbligato voices makes an appearance, and Bach fully exploits keys (for commercial reasons, short of the well-tempered system) and the principal church modes. Finally, the collection presents tremendous challenges to the performer, since there are no easy pieces included. On the contrary, with its use of advanced keyboard technique (from *pièces croisées* requiring hand-crossing skills to the most complex double-pedal technique), the *Clavier-Übung* sets new performance standards that match the rigorous principles of compositional organization.

The partitas of part I were followed in the spring of 1735 by the *Italian Concerto* and *French Overture* of part II, now published by Christoph Weigel, Jr. The concerto recalls Bach's Weimar keyboard settings of Italian instrumental concertos by Vivaldi and others, while the overture (suite) has no direct counterpart in Bach's previous work in its imaginative exhibition of French manners of genre and style. That the *Italian Concerto* in particular was enthusiastically received is indicated by a 1739 review written by Johann Adolph Scheibe, who two years earlier had attacked Bach's compositional style for demanding "that singers and instrumentalists should be able to do with their throats and instruments whatever he can play on the clavier."[84] Now Scheibe wrote—perhaps in an attempt to repair the damage he had done previously—that

preeminent among works known through published prints is a clavier concerto of which the author is the famous Bach in Leipzig. . . . Since this piece is arranged in the best fashion for this kind of work, I believe that it will doubtless be familiar to all composers and experienced clavier players, as well as to amateurs of the clavier and music in general. Who is there who will not admit at once that this clavier concerto is to be regarded as a perfect model of a well-designed solo concerto? But at the present time we shall be able to name as yet very few or practically no concertos of such excellent qualities and such well-designed execution. It would take as great a master of music as Mr. Bach, who has almost alone taken possession of the clavier.[85]

With part III, Bach returned to the principle of self-publishing, but he apparently ran into some production problems with the Krügner engraving firm so that the publication date had to be postponed from the Easter Fair in 1739 to the St. Michael's Fair half a year later. Devoting this installment entirely to organ music, Bach created his own version of the *Livre d'orgue* like those by Nicolas de Grigny, Pierre Du Mage, and others, with which he was familiar. Picking up on these French models, he included free pieces (prelude, fugue, duets) and chorale settings of general applicability (the Kyrie and Gloria hymns of the Mass and the classic Lutheran Catechism hymns), shunning hymns with specific themes that tied them to the ecclesiastical year, such as those in the *Orgel-Büchlein* and in the "Great Eighteen" Chorales.[86] The conception of part III also relates to Bach's growing interest in broadening the stylistic spectrum from old techniques of motet style (which he adopted for the large Kyrie settings and "Aus tiefer Not") and ancient church modality[87] to the most modern musical idioms (epitomized in the organ Chorales "Vater unser im Himmelreich" and "Jesus Christus, unser Heiland"). In part III, Bach created not only his most extensive but also his most significant organ work. Lorenz Christoph Mizler correctly remarks in his 1740 review: "The author has here given new proof that in this field of composition he is more practiced and more fortunate than many others. No one will surpass him in it, and few will be able to imitate him." Mizler then states, in direct reference to Scheibe's criticism, that "this work is a powerful refutation of those who have made bold to criticize the composition of the Honorable Court Composer,"[88] but fails to observe the practical side that Georg Andreas Sorge addresses in the preface to his own 1750 collection of chorale preludes: "The preludes on the Catechism Chorales by Capellmeister Bach in Leipzig . . . deserve the great renown they enjoy"; at the same time, they "are so difficult as to be all but unusable by young beginners and others who may lack the considerable proficiency they require."[89]

The concluding part IV was published (like part II, in Nuremberg) in the fall of 1741. Forkel relates the anecdote that the work came into being at the request of Hermann Carl von Keyserlingk in Dresden, who "once said to Bach that he should like to have some clavier pieces for his [house harpsichordist, Johann Gottlieb] Goldberg, which should be of such a soft and somewhat lively character that he might be a little cheered up by them in his sleepness nights."[90] However, all internal and external clues (lack of any formal dedication to Keyserlingk as required by eighteenth-century protocol, and Goldberg's tender age of fourteen) indicate that the so-called *Goldberg Variations* did not originate as an independently commissioned work, but were from the outset integrated into the overall concept of the *Clavier-Übung* series, to which they constitute a grandiose finale. The variations are based on a thirty-two-measure theme, exposed in the ostinato bass line of an aria and in its first eight measures identical with the theme of Handel's *Chaconne avec 62 variations,* HWV 442, a work dating from 1703–6 that was published later in his 1733 *Suites de Pièces pour le clavecin.* The chaconne had already been printed separately around 1732 by Witvogel in Amsterdam, a publisher known to have used Bach as a distributor of the harpsichord works of the German-Dutch virtuoso Conrad Friedrich Hurlebusch (according to an announcement of 1735–36, Hurlebusch's *Compositioni musicali per il Cembalo* were available "from Capellmeister Bach at the St. Thomas School in Leipzig").[91] Bach would have known Handel's chaconne from either the Amsterdam or London edition, and he must have noticed the simple two-part canon forming the final variation (as well as flaws in its contrapuntal design). His considering the traditional eight-note ostinato model that Handel used as a ground triggered the kind of complex chain reaction described in the Obituary: "He needed only to have heard any theme to be aware—it seemed in the same instant—of almost every intricacy that artistry could produce in the treatment of it."[92] So Bach's investigation into the canonic potential of the eight-note subject resulted in a series of *Fourteen Canons,* BWV 1087, which he later entered into his personal copy of *Clavier-Übung* IV. For the variation cycle itself, Bach decided not to stick with the limiting straitjacket of the eight notes nor with the confining notion of a totally canonic work. He thus expanded the original ostinato bass significantly so that it could provide the harmonic underpinning of an aria whose captivating melody ingeniously distracts from its bass and thereby from the true structural backbone of the variation cycle. And he interspersed the canonic movements systematically but as unobtrusively as possible, with the apparent aim of leveling the performer's and the listener's perception of canonic versus noncanonic counterpoint—a powerful demonstration of his ideal that artful design and natural appeal need not be mutually exclusive.

The well-thought-out design of the *Clavier-Übung* series is mirrored in the careful planning of its individual parts (Table 10.7), each of which represents a well-rounded entity often featuring fine-tuned subunits. In part I, all six partitas conform to the same basic suite scheme (Allemande-Courante-Sarabande-Gigue), but each one pursues the principle of variety in its own way; each begins with a distinctive opening movement (from Praeludium to Toccata) and then presents different choices of gallantry pieces (from dances to character pieces such as Scherzo and Burlesca). In part II, the two predominant national styles are contrasted in more than one way: three-movement concerto form versus eleven-movement suite structure; F major versus B minor, that is, opposite modes compounded by the tritone interval between them (attained by transposing the earlier C-minor version of the *French Overture*). Part III exhibits a multilevel formal organization, held together by the frame of an overture-like prelude and a fugue with three subjects, both for full organ. Corresponding to these two pieces are four duets for organ without pedal, in ascending keys (E to A, in symmetric modes). The overall framing device embraces twenty-one chorales. A first group consists of nine settings of strophic German versifications of the Kyrie "fons bonitatis" (three large *stile antico* chorales with migrating cantus firmi from soprano to pedal, followed by three miniature settings of the same melodies) and the Gloria (three trios in ascending keys, from F to A), with the central piece a pedal trio. A second group of twelve chorales (each of the six large-scale Catechism hymns with a corresponding small-sized pendant) features a subgroup comprising two canonic cantus firmus settings and a setting for full organ as centerpiece, and a second subgroup comprising two pieces with pedal cantus firmus and another centerpiece with full organ. The inclusion of smaller, less demanding settings made the collection more accessible to a broader circle of customers. Finally, part IV as a large-scale but unified performing cycle contrasts with the character of the preceding parts. Here, a chain of thirty variations is placed between an opening aria and its repetition at the end, which mark both the point of departure and the point of arrival for the work. An overture designates the beginning of the second half of the cycle (thereby fulfilling the same "symbolic" function as the overture opening Partita No. 4 does in part I). The internal variations are punctuated by canons that end each of the ten threefold groups of pieces; the canons themselves are arranged in ascendingly ordered imitation intervals, from unison to ninth, leading up to the quodlibet, with its several tuneful melodies fancifully combined, as a relaxed culmination.

The overall circulation of the *Clavier-Übung* series must have been considerable, with single print runs of at least one hundred copies keeping the process profitable.[93] For parts III and IV, we know of only one printing; parts I and II had two printings each, part I possibly even three. The price of engraved music was relatively high: for example, part I sold for 2 talers (the same price as Heinichen's thoroughbass treatise, 994 typeset pages long) and part III for 3 talers, figures that prohibited distribution beyond the circle of genuinely interested parties. Nevertheless, copies of parts I and III found their way, for instance, into the hands of Giambattista Martini in Bologna. While Padre Martini knew much more about Bach than what is contained in the two *Clavier-Übung* volumes,[93] he recognized the significance of this particular collection of clavier and organ music, which had, in its far-ranging and all-encompassing form, no precedent or parallel. Indeed, with his kaleidoscope of published keyboard music, Bach had erected nothing short of a monument to his own artistry, anticipating the Obituary's declaration that he was "the greatest organ and clavier player that we have ever had."

## TABLE 10.7. The *Clavier-Übung* Series, 1731–41

**Part I:** *Preludes, Allemandes, Courantes, Sarabandes, Gigues, Minuets, and Other Gallantries* (Leipzig, 1731), 73 pages of music: BWV 825–830

| | |
|---|---|
| Partita 1 in B-flat major: | Praeludium, Allemande, Corrente, Sarabande, Menuet I/II, Giga |
| Partita 2 in C minor: | Sinfonia, Allemande, Courante, Sarabande, Rondeaux, Capriccio |
| Partita 3 in A minor: | Fantasia, Allemande, Corrente, Sarabande, Burlesca, Scherzo, Gigue |
| Partita 4 in D major: | Ouverture, Allemande, Courante, Aria, Sarabande, Menuet, Gigue |
| Partita 5 in G major: | Praeambulum, Allemande, Corrente, Sarabande, Tempo di Minuetta, Passepied, Gigue |
| Partita 6 in E minor: | Toccata, Allemande, Corrento, Air, Sarabande, Tempo di Gavotta, Gigue |

**Part II:** *A Concerto after the Italian Taste and an Overture after the French Manner* (Christoph Weigel, Jr.: Nuremberg, 1735), 27 pages: BWV 971, 831

Concerto in F major: [Allegro], Andante, Presto
Overture in B minor: Ouverture, Courante, Gavotte I/II, Passepied I/II, Sarabande, Bourrée I/II, Gigue, Echo

**Part III:** *Various Preludes on the Catechism and Other Hymns* (Leipzig, 1739), 77 pages: BWV 552, 669–689, 802–805

| (for large organ:) | (for small organ:) |
|---|---|
| Prelude in E-flat major | |
| Kyrie, Gott Vater in Ewigkeit )<br>(cantus firmus in soprano | Kyrie, Gott Vater in Ewigkeit |
| Christe, aller Welt Trost (c.f. in tenor) | Christe, aller Welt Trost |
| Kyrie, Gott heiliger Geist (c.f. in pedal,<br>*organo pleno*) | Kyrie, Gott heiliger Geist |
| | Allein Gott in der Höh sei Ehr (F major) |
| Allein Gott in der Höh sei Ehr (G major;<br>*2 clav. e ped.*) | Allein Gott in der Höh sei Ehr (A major) |
| Dies sind die heilgen zehn Gebot<br>(c.f. *in canone*) | Dies sind die heilgen zehn Gebot |
| Wir glauben all an einen Gott<br>(*organo pleno*) | Wir glauben all an einen Gott |
| Vater unser im Himmelreich<br>(c.f. *in canone*) | Vater unser im Himmelreich |
| Christ, unser Herr zum Jordan kam<br>(c.f. in ped.) | Christ, unser Herr zum Jordan kam |
| Aus tiefer Not schrei ich zu dir<br>(*organo pleno*) | Aus tiefer Not schrei ich zu dir |
| Jesus Christus unser Heiland<br>(c.f. in ped.) | Jesus Christus unser Heiland<br>Duets: E minor, F major, G major, A minor |
| Fugue in E-flat major | |

**Part IV:** *Aria with Divers Variations* (Balthasar Schmid: Nuremberg, [1741]), 32 pages:
    BWV 988

Aria

| Variatio 1, 2, 3 (canon at the unison), | 16 (Ouverture), 17, 18 (canon at the sixth), |
|---|---|
| 4, 5, 6 (canon at the second), | 19, 20, 21 (canon at the seventh), |
| 7, 8, 9 (canon at the third), | 22, 23, 24 (canon at the octave), |
| 10, 11, 12 (canon at the fourth), | 25, 26, 27 (canon at the ninth), |
| 13, 14, 15 (canon at the fifth), | 28, 29, 30 (Quodlibet) |
| Aria | |

## AT THE COMPOSER'S DESK

One of the most remarkable chapters of Forkel's 1802 biography deals with Bach as "the reviser of his own works."[94] Here Forkel draws on his philological experience as an adviser to Hoffmeister and Kühnel's projected complete edition of Bach's keyboard works, which was begun in 1800 and which led him to consult many unpublished manuscripts. "I have had opportunities," he writes, "of comparing together many copies of his principal works, written in different years, and I confess that I have often felt both surprise and delight at the means with which he employed to make, little by little, the faulty good, the good better, and the better perfect." Unfamiliar with Bach's handwriting development and not always correctly differentiating between autographs and scribal copies, Forkel often arrives at problematic conclusions and attributes certain major changes to fleeting fashions and tastes. On the other hand, Bach's sons may have pointed him in the right direction because he so clearly recognized one of the most characteristic traits of Bach's compositional activities: the never-ending process of reviewing and improving his musical scores:

Unity of style and character are often achieved by the alteration of a single note against which, in its former situation, the most rigid musical grammarian could not make any objection, but which yet did not entirely satisfy the connoisseur. Even commonplace passages are frequently changed into the most elegant by changing, taking away, or adding a single note. In these cases only the most thoroughly trained feeling and the finest, most polished taste can decide. This fine feeling and polished taste were possessed by Bach in the greatest perfection. He had gradually so improved both that at last no thought could occur to him which, in all its properties and relations, did not accord with the whole as it should and must. His later works, therefore, are all as if they were one cast: so gentle, soft, and even flows the inconceivably rich stream in them of the most diversified ideas blended together. This is the lofty summit of perfection in art which, in the most intimate union of melody and harmony, nobody besides Johann Sebastian Bach has ever yet attained."

Forkel does not exaggerate. Although he provides no examples, there are numerous instances where indeed the change of a single note makes a tremendous difference. One need only compare the initial melodic contour of the principal theme of the "Confiteor" fugal movement from the *B-minor Mass,* BWV 232/20, as notated in the autograph score with its final shape (Ex. 10.1). Here Bach changed the third note in order to avoid undue emphasis on the third syllable "confiteor," thereby also mollifying the melodic flow of the subject. A revision like this is not driven by any other than a purely musical consideration, and illustrates Bach's fine sensitivity. It shows the degree of attention he paid to the most subtle details of his scores, increasingly with advanced age and growing experience as a teacher-composer.[96]

In sheer compositional prowess, Bach moved at the highest levels of artistic achievement beginning in the later Arnstadt years, gradually conquering technique after technique, genre after genre, and quickly gaining complete control over the material he tackled. We can, however, observe a noticeable change in his attitude that emerged in the late 1720s and prevailed from the 1730s on. This change seems related to, or may even have been prompted by, Bach's having a large repertoire of vocal and instrumental compositions on hand for reuse and repeat performances. Now his composing and performing of new works stood side by side with re-performances of older works, primarily church compositions and keyboard music—a situation by no means typical of other composers, who for the most part opted for composing more new works. Thus, Telemann wrote over a thousand sacred cantatas, and Johann Friedrich Fasch and Gottfried Heinrich Stölzel produced no fewer, but neither of them taught to the extent Bach did. Regularly turning to *The Well-Tempered Clavier,* for example, sharpened his eye and ear for compositional choices that are reflected in his continued revisions—a steady stream of minor and major changes made in the autograph score or entered into student copies. It is futile in this case, as in most of his keyboard works, to differentiate between distinct layers or versions because the situation cannot be compared with the careful revisions he undertook, for example, in the *St. John Passion.* In the pieces he tended to use for teaching purposes, Bach's never-ending review process was more haphazard than systematic, often affecting only a short passage or a single detail (see Ex. 10.2)—perhaps one flaw detected and "corrected" on the spot in the course of a lesson.

Considering Bach's immense facility at the organ and clavier, it may come as a surprise to learn that he ordinarily composed away from the keyboard, as son Carl testified in 1775: "If I exclude some (but, *nota bene* not all) of his clavier pieces, particularly those for which he took the material from improvisations on the clavier, he composed everything else without instrument, but later tried it out on one."[97] Many initial corrections may have resulted from

Bach's checking his scores at the keyboard or—depending on the kind of work or passage—on the violin or some other instrument. The essential work, however, took place at the desk in his studio, which provided him with all he needed: stacks of paper; black (or dark-brown) and red ink pots and a supply of copper-gallic ink powder to be mixed with water;[98] raven quills and a knife for preparing and sharpening quill pens (the same knife was used also for erasing mistakes after the ink had dried); single and double *rastrals* for ruling individual five-line staves or double (keyboard) staves; a straight ruler for drawing long bar lines in fair-copy scores; a box of fine sand to blot the ink; and (though rarely used) lead pencils. Bach clearly preferred to plan the layout of a page according to the structural needs of the music, so he avoided pre-ruled music paper. In this way, he also saved on the expensive commodity of paper suitable for music, which had to be more opaque than that used for correspondence and printing, and heavier because the sheets had to hold up on music stands. Bach's autograph scores invariably reflect the composer's space-saving efforts—for example, running a two-stave recitative underneath a multiline chorus score.

The 1730s prompted from Bach an unusually large number of works, although their texts usually made specific references to this king's name day or that prince's birthday, rendering them unsuitable for repeat performances. Since these works invariably required considerable effort on the part of the composer, Bach had an understandable interest in rescuing the music he created for unique occasions and granting it a permanent place in the repertoire, albeit with a different text. More often than not, this meant converting secular works to church music. Since the Renaissance era, parody techniques had been widely employed for the adaptation, with new text underlay, of secular works for sacred music, and, like his contemporaries, Bach made use of the practice: as when, for example, he integrated Cöthen serenades into the first cycle of Leipzig church cantatas in 1724.

The parody process involved not only careful fitting of a new text to the old music, but also close attention to the relationship between the meaning of the words and the affect and character of the music. Other considerations, such as scoring and key changes, also played a role when a single movement was placed in a new context (rarely could a complete work be transformed into another complete work; BWV 173 of 1724 is one such rare instance). As a case in point, the *Christmas Oratorio*, BWV 248, one of the principal works to benefit from the availability of recent adaptable secular music, demonstrates Bach's imaginative musical selection and technical manipulation. His reuse of his own composition was motivated not by any intention of cutting corners—that is, turning to existing music out of convenience—but by rescuing important material for a more durable purpose. Hence, virtually all choruses and arias from the congratulatory birthday cantatas, the *drammi per musica* BWV

213–214 of September and December 1733, were adopted in late 1734 for the oratorio; only recitatives and chorales had to be newly composed, and Bach used these to create fresh and compelling connections between movements that had originally known a different sequence of textual content and musical ideas.

Nothing made more sense to Bach than to use the birthday music for a royal family as music to celebrate the nativity of Christ, the king of heaven. The common themes of praise and rejoicing readily applied to both events. Likewise, as the treatment of allegorical and mythological figures did not in principle differ from that of biblical characters, the lullaby for a son of the gods from the *Hercules Cantata* BWV 213 could address the Christ child equally well. As the musical forms and idioms of secular and sacred cantatas were generally identical, the broader palette of musical affects and expressive devices matched as well. But in order to write new poetry for existing music, the meter and rhyme of the verse and the lyrical form had to correspond, as shown by the opening chorus of the *Christmas Oratorio* and its model, where dactylic meter (long, short, short), weak and strong line endings (ws-ws-ww), rhyme scheme (ab-ab-cc), and da capo structure (**A-B-A**) completely conform:

| Secular cantata, BWV 214/1 | | | *Christmas Oratorio,* BWV 248/1 |
|---|---|---|---|
| Tönet, ihr Pauken! Erschallet, Trompeten! | **A** | w a | Jauchzet, frohlocket, auf preiset die Tage! |
| Klingende Saiten, erfüllet die Luft! | | s b | Rühmet, was heute der Höchste getan! |
| Singet itzt Lieder, ihr muntren Poeten! | | w a | Lasset das Zagen, verbannet die Klage, |
| Königin lebe! wird fröhlich geruft. | | s b | Stimmet voll Jauchzen und Fröhlichkeit an! |
|    Königin lebe! dies wünschet der Sachse, | **B** | w c |    Dienet dem Höchsten mit herrlichen Chören, |
|    Königin lebe und blühe und wachse! | | w c |    Laßt uns den Namen des Herrschers verehren! |
| *da capo* | **A** | | *da capo* |

While the overall character of praise determines the content of both the original poem and its parody, Bach's score translates the opening phrase of the secular poem ("Sound, ye drums! Ring out, trumpets! Resonant strings, fill the air!") literally into music: the timpani start the piece, trumpets follow suit, then the strings enter. This detail is lost in the musical parody, as Bach generally—and in his sacred music especially—stresses "the sense of the whole" over punctuation on individual words. Carl Philipp Emanuel explained to Forkel in 1774: "As to the church works of the deceased, it may be mentioned that he worked devoutly, governing himself by the content of the text, without any strange misplacing of the words, and without elaborating on the individual words at the expense of the sense of the whole, as a result of which ridiculous thoughts often appear, such as sometime arouse the admiration of people who claim to be connoisseurs and are not."[99]

More complex compositional concerns were reflected in the internal musical logic of the "new" work, as Bach's key organization, transpositions, and scoring changes make clear (see Table 10.8). In the secular cantata BWV 213, in F major, Bach uses the sequence of its arias most effectively to contrast flat and sharp keys, thereby supporting the theme of this dramatic cantata, *Hercules at the Crossroads,* by means of musical allegory (Table 10.8B). He alters this scheme, which would be entirely unsuitable for the *Christmas Oratorio,* by transposing all the arias into a completely new tonal design that gives the six-part oratorio its own, internally coherent key structures and scoring devices. This coherence is displayed, for example, in the symmetry of parts I–III, to be performed on the three days of Christmas, with identical brass scoring and

### TABLE 10.8. Key Structure and Scoring Changes in the *Christmas Oratorio* and Its Models

**A. *Christmas Oratorio,* BWV 248**

| Part I: | SATB | 3 trumpets/timpani, 2 flutes, 2 oboes (d'amore), strings, continuo | D major (D-a-G-D) |
|---|---|---|---|
| Part II: | SATB | 2 flutes, 2 oboi d'amore, 2 oboi da caccia, strings, continuo | G major (G-e-C-G) |
| Part III: | SATB | 3 trumpets/timpani, 2 flutes, 2 oboes (d'amore), strings, continuo | D major (D-A-b-G-f♯-D) |
| Part IV: | SATB | 2 horns (corni da caccia), 2 oboes, strings, continuo | F major (F-C-d-F) |
| Part V: | SATB | 2 oboi d'amore, strings, continuo | A major (A-f♯-b-A) |
| Part VI: | SATB | 3 trumpets/timpani, 2 oboes (d'amore), strings, continuo | D major (D-A-G-b-D) |

**B. BWV 213**  →  **BWV 248**

| (original movement sequence) | | (broken-up sequence, parts I–IV) | |
|---|---|---|---|
| 1. Chorus: Laßt uns sorgen | F major | 36.[IV] Fallt mit Danken | F major |
| 3. Schlafe, mein Liebster (S, str, bc) | B-flat major | 19.[II] Schlafe, mein Liebster (A + fl, str + ob) | G major |
| 5. Treues Echo (AA, ob d'am, bc) | A major | 39.[IV] Flößt, mein Heiland (SS, ob) | C major |
| 7. Auf meinen Flügeln (T, ob, v, bc) | E minor | 41.[IV] Ich will nur dir zu Ehren (T, 2v) | D minor |
| 9. Ich will dich nicht hören (A, v, bc) | A minor | 4.[I] Bereite dich, Zion (A, ob d'am + v) | A minor |
| 11. Ich bin deine (AT, 2va, bc) | F major | 29.[III] Herr, dein Mitleid (SB, 2ob d'am) | A major |

home keys (D major) for the framing parts. Part IV, then, marks New Year's Day with both a new key and the introduction of horns in the orchestral ensemble; part V, for the lesser feast on the Sunday after New Year's, tones down the instrumental scoring but counterbalances the subdominant G-major key of part II (with its pastoral woodwind ensemble) with the dominant A major of the main key, D major, which returns, along with trumpets and timpani, in the concluding part VI for the glorious feast of Epiphany.

From the eloquent musical architecture of the *Christmas Oratorio,* we can see that the parody projects that engaged Bach during the 1730s involved multidimensional tasks, of which the mere process of musical transcription was usually the least important. Going back to a piece of music written earlier was invariably turned by Bach into an opportunity to carefully review the work and revise and improve the score. This was especially the case when, rather than adopting a secular occasional piece for the sacred repertoire, he converted a movement from a church cantata into another sacred work. Examples can be found in the Kyrie-Gloria Masses, which are based prevailingly on sacred compositions. For all five Masses, Bach selected cantata movements of particularly refined and sublime qualities. A different parody technique was required, since the asymmetric Latin prose of the Mass text was fundamentally different from German metrical poetry. A striking example of Bach's enhancing a movement already possessed of extraordinary quality occurs in the "Qui tollis" movement of the Mass in F major, BWV 233, which is based on an aria from the cantata "Herr, deine Augen sehen nach dem Glauben," BWV 102, of 1726:

| Cantata, BWV 102/3 | Mass, BWV 233/4 |
|---|---|
| Weh der Seele, die den Schaden | Qui tollis peccata mundi, |
| Nicht mehr kennt. | Miserere nobis. |
| Und, die Straf auf sich zu laden | |
| Störrig rennt, | |
| Ja, von ihres Gottes Gnaden | |
| Selbst sich trennt. | |

The expressive qualities of the entire cantata movement concentrate in the initial outcry "woe" ("Weh"), translated by Bach into a wailing oboe solo that, with its parallel vocal response, serves the image of suffering in the "Qui tollis" Mass section equally well (Ex. 10.3). Bach has much less text to distribute under the vocal part of the Mass movement, which is kept at exactly the same length. But the declamatory style of the instrumental and vocal gestures are modified in order to generate a more intense expressive rhetoric and, at the same time, greater textural transparency, notably by means of a delicately withdrawn continuo line. The result is a simpler and airier trio in a stylistically more forward-looking setting, typical of Bach's music throughout the 1730s. The composer was constantly adjusting to influences and challenges from outside, especially within the context of an ongoing public concert series that featured modern instrumental and vocal works, including novel, freshly imported Italian solo cantatas by Nicola Porpora.[100] But while the signs of growth and development in his music from the 1730s were an outcome of his exposure to new music of other composers, they were equally the result of an abiding confrontation with his own creative efforts.

It is the combination of external influences and constant refinement, compounded by his sustained teaching activities, that raised the level of Bach's compositional art by yet another noticeable margin. Nowhere is this elevation more immediately perceptible than in his four-part chorales. Bach's chorale style in his first dozen Leipzig years cogently documents the changes in his principles of composition. If we view his chorale settings in their original context as part of the cantata repertoire, we cannot help but discern a line of development that culminates in the *Christmas Oratorio* of 1734–35. Having harmonized over the decades hundreds of chorales and having taught the skill to scores of students, Bach still found it possible to break through even his own conventions. For the chorale settings of the *Christmas Oratorio* reveal a new degree of polyphonic sophistication, elegance of voice leading, and immediacy of expression. A comparison between the first chorale of the oratorio and a setting of the same tune from the first Leipzig cantata cycle underscores the difference (Ex. 10.4). Note-against-note style has virtually disappeared, as the melodic-rhythmic profiles of all four actively participating voices—with a balanced distribution of passing tones, suspensions, and syncopation—join in an even flow whose musical message both encapsulates and highlights the textual meaning of the whole stanza.

Bach, predisposed from the very beginning toward traversing conventional boundaries, nevertheless preferred to work within a given framework and accept the challenges it posed. He never tired of exploring the material at hand on yet a deeper level—whether it was a melody from a hymnbook, music written by someone else, or one of his own compositions. Multiple examples exist for all three:

(1) *Clavier-Übung* III demonstrates Bach's abiding interest in elaborating the classic hymn melodies, inventing suitable counterpoints for compact or extended settings, and probing various techniques of cantus firmus treatment in different voice ranges, stylistic configurations, or canonic imitation. His affinity for polyphonic complexities enticed him to apply contrapuntal designs even where they had no natural home. He thus managed to enhance a perfect

*cantabile*-style melody such as that of the Air in the orchestral Suite in D major, BWV 1068—not by repressing the second violin and viola parts but by activating them contrapuntally against the first violin, which carries the melody. Similarly, he gives greater weight to the leading upper voice (transverse flute doubled by violin I) of the Sarabande in the orchestral Suite in B minor, BWV 1067, by running a strict canonic imitation of it in the basso continuo, at the distance of one measure and the interval of a fifth (a canon that is, incidentally, so smoothly conceived that even a well-trained ear can easily miss it).

(2) Bach's copies of a Magnificat by Antonio Caldara and of the Stabat Mater by Giovanni Battista Pergolesi reveal his curiosity in finding out whether certain sections might be improved, from his perspective at least, by creating a denser texture resulting from added voices. Caldara's "Suscepit Israel" for four voices and continuo, for example, is supplied with two violin parts in Bach's arrangement, BWV 1082, of 1739–42, which significantly expands the polyphonic texture of the setting; yet it does so without affecting the compositional substance of the score, because the new parts are derived from the substance of the old. Likewise, Bach supplements the essentially three-part texture in Pergolesi's instrumental score by inserting a contrapuntal viola part at certain sections in his arrangement, BWV 1083 (from the same period). Here, Bach is exercising constructive criticism on the Italian's (unquestionably deliberate) lightening of the instrumental accompaniment by leading the viola part parallel to the continuo. Bach clearly enjoyed toying with other composers' scores; as Carl Philipp Emanuel reported in 1774 about his father, "He accompanied trios on more than one occasion on the spur of the moment and, being in a good humor and knowing that the composer would not take it amiss, and on the basis of a sparsely figured continuo part just set before him, converted them into complete quartets, astounding the composer of the trios."[101] The Trio for violin and harpsichord in A major, BWV 1025, from around 1740, is a good example. Here Bach expands on a lute suite by Silvius Leopold Weiss of the Dresden court capelle by adding a contrapuntal line to the original lute part that alternates between the violin and the right hand of the keyboard.

(3) Beyond the more conventional processes of transcribing an existing concerto for a different medium, revising and improving a keyboard, vocal, or instrumental score, or parodying a secular or sacred cantata, Bach's rewriting of his own music often resulted in a thorough and complete transformation of the original. One of the most remarkable examples of this kind is represented by the sinfonia to cantata BWV 29, for concertato organ, 3 trumpets, timpani, 2 oboes, strings, and continuo, first performed at the annual city council election service on August 27, 1731. The work, based on the opening Preludio of Partita No. 3 in E major for unaccompanied violin, BWV 1006, is a brilliant and complete transformation of a piece originally conceived for a single instrument and no-

tated on a single staff into a fully scored ten-part ensemble work. As Bach was well aware that the original solo composition represented the most advanced kind of violin writing, he made sure that he would not lose that quality in the cantata sinfonia by adding the obbligato organ, an equally novel idea.[102] The cantata sinfonia belongs in the wider context of Bach's keyboard concerto writing that flourished throughout the 1730s and that paved the way for the clavier concertos produced by the generation of his sons and students. Thought out at the composer's desk, but with the results tested on the keyboard itself, a work like the Harpsichord Concerto in E major, BWV 1053, impressively demonstrates the emancipation of the left hand; we need only compare the rewritten bass part with its model, the sinfonia of cantata BWV 169 (Ex. 10.5 a and b). The many figurative refinements of the original continuo part take on the qualities of wholly idiomatic keyboard writing, something indeed "not yet heard."

What becomes evident here is that in the 1730s, Bach's composing desk became the work site for a creative mind more exploring, self-critical, and far-ranging than ever before. His continuing output of new works was complemented by an intensified review of the extant repertoire, a persistent process of improving smaller and larger details, and a systematically cultivated campaign of parodying and arranging—with the goal not of exploiting or multiplying extant works but rather of opening new horizons for them. For Bach, however, the term "new" was not necessarily synonymous with "progressive," although he became, notably as a result of the Scheibe attack of 1737, more sensitive and more consciously receptive in this regard. Mizler's review of the homage cantata BWV Anh. 13 of 1738 specifically emphasizes Bach's pursuit of the "newest taste" and the intention to "accommodate his listeners."[103] But since the music of this key work is lost, we must depend on inadequate yet critical substitutes, like the Prelude, Fugue, and Allegro in E-flat major for lute, BWV 998 (from the late 1730s), or several chorale settings and the four duets from *Clavier-Übung* III and the *Goldberg Variations* from part IV. At the same time, the two *Clavier-Übungen,* notably part III, document the genuine multidirectional approach taken by Bach. Just as he put himself, with carefully chosen examples, at the forefront of contemporary musical styles, he used other examples to demonstrate to himself, his students, and his audience that traditional genres, styles, and techniques—even such historically distant *stile antico* settings in the Phrygian mode as the Kyrie chorales, BWV 669–671—still offered many challenges to be mastered. In uncompromising refutation of "those who either do not understand the rules of composition or do not know how to employ them properly," Bach the scholar and prototype of a composition professor conceived his music for the benefit of those who did not "confuse important ideas with childish notions" and "whose musical hearing is not spoiled by . . . newfangled taste."[104]

Rear view of the St. Thomas School in winter, largely as it was during Bach's time, with St. Thomas's Church, the St. Thomas gate, the St. Thomas mill, and the Pleisse River, in a watercolor by Felix Mendelssohn Bartholdy (1838), executed from his apartment across the mill stream and opposite the school. Visible are three windows of Bach's second-floor study at the southwest (right) corner of the school building (above and to the left of the gate).

# ~ 11 ~

# A Singing Bird and Carnations for the Lady of the House

## DOMESTIC AND PROFESSIONAL LIFE

### FAMILY AND HOME

When portrait painter Elias Gottlob Haußmann depicted the Leipzig town council in 1746, he painted the councillors in their official likenesses—in serious pose, formal attire, periwig, and sometimes with specific attributes identifying their function. So councillor and city librarian Professor Mascov (1749) is posed against a background of library shelves, standing at his desk with ink pot and writing utensils, clutching a closed book in his left hand and pointing at it with his right, thereby identifying himself as an author.[1] The same pattern applies to Haußmann's portrait of Bach (see frontispiece), in which the subject's right hand holds a page of music, but not just any old music. The cantor shows us a sheet inscribed with three short lines of musical notation and the inscription *Canon triplex à 6 Voc[ibus]* | *per J. S. Bach* (triple canon for six voices, by J. S. Bach),[2] an encoded text whose complex musical contents would remain obscure to the general viewer and challenge even the well-versed musician. A similar portrait by Haußmann of Johann Gottfried Reiche (1727), senior member of the town music company, shows Reiche holding his trumpet and a sheet of music bearing an extremely difficult passage—one that probably only he could play.[3] Bach displays what he considers his trademark, the short but highly sophisticated canon BWV 1076, an emblem of his erudite contrapuntal art. By not having a keyboard instrument included in the picture, he chose to disclaim his fame as a virtuoso performer. And by not clasping a paper roll, the conductor's attribute (as Johann Hermann Schein, an earlier Thomascantor, does in his portrait),[4] Bach elected to play down his office as cantor and music director. The austere expression worn by the composer in this only authentic portrait corresponds well to the musical statement.

In the portrait, Bach the man takes a back seat to his work, and that is how we have always understood him and how we ordinarily see him: compared with his imposing oeuvre, the human being seems of secondary importance. It is, indeed, as hard to gain insight into Bach's character as it is difficult to glean much detail about his family and everyday life, the environment within which he moved, the external conditions under which he worked, details concerning his professional engagements and private activities. Compounding the scarcity of pertinent historical information is the paucity of personal writings and letters. While the rich correspondence of the Mozart family, for example, opens up many aspects of the composer's life, thoughts, and experiences, the few extant Bach letters do not, though they raise some questions. Did Bach really limit his writings to organ reports, student recommendations, petitions, and financial receipts? If so, how would we explain the noticeable difference between Bach and his second son, Carl, whose copious body of correspondence ranks among the more interesting and important of such eighteenth-century collections? And if Bach did not engage much in personal correspondence, why did he use a private secretary between 1737 and 1742?

Nephew Johann Elias Bach of Schweinfurt, a grandson of Georg Christoph, Ambrosius Bach's brother, was a theology student at Jena University when he ran out of money and was hired in the fall of 1737 by Johann Sebastian as his personal secretary and as tutor for his children (two years later, he resumed his theology studies at Leipzig University).[5] Elias's correspondence on behalf of his uncle survives in a copybook, from which we learn about Bach's travels, publication plans, and lending out of music, among other matters.[6] Considering the Thomascantor's busy schedule, he likely required secretarial assistance both before and after Elias's stint.[7] Moreover, he probably maintained records of his correspondence and kept copybooks, as a letter of October 28, 1730, to his old classmate Georg Erdmann suggests; there Bach writes: "It must be nearly four years since Your Honor favored me with a kind answer to the letter I sent you."[8] Bach had written to Erdmann on July 28, 1726,[9] and though Erdmann's reply has not survived, a note of his on Bach's letter shows that he answered it on October 22, 1726.[10] Bach would have received Erdmann's reply around November 1, a perfect match for Bach's reference on October 28, 1730, to "nearly four years" ago. That Bach could pinpoint the date so precisely indicates that he was able to check the dates and contents of earlier letters. We can assume, then, that his correspondence amounted to much more than what has come down to us, that he maintained copybooks of his letters, and that, sadly, the extant materials represent merely haphazard remnants of what once existed.

The entries in Elias Bach's copybook provide ample evidence of his uncle's extremely busy schedule. In September 1739, for example, he begs Johann Wilhelm Koch, cantor in Ronneburg,

Not to take it amiss that, on account of the accumulation of work, he cannot thank you
with a note of his own this time, since he will begin the Collegium Musicum this Friday and will perform some music in the first week of the Fair for the birthday of His
Royal Majesty; it will certainly be worth listening to, and if my Brother could get away,
he would certainly not regret having been in the audience. Concerning Your Honor's
first letter, I must report in most obedient reply that the church piece he sent back was
duly received, together with the 10 gr., and also that the work of my honored Cousin,
engraved on copper, is now ready, and may be obtained from him à 3 rthl. per copy.[11]

Here, apologies for the impersonal thank-you note are combined with an invitation to a Collegium concert, acknowledgment of a returned cantata and its
rental fee, and a suggestion to purchase Bach's newly published *Clavier-Übung,*
part III. Another letter to the same cantor Koch, this one from January 1741,
again concerns borrowed music from Bach, and also refers to canons that Koch
had sent, with questions about their resolutions. Elias writes on behalf of his
uncle: "There is no magic involved here, as he put it, and he has written a comment on the large one." The reference to this comment, which has not survived,
is a tantalizing hint of what written documents must once have existed. Completely lost, too, are all family letters. We know, for example, that Bach wrote
to his wife during a trip to Berlin in the summer of 1741, when she was pregnant with her last child and apparently became seriously ill. As Elias's letter
of August 9 to Bach in Berlin relates:

Our honored Cousin has been good enough to send his beloved wife another good report, to the relief of us all, and to set the date of his departure [from Berlin]; but great
as was the pleasure we derived from this, just so great must be the pain we feel about
the increasing weakness of our most honored Mama, for the latter has for a fortnight
now not had a single night with one hour's rest, and cannot either sit up or lie down,
so that during last night I was called, and we could not help thinking that, to our great
sorrow, we would lose her.[12]

It is not hard to imagine how alarmed Bach would have been on receiving such
news from home; it must have reminded him vividly of the death of his first
wife, Maria Barbara, during his stay with Prince Leopold in Carlsbad. Bach returned, and Anna Magdalena recovered slowly, eventually giving birth to a
healthy daughter—Regina Susanna—the only one of the Bach children who
lived into the nineteenth century. Even so, Anna Magdalena had to cancel a trip
to her relatives in Weissenfels, planned for September, as secretary Elias's draft
of a letter for her specifies: "My past and continuing sickly condition robs me,
alas, of such pleasant hours, and the advice of my family forbids me to undertake such a journey, on which, in their opinion, might hinge either a noticeable improvement or the complete ruin of my health."[13]

Bach's devotion to Anna Magdalena and their affectionate relationship is evidenced, from the very beginning of their marriage, by the two Clavier Books of 1722 and 1725 dedicated to her. The second continued to be filled until the early 1740s,[14] with early compositional attempts by the young Johann Christian among the later entries. Around 1741, Anna Magdalena herself copied into it the Aria of the *Goldberg Variations,* apparently one of her favorite pieces, changing the notation of the right-hand part from treble to soprano clef in order to make it easier for her, a soprano singer, to play the piece. And a charming love song such as Giovannini's aria "Willst du dein Herz mir schenken, so fang es heimlich an" (If you want to give me your heart, you must begin so in secret), even though not entered by Bach himself, helps to convey the intimate character of the album. Further, Elias Bach's copybook—despite the formalities of eighteenth-century correspondence conventions—permits occasional glimpses of Bach's attentiveness and loving care toward his wife, small yet meaningful gestures to make the lady of the house happy. So a letter of June 1740 to Johann Georg Hille, cantor in Glaucha near Halle, tells us that he had "reported to his beloved wife . . . that Your Honor possessed a linnet which, as a result of the skillful instruction of its master, made itself heard in particularly agreeable singing. Now, since the honored lady my cousin is a particular lover of such birds . . . I should inquire whether Your Honor would be of a mind to relinquish this singing bird to her for a reasonable sum, and to send it to her by some sure means."[15]

A few months later, Anna Magdalena received a gift of "six most beautiful carnation plants" that gave her the greatest pleasure, as the secretary's acknowledgment testifies: "With an extended description of the joy that was given thereby to the said lady my cousin I will not burden Your Honor, but will mention only this: that she values this unmerited gift more highly than children do their Christmas presents, and tends them with such care as is usually given to children, lest a single one wither."[16] The flower plants were sent by Simon Friedrich von Meyern of Halle, who apparently had learned from Bach about Anna Magdalena's desires. Elias himself also knew well what his aunt liked. In a letter he wrote to his mother in Schweinfurt, he asks her to send him a present intended for his substitute parents in Leipzig as an expression of his gratitude: "for my honored cousin a bottle of the brandy made with rose hips and a few, *notabene,* yellow carnations for our honored aunt, a great connoisseur of gardening." He did not need to explain that the "Herr Vetter," his Leipzig cousin, was a great friend of alcoholic libations. Indeed, Bach followed his father's example by maintaining a special relationship with the folks on the Main, in the center of the Franconian wine region beyond the Thuringian Forest. Bach's liking for strong waters led to an episode addressed in a letter he wrote later to Elias, who by then had been appointed cantor at St. John's in his hometown Schweinfurt and had cultivated his own vineyard there:

That you and also your dear wife are still well I am assured by the agreeable note I received from you yesterday accompanying the excellent little cask of wine you sent me, for which I send you herewith the thanks I owe you. It is, however, greatly to be regretted that the little cask was damaged, either by being shaken up in the wagon or in some other way, for when it was opened for the usual customs inspection here it was almost two-thirds empty, and according to the inspector's report contained no more than six quarts; and it is a pity that even the least drop of this noble gift of God should have been spilled. . . .

Although my Cousin kindly offers to oblige with more of the liqueur, I must decline his offer on account of the excessive expenses here. For since the carriage charges cost 16 groschen, the delivery man 2 groschen, the customs inspector 2 groschen, the inland duty 5 groschen 3 pfennig, and the general duty 3 groschen, my honored Cousin can judge for himself that each quart cost me almost 5 groschen, which for a present is really too expensive.[17]

Anna Magdalena, sixteen years Bach's junior, came from a family of musicians and brought to the marriage the background and orientation of a professional singer. Indeed, she regularly performed with her husband in Cöthen and elsewhere until 1725,[18] and from the time public singing engagements are no longer recorded, her collaboration as a copyist is well documented. Until the early 1740s, her hand shows up in a variety of manuscripts containing Bach's music. She prepared, in particular, fair copies of the Cello Suites, BWV 1007–1012; the Violin Partitas and Sonatas, BWV 1001–1006; the organ Trio Sonatas, BWV 525–530; major sections of *The Well-Tempered Clavier,* parts I and II; the Kyrie and Gloria of the *B-minor Mass;* several cantatas; and other vocal and instrumental works.[19] By comparison, Maria Barbara, Bach's first wife, left few traces. Although she was the product of a musical family as well, there are no references whatsoever to her performing activities, secretarial assistance, or any other semiprofessional ventures, but it is hard to imagine that she would not have been engaged in any.

Although Anna Magdalena in all likelihood continued her professional singing career after 1725, she would have done so on a greatly reduced scale. Opportunities existed in Leipzig within the Collegium Musicum series and in private homes such as the Bose family mansion at the Thomaskirchhof,[20] and elsewhere when she accompanied Bach on various trips, especially to her hometown Weissenfels and perhaps also to Dresden.[21] An entry by Anna Magdalena in her Clavier Book—an arrangement for soprano solo of the recitative and aria "Ich habe genung" / "Schlummert ein, ihr matten Augen," from cantata BWV 82 of 1727 for solo bass, transposed from C minor/E-flat major to E minor/G major—suggests that she was preparing the piece for public or private performance. Within the family circle, there were unlimited performance possibilities. In his 1730 letter to Erdmann, Bach proudly mentions that his children "are all born musicians, and I can assure you that I can already form an ensemble both *vocaliter* and *instrumentaliter* within my family, particularly since my present wife sings a good, clear soprano, and my eldest daughter, too, joins in not badly."[22]

Anna Magdalena fulfilled many roles over the years: companion, professional partner, assistant, keyboard student, and maybe also critic, but above all she mothered a large and steadily increasing family. In marrying Bach, she took on a widower with four small children ranging in age from eleven to six. She then gave birth to thirteen children over nineteen years (see Table 11.1), averaging one a year for most of that span. The baptisms were witnessed by godparents chosen by Bach and his wife from their close family circle and from among good friends, sometimes also to satisfy social honor codes—as, for example, when Prince Leopold and Burgomaster Lange, respectively, stood godfather to the firstborns in Cöthen and Leipzig. Since, by convention, the same person was rarely chosen twice within a family to further as godfather or godmother a child's Christian upbringing—Anna Magdalena's *Herzens Freundin* (friend of heart) and neighbor, Christiana Sybilla Bose,[23] being an exception—the overall company of godparents reflects a broad range of personal ties and social connections maintained by the Bach family. Only six of Anna Magdalena's children outlived early childhood, as did four of Maria Barbara's. Infant mortality was then a normal fact of life, and staying alive was considered a godsend. Joy and sorrow always stood side by side, with experiences of hardship, illness, and pain usually prevailing. Thus, Bach shared worries and much grief with both of his wives. But in addition to mourning the deaths of so many offspring, he and Anna Magdalena were also deeply concerned about two of their adolescent sons.

## TABLE 11.1. Johann Sebastian Bach's Children

*With Maria Barbara*

1. **Catharina Dorothea,** baptized Weimar, December 29, 1708; died Leipzig, January 14, 1774.
Godparents: D. Georg Christian Eilmar (pastor in Mühlhausen), Martha Catharina Lämmerhirt (widow of Tobias Lämmerhirt, brother of Bach's mother, in Erfurt), Johanna Dorothea Bach (wife of Bach's elder brother in Ohrdruf).

2. **Wilhelm Friedemann** ("Friedemann"), born Weimar, November 22, 1710; d. Berlin, July 1, 1784.
Godparents: Wilhelm Ferdinand Baron von Lyncker (ducal chamberlain in Weimar), Anna Dorothea Hagedorn (daughter of pastor Eilmar of Mühlhausen), D. Friedemann Meckbach (attorney in Mühlhausen).

3. Maria Sophia, b. Weimar, February 23, 1713; d. March 15, 1713.
Godparents: Martha Regina Heintze (wife of S. Heintze of Suhl, J. G. Walther's predecessor

as town organist in Weimar), Margaretha Hoffmann (wife of J. C. Hoffmann of Suhl, great-grandson of the town piper Hoffmann, father-in-law of Johann Bach [4]), Georg Theodor Reineccius (cantor in Weimar).

4. Johann Christoph, b. February 23, 1713; d. at birth (received emergency baptism).

5. **Carl Philipp Emanuel** ("Carl"), b. Weimar, March 8, 1714; d. Hamburg, December 14, | 1788.
Godparents: Adam Immanuel Weldig (master of the pages and court singer), Georg Philipp Telemann (capellmeister), Catharina Dorothea Altmann (wife of C. F. Altmann, princely chamberlain at Arnstadt).

6. **Johann Gottfried Bernhard,** b. Weimar, May 11, 1715; d. Jena, May 27, 1739.
Godparents: Johann Andreas Schanert (county registrar in Ohrdruf), Johann Bernhard Bach (organist in Eisenach), Sophia Dorothea Emmerling (wife of the court chef in Arnstadt and cousin of Maria Barbara's).

7. Leopold Augustus, b. Cöthen, November 15, 1718; d. September 28, 1719.
Godparents: Prince Leopold of Anhalt-Cöthen, Augustus Ludwig, prince of Anhalt-Cöthen, Duchess Eleonore Wilhelmine (wife of Duke Ernst August of Saxe-Weimar), Christoph Jost von Zanthier (privy councillor at the Cöthen court), Juliana Magdalene (wife of G. von Nostiz, principal court steward).

*With Anna Magdalena*

8. Christiana Sophia Henrietta: bapt. spring 1723 (baptism not recorded); d. June 29, 1726.

9. **Gottfried Heinrich,** bapt. Leipzig, February 27, 1724; buried Naumburg, February 12, 1763.
Godparents: D. Gottfried Lange (burgomaster of Leipzig and chair of St. Thomas's), Regina Maria Ernesti (wife of J. H. Ernesti, rector of the St. Thomas School), D. Friedrich Heinrich Graff (attorney in Leipzig).

10. Christian Gottlieb, bapt. Leipzig, April 14, 1725; d. September 21, 1728.
Godparents: Christian Wilhelm Ludwig (electoral Saxon official and singer, Leipzig), Maria Elisabeth Taubert (wife of J. Taubert, merchant in Leipzig), Gottlieb Christian Wagner (city official and son of the former burgomaster).

11. **Elisabeth Juliana Friderica** ("Lieschen"), bapt. Leipzig, April 5, 1726; d. Leipzig, August 24, 1781.
Godparents: Christina Elisabeth Küstner (wife of D. G. W. Küstner, city councillor), D. Johann Friedrich Falckner (attorney in Leipzig), Juliana Romanus (wife of D. C. F. Romanus, city judge in Leipzig).

12. Ernestus Andreas, bapt. Leipzig, October 30, 1727; d. November 1, 1727.
Godparents: D. Johann Ernst Kregel (judge at the electoral court, Leipzig), Magdalena Sibylla Baudis (wife of law professor and city councillor D. G. Baudis in Leipzig), D. Andreas Rivinus (professor of law in Leipzig).

13. Regina Johanna, bapt. Leipzig, October 10, 1728; d. April 25, 1733.
Godparents: Anna Katharina Meissner (wife of G. C. Meissner, court trumpeter in Weissenfels, and sister of Anna Magdalena), Johann Caspar Wilcke (court trumpeter in Zeitz, brother of Anna Magdalena), Johanna Christina Krebs (wife of J. A. Krebs, court trumpeter in Zeitz, sister of Anna Magdalena).

14. Christiana Benedicta, bapt. Leipzig, January 1, 1730; d. January 4, 1730.
Godparents: Benedicta Carpzov (daughter of D. J. G. Carpzov, archdeacon at St. Thomas's),
D. Christian Gottfried Moerlin (attorney in Leipzig), Catharina Louisa Gleditsch (wife of J.
G. Gleditsch, bookseller in Leipzig).

15. Christiana Dorothea, bapt. Leipzig, March 18, 1731; d. August 31, 1732.
Godparents: Christiana Sybilla Bose (daughter of G. H. Bose, merchant in Leipzig), M. An-
dreas Winckler (theologian and orientalist, Leipzig), Christiana Dorothea Hebenstreit (wife of
M. J. C. Hebenstreit, conrector at St. Thomas's).

16. **Johann Christoph Friedrich** ("Friederich"), bapt. Leipzig, June 23, 1732; d. Bückeburg,
    January 26, 1795.
Godparents: Johann Sigismund Beiche (chamber commissioner in Pegau), Dorothea Sophia
Weiss (daughter of C. Weiss, pastor at St. Thomas's), D. Christoph Donndorf (attorney in
Leipzig, in 1731–32 Bach's interim landlord).

17. Johann August Abraham, bapt. Leipzig, November 5, 1733; d. November 6, 1733.
Godparents: M. Johann August Ernesti (conrector at St. Thomas's), Elisabeth Caritas Gesner
(wife of J. M. Gesner, rector at St. Thomas's), M. Abraham Kriegel (*collega tertius* at St.
Thomas's).

18. **Johann Christian** ("Christel"), bapt. Leipzig, September 7, 1735; d. London, January 1,
    1782.
Godparents: M. Johann August Ernesti (rector at St. Thomas's), Christiana Sybilla Bose
(daughter of G. H. Bose, merchant in Leipzig), D. Johann Florens Rivinus (professor of law,
Leipzig).

19. **Johanna Carolina,** bapt. Leipzig, October 30, 1737; d. Leipzig, 18, 1781.
Godparents: Sophia Carolina Bose (daughter of G. H. Bose, merchant of Leipzig), M. Christ-
ian Weiss (deacon at St. Nicholas's), Johanna Elisabeth Henrici (wife of C. F. Henrici Leipzig,
[Picander], post office commissioner in Leipzig).

20. **Regina Susanna,** bapt. Leipzig, February 22, 1742; d. Leipzig, December 14, 1809.
Godparents: Anna Regina Bose (daughter of G. H. Bose, merchant in Leipzig, engaged to be
married to F. H. Graff), D. Friedrich Heinrich Graff (attorney in Leipzig), Susanna Elisabeth
Bose (daughter of G. H. Bose).

---

*Note:* Boldface type identifies individuals who lived to adulthood.

Bach's Genealogy describes Anna Magdalena's oldest, Gottfried Heinrich,
as "inclined toward music, particularly clavier-playing," but Carl later refers
to him as "a great genius who didn't fully develop."[24] Suffering from some
learning disability or mental deficiency, the youngster was unable to attend the
St. Thomas School and instead received private tutoring. At fifteen, he was described by Johann Elias Bach as being "in great need of solid and consistent instruction."[25] Both parents evidently tried to further his unquestionable musical
talents. Indeed, it may have been Gottfried Heinrich who entered—and possibly composed—the delightful little aria "So oft ich meine Tobacks-Pfeife mit
gutem Knaster angefüllt" (Whene'er I take my pipe and stuff it full of good

tobacco), BWV 515, into his mother's Clavier Book, as the childlike notation of the two-part song score (without words) suggests. Mother and father each lent a helping hand: she by copying the melody onto the opposite page, transposing it from D minor into the singable range of G minor and providing the text underlay; and he by significantly improving the bass line and fixing the first and second endings of the bipartite song structure.[26]

A more difficult and, in the end, tragic case was Johann Gottfried Bernhard, Maria Barbara's third son, doubtless an intelligent young man and a gifted musician but also an apparent ne'er-do-well. After graduating from the St. Thomas School in 1735, he applied for the organist post at St. Mary's in Mühlhausen. Johann Sebastian had learned that his former colleague Johann Gottfried Hetzehenn had died that April, and using his long-established connections and writing directly to the burgomaster, Bach managed to get his son scheduled for an audition.[27] Early June saw both father and son traveling to Mühlhausen, where Bernhard auditioned for the opening and was elected for the job by the town council on June 16. Meanwhile, Bach had offered free advice on the rebuilding of the organ at St. Mary's, under contract with Johann Friedrich Wender and his son Christian Friedrich. Then, on the evening of the organist election, Bach and his son were wined and dined by the town council.[28] But Bernhard did not remain in the Mühlhausen post for very long. Sixteen months later, Bach contacted Johann Friedrich Klemm of Sangerhausen, son of Johann Jacob Klemm, with whom he had dealt way back in 1702 as a candidate for the post of town organist in Sangerhausen. "I have dared," he wrote, "to take the liberty (since I have heard that the organist of the Lower Church has died and the vacancy will probably soon be filled) of obediently asking you . . . not only for your gracious patronage on behalf of a person who is very close to me, but also to show me in this matter the special *faveur* of sending me most kindly a gracious note on the salary of the vacant post."[29] Additional correspondence with Sangerhausen followed, and again, thanks to his father's intervention, Bernhard was invited to audition on January 13, 1737, was elected the following day, and quit his Mühlhausen post about a month later.

No doubt an excellent organist who easily passed an audition, Bernhard had a very fine instrument at his disposal in Sangerhausen: the old organ his father had played in 1702 had by then been replaced by a new instrument by Zacharias Hildebrandt of Leipzig, a frequent collaborator with Bach, onetime apprentice of the renowned Gottfried Silbermann, and now ducal Saxe-Weissenfels court organ builder. But not even this attractive organ could bind the unsteady and restless Bernhard to Sangerhausen. In the spring of 1738, he suddenly disappeared from the scene without informing anyone of his whereabouts. The embarrassed and disappointed father expressed his despair in a letter that May to Friedrich Klemm:

With what pain and sorrow . . . I frame this reply, Your Honor can judge for yourself as the loving and well-meaning father of Your Honor's most beloved offspring. Upon my (alas! misguided) son I have not laid eyes since last year, when I had the honor of enjoying many courtesies at Your Honor's hands. Your Honor is also not unaware that at that time I duly paid not only his board but also the Mühlhausen draft (which presumably brought about his departure at that time), but also left a few ducats behind to settle a few bills, in the hope that he would now embark upon a new mode of life. But now I must learn again, with greatest consternation, that he once more borrowed here and there and did not change his way of living in the slightest, but on the contrary has even absented himself and not given me to date any inkling as to his whereabouts. What shall I say or do further? Since no admonition or even any loving care and assistance will suffice any more, I must bear my cross in patience and leave my unruly son to God's Mercy alone, doubting not that He will hear my sorrowful pleading and in the end will so work upon him, according to his Holy Will, that he will learn to acknowledge that the lesson is owing wholly and alone to Divine Goodness.[30]

For quite a while, Bernhard left no trace; no one could find him—according to an inquiry by the town council, "not even his father, the *Capell Director* in Leipzig."[31] The distressed parents may not even have become aware of their lost son's matriculation in January 1739, as a law student at Jena University—an attempt on the part of the gifted young man struggling with obligation and inclination, intimidated son of a powerful father and uncertain of his own place in life, to turn things around? But only four months later, on May 27, shortly after his twenty-fourth birthday, Bernhard died "from a hot fever."[32] Nothing beyond this is known of his illness, death, or burial.

The educational opportunities in Leipzig for all the Bach children were rich and manifold. And there is no reason to doubt that the daughters, though at the time Latin schools and universities were closed to them, received the kind of schooling that would not have been so readily available to them in other places. Anna Magdalena may have played the major role in their musical training, and it is worth noting that in his letter to Erdmann Bach does not exempt his daughters from the vocal-instrumental family ensemble. On the contrary, he names only his wife's "clear soprano" and his eldest daughter, who "joins in not badly"—the sons remain unmentioned. There is no indication, however, that Catharina Dorothea or any of her sisters were guided toward a musical career. As professional career choices for women were generally extremely limited,[33] Bach, in line with both social convention and family tradition, focused on the professional development of his sons and took their education very much to heart. He saw to their musical training himself, particularly their keyboard skills and exercises in composition.

The father's pedagogical investment in the future of his sons is best represented by the Clavier Book for his oldest, Wilhelm Friedemann.[34] Although

no comparable material has survived for any of the other children, their musical upbringing could hardly have differed much, as their various creative lives
amply manifest. Bach also helped launch their careers; his efforts on behalf of
the unhappy Johann Bernhard were by no means exceptional. He often took
the crucial initiative. For example, he composed and wrote the letter that Wilhelm Friedemann submitted in 1733 to the Dresden city council in applying
for the organist post at St. Sophia's Church (even the signature is in the father's
hand!); on the same day, June 7, he also sent a letter of recommendation for his
son to the church consistory member in charge of the appointment.[35] Moreover,
Bach copied out the audition piece for his son: the Prelude and Fugue in G
major, BWV 541.[36] The question arises: was all this done by an overzealous father with an overprotective attitude? Bach also called on his musical and political connections to secure a place for Carl Philipp Emanuel, who in 1738
joined the private capelle of crown prince Friedrich, the later king of Prussia.
Helpful go-betweens were most likely Johann Joachim Quantz and the brothers Graun, Carl Heinrich and Johann Gottlieb, all close acquaintances of Bach's
who had been hired by the musically ambitious crown prince. As an alternative, Carl Philipp Emanuel was given the opportunity, after completing his
university studies at Frankfurt on the Oder, to escort "a young gentleman" on
a grand tour through Austria, Italy, France, and England.[37] The gentleman was
none other than the son of Count Keyserlingk in Dresden, one of Bach's most
important patrons, and the scheme had clearly been worked out by the two fathers. Finally, the appointment in 1749 of the seventeen-year-old Johann
Christoph Friedrich to the court at Bückeburg bears the father's mark as well.
Bach sent his second youngest on his way with an accompanying note to Count
Wilhelm of Schaumburg-Lippe: "Since Your Imperial Highness has deigned to
honor one of my family to be in the service of Your Highness, I send with this
my son, hoping that he may be able to offer Your Imperial Highness complete
satisfaction."[38] Count Wilhelm's father had earlier married the widow of Prince
Leopold of Anhalt-Cöthen[39]—old, established connections apparently still
worked well.

      Bach had every reason to be proud of his sons, but he may not have been an
"easy" father. The information we have about his behavior is too fragmentary
to allow for any judgments about his character. But from his defiant attitude
in matters of accompanying congregational hymn singing and the violent
brawl with Geyersbach back in Arnstadt to the insubordinate demeanor that
led to his detention in Weimar and in Leipzig (according to rector Ernesti) to
his chasing the prefect Krause "out of the choir loft with much shouting and
noise,"[40] we can deduce that he was impatient, often unyielding, and irascible
when provoked. Bach is said to have conducted himself in a generally "peace-
ful, quiet, and even-tempered way" in the face of all kinds of unpleasantness

"as long as it concerned only his own person," but the same source acknowledges that he "became a very different man if he felt threatened in his art, which he held sacred, and that he then became mightily enraged and in his zeal sought to find vent by the strongest expressions."[41] He probably had few reasons to argue with his sons over matters of musical substance and artistic conviction, although he saw all four of them go their own ways, distinct from that of their father. Indeed, that met with Bach's approval, as none of them were trained to imitate his musical orientation. Thus, each of the four composing brothers followed his personal stylistic preferences and each eventually developed a musical language that confirmed his father's ideals of individuality.

We must apply several grains of salt before we swallow a 1792 report by Carl Friedrich Cramer that Bach "was satisfied only with Friedemann, the great organist. Even of Carl Philipp Emanuel he said (unjustly!), ''Tis Berlin Blue! It fades easily!' He always applied to the London Chrétien Bach the verse by Gellert: 'The boy progresses surely by his stupidity!' Actually this one of the three Bachs made the greatest progress."[42] Cramer claimed to have received the statement "direct from the mouth of Friedemann," and precisely therein lies a problem—the self-serving nature of Friedemann's testimony. On the other hand, there is sufficient evidence that the oldest son received preferential treatment, that Sebastian and Friedemann were musically and intellectually close, and that Carl was the more independent of the two older sons. The reference to the youngest may reflect critical comments on Christel's progress in school, about which nothing is known today, but then he expressed his love and support by making him a gift of three harpsichords.[43]

Like the rector of St. Thomas's, the cantor and his family occupied a spacious apartment in the school building right next to the church on its south side. We have detailed information about Bach's Leipzig living quarters (corresponding knowledge is completely lacking for any of Bach's earlier life stations). The specific facts about the layout of the cantor's apartment before and after the 1731–32 renovation of the school building are based primarily on drawings by the master mason George Werner, reports on the building project, and later descriptions of the cantor's apartment in the building,[44] which was pulled down in 1902. Before 1731, the apartment was considerably smaller, the old school building having only three stories where the new one had five. Disruptions during the construction phase between May 1731 (after the Easter Fair) and April 1732 must have been considerable. The Bach household had to relocate, and in late June 1731 the family took up temporary quarters in a house at Hainstrasse 17 belonging to the law professor Dr. Christoph Donndorf (the annual rent of 120 talers, covered by the city, hints at the magnitude of the free-housing benefit as part of the cantor's compensation).[45] When the family returned to their apartment on April 24, 1732, they had gained an enlarged, heated living room and a new bedroom on the third floor, which had previously held only one living room; another heated living room was available on the newly built fourth floor, along with a large bedroom in the second attic under the new curb roof (see Table 11.2, p. 406).

The imposing building of the St. Thomas School closed the west flank of St. Thomas Square, running parallel and close to the inside of the old city wall; the external walls of the school building were particularly thick and used as an extra fortification in earlier times against attack from outside. A small gate near the southwest corner of the school building, the so-called *Thomas-Pförtchen* (little gate), provided an opening through the city wall for pedestrian traffic. The cantor's apartment took up a major part of the building's south wing, while the rector's quarters lay in the north wing. Approaching the school building from St. Thomas Square, one entered the cantor's apartment through a door on the left side, ascending two steps. To answer the doorbell, the front door could be opened by a pull mechanism from the second-floor living room immediately above that looked out onto the square and allowed the scanning

Renovated façade of the St. Thomas School, Leipzig, in an engraving made by Johann Gottfried Krügner, Sr. for the school's rededication (1732).

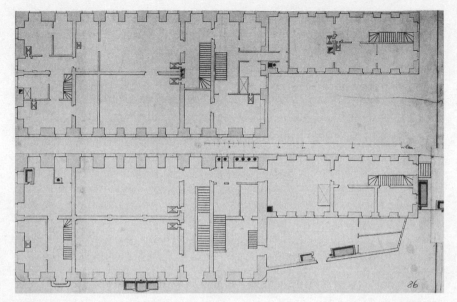

Floor plans of the St. Thomas School, drawn up by the master builder George Werner for the 1732 renovation of the building, showing the first, or street-level, floor (above) and the second floor (top) with the cantor's apartment in the south wing (left), classrooms (center), and the rector's apartment in the north wing (right).

of visitors. The tiled ground floor—that is, the first floor—contained two rooms, one heated and one unheated; the corner living room downstairs apparently provided study space for the school-age children.[46] The front section of the ground floor opened to a split-level structure in the back: four steps down led to the laundry, with a built-in copper wash basin and a door to the outside, and the cellar, with two beer caches and other storage facilities; several steps up led to the maids' room and the privy. A straight staircase connected the ground floor with the second, which contained a spacious landing, the cantor's office, the kitchen, the main living room, and the master bedroom. The third and fourth floors were reached by a winding staircase that also led up to a bedroom and drying loft in the attic. According to eighteenth-century urban apartment design, unheated rooms—that is, bedrooms—were ordinarily inaccessible from hallways but could be entered only through the adjacent living rooms, whose stoves were stoked with fuel from the hallway. The cantor's apartment was equipped with ample built-in closet space, which explains why the 1750 inventory of Bach's estate enumerates only one dresser, one linen chest, and one wardrobe; other furnishings included six tables, eighteen leather chairs, seven wooden bedsteads, and one writing desk with drawers—undoubtedly Bach's working desk.[47]

The cantor's office suite consisted of the composing studio, a heated corner room with windows facing south and west, and an adjacent chamber as additional work space. From the west window of this corner room, Bach could look out over the city wall to the Pleisse River and the flat countryside; on clear days, the silhouette of the cathedral and castle of Merseburg would have been visible. A large iron stove in the southeast corner of the room was fired from the hallway outside, to the left of the office door; to its right, also outside the door, stood a large book cabinet, with many shelves protected by four lockable doors. How the office suite was furnished is unknown, but besides Bach's working desk it would surely have contained chairs, musical instruments, and bookshelves. From the hallway in front of his office, Bach could enter the

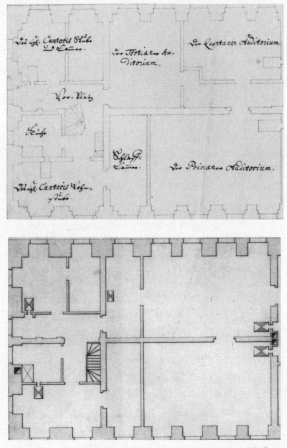

The cantor's apartment and adjoining classrooms on the second floor, shown before (top) and after the 1732 renovation.

school's music library, a newly created heated room whose four walls had built-in shelves that accommodated the old St. Thomas library, with its 500-plus ti-tles and 4,500 partbooks, and perhaps also the bulk of Bach's own sacred compositions. From the library, which may also have served as the principal workplace for Bach's copyists, a lockable door opened into the auditorium of the *secunda* class, a large room with four windows facing west that also served as one of Bach's main teaching and rehearsal spaces. The cantor's apartment provided access to the school's classroom from the third and fourth floors as well, similarly to the dormitory of the choral scholars situated on the fifth (mezzanine) floor and on the first and second attic.

The total space of the cantor's apartment amounted to about 10 by 23.5 Saxon ells; that is, 74.5 square meters (5.6 × 13.3 m.) or 802 square feet (18.4 × 43.6 ft.); the largest room in the apartment, the second-floor living room, was barely 23.5 square meters or 253 square feet, and Bach's composing stu-dio amounted to little more than half of that. By eighteenth-century bourgeois standards, the Bach family lived in a big house, though it must have felt crowded, considering the large brood of children and the nonfamily traffic that traipsed through daily. The management of the household fell to Anna Magdalena Bach. In addition to the customary maid service, she was probably helped by Friedelena Margaretha Bach, Maria Barbara's sister, who had lived in the household ever since 1708. When she died on July 28, 1729, at the age of fifty-three, her functions were likely absorbed by Bach's oldest daughter, Catharina Dorothea, then almost twenty-one. Like two of her stepsisters,

## TABLE 11.2. Layout of the Cantor's Apartment, 1732

| | |
|---|---|
| Ground floor | Main level, east section: entrance hall (door), *room* (1E, 1S), bedroom (1S) |
| | Sunken level, west section: wash house/laundry (door/S), 2 beer caches |
| | Raised level, above sunken level, west section: maids' room (1S), pantry, privy (1W) |
| Second floor | *Living room* (2E, 1S), master bedroom (1E), kitchen (1S), office suite: composing studio (1S, 1W), work room (1W), landing (1S) with access door to library and classrooms |
| Third floor | *Room* (2E, 1S), bedroom (1E), landing (1S) with access door to library and classrooms |
| Fourth floor | *Room* (2E, 1S), landing (1S) |
| Fifth floor (mezzanine) | — |
| First attic | — |
| Second attic | Bedroom (1S, 2 dormers W/E?) |
| Third attic | Drying loft |

*Note:* The number and direction of windows are in parenthesis; italics indicate that the room was heated.

Catharina remained single; in fact, the only one of the four Bach daughters who married was Lieschen, who on January 20, 1749, celebrated her wedding with Johann Christoph Altnickol, one of her father's best students.

Altnickol matriculated at Leipzig University in 1744 and quite possibly numbered among the cantor's select few pupils who received free tuition, room, and board—as is documented for Bach's Weimar student, Philipp David Kräuter, and his very last student, Johann Gottfried Müthel. Müthel, a young and gifted court organist with Duke Christian II Ludwig of Mecklenburg-Schwerin, received a stipend from his duke to study with Bach in Leipzig. The court issued a passport, on May 5, 1750, and a letter of introduction to Bach that was personally signed by the duke "for the organist Müthel, who will take a leave of absence for a year and go to Leipzig to the famous organist and composer Bach in order to perfect himself in his metier."[48] It was later reported that "the Capellmeister Bach accepted him graciously and provided him with a place in his house, and that Müthel availed himself of his instruction with the greatest attentiveness."[49] As Bach was to die two months later, Müthel could benefit only briefly from Bach's teachings, though he apparently developed close relations with the family.[50]

From Kräuter, who studied with Bach back at Weimar in 1712–13, we receive a much more detailed account of a live-in student-apprentice. Kräuter's stipend was provided by the city of Augsburg. His first report to the scholarship committee, dated April 30, 1712, shortly after his arrival in Weimar, ends with an enthusiastic report about the multifaceted learning experience under Bach's tutelage:

I shall report, according to your kind instruction, how I have used these funds and how I have duly arranged with my new teacher, Mr. Bach in Weimar, for a year's board and tutelage. The traveling expense was between 25 and 26 florins, since the roads were very bad and I had to give the coachman almost twice the normal compensation. I gave 4 florins to Mr. Bach for half the month of April, since I was concerned that he might count the entire month as part of the year that now is to commence with the month of May. He had initially asked for 100 reichsthaler to cover the year, but I was able to lower it to 80 thlr., against which he will offer me board and tuition. . . . It is assuredly six hours per day of guidance that I am receiving, primarily in composition and on the keyboard, at times also on other instruments. The rest of the time I use by myself for practice and copying work, since he shares with me all the music I ask for. I am also at liberty to look through all of his pieces.[51]

Bach basically continued the practice he had grown up with in his parents' home in Eisenach, where his father's apprentices lived with the family while studying with and assisting their master. During Kräuter's time in Weimar, Johann Martin Schubart, a pupil of Bach's from Mühlhausen days, was also studying with Bach and may have been boarding with the family as well.[52]

After the Bachs moved to Cöthen and then to Leipzig, more than one live-in student-apprentice at any given time seems improbable, especially in view of the family's growth.

Carl Philipp Emanuel remembered the Bach household during the Leipzig years as a "pigeonry," with people swarming in and out all the time. He invoked that picture to help him explain to Forkel the dire lack of information about the simple facts of his father's life, let alone his thoughts: "With his many activities he hardly had time for the most necessary correspondence, and accordingly would not indulge in lengthy written exchanges. But he had the more opportunity to talk personally to good people, since his house was like a pigeonry, and just as full of life. Association with him was pleasant for everyone, and often very edifying. Since he never wrote down anything about his life, the gaps are unavoidable."[53] What does come through clearly in Carl's description, however, is the outgoing attitude of his father and the convivial and stimulating atmosphere he created, his taking the time to talk with people. Johann Sebastian and Anna Magdalena Bach kept an open house where they welcomed many friends and colleagues from near and far. "No master of music," the Hamburg Bach later recalled, "was apt to pass through this place [Leipzig] without making my father's acquaintance and letting himself be heard by him."[54] Guests included some of the leading figures in contemporary German musical life, among them Carl Heinrich and Johann Gottlieb Graun, Jan Dismas Zelenka, Franz Benda, Johann Joachim Quantz, and the husband-and-wife team of Johann Adolph Hasse and the celebrated Faustina Bordoni, who came to Leipzig several times.[55] Visits of individual musicians, such as that of the Dresden flutist Pierre-Gabriel Buffardin, are usually undatable and reported only coincidentally, mostly for secondary reasons (Buffardin told Bach about meeting and teaching his brother, Johann Jacob, at Constantinople)[56] or to make a particular point. For example, about the visit in the 1730s of the erstwhile royal Swedish court capellmeister, Conrad Friedrich Hurlebusch, Forkel relates that this "conceited and arrogant clavier player" came to Leipzig not to hear Bach "but to let himself be heard. Bach received him kindly and politely, listened to his very indifferent performance with patience; and when Hurlebusch, on taking leave, made the eldest sons a present of a printed collection of sonatas, exhorting them to study them diligently (they who had studied very different things), Bach only smiled to himself and did not at all change his friendly behavior to the stranger."[57]

When the Bachs entertained at home, they arranged for house concerts, when the occasion arose. Johann Elias Bach tells of such an incident in a letter draft where he mentions that Wilhelm Friedemann "was here for over four weeks, having made himself heard several times at our house along with the two famous lutenists Mr. [Silvius Leopold] Weiss and Mr. [Johann] Kropffgans" from Dresden.[58] But the welcoming hospitality of the cantor and his wife surely extended beyond amusing their musical guests. What would their ample and costly supply of silverware have been used for other than dinner parties?[59] What purpose would two silver coffee pots, big and small, a tea pot, and two sugar bowls, larger and smaller, with spoons (valued at over 65 talers), have served other than drinking coffee and tea with friends? What use would Bach have had for four *tabatières* (probably gifts, valued at over 54 talers) other than stuffing and smoking a pipe or taking snuff in a gregarious circle of colleagues and friends? When Bach retreated into the solitude of his composing studio, all by himself, he apparently preferred to do so with a bottle of brandy.

## BALANCING OFFICIAL DUTIES AND PRIVATE BUSINESS

For the Bachs, living in the St. Thomas School building meant that the regular school rhythm governed much of their daily lives. As part of the cantor's obligations, he, the rector, the conrector, and the *tertius* took turns as inspector for the week. The school regulations prescribed that

the Inspector conducts morning and evening prayers. . . . He see that the school is called at 6 A.M. in winter, at 5 A.M. in summer, and that fifteen minutes later all are assembled for prayers in the auditorium downstairs. He says prayers again at 8 P.M., and is careful to note that none is absent and that no lights are taken into the dormitories. At meals he must see that there is no boozing, that Grace is said in German before and after meal, and that the Bible or a history book is read during the repast. It is his duty to make sure that the scholars return in full number and at the proper hour from attending funerals, weddings, and especially the winter *currende* singing; particularly must he satisfy himself that none comes home having drunk too much. . . . The Inspector holds the key to the infirmary and visits the patients in it. Absence from his duty during the day entails a fine of four groschen, and at night of six.[60]

There was no way around the inspector's service, so Bach had to take on this responsibility once a month throughout his twenty-seven-year tenure, a burden not exactly conducive to musical creativity. Largely parallel to the school rhythm, his own workday began at 5 A.M. (6 in winter), a lunch break came at 11, and dinner was held at 6 P.M. Even if he observed the 9 P.M. bedtime of the school dormitory—which he probably did not—his workday would have lasted fifteen to sixteen hours. With daily singing exercises from noon to 1 P.M.,[61] private vocal and instrumental lessons (outside the academic lecture periods of 7–10 A.M. and 1–3 P.M.), and other obligations, he was caught in a tight schedule of the kind he had never before experienced. He surely had not been used to anything like it in his previous court positions at Weimar and Cöthen. But the unfamiliar discipline clearly did not deter him, for example, from his ambitious project of putting together a new and large repertoire of church music that would serve for decades to come. What Bach actually invested in the St. Thomas cantorate was known only to him and was certainly not measurable by the conventional means applied by his superiors, who thought he was cutting corners when he skipped a singing class or had a choral prefect take it over.[62] Whatever reduction of his brutal schedule Bach managed to achieve—always at the expense of being considered irresponsible—the everyday obligations of his office remained as arduous as they were inexorable.

To some extent, the relentless school timetable is replicated in Bach's own cantata production schedule, certainly during the periods when he engaged in weekly composition. The process from the beginning of the preparatory work to the performance of the completed piece followed a regular pattern:

1. Select or have selected (by clergy) the text (also arrange texts—approximately six per cantata booklet—and prepare about twelve such booklets per year for publication).
2. Compose choruses, arias, recitatives, and chorales—generally in that order (beginning on Monday, if not before);[63] prepare the music paper and score, and write the more elaborate movements first, to allow enough time for copying and rehearsing.
3. Organize and supervise the copying effort to make performance parts (assemble the copyists around tables in the cantor's office and the library).
4. Review the performance materials (proofread, correct, enter articulation and other performance markings).
5. Conduct rehearsals (generally no more than one complete read-through on Saturday).

This process was interrupted not only by teaching and being on duty every Friday from 7 to 8 A.M. for the weekly prayer service, but also by weddings and funerals. As a requirement of the city, the school had to participate in all public funerals. These took place after 3 P.M. so that instruction would not be hindered, with the number of participating students depending on the bereaved family's ability to pay. For both students and teachers a major source of income, funerals involving the "Whole School" (all classes) were the most expensive, and those requiring a "Larger Half School" (*prima, secunda, tertia,* and *quinta*), a "Smaller Half School" (*prima* and *tertia,* or *secunda* and *quarta*), or a "Quarter School" (one of the lower classes) less costly. Independent of its size, the school choir was escorted by members of the faculty, who collected fees commensurate with their rank and function: for a Whole School, the rector received 1 taler, the conrector 8 groschen, the cantor 15 groschen, and so forth; for a Larger Half School, the rector was paid 15 groschen, the conrector 6 groschen, the cantor 1 taler; and for a Quarter School, the rector earned 1 groschen 6 pfennig, the conrector 3 pfennig, and the cantor 6 pfennig. The musical assignments varied according to what was ordered, from elaborate motets (such as "O Jesu Christ, meins Lebens Licht," BWV 118, dating from around 1736, with portable instruments for the funeral procession: 2 *litui* [special trumpets], cornetto, and 3 trombones)[64] to simple unison chorales without accompaniment. Wedding ceremonies, where school participation was not compulsory, occurred less frequently and were handled more flexibly. They also were divided into two categories: a full wedding Mass involved a cantata performance (BWV 34a, 120a, 195, and 197, for instance), while a half wedding Mass required only four-part chorales (BWV 250–252 represent a sample from after 1730). Altogether, funerals and weddings took up a considerable amount of time every week.

Considering these additional obligations, it is truly remarkable that Bach was able to manage, on the side, so to speak, such demanding activities as the directorship of the Collegium Musicum—if only after largely completing the cantata repertoire for the school—and practicing and preparing for recitals, let alone teaching private pupils. Those who came to him for private studio instruction fell into two groups: professional students, whom he usually taught in exchange for services and a modest fee, and wealthy amateurs, mostly from among aristocratic students at the university, who paid a hefty fee. The latter provided him with considerable extra income; for a keyboard lesson he gave in 1747 to Eugen Wenzel Count of Wrbna, Bach received 6 talers, or six times the highest fee charged for a funeral or wedding.[65] In addition, he rented the count a clavier for several months at a monthly fee of 1 taler 8 groschen.

Bach kept a sizable collection of instruments in his home. His estate catalog lists no fewer than eight harpsichords, one pedal harpsichord, two lute claviers, one spinet, two violins, a piccolo violin, three violas, a *Bassetchen* (viola pomposa), two cellos, a viola da gamba, and a lute.[66] Some of these instruments he needed for his own, his wife's, and his children's use, for instructional purposes, for performances at home, and for supplementing Collegium and church instruments. Others, however, especially keyboard instruments, were available for rent. A dunning letter to the Leipzig innkeeper Johann Georg Martius (or his son), who specialized in funeral and wedding parties, sheds light on Bach's instrument-rental business. An obviously angry cantor wrote on March 20, 1748, to his debtor:

Mr. Martius,
My patience is now at its end. How long do you think I must wait for the harpsichord? Two months have passed, and nothing has changed. I regret to write this to you, but I cannot do otherwise. You must bring it back in good order, and within five days, else we shall never be friends. Adieu.

*Joh: Sebast: Bach*[67]

Through his widespread connections, Bach also functioned as sales agent for instrument makers. Thus, at the time of the Easter Fair in 1749, Bach sold a very expensive fortepiano to a Polish nobleman—apparently on commission from the Dresden organ builder Gottfried Silbermann, at the time the only maker of this kind of instrument. Bach's receipt for his payment provides the necessary details:

That to me, the undersigned, the payment of 115 rthl., written out one hundred and fifteen rthl. in *Lui blanc* [= 23 louis d'or], for an instrument called Piano et Forte which shall be delivered to His Excellency Count [Jan Casimir von] Branitzky in Bialystok, was properly handed over by Mr. [Barthelemy] Valentin here, I herewith attest. Leipzig, May 6, 1749.

> *Joh: Sebast: Bach*
> Royal Polish and Electoral Saxon
> Court Composer

In addition to his instrument-rental and commission sales business, the eminently practical, versatile, and entrepreneurial Bach—the "compleat musician" par excellence—ran a small book and music sales operation. Available for purchase were not only his own publications, such as the volumes from the *Clavier-Übung* series, but also works by his sons, students, and colleagues. In the spring of 1729, for example, German newspaper advertisements informed the public that important new music books such as Johann David Heinichen's *Der General-Bass in der Composition* of 1728 and Johann Gottfried Walther's *Musicalisches Lexicon* of 1731 were available under commission "in Leipzig from Capellmeister Bach" (as in Hamburg from Johann Mattheson, in Darmstadt from Christoph Graupner, and so forth).[68] Moreover, the title pages of Wilhelm Friedemann Bach's keyboard publications dating from 1745 to 1748 invariably indicate that the works were obtainable not only "from the author" in Dresden and Halle, but also "from his father in Leipzig, and from his brother in Berlin." Similar references to Bach's music business can be found on keyboard publications of 1735 and 1736 by Conrad Friedrich Hurlebusch and on the *Clavier-Übung* of 1741 by Bach's student Johann Ludwig Krebs.[69] The sales venture was complemented by a manuscript-copying service and by the rental of manuscript parts of his own works. For example, the autograph score of the Sanctus in D major, BWV 232[III], bears the notation "NB. The parts are in Bohemia with Count Sporck"[70]—referring to Franz Anton Count Sporck of Lissa and Prague, with whom Bach maintained contact; the parts were apparently never returned, so that a replacement set had to be copied out.

Bach's multifarious connections with instrument makers allowed him to experiment with new instrument designs, less for commercial reasons than out of a genuine interest in the technology of musical instruments. Directly related to his activities as keyboard virtuoso were, of course, his services as a consultant and organ expert, an area in which he had virtually no peers. But not only did he design and test organs, he also played a significant role in the development of new keyboard instruments, most notably the lute-clavier, a gut-strung variant of the traditional harpsichord, and the fortepiano, the prototype of the modern piano. Possibly inspired by the work of his elder cousin Johann Nicolaus Bach of Jena, who had built lute-clavier instruments,[71] Bach himself toyed with this hybrid instrument type. Johann Friedrich Agricola later recalled "about the year 1740, in Leipzig, having seen and heard a lute-harpsichord designed by Mr. Johann Sebastian Bach and executed by Mr. Zacharias Hildebrandt, which was of smaller size than the ordinary harpsichord."[72] Among the works intended for this instrument is the Prelude, Fugue, and Allegro in E-flat major, BWV 998, dating from the late 1730s, and according to its autograph title written "pour la Luth ò Cembal." However, much more consequential than his association with this short-lived keyboard type was Bach's involvement with Gottfried Silbermann's important refinement of the fortepiano, a keyboard instrument with controllable hammers that permitted an infinitely variable differentiation between *forte* and *piano* dynamics. The Saxon organ builder improved Bartolomeo Cristofori's original design, in particular its hammer action and sound quality, and for both he received critical advice from Bach,[73] as the same Agricola reported:

Mr. Gottfried Silbermann had at first built two of these instruments. One of them was seen and played by the late Capellmeister, Mr. Joh. Sebastian Bach. He praised, indeed, admired, its tone; but he complained that it was too weak in the high register and too hard to play. This was taken greatly amiss by Mr. Silbermann, who could not bear to have any fault found in his handiworks. He was therefore angry at Mr. Bach for a long time. And yet his conscience told him that Mr. Bach was not wrong. He therefore decided—greatly to his credit, be it said—not to deliver any more of these instruments, but instead to think all the harder about how to eliminate the faults Mr. J. S. Bach had observed. He worked for many years on this. And that this was the real cause of this postponement I have the less doubt since I myself heard it frankly acknowledged by Mr. Silbermann. . . . Mr. Silbermann also had the laudable ambition to show one of these instruments of his later workmanship to the late Capellmeister Bach, and have it examined by him; and he received, in turn, complete approval from him.[74]

Silbermann had developed his original model in the early 1730s, but withdrew it after it was not fully approved by Bach; he introduced his new and better version in the mid-1740s. Bach then played on the new fortepianos at the court of King Friedrich II of Prussia in 1747. Reportedly, the improved instruments manufactured by Silbermann—the kind Bach helped market at the Leipzig trade fair—"pleased the king so much that he resolved to buy them all up. He collected 15."[75]

Contemporary reports also link Bach to the design of the viola pomposa (or violoncello piccolo, or *Bassetchen*), a higher-range bass string instrument. In 1782, Forkel discussed the reasons for what seems to have been Bach's own modification—not properly an invention—of existing prototypes of the violoncello piccolo.[76] Forkel cites the dilemma in making the proper choice of an instrument that is either too low (cello) or too high (violin) for accompanying certain lines in a flexible manner: "In order to find a way out of this situation, and to avoid both extremes, the former Capellmeister in Leipzig, Mr. Joh. Seb. Bach, invented an instrument that he called viola pomposa. It is tuned like a violoncello but has one string more at the top, is somewhat larger than a viola, and is so attached with a ribbon that it can be held on the arm in front of the chest."[77] Bach made use of this five-string viola pomposa in the Suite in D major, BWV 1012, specifically designated "a cinq cordes" within the set of solo cello suites. For accompanimental purposes, he required it in several cantatas written between 1714 and 1726 (BWV 199/second version, 5, 180, 115, 139, 41, 6, 85, 183, 68, 175) and also in the A-major Mass, BWV 234, for a performance in the 1740s. Bach's keen interest in exploring unconventional sonorities is particularly well documented in his early Leipzig cantatas. The oboe d'amore, for example, not traceable anywhere before 1720, is integrated into his Leipzig instrumental ensemble from the very beginning; in fact, his audition piece apparently introduced the instrument into the Leipzig church music repertoire. A bit later, beginning in 1724, Bach promoted the invention of the oboe da caccia, a hybrid tenor-range oboe with a wooden shaft and a brass bell, by the Leipzig instrument maker Johann Heinrich Eichentopf. The instrument is featured most prominently in the pastoral sinfonia that opens part II of the *Christmas Oratorio,* which combines a pair of oboi da caccia with a pair of oboi d'amore.

Eichentopf, perhaps the most eminent German woodwind instrument maker of his time, was also among the few who tried their hand at producing contrabassoons. Bach called for one in the 1749 version of his *St. John Passion* and, most likely, used an Eichentopf instrument for that performance. Eichentopf lived and worked with other instrument makers in the Stadtpfeifergasse, the street where the Leipzig town musicians received free or subsidized housing. The distinguished violin maker Johann Christian Hoffmann lived there as well, and the Bach family maintained particularly close connections with him,[78] apparently from the beginning. In 1729, Bach purchased from Hoffmann a new quartet of string instruments, complete with bows, for St. Thomas's.[79] Hoffmann, who held the privilege of Royal Polish and Electoral Saxon Court Instrument and Lute Maker and was charged with maintaining the string instruments that belonged to St. Thomas's and St. Nicholas's, probably worked with Bach on the construction of the viola pomposa. He listed Bach among the beneficiaries of his estate, and when he died in January 1750, Bach passed his portion—an unspecified musical instrument—on to his second youngest, Johann Christoph Friedrich, who probably made good use of it, as the seventeen-year-old was entering his first employment as Schaumburg-Lippe court musician.[80]

Close personal working relationships with organ builders and string and wind instrument makers must have meant a great deal to Bach. Besides being congenial company, they never held his own craftsman's origin in contempt. Mechanically skillful, always attracted by technological tasks, and a quick problem solver, Bach never felt that personally maintaining and repairing his instruments was beneath him; he even worked on those that were merely under his purview, such as the instruments at the Weimar and Cöthen courts and, at least initially, the church instruments at St. Thomas's and St. Nicholas's.[81] "Nobody," wrote Forkel, "could install the quill plectrums of his harpsichord to his satisfaction; he always did it himself. He also tuned both his harpsichord and his clavichord himself, and was so practiced in the operation that it never cost him above a quarter of an hour."[82] All of this extra work, of course, made for an even tighter professional schedule, and the kind of balancing act that Bach had to manage on a daily basis is indeed hard to imagine. On the other hand, he never became a slave to his office and his assigned responsibilities. Instead, he devoted himself to his musical science in the broadest possible sense, to exploring the full range of musical composition and performance—up to but not exceeding the limits imposed by the physical, acoustical, mechanical, and physiological conditions of actual music making. When it came to the business of commission sales and instrument rentals, he merely adopted the practices that others exercised as well. But there was hardly anyone among his composer peers who cared so much about and spent so much time involved with instrumental sound production, the mechanics and ergonomics of performance, and the thorny issues surrounding musical temperament. Somehow, what looks to us like a totally unmanageable workload left room not only for an unrivaled creative output, but also for such matters as procuring a singing bird and carnations for the lady of the house.

Autograph score of "Et incarnatus est" (1749) from the *Mass in B minor*, BWV 232.

# 12

## Contemplating Past, Present, and Future

### THE FINAL DECADE: THE 1740s

RETREAT BUT NO REST

Ever since Johann Kuhnau's 1721 Passion performance at the newly established Good Friday Vespers, the annual presentation of the Passion had been the highpoint of Leipzig's church music calendar. And from 1724 on, Bach had single-handedly shaped that tradition, so it must have come as a shock to him when, after fifteen years, the city council interdicted the Passion performance planned for Good Friday, March 27, 1739. Bach himself apparently did not know the reasons for the council's decision. The only report we have of the clearly unpleasant incident was written by the assistant city clerk on March 17:

Upon a Noble and Most Wise Council's order I have gone to Mr. Bach here and have pointed out to the same that the music he intends to perform on the coming Good Friday is to be omitted until regular permission for the same is received. Whereupon he answered: it had always been done so; he did not care, for he got nothing out of it anyway, and it was only a burden; he would notify the Superintendent that it had been forbidden him; if an objection were made on account of the text, [he remarked that] it had already been performed several times.[1]

The council's interference in this matter and the background for their claiming the permission rights raises many questions: What triggered the intrusion? The church administration was clearly not involved, but who actually was? Which faction of the city council prevailed? Did rector Ernesti play a role? Was someone jealous of the cantor's prominent exposure at the musical event of the year in Leipzig? The work scheduled by Bach for performance at St. Nicholas's was probably the *St. John Passion,* which he had indeed performed "several times." Moreover, the only surviving fair copy of the score, an autograph manuscript that Bach started copying and revising for a re-performance of the work in the late 1730s, breaks off abruptly in the middle of recitative no. 10, on page 20; Bach never returned to the task beyond that point.[2] If it was indeed the *St. John Passion* that was canceled in 1739, we can understand Bach's anger and frustration over an issue he did not quite fathom. He chucked the whole business because "it was only a burden."

Whatever musical work replaced the Passion on Good Friday 1739, Bach resumed Passion performances in the following years: the *St. Matthew* in 1740 or 1742 and the *St. John* in 1749. Nevertheless, the 1739 prohibition marked a defining moment for Bach in the conduct of his office during the final decade of his life. Retirement from his post was inconceivable—he was only fifty-five and in good health—and permission to retire in good standing was granted only under the most extraordinary circumstances. But the combination of discouraging experiences with the civic administration and the strained relationship with the rector of the St. Thomas School on the one side, and his protected status as royal court *compositeur* on the other, led him to devise a scheme of limited withdrawal from the pandemonium of the school office. At the same time, he must have realized that he had brought on the greatest amount of pressure himself by undertaking to compose a new cantata nearly every week for a considerable stretch of time in the 1720s. He knew that he completely controlled his actual workload at St. Thomas's and St. Nicholas's. His office required of him neither weekly delivery of new pieces nor technically demanding performances of large-scale works. Exceeding the expectations of the office on the scale he did was entirely his own decision, one he surely never regretted, though the lack of genuine recognition by his superiors rankled.

Now disillusioned and dispirited, the cantor retreated a step further from what had already become a reduced level of creative activity for the church music repertoire ever since 1729, when he had assumed the directorship of the Collegium Musicum. He still fulfilled his duties as music director of the Leipzig main churches in traditional capellmeister style, performing the accustomed repertoire of intricate works that continued to challenge his performers, many of whom—though none of the singers—were the same as before. In other words, he kept introducing what to his choir and instrumental ensemble were indeed "new" cantatas and related works, but he expanded the church repertoire only minimally after 1739–40. In fact, the only evidence we have of a newly composed cantata movement after 1740 is the single aria "Bekennen will ich seinen Namen," BWV 200, dating from around 1742. All other compositional activity in the realm of church cantatas was limited to modifying older pieces, for example, by reassigning certain instruments to accommodate changing performance conditions. One of the few revisions or reworkings that do reflect changes in musical aesthetics involves the cantata "Dem Gerechten muß das Licht immer wieder aufgehen," BWV

195—characteristically, a work not intended for the regular Sundays and feast days but composed for a special occasion, a wedding Mass. In 1748–49, for a performance of a work that was some twenty years old, Bach wrote two new recitatives (nos. 2 and 4) that reveal a remarkable level of heightened compositional sophistication. Movement 4 in particular, an accompanied recitative scored for soprano, 2 transverse flutes, 2 oboi d'amore, and continuo, exhibits an exceptionally refined sense of declamatory intensity, enhanced by the rich textures of colorful yet well-blended instrumental sonorities. This kind of substantive revision in the cantata repertoire is rare, though, and new adaptations from earlier compositions occur even less frequently. One such instance is a festive Latin work for Christmas Day, "Gloria in excelsis Deo," BWV 191, based on three movements (nos. 4, 8, and 12) from the Mass in B minor of 1733 and presented sometime between 1743 and 1746. However, the most eloquent testimonial for Bach's markedly scaled-back efforts in music for the ecclesiastical year is the fragmentary revision of the *St. John Passion,* a major project broken off in 1739 and never resumed, even though Bach presented a performance of the Passion on Good Friday 1749.[3]

Yet however sharply Bach reduced his creative investment in the functions of cantor at St. Thomas's and music director at the main churches, he did not withdraw from the responsibilities of his appointment. As before, he apparently made optimal use of the choral prefects at his disposal for much of the daily school routine while personally seeing to the essential singing exercises and rehearsals, private lessons for the most gifted students, the rotating four-weekly inspector's duties, and the regular church performances. He thus found a way to administer the office, achieve the objectives of the cantorate, and avoid problems within his control. Seen from the vantage point of the 1740s, it becomes clear that the two earlier instances of Bach's arguing with his superiors represented challenges to the authority of his office: in one case, the cantor's customary prerogative of choosing the hymns for the divine service, in the other, his right to appoint the choral prefects.

Unlike any of his predecessors or successors, Bach never needed to depend entirely on his appointment as cantor and music director at St. Thomas's. His stature as a keyboard virtuoso without peer, a widely recognized organological expert, an accomplished composer versed in all musical genres, an experienced leader of high-profile performances, and a sought-after private teacher—all buttressed by his titles of distinguished court capellmeister and court composer—provided him with a choice of outside options and guaranteed him considerable latitude in conducting his Leipzig office. This freedom allowed him to subordinate the cantorate's established functions to his own interests. At times he demanded the utmost of his singers and instrumentalists by performing church music of unprecedented complexity, and at other times he scaled back his activities by programming less taxing works, mostly by other composers. The same freedom allowed him time off to pursue other professional activities and, if necessary, call on substitutes to take over school duties and direct church performances. Atypically for his time, Bach had managed throughout his career to carry out several projects at once, ranging from those that enhanced the scope of his position to those entirely outside his official obligations but consistent with the pursuit of his own artistic goals.

The award in 1736 of the prestigious title Electoral Saxon and Royal Polish Court *Compositeur,* which carried no specific obligations but gave Bach the stamp of royal approval with the privileges of courtly affiliation and protection, pleased him to a degree that cannot be overestimated. The honorary title emphatically recognized Bach's calling and accomplishments as composer, and at that point in his career, this aspect of his musicianship meant more to him than any other. Organ and clavier virtuoso, capellmeister, cantor and music director—these activities had played an important role in his professional life and, to be sure, continued to do so, though on a reduced scale (even his resumption of the Collegium directorship in 1739 lasted only for some three years, and his public appearances as a keyboard performer became rare).[4] What never changed were the time and effort spent at his desk in his composing room, in the southwest corner on the second floor of the St. Thomas School building, where little could disturb him.

Here at his desk, Bach was surrounded by shelves bearing the bulk and weight of the products of his creative mind, forcefully affirming the notion that his primary calling was that of a composer. This view was strengthened when he looked at the compositions by his ancestors that had found their way into a collection he maintained. Carl Philipp Emanuel, who later inherited this material, called it the Old-Bach Archive, a term the father may already have coined. The Archive contained most of the surviving compositions produced by the older generations of the Wechmar line Bach family (see Table 1.1), notably works of Johann *(4),* Heinrich *(6),* Christoph *(13),* and Michael *(14).* It happened that Bach amassed the Archive at about the time that he witnessed, with pride, his older sons leaving the parental home and taking up careers as professional musicians in their own right. It became obvious that the stream of "members of the Bach family who have excelled in practical music"[5] would continue in the younger generation. It was in this setting, in about 1735, that Bach undertook a careful documentation of both a family tree and a Genealogy that contained a brief commentary on each male member—virtually all of them musicians—to complement the Archive. Bach, at the age of fifty, was opening a broad historical spectrum that induced him to look in two directions: the musical past of the family and its future—ancestors on one side and his own children on the other—with himself in the middle. The past, present, and future of the family tangibly mirrored the past, present, and future of music within his realm and reach. His own music would now serve as a foundation for the music of the new generation, which also included his students. The gradual "changing of the guard" may have helped Bach gain a sound balance between deliberately distancing himself from official duties and intensifying his compositional introspection. So he embarked on a journey of reflection to critically survey his major works and set the stage for such large-scale projects as *The Art of Fugue* and the *B-minor Mass.*

Still, Bach was no dissociated or estranged character who isolated himself in his composing studio: he took on, for example, more instrument projects in the 1740s than ever before. He tested the new organ by Johann Scheibe of Leipzig for St. John's, a church (no longer standing) surrounded by the large municipal cemetery just outside Leipzig's walls. The instrument (with twenty-two stops on two manuals and pedal) was dedicated in December 1743 and "deemed flawless by Capellmeister Bach and Mr. Zacharias Hildebrandt, after the strictest examination that an organ was perhaps ever subjected to."[6] Bach collaborated again with Hildebrandt on a new instrument for St. Wenceslas's Church in Naumburg, the largest organ design and construction project of the Leipzig organ builder's career. For four days in late September 1746, Bach and Gottfried Silbermann examined the instrument (with fifty-three stops on three manuals and pedal) and wrote a highly favorable report for the Naumburg town council.[7]

Throughout the decade, Bach maintained an intense professional life on several fronts and cultivated his many musical and social contacts. He had outstanding private students, notably Johann Friedrich Agricola, Johann Philipp Kirnberger, Johann Christoph Altnickol, Johann Christian Kittel, and Johann Gottfried Müthel—all of whom later assumed influential musical positions and, through their own teachings and writings, solidified the tradition of a "Bach School." Bach's reputation, gregarious character, and discursive manner lured many a musician and musical connoisseur to make contact with him, and the bustling life of the commercial city and university town offered plentiful opportunities for such relationships. Tangible evidence for these contacts survives in the form of short album entries, for which Bach invariably chose a canon in enigmatic notation. Only three of these dedicatory canons are dated: BWV 1075 of 1734 for an unknown visitor, BWV 1077 of 1747 for the theology student Johann Gottfried Fulde, and BWV 1078 of 1749 for a person by the name of Faber.[8] These and other such contrapuntal pieces shed light on the atmosphere in which these encounters took place, in that they induced the learned composer to challenge his visitors with simple-looking yet complex vignettes of musical logic. Although we can identify few of the musical gentlemen undoubtedly held spellbound by his scholarship and artistry, we do know that the young composer and theorist Friedrich Wilhelm Marpurg—most likely on his return from Paris to Berlin between 1747 and 1749—spent time with Bach and consulted with him on fugal composition.[9] The visit, which must have occurred just when Bach was preparing his *Art of Fugue* for publication, was apparently a crucial background event for Marpurg's planning of his two-volume essay *Abhandlung von der Fuge* of 1753–54—the first-ever systematic treatise on fugal composition—which in many ways takes Bach's *Art of Fugue* as a point of departure. Marpurg's Leipzig visit and personal exposure to the old fugue master explains why the Bach heirs turned to him in 1752 for writing a preface to the second edition of *The Art of Fugue,* thereby tying the practical tour de force with the theoretical one.

In June 1747, Lorenz Christoph Mizler passed through his old stomping grounds, on his way from Erfurt, where he took his doctorate in medicine, to Warsaw, where he would work mainly as a practicing physician. During his stopover in Leipzig, he finally managed to persuade his former teacher, the Thomascantor, to join the Society of Musical Science, a loose association of intellectually minded musicians that Mizler had founded in 1738. Bach became the fourteenth member of this exclusive corresponding society,[10] which aimed at fostering contacts among the regular members by mailing twice a year, at around Easter and St. Michael's Day, a circular containing musical news, essays, and practical and theoretical works contributed or selected by the membership. Bach made quick use of this convenient means of communication among colleagues. In the packet mailed from Leipzig after St. Michael's Day 1747, he sent around copies of the Triple Canon for six voices, BWV 1076, the piece depicted on the Hausmann portrait and also issued by Bach as a separate print. Father Meinrad Spiess of the Benedictine Abbey of Yrsee in southern Germany, a member of the society, attached a copy of BWV 1076 (one of only two that survive) to his working exemplar of his own treatise on practical musical composition.[11] Spiess probably found in the same circular a copy of the *Musical Offering,* BWV 1079, for Mizler had reported to him on September 1: "On my return by way of Leipzig spoke to Capellmeister Bach, who told me of his Berlin journey and the story of the fugue he played before the king, which will shortly be engraved in copper and a copy of which will appear in the packet of the Society. I have already seen the beginning of it."[12] Later, Bach mailed the *Canonic Variations on "Vom Himmel hoch,"* BWV 769, "fully worked out," as Mizler testifies in a concluding paragraph to Bach's Obituary. He also presented to the society a reprint of the canon BWV 1076, and, according to Mizler, "he would undoubtedly have done much more had not the shortness of time—he was member for only three years—prevented him from doing so."[13]

Mizler makes no mention, however, of a conflict Bach had with Johann

Gottlieb Biedermann, rector of the gymnasium in Freiberg, which erupted in 1749 over the role of music and musicians at Latin schools and which created a major stir well beyond the Saxon borders and also touched the society's interests. The conflict resulted from a performance at the gymnasium of a singspiel composed by Bach's former student Johann Friedrich Doles, cantor at Freiberg (and Bach's second successor as Thomascantor). Under the heading *De Vita musica* (Of Musical Life), Biedermann published a school pamphlet in May 1749 in which he took pleasure in referring to all musicians, without exception, as depraved and wicked. The article, sent to Leipzig probably by Doles himself, infuriated Bach. He commissioned the organist, writer, and instrument maker Christoph Gottlieb Schröter of Nordhausen, with whom he had been in contact for over thirty years, to review and refute the Biedermann piece, and offered to get the review published "in the learned journals"—an allusion to Mizler's *Musikalische Bibliothek.* Schröter, likewise a member of the Society of Musical Science, accepted the task, acknowledging that the pamphlet's "principal aim, despite its title, was not at all directed to the praise of music and its kindred arts" but openly revealed the rector's "unfriendly attitude toward the innocent art of music." In a letter of December 10, 1749, to another colleague, Georg Friedrich Einike of Frankenhausen, Bach stated that "Schröter's criticism is well written, and to my taste, and will soon make its appearance in print." He concluded, almost surely with a sidelong glance at Thomasrector Ernesti, with the bitingly sarcastic remark that, with further refutations to be expected, "the rector's dirty ear will be cleansed and made more fit to listen to music."[14] The remark was also a kind of pun: the term for "dirty ear," *Dreck-ohr,* resembles that for "rector" *(Rec-dor)* as pronounced in the Saxon dialect. Some details of the affair were reported in 1751 by Johann Mattheson, who also included Bach's derogatory pun with the fastidious comment (in French): "A base and disgusting expression, unworthy of a Capellmeister; a poor allusion to the word *rector.*"[15]

Bach let himself be drawn even more deeply into the matter and, in some ways, managed to make the Biedermann affair very much his own case. Despite the statement about Schröter's "well-written" review, he considered it much too mild. He therefore added his own sharp-tongued comment on the text and, as Einike later reported,

sent on a few copies of the said review, but in such form that . . . it no longer resembled Mr. Schröter's original in the least but had many additions and many changes. Mr. Schröter, when he saw this gruesome mixture, could not help being offended about it and . . . bade me inform Mr. Bach "that the violent changes made in his criticism had offended him deeply"; further, "that his consolation in the matter was that no reader who was familiar with his way of writing or thinking, from other sources, could consider him the author of such a mixture, not to mention the unhappy title *Christian Reflections* upon, etc."

Although no copy of the review with Bach's hot-tempered emendations and the unauthorized heading "Christian Reflections" has turned up, it is easy to imagine that what affected Bach's sensitivities so strongly and provoked his apparently unmeasured response was a matter of school politics. Given the parallels between the Freiberg and Leipzig situations, specifically between the rectors Biedermann and Ernesti, Bach felt that he had to throw his weight behind a defense of the cantorate. He may have tried to explain just that to his irritated colleague in Nordhausen, Schröter, who complained to Einike on June 5, 1750—less than two months before the Thomascantor's death—that "Capellmeister Bach remains at fault, no matter how he twists or turns, now or in the future." While intending a counterattack on Biedermann's assault, Bach had unintentionally managed to insult his own ally.

Bach's principled defense of the cantorate squares well with his position in the prefect dispute of the late 1730s, even to the extent that in both cases his ardor led him to get carried away and overshoot the mark. Despite his often negative experiences, Bach had the highest esteem for his school and church offices throughout his Leipzig tenure. And it seems that when he self-consciously steered his own course, he did so in justice to himself, to his cantorate, and, by extension, to his function as capellmeister and his calling as composer. Hence, he saw no conflict in the 1730s between school and church on the one hand and the Collegium Musicum on the other, nor in the balancing act of administering the cantorate and pursuing his compositional interests. In the 1740s, these interests ranged conceptually and stylistically from the commissioned 1742 burlesque cantata "Mer han en neue Oberkeet," BWV 212, with a comical text written in dialect, to the introspective and abstract contrapuntal perspectives of *The Art of Fugue*, BWV 1080, an entirely self-determined project.

The number of commissioned works originating from the 1740s is understandably very small, since Bach had few incentives to seek them after he gave up the Collegium directorship, and little opportunity to perform vocal compositions outside the Leipzig churches. Bach seems also to have reduced his public appearances for keyboard and chamber performances, at least during the second half of the 1740s. Johann Friedrich Wilhelm Sonnenkalb, a choral scholar at St. Thomas's who was close to the Bach family, reported in 1759 that "this great artist did not let himself commonly be heard outside of his own house; but there concerts were held quite often." He also relates that those performances involved not only the two youngest sons but also their older step-brothers, when they visited, and Bach's assistant and later son-in-law Alt-nickol.[16] Guest performances outside Leipzig were even rarer, but we must assume that any travels by Bach, notably the two trips to Berlin in 1741 and 1747, were undertaken with official invitations.

We know about the first of those trips only because Bach wrote from Berlin to his family at the beginning of August 1741 and Johann Elias Bach wrote him there on August 5 and 9.[17] He had returned by August 25, in time for the performance of the cantata for the city council election. The Berlin sojourn may have been related to Carl Philipp Emanuel Bach's employ in the court capelle of Friedrich II, who had acceded to the Prussian throne in 1740. An official court visit, which Bach may well have envisioned in planning the journey, did not materialize. Bach apparently stayed with the physician Georg Ernst Stahl, privy councillor at the court and a family friend,[18] who seems to have played a role in arranging for the trip and whose house was located on Unter den Linden, the avenue in the center of Berlin that led up to the royal palace. Though Bach was not granted an encounter with the king, he must have met Michael Gabriel Fredersdorf, the king's chamberlain and, like the king, an accomplished flutist: an early manuscript copy of the Flute Sonata in E major, BWV 1035, bears the remark "after the [lost] autograph by the composer, which was written anno 17 , when he was at Potsdam, for privy chamberlain Fredersdorff."[19] The digits missing from the year can be filled in to read either 1741 or 1747, but considering Bach's tight schedule in 1747 and also for stylistic reasons, 1741 is the more plausible date.

The second trip to Berlin and Potsdam in May 1747 turned into one of the most important events of Bach's life. It was also the high-water mark of his public recognition when German newspapers in Berlin, Frankfurt, Hamburg, Leipzig, Magdeburg, and probably elsewhere picked up the official Potsdam press release of May 11:

One hears from Potsdam that last Sunday [May 7] the famous Capellmeister from Leipzig, Mr. Bach, arrived with the intention to have the pleasure of hearing the excellent Royal music there. In the evening, at about the time when the regular chamber music in the Royal apartments usually begins, His Majesty was informed that Capellmeister Bach had arrived at Potsdam and was waiting in His Majesty's antechamber for His Majesty's most gracious permission to listen to the music. His August self immediately gave orders that Bach be admitted, and went, at his entrance, to the so-called Forte et Piano, condescending also to play, in His Most August Person and without any preparation, a theme for the Capellmeister Bach, which he should execute in a fugue. This was done so happily by the aforementioned Capellmeister that not only His Majesty was pleased to show his satisfaction thereat, but also all those present were seized with astonishment. Mr. Bach found the theme propounded to him so exceedingly beautiful that he intends to set it down on paper as a regular fugue and have it engraved on copper. On Monday, the famous man let himself be heard on the organ in the Church of the Holy Spirit at Potsdam and earned general acclaim from the listeners attending in great number. In the evening, His Majesty charged him again with the execution of a fugue, in six parts, which he accomplished just as skillfully as on the previous occasion, to the pleasure of His Majesty and to the general admiration.[20]

This time around, we can be sure that a court visit was carefully prepared through diplomatic channels, most likely the good services of Count Hermann Carl von Keyserlingk, Bach's longtime champion, who was then serving as Russian ambassador in Berlin. Keyserlingk's 1746 reassignment from Dresden to Berlin reflected a major political power shift in Europe that resulted from a bold move made in the 1740s by the young Prussian king: in order to expand and secure his territory, he fought two wars against the allied forces of Saxony, Poland, and Austria. During the Second Silesian War, Prussian troops under Leopold of Anhalt-Dessau took Leipzig on November 30, 1745, and occupied it for a month. On December 25, 1745, at the Peace of Dresden, Empress Maria Theresa confirmed the cession of Silesia, and in a 1748 letter Bach recalled the period as "the time we had (alas!) the Prussian Invasion."[21] Hence, the trip of the Leipzig cantor and Dresden court composer to the Prussian capital and, especially, his personal reception by the king—exactly six months after Prussian troops had withdrawn from Leipzig—occurred at a sensitive political moment and surely had implications that would make the people of Saxony, notably the Leipzig city council and the Dresden court, prick up their ears: his musical eminence, the Thomascantor of Leipzig, had gone to Berlin as a true ambassador of peace.

Bach was accompanied on this trip by his oldest son, who had left Dresden the year before to become organist and music director of Our Lady's in Halle—on Prussian territory. Wilhelm Friedemann later provided Forkel with some further details of the Berlin visit. Since Friedemann's story as related by Forkel confirms and amplifies the Berlin press release, we may take the biographer's 1802 account as reliable. According to Forkel, Bach's visit took place largely at the request of the king himself:

The reputation of the all-surpassing skill of Johann Sebastian was at this time so extended that the King often heard it mentioned and praised. This made him curious to hear and meet so great an artist. At first he distantly hinted to the son his wish that his father would one day come to Potsdam. But by degrees he began to ask him directly why his father did not come. The son could not avoid acquainting his father with these expressions of the King's; at first, however, he could not pay any attention to them because he was generally too overwhelmed with business. But the King's expressions being repeated in several of his son's letters, he at length, in 1747, prepared to take this journey.[22]

The simple fact is, of course, that it would have been utterly inappropriate for Bach to appear at the Prussian court during the Prussian occupation of Leipzig.

Bach and his son Friedemann may have stayed once again at the house of Dr. Stahl, at least for the Berlin part of the trip; but their first call was Potsdam, eighteen miles southwest of Berlin, the preferred residence of Friedrich II. The construction of "Sanssouci" Castle had just been completed and dedicated on May 1, 1747, but the encounter between the king and Bach took place in the Potsdam city palace (destroyed in World War II), where chamber music was ordinarily played from 7 to 9 P.M. daily. Forkel's account continues:

The king used to have every evening a private concert, in which he himself generally performed some concertos on the flute. One evening, just as he was getting his flute ready and his musicians were assembled, an officer brought him the written list of the strangers who had arrived. With his flute in his hand, he ran over the list, but immediately turned to the assembled musicians and said, with a kind of agitation: "Gentlemen, old Bach is come." The flute was now laid aside; and old Bach, who had alighted at his son's lodgings, was immediately summoned to the Palace.

. . . the King gave up his concert for this evening and invited Bach . . . to try his fortepianos, made by Silbermann, which stood in several rooms of the Palace. The musicians went with him from room to room, and Bach was invited to try them and to play unpremeditated compositions. After he had gone on for some time, he asked the King to give him a subject for a fugue in order to execute it immediately without any preparation. The King admired the learned manner in which his subject was thus executed extempore; and, probably to see how far such art could be carried, expressed a wish to hear also a fugue with six obbligato parts. But as not every subject is fit for such full harmony, Bach chose one himself and immediately executed it to the astonishment of all present in the same magnificent and learned manner as he had done that of the King.

The twenty-plus musicians King Friedrich had assembled for his capelle were among the very best to be found anywhere and included such distinguished figures as the brothers Carl Heinrich and Johann Gottlieb Graun (capellmeister and concertmaster), the brothers Franz and Johann Georg Benda, and Johann Joachim Quantz—all well known to Bach. The Grauns had been trained in Dresden, and Johann Gottlieb, previously concertmaster in Merseburg, had been Friedemann's violin teacher. The Bendas had been members of the Dresden court capelle before accepting positions as violinist and violist in the newly formed ensemble of then crown prince Friedrich; Quantz joined them from Dresden in 1741. They could now hear the Leipzig capellmeister play on the new fortepianos built by Silbermann with considerable technical input from Bach; they also witnessed Bach's command performance of a fugue on the "royal theme."

On the following day, May 8, again at the request of the king and in his presence, Bach played the organ at Potsdam's Holy Ghost Church, a medium-size instrument built in 1730 by Johann Joachim Wagner. According to Forkel, "Bach was taken to all the organs in Potsdam," so he would also have performed—though not, apparently, in the king's presence—on the organs at the Garnison Church (a larger Wagner instrument of 1732, with forty-two stops on three manuals and pedal) and St. Nicholas's (an instrument by Johann Michael Röder, with twenty-three stops on two manuals and pedal). The composer then went on to Berlin, where he visited the four-year-old royal opera house Unter den Linden, built by the eminent architect Georg Wenzeslaus von Knobelsdorff. As Carl Philipp Emanuel later wrote to Forkel:

He came to Berlin to visit me; I showed him the new opera house. He perceived at once its virtues and defects (that is, as regards the sound of music in it). I showed him the great dining hall; we went up to the gallery that goes around the upper part of that hall. He looked at the ceiling, and without further investigation made the statement that the architect had here accomplished a remarkable feat, without intending to do so, and without anyone's knowing about it: namely, that if someone went to one corner of the oblong-shaped hall and whispered a few words very softly upward against the wall, a person standing in the corner diagonally opposite, with his face to the wall, would hear quite distinctly what was said, while between them, and in the other parts of the room, no one would hear a sound. A feat of architecture hitherto very rare and much admired! This effect was brought about by the arches in the vaulted ceiling, which he saw at once.[23]

So it did not escape Bach's remarkable power of observation that the dining hall of the Berlin opera house possessed the same peculiar acoustical qualities that he apparently remembered from the "mathematical art chamber," or *turris echonica* (echo tower), at the palace church in Weimar.[24]

Bach returned to Leipzig by May 18, when he is listed as a communicant at St. Thomas's. He then lost no time setting out to fulfill the promise made in Potsdam, which had already been carried by the press release of May 11, to set down the royal theme "on paper as a regular fugue and have it engraved on copper." We have every reason to believe that the theme Bach elaborated on and published as *Thema Regium* is substantially what the king presented to him on that memorable evening, even if its final version suggests Bach's polishing hand. And what was originally planned to be the published version of the fugue improvised before the king turned into a greatly expanded, multipart composition dedicated to his royal host under the title *Musical Offering,* BWV 1079 (see Table 12.1).

## TABLE 12.1. *Musical Offering,* BWV 1079: Contents

I. Two fugues *(Regis Iussu Cantio Et Reliqua Canonica Arte Resoluta):* keyboard
      Ricercar a 3, Ricercar a 6

II. Sonata: transverse flute, violin, continuo
      *Sonata sopr' Il Soggetto Reale*
      Largo—Allegro—Andante—Allegro

III. Various canons *(Thematis Regii Elaborationes Canonicae):* flute, violin, keyboard

| | |
|---|---|
| Canon 1. *a 2* (in retrograde motion) | *Fuga canonica* |
| Canon 2. *a 2* (in unison) | *Canon perpetuus* |
| Canon 3. *a 2* (in contrary motion) | *Canon perpetuus* |
| Canon 4. *a 2* (augmenting, in contrary motion) | *Canon a 2* |
| Canon 5. *a 2* (modulating) | *Canon a 4* |

The Potsdam event had a lasting effect on the wider concept of the work. Not only does the three-part Ricercar reflect the qualities of an improvised fugue, with traces of free paraphrasing between the more concentrated fugal expositions, Bach's choice of the term "ricercar" (from the Italian for "to search and research") as a heading was related to an ingenious Latin acrostic he designed to summarize the origin and character of the whole work: ***Regis Iussu Cantio Et Reliqua Canonica Arte Resoluta,*** meaning "At the king's demand, the song [that is, the fugue] and the remainder [the canonic movements] resolved with canonic art." Moreover, the motivic material of the interludes in the three-part Ricercar, significantly distinct from Bach's other keyboard works, was inspired by and conceived for the fortepiano and its new—unlike the harpsichord's—dynamically flexible sound. The six-part Ricercar is none other than the "fugue with six obbligato parts" requested by the king at the time, the improvisation of which Bach felt capable of approaching only with a theme he had chosen himself. The Trio Sonata must be understood as a special gift to the flute-playing monarch to enrich his chamber music repertoire, and the canonic settings are exemplary samples of Bach's contrapuntal craftsmanship, which called forth the king's and his musicians' great admiration. And two of the canons gave him the opportunity for emblematic references; in the king's dedication copy, Bach added by hand two meaningful Latin marginalia to the augmentation and modulation canons: "Notulis crescentibus crescat Fortuna Regis / Ascedenteque Modulatione ascendat Gloria Regis" (May the king's happiness grow with the augmenting notes, and with the rising modulation may the king's fame increase).

Bach completed the complex project in a relatively short time. The dedicatory preface dates from July 7, 1747, exactly two months after the Potsdam event, and respectfully addresses the "Monarch whose greatness and power, as in all the sciences of war and peace, so especially in music, everyone must admire and revere"—without missing an opportune moment to subtly link music and peace. The entire publication was ready by September 30, when the following announcement appeared in the newspapers:

Since the Royal Prussian Fugue Theme, as announced on May 11 of the current year by the Leipzig, Berlin, Frankfurt, and other gazettes, has now left the press, it shall be made known that the same may be obtained at the forthcoming Michaelmas Fair from the author, Capellmeister Bach, as well as from his two sons in Halle and Berlin, at the price of 1 imperial taler. The elaboration consists 1.) In two fugues, one with three, the other with six obbligato parts; 2.) In a sonata for transverse flute, violin, and continuo; 3.) In diverse canons, among which is a *fuga canonica*.[25]

The *Musical Offering* is not a cyclical work with a binding movement sequence, but rather comprises various solo and ensemble pieces, with each individual setting based on the royal theme. It was the composer's aim to treat this theme in the most varied manner, from free-style to the very strictest contrapuntal technique, from old-style counterpoint (notably in the six-part Ricercar) to the most modern mannerisms. The slow middle movement of the sonata in particular, with its melodically twisted, rhythmically differentiated, harmonically surprising, and dynamically shaded gestures, demonstrates impressively how Bach could easily match the musical language of *Empfindsamkeit* (sensitivity), so fashionable among his younger Berlin colleagues, and even outclass them. As a whole, the *Musical Offering* proves that "the old Bach," as he was received in Potsdam, did not just dreamily follow esoteric arts but was still the brilliant virtuoso musician and the master of all compositional methods. In some ways, the work conceals a musical self-portrait: of a composer in his capacity as keyboard genius and master of fugue, capellmeister and chamber musician, contrapuntalist and musical scholar.

There is no record of Bach's having received from the Prussian court any kind of acknowledgment, let alone monetary present, for his dedication, as the custom of the time would have dictated, though he may have been given a present while still in Potsdam. We know, however, that he ordered a print run of two hundred copies, absorbed all the costs, distributed most of them *"gratis* to good friends" (as Bach put it a year later), and sold the remainder for 1 taler per copy so that he would make at least a small profit.[26]

The opportunity for much more lucrative business, however, lurked behind contacts that emerged in the spring of 1749 with Johann Adam von Questenberg, a cultured and immensely wealthy patrician with residences in the Moravian countryside, Prague, and Vienna. Himself a practicing lutenist,

Questenberg had musical connections with Johann Joseph Fux, Antonio Caldara, Francesco Conti, and later also with Christoph Willibald Gluck. At his main residence some sixty miles northwest of Vienna, the large palace in Jaromerice, the imperial count maintained a substantial ensemble that regularly played chamber music and also performed operas and oratorios.[27] Questenberg asked the young Moravian count Franz Ernst von Wallis, an acquaintance who was studying law at Leipzig University, to get in touch with Bach on his behalf. On April 2, Wallis informed Questenberg that the mission was accomplished: "I inquired in different places about Mr. Bach's residence and, the information having been obtained, the Lieutenant went to him in person in order to transmit the messages, as reported in the letter. He was greatly pleased to receive news from your Excellency, as his generous benefactor, and asked me to forward the enclosed letter. . . . The letter of the Herr *Musique-Director* will convey the various matters that Your Excellency has wanted to know."[28] The wording of the letter, especially Bach's reference to "his generous benefactor," suggests a relationship with the count of longer standing. Nevertheless, whatever Questenberg actually wanted from Bach—probably a commissioned piece or a performance, doubtless for a substantial fee—serious health problems that Bach developed toward the middle of 1749 thwarted any plans in the making.

## THE ART OF FUGUE, THE B-MINOR MASS, AND A PLACE IN HISTORY

Between 1737 and 1739, off and on, Bach was drawn into the aesthetic dispute, provoked by Johann Adolph Scheibe, over his music and artistry. As much as bystanders may have viewed the literary battle between Scheibe and Birnbaum (on Bach's behalf) as a tempest in a tea pot,[29] Bach did not remain unaffected by it. Also, and to Bach's annoyance, the controversy was unduly kept alive for an extended period by Scheibe, who reprinted most of the exchange in 1745 in his periodical *Der Critische Musicus.* In this dispute, the decisive issue for Bach was his concept of the nature of music, as formulated by Birnbaum:

The true amenity of music consists in the connection and alternation of consonances and dissonances without hurt to the harmony. The nature of music demands this. The various passions, especially the dark ones, cannot be expressed with fidelity to Nature without this alternation. One would be doing violence to the rules of composition accepted everywhere if one wished to slight it. Indeed, the well-founded opinion of a musical ear that does not follow the vulgar taste values such alternation, and rejects the insipid little ditties that consist of nothing but consonances as something of which one very soon becomes tired.[30]

In Bach's view of nature and harmony, the connection and alternation of consonances and dissonances was governed by counterpoint. And it is the timeless value of counterpoint, way beyond the scope of old and new techniques, styles, or manners of composing, that he thought needed to be upheld. Through Birnbaum, the royal court *compositeur* spoke with authority, and, perhaps even more than before, Bach's compositions written or revised during and after the Scheibe-Birnbaum controversy reflect a deliberate emphasis on the principles of counterpoint. As demonstrated in the concluding quodlibet of the *Goldberg Variations,* even popular tunes could be governed and indeed enhanced by these time-tested rules.

Nowhere, however, could the principles of counterpoint be more richly applied than in the composition of fugue. In this genre, Bach not only excelled, peerlessly, but set new standards of technique, form, and performance. Characteristically, King Friedrich asked him to improvise a fugue, so commonly identified was Bach with the genre. Bach knew both what had been achieved by others in this branch of composition and where his own contributions had a particular impact. He could see that to a considerable extent, his place in history would be that of "fugue master." Thus, it should hardly surprise us that he devised a plan that would center systematically on fugal composition—unlike *The Well-Tempered Clavier,* without preludes—something neither he nor anyone else had ever done before. Moreover, in designing something like a vocal counterpart, he turned to the timeless genre of the Mass as the type of composition that would most readily lend itself to exclusively contrapuntal treatment.

*The Art of Fugue* and the *B-minor Mass* conform to the ever-present Bachian intention of excelling beyond himself and others. *The Art of Fugue,* though linked to earlier fugue compositions, moves to a level that is utterly novel. The entire multisectional work is derived from the same thematic material, a musical plan that presupposes a far-reaching thought process regarding the harmonic-contrapuntal implications of the chosen theme. The result is more than a study of fugue: it is a compendium of the range offered by the utmost concentration and the highest technical demands of instrumental counterpoint. The *B-minor Mass* figures as a fully comparable counterpart. Its dimensions correspond to those of the *St. Matthew Passion,* but the Mass stands out, not just for its dominant choral fugues but for its exclusive focus on contrapuntal settings. It features a dynamic interplay of unparalleled dimensions, pitting vocal against instrumental counterpoint and vice versa, exposing styles conceived both vocally and instrumentally, and integrating many different vocal textures, with and without obbligato instruments, into a large-scale, complex score that has no room for such "lower" categories as recitatives and note-against-note chorale settings.

Two compositional projects played a major role in shaping Bach's work on

*The Art of Fugue: The Well-Tempered Clavier,* whose score accommodated many but not all fugal devices, and the *Goldberg Variations,* which exhibited the potential of a multimovement monothematic cycle. Thus, in the absence of a datable composing score of *The Art of Fugue,* we can logically trace its true genesis to the beginning of the 1740s, when the composition of both part II of *The Well-Tempered Clavier* and part IV of the *Clavier-Übung* were completed. Indeed, an early version of *The Art of Fugue* emerged by around 1742, when Bach made a fair copy of the work.[31]

The governing idea of the work, whose title came later (the title page of the autograph fair copy was originally left blank), was an exploration in depth of the contrapuntal possibilities inherent in a single musical subject. The carefully constructed subject would generate many movements, each demonstrating one or more contrapuntal principles and each, therefore, resulting in a self-contained fugal form. Bach selected the key of D minor (closely related to the traditional first, or Dorian, mode) and crafted an easily identifiable subject with distinct melodic contours and a sharp rhythmic profile, whose regular and inverted versions, if sounding together in a contrapuntal relationship, resulted in flawless and attractive harmony, and whose chordal structure presented a pivotal cadential scheme (Ex. 12.1).

In the course of the work, the main subject (theme) would be joined by various kinds of derived and freely invented counterpoints, would itself be gradually subjected to variation, and would also be combined with contrasting countersubjects (new themes).

The early version of *The Art of Fugue* (still without title)[32] comprised a total of fourteen movements (also lacking headings), which can be regarded as a complete cycle in that the twelve fugues and two canons present a rational order and well-rounded structure (the first column in Table 12.2 indicates the movement sequence in Roman numerals). Its overall organizational design is based on two points.

First, types of counterpoint are introduced according to increasing difficulty and complexity, and sometimes—if particularly significant—are designated in customary Latin or Italian terminology (in the later printed edition): *per augmentationem et diminutionem* = with the subject in augmented (doubled) and diminished (halved) note values; *in contrario motu* = with the entire part in contrary motion; *contrapunctus inversus* = the entire setting inverted, that is, read in mirror image; *in contrapunto alla terza, quinta, decima,* or *duodecima* = the distance between the subject and its counterpoint at the interval of the third, fifth, tenth, or twelfth.

Second, Bach gradually increases the animation of the subject, giving us a sense of developing variations, with the rhythmic-metric arrangement adding a new dimension to the compositional makeup of the movements.

The changing rhythmic-melodic textures contribute significantly to the overall stylistic variety of the work, which takes as its point of departure the classic simplicity reminiscent of sixteenth-century counterpoint, then touches on prominent models such as the French style, and proceeds to the most so-

TABLE 12.2. *The Art of Fugue,* BWV 1080: Synopsis of Earlier and Later Versions

| Earlier Version: Autograph MS (1742)[a] | Later Version: Original Edition (1751) | Structural Design of Later Version |
|---|---|---|
| I | *Contrapunctus 1* | Simple fugues: main theme |
| III | *Contrapunctus 2* | introduced in regular |
| II | *Contrapunctus 3* | or inverted form |
| — | *Contrapunctus 4* | |
| IV | *Contrapunctus 5* | Counterfugues: main |
| VII | *Contrapunctus 6 a 4 in Style Francese* | theme introduced together with its inversion |
| VIII | *Contrapunctus 7 a 4 per Augment: et Diminut:* | |
| X | *Contrapunctus 8 a 3* | Fugues with multiple themes: main theme |
| V | *Contrapunctus 9 a 4 alla Duodecima* | combined with countersubjects |
| VI | *Contrapunctus 10 a 4 alla Decima*[b] | |
| XI | *Contrapunctus 11 a 4* | |
| XIII | *Contrapunctus inversus 12 a 4* | Mirror fugues: complete |
| XIV | *Contrapunctus inversus 13 a 3* | score inverted |
| IX | *Canon alla Ottava* | Canons |
| — | *Canon alla Decima in Contrapunto alla Terza* | |
| — | *Canon alla Duodecima in Contrapunto alla Quinta* | |
| XII | *Canon per Augmentationem in Contrario Motu*[c] | |
| — | *Fuga a 3 Soggetti [Contrapunctus 14]*[d] | [Fugue with multiple themes] |

[a]Movement sequence indicated by Roman numerals.
[b]Original edition: In addition to the later version, the earlier version is erroneously included.
[c]Original edition: The augmentation canon is erroneously placed at the beginning of canon group.
[d]Original edition: Incomplete (quadruple) fugue, followed by the chorale "Wenn wir in höchsten Nöthen sein."

phisticated contemporary mannerisms, as exposed particularly in the translucent web of the capricious two-part canons:

| Movements of earlier version | | Movements of later version |
|---|---|---|
| I, II | *[musical notation in cut time]* | 1, 3, 4 |
| III | *[musical notation in cut time]* | 2 |
| IV | *[musical notation in cut time]* | 5 |
| V | *[musical notation in common time]* [c 𝅝 \| 𝅝 \| etc.] | 9 |
| VI | *[musical notation in common time]* ← | 7 |
| VII | *[musical notation in common time]* | 6 |
| VI, VII, VIII | *[musical notation in common time]* ← (dim.) [c ♩ ♩. ♪ \| ♩. ♪♪ ] | 6, 7, 10 |
| VIII | *[musical notation in common time]* ← (augm.) | 7 |
| IX | *[musical notation in 9/16]* | (14) |
| X, XI | *[musical notation in 2/4]* [¢ 𝄾 ♩♩♩ \| 𝄾 ♩♩♩ \| etc.] | 8, 11 |
| XII | *[musical notation in common time]* [¢ ♫♩ ♩ ♫ etc.] | (17) |
| XIII | *[musical notation in 3/4]* [3/2 ♩ 𝅝 \| etc.] | 12 |
| XIV | *[musical notation in 2/4]* [c ♩ \| ♩ ♩♫ etc.] | (13) |
| | *[musical notation in 12/8]* | (15) |
| | *[musical notation in cut time]* | (16) |

The autograph fair copy from around 1742 represents *The Art of Fugue* in this fourteen-movement version. Bach, however, clearly fascinated by the work's perplexing challenges and unique opportunities, continued to develop it. Between 1742 and 1746, he revised and expanded individual movements—notably the fugues nos. I–III, which received longer concluding sections, and the augmentation canon no. XII, which was completely rewritten. He also added four entirely new movements, two fugues and two canons. The revisions and additions considerably broadened the conceptual and compositional dimensions of the work. For example, the newly composed Contrapunctus 4, added to the group of simple fugues, introduced a highly innovative modification of the inverted theme by breaking traditional rules of interval order (Ex. 12.2).

This change allowed the subject to trigger modulations, within the key of

D minor, to E major and B major, an unprecedented expansion of the harmonic spectrum. Bach also added a quadruple fugue (mislabeled "Fuga a 3 soggetti" in the original edition) in which he presented, as the third theme, a subject constructed on the musical letters of his own name: B-A-C-H (B and H being the German note names for B-flat and B-natural).[33] This chromatic motive permitted him to explore chromatic harmony, prevalent in a number of movements, on a plain thematic level as well—apart from the fact that the B-A-C-H theme emphatically personalized the work. But, most important, Bach completely reorganized the work so that the various movements make up a practical textbook on fugue in five chapters: simple fugues, counterfugues, multiple-theme fugues, mirror fugues, and canons—remarkably predating any theoretical textbook on the subject.

It was at this point, in 1747 or later, that Bach formulated the title *Die Kunst der Fuga* (added in the hand of his son-in-law Altnickol to the autograph fair copy of the earlier version) or, entirely Germanized, *Die Kunst der Fuge* (the title of the 1751 edition).[34] Although the title does not appear in Bach's own hand, there is no reason to doubt its authenticity. Moreover, the fact that he used the term "contrapunctus" for the individual fugues indicates that he wanted the pieces to be seen not exclusively as fugues but, more generally, as examples of contrapuntal settings.[35] Bach intended, probably from the start, to publish the work. However, not before 1748, and definitely after the publication of the *Musical Offering,* the *Canonic Variations on "Vom Himmel hoch,"* and the Schübler Chorales, was *The Art of Fugue* ready to go into production. For the most part, Bach was able to supervise the engraving process, even though he would not see it through to the end. A note written posthumously on the proof sheets by his second-youngest son, Johann Christoph Friedrich, indicates how meticulously Bach went about movement headings:

Canon p[er] Augmentationem contrario motu.
NB: The late Papa had the following heading engraved on the plate: "Canon per Augment: in Contrapuncto all ottave," but he had crossed it out on the proof plate and put it in the above-noted form.[36]

Bach apparently composed the quadruple fugue as an afterthought while the engraving of *The Art of Fugue* was already in progress. The composing manuscript, which dates from 1748–49, belongs among the latest musical manuscripts from Bach's hand, and its unfinished state (it breaks off after 239 measures) may tempt us to think that death stayed the composer's pen. Even Carl Philipp Emanuel was misled, as shown in a note he appended many years later to the last manuscript page: "NB. While working on this fugue, in which the Name BACH appears in the countersubject, the author died."[37] But the incomplete form in which the fugue has been transmitted does not correspond to what actually existed at the time of Bach's death. Before composing the quadruple fugue, Bach would have had to test the combinatorial possibilities of the four themes. His draft of such contrapuntal combinations has not survived, but a description, at least, of the composer's intentions is included in the Obituary, which mentions the "draft" for a fugue that "was to contain four themes and to have been afterward inverted note for note in all four voices."[38] From this statement, we can reasonably surmise that *The Art of Fugue* at the time of Bach's death was less incomplete than what has come down to us. But whatever the lost draft contained, it must not have been sufficiently worked out to bring the quadruple fugue to an end.

Nevertheless, even in its unfinished state, *The Art of Fugue* stands before us as the most comprehensive summary of the aged Bach's instrumental language. At the same time, it is a highly personal statement; the letters BACH woven into the final movement represent much more than a fanciful signature. Theory and practice merge in this work. By letting the substance of the musical subject be logically uncovered and systematically exhausted, by employing traditional and novel techniques of composition as well as old and new elements of style, Bach created an autonomous work of art that embodies the character and universality of his art. The significance of the work at an important historical moment was captured well by Marpurg in dedicating the second volume of his own fugal treatise to the two elder Bach sons:

I take the liberty of laying before Your Honors the principles of an art that owes its improvement particularly to the excellent efforts of your famous Father. One need not look back even half a century to discover the happy moment when a beginning was made of combining imaginative harmonic changes with an agreeable and unified melody [referring to the new Italian style of the Vivaldi generation]. At the very time when the world was beginning to degenerate in another direction, when light melody making was gaining the upper hand and people were becoming tired of difficult harmonies, the late Capellmeister was the one who knew how to keep to the golden mean, and taught us how to combine an agreeable and flowing melody with the richest harmonies.[39]

The grand-scale project of *The Art of Fugue* seems to have occupied the composer's mind throughout the last decade of his life. Seen in this light, however, the work is less the crowning conclusion of a representative series of monothematic compositions (beginning with the *Goldberg Variations* and including the *Musical Offering* and the *"Vom Himmel hoch" Variations*) than the conceptual background and theoretical underpinning for many of Bach's works written during the 1740s. Yet the language of *The Art of Fugue,* despite its remarkably broad stylistic palette, is marked by significantly greater systematization, concentration, and abstraction than any of the other monothematic instrumental cycles, let alone the magnificent *B-minor Mass*. Nevertheless, the Mass similarly reflects a long-term engagement and—within the limitations dictated by vocal composition, a fixed liturgical genre, and a long historical tradition—a comparable systematic musical exploration that Bach defined for himself.

Bach's grandiose plan to set a solemn Mass can already be discerned in the layout of the Kyrie-Gloria Mass of 1733 (Table 12.3). This aim is apparent in the five-part texture of the vocal writing, the large orchestral contingent, and especially the sophisticated design of its individual movements. The opening three-movement Kyrie group clearly proclaims the composer's ambition: Kyrie I is an extended fugue with obbligato orchestra, the Christe adopts the style of a contemporary opera duet, and Kyrie II draws on retrospective vocal counterpoint, thereby relegating the orchestra to the role of doubling the choral parts. The entire Kyrie complex shows the great value Bach placed on highly contrasting compositional styles and techniques. Its movements also outline a sequence of keys from B minor to D major to F-sharp minor, forming a B-minor triad, thereby signaling a broadly conceived harmonic scheme for the entire work that centers on D major (the trumpet key).

The Gloria complex of the musically self-contained Kyrie-Gloria Mass of 1733 resolutely builds on the stylistic variety of the Kyrie group by offering four large-scale choruses ("Gloria in excelsis / Et in terra pax," "Gratias agimus tibi," "Qui tollis peccata mundi," "Cum sancto spiritu") interspersed with four equally large-scale solo movements with obbligato instruments, each with a full polyphonic orchestral accompaniment. Thus, the Gloria section gives a solo aria to each concertist of the five-voiced choir and an obbligato part to each family of instruments in the orchestra (strings, flutes, reeds, and brass): combining solo soprano II with solo violin ("Laudamus"), soprano I and tenor with flute ("Domine Deus"), alto with oboe d'amore ("Qui sedes"), and bass with horn ("Quoniam").

When did Bach begin to expand his Kyrie-Gloria Mass into a complete setting of the Mass? A possible clue lies in an early version of the Credo intonation,[40] but this merely indicates that the Credo added to the Mass during the years 1748–49 had a prehistory. We do know that in the late 1730s and early 1740s, Bach copied, performed, and examined numerous Masses by composers ranging in time from Palestrina to his own contemporaries.[41] For example, he performed the six-voice *Missa sine nomine* by Palestrina, with added cornettos, trombones, and continuo, and the *Missa sapientiae* by Antonio Lotti. And compositional studies with a direct impact on the *B-minor Mass* include a "Credo in unum Deum" intonation, BWV 1081, added to a Mass in F major by Giovanni Battista Bassani, and a contrapuntal expansion of the "Suscepit Israel"

## TABLE 12.3. *Mass in B Minor*

| Movement (solo: indented) | Key | Scoring | Adapted from: |
|---|---|---|---|
| **No. 1. Missa** [1733]: SSATB; 3tr/ti, cor da caccia, 2trav, 2ob (d'am), 2bs, str, bc | | | |
| (1) Kyrie eleison | B minor | tutti [- brass] | Kyrie (?) in C minor |
| (2) Christe eleison | D major | S1–2 + v1–2, bc | |
| (3) Kyrie eleison | F-sharp minor | tutti [-brass], instruments *colla parte* | |
| (4) Gloria in excelsis | D major | tutti | |
| (5) Et in terra pax | D major | tutti | |
| (6) Laudamus te | A major | S2 + v solo, bc | |
| (7) Gratias agimus tibi | D major | tutti | BWV 29/1 |
| (8) Domine Deus | G major | S1, T + trav solo, str, bc | |
| (9) Qui tollis | B minor | choir + 2trav, str, bc | BWV 46/1 |
| (10) Qui sedes | B minor | A + ob d'am solo, bc | |
| (11) Quoniam | D major | B + cor da caccia, bs 1–2, bc | |
| (12) Cum Sancto Spiritu | D major | tutti | |
| **No. 2. Symbolum Nicenum** [1748–49]: SSATB; 3tr/ti, 2trav, 2ob (d'am), str, bc | | | |
| (13) Credo in | A-Mixolydian | choir + 2v, bc | Credo in G-Mixolydian |
| (14) Patrem | D major | tutti | BWV 171/1 |
| (15) Et in unum | G major | S1, A + ob d'am 1–2, str, bc | |
| (16) Et incarnatus est | B minor | choir + 2v, bc | |
| (17) Crucifixus | E minor | choir + 2trav, str, bc | BWV 12/2 |
| (18) Et resurrexit | D major | tutti | BWV Anh./9/1 (?) |
| (19) Et in Spiritum | A major | B + ob d'am 1–2, bc | |
| (20) Confiteor | F-sharp minor | choir + bc | |
| (21) Et expecto | D major | tutti | BWV 120/2 |
| **No. 3. Sanctus** [1724]: SSAATB; 3tr/ti, 3ob, str, bc | | | |
| (22) Sanctus | D major | tutti | Sanctus (SSSATB), 1724 |
| **No. 4. Osanna, Benedictus, Agnus Dei and Dona nobis pacem** [1748–49]: SATB I, SATB II; 3tr/ti, 2trav, 2ob, str, bc | | | |
| (23) Osanna | D major | tutti | BWV Anh. 11/1 |
| (24) Benedictus | B minor | T + trav solo, bc | |
| (25) Osanna (rep.) | D major | tutti | |
| (26) Agnus Dei | G minor | A + 2v, bc | BWV Anh. 196/3 |
| (27) Dona nobis pacem | D major | tutti | BWV 232/7 |

movement, BWV 1082, in a Magnificat setting by Antonio Caldara. In its first version, the Symbolum Nicenum (Credo section) of the *B-minor Mass* comprised only eight movements, as the duet setting of "Et in unum Dominum" also incorporated the text portion "et incarnatus est . . ." After finishing this duet, however, and possibly after finishing the entire score of the Symbolum, Bach decided to reapportion the text underlay of the duet, free up the "et incarnatus est" section, and compose a separate movement for this liturgically pivotal text traditionally treated with special musical emphasis. In its overall design, now comprising nine movements, the Symbolum gained a strengthened symmetrical layout. Bach turned what had been a 2+1+2+1+2 design (eight movements, choruses boldface) into an architecture of 2+1+3+1+2.

The Symbolum opens and closes with a pair of contrasting choruses: "Credo" (motet, on the liturgical chant) together with "Patrem omnipotentem" (concertato fugue) at the start, and "Confiteor" (likewise on the liturgical chant) together with "Et expecto" (again, concertato fugue) at the end. By including two settings in an emphatically retrospective style ("Credo" and "Confiteor") based on medieval chant, Bach added a theological, historical, and compositional dimension that the Kyrie-Gloria Mass of 1733 lacked. Thus, in setting the chants, Bach uses the (musical) canon technique in order to accent the (liturgical) canonical value of the Mass text in general and the Nicene Creed in particular, while the archaic style of the two cantus firmus settings allows the work to embrace a wide span of the compositional history of the Mass genre. In the theological realm, we find that following the "Confiteor," which is set in imitative counterpoint, two different settings of the text "Et expecto resurrectionem" (And I await the resurrection) draw a line between "the expecting" and "the expected": an expressive Adagio, filled with unprecedented chromatic and enharmonic devices that illustrate the suffering in this world, contrasting with an upbeat Vivace that portrays, in anticipation, the life of the world to come. The two framing choral pairs of the Symbolum are each adjoined by two arias that function as connecting links to the central choral complex. This center emphasizes in a musically persuasive way the Christological core of the Nicene Creed: "And he was made incarnate," "He was crucified," "And he was resurrected."

This central group of three choruses includes both the oldest and the most recent compositions of the entire Mass: "Crucifixus," a movement based on the chorus "Weinen, Klagen, Sorgen, Zagen" from cantata BWV 12 of 1714, and "Et incarnatus est," an inserted afterthought and apparently Bach's last choral setting, dating from 1749. In the scheme of things, the "Crucifixus" coming immediately after "Et incarnatus est" would seem to threaten a stylistic and aesthetic clash of incompatible music.[42] Bach, however, avoids such a conflict: he subtly links the two movements by providing both with a similar structural underpinning, and unifies them by using a repeated melodic pattern in each. The six-note violin figure that shapes the "Et incarnatus est" from beginning to end (and, for the concluding measures, even slips into three-part canonic counterpoint) gives way to the seven-note ostinato bass line of the "Crucifixus."

The Sanctus and the movements that follow it date from the time the score of the Mass was completed in 1748–49. All of them, however, derive from earlier works. The Sanctus was originally written for Christmas 1724, though in a slightly different scoring for three sopranos, alto, tenor, and bass. The "Osanna" derives from a secular cantata movement dating from 1732, and the Benedictus from an unknown original. Even the Agnus Dei is a parody of a 1725 cantata movement; however, not only does it evince substantive changes, it also contains newly composed passages, such as the entrance of the alto in canon with the unison strings, a genuine tour de force in enhancing a parody with new material.[43] This case strikingly documents Bach's intention to improve where necessary, the contrapuntal structure of the work. Finally, the "Dona nobis pacem," being a musical reprise of the "Gratias agimus tibi," shows evidence both of Bach's understanding of this final section of the Ordinary of the Mass—a song of thanksgiving—and of his artistic intention to round off a work that originated over decades, but whose separate sections were now put together to form a whole. Even so, the paper dividers—that is, the numbered autograph title pages inserted for all four Mass sections (Table 12.3, boldface subheadings)—and the noticeable differences in the scoring of the various sections preserve traces of the work's genesis.

In the completed score, which embraces a wide spectrum of vocal-instrumental polyphony, Bach was able to underline what he perceived as the timeless validity of the liturgical and musical meaning of the ancient Mass. Hence, the multiple compositional styles that constitute the B-minor Mass cannot be reduced to a mere historical anthology of exemplary settings. True, where Bach borrowed from existing music, he selected from among the best he had. To some extent, he may also have been guided by the aspect of preservation, for he could see very well the difference between the short-lived fashions of the German cantatas on the one hand and the longevity of the Latin Mass on the other—not to mention the parochial qualities of the cantatas vis-à-vis the universality of the Mass. So he chose this most historical of all vocal genres to embody the *summa summarum* of his artistry, that of the capellmeister-cantor.

We know of no occasion for which Bach could have written the B-minor Mass, nor any patron who might have commissioned it, nor any performance of the complete work before 1750. Thus, Bach's last choral composition is in many respects the vocal counterpart to *The Art of Fugue,* the other side of the composer's musical legacy. Like no other work of Bach's, the *B-minor Mass* represents a summary of his writing for voice, not only in its variety of styles, compositional devices, and range of sonorities, but also in its high level of technical polish. The Mass offers a full panoply of the art of musical composition, with a breadth and depth betraying not only theoretical perspicacity but also a comprehensive grasp of music history, particularly in its use of old and new styles. Just as theological doctrine survived over the centuries in the words of the Mass, so Bach's mighty setting preserved the musical and artistic creed of its creator for posterity.

## THE END

As far as we know, Bach suffered no serious illness at any point in his life, with the striking exception of the final year. A fever he ran in the summer of 1729 that prevented him from meeting Handel in Halle remains a minor isolated incident not linked to any continuing health pattern.[44] Indeed, the Obituary expressly emphasizes Bach's "thoroughly healthy" disposition.[45] Therefore, it comes as a total surprise when a letter of June 2, 1749, from the Saxon prime minister Heinrich von Brühl to the Leipzig burgomaster Jacob Born anticipates Bach's death—if not imminent, then eventual. Count Brühl did not mince words in requesting that the director of his private capelle, Gottlob Harrer, be considered for filling the post of *Capell-Director* in Leipzig, "upon the eventual . . . decease of Mr. Bach."[46] The bearer of the letter was none other than Harrer himself, who, as Brühl wrote, was "the candidate I recommended to Your Honor when I was in Leipzig." Clearly, Bach's succession had already been discussed, so the Leipzig city council could swiftly respond to the mighty Dresden minister. Paying no attention to issues of propriety (mixing private and government business) or of tact and taste (bypassing the ill incumbent), the council quickly obliged and arranged for an almost immediate audition. Harrer had brought along an audition piece whose reception was more or less pre-programmed, as Brühl, in a postscript, expressed no doubt that "the trial music to be performed . . . will meet with approbation." An irony of history seems to have been at work here: the city council, which had taken the clergy by surprise in putting through its own candidate as Kuhnau's successor, now found itself being steamrolled by the Saxon prime minister.

By order of the council, Harrer's pro forma audition took place on Wednesday, June 8, at the Three Swans, a concert hall on the avenue Am Brühl generally used by the Grand Concert organization. Most council members attended what was billed as a "trial performance for the future appointment as Cantor of St. Thomas's, in case the Capellmeister and Cantor Mr. Sebastian

Bach should die."[47] The candidate presented his cantata "Der Reiche starb und ward begraben" (The rich man died and was buried),[48] a work that to no one's surprise met "with the greatest applause." Harrer returned to Dresden with a certificate assuring him that "in the said eventuality" he would "not be passed over"[49]—which indeed he would not, although the said eventuality occurred a full thirteen months later. The premature audition was extraordinary in every respect. The cantata performance had to take place on a weekday and outside the church because the incumbent cantor was still in charge of the regular church music program, and if he himself was unable to conduct, his first prefect would step in for him. Moreover, it is unlikely that Harrer had access to the first choir of the St. Thomas School for his audition, and the availability of Bach's best instrumentalists was questionable too, as the cooperation of Bach loyalists in general and the cantor in particular—no matter how ill and weak he may have been— could hardly have been expected. Bach had little choice but to perceive the whole affair as a humiliating gesture by the city council. He may not have been aware that the council had acted under direct pressure from Dresden; had he learned about it early on, he might have been all the more disgusted with the council's spineless action. He eventually realized what had happened, or was told about Count Brühl's role, a fact that did not encourage him to develop a forgiving attitude toward the council.

Bach's health must have quickly reached a crisis in the late spring of 1749. For the city of Leipzig, the matter was so important that Burgomaster Born reported it to the Saxon prime minister; and even if the city council clearly overreacted, we have no reason to believe that they were misled by an exaggerated assessment of Bach's illness, whose exact nature still lies in the dark. The Obituary writers are of little help in relating that "his naturally somewhat weak eyesight, further weakened by his unheard-of zeal in studying, which made him, particularly in his youth, sit at work the whole night through, led in his last years, to an eye disease."[50] Forkel reports that the weakness of his eyes "continually increased in his later years till at length it brought on a very painful disorder in the eyes."[51] But although overstressing the eyes over a long period of time may indeed cause serious damage, it would hardly bring on a life-threatening illness. No reliable medical diagnosis can be made in retrospect on the basis of such scanty information, but the most convincing hypothesis suggests an old-age-related diabetic condition as the origin of Bach's final illness.[52] Untreated diabetes may result in neuropathy, encephalosis, eye pains, vision problems, inflammation of the optic nerves, glaucoma, cataracts, or blindness. Intermittent hypoglycemia, which characteristically leads to an alternating intensifying and subsiding of the various symptoms, would account for temporary improvements reported in Bach's deteriorating eyesight and the observable changes in his handwriting.

Whatever condition it was that afflicted Bach does not appear to have reduced his capacity for work before 1749. A letter of November 2, 1748, to his cousin Elias seems to have been written in a relaxed mood. Besides bringing up the mishap with the wine shipment from Franconia (see Chapter 11), he regrets the great distance between Leipzig and Schweinfurt,[53] writing that "otherwise I should take the liberty of humbly inviting my honored Cousin to the marriage of my daughter Lieschen, which will take place in the coming month of January 1749, to the new organist in Naumburg, Mr. Altnickol."[54] Bach also mentions the fact that recently "Magister Birnbaum was buried," but says not a word about eye pains or any other health troubles that might cast in doubt his enjoyment of the forthcoming wedding—the first one for any of his daughters. But the letter clearly shows a sudden worsening of his handwriting style, with irregular lettering, frequently slurred abbreviations, and a noticeable stiffness.[55] On the other hand, we have no evidence that any developing health problem affected his official duties and private business through much of the spring of 1749. The letter of April 2, 1749, written by Franz Ernst von Wallis, whose lieutenant had contacted Bach on behalf of Count Questenberg, reports nothing about his being ill.[56] Two days later, Bach performed his *St. John Passion* with an increased ensemble. In the same month, he also held a conference at his house with the organ builder Heinrich Andreas Cuntzius,[57] and on May 6 he issued a receipt to a Polish nobleman for the sale of a fortepiano.[58] However, that Bach put only his signature on this document, which was otherwise written by his son Friederich, indicates that he was avoiding an unnecessary task. We can conclude, then, that Bach's work capacity became truly diminished in April 1749 and that toward the middle of May his health deteriorated so rapidly and alarmingly that city officials considered making provisions in case he should die.

But Bach pulled through this first serious health crisis, and did so soon after the ill-conceived audition of Harrer for the cantorate. For only twelve days later, on June 19, the second Sunday after Trinity, he partook of the Lord's Supper at St. Thomas's together with his sons Friederich and Christian.[59] Then on August 25, for the annual city council election service, he performed one of his most ambitious works ever written for this purpose, the cantata "Wir danken dir, Gott, wir danken dir," BWV 29, a piece involving not only a large orchestra with trumpets and timpani but also, in the opening sinfonia, concertato organ. Bach conceivably played the ambitious solo part himself, if only to show the assembled town officials and representatives from Dresden that he was not only still around but fully capable of demonstrating the unmatched quality of his art. In preparing the performance material for this cantata, he wrote out—in what was by now his clumsy hand—a new set of figures for the continuo part of the sinfonia (indicating that he himself certainly did not play that part) and had his youngest son Christian write out a second continuo part (suggesting that the fourteen-year-old was also to be involved in the performance). In selecting this work, Bach would unquestionably have related the opening words of the cantata text, "We give thee thanks, God, and proclaim to the world thy wonders" (Psalm 72:2)[60] to his own recovery from serious illness and to God Almighty's being above any worldly authority.

The late summer or fall of 1749 saw Bach involved in another musical demonstration, apparently in direct response to the Biedermann affair and at the same time to the audition of Count Brühl's protégé Harrer. Considering the circumstances, Bach's re-performance of "The Contest between Phoebus and Pan," BWV 201—a work exposing both high and low musical art and good and poor artistic judgment—was most fitting, and the composer, at his feisty best, took the opportunity to provide a scarcely hidden autobiographical undertone. Bach must have been able to mobilize what was now the "Gerlachische" Collegium Musicum, the ensemble of his associate and former student Carl Gotthelf Gerlach. Gerlach also functioned as first violinist of the Grand Concerts—the concert series usually held at the Three Swans—and it would indeed have been an ironic turn of events had Bach performed his Phoebus-and-Pan cantata in the same hall that had witnessed the presentation by Harrer.

The whole performance appears to have been deliberately planned down to the smallest detail by the deeply hurt Bach together with his family, students, and friends. The cantata's autograph score and a manuscript copy of Picander's libretto, written by the two youngest Bach sons, both contain a significant text variant in the concluding lines of the final recitative, in which Phoebus, the winner of the contest, is encouraged to embark on further efforts. The text change, made by Bach himself, shows his polemic bent (when called for) and his poetic vein, and even more his intimate familiarity with classical Latin literature. He invokes two infamous if rather obscure figures: Quintus Hortensius Hortalus (a Roman orator known for his overly profuse style and defeated by Cicero in the trial against Verres) and Lucius Orbilius Pupillus (Horace's teacher, known for beating up his students).[61]

*Picander's original:*

| | |
|---|---|
| Ergreiffe Phoebus nun die Leyer wieder, | Now, Phoebus, take up your lyre again; |
| Es ist nichts lieblicher als deine Lieder. | There is nothing lovelier than your songs. |

*Changed by Bach to:*

| | |
|---|---|
| Verdopple, Phöbus nun Musik und Lieder | Now, Phoebus, redouble music and songs, |
| Tobt gleich Hortensius und ein Orbil darwider. | Despite Hortens and Orbil raging against it. |

Here Bach introduces two truly historical figures as antagonists of the endangered species of music that Phoebus stands for. But the composer could not resist sharpening the punch line further just before the concluding chorus: he changed the last line once more to read "Tobt gleich Birolius und ein Hortens darwider." Just as he had played linguistically with the word "rector" in the Biedermann affair, he now manipulated the name Orbil(ius) into an anagram, Birolius—sounding awfully close to a dog-Latin version of the Saxon prime minister's name, Brühl.[62] There must have been enough people in the audience to get the wittily disguised innuendo so that Bach once again had the last laugh, this time in a double sense.

In a further response to the Harrer audition, probably considered by many in Leipzig to be an inappropriate if not illegitimate move, Bach seems to have organized a sort of counteroffensive by inviting his two older sons to present their own church compositions at St. Thomas's and St. Nicholas's on prominent feast days. Friedemann, by now established as organist and music director at Our Lady's in nearby Halle, performed his cantata "Lasset uns ablegen die Werke der Finsternis," Fk 80, on the first Sunday in Advent 1749.[63] Carl, harpsichordist of the Prussian court capelle in Berlin, composed—possibly at the request of his father for an anticipated Leipzig audition—his first sacred work, the Magnificat in D major, Wq 215. A St. Thomas pupil and participant in the performance, Johann Friedrich Sonnenkalb, recalled that it took place "at a Marian feast" and "still during his late father's lifetime."[64] Since Friedemann likely preceded his younger brother in performing his cantata, Carl's presentation would have occurred on either the Feast of Purification, February 2, or the Feast of the Annunciation, March 25, 1750.[65]

Apart from the politics, the two performances by Friedemann and Carl also helped unburden their ailing father from his regular duties, although Carl Gotthelf Gerlach, organist at the New Church, was available to support or substitute for the cantor, as was the erstwhile first prefect, Johann Nathanael Bammler, now a theology student at Leipzig University, who continued to serve as a copyist for Bach.[66] Beginning in 1747, Bach had entrusted Bammler with the cantor's duties whenever he was unable to conduct, as, for example, during his 1747 trip to Potsdam and Berlin. On April 12, 1749, Bach wrote him a good reference—the last extant document written entirely in Bach's hand[67]—in which he stated that "as a prefect he applied himself well both *vocaliter* and *instrumentaliter.*" Eight months later, Bach testified that he "could fully entrust him [Bammler] with the prefect's office for the choirs, as he directed the church music of the second choir for three years and, for his last year in school, likewise served as prefect of the first choir, too, and conducted not only the motets but also, in my absence, the entire church music."[68]

This letter, dated December 11, bears Bach's last known signature and as such represents the last dated bit from his pen; the document itself was not written by Bach but dictated by him. On the next (and last) known document dictated by Bach, dated December 27—a letter of thanks to Count Wilhelm of Schaumburg-Lippe for having accepted his son Johann Christoph Friedrich into his service—the signature was supplied by a scribal hand.[69] The signature on the December 11 letter in Bach's now stiff and clumsy handwriting indicates that writing gave him considerable trouble, raising the question of whether Bach was capable of composing and writing for much longer after that date.[70] We may then surmise that the last musical scores to stem from Bach's hand—parts II–IV of the *B-minor Mass* and the unfinished quadruple fugue from *The Art of Fugue*—were written no later than the first weeks of 1750. Only some of the earlier work on the Mass and *The Art of Fugue*, dating mainly from 1748–49, involved new composition, the rest consisting of parody and revision. Apart from inserted canonic sections of the Agnus Dei, the "Et incarnatus est" movement of the *B-minor Mass* is the last newly composed vocal setting by Bach. Its irregular, daringly innovative, and unique treatment of polyphonic imitation (Ex. 12.3) demonstrates Bach's unbroken creative ingenuity, contrapuntal command, and technical control in uncharted musical territory. Only one parallel case exists: Contrapunctus 4 of *The Art of Fugue,* with its similarly irregular but less pointed thematic treatment (see Example 12.3). Contrapunctus 4 together with the unfinished fugue and "Et incarnatus est," representing the final layer of original composition in Bach's creative life, probably date from the fall of 1749 to the turn of the year. But considering the apparent ups and downs in Bach's condition, some limited and unstressful work may have continued until about Easter 1750. In any case, the last traces of performances in which Bach had a hand appear in the form of minor changes entered by the composer in the original performance materials for the New Year's cantata BWV 16 and the *Easter Oratorio,* BWV 249, both of which may belong to either 1749 or 1750.

Bach was not totally incapacitated through much of the spring of 1750, but, as the Obituary relates, his eye troubles apparently became so serious and the pain so unbearable that

he wished to rid himself of this by an operation, partly out of a desire to be of further service to God and his neighbor with his other spiritual and bodily powers, which were still vigorous, and partly on the advice of some of his friends, who placed great confidence in an oculist who had recently arrived in Leipzig. But the operation, although it had to be repeated, turned out very badly. Not only could he no longer use his eyes, but his whole system, which was otherwise thoroughly healthy, was completely overthrown by the operation and by the addition of harmful medicaments and other things, so that, thereafter, he was almost continually ill for full half a year.[71]

Clearly, Bach was not ready to give up, and he possessed physical strength, psychic determination, faith in God, and great confidence in the most modern medical procedures. He offered himself as a patient to the famous English oculist Sir John Taylor, who in March 1750 came to the university town of Leipzig in order to lecture on and demonstrate his ophthalmological expertise and surgical skills. The first operation took place after March 28—when Taylor arrived in Leipzig—and before April 1, when the local newspapers reported:

This Saturday past, and again last night, the Chevalier Taylor gave public lectures at the concert hall in the presence of a considerable assembly of scholars and other important persons. The concourse of people who seek his aid is astonishing. Among others, he has operated upon Capellmeister Bach, who by constant use of his eyes had almost entirely deprived himself of their sight, and that with every success that could have been desired, so that he has recovered the full sharpness of his sight, an unspeakable piece of good fortune that many thousands of people will be very far from begrudging this world-famous composer and for which they cannot sufficiently thank Dr. Taylor.[72]

Taylor, a specialist in cataract operations, was well respected and by no means a medical charlatan. The operation performed on Bach seemed to have been successful, for the newspapers reported on April 4 that "his cures of the *medico* Dr. Koppen, of Capellmeister Bach, and of the merchant Mr. Meyer have been so particularly successful as to do him honor. The many patients who call upon him have caused him to postpone his departure until next Tuesday morning, when he proposes to leave for Potsdam, and to reach Berlin the following day."[73] As it turned out, however, the success was short-lived, as the operation had failed to produce the desired result. Between April 5 and 8 (Taylor's departure), Bach underwent a second operation, which, as the Obituary states, failed; matters were made worse by "harmful medicaments and other things," possibly including rubbing the eye with a brush and draining the eye and its surrounding area of blood, up to half a teacup full—treatments known to have been applied by Taylor.[74] A bulletin issued in May 1750 by the Leipzig Faculty of Medicine expresses restrained criticism of Taylor's operations,[75] focusing on the three prominent patients mentioned in the April 4 newspaper report. Accordingly, the operations on Kopp and Meyer were at least partially successful, whereas Bach was "suffering from bouts of inflammation and the like."[76] Taylor, who later operated on Handel as well, reported in 1761 on the operation he had performed on Bach. His account, though not exactly self-critical, let alone flawless, is still illuminating, in spite of its beginning with unconsciously comical analogies:

I have seen a vast variety of singular animals, such as dromedaries, camels, etc., and particularly at Leipsick, where a celebrated master of music, who had already arrived to his 88th [actually 66th] year, received his sight by my hands; it is with this very man that the famous Handel was first educated [erroneously taking Bach for Handel's teacher Zachow], and with whom I once thought to have had the same success, having all circumstances in his favor, motions of the pupil, light, etc., but upon drawing the curtain, we found the base defective, from a paralytic disorder.[77]

After the second operation, Bach's entire physical system fell into disarray, and he was "almost continually ill"—not for full half a year, as stated in the Obituary, but for a quarter. Nevertheless, his acceptance of Johann Gottfried Müthel, who arrived in Leipzig on May 4, as a boarding student again evinces his hopes of getting better; indeed, he probably found some welcome distraction by working with a good private pupil. Presumably, Bach was completely blind from early April until mid-July. Then,

ten days before his death his eyes suddenly seemed better, so that one morning he could see quite well again and could also again endure the light. But a few hours later he suffered a stroke; and this was followed by a raging fever, as victim of which, despite every possible care given him by two of the most skillful physicians of Leipzig, on July 28, 1750, a little after a quarter past eight in the evening, in the sixty-sixth year of his life, he quietly and peacefully, by the merit of his Redeemer, departed this life.[78]

From this report, it seems that Taylor's operation itself had not damaged Bach's eyes but that the postoperative treatment and subsequent inflammations had affected his whole body, which in addition may have been weakened by untreated diabetes. The two skilled physicians who were brought in—surely including Professor Samuel Theodor Quellmaltz, head of the Faculty of Medicine and a distinguished surgeon and ophthalmologist—were apparently unable to reverse Bach's decline.

In the immediate aftermath of the stroke that hit him on July 20, Bach realized that his end was near. Two days later, on the Wednesday following the eighth Sunday after Trinity, his longtime father confessor, D. Christoph Wolle, archdeacon at St. Thomas's, visited the cantor at his bedside and administered the sacrament. During his final week, Bach thought of his organ chorale "Wenn wir in höchsten Nöten sein" (When we are in the greatest distress), BWV 668. Having set the piece long before and knowing his hymnal better than most, he realized that its original sixteenth-century melody also used to be sung to the text of "Vor deinen Thron tret ich hiermit" (Before your throne

I now appear), a prayer hymn first published in 1646 for morning, midday, and evening use.[79] He had originally composed "Wenn wir in höchsten Nöten sein" in Weimar for his *Orgel-Büchlein* and then expanded the twelve-measure chorale (BWV 641) to a setting of forty-five measures, under the same title (BWV 668a). In this version, it belonged to the collection of large-scale organ chorales known as the "Great Eighteen," which he revised later in Leipzig, mainly in the years 1739–42. The texts of the two hymns complement each other, so that the expressive character of Bach's setting fits both equally well. But the text that went through Bach's mind, in the face of near death, especially the first and last stanzas of the prayer hymn, may have redefined the setting and its function for a moment he had not anticipated earlier:

| | |
|---|---|
| Vor deinen Thron tret ich hiermit | Before your throne I now appear, |
| O Gott, und dich demütig bitt | O God, and bid you humbly, |
| wend dein genädig Angesicht | turn not your gracious face |
| von mir, dem armen Sünder nicht. | From me, a poor sinner. |
| | |
| Ein selig Ende mir bescher, | Confer on me a blessed end, |
| am jüngsten Tag erwecke mich, | on the last day awaken me, |
| Herr, daß ich dich schau ewiglich: | Lord, that I may see you eternally; |
| Amen, amen, erhöre mich. | Amen, amen, hear me. |

We cannot reconstruct what actually happened on Bach's deathbed, but the "notice" on the back of the title page of the posthumous first edition of *The Art of Fugue,* which incorporates the chorale under the heading "Wenn wir in höchsten Nöten sein," should not be taken literally: "The late Author of this work was prevented by his disease of the eyes and by his death, which followed shortly upon it, from bringing the last Fugue, in which at the entrance of the third subject he mentions himself by name, to conclusion; accordingly, it was wished to compensate the friends of his muse by including the four-part church chorale added at the end, which the deceased man in his blindness dictated on the spur of the moment to the pen of a friend."[80] The chorale could not have been dictated on the spur of the moment because it existed before, apparently for quite some time. There must, nevertheless, be a kernel of truth in this notice.

Although the pertinent source materials have not been completely preserved, the following picture emerges: Bach asked "a friend"—whose identity, beyond the fact that he must have been an organist, remains open[81]—to play for him, on his pedal harpsichord, the chorale "Wenn wir in höchsten Nöten sein," BWV 668a, now hearing it as a setting of "Vor deinen Thron tret ich hiermit."[82] Listening to the piece, he realized that it could benefit from some improvements in a number of contrapuntal, melodic, and rhythmic details. He then asked the friend to change the heading of the chorale to "Vor deinen Thron tret ich hiermit" and dictated the changes deemed necessary in order for him to be ready to appear before his Creator's throne. In this form, with the composer's final edits, the chorale (BWV 668) was entered as a fair copy by an unnamed copyist[83] (possibly the same person who took Bach's dictation) at the very end of the partial autograph manuscript that already contained, among other organ works, seventeen of the Great Eighteen chorales in revised form and the *"Vom Himmel hoch" Variations.*[84] Not knowing this revised version but aware that Bach on his deathbed had tinkered with the piece, the editors of *The Art of Fugue* incorporated the earlier version (BWV 668a), headed differently. The extant sources for this extraordinary organ chorale, in its three versions, indisputably verify the composer's involvement, both spiritual and artistic, with the larger setting close to his end. They offer a true glimpse at Bach's deep-rooted devoutness. At the same time, the emendations that elevate the final version, "Vor deinen Thron tret ich hiermit," from the earlier "Wenn wir in höchsten Nöten sein" represent a final instance of a lifelong striving for musical perfection.

Johann Sebastian Bach died on July 28, a Tuesday, a little after 8:15 P.M. The funeral took place three days later. Following the custom for the death of a school colleague, the entire faculty and student body headed the funeral procession through the Grimma Gate as family, friends, and others followed the oaken casket.[85] For the cantor, whose office had obliged him to participate in all funerals for twenty-seven years, the hearse was provided *gratis* and no fees had to be paid to the St. Thomas School. Other than that, no further details are known—nothing about a possible memorial service at St. Thomas's or St. Paul's or the music sung at the school when the casket was carried down from the cantor's apartment and at St. John's cemetery, where the body was buried on the south side of St. John's Church.

Nevertheless, we have indirect evidence that a piece from the Old-Bach Archive, the double-choir motet "Lieber Herr Gott, wecke uns auf " by Johann Christoph Bach, may have been sung at Bach's funeral. Johann Sebastian owned a score of his ingenious uncle's composition, dated December 1672, and a set of vocal parts, both copied by Christoph Bach's father, Heinrich Bach of Arnstadt. Late in 1749 or in the spring of 1750, Johann Sebastian prepared a set of instrumental parts doubling the vocal parts. The extant sources not only document what appear to be among the latest samples of Bach's handwriting,[86] they also reveal that the ailing old man clearly had trouble writing: the lettering is unwieldy—uneven, stiff, disproportionately large, and disjunct. Bach also limited himself to writing the absolute minimum, inscribing the complete title only for the wrapper of choir I, writing the instrumental designation at the top of every part (*Coro I: Violino 1–2, Viola, Violoncello, Organ; Coro II: Hautbois 1–2, Taille, Basson, Violone*), indicating the transpos-

Johann Christoph Bach, motet "Lieber Herr Gott, wecke uns auf," from the Old-Bach Archive. Choir I title page, written by Johann Sebastian Bach (1749–50, facing page) and choir II taille, or 3rd oboe, part (above), in the hand of Bach's last prefect and substitute, Johann Nathanael Bammler. The heading (*Taille*), the transposing indication (*Tief Cammerthon,* or low chamber pitch), the initial clef, and the first notes were written in by Johann Sebastian Bach (1749–50). Tempo designation "Langsam" added later by C.P.E. Bach.

ing mode so that the G-minor work could be performed in E minor (*tief Cammerthon,* that is, low chamber pitch), and notating the clef followed by a few notes at the beginning of the first staff of each part—specifying just enough so that his assistant, Johann Nathanael Bammler, could copy the parts (see illustrations). Bach had decided on a supporting instrumental complement that required the participation of school's first and second choirs (the only parallel case being the motet BWV 226 sung in 1729 at the funeral of Rector Ernesti). Though neither the time nor the occasion can be determined exactly, it is hard to imagine, considering the circumstances, that Bach would undertake such a project unless it meant a lot to him. Conceivably, then, feeling that his end was near and wanting to make deliberate contingency plans, he selected a work by his most distinguished ancestor that set to music a traditional prayer text whose words anticipated life after death:[87]

Lieber Herr Gott, wecke uns auf,                    Dear Lord God, wake us up,
daß wir bereit sein, wenn dein Sohn kömmt,          so that we are prepared when Thy son comes,

| | |
|---|---|
| ihn mit Freuden zu empfahen | to receive him with joy |
| und dir mit reinem Herzen zu dienen | and to serve Thee with a pure heart, |
| durch denselbigen, deinen lieben Sohn, | by the same, Thy dear son, |
| Jesum Christum. Amen. | Jesus Christ. Amen. |

No gravestone or other marker signified Bach's final resting place—at least, none was extant by the mid-nineteenth century—but groups of St. Thomas choral scholars paid tribute to their great cantor every year on July 28 for more than a century after Bach's death. It was they who established a tradition that the grave was located about six paces from the southern church door.[88]

On July 31, the day of the funeral, at the Friday afternoon prayer service, an announcement was read from the pulpit of St. Thomas's: "The Esteemed and Highly Respected Mr. Johann Sebastian Bach, Court Composer to His Royal Majesty in Poland and Serene Electoral Highness in Saxony, as well as Capellmeister to the Prince of Anhalt-Cöthen and Cantor in the St. Thomas School, at the Square of St. Thomas's, peacefully and blissfully departed in God; his dead body was this day, in accordance with Christian usage, committed to the earth."[89] With the date of the funeral, newspapers in Leipzig, Berlin, and elsewhere published a short notice that indicates the cause of death but also refers to the eminence of the deceased and to the import of this event in musical circles:

Leipzig, July 31. Last Tuesday, that is, the 28th instant, the famous *Musicus* Mr. Joh. Seb. Bach, Royal Polish and Electoral Saxon Court Composer, Capellmeister of the Princely Court of Saxe-Weissenfels and of Anhalt-Cöthen, Director Chori Musici and Cantor of the St. Thomas School here, in the 66th year of his age, from the unhappy consequences of the very unsuccessful eye operation by a well-known English oculist. The loss of this uncommonly able man is greatly mourned by all true connoisseurs of music.[90]

The unknown author of this press release apparently knew well that despite the various distinguished titles he carried, Bach understood himself first and foremost as *musicus,* a practical musician of all trades but one who possessed the deepest understanding of music and, until the very end, was still searching for the truth—a genuine musical scholar.

On July 29, the day immediately following Bach's death, the inner city council briefly discussed six applicants for his post: Carl Philipp Emanuel Bach of Berlin, Johann Trier of Leipzig, Johann Gottlieb Görner of Leipzig, Gottlob Harrer of Dresden, August Friedrich Graun of Merseburg, and Johann Ludwig Krebs of Zeitz. With Burgomaster Born's statement, however, that "he could hardly disregard the recommendation" of Prime Minister Brühl, the stage was set for the decision to be made later by the entire council. Second burgomaster Stieglitz added a little more flavor: "The School needed a Cantor and not a Capellmeister, although he must understand music. Harrer had made excellent promises and had declared himself agreeable to everything required of him."[91] On August 7, the formal election took place with the expected result, and with little delay, Gottlob Harrer was formally installed on the following St. Michael's Day, September 29—only two months and one day after the death of his predecessor.

ESTATE AND MUSICAL LEGACY

At his death, Bach left behind his wife and nine children, four of them minors. Wilhelm Friedemann, Carl Philipp Emanuel, and Johann Christoph Friedrich were gainfully employed, Elisabeth Juliana Friderica was married, but Anna Magdalena, his forty-eight-year-old widow with two sons and three daughters, was unprovided for. On August 15, 1750, she petitioned the Leipzig city council for a bounty, the traditional half-year's grace payment. After some bureaucratic details were clarified, she received two late quarterly installments of the deceased cantor's base salary in September 1750 and January 1751.[92] The widow—in consultation with Leipzig University, the appropriate venue of jurisdiction for the Bach family—also arranged for guardianship of her minor children, for which the family friend and Thomas-organist Johann Gottlieb Görner was appointed on October 21, 1750; for the feeble-minded Gottfried Heinrich, the family friend and theology student Gottlob Sigismund Hesemann was appointed trustee.[93] In all these arrangements, Anna Magdalena was assisted by a good family friend and godfather of two Bach children, the attorney Dr. Friedrich Heinrich Graff, judge at the Saxon Superior Court in Leipzig. Meanwhile, the large household had to be dissolved as the family needed to vacate the apartment in the St. Thomas School within the statutory six months—no minor task.

On the basis of a detailed inventory, the value of Bach's possessions—including cash; silverware and valuables; pewter, copper, and brass objects; clothing; home furnishings; and theological books—was determined by the university probate court. The hearing took place on November 11, 1750, in the presence of the entire family: Anna Magdalena, who was present but, as a woman, could not legally speak for herself, was represented by Graff as trustee; Carl, who could not attend, was represented by Friedemann as trustee; Lieschen was represented by her husband Johann Christoph Altnickol as trustee; Gottfried Heinrich was represented by Hesemann, and the four minors by Görner.[94] Bach had not died a poor man—he even owned a share, valued at 60 talers, in a small mining business—but neither was he wealthy. At the end, he held 231 talers in cash, more than double his annual base salary. His salary and additional earnings had easily supported his large family, and while he could have used excess funds to build up some savings, he chose not to do so. Instead, he bought books and instruments, and surely helped finance his ambitious performances. The grand total of the Bach estate (money, securities, and all movable goods, with the notable exception of music and books on music) came to almost 1,160 talers, from which liabilities of some 152 talers had to be subtracted. Of the entire estate, the widow received one-third, with the remaining two-thirds divided equally among the children.[95]

The legal procedures of November 11 seem to have gone smoothly and amicably, apart from a minor dispute recorded in the court papers. The three siblings from Bach's first marriage questioned the claim of their youngest stepbrother, Johann Christian, that his father had given him, during his lifetime, three claviers and a set of pedals. (These four instruments had, for this reason, not been included in the inventory's list of seven keyboard instruments.) But since Christel's claim was verified by witnesses (his mother, Altnickol, and Hesemann), the matter was quickly put to rest.[96]

After Bach's death—perhaps even before, with him having some say—it was arranged that Gottfried Heinrich would live in the Altnickol household at Naumburg, where he died in 1763 at the age of thirty-nine; and that Johann Christian would move with Carl to Berlin, where he remained until 1755, when he left for Italy. Anna Magdalena remained in Leipzig with three daughters, Catharina Dorothea, Johanna Carolina, and Regina Susanna. Next to nothing is known about their lives after Bach's death, but the women seem to have eventually lived together in rather poor circumstances. The inheritance was soon used up, and a payment of 40 talers that the widow received from the city council in 1752 for her gift of several copies of *The Art of Fugue* would not have lasted long either.[97] (The figure represented 40 percent of Bach's base salary, though, and the city council's generosity—no matter of course—shows their respect for the deceased.) Anna Magdalena lived on the Hainstrasse, apparently in an apartment at the house of the attorney Graff, where she died on February 27, 1760, at the age of fifty-nine. Listed in the burial registry as *Almosenfrau,* a woman supported by charity, she had, after her inheritance and other means were used up, received some income from the welfare bureau maintained by the city council.[98] A mere Quarter School escorted her casket to the same cemetery where, almost ten years earlier, her husband had been buried. In later years, the Bach daughters received monetary support from their brother Carl in Hamburg, who arranged for the payments through his publisher, Johann Gottlob Immanuel Breitkopf.[99] However, when the youngest, Regina Susanna, survived all her sisters and brothers, there was no one to support her until Friedrich Rochlitz, the first editor of the Leipzig *Allgemeine Musikalische Zeitung* and a former choral scholar at the St. Thomas School under the cantor Doles, published a call in the May 1800 issue of his periodical to support the last surviving daughter of the "great Sebastian Bach." The plea did not fall on deaf ears, and a considerable amount was collected on her behalf by Breitkopf & Härtel (Beethoven never realized his promise to dedicate the proceeds from a publication or concert to this purpose). In the journal's issue of the following May, Regina Susanna publicly and "with tears of joy" expressed her thanks. She died eight years later.

It seems highly peculiar that the most important part of Bach's estate, his compositions and his complete music library (manuscript and printed music, books on music and music theory), were omitted from the estate inventory. We must conclude, then, that these materials were neither evaluated nor distributed according to the established scheme of division. The collection is also conspicuously absent in the probate hearing record. While the documentation of a separate procedure dealing with Bach's compositions and music library may conceivably have been lost, the complete lack of any cross-reference within the detailed court documents speaks against it. We can presume, then, that the distribution of the musical estate was settled separately beforehand, and, more likely than not, was guided by Bach himself. He apparently left no written will, or else the dispute over the keyboard instruments claimed by Johann Christian would hardly have arisen. This son's witnessed statement, on the other hand, that he had received them as a gift from his father indicates that before his death, Bach had made some decisions about what to leave to whom. For the composer himself, there was no question that the musical estate was by far the most valuable part of his bequest. It actually made good sense that the musical instruments, the only portion of the musical estate whose material value could be appraised, were treated as part of the whole estate (and actually made up roughly one-third of its grand total). Similarly, the theological books were added to the saleable part (valued about one-tenth of the instrument collection), whereas the musical treatises and other books on music had an ideal value that, from a musician's point of view, far exceeded their material value. Bach seems to have thought carefully about his musical bequest and perhaps even compared notes with the Leipzig luthier Johann Christian Hoffmann, who was formulating a will in 1748 that included Bach.[100] How much easier it was to deal with items such as lutes, violins, strings, bows, tools, and wood!

As Bach had himself inherited music from his ancestors and placed great value on it, he could reasonably expect that his children would do the same for his own work and that it would, in fact, become the newest and largest section of the Old-Bach Archive. He may have had this thought in mind when he prepared fair, or "archival," copies of his principal works, such as the unaccompanied violin pieces, *The Well-Tempered Clavier,* and the *St. Matthew Passion,* and when he made or arranged for duplicate copies of his works. He could feel reasonably sure that the musical tradition would carry on in his family and, considering the stream of students he had taught, that his own work would indeed have a future well beyond the realm of the family.

For various reasons, it makes good sense to assume that the division of the musical estate was determined, at least to a large extent and in its basic outlines, by Bach himself and that the family members willingly followed his guidelines. The fact that no dispute seems to have arisen over a matter as crucial as this one speaks for it. Everyone in the family was aware that the musical estate was a veritable treasure chest, even though it could hardly be cashed—at least not for its ideal value, as Anna Magdalena learned when her offer to the St. Thomas School of the performing parts of the chorale cantata cycle was accepted for what was certainly a fraction of their worth. (But she at least fared better than the widow of Johann Kuhnau, for whose musical estate the cantor Bach had expressed no interest.) Moreover, the cantata repertoire was divided up in a way designed to maximize the material, a plan that could hardly have been developed during the few days surrounding the funeral, the only period after Bach's death when the entire family was assembled. Finally, the time frame within which the division of the musical estate was decided was much too short for serious consultations among family members in and out of Leipzig. Anna Magdalena's discussion with the Thomasrector Ernesti about acquisition by the St. Thomas School of the chorale cantatas took place before August 29, 1750,[101] indicating that the widow knew by then which portion of the music was hers. It seems plausible, therefore, that the musical estate was basically settled by the time of the funeral, a circumstance that could hardly have been achieved without clear oral or written instructions from the deceased. More likely than not, the health crisis of May–June 1749 impressed on Bach the necessity of providing for the future—of his music, as well as his family's. Much of his life's work, definitely the great bulk of the vocal oeuvre, including Passions and oratorios, existed as unique materials on his music shelves and had never been copied for outside use. And as both older sons had come to visit their father at least once during the fall, winter, and spring of 1749–50, there would have been ample time for Bach to consult with them on this all-important matter.

In the absence of any documentation, we must look at transmission patterns to determine how the musical estate was divided. The cantata manuscripts, for example, were split up so that each *Jahrgang* (annual cycle) would be shared by at least two heirs:[102]

*Jahrgang I:* Alternating scores and parts to Carl Philipp Emanuel; complementary parts and scores probably to Johann Christoph Friedrich ("Friederich" on the wrapper to parts of the cantata BWV 76, the first of cycle I).

Carl's portion of the first cycle has survived; much of his own estate that included his father's works ended up first in the hands of the collector Georg Poelchau, then went to the Berlin Singakademie. From there, the cantatas were acquired in 1854 by the Royal Library, Berlin (today Staatsbibliothek zu Berlin).[103] Friederich's portion of the cycle has been lost.

*Jahrgang II:* Parts to Anna Magdalena; scores and duplicate parts to Wilhelm Friedemann.

Bach's widow gave her portion (altogether forty-four sets of parts) to the St. Thomas School, where they have survived. Friedemann sold some of the scores to Johann Georg Nacke, cantor in Oelsnitz; most of them ended up later in the collection of Franz Hauser and eventually in the Royal Library, Berlin. The remainder of the scores are, for the most part, lost.

*Jahrgang III:* Heir of parts is unknown; scores and duplicate parts to Carl Philipp Emanuel and Johann Christian ("Carl u Christel" on wrapper to parts of the cantata BWV 39, the first of cycle III).

After Christel's departure from Berlin, Carl's collection incorporated his brother's materials, probably by purchasing them from him so that the twenty-year-old could finance his trip to Italy. The complementary portion of the cycle has not survived.

Friedemann apparently also had the privilege of picking from *Jahrgang* I and III pieces for the high feast days on which he had to present performances in Halle.[104] For the relatively small number of cantatas not belonging to the three cycles listed above, no transmission pattern emerges that would permit us to draw further conclusions about the division of Bach's estate. The same holds true for the Passions, Masses, and oratorios. For example, the complete scores and parts for the *St. Matthew* and *St. John Passions* and for the *Christmas Oratorio* came into Carl's possession, probably to be shared with Christel, who never returned to a position in Germany. Carl also held the score of the *B-minor Mass.* Considering this fact, together with Forkel's statement that the annual sets of cantata materials "were divided after the author's death between the elder sons, and in such a manner that Wilhelm Friedemann had the larger share,"[105] we may ask which large-scale works Carl's brothers received. Besides the *St. Mark Passion,* for which only the libretto survives, what other large-scale works may have been lost?

Most everything that went to Bach's second son—the most careful curator of his father's materials—has survived,[106] while Friedemann's share of the estate has come down to us in incomplete and scattered form,[107] because after resigning his post at Our Lady's in Halle and never again taking up employment, he invariably found himself in economic trouble and gradually sold off his inheritance. He once offered the bulk of the scores of the chorale cantata cycle to Forkel for 20 louis d'or, but Forkel did not have the money for the purchase.[108] In 1778, Friedemann asked Johann Joachim Eschenburg of Brunswick to auction off the remainder of his part of the estate: *"À propos,* did Your Honor give Your *Musicalia* into auction? My departure from Braunschweig was so hasty that I could not compile a catalog of my relinquished music and books. I do remember *The Art of Fugue* by my father and Quantz's manual for the flute. Your honor has kept in good faith the other church *Musiquen* and annual cycles, as well as books, and promised me to convert them, with the advice of a knowledgeable musician, into cash through auction."[109] The fate of these materials apparently sold on Friedemann's behalf remains completely unknown. And what happened to Johann Christoph Friedrich's inheritance is another sad story. After Friederich's death in 1795, his son Wilhelm Friedrich Ernst (capellmeister in Berlin) received little or nothing. Later, the widow seems to have sold off most of the inheritance: when the collector Georg Poelchau went to Bückeburg in 1817, he found among the meager leftovers only three autograph manuscripts by Johann Sebastian.[110]

The survival rate of the instrumental music in Bach's estate likewise differs according to the individual heirs. Again, Carl's share is the most complete (including the autograph of the organ trio sonatas and *The Art of Fugue*), Friedemann's greatly diminished and scattered, Friederich's almost nonexistent (only the autograph of the unaccompanied violin works survives), and Christel's minimal (and probably for the most part merged with Carl's; among the very few identifiable items from Christel's share is the autograph of the organ Prelude and Fugue in B minor, BWV 544). Taking all shares together, the majority of the autograph scores of the instrumental works, including keyboard music, have not survived. Among the few instrumental autograph sources that survived entirely outside of the Bach estate is the score of the *Brandenburg Concertos,* dedicated and sent to the margrave of Brandenburg in 1721. In the realm of keyboard music, however, Bach's extensive teaching activities opened important secondary channels of transmission. Most of the keyboard works were copied by students, beginning with the Weimar pupils Johann Caspar Vogler and Johann Tobias Krebs. Therefore, very few if any keyboard works, especially those composed after 1714, have been lost. That is not true of the earlier works, which, after about 1710, Bach no longer considered useful as teaching models because he deemed them technically and stylistically outdated. Typically, many early works, such as the Toccata in D minor, BWV 565, and also vocal works such as the *Actus tragicus,* BWV 106, became accessible only after Bach's death in sources originating after 1750.[111]

Considering the extant manuscript and printed repertoire stemming directly from Bach's library (including works by other composers copied by him or in his possession and books on music) and the complex issue of provenance, many questions remain open. Presumably, the bulk of the estate went to the four musical sons. But did Anna Magdalena really receive only the parts for the chorale cantatas? Could Gottfried Heinrich have ended up completely empty-handed? What about the Bach daughters and the son-in-law Altnickol?[112] Most such questions cannot be answered, but a picture emerges of a musical estate that is much larger than we generally imagine.

The transmission of Bach's estate was influenced not only by the fate and the actions of the direct heirs but also by other factors. For example, the process of historical selection always favors works that show innovative features; more conventional items tend to become marginalized. Already the summary worklist of the Obituary falls victim to this principle. It lists specifically the works that have no or few counterparts: organ trio sonatas or other works with obbligato pedal, preludes and fugues through all twenty-four keys, pieces for un-accompanied violin and cello, concertos for one to four harpsichords, and the like. But ordinary concertos, suites, and sonatas are covered by the catch-all category "a mass of other instrumental pieces of all sorts and for all kinds of instruments."[113] Typically, Carl Philipp Emanuel wrote in 1774: "The 6 Clavier Trios [BWV 1014–1019, not even listed in the Obituary's summary catalog] . . . are among the best works of my dear departed father. They still sound excellent and give me much joy, although they date back more than fifty years. They contain some *Adagii* that could not be written in a more singable manner today."[114] In comparison, ordinary trios such as sonatas for two violins and continuo would not have deserved any special mention; consequently, their chances for survival were considerably smaller. No wonder that very few works of this type have been preserved, although Bach almost certainly produced dozens of them, mainly before 1723. Some relics have been found in recycled and revised versions among the organ trio sonatas; perhaps even the composer himself may have lacked any interest in keeping the more conventional earlier versions. It must be stressed, though, that simply equating the survival of a work with its artistic quality distorts the truth. The two *Passions According to St. Matthew* and *St. Mark* offer a case in point. It is inconceivable that the lost *St. Mark Passion* surpasses, in compositional and aesthetic terms, the *St. Matthew*. But does this diminish the value of the former and reconcile us to the loss? The *St. Mark* of 1731, composed four years after the *St. Matthew,* in all likelihood incorporated a more modern vocal style—in recitatives, arias, and choruses, including those adopted from other works—and certainly also an up-dated style of chorale harmonization. Its loss means that our understanding of Bach's vocal music of the 1730s remains highly fragmentary.

Another example pertains to vocal works written for special occasions, containing direct textual references to the unique event. The two large-scale works written for the funeral of Prince Leopold of Cöthen had no practical value after 1729—not even for the composer, except that of a potential musical quarry. We should not be surprised that the rate of loss among the secular congratulatory cantatas and similar compositions is proportionately the greatest by far. For instance, of twenty-four documented cantatas in honor of members of princely courts, the music for only ten scores has survived. There is no question, however, that the truly significant losses of Bach's music in all genres were caused by the division of his musical estate into multiple shares. And these losses would have been even greater, especially in the realm of keyboard music, had there not been a secondary transmission through the activities of Bach's students and others.

Throughout the second half of the eighteenth century—the most decisive period for Bach's reception—no one, not even his own sons, had a real grasp of the size of Bach's oeuvre, let alone comprehensive insight into the materials. Not counting potential losses prior to 1750, the corpus of Bach's creative output as a unit was destroyed with the division of the estate, and its structure was distorted once and for all. However, the limited knowledge of the works that were available after 1750 only magnified the effect of individual compositions as their musical essence and compositional makeup were contemplated. Bach's music immediately established new benchmarks of compositional artistry and technical perfection. Its exemplary value was recognized, as each work soon became a touchstone for performers, composers, and theorists alike—a distinction the pieces hold to this day. After Bach, music was no longer the same. A paradigm shift had taken place and gradually took hold, comparable to what happened in philosophy (which included mathematics and physics) as a result of Newton's work. Certainly by coincidence but exactly a month after Bach's death, in an article dated August 28, 1750, Bach's former student Johann Friedrich Agricola, who had become a respected composer, performer, and theorist in Berlin, drew an analogy for the first time between Newton and Bach, pointing out their deep involvement with the "profound science" of their respective fields. And it appears utterly appropriate to see Bach's musical advances in the light of Newton's philosophical achievements. The two men reached pinnacles of a very different kind, but they lived, thought, and worked in the same intellectual climate of scientific discovery and empirical testing of fundamental principles.

Just as no one in 1728 could know Newton *in toto,* no one in 1750 knew all of Bach, but the main ideas for which their life's work stood were clearly present, even already at work. Therefore, the unfortunate fate of Bach's musical estate had virtually no effect on his musical legacy, either in the 1750s and 1760s or later. Surely, any lost work of Bach's would, if retrieved, significantly broaden the scope of the surviving repertoire and add new facets as well. At the same time, such a find would in no way alter our perception of the principled nature of Bach's compositional art—principled yet moving, scientific yet human—the true core of his musical legacy.

Even before 1750, that legacy had begun to spread, slowly but steadily and irreversibly, primarily through his students and his sons, and first and foremost in circles of professional musicians. But knowledgeable admirers of Bach's art could be found outside German lands as well. A representative voice in this regard is that of the composer and theorist Padre Giovanni Battista Martini in Bologna, who wrote to a German colleague in April 1750, more than three months before Bach's death: "I consider it superfluous to describe the singular merit of Sig. Bach, for he is thoroughly known and admired not only in Germany but throughout our Italy. I will say only that I think it would be difficult to find someone in the profession who could surpass him, since these days he could rightfully claim to be among the first in Europe."[115] Martini's words demonstrate the growth of Bach's influence far away from his geographic home. Leipzig, however, continued to play a prominent role in the further dissemination of his music, especially as a result of the manuscript-copying services of the Breitkopf firm throughout the second half of the eighteenth century.

As for the St. Thomas School, so long Bach's principal place of operation, Gottlob Harrer's cantorate was solid if uneventful. He composed a great deal of music for the Leipzig churches but also paid considerable attention to other composers' music. He cultivated in particular the Masses of Palestrina and the chorale cantatas of his immediate predecessor, using the original performance materials for the latter.[116] However, after holding the office for less than five years, Harrer died on July 9, 1755. The council then proceeded to elect Johann Friedrich Doles,[117] who had been thoroughly trained by Bach and who occupied the office for thirty-three years, from 1756 to 1789—even longer than his teacher. It was also Doles who laid the cornerstone of what can be called a Leipzig Bach tradition. In 1789, when Mozart traveled from Vienna to Leipzig and, on the initiative of Doles, visited the St. Thomas School,

the choir surprised Mozart with the performance of the double chorus motet *Singet dem Herrn ein neues Lied* by Sebastian Bach. Mozart knew this master more by hearsay than by his works, which had become quite rare; at least his motets, which had never been printed, were completely unknown to him. Hardly had the choir sung a few measures when Mozart sat up, startled; a few measures more and he called out "What is this?" And now his whole soul seemed to be in his ears. When the singing was finished he cried out, full of joy: "Now there is something one can learn from!"[118]

# Epilogue
## Bach and the Idea of "Musical Perfection"

Bach must have derived considerable satisfaction on reading, in January 1738, the defense against the attack on him that Johann Adolph Scheibe had launched the previous year. The essay, written by Magister Johann Abraham Birnbaum (doubtless with Bach's assistance),[1] replaces Scheibe's image of Bach the music maker with that of Bach the virtuoso. The article also refers to Bach consistently as "the Hon. Court Composer"—a formulaic reverential gesture, to be sure, but an appellation that emphasizes the significance of Bach the composer.[2] Since, however, Birnbaum deliberately appealed to a discriminating audience, in particular to the "real connoisseur of true musical perfections," he placed the bar as high as possible in addressing the "remarkable perfections that indisputably belong to the Hon. Court Composer alone." Here Birnbaum revealed himself as a true and resourceful threesome—rhetorician, legal scholar, and philosopher—and overpowered his opponent by introducing into the discussion the concept of "musical perfection," a notion as abstract as it is irrefutable.

While perfection had traditionally been considered the exclusive property of God and His creation, the perfectibility of man became an idea of the Enlightenment that was able to cross the newly lowered theological barriers. Therefore, Birnbaum's attribution of "remarkable perfections" to Bach could no longer be considered blasphemous, even though the remark that these perfections "indisputably" belonged to him brought Birnbaum dangerously close to declaring Bach godlike, surely an unintended comparison. Yet Birnbaum clearly meant to place Bach on a pedestal of uniqueness, a judgment Bach could comfortably accept and a view later echoed in the Obituary statement that Bach's music resembled that of "no other composer." This appraisal resulted neither from blunt arrogance nor from unreasonable exaggeration, since the principal subject of the debate, musical composition—referred to by its ancient Greek synonym *harmonia*—had prompted discussion of the term "perfection" in the first place.

According to both Pythagorean philosophical doctrine and medieval the-ology, the harmony of the spheres produced consonant (if hidden) music, which reflected the perfection of the celestial world—a view that neither Kepler nor Newton disputed, leaving it one of the few fundamental truths still upheld by both philosophers and theologians of Bach's time. Not surprisingly, all-encompassing philosophical concepts from Marin Mersenne's "universal har-mony" to Gottfried Wilhelm Leibniz's "prestabilized harmony" invariably draw on this genuinely musical term because of its fundamental implications. As Georg Venzky, like Bach a member of Lorenz Christoph Mizler's Society of Musical Science, put it, "God is a harmonic being. All harmony originates from his wise order and organization . . . Where there is no conformity, there is also no order, no beauty, and no perfection. For beauty and perfection consists in the conformity of diversity."[3]

The principle of unity in diversity, derived from the theocentric concept of the harmony of the spheres, provided the basis for Birnbaum's definition of musical perfection:

Now the idea that the melody must always be in the upper voice and that the constant collaboration of the other voices is a fault, is one for which I have been able to find no sufficient grounds. Rather it is the exact opposite that flows from the very nature of music. For music consists of harmony, and harmony becomes far more complete if all the voices collaborate to form it. Accordingly this is not a failing but rather a musi-cal perfection. . . . The author need only look into the works of Palestrina, among the old composers, or Lotti among the more modern ones, and he will find not only that the voices are continuously at work but also that each one has a melody of its own that harmonizes quite well with the others.[4]

For Birnbaum and Bach, two points were of particular importance: the nature of music and the continuity of its history. As to first, the issue of art versus na-ture, Birnbaum explains at a later point in greater detail:

The essential aims of true art are to imitate Nature, and, where necessary, to aid it. If art imitates Nature, then indisputably the natural element must everywhere shine through in works of art. . . . Now, the greater the art is—that is, the more industri-ously and painstakingly it works at the improvement of Nature—the more brilliantly shines the beauty thus brought into being. Accordingly, it is impossible that the greatest art should darken the beauty of a thing. Can it be possible, then, that the Hon. Court Composer, even by the use of the greatest art he applies in the working out of his musical compositions, could take away from them the natural element and darken its beauty?"[5]

The concept of nature to which Birnbaum and Bach adhered owed a large debt to seventeenth- and early eighteenth-century thinking; it was as far removed from later thought as a French Baroque garden with its formality and decor (that is, its need for artful "improvement of nature") was from the later eighteenth-century English garden with its naturalistic landscape. Regarding the second point, Birnbaum's references to older masters stress the importance to Bach of an unbroken tradition of the art of counterpoint, according to the notion that "natural and cogent thoughts maintain their worth in all times and places."[6] At the same time, both Palestrina and Lotti, along with de Grigny's and Du Mage's *Livres d'orgue* (cited by Birnbaum elsewhere in the essay), were composers and works represented in Bach's library, confirming his direct input in building the argument for the validity of contrapuntal style.

Birnbaum's description of harmony as accumulated counterpoint goes well beyond mere functionality when, in one of the most thoughtful and poetic descriptions of the inner workings of Bach's harmonious polyphony, he addresses the essential aesthetic aspects of a contrapuntally conceived harmonic structure:

Where the rules of composition are most strictly preserved, there without fail order must reign. . . . It is certain . . . that the voices in the works of this great master of music work wonderfully in and about one another, but without the slightest confusion. They move along together or in opposition, as necessary. They part company, and yet all meet again at the proper time. Each voice distinguishes itself clearly from the others by a particular variation, although they often imitate each other. They now flee, now follow one another without one's noticing the slightest irregularity in their efforts to outdo one another. Now when all this is performed as it should be, there is nothing more beautiful than this harmony.[7]

Birnbaum then poses a whole series of questions pointing to the uniquely high degree of individuality exhibited by Bach's musical language: "Why does he [Scheibe] not praise the astonishing mass of unusual and well-developed ideas? the development of a single subject through the keys with the most agreeable variations? the quite special adroitness, even at the greatest speed, in bringing out all the tones clearly and with uninterrupted evenness? the uncommon fluency with which he plays in the most difficult keys just as quickly and accurately as in the simplest? and in general an amenity that is everywhere joined with art?"[8]

From a modern perspective, it is not difficult to assign Bach a special place in his time. It is most unusual, however, that Bach's contemporaries recognized and articulated that his music was distinctly different. "No one ever showed so many ingenious and unusual ideas as he in elaborate pieces such as ordinarily seem dry exercises in craftsmanship," reads the Obituary, which continues even more explicitly: "His melodies were strange, but always varied, rich in invention, and resembling those of no other composer."[9] Indeed, the quality of originality in Bach's music was identified early, much earlier than is generally assumed, and culminated in Christian Friedrich Daniel Schubart's 1784–85 pronouncement: "Johann Sebastian Bach was a genius of the highest degree; his spirit is so unique and individual, so immense that it will require centuries to really reach him. . . . The original genius of Bach is readily recognizable."[10]

The term "original genius" became fashionable only after Bach's lifetime. The triumph of individual spontaneity over codified rules cannot be properly applied to him, even though by the end of the eighteenth century Bach frequently served as the model of original genius in German aesthetics, much as Shakespeare did in England.[11] But Schubart formulated in the nomenclature of his day (thirty-five years after Bach's death) only what both the Obituary and Birnbaum had anticipated in stressing the phenomena of individuality and uniqueness. And neither Schubart nor the others saw any incongruity between the two images of Bach, as someone strictly adhering to the established rules of composition and as someone setting his own rules. Indeed, they understood his art as a paradigm for reconciling what would ordinarily be conflicting stances. And when the authors of the Obituary speak of Bach's "ingenious and unusual ideas" on the one hand and his extraordinary command of the "hidden secrets of harmony" on the other, they identify an essential element in Bach's approach to musical composition: the tension between protecting objective precepts and pursuing subjective goals. Bach, for whom the "invention of ideas" constituted a fundamental requirement ("anyone who had none he advised to stay away from composition altogether," as his son later recounted),[12] understood the elaboration of musical ideas not as an act of free creation but rather as a process of imaginative research into the harmonic implications of the chosen subject matter.

The "astonishing mass of unusual and well-developed ideas" praised by Birnbaum depends little on the traditional art of devising motifs and themes based on rhetorical models. Instead, Bach's "strange" melodies move strongly in the direction of original though not unbridled creation. Just as he conceives of harmony as a nature-given essence whose secrets are to be explored, his invention is always derived from given premises, expanding on which he accepts as a challenge. In this connection, a report from a certain M. Theodor Pitschel of Leipzig, dated 1741, seems particularly illuminating, for Bach's art of improvising and composing is always determined by concrete points of references:

The famous man who has the greatest praise in our town in music, and the greatest admiration of connoisseurs, does not get into condition, as the expression goes, to delight others with the mingling of his tones until he has played something from the printed or written page, and has thus set his powers of imagination in motion. . . . The able man . . . usually has to play something from a page which is inferior to his own ideas. And yet his superior ideas are the consequences of those inferior ones.[13]

Characteristic of Bach's manner of composing is a way of elaborating the musical ideas so as to penetrate the material deeply and exhaustively. As Carl Philipp Emanuel Bach points out, the approach taken by his father never reflected the tensed-up, arduous, and compulsive attitude of a fanatic but served, instead, to provide him with fun and, often, a playful intellectual pastime: "Thanks to his greatness in harmony, he accompanied trios on more than one occasion on the spur of the moment and, being in good humor, . . . converted them into complete quartets. . . . When he listened to a rich and many-voiced fugue, he could soon say, after the first entries of the subjects, what contrapuntal devices would be possible to apply and which of them the composer by rights ought to apply."[14]

So it appears that uncovering secrets implicated in harmony was a veritable passion that had its roots in the youth of this essentially self-taught composer, whose "own study and reflection alone" made him such a "pure and strong fugue writer."[15] From the outset, the contrapuntal elaboration of a theme held his intense interest, and given his phenomenal gift of combination, it became immaterial whether the theme was his own or that of another composer. In every instance, the theme presented a challenge to uncover its latent harmonic qualities so that in the final setting, all parts worked "wonderfully in and about one another, but without the slightest confusion" and, therefore, truly represented unity in diversity, or musical perfection.

In striving for musical perfection, the principle of elaboration is an integral factor, whatever the genre, and this principle determines like nothing else Bach's art and personal style. Elaboration takes many forms, as it involves counterpoint, variation, and basic components of musical design such as melody, harmony, and rhythm. Elaboration affects all aspects of the compositional process and the continuing search for improved or alternate solutions, from sketch, draft, harmonization, and orchestration to correction, revision, and parody. Elaboration requires the concrete application of musical science, that is, the knowledge of all possible implications held by a musical idea, as well as how and why they are possible. The most important aspect of elaboration, however, is that it provides a method for working "industriously and painstakingly . . . at the improvement of nature"[16]—for seeking, in other words, musical perfection.

Not surprisingly, the unmistakable qualities of Bach's music find their equivalent in his strong and highly individual artistic personality. His life story reveals an extremely self-aware manager who looked out for his own interests and knew how to protect them. Furthermore, in more than fifty years of intense compositional activity, Bach underwent an evolution that is without parallel among his contemporaries. Comparing the first fruits of early mastery such as the Passacaglia in C minor, BWV 582, and the *Actus tragicus,* BWV 106, with such late works as *The Art of Fugue* or the *B-minor Mass* exposes an extraordinarily broad spectrum of artistic development and technical and stylistic advances, continually setting new benchmarks.

The rapid rate of change and progress in Bach's compositional development is all the more remarkable in that his geographical horizon and his exposure to contemporaneous European musical life remained quite constricted. Still, the breadth of his knowledge and his intimate familiarity with the music literature both of his day and of the past was unusual if not unique among his contemporaries. He was certainly unsurpassed in his ability to absorb new insights and experiences in his compositions as elements of enrichment and reorientation. The overall development of Bach's musical language clearly reflects his immense curiosity, openness toward change, and power of integration.

The permutations in Bach's style are regulated by one dominating element of stability and continuity, and that is his thoroughly virtuosic disposition. Having grown up in a family of musicians provided him with a professional outlook that he never shook off. Accordingly, making concessions to nonprofessional music making was for him unthinkable. More often than not, his technical requirements push the limits of both performance and compositional complexity, whether the work is a church cantata, a keyboard piece, or an instrumental concerto. The high standards and demands are typical of the young, middle, and old Bach—in fact, they represent one of his most characteristic trademarks and one that brought him much admiration during his lifetime as well as considerable disapproval (he was accused of requiring that the throats of his singers have the same facility that his own fingers had at the keyboard).

Bach's idea of musical perfection, as Birnbaum affirmed, included the goal of perfect execution. He was well aware, however, that performances, especially of larger ensemble works, would not necessarily match the degree of perfection represented in the musical composition. It is this aspect that prompted him to have Birnbaum, in a 1739 supplementary essay, raise a crucial point: "It is true, one does not judge a composition principally and predominantly by the impression of its performance. But if such judgment, which indeed may be deceiving, is not to be considered, I see no other way of judging than to view the work as it has been set down in notes."[17]

This statement is significant since it points to the value of the notated score of a composition, above and beyond its performance. It is, after all, the written text that establishes the only reliable document of the composer's ideas and intentions, and that is particularly true of a work displaying Bach's "unusual musical perfections." And as a performance may only represent an approximation, the dilemma between the perfection of the idea and the perfection of its realization may remain unresolved but still provide a stimulating incentive for perfectibility. In the final analysis, only the idea can claim to be truly perfect, and Bach knew it.

His music, because it represented the idea of musical perfection in such a striking and paradigmatic way, became the model for an ideal very early on. The exemplary quality of his keyboard fugues and his four-part chorales in particular were well recognized in the immediate decades after his death. But it was the singular combination of Bach as an authority in the later eighteenth-century treatises on musical composition and his impact on Viennese Classicism, notably on the works of Mozart and Beethoven, that sealed the historical significance of his art. That Bach's music could engender theory without freezing into theory demonstrates the strength of its scientific underpinning and the stirring power of its expressive message. Moreover, that it could help lift a piece such as the finale movement of Mozart's *Jupiter* Symphony to sublime heights proves its strength as an all-encompassing and stimulating catalyst. And when Beethoven called Bach the "progenitor of harmony," he echoed what the Berlin capellmeister Johann Friedrich Reichardt had proclaimed in 1784: Bach was "the greatest harmonist of all times and nations."[18] Beethoven doubtless shared Reichardt's judgment expressed in an 1805 review of the first edition of Bach's solo works for violin, that these works were "perhaps the greatest example in any art form of a master's ability to move with freedom and assurance, even in chains."[19]

Perfectly constructed and unique in sound, Bach's compositions offer the ideal of bringing into congruence original thought, technical exactitude, and aesthetic beauty. Whatever the category of music and whatever the level of achievement, the two-part *Inventions* or *The Well-Tempered Clavier,* a four-part chorale or an eight-part motet, an unaccompanied cello suite or a concerto for multiple instruments, individually and collectively Bach's works demonstrate the musical realization of unity in diversity, of musical perfection. But the dialectic of divine perfection and human originality that manifests itself in Bach's oeuvre so strongly and influentially has never been formulated more poignantly or more aptly than by Johann Nicolaus Forkel at the end of his 1802 biography. It seems worth repeating, despite its flourishes of Romantic diction, because it preserves the atmosphere of the immediate post-Bach generation of the eighteenth century that once set the stage for an ongoing post-Bach era now poised to transcend the millennium:

It is owing to this genuine spirit of art that Bach united his great and lofty style with the most refined elegance and the greatest precision in the single parts that compose the great whole, which otherwise are not thought so necessary here as in works whose only object is the agreeable; that he thought the whole could not be perfect if anything were wanting in the perfect precision of the single parts; and, last, that if, notwithstanding the main tendency of his genius for the great and sublime, he sometimes composed and performed something gay and even jocose, his cheerfulness and joking were those of a sage.

It was only through this union of the greatest genius with the most indefatigable study that Johann Sebastian Bach was able, whichever way he turned, to extend so greatly the bounds of his art that his successors have not even been able to maintain this enlarged domain to its full extent; and this alone enabled him to produce such numerous and perfect works, all of which are, and ever will remain, true ideals and imperishable models of art.[20]

# Notes

### Prologue

1. *NBR,* no. 343.
2. *NBR,* no. 344.
3. Ibid.
4. Johann Mattheson, *Grundlage einer Ehrenpforte* (Hamburg, 1740), pp. xxxiiif.
5. *NBR,* no. 318.
6. *NBR,* no. 303.
7. *NBR,* no. 306.
8. *NBR,* no. 162.
9. *NBR,* no. 303, nos. 13–14.
10. *NBR,* no. 162.
11. *NBR,* no. 306.
12. *NBR,* no. 344.
13. "Therefore, Joseph, you will strive in time with all your might for novelty and invention; but by no means overturn the rules of art, which imitates and perfects nature, but never destroys it. If you master all this through continuous practice and if you acquire skill, Joseph, I trust you will have all you need to become famous as an exceptional composer." Translated from the annotated German translation published by Bach's student Lorenz Christoph Mizler (Leipzig, 1742), p. 196.
14. Beißwenger 1992, p. 285.
15. Cf. Butt 1994; Dammann 1985; Leisinger 1994.
16. *Musicalische Bibliothek,* V (Leipzig, 1738), p. 72.
17. *Kurze doch deutliche Anleitung zu der lieblich- und löblichen Singekunst* (Mühlhausen, 1690, 1704) (Butt 1994, p. 37).
18. *De usu atque praestantia Philosophiae in Theologia, Iurisprudentia, Medicina* (Leipzig, 1736) (Leisinger 1994, p. 66).
19. Wilson 1998, p. 14.
20. *NBR,* no. 349.
21. Fabian 1967, pp. 61ff.
22. "Anfangsgründe des General-Basses," in: *Musikalische Bibliothek,* II/1 (Leipzig, 1740), p. 131.
23. The Leipzig periodical *Acta eruditorum* published in 1714 one of the most important early reviews of Newton's principal opus, with a careful collation of the 1687 and 1713 editions of the *Philosophiae Naturalis Principia Mathematica.* See Cohen 1978, pp. 6f. and 254.

24. For a summary of Newton's intellectual achievements, see Cohen 1985, pp. 161–65.
25. On the "Newtonian style," see Cohen 1985, pp. 165–70.
26. Dobbs-Jacob 1995, pp. 8–12.
27. Cohen 1985, p. 161.
28. Book III of the *Principia:* "De mundi systemate."
29. For Newton's Kepler critique, see Cohen 1985, p. 144.
30. *Precepts and Principles for Playing the Thorough-Bass* (Leipzig, 1738), translated with a commentary by Pamela L. Poulin (Oxford, 1994), p. 11.
31. Unlike, for example, Jean-Philippe Rameau, a true representative of the Age of Reason, who wrote a *Traité de l'harmonie* (Paris, 1722) that included general statements such as "Music is a physico-mathematical science; sound is its physical object, and the ratios found between different sounds constitute its mathematical object." However, this kind of musical science had very little if any bearing on actual compositional practice. Denis Diderot hoped, therefore, that "someone would bring [Rameau's system] out from the obscurities enveloping it and put it within everyone's reach" (1748; cited by Lester 1992, p. 143). This did not happen, and by 1800 Rameau had almost completely fallen into obscurity.
32. *NBR,* no. 281.
33. *Vierstimmige Choralgesänge,* 2 vols. (Berlin, 1765–69), incomplete; and 4 vols, ed. Carl Philipp Emanuel Bach and Johann Philipp Kirnberger (Leipzig, 1783–87).
34. *AMZ,* 3 (1801): col. 259 (*Documenta,* p. 79).
35. §53 (cf. Dahlhaus 1978)—anticipated by Kirnberger's "art of pure composition" (*Die Kunst des reinen Satzes in der Musik,* Berlin 1771), a treatise largely based on Bach's teachings. Not insignificantly, Kirnberger's use of "rein" is terminologically consistent with that of Immanuel Kant in his *Kritik der reinen Vernunft* (Königsberg, 1781).
36. *NBR,* no. 373.
37. *NBR,* no. 306.
38. *NBR,* no. 344. Cf. Mattheson's brief critical comment on Bach's assertion, *BD* II, no. 464.
39. The thesis forms part of the title of the book.

CHAPTER 1

1. For the entry in the baptismal register, see *NBR,* no. 2.
2. Cf. *BD* II, no. 59; the baby was baptized on September 7, 1713.
3. Cf. Hübner 1998.
4. *NBR,* no. 7.
5. Brück 1990, 1996.
6. Oefner 1996, p. 19.
7. Rollberg 1927, p. 141.
8. *NBR,* no. 1 (no. 20 of the Genealogy, *NBR,* no. 303).
9. Freyse 1955.
10. Schulze 1985, pp. 61f.
11. Oefner 1996, p. 28.
12. The appearance of Johann Nicolaus in the Eisenach school records created much confusion in the Bach family literature; for some time it was speculated that he was a ninth child of Ambrosius Bach (Helmbold 1930, p. 55). Although he can be related to No. *20* in the Genealogy (*NBR,* no. 303) by implication only, this identification seems justified on many grounds.
13. The "Bachhaus" (Frauenplan 21) was ruled out long ago as Bach's birthplace; in the late seventeenth century, it belonged to Heinrich Borstelmann, rector of the Latin school. Ambrosius's citizenship entry in the Eisenach *Bürgerbuch* reads: "Ambrosius Bach, Haußman, along with his wife and children, on April 4, 1674."
14. *NBR,* no. 89; Brück 1996, p. 113.

15. Freyse 1956.
16. Rollberg 1927, pp. 144f.
17. Of this ensemble of buildings, only the old town hall no longer stands; it was torn down in 1745 after the town council moved to the old "Brothaus" on the east side of the market square, which functions as town hall to this day.
18. Rollberg 1927, p. 135.
19. On the history of the Eisenach court capelle, see Claus Oefner, *Telemann in Eisenach: Die Eisenacher Musikpflege im 18. Jahrhundert* (Eisenach, 1980), pp. 43–48.
20. Nuremberg, 1675.
21. Freyse 1933, p. 8.
22. *Census-Catalogue of Manuscript Sources of Polyphonic Music, 1400–1550* (Stuttgart, 1979), 1:204.
23. Schadaeus, *Promptuarium musicum,* 1611–13 (motets for the church year); Franck, *Threnodiae Davidicae,* 1615; Scheidt, *Geistliche Concerte,* 1634–40, and *Neue Geistliche Concerte,* 1631; Profe, *Geistliche Concerte und Harmonien,* 1641–46.
24. See note 13.
25. Kaiser 1994, p. 180.
26. Of Sebastian's brothers, Johann Christoph entered the *quarta* in 1680 when he was ten, moved on to the *tertia* in 1683 for two years, and left school after graduating in 1685. Johann Balthasar began at eight together with his older brother, but in the *sexta* (1680/81–82), spent two years each in the *quinta* (1683–84), *quarta* (1685–86), and *tertia* (1687–88), and then left school. Johann Jonas entered the *quinta* in 1684 at nine, was promoted after one year, but died a few months into the *quarta*. Finally, Johann Jacob spent three years in the *sexta* (1689–92) and at eleven joined his brother Sebastian in the fifth (1693–94) and fourth (1695) classes. *NBR,* no. 6, and Helmbold 1930.
27. For details, see Petzoldt 1985.
28. *NBR,* no. 6.
29. *NBR,* p. 424.
30. *NBR,* no. 306, p. 298.
31. For a worklist, see Wolff, *Die Bach Familie* (Stuttgart, 1993), pp. 43–45.
32. Freyse 1956, pp. 36–51; Oefner 1996, pp. 48–61.

CHAPTER 2

1. *NBR,* no. 3.
2. *NBR,* nos. 303, 283.
3. Kock 1995, p. 172.
4. *NBR,* no. 4.
5. Helmbold 1930, p. 55.
6. He apparently returned to relatives in Erfurt and eventually studied medicine there. J. S. Bach kept track of his cousin and classmate from Eisenach days; he reports in the Genealogy (*NBR,* no. 303) that Johann Nicolaus (No. *20*) ended up as a *chirurgus* near Königsberg in east Prussia.
7. *NBR,* no. 5.
8. *BD* II, no. 3; *NBR,* no. 7 (excerpt).
9. For biographical details, see Schulze 1985a.
10. *NBR,* no. 9.
11. For the specifications, see *NBR,* no. 10.
12. Küster 1996, p. 74.
13. Discussed in detail by Junghans 1870, p. 8.
14. *NBR,* no. 8f.
15. *NBR,* no. 9.
16. Among Bach's cousins, only the oldest son of Johann Christoph Bach *(13),* Johann

Nicolaus, completed Latin school; he graduated in 1689 from the *prima* of the Eisenach school and then enrolled for a short period at Jena University.

17.  *NBR,* no. 279.

18.  For a representative choral repertoire from the Gotha region, see the Eccard inventory in Wollny 1997a. Virtually no comparable inventories of choral libraries from seventeenth- or eighteenth-century Thuringia have survived; cf. Friedhelm Krummacher, *Die Überlieferung der Choralbearbeitungen in der frühen evangelischen Kantate* (Berlin, 1965), pp. 193f.

19.  *NBR,* no. 306.

20.  *NBR,* no. 304.

21.  See Wolff 1986, pp. 374–86.

22.  Ibid., p. 382.

23.  *NBR,* no. 306, p. 299.

24.  Complete inventories in *Keyboard Music from the Andreas Bach Book and the Möller Manuscript,* ed. Robert Hill, Harvard Publications in Music, vol. 16 (Cambridge, 1991), pp. xxix–xlvi. The exact dating of the two manuscripts is problematic, but the Möller Manuscript (MM), at least in part, most likely preceded the Andreas Bach Book (ABB). Schulze 1984a, who first identified the principal scribe, dates both in the period 1705–13, with later entries by scribes other than Johann Christoph Bach; Hill dates MM c. 1703–7 and ABB c. 1708–13 and beyond. There are, however, neither philological nor codicological reasons that speak against the possibility of assuming slightly earlier dates for the beginning of both manuscripts, especially for ABB. See also the discussion on pp. 30–56.

25.  One item from Johann Christoph Bach's collection (his copy of Buxtehude's Prelude in G minor, BuxWV 148) ended up in the United States; cf. Hans-Joachim Schulze, "Bach und Buxtehude. Eine wenig beachtete Quelle in der Carnegie Library zu Pittsburgh/PA," *BJ* 1991: 177–81. The copy most likely originates from before 1700 and might include, as Schulze surmises, a section (fol. 2r) copied by Johann Sebastian in Ohrdruf. This would then represent his earliest autograph sample.

26.  Schulze 1985a, p. 77.

27.  See Hill 1985; *HWV,* vol 3.

28.  Mainwaring, p. 35.

29.  *The Letters of C. P. E. Bach,* trans. and ed. Stephen Clark (Oxford, 1997), no. 287; see also the corresponding remark in Bach's autograph catalogue of his keyboard works (1772), cited in Wolff 1999.

30.  Johann Pachelbel, *Orgelwerke,* ed, Max Seiffert. Denkmäler der Tonkunst in Bayern, IV/1 (1903), no. 66.

31.  Cf. *BJ* 1997: 158–59.

32.  *NBR,* p. 459.

33.  *NBR,* p. 456.

CHAPTER 3

1.  Herda (1674–1728) had served toward the end of his Lüneburg years as a bass *concertist.* He then studied theology at Jena University for two years, taught briefly in Gotha, and became cantor in Ohrdruf in January 1698; cf. Fock 1950, p. 38.

2.  Ibid., p. 38.

3.  Indicated by the wording in the Obituary of 1750/54: "Johann Sebastian betook himself, in company with one of his schoolfellows, named Erdmann" (*NBR,* no. 306, p. 299); see also *NBR,* p. 35.

4.  In a letter of 1726 to Erdmann (*NBR,* no. 121).

5.  One of the very few descendants of Veit Bach's second son, mentioned in the Genealogy (*NBR,* no. 303, p. 286).

6.  They must have arrived in time for the beginning of the special rehearsal period for

Easter. According to the school's regulations, "at Easter, the choral rehearsals began on the Thursday before Palm Sunday [which fell that year on April 1] and lasted until the Wednesday before Maundy Thursday" (Fock 1950, p. 71).

7. On the organization of services and music, see Fock 1950 (which includes a 1655 schedule for Vespers and Matins).

8. First Sunday in Advent, three Christmas feast days, New Year's Day, Epiphany, Estomihi Sunday, Good Friday, three Easter feast days, Jubilate Sunday, Ascension Day, three Pentecost feast days, Trinity Sunday, tenth and eleventh Sundays after Trinity, St. Michael's Day, and the three Marian feasts. Cf. Fock 1950, p. 27.

9. Letters and other documents show that Bach possessed at least an elementary facility in French; the most extensive document in French is his 1721 dedication of the *Brandenburg Concertos* (*NBR*, no. 84), for which he may have received some expert linguistic assistance. See Chapter 7, note 50.

10. Published in Fock 1950, pp. 114–15. Other compositions are contained in the inventory of the St. Michael's choir library; cf. note 11.

11. For inventories, see Seiffert 1907–8 and Schering 1918–19; the Leipzig collection has not survived.

12. *NBR*, no. 306, p. 298.

13. See Küster 1996, pp. 87–97, although Küster's efforts in postulating that Bach never sang soprano in Lüneburg and was actually hired as bassist fail to convince; see review by Schulze in *BJ* 1997: 204.

14. *NBR*, no. 394, p. 397.

15. Spitta I, pp. 187f.

16. *NBR*, p. 426.

17. The school owned at least one harpsichord, a regal (reed organ), and a relatively new *positiv* organ (with four stops) that was purchased in 1662; cf. Fock 1950, p. 81. St. Michael's had owned two organs since 1474. The larger instrument, expanded and rebuilt several times, had thirty-two stops (three manuals and pedal) around 1700 but was in a poor state of repair. According to an expertise prepared c. 1704–5 by Matthias Dropa, a pupil of the renowned organ builder Arp Schnitger, only twenty-five stops were then playable. Subsequently, a completely new organ was commissioned from Dropa and built by him in 1705–8. Cf. Fock 1974, pp. 120–23; Petzoldt 1992, p. 122.

18. Fock 1950, pp. 81f.

19. Morhardt, son of Peter Morhardt (d. 1685), the distinguished previous organist at St. Michael's from 1662, was provisionally entrusted with the position after his father's death "until another able organist can again be appointed" (Petzoldt 1992, p. 113). This had to wait until 1707, when, after a thorough renovation of the organ, Gottfried Philipp Flor was appointed. On the older Morhardt, see *New Grove* 12:573f.

Löwe, who signed himself "Löw von Eysenach," was born in Vienna, where his father, a native of Eisenach, served as a diplomat. He had studied with Heinrich Schütz and served as capellmeister in Wolfenbüttel and Zeitz before taking up the organist post in Lüneburg in 1683. Most of his vocal and instrumental compositions and all of his publications appeared before his Lüneburg period.

Flor was the oldest son of the prominent composer Christian Flor, organist at St. John's in Lüneburg from 1668 (deputy) and 1676. The second son, Gottfried Philipp (1682–1723), became organist at St. Michael's in 1707 (see note 20).

20. *BD* II, no. 224.

21. *NBR*, no. 395.

22. As stated at the opening of the Obituary; see *NBR*, no. 306.

23. Johann Christoph Graff reportedly studied composition with Böhm in Lüneburg (Walther 1732, p. 288). Previously he had been a pupil of Johann Pachelbel in Erfurt, at the same time as the Ohrdruf Johann Christoph Bach (Schulze 1985a, p. 66).

24. Altogether ten suites plus one overture (copied by J. C. Bach) represent virtually everything Böhm wrote in this genre.

25. Zehnder 1988, pp. 76f.
26. *NBR*, no. 306, p. 303.
27. *NBR*, no. 397. Friedrich Wilhelm Marpurg, who reported the anecdote in 1786, personally knew Bach and his two oldest sons.
28. Johann Ernst, son of Johann Christoph, Ambrosius Bach's twin brother, succeeded Sebastian in 1707 as organist of the Arnstadt New Church.
29. *Arnstädter Bachbuch,* p. 63.
30. See *NBR,* no. 12.
31. *NBR,* nos. 358a, 358b.
32. Cf. Wolff, *Essays,* p. 64; Wolff 1995, pp. 24f.
33. See Wolff, *Essays,* pp. 65–71.
34. See Walker 1989.
35. Carl Philipp Emanuel Bach later reports that his father held Keiser in high esteem but did not know him personally (*NBR,* no. 395, p. 400).
36. *NBR,* no. 306, p. 300.
37. See *BJ* 1985: 107, reprinted in Wolff, *Essays,* p. 62. Beginning with Spitta and continuing to 1985, the Bach literature consistently interpreted this passage as referring to Bach's trips to the town of Celle.
38. Cf. Fock 1950, pp. 44f.
39. Fock 1950 was the first to reject the prevailing earlier view that Bach remained at St. Michael's through much of 1702, and makes the case for Bach's graduation in the spring of 1702. The pertinent Lüneburg school registers have not survived, but considering Bach's outstanding academic achievements at the Ohrdruf Lyceum, he should have had no trouble in meeting St. Michael's requirements in the customary four semesters, to which one semester from the Ohrdruf *prima* must be added.
40. Traditional Bach biographies, including Küster 1996, assume a course that led more or less directly from Lüneburg to Weimar, without an extended stay with the family in between.
41. All notions of tension between the two brothers, often assumed in the older Bach literature, were dispelled by Schulze 1985a.
42. See Schulze 1985a, pp. 73–75; Johann Christoph Bach's autobiographical note (*NBR,* no. 9) belongs in this context.
43. *NBR,* no. 303.
44. *NBR,* no. 395.
45. *NBR,* no. 189.
46. The organ was built in 1603 by Ezechiel Greutscher of Eisleben. A new, two-manual instrument by Zacharias Hildebrandt (with twenty-eight stops) was dedicated on June 1, 1728, in the presence of Duke Christian, Bach's later patron and younger brother of Duke Johann Georg (see Schmidt I, pp. 702–3).
47. Sangerhausen church records of 1703 as quoted in Schmidt I, pp. 722–25; Werner 1911, p. 78. Kobelius later wrote numerous works for the Weissenfels court, and from 1716 regularly composed operas for the court under Duke Christian, one of Bach's major princely patrons beginning in 1713 (see Werner 1911, p. 119). In 1724, Kobelius succeeded Krieger as court capellmeister in Weissenfels, and in 1729 (two years before Kobelius's death) Bach was appointed titular capellmeister to the duke of Weissenfels—a curious if coincidental knotting together of two musical fates.
48. *NBR,* no. 188.
49. Genealogy, *NBR,* no. 303.
50. *NBR,* no. 13.
51. Ibid.
52. See the Genealogy entry under no. 24 in *NBR,* no. 303.
53. Forkel, on the other hand, reported in 1802 that "he was engaged to play the violin" (*NBR,* p. 426), but it is unclear where he obtained such information, and furthermore,

the remark is contradicted in a reference to Bach as "Court Organist to the Prince of Saxe-Weimar" in the records of Bach's Arnstadt organ examination of July 1703 (*NBR*, no. 15). That reference, however, may have been a free invention of the Arnstadt burgomaster or a minor act of misrepresentation by Bach himself.

54. Whether the lackey Hoffmann at the Weimar court was a descendant of the town musician and *Hausmann* Johann Christoph Hoffmann of Suhl and therefore a distant relative of Bach's (as surmised by Jauernig 1950, p. 52) cannot be ascertained.

55. For the little-known details of Effler's biography, see Javernig 1950.

56. The cost for the instrument was covered by a bequest of 800 florins; the detailed contract drawn up for the organ builder was signed October 17, 1699 (see *Arnstädter Bachbuch* 1950, pp. 81–84). For the most complete list available of Wender organs, see Kröhner 1995, p. 85.

57. *Arnstädter Bachbuch* 1950, pp. 87, 84.

58. Expanded version of Werckmeister's earlier *Orgelprobe, oder kurze Beschreibung, wie . . . die Orgelwerke . . . annehmen, probiren, untersuchen . . . solle* (Frankfurt/Main and Leipzig, 1681).

59. *NBR*, no. 31.

60. Cf. Williams 1982, p. 185.

61. *NBR*, no. 15.

62. *NBR*, p. 41.

63. "Every year at the Feast of St. John the Baptist he shall play at the close of the afternoon service for a half hour the full organ with all its stops and voices in pleasing and harmonious concord, in remembrance of his installation as organist, and thus at the same time give proof to the whole Christian congregation of how he has improved himself in his office during the year." Cf. Ziller 1936, p. 127.

64. The notion of Bach as a late starter goes back to Spitta, and the fact that even Bach's Weimar cantatas of 1714–17 have long been considered among his "early" works reinforced the idea.

65. After 1750; see BWV², p. 530.

66. *NBR*, no. 303, p. 289.

67. *NBR*, no. 121.

68. The Toccata in D minor, "In honorem delectissimi fratris Joh. Christ, Bach Ohrdruffiensis," BWV 913, seems to belong in this same context, perhaps somewhat later; see *NBA/KB* V/9.1 (Wollny).

CHAPTER 4

1. *NBR*, no. 306, p. 300.

2. *NBR*, no. 16; *BD* II, no. 11.

3. Spitta I, pp. 223f; Schiffner 1995, pp. 9f.

4. The counts of Schwarzburg also ruled in two other Thuringian principalities, with residences in Rudolstadt and Sondershausen.

5. Next to the Naumburg and Magdeburg cathedrals the most significant medieval sacred structure in Thuringia and Saxony.

6. *Arnstädter Bachbuch*, p. 95. For comparison, the superintendent and senior minister Olearius earned a salary of 100 florins. Not included in any of the figures are additional payments in kind and benefits.

7. Schiffner 1995, p. 5.

8. *NBR*, no. 16.

9. *NBR*, no. 17; the cash supplement for room and board compared extremely favorably with the payments in kind received instead by the interim organist Börner, 1702–3, and by Johann Ernst Bach, from 1707 (three and one and a half, respectively, bushels of grain).

10. Bach's compensation came from three different sources, reflecting joint responsibil-

ity of church and town for his position: 25 florins from the cash box of the New Church, 25 florins from the beer taxes, and 30 talers from St. George's Hospital.

11. *Arnstädter Bachbuch*, p. 54.

12. The Wender organ has long been replaced by enlarged successor instruments, but much of the original case and facade have been preserved.

13. For the original specification, identical with that of the organ contract of 1699, and a detailed description of the authentic console of the Wender organ (removed in 1864, now kept in the Bach Memorial at the Arnstadt Museum), see Wenke 1995; all previous descriptions of the organ contain numerous errors.

14. Werckmeister's *Erweiterte und verbesserte Orgelprobe* (Quedlinburg, 1689), p. 79, deemed the tuning system "a good adequate temperament"; the term "wohl temperiret" appears already on the title page of the 1681 edition of his *Orgelprobe*. Cf. Williams 1984, III, p. 184.

15. The exact pitch and the actual tuning are not known.

16. *Harmonologia musica* (Quedlinburg, 1702).

17. Schiffner 1985, p. 51.

18. *Biblische Erklärung* (Leipzig, 1679–81); cf. *NBR*, no. 279. The son of the Arnstadt superintendent, Johann Christoph Olearius, served before Bach's time as preacher at the New Church and also wrote a town chronicle, *Historia Arnstadiensis* (Arnstadt, 1701).

19. Excerpts in *BJ* 1995: 101–2.

20. See Petzoldt 1997, pp. 129–31.

21. Schiffner 1985, p. 15. Gleitsmann's appointment letter required him to present new compositions for all Sundays and feast days and to rehearse those extensively.

22. *NBR*, no. 19.

23. For the ages of the other Lyceum students involved in the Geyersbach affair, see *BD* II, no. 14.

24. *NBR*, no. 20.

25. Ibid.

26. Ibid.

27. Schiffner 1995, pp. 24f.

28. *NBR*, no. 7.

29. Fuhrmann 1995, p. 28.

30. *BD* II, no. 14, p. 17.

31. In 1705, the capelle numbered twenty-two, but in the absence of name lists, its exact membership during the Gleitsmann years (1701–10) cannot be determined; see *Arnstädter Bachbuch*, pp. 68–78.

32. Composer(s) and performers are unknown; see *Arnstädter Bachbuch*, p. 75.

33. Schiffner 1995, p. 5.

34. *NBR*, no. 21.

35. Spitta I, p. 328, hypothetically identified Maria Barbara as the *frembde Jungfer*.

36. Schiffner 1995, p. 51.

37. *Arnstädter Bachbuch*, p. 38.

38. *BD* II, no. 26.

39. *NBR*, no. 22a.

40. *NBR*, no. 26.

41. *NBR*, no. 303.

42. Spitta I, p. 369 proposes as occasion for this work the wedding of Johann Lorenz Stauber and Regina Wedemann in Dornheim; Küster 1996, p. 171, dates BWV 196 for stylistic reasons to the early Weimar years.

43. The text includes, for example, the names "Salome" and "Dominus Johannes," which may refer to Bach's sister Marie Salome and the parson Johann Lorenz Stauber; "ancillam in corona aurea" may refer to a maid (any of the Michael Bach daughters?) at the Golden Crown *(Güldene Krone),* the house of Burgomaster Feldhaus.

44. *NBR,* no. 306, p. 300.
45. *NBR,* no. 395.
46. See repertoire in Andreas-Bach-Book and Möller Manuscript (Hill 1991) as well as Bach's elaborations on Legrenzi and Corelli, BWV 574 and 579.
47. *NBR,* no. 395.
48. The most prominent autograph is that of BWV 739; see *NBR,* no. 286.
49. Ever since Spitta I, book 2.
50. Included in Neumeister Collection; see Wolff, *Essays,* p. 120.
51. Johann Mattheson, *Grundlage einer Ehrenpforte* (Hamburg, 1740); reprint, ed. M. Schneider (Kassel, 1969), p. 94.
52. Proceedings, *NBR,* no. 20.
53. *BD,* no. 1; the calculation of c. sixteen weeks (about four times four weeks) is based on the rebuke to Bach for his prolonged absence, *NBR,* no. 20.
54. *NBR,* no. 21.
55. Walther to Johann Mattheson; Johann Gottfried. Walther, *Briefe,* ed. Klaus Beckmann and Hans-Joachim Schulze (Leipzig, 1987), pp. 219f.
56. J. G. Ahle received his laureateship in 1680 from Emperor Leopold I.
57. In the concluding chorale of cantata BWV 60, "Es ist genung" (1723), Bach makes use of J. R. Ahle's aria melody, including its ascent to the augmented fourth (A/B/C-sharp/D-sharp), from the latter's *Drittes Zehn Neuer Geistlicher Arien* (Mühlhausen, 1662).
58. *NBR,* no. 22a.
59. The sources of the first Leipzig re-performance of this piece reflect a number of substantive changes, such as the apparent replacement of the original final movement by a newly composed four-part chorale; see BC A 54a–b.
60. *NBR,* no. 24.
61. *BD* II, nos. 22–23.
62. Bach started with a rather busy weekend, for the festival of Visitation (July 2) fell on a Saturday. M. Petzoldt (1992, pp. 135f.) makes a case for Bach having performed the cantata BWV 223 on the Marian feast day, based on some connections between the (incomplete) text of the (fragmentary) cantata and the outline of a sermon held on this day by pastor Eilmar. The question is, however, whether there was really sufficient time for communicating with Eilmar, moving from Arnstadt to Mühlhausen, and preparing a performance.
63. Cf. *BD* II, commentary to no. 26 and nos. 34–35.
64. Petzoldt 1992, p. 130.
65. Ibid., p. 138.
66. *NBR,* no. 23.
67. *NBR,* no. 22b.
68. Cf. Ernst 1987.
69. The nunnery was torn down after 1884, but the Wender organ survives in part at the village church of Dörna near Mühlhausen, Wender's birthplace; cf. Ernst 1987, pp. 80f.
70. Ibid., p. 77.
71. For example, the organist's fee at St. Blasius's for a wedding Mass with a piece of concerted music ("so figural musiciret wird") amounted to 9 groschen; see ibid.
72. Walther, *Lexicon,* p. 557.
73. Reported by Forkel, *NBR,* p. 456.
74. Exemplars of both formularies are to be found in the Mühlhausen church archives; cf. Petzoldt, *WBK* 1: 131–33.
75. *BD* I, p. 154; Petzoldt 1992, pp. 142f.
76. *NBR,* no. 31.
77. *NBR,* no. 358b.
78. Cf. the historical description of the ceremony (1705) in *NBA/KB* I/32.1, pp. 59f.

79.   *NBR,* no. 28a.
80.   *NBR,* no. 28d.
81.   *NBR,* no. 27.
82.   *NBR,* comments to no. 54.
83.   Rondeau from Jean-Baptiste Lully's 1686 opera *Armide,* also disseminated after 1700 as a keyboard suite; cf. Wolff 1995a, p. 27.
84.   *BD* III, p. 638. Eilmar was present in Weimar on December 29, 1708, at the christening of Catharina Dorothea Bach, along with godmothers Martha Catharina Lämmerhirt (widow of Bach's late uncle Tobias Lämmerhirt) and Johanna Dorothea Bach, wife of his Ohrdruf brother Johann Christoph. See *BD* II, no. 42.
85.   Jauernig 1950, pp. 53f.; Schrammek 1988, pp. 100f.
86.   *NBR,* no. 306, p. 300.
87.   Jauernig 1950, p. 55. Effler died 1711 in Jena, where his children lived.
88.   *NBR,* no. 35.
89.   This view, summarized by W. Emery in *New Grove,* 1: p. 58, goes back to Spitta I, pp. 358–64. Petzoldt 1992, pp. 133–35, corrects the picture of a supposedly anti-orthodox Frohne but does not draw any conclusions about Bach's move from Mühlhausen to Weimar.
90.   Petzoldt 1992, pp. 133f.
91.   See Bunners 1966.
92.   Beißwenger 1992, pp. 46ff. The only very early example, albeit a secular one, is the autograph copy of a cantata by Biffi; see above, p. 88. Peter Wollny has made a plausible case for the transmission of what constitutes today the bulk of the *Alt-Bachisches Archiv* via the Arnstadt cantor Heindorff, a close friend of the Bach family (see Wollny 1998).
93.   *NBR,* no. 33.
94.   *NBR,* no. 34.
95.   *BD* II, no. 51.
96.   *BD* II, no. 365.

CHAPTER 5

1.    *NBR,* no. 36.
2.    *BD* II, no. 45. 1709 census listing: "The organist Johann Sebastian Bach, with his sweetheart and her sister."
3.    For Bach's total compensation and ducal gifts, 1708–13, see *NBR,* nos. 35–39; *BD* II, no. 48; cf. also Jauernig 1950, pp. 51–58.
4.    Jung 1985, p. 11.
5.    *BD* II, no. 56.
6.    *BD* II, no. 58.
7.    Jung 1985, pp. 5f.; Glöckner, *Bachfest* 1985.
8.    *NBR,* no. 38.
9.    His collections included, for example, a viola da gamba by the famous Hamburg instrument builder Joachim Tielke, with marvelous ornamental inlay of ivory; see Günther Hellwig, *Joachim Tielke, ein Hamburger Lauten-und Violenmacher der Barockzeit* (Frankfurt, 1979), p. 97.
10.   *NBR,* no. 43.
11.   S. E. Hanks, *New Grove,* 9: 659.
12.   *NBR,* no. 395.
13.   *NBR,* no. 39f–g. Bach's base salary was paid by the joint ducal treasury.
14.   Jung 1985, p. 36.
15.   Walther, *Lexicon,* p. 331.

16.   Jauernig 1950, p. 52, suggests that he may be related to the Hoffmann family of musicians from Suhl (Thuringia), who were in turn related to several Bach family members by marriage. The godmother of Bach's daughter Maria Sophia, born in 1713, was the wife of Johann Christoph Hoffmann from Suhl, great-grandson of the old town piper of Suhl (*NBR*, no. 303, pp. 286f).

17.   Küster 1996, pp. 190f. Bach's appointment in 1703 may have been facilitated by the younger Drese's absence.

18.   Dimensions: height: 7 + 7.5 + 5m (ceiling); 4.75 + 3.5m (*Capelle* + cupola). Jauernig 1950, p. 60; Schrammek 1988, p. 99. See also Chapter 12, footnote 24, regarding the "echo tower" effect of the *Capelle*.

19.   Gottfried Albin Wette, *Historische Nachrichten von der berühmten Residenz-Statt Weimar*, vol. 1 (Weimar, 1737).

20.   In 1638, Compenius built the large instrument for Johann Bach at the Prediger Church in Erfurt. For details regarding the history of the Weimar palace organ, see Schrammek 1988.

21.   Schrammek 1988, pp. 103–5.

22.   Jauernig 1950, p. 73. J. Adlung (*Anleitung zu der musikalischen Gelahrtheit*, Erfurt, 1758, p. 425) reports that the carillon of the Weimar court organ extended through all keys of one manual.

23.   Jauernig 1950, p. 74.

24.   *NBR*, no. 312c.

25.   The full contractual payment for the organ, however, did not occur until September 15, 1714.

26.   For a student list, see *NBR*, pp. 315–16; for J. B. and J. L. Bach, see *BD* II, nos. 82 and 277.

27.   Schulze, *Bach-Überlieferung*, pp. 158–59; on the de Graaf connection, pp. 156–58.

28.   Also works by Dieupart and other French masters; see Horn 1986.

29.   *NBR*, no. 69.

30.   Chronology according to Wolff, Stinson 1996.

31.   Facsimile edition (Leipzig, 1981).

32.   *NBR*, no. 35.

33.   Kobayashi 1995, p. 304, dates BWV 199 to August 27, 1713; for BWV 54, see *NBA/KB* I/8 (Wolff), p. 89.

34.   Reported by P. D. Kräuter in 1713 (*NBR*, no. 312c).

35.   See Melamed-Sanders 1999; previously attributed to Reinhard Keiser. An extant libretto of the Passion points to a 1707 performance in Hamburg under Brauns.

36.   On March 22, 1714, Bach stood godfather for a son born to Weldig in Weissenfels (*BD* II, no. 68).

37.   *BD* II, no. 39, p. 36.

38.   *NBR*, no. 312c.

39.   See *NBR*, no. 59.

40.   *NBR*, p. 307.

41.   *NBR*, no. 350.

42.   Beißwenger, 1992, nos. I/A/2, I/F/2.

43.   *NBR*, p. 435. The possibility of the friend's being Walther was suggested by Spitta I, p. 388.

44.   Primarily C. P. E. Bach and J. J. Quantz.

45.   *NBR*, p. 434.

46.   *NBR*, pp. 432–34.

47.   *NBR*, pp. 438–39.

48.   *NBR*, no. 306, p. 306.

49.   *NBR*, p. 440.

50. *NBR,* no. 31.
51. *NBR,* no. 236.
52. *NBR,* no. 72.
53. *NBR,* p. 440.
54. *Dresdner Gelehrten Anzeigen,* 1798, no. 7 (*BJ* 1983: 103).


CHAPTER 6

1. *NBR,* no. 51.
2. *Der vollkommene Capell-Meister* (Hamburg, 1739), p. 483.
3. "The courier to the organist in Weimar" received "fee and waiting money" (*NBR,* no. 46a).
4. *NBR,* no. 491
5. *BD,* pp. 24f.
6. Only ten miles south of Halle, up the Saale River and on the way to Weimar, Johann Friedrich Wender of Mühlhausen was at the time building his largest instrument ever (with sixty-six stops on four manuals and pedal) at the cathedral of Merseburg (see Kröhner 1995, p. 85). As Wender and Bach had known each other well since Arnstadt, Bach would have been aware of the Merseburg project. The cathedral organist and music director of the duke of Saxe-Merseburg was Georg Friedrich Kauffmann, a former student of Johann Heinrich Buttstedt in Erfurt and later among Bach's competitors for the St. Thomas cantorate in Leipzig.
7. Friedrich Chrysander (*G. F. Händel,* vol. 1, Leipzig, 1858; "Joh. Seb. Bach und sein Sohn Wilhelm Friedemann in Halle, 1713–1768," *Jahrbücher für musikalische Wissenschaft,* vol. 2, Leipzig, 1867) was the first to suggest Bach's involvement with the Halle organ project, and he even suggested that Bach wrote the specifications. Spitta (I, p. 521) points out that there is no evidence for the latter claim. There are, however, two related specification drafts, an anonymous one dated 1712 *(Dispositio eines großen 16 füßigen Orgelwerckes)* and a later one signed by Cuntzius; see *BD* I, p. 160. Vladimir Stadnitschenko ("Studien zur Vokalmusik Friedrich Wilhelm Zachows," Ph.D. diss., University of Freiburg/Breisgau, 1998, pp. 242–44) identifies some important concordances between Bach's Mühlhausen organ renovation plan and the Halle project, strongly suggesting that Bach indeed had some influence on the design of the Halle organ. Serauky 1939, pp. 479–83.
8. *NBR,* no. 46b.
9. *NBR,* no. 50.
10. *NBR,* nos. 46a and 47.
11. None of the pieces that have for various reasons been considered (BWV 21, 61, and 63) show any evidence of originating in conjunction with Bach's Halle audition; for details, see Wollny 1994.
12. Ibid., p. 31.
13. *NBR,* no. 48.
14. *NBR,* no. 306, p. 300.
15. *NBR,* no. 50.
16. See *NBA/KB* I/8 (Wolff), p. 114. On Franck's poetry, see Schulze, *WBK* 1: 105–7.
17. List b is undated, but must have originated from late 1714 or early 1715 because it includes Christoph Alt, who died in 1715. His son Philipp Samuel as well as Gottfried Blühnitz, though both on list a, do not appear on list b; they may not have counted among the full-time members.
18. Terry 1993, pp. 91f.
19. Cf. Johann Gottfried Walther, *Briefe,* ed. Klaus Beckmann and Hans-Joachim Schulze

(Leipzig, 1987), p. 72, where the town organist reports about his playing the violin at court. Eight choirboys were regularly paid by the court treasury for handling the liturgical chant *(Choralsingen);* see Jauernig 1950, p. 71.

20. *NBR,* no. 394.

21. See *NBA/KB* I/8.1–2 (Wolff), p. 104. In 1713–15, Schubart was officially paid by the court of Duke Ernst August for copying services *(Musicalienschreiben).*

22. *BD* II, nos. 69, 80; *NBR,* no.53.

23. To the original four-part string score of the sonata (v, va 1–2, vc), Bach added a separate part for *ripieno* violin, either immediately before the first performance or for a later Weimar performance. For this version, the string ensemble required six players; recorder and organ would bring the minimum total number to eight. Still more would be needed if the continuo group were to include bassoon and/or violone.

24. Twenty-two trees were needed for beams and timberwork; the entire project was completed by December 1714 with the finishing of a copper roof (Jauernig 1950, pp. 64f.).

25. A pound of soap purchased in July 1712 helped grease the machinery; see ibid., p. 63.

26. Ibid., pp. 63f.

27. In 1718, "six red-painted benches" were newly acquired for the *Capelle,* apparently to replace old ones (ibid., p. 70).

28. As quoted by Schrammek 1988, p. 99.

29. *Gottgefälliges Kirchen-Opffer* (Darmstadt, 1711). On Lehms and Neumaster texts, see Schulze, *WBK* 1: 101–5.

30. *Geistliches Singen und Spielen* (Gotha, 1711).

31. The court paid the members of the court capelle for mourning clothes *(BD* II, no. 75).

32. A calligraphic copy of the text has survived. On April 4, 1716, Franck, Bach, and two other court officials received, in conjunction with the preceding funeral service, unspecified shares of a substantial payment from the treasury of the Red Palace, totaling 45 florins 15 groschen (Glöckner 1985, p. 163).

33. Cf. Dürr 1976, Hofmann 1993, Kobayashi 1995.

34. On the early history of BWV 21, see BC A99a and Wolff 1996b.

35. Cf. Dürr 1977, pp. 65 and 69; also Hofmann 1993, p. 29.

36. *NBR,* no. 54.

37. Cf. *NBA* IX/2; Beißwenger 1992; Kobayashi 1995; and Peter Wollny, book review in *BJ* 1998: 209.

38. *NBR,* no. 306, p. 300.

39. This and the following quotations in *NBR,* pp. 441f. Quotations, like the others in this volume, are rendered in the 1820 English translation by A. F. C. Kollmann, which is reproduced in its entirety on pp. 419–82.

40. See BWV 2, p. 530.

41. In Birnbaum's reply to Scheibe: "Harmony becomes far more complete if all the voices collaborate to form it" *(NBR,* no. 344, p. 347); cf. Epilogue.

42. For a more thorough analysis, see Wolff, *Essays,* Chapter 7.

43. *NBR,* no. 395.

44. *NBR,* p. 436. Mozart also used the clavichord to check the results of his composing activities.

45. *NBR,* no. 57.

46. Jauernig 1959, pp. 102–4.

47. Glöckner 1988, pp. 138.

48. *BD* II, no. 81.

49. Jauernig 1950, p. 99.

50. See Glöckner 1985, pp. 159–64, for the events related to Prince Johann Ernst's death, and Melamed 1993 for the possible performance on November 10 of the (lost) cantata "Wir haben nicht mit Fleisch und Blut."

51. *BD* II, no. 77 (for the correct identification of the document, see Glöckner 1985).

52. Smend, 1985, p. 187.

53. Duchess Eleonore Wilhelmine herself may also have contributed to furthering connections between her brother and Bach; in August 1718, Bach asked her to be godmother to his son Leopold Augustus (*BD* II, no. 94).

54. *NBR*, no. 60.

55. *NBR*, nos. 63–65.

56. See Glöckner 1995.

57. Cf. BC D 1.

58. See Telemann's autobiography, in Johann Mattheson, *Grundlage einer Ehrenpforte* (Hamburg, 1740), p. 364.

59. *NBR*, no. 70b.

60. *NBR*, no. 318.

61. The oldest report appears in Birnbaum's "Defense" (*NBR*, no. 67). The most detailed source is the Obituary (*NBR*, pp. 301–2). And Marpurg indicated in 1786 that he heard the story directly from Bach. For a comparative reading of the reports, see Breig 1998.

62. *NBR*, no. 396, p. 408.

63. Mattheson, *Grundlage einer Ehrenpforte* (Hamburg, 1740), p. 396.

64. Fürstenau, 2:122. A medal bearing the image of King Augustus the Strong is listed in Marchand's estate (Busch 1996, p. 175).

65. *NBR*, pp. 300–2.

66. Titon du Tillet, *Le Parnass françois* (Paris, 1732), p. 658: "Il ne dependoit que de lui de faire une fortune considerable, mais son esprit incertain et sa conduite des plus singulieres lui empêcherent des profiter de toutes les occasions favorables qui se presentoient"—quoted after Busch 1996, p. 175.

67. *NBR*, no. 67; cf. also *BD* I, no. 6. Forkel apparently errs when he reports that Bach "was not the challenger in this case, but the challenged" (*NBR*, no. 459).

68. Probably Guillaume Marchand (see D. Fuller, in *New Grove* 11:655).

69. Fürstenau, 2: 101–21.

70. *NBR*, no. 395.

71. *NBR*, no. 68.

72. The pertinent records, referred to ("vid. acta") in the document cited, are lost. Points of contention might have been Bach's participation and nonparticipation, respectively, in the bicentennial celebrations of the Lutheran Reformation in late October 1717 and in the upcoming Christmas services.

73. The document regarding Bach's arrest, unknown to Spitta, was found by Paul von Bojanowsky (*Das Weimar Johann Sebastian Bachs*, Weimar, 1903) and then first used in Albert Schweitzer's 1905 biography. Terry 1993, p.114, speculates (erroneously) that Bach wrote the *Orgel-Büchlein* in jail.

74. See *NBR*, no. 315; *NBR*, no. 370; see also *NBA/KB* V/6.1, p. 187.

75. *NBR*, nos. 71–73.

76. Küster 1996, pp. 202f.


CHAPTER 7

1. *NBR*, no. 72.

2. Court councillor and chamberlain Johann Christoph Laurentius, the highest paid official, earned 540 talers; only privy councillor von Zanthier (500) and court marshal von Nostiz (484) earned more than the capellmeister (see Hoppe 1986, p. 39).

3. *NBR,* no. 70.
4. That is, twice Stricker's salary; Cöthen salary payments were made at the end of every month, not quarterly. Extra allowances brought Bach's salary up to about 450 talers.
5. On Bach's Cöthen lodgings, see Hoppe 1994.
6. Hoppe 1997, p. 65.
7. Hoppe 1986, p. 148.
8. Bunge 1905, p. 19; Hoppe 1997, p. 66 (facsimile from the diary). Zanthier later became princely court councillor and director of the administration of the principality of Anhalt-Cöthen.
9. Spitta II, p. 1, took the dates from Leopold's diary.
10. Especially French and Italian music (including three operas by Lully and cantatas by Francesco Mancini); see Hoppe 1986, p. 27.
11. Ibid., p. 28.
12. Reprinted in Johann Adam Hiller, *Lebensbeschreibungen berühmter Musikgelehrten und Tonkünstler neuerer Zeit* (Leipzig, 1784), p. 135.
13. Bunge 1905, p. 19.
14. *NBR,* no. 152.
15. See Michael Tilmouth, "Gottfried Finger," *New Grove* 6: 565–66; Christoph Schubart, "Augustin Reinhard Stricker," *MGG* 12 (1965): cols. 1603–5.
16. *BD* II, no. 99.
17. Based on information provided by Hoppe 1986 and *BD* II, nos. 86, 99, 108, 277.
18. *BD* II, no. 91.
19. The manuscript inventory of the music library at the neighboring ducal castle of Zerbst offers welcome insight into the rich and diversified vocal-instrumental repertoire maintained at a small court. The instrumental genres represented on twenty-four densely filled pages include concertos (for violins, flutes, recorders, oboes, and bassoons), overtures and symphonies for large orchestra, and sonatas for four, three, and two players. See *Concert-Stube des Zerbster Schlosses. Inventarverzeichnis aufgestellt im März 1743,* facsimile edition (Michaelstein, 1983).
20. *Auserlesene und theils noch nie gedruckte Gedichte,* vol. 2 (Halle, 1719).
21. *NBR,* no. 78.
22. *BD* II, no. 96.
23. *BD* II, no. 103.
24. *BD* II, no. 92.
25. Contrary to references in the older literature, neither the specifications nor the manual and pedal ranges of the old St. Agnus organ are known (Henkel 1985, pp. 5, 22).
26. *BD* II, no. 116.
27. On Spieß as composer, see Hoppe 1998, p. 34.
28. Smend 1951/E, p. 34.
29. Smend 1951/E, p. 189.
30. *BD* II, no. 115.
31. *NBR,* no. 76. The visiting musicians listed under the December 1718 date (Johann Gottfried Riemschneider, concertmaster [N. N.] Lienicke [surely a relative of the Cöthen chamber musician and member of the Lienicke family of musicians], Johann Gottfried Vogler, and Emanuel Preese) may have participated in the performance of the cantata BWV Anh. 5 and BWV 66a on the occasion of the prince's birthday.
32. *OPERA PRIMA | Erster Theil: | Bestehet in 6. Italienischen | CANTATEN | à | VOCE SOLA | Worzu | Violino oder Hautbois Solo accompagniret | Von | Augustino Reinhardo Stricker, | HochFürstl. Anhaltscher Capellmeister in Cöthen* (Cöthen, 1715); the collection is dedicated to Prince Leopold.
33. According to Walther, *Lexicon,* p. 527. Riemschneider used to be a member of the Leipzig Collegium Musicum; see Andreas Glöckner, "Musikalisches Leben am Köthener Hof," in *WBK* 2, p. 110.

34. *Händel-Handbuch,* vol. 4: *Dokumente zu Leben und Schaffen* (Leipzig, 1985), p. 173; in 1739, Riemschneider became cantor at the cathedral in Hamburg.
35. *NBR,* no. 152.
36. Table 7.4 provides a summary of detailed financial information analyzed by Hoppe 1986.
37. Still, this percentage rate is relatively high. In comparison, the neighboring princely court of Anhalt-Zerbst, with a total income of 107,618 talers, spent 1,322 talers (1.2 percent) for music (figures for 1723–24). See Hoppe 1986, p. 61.
38. Based on expeditures for 1723–24; see ibid., pp. 43f.
39. See ibid., pp. 31–33.
40. Cited ibid., p. 34.
41. In 1719, Leopold established a palace library and appointed his French tutor from childhood days, Gustave Adolphe Allion de Maiseroy, as first librarian; see ibid., pp. 36, 53.
42. Among other things, many of which related to religious quibbles over Calvinist versus Lutheran dominance, Prince Leopold in particular never overcame the long-lasting negative effects of his decision to deprive Wilhelm Heinrich von Rath, his mother's brother, of his power. Upon his accession in 1716, Leopold dismissed his uncle from the influential position as court and chamber councillor. Domestic and dynastic disputes overshadowed Leopold's administration from beginning to end.
43. *NBR,* no. 128.
44. *NBR,* no. 117; *BD* II, no. 184.
45. *NBR,* no. 117.
46. A detailed description of the funeral rites, based on court documents, is in Smend 1951, pp. 164–67.
47. *NBR,* no. 396 (pp. 407f.). Handel's visits to his hometown are documented for May–June 1719, June 1729, and August 1750 (cf. *Händel-Handbuch,* 4: 82, 173, 442).
48. *NBR,* no. 77.
49. Although no details are known, Immanuel Heinrich Gottlieb Freitag of the Cöthen court capelle probably played in 1720–21 in the margrave's capelle.
50. *NBR,* no. 84. The dedication is written in a French translation that was probably provided by the Cöthen court librarian, Gustave Adolphe Allion (see note 41). In French, "une couple d'années" refers to a period of two years. The date of the dedication (March 24, 1721) is exactly two years after Bach's Berlin visit of March 1719.
51. Hoppe 1986, p. 16.
52. Guest lists are provided in *Neu-verbessert und vermehrtes denckwürdiges Kayser Carls-Baad* (Nuremberg, 1731), pp. 79f. For 1718 the guests listed, by name or title, include Prince Leopold and his brother ("with their princely household"), the cardinal of Saxe-Zeitz, and Princess Elisabetha von Lamberg; for 1720, again Prince Leopold "with his princely household" but without his brother, and then only "Her Royal Majesty, the Queen of Poland and Electoress of Saxony, with her high royal household"—possibly the first time for Bach to encounter Dresden royalty. For both years, general references are made to other high religious officials and secular dignitaries from many different provinces and countries.
53. *BD* II, p. 68.
54. See postscript by Christoph Wolff in Plichta 1981, p. 29.
55. Named after Prince Leopold and his brother August Ludwig. Both princes as well as their sister Eleonore Wilhelmina, duchess of Saxe-Weimar, served as godparents, along with the director of the Cöthen-Anhalt government and the wife of the prince's steward. The baptism with its prominent attendance took place on November 17, 1718, at the castle church (*NBR,* no. 78).
56. *NBR,* no. 306, pp. 304f.

57. *NBR,* no. 80.

58. On Telemann's Hamburg appointment, see *MGG* 13 (1966): col. 187. It remains noteworthy that the reputation Bach earned in 1713 in Halle and 1720 in Hamburg helped pave the way, a generation later, for his son Wilhelm Friedemann to succeed Ziegler in Halle and for Carl Philipp Emanuel to obtain Telemann's position in Hamburg.

59. *NBR,* no. 306, p. 302. Besides a city dwelling, the affluent Reinken owned a suburban lodge; in one of his homes he kept the group portrait (with himself, Buxtehude, and other musicians) that he had commissioned from Jan Voorhout in 1674; see Wolff 1989.

60. For a corresponding quotation from Quantz (1752), see Chapter 5, p. 136f.

61. Not limited to the opening chorus (Psalm 94:19), the other cantata movements also focus on expressions of grief and consolation, as the text incipits indicate: aria no. 3, "Seufzer, Tränen, Kummer, Not" (Sighs, tears, sorrow, need); aria no. 5, "Bäche von gesalznen Tränen" (Streams of salty tears); duet no. 8, "Komm, mein Jesu, und erquicke" (Come, my Jesus, and refresh); chorale no. 9, "Was helfen uns die schweren Sorgen" (What do heavy sorrows help us).

62. *NBR,* no. 319.

63. *BD* II, no. 302. See BWV$^k$, p. 317, for the possibility of Weimar origin of BWV 542/2.

64. Fitting well into the context of Bach's manifold explorations of the tonal spectrum (*Well-Tempered Clavier, Chromatic Fantasy and Fugue,* etc.).

65. Cf. Wolff 1989.

66. *NBR,* no. 81. The St. Jacobi church body authorized to make the appointment consisted of the senior minister (Neumeister), two town council members residing in the parish, and four sworn members; see Kremer 1993, p. 217.

67. The others being Matthias Christoph Wiedeburg of Gera, Heinrich Zinck of Itzehoe, Vincent Lübeck of Hamburg, Johann Joachim Heitmann of Hamburg, Johann Heinrich Frenkel of Ratzeburg, Hans Heinrich Lüders of Flensburg, and Johann Georg Hertzog of Hamburg.

68. Cantor Joachim Gerstenbüttel and the organists of St. Catharine's (Johann Adam Reinken), St. Peter's (Andreas Kniller), and Holy Spirit (Georg Preuß); see *NBR,* no. 81.

69. See also *BD* II, p. 79, and Kremer 1993.

70. *NBR,* no. 82. Mattheson's reference to Bach's playing "on the most various and greatest organs" may refer to Bach's undertaking a tour of the city's organ landscape, probably in the company of a group of musicians and some curious bystanders.

71. See *BD* II, no. 108. The other godparents included Bach and the chamber musician Lienicke.

72. Personal and family trips are usually not documented. But Bach may have attended the funeral of his oldest brother, Christoph, who died on February 22, 1721, at age forty-nine in Ohrdruf, a two-day trip away from Cöthen. In the spring of 1722, he learned of the death of his brother Jacob in faraway Stockholm, where he had served as royal Swedish court musician.

73. *NBR,* no. 85. Bach was in Schleiz for several days in early August and stayed at the Inn of the Blue Angel, all expenses paid. The court account books do not specify the purpose of his visit, indicating only that Bach received his fee on August 7, his hotel bill was paid on the 11th (a Monday), and his mail-coach fare on the 13th. The visit probably involved a church performance on August 10 (ninth Sunday after Trinity), especially since the cantor of the Schleiz palace church, Johann Sebastian Koch, seems to have been an old acquaintance of Bach's; prior to 1711, Koch had served as choir prefect in Mühlhausen.

74. Schubart 1953, p. 48.

75. The Monjou daughters were employed on a part-time basis; see also Smend 1951, p. 35.
76. Schubart 1953, p. 46.
77. Bach is known to have played a guest performance of the cantata "Overgnügte Stunden" (not listed in BWV) on August 9, 1722, the birthday of Prince Johann August, just a few weeks before Johann Friedrich Fasch became capellmeister in Zerbst (BD II, no. 114), but Bach may well have visited and performed in Zerbst before.
78. Indicative of the numerous interfamily connections is the fact that Adam Imanuel Weldig, Bach's colleague at the Weimar court capelle and later a member of the Weissenfels capelle, was godfather in 1713 to a child born to the Weissenfels trumpeter Georg Christian Meissner and Anna Magdalena's sister Katharina. A year later, Bach and Weldig exchanged godparentships: Weldig as godfather to Carl Philipp Emanuel Bach, Bach to Johann Friedrich Immanuel Weldig (see BD II, nos. 67–68).
79. Within a few months, her salary matched that of the highest-paid chamber musician, Joseph Spieß (300 talers).
80. BD II, no. 106.
81. NBR, no. 86.
82. BD II, no. 111. On September 26, 1721, the reading of the will of Martha Katharina Lämmerhirt, widow of Bach's uncle Tobias Lämmerhirt, took place. Bach's share came to about 50 florins, but it was not paid out to him until 1722. Regarding the complex partition of the Lämmerhirt estate, see BD I, no. 8; BD II, nos. 109, 112, 117, and 118; and NBR, no. 89.
83. Hoppe 1986, pp. 16, 31ff.
84. BD II, no. 158.
85. See Zimpel 1979, p. 104.
86. NBR, no. 152.
87. On Telemann's Leipzig activities, see Glöckner 1990, pp. 18–39.
88. For the details of the process leading to Bach's appointment, see Schulze 1977; Schulze 1988; the commentaries to BD I, no. 91, and BD II, nos. 119, 121, 121–125, 127; and NBR, nos. 93–95.
89. NBR, no. 94a.
90. BD II, no. 129.
91. Details about their auditions are conflicting. According to the Hamburg newspaper, Der Hollsteinsche Correspondent, Duve and Kauffmann auditioned on November 29 (First Sunday in Advent) at St. Nicholas's, presenting their cantatas before and after the sermon, while Schott performed his piece on the same day in the Vespers at the New Church. A later issue of the same paper announces for the upcoming period of the New Year's trade fair the trial performances of Graupner, Kauffmann, and— oddly enough—the Dresden court organist Christian Petzolt, whose candidacy is mentioned nowhere else. See Schulze 1988, p. 3.
92. NBR, no. 94b.
93. First suggested by Hans-Joachim Schulze; BWV 75–76, Bach's first Leipzig cantatas, seem to have the same author as well. For further details, also regarding the genesis of BWV 22–23, see NBA/KB I/8 (Wolff), p. 23.
94. NBR, no. 152.
95. NBR, no. 95.
96. NBR, no. 94c.
97. NBR, no. 97.
98. NBR, no. 96.
99. NBR, no. 98.
100. NBR, p. 103.
101. NBR, no. 152.

102. *Aufrichtige Anleitung,* comprising fifteen inventions and fifteen sinfonias, is the title of the collection and not, as usually rendered, the heading of a preface.
103. The 1730 renovation plans for the St. Thomas School provided that "each alumnus receives a sizable cubicle where he can study and, in addition, keep his clavier." See Braun 1995, p. 55.
104. As reported by his pupil Johann Philipp Kirnberger (*NBR,* no. 363).
105. See Heinichen, *Der General-Bass in der Composition* (Dresden, 1728), p. 837.
106. Mattheson, *Das beschützte Orchestre* (Hamburg, 1717), p. 437.
107. *NBR,* no. 306, p. 304.
108. The lost autograph of the cello suites would have been called *Libro Secondo,* corresponding to the *Libro Primo* (= BWV 1001–1006).
109. On the flauto d'echo, see Rampe-Zapf 1997–98.
110. See Dirksen 1992.

### Chapter 8

1. *NBR,* no. 102. Cited from the Hamburg *Staats- und Gelehrte Zeitung,* but similar reports appeared in various papers.
2. Roth's application letter for the Grimma cantorate specified, "I have not only occupied the *Praefectur* at the St. Thomas School for 4 years, but also taken over the [music] directorship at both churches for a whole year—if modesty permits, much to the pleasure of the entire citizenry, of each and every high and low inhabitant—after the death of the late music director, Mr. Kuhnau." The outstanding quality of the prefect is acknowledged in an accompanying recommendation by Christian Ludovici, rector of Leipzig University and former conrector of the St. Thomas School, who points out Roth's "exceptional experience in instrumental and especially in vocal music, the more so as he conducted the music at the churches here, during the vacancy [after the death] of the late Kuhnau, to the greatest pleasure of the patrons" (Schulze 1998, p. 106). It seems likely that Roth continued as prefect for a while under Bach. From March 1725 to Easter 1726 (when he left for Geringswalde), he studied theology at Leipzig University. Although a pertinent testimonial by Bach is not known, he may have served Bach's ensemble for almost three years.
3. Czok 1985, p. 146.
4. In 1765, fifty-six publishers and booksellers had their business in Leipzig, in addition to numerous printers, engravers, and bookbinders (Czok 1985, pp. 150, 161).
5. A census of 1753 counted 32,384 permanent residents, leading to a general estimate of between 32,000 and 35,000 for the second quarter of the eighteenth century. In comparison, Dresden had about 52,000 inhabitants in 1750 (c. 46,500 in 1727), and among the 147 cities in electoral Saxony, Chemnitz (population 10,400) followed as a distant third. See Czok 1982; Czok 1985, p. 163.
6. By 1747, local industry comprised nineteen factories, indicating a shift toward increased manufacturing. The printing business and book trade, strongly identified with Leipzig since the fifteenth and sixteenth centuries, assumed major importance. Cf. Czok 1985, pp. 150ff.; for a detailed summary, see also Stauffer 1994. On Leipzig architecture, see Pevsner 1928.
7. Johann Ernst Hebenstreit, *Museum Richterianum* (Leipzig, 1743), serves as a catalog of the collection and includes an engraving with an interior view of the museum (reproduced in Wustmann 1897, p. 75).
8. Catalog: *Historische Erklärungen der Gemälde, welche Herr Gottfried Winckler in Leipzig gesammelt* (Leipzig, 1768).
9. Czok 1985, pp. 175f.
10. First documented in 1768, cited later in Goethe's *Faust;* see Gustav Wustmann, *Bilderbuch aus der Geschichte der Stadt Leipzig* (Leipzig, 1897), p. 99.

11. The history of the Leipzig Collegia Musica that begins in the early seventeenth century is not without interruptions. Görner's Collegium seems to be the one whose actual origins predate 1700 and that in the 1680s and 90s was under the direction of Kuhnau, when he was a law student at Leipzig University and from 1684 organist at St. Thomas's.

12. Petzoldt 1998.

13. *NBR*, no. 101.

14. *BD* II, no. 135.

15. Theological charter of June 25, 1580, summarizing the central doctrines of the Lutheran Reformation.

16. *BD* II, no. 136.

17. *BD* II, nos. 143–146, 148, 152, 175, 177, 178.

18. *NBR*, nos. 106f.

19. Bach specifically wrote, "I entered upon my university functions at Whitsunday, 1723" (*NBR*, no. 119c, p. 124).

20. First proposed by Arnold Schering, *BJ* 1938: 75f.

21. Payable throughout the year; for example, from the Lobwasser legacy he received 2 florins annually; from the Sinner legacy, 10 talers; and from the Mentzel endowment, 2 talers 16 groschen. Most of the legacies related to endowed performances were to take place under the cantor's direction, so the Rettenbach legacy, for instance, paid for the singing of motets and hymns four times a year in memory of various family members (on January 18, Jacob Handl's motet "Ecce quomodo moritur"; on April 24, the hymn "Herr Jesu Christ, meins Lebens Licht"; on September 9, the hymn "Freu dich sehr, o meine Seele"; and on October 26, the hymn "Herzlich lieb hab ich dich, o Herr"). The Bose legacy funded the singing of the motet "Turbabor sed non perturbabor" on the donor's name day. See *NBR*, no. 109.

22. *NBR*, no. 110; *BD* II, nos. 160–161. From 1733 and 1734–35, respectively, Bach no longer received these payments; others were hired for the task.

23. *NBR*, no. 108.

24. In a memorandum of October 15, 1722, Telemann compares his Frankfurt and Hamburg income with what he was promised in Leipzig ("never under 1,000 talers annually, but ordinarily 1,200 talers and above"), and Graupner's new salary order at the Darmstadt court of May 3, 1723, makes reference to a Leipzig offer of 1,000 talers as well (see Schulze 1998, p. 104).

25. Cf. Hans-Joachim Schulze, in *WBK* 3: 111.

26. Cited from the Hamburg *Relationscourier; NBR*, no. 105.

27. *NBR*, no. 103.

28. *NBR*, no. 104.

29. By contract, the cantor was required "not to take any boys into the School who have not already laid a foundation in music, or are not at least suited to being instructed therein" (*NBR*, no. 100).

30. *NBR*, nos. 141–145.

31. *NBR*, no. 151, p. 150.

32. *Thomana Ordnungen*, 1723 (facsimile edition), p. 12.

33. Transmitted in a copy made in 1738 by Carl August Thieme, pupil at St. Thomas's in 1735–45. See *J. S. Bach's Precepts and Principles . . . ,* translated with facsimile, introduction, and explanatory notes by Pamela L. Poulin (Oxford, 1994).

34. *NBR*, no. 150

35. *Thomana Ordnungen*, 1733 (facsimile edition), p. 23.

36. Ibid., p. 22.

37. *NBR*, no. 100.

38. The 1,500 is a rough estimate, based on some 1,630 regular Sundays and religious feast days celebrated in Leipzig during Bach's tenure (not including special feasts and

events) and taking into consideration occasional absences, illnesses, and two state mourning periods, one of four months' duration in 1727–28 and another of six months' in 1733. During Bach's time, St. Thomas's had a seating capacity of 2,000–2,100, not counting the considerable standing room; St. Nicholas's held slightly more. Both churches were ordinarily filled to capacity. See Stiehl 1984, p. 13.

39. *NBR,* no. 274a.

40. Facsimile in Neumann *Texte,* pp. 448–55.

41. *NBR,* no. 113.

42. At the Leipzig main churches, the organ preluded before the congregational hymns, but ordinarily did not accompany them—with the exception of the hymn before the sermon. See Petzoldt in *WBK* 3: 88.

43. This practice was still being upheld when Lowell Mason reported in 1852 on music in the Leipzig services. After the reading of the Gospel, "the organ burst out in a loud minor voluntary [prelude in the minor key of the following piece], which continued three or four minutes, during which time the violins, violoncellos, double basses, and wind instruments tuned. Yet so carefully was this done, that it was hardly perceptible, for the organ was giving out its full progressive chords, so as to nullify the tuning process, at least upon the ears of the people" (*NBR,* no. 412, p. 523).

44. For details, see Stiller 1970 and Petzoldt in *WBK* 3.

45. Sermons at St. Nicholas's and St. Thomas's for the Sunday and weekday services were assigned according to a fixed schedule. For example, the sermons at the main service on Sundays and feast days were always preached by the senior minister or pastor; archdeacon, deacon, and subdeacon assisted as ministrants for the liturgy of the main service and the administration of the sacrament. The archdeacon at St. Nicholas's preached on Mondays, the archdeacon at St. Thomas's on Tuesdays; the deacon at St. Nicholas's on Fridays, the deacon at St. Thomas's at Vespers on Sundays and feast days; the subdeacon at St. Nicholas's was the Vespers preacher and the subdeacon at St. Thomas's preached the noon sermon on Sundays (see Stiller 1970, pp. 56–58). Except for Vespers, no polyphonic music was sung at these services.

While D. Salomon Deyling served throughout Bach's Leipzig tenure as senior minister (pastor and superintendent, 1720–55) at St. Nicholas's, St. Thomas's had five senior ministers: D. Christian Weiß, 1714–36; Friedrich Wilhelm Schütz, 1737–39 (archdeacon at St. Nicholas's, 1721–37; subdeacon and deacon at St. Thomas's, 1709–21); D. Urban Gottfried Sieber, 1739–41; Gottlieb Gaudlitz, 1741–45; and Romanus Teller, 1745–50 (subdeacon and deacon, 1737–40). Archdeacons at St. Thomas's: Johann Gottlob Carpzov, 1714–30; D. Urban Gottfried Sieber, 1730–39 (subdeacon and deacon, 1710–30); Gottlieb Gaudlitz, 1739–41 (deacon, 1731–39; subdeacon at St. Nicholas's, 1726–31); and Christoph Wolle, 1741–61 (subdeacon, 1739–40).

The St. Thomas Church registered annually between 10,000 and 20,000 communicants, averaging between 150 and 300 per Mass service on Sundays and feast days, fewer at the weekly Mass service (without sermon and music) on Thursdays. Bach and his family took communion at St. Thomas's about twice a year and always at the Thursday Mass—for the first time in the week of the Twenty-second Sunday after Trinity, 1723, and for the last time in the week after the Third Sunday in Advent, 1749 (then with two of his sons). He signed up in advance with his confessors: 1723–36, pastor D. Christian Weiß; 1737–40, deacon M. Romanus Teller; 1740–41, subdeacon M. Johann Paul Ram; and 1741–50, archdeacon Christoph Wolle. See *BD* II, no. 162, and Petzoldt 1985.

46. *NBR,* no. 137.

47. *NBR,* no. 138.

48. Facsimiles in Neumann *Texte,* pp. 422–47. An additional booklet, with texts from the Twenty-second to the Twenty-fifth Sunday after Trinity and the First Sunday in Ad-

vent, 1724, has been missing from a St. Petersburg collection since 1919; see Hobohm 1973, p. 7.

49. Details about printrun and sales of regular cantata booklets are not available, but information about a passion booklet printed for a Good Friday performance in 1738 suggests that Bach counted on three hundred salable copies (*BD* II, no. 416). In 1738, he was invoiced by Breitkopf for 5 talers (paper and printing) and sold these copies at a profit of probably 10 talers or more. Telemann's Hamburg correspondence reports on his income from similar sales of cantata booklets; see Georg Philipp Telemann, *Briefwechsel,* ed. Hans Große and Hans Rudolf Jung (Leipzig, 1972), pp. 28–54.

50. The stipends are documented for 1724–29, 1731, and 1745; see Schulze 1984a.

51. Cf. *NBR,* no. 142.

52. Bach's own soprano voice changed in Lüneburg, after his fifteenth birthday. Nineteenth-century improvements in nutrition accelerated physical growth and caused boys' voices to change much earlier. See Behrendt 1983.

53. *NBR,* no. 151.

54. Schering 1941, p. 150.

55. For instance, the son of town piper Gleditsch, Christian Wilhelm, who later became an art fiddler, would have been performing with his father for many years; town piper Reiche is known to have had among his adjuncts a Johann Ferdinand Bamberg, who in 1737 unsuccessfully auditioned for a Leipzig town music position (*BD* II, no. 405a).

56. *NBR,* no. 234.

57. See Schulze 1985.

58. Schulze 1984, p. 52.

59. *NBR,* no. 134.

60. *NBR,* no. 131.

61. *NBR,* no. 183, p. 176.

62. The schedule for alternating locations of the performances can be determined on the basis of the extant original booklet for the 2nd Sunday after Epiphany to Purification, 1724; see Neumann, *Texte,* p. 423.

63. Detailed descriptions provided by Stiehl 1984. St. Nicholas had a large organ, originally by Johann Lange (1597–98) and substantially rebuilt by Zacharias Thayssner (1693–94): thirty-six stops on three manuals and pedal. St. Thomas also had a large instrument by Lange (1598–99) that was enlarged by Christoph Donat in 1670–71 and renovated by Johann Scheibe in 1721–22. It then also had thirty-six stops on three manuals and pedals. The small (swallow's nest) organ at St. Thomas was originally built in 1489 and enlarged in 1630 by Heinrich Compenius. Scheibe repaired the instrument, which had twenty-one stops on two manuals an pedal, in 1720–21, but in 1741 the organ was torn down. See Dähnert 1980, pp. 180f.

64. Stiehl 1984, p. 16.

65. It is conceivable that the number of cantata cycles indicated by the authors of the Obituary is erroneous and that the three nearly intact annual cycles basically represent the composer's cantata output. On this controversial point, see Scheide 1961 and Dürr 1961. Among other points, Scheide refers to an early nineteenth-century report by Friedrich Rochlitz according to which Bach supposedly would "usually" submit three cantata texts to superintendent Deyling, out of which one was chosen.

66. The only chorale cantata of the 1724–25 cycle with pure hymn text *(per omnes versus)* is BWV 107. See, however, the pertinent examples in Table 8.9.

67. It is likely that the composition of some large chorale choruses, BWV 138/1 and 95/1 in September 1723 and BWV 73/1 in January 1724, had a stimulating effect on Bach's emerging concept of a chorale cantata cycle.

68. See Schulze in *WBK* 3: 115f.

69. For an analytical discussion of the chorale cantata cycle, see Krummacher 1995.
70. Two of them, BWV 128 and 68, open with a chorale chorus. Whether this happened by coincidence or by Bach's request, Ziegler did not pursue the chorale cantata concept.
71. *Versuch in gebundener Schreib-Art* (Leipzig, 1729).
72. Bach and his wife had concerts in Cöthen; see *NBR,* no. 117.
73. Dürr 1985, p. 56.
74. Christoph Wolff, "Bachs Leipziger Kirchenkantaten: Repertoire und Kontext," in *WBK* 3, p. 17
75. *BD* II, no. 243; Spitta II, p. 345.
76. For example, Picander's cantata for the First Sunday in Advent concludes with the chorale "Gottes Sohn ist kommen," a setting of which (BWV 318) can be found in the 1765 edition of the four-part chorales (no. 21); none of Bach's extant cantatas includes this hymn. Moreover, the style of the harmonization resembles that of Bach's later (post–*Jahrgang* III) chorale settings.
77. *NBR,* no. 146.
78. *BD* II, no. 452.
79. See facsimile in *NBA/KB* II/5, p. 61.
80. Quote 1717
81. See also Johann Kuhnau, Magnificat in C major, ed. Evangeline Rimbach. Madison, Wisc., 1980.
82. We don't know how regularly or often Bach performed his Magnificat on the high feast days of the ecclesiastical year, but we do know that at least occasionally he performed Magnificat settings by other composers; see Cammarota 1986.
83. In the liturgy of the Good Friday morning service, Walter's *St. John Passion* stood in place of the Gospel lesson and followed the chanting of Psalm 22 or Isaiah 53 (instead of the Epistle lesson). The performance of the Passion was framed by two hymns, "Da Jesus an dem Kreuze stund" and "O Traurigkeit, o Herzeleid"; see *BJ* 1911: 58f.
84. Glöckner 1990, p. 79.
85. Schering 1926, pp. 23–25.
86. *NBR,* no. 114.
87. Schering 1926, pp. 25–33.
88. *NBR,* no. 115. Only over a year later, in June 1725, was Bach reimbursed 3 talers 8 groschen for printing costs and harpsichord repair (*BD* II, no. 190).
89. In BWV 245, Bach apparently used transverse flutes for the first time in his Leipzig church music.
90. The five "new" movements in version II of the *St. John Passion* do not represent new compositions but seem to stem from the 1717 Passion; see BC D1.
91. None of the available editions of the *St. John Passion,* including *NBA* II/4, properly differentiate between the unfinished revision and the 1749 version of the work; see BC D 2a–e.
92. *NBR,* no. 208.
93. See Glöckner 1977.
94. Reference is made there to "Five Passions, of which one is for double chorus" (*NBR,* no. 306, p. 304).
95. Spitta II, pp. 340–45.
96. Leaver 1983.
97. None of the composers who set the Brockes Passion to music made use of a double choir.
98. The two extant original performing parts marked "Soprano in Ripieno" suggest that about six singers participated (*NBA/KB* II/5, p. 49).
99. *NBR,* no. 114.
100. See Dürr 1963/64: 47–52.

101.  1736 revision: choir I: SATB (solo, *ripieno,* including Evangelist and *soliloquentes:* An-
      cilla 1–2, Uxor Pilati, Jesus, Judas, Pontifex 1–2, Petrus, Kaiphas, Pilatus); 2rec,
      2trav, 2ob (d'amore, da caccia), 2v, va, va da gamba, bc (vc, vne, org); choir II: SATB
      (solo, *ripieno*), including Testis 1–2; 2trav, 2ob (d'amore), 2v, va, bc (vc, vne, org); choir
      III: S in *ripieno.* Prior to 1736: one continuo group for choir I/II; lute instead of va da
      gamba for nos. 56–57; 1742: va da gamba for nos. 34–35, cemb instead of org for nos.
      1–68 (choir II).

102.  When Bach was elected to the post of cantor, consul Steger had requested that he
      "make compositions that were not theatrical" (*NBR,* no. 98).


CHAPTER 9

  1.  The reference to the "pater organistarum in Germania" occurs within a brief discus-
      sion of music of the Protestant Germans; see *BD* III, no. 798. The poem appears in
      Guido's *Regulae musicae rhythmicae.*
  2.  *NBR,* nos. 343–346.
  3.  Bach never even responded to Mattheson's requests in 1719 and 1731 to contribute
      an autobiography; see Schulze 1981.
  4.  Marpurg, who wrote the preface to the second (1752) edition of *The Art of Fugue,* refers
      in 1750 to a personal encounter with Bach (*BD* III, no. 632) that most likely occurred
      on his return from Paris, in 1746.
  5.  The chorales to follow more than a decade later, in 1765 and 1769, in two volumes:
      *Johann Sebastian Bachs vierstimmige Choralgesänge.* On the manuscript and printed tra-
      dition, see BC, I/4, pp. 1288–90.
  6.  *NBR,* no. 376.
  7.  *NBR,* no. 374.
  8.  *NBR,* no. 281.
  9.  From the preface to the first edition; *NBR,* no. 378.
 10.  Prefaces to the *Orgel-Büchlein, Aufrichtige Anleitung,* and advertisement for *The Art of
      Fugue: NBR,* nos. 69, 92, and 281.
 11.  Bach after Niedt (*NBR,* pp. 16f.); see note 12.
 12.  J. S. Bach, *Precepts and Principles,* facsimile edition, ed. Pamela Poulin (Oxford, 1994).
 13.  Niedt, *Musicalische Handleitung,* 3 vols. (Hamburg, 1710, 1717, and 1721); facsim-
      ile edition (Buren, 1976). See also Poulin (note 12), pp. 10f. and 66.
 14.  Niedt's text reads: "The thoroughbass is the most complete foundation of music. It
      is played with both hands on a keyboard instrument in such a way that the left hand
      plays the prescribed notes, while the right hand strikes consonances and dissonances,
      so that this results in a well-sounding *Harmonie* for the Honour of God and the per-
      missible delight of the soul" (Pamela Poulin, trans.; F. E. Niedt, *The Musical Guide*
      [Oxford, 1989], p. 28).
 15.  See Jacob and Wilhelm Grimm, *Deutsches Wörterbuch,* vol. 9 (Leipzig, 1935; reprint
      1984), cols. 891f. The Leipzig-trained Johann Adolph Scheibe, in *Critischer Musikus*
      (Hamburg, 1737), p. 33, discussed the science of musical composition in terms of "the
      principles on which the whole harmonic structure is based."
 16.  For example, Johann Christoph Gottsched's "principles of philosophy" (*Erste Gründe
      der gesamten Weltweisheit* [Leipzig, 1733]).
 17.  Mizler, *Musikalischer Staarstecher* (Leipzig, 1739–40), p. 9; the following citation, p.
      83. See also Leisinger 1994, pp. 75–77.
 18.  Music lost, text extant.
 19.  Kuhnau's successors as organists were Johann Adam Stolle (1710–13), N. Pitzschel
      (1713–14), Johann Zetzsche (1714–16), Johann Gottlieb Görner (1716–21; there-
      after organist at St. Nicholas's), and Johann Christoph Thiele (1721–74).
 20.  Schering 1941, p. 17.

21. Görner received 2 talers 15 groschen per quarter; see ibid., p. 104.

22. *BD* I, p. 44.

23. For the extensive documentation of this affair, see *NBR,* nos. 119–20, and *BD* I, nos. 9–12.

24. Incidental fees and other income derived from university connections not included. Records of the annual fee collected by Bach (discovered in 1985 in the Leipzig University archives) completely changed the previously held view that Bach had ended his academic service by the beginning of 1726, that is, following his unsuccessful appeal to the king; see Szeskus 1987.

25. The traditional view (since Spitta II, pp. 210–12) of Görner as a bitter and incompetent rival is purely fictional.

26. *NBR,* no. 279, p. 255.

27. The basic liturgical framework of the academic service at St. Paul's (Christian Ernst Sicul, *Neo annalium Lipsiensium continuatio,* II [Leipzig, 1715–17], §16): organ prelude; hymn "Allein Gott in der Höh sei Ehr"; hymn (selected); hymn "Wir glauben all an einen Gott"; sermon on the Gospel lesson; Collect, prayers, announcements, Benediction; hymn (selected). On high feasts and on Sundays during the fair only, a cantata was followed by the hymn stanza "Gott sei uns gnädig."

28. *BD* II, no. 156.

29. According to the index in Johann Adolph Scheibe, *Critischer Musikus* (Leipzig, 1745), "ein elender Componist."

30. *BD* II, no. 226; nos. 225–228 cover the pertinent squabble.

31. *NBR,* no. 135.

32. *NBR,* no. 136.

33. Professor Jöcher, a philosopher, historian, and bibliographer, had in 1714 been a respondent to a medical dissertation on the effect of music on man.

34. *BD* II, no. 415; see also nos. 422, 424, and 424a; *NBR,* nos. 199–201.

35. An instrument acquired in 1678–79 (Dähnert 1980, p. 184) and, like the organs in the Leipzig main churches, tuned to choir pitch, a whole tone above chamber pitch; the organ part of BWV 228 is therefore notated in A-flat major.

36. The instrument cost more than 3,000 talers (the original organ contract with Scheibe of 1711 refers to a purchase price of 2,926 talers); for specifications, see *BD* I, p. 167, and Dähnert 1980, pp. 183–84. Gottfried Silbermann received the sum of 2,000 talers for the thirty-one-stop organ at St. Sophia's in Dresden, completed in 1720.

37. *BD* I, pp. 166f.

38. Unlike the old small choir organ, the new Scheibe organ was tuned to chamber pitch.

39. The organ fugue BWV 537/2 makes use of a not fully evolved da capo form, whereas the lute fugue BWV 998/2 from the mid-1730s picks up the strict da capo principle from BWV 548/2.

40. *NBR,* no. 118.

41. All other hypothetical "original" solo instruments heretofore proposed for this work present serious problems; if the finale movement, for example, is played by a transverse flute or oboe, there is hardly a spot for taking a breath.

42. Like the Scheibe organ at St. Paul's, the Silbermann organ at St. Sophia's was tuned to chamber pitch.

43. The scholarly careers and publications of the academics are described in Jöcher 1750–51.

44. Schering 1941, p. 101.

45. *NBR,* no. 328.

46. *Dichtung und Wahrheit* (1811), book VI.

47. See Lloyd Espenschied, "The Electrical Flare of the 1740s," *Electrical Engineering* 74 (1955): 392–97, and Cohen 1990, pp. 64, 113.

48. See note 46.
49. Referred to above; see Söhnel 1983, p.16.
50. *BD* II, no. 162.
51. Ibid.; Petzoldt 1985.
52. See *BD* II, nos. 405a, 418, 426, 577.
53. *BD* II, no. 249; see also no. 483.
54. Stiller 1976.
55. *BD* II, no. 309. The Partita in C minor, BWV 826, in this collection contains a capriccio.
56. The canonic voice responds at half speed; *NBR,* no. 220.
57. Neumann 1970.
58. *BD* II, no. 505.
59. According to 1756 statistics, five in the Faculty of Theology, fourteen in Law, eight in Medicine, and seventeen in Philosophy; see Müller 1990, p. 60.
60. Numbers vary greatly. The 1723–50 matriculations: maximum, 338 (winter 1727) and 165 (summer 1727); minimum, 215 (winter 1749) and 65 (summer 1734); see Schulze 1802, pp. 70–71.
61. Rent from seats, pews, and boxes (built-in and often heatable, called "chapels") were the churches' major source of income.
62. The numerous published sermons by Deyling provide welcome insight into the learned exegetical and hermeneutical approach and polished pulpit rhetoric. The collection of essays in Petzoldt 1985 deal with sermon styles and interpretive traditions in Bach's time.
63. It must be noted that the population nearer the bottom of the social scale attended services at the churches with "free" seating and with no musical program, such as St. Peter's in Leipzig.
64. *NBR,* no. 151.
65. Bach referred to it as *privat information;* see *NBR,* no. 231.
66. See the list in *NBR,* pp. 316–17.
67. *NBR,* no. 148.
68. *NBR,* no. 252.
69. *NBR,* no. 395.
70. See *NBA/KB* III/2.1 (Frieder Rempp, 1991), pp. 21ff.
71. See BC I/4, pp. 1271ff.
72. *NBR,* no. 378.
73. See Chapter 8, p. 263.
74. *NBR,* no. 315.
75. See Dürr 1978.
76. The "canon" of six *English* and six *French Suites* was established only after 1724.
77. Begun November 21, 1725.
78. Published in Spitta II, appendix, pp. 1–11.
79. *Abhandlung vom harmonischen Dreiklang* (unpublished treatise, announced in 1758 in Leipzig newspapers); manuscript (begun c. 1754) lost.
80. *NBR,* no. 168.
81. *NBR,* no. 306, p. 302.
82. "Good store [*apparat*] of the choicest church compositions" (*NBR,* no. 32); "artfully composed things [*Sachen*]" (J. S. Bach, *Precepts and Principles,* ed. Poulin, p. 66).
83. Listed 1697 in a *Catalogus Librorum Musicorum Scholae Thomanae* by Johann Schelle, with a 1702, supplement by Johann Kuhnau. A substantial addition had occurred in 1712, when on Kuhnau's recommendation the musical estate (375 items) of cantor Johann Schelle was purchased for 40 talers, with funds from the city. For a historical inventory, see Schering 1919.

84. In 1729 and later, however, Bach used municipal funds to acquire new editions of Erhard Bodenschatz's classic motet collection, *Florilegium Portense* (1618), for regular use at St. Nicholas's and St. Thomas's; see *BD* II, nos. 271–272.
85. Küster 1991.
86. A reconstruction has been attempted by Beißwenger 1992; see also Wolff 1968.
87. As in the case of Lotti's *Missa sapientiae,* which Bach seems to have obtained from him; see Beißwenger 1992, p. 304.
88. Wolff 1968, p. 227.
89. *NBR,* no. 279.
90. The only extant hymnal from Bach's library (University of Glasgow); see BC I/4, p. 1273.
91. *NBR,* no. 228.
92. The *Großes vollständiges Universal Lexicon aller Wissenschafften und Künste,* the largest and most influential eighteenth-century German scholarly reference work (Leipzig, 1732–52), appeared almost twenty years earlier than the great French *Encyclopédie,* begun in 1751.
93. Volume 22 (Leipzig, 1739), col. 1388, article "Musik."
94. *NBR,* no. 306, p. 305.
95. Cf. the canons BWV 1073–1078; *NBR,* nos. 45, 133, 166, 242, 251, 259.
96. *NBR,* no. 259.
97. Athanasius Kircher, *Musurgia universalis* (German edition) (Schwäbisch Hall, 1662), p. 364.
98. "Avertissement" of *The Art of Fugue,* May 1751; *NBR,* no. 281.
99. Analogous to *scientia possibilium,* the science of the possible, as propagated by Christian Wolff; see H. Seidl, "Möglichkeit," *Historisches Wörterbuch der Philosophie,* ed. Joachim Ritter and Karlfried Gründer, vol. 6 (Basel, 1984), col. 86.
100. Johann Abraham Birnbaum on Bach, 1739; *BD* II, no. 441, p. 353.
101. Westfall 1995, p. 357.
102. Jacob and Wilhelm Grimm, *Deutsches Wörterbuch,* vol. 1 (Leipzig, 1854), article "Andacht, andächtig (attentus, intentus, pius, devotus)," cols. 302–3.

CHAPTER 10

1. The actual birthday was February 23, but Bach, like other musicians, was provided lodging "for several days," suggesting lavish festivities. Guest musicians included Anna Magdalena Bach; her sister and sister's husband, the Zeitz court trumpeter Johann Andreas Krebs; Carl Gotthelf Gerlach as alto singer; and three others (see *BD* II, no. 254).
2. Bach's biography (completed before August 1729) in Walther *Lexicon,* p. 64, contains the first reference to the new title. On January 18, 1729, Bach still used his Cöthen title (*BJ* 1994: 15), indicating that he did not receive the appointment in conjunction with the duke's January visit in Leipzig.
3. In the 1720s, the court capelle under the direction of Johann Gotthilf Krieger employed thirty musicians, among them Anna Magdalena Bach's father, Johann Caspar Wilcke.
4. *BD* II, no. 278.
5. Spitta II, p. 256.
6. *NBR,* no. 152.
7. *NBR,* no. 121.
8. Franz Keßler, "Freißlich," *MGG* 16: cols. 355–358.
9. *NBR,* no. 151, p. 150.
10. Minutes of the meeting in *NBR,* no. 150.

11. *BD* II, no. 282.
12. Spitta II, p. 242.
13. Gesner wrote a new set of school regulations, *Gesetze der Schule zu St. Thomae* (Leipzig, 1733), which contained a separate section on music and illuminates his interest in musical education and practice; *Thomana Ordnungen,* pp. 22–23.
14. *BD* II, no. 291; Braun 1995, p. 58.
15. *NBR,* no. 328. As for the hypothetical postulation of different and much smaller numbers, see my brief comments in *Early Music,* 26 (1998): 540 and 27 (1999): 172.
16. *NBR,* no. 151, p. 147.
17. Leipzig town musicians received an annual salary of 42 florins and free housing, adding up to about 50 talers; see Richter 1907, p. 36.
18. *NBR,* no. 151, p. 150.
19. Johann Friedrich Köhler, after 1776; *BD* III, p. 315.
20. *BD* II, no. 355.
21. *NBR,* no. 183.
22. According to the school regulations, the cantor was regularly assisted by three prefects from the Sunday after Easter through the first Sunday in Advent and by four prefects during the busy season from Christmas through Easter.
23. *NBR,* nos. 181–186, 192–196; for an analysis of the affair pertaining to the school regulations, see *Thomana Ordnungen,* Nachwort (Schulze), pp. 2–3.
24. Johann August Abraham (baptized November 5, 1733) and Johann Christian (baptized September 7, 1735).
25. *NBR,* no. 196.
26. *NBR,* no. 180.
27. *NBR,* no. 130.
28. In Johann Mattheson, *Grosse General-Baß-Schule* (Hamburg, 1731), p. 173.
29. Glöckner, *WBK* 3: 106f.
30. Ibid., p. 111.
31. *NBR,* no. 186, p. 184.
32. *NBR,* no. 132.
33. *NBR,* no. 315.
34. Connections with the Collegium predated Bach's Leipzig years. In Cöthen, Bach performed with Gottfried Riemschneider (member of the Collegium under Hoffmann) and with Johann Gottfried Vogler, director of the Collegium, 1716–18. Moreover, it is conceivable that Bach performed at Collegium concerts during visits to Leipzig from Cöthen.
35. *NBR,* no. 187.
36. *NBR,* no. 207.
37. Neumann 1960, pp. 6f.
38. In 1737–39, Bach was involved with *Clavier-Übung* III, the Eighteen Chorales, *The Well-Tempered Clavier* II, and other projects, apart from his regular Sunday and feast day performance schedule.
39. *NBR,* no. 346.
40. *BD* II, no. 457.
41. Rudolf Eller, "Leipzig," *MGG* 8: col. 555. The Grand Concerts were the immediate forerunner of the Gewandhaus concerts that began in 1781.
42. After 1743, the Grand Concerts presented Passion oratorios regularly during Lent; the Riemer chronicle mentions, for example, the performance on March 31, 1749, of a "passionalisches Oratorium" for an audience of more than three hundred (Wustmann 1889, p. 430). It seems likely that Bach's performances of works that did not meet the liturgical requirements for the Leipzig main churches, such as Handel's *Brockes Passion* (1746–47), a Keiser-Handel Passion pasticcio (1747–49), a Passion oratorio

by Graun (~1750), and a Graun-Telemann-Bach-Kuhnau-Altnickol Passion pasticcio (before 1750), were presented at the Grand Concerts. See Glöckner 1977, p. 107.

43. *NBR,* no. 197.
44. Glöckner 1990, pp. 89f.
45. See Ranft, BzBf 6: 10. Bach lent Büchner the parts of a solo cantata (probably BWV 82); *NBR,* no. 219.
46. Glöckner 1981, pp. 68ff.
47. *BD* II, no. 425.
48. After Carl Gotthelf Gerlach's death in 1761, the Leipzig printer Gottlob Immanuel Breitkopf acquired his extensive music library, which formed the early nucleus of Breitkopf's music business. Since Gerlach seems to have functioned for a long time as the Collegium's librarian, the Breitkopf music catalogues published from 1762 may give a reasonable overview not only of what was available in Leipzig by that time (even though the Gerlach provenance is not always clear) but also what was likely to be performed at the Collegium series from the 1720s on.
49. See BC G 46.
50. See Wolff, *Essays,* Chapter 17.
51. *NBR,* nos. 172 and 201.
52. See BC I/4, pp. 1487–1500.
53. *NBR,* no. 173.
54. Ibid.
55. A sole example of an outdoor processional piece by Bach has survived in the *Marche* of cantata BWV 207.
56. *BD* II, no. 352, p. 251.
57. *NBR,* p. 461.
58. Dreyfus 1987, p. 60. Ulrich Leisinger (private communication) suggests a performance of *Jahrgang* II, 1732–33, up to the state mourning period (February 15), and the composition of new chorale cantatas for 1734–35.
59. Princess Maria Amalia, born in 1724, stood out as a particularly accomplished performer on the keyboard.
60. Fürstenau 1862, pp. 180f.
61. Single Sanctus settings (from 1720s) appended, for completion of Latin repertoire:

| BWV 237 | Sanctus in C major | SATB, 3tr/ti, 2ob, str, bc | 1723 (St. John's Day, June 24) |
| BWV 238 | Sanctus in D major | SATB, str, bc | 1723 (Christmas Day) |
| BWV 232ᴵᴵᴵ | Sanctus in D major | SSSATB, 3tr/ti, 3ob, str, bc | 1724 (Christmas Day) |

62. *NBR,* no. 307.
63. Horn 1987, p. 121.
64. Aside from the Magnificat, his Latin pieces consisted solely of individual Sanctus settings he needed in 1723–24 for the main services on high feast days in Leipzig. For the concerted Kyrie and Gloria likewise required for Leipzig (Table 8.3), he usually turned to works by other composers. For the Leipzig repertoire of the 1720s (which included works by Johann Christoph Pez and Johann Hugo von Wilderer), see Wolff 1968, pp. 159–72, and Beißwenger 1992.
65. The more private but also suspended Collegium concert series was permitted to start earlier, on July 17, 1733; *NBR,* no. 160.
66. See the report in the Riemer chronicle, Wustmann 1889, 2:286–89.
67. Facsimile edition, with a commentary by Hans-Joachim Schulze (Leipzig, 1983).

68. *NBR,* no. 161, with facsimile of the title wrapper.
69. Facsimile, *BJ* 1994: 11. In exact juxtaposition, the two dedications read:

    | bezeigte mit inliegender | Bezeigte in einer |
    |---|---|
    | MISSA | CANTATA |
    | seine unterthänigste *Devotion* | seine unterthänigste *Devotion* |
    | der Autor | Johann Sebastian Bach |
    | J. S. Bach | |

    For similar dedications, see *BD* II, nos. 221, 402.
70. St. Sophia's was the church generally frequented by the Lutheran court officials. In 1737, the Lutheran court service was officially moved there after the old palace church had been converted into apartments.
71. The coronation as king of Poland would take place on January 17, 1734.
72. *NBR,* no. 162.
73. *BD* I, p. 75.
74. *BD* I, no. 36.
75. *NBR,* no. 190.
76. *NBR,* no. 191.
77. It is also possible that BWV 906 was added to the library at a later point. See commentary by Hans-Joachim Schulze, facsimile edition of BWV 906 (Leipzig, 1984).
78. Ibid., pp. 6f.
79. Handel's Organ Concertos Op. 4 (1738) and Op. 7 (1761), originally performed by the composer during oratorio intermissions, reflect a similar idea but don't develop a comparable kind of concerto structure and texture.
80. See Stauffer 1996, p. 1.
81. *NBR,* no. 179.
82. For the printing history and other details, see the commentary to the facsimile edition of the entire *Clavier-Übung,* ed. Christoph Wolff (Leipzig, 1984).
83. *BD* II, no. 224.
84. *NBR,* no. 343.
85. *NBR,* no. 331.
86. The revision of the Eighteen Chorales, largely during the years 1739–42, may have been prompted by *Clavier-Übung* III.
87. Dorian: "Wir glauben all an einen Gott"; "Christ unser Herr zum Jordan kam"; "Vater unser im Himmelreich"; "Jesus Christus, unser Heiland." Phrygian: "Kyrie, Gott Vater" (three strophes); "Aus tiefer Not." Mixolydian: "Dies sind die heilgen zehn Gebot." In his discussion of *Clavier-Übung* III, Johann Philipp Kirnberger stressed in 1771 that "the most delicate of modern composers, J. S. Bach, considered it necessary to know the method of composing in the old church modes" (*BD* III, no. 767, p. 221).
88. *NBR,* no. 333.
89. *NBR,* no. 342.
90. *NBR,* pp. 464–65.
91. See Wolff 1996a, pp. 119–21.
92. *NBR,* no. 306, p. 305.
93. Corroborated by known figures from the *Musical Offering* of 1747 (front matter, two hundred copies; first print run of engraved music, one hundred copies); see *NBR,* nos. 246, 257.
94. See *NBR,* no. 385.
95. *NBR,* pp. 474–76.
96. The "Confiteor" setting was written in the late 1740s.
97. *NBR,* no. 395, p. 399.
98. The high proportion of gallic acidity in Bach's ink is primarily responsible for the phenomenon of ink bleeding through the page; this is gradually destroying the paper on which his compositions are written.

99. *NBR,* no. 394, p. 396.
100. A one-time contender for the Heinichen succession in Dresden; see Walther, *Lexicon,* p. 488.
101. *NBR,* no. 394, p. 397.
102. Yet another arrangement from 1736–37 transcribes the work for lute, as the opening movement of the Suite in E major, BWV 1006a.
103. *BD* II, no. 436.
104. *NBR,* no. 344, p. 343.

CHAPTER 11

1. *BD* IV, p. 160.
2. The portrait survives in two authentic versions. The earlier one, painted in 1746 and now at the Stadtgeschichtliches Museum in Leipzig (formerly at the St. Thomas School), suffered serious damage over the years and bears several layers of problematic restorations. The replica of 1748, which is very well preserved, is owned by William H. Scheide (of Princeton, New Jersey), who has kindly permitted me to reproduce it as a frontispiece for this book.
3. 1726–27; *BD* IV, p. 234.
4. *MGG,* vol. 11 (1963), plate 81.
5. *BD* I, p. 118.
6. See Odrich-Wollny 1999, no. 58.
7. Johann Elias Bach's predecessor as tutor for the Bach children, Bernhard Dietrich Ludewig, left Leipzig in October 1737; he had studied theology at Leipzig University from 1731. In a testimonial of October 10, 1737, Bach mentioned "the diligent instruction he has given my children and the assistance he has lent to both church and other music, vocally as well as instrumentally" (*NBR,* no. 198). Ludewig may also have acted as private secretary.
8. *NBR,* no. 152.
9. *NBR,* no. 121.
10. On October 22, he replied via Catterfeldt ("den 22 8br. per Catterfeldt beantwortet"); see facsimile, *BJ* 1985: 84.
11. *NBR,* no. 210.
12. *NBR,* no. 223.
13. *NBR,* no. 224.
14. See facsimile edition (with afterword) of the 1725 album, ed. Georg von Dadelsen (Kassel, 1989).
15. *NBR,* no. 217.
16. *NBR,* no. 218.
17. *NBR,* no. 258.
18. Joint guest performance of Anna Magdalena and Johann Sebastian Bach in Cöthen, December 1725; *NBR,* no. 117.
19. List of Anna Magdalena Bach's copies in Dadelsen 1957, pp. 34–37.
20. She was a close friend of Christina Sybilla Bose, ten years her junior, who died in 1749. See Schulze 1997.
21. In 1731, Anna Magdalena traveled with her husband to Kassel, where he examined the organ at St. Martin's, an unlikely occasion for her to perform.
22. *NBR,* no. 152.
23. On the friendship between the two women, see Schulze 1997.
24. *BD* I, no. 184, p. 267; *NBR,* no. 303, p. 293.
25. *BD* II, no. 443.
26. See facsimile edition (note 14 above), pp. 68–69, and afterword, p. 13.
27. *NBR,* nos. 175–176.

28. *BD* II, no. 365.
29. *NBR*, no. 188.
30. *NBR*, no. 203.
31. *BD* I, p. 109.
32. *NBR*, no. 305.
33. Johann Pachelbel's daughter Amalia (1688–1723) is a notable exception in an early eighteenth-century musical family. She became a successful and well-known painter and draughtswoman in Nuremberg. See Ulrich Thieme and Felix Becker, eds. *Allgemeines Lexikon der bildenden Künstler von der Antike bis zur Gegenwart*, vol. 25. Leipzig, 1932, p. 120.
34. Facsimile edition (New York, 1979); see also Chapter 2.
35. *BD* I, nos. 25–26.
36. See the commentary (by H.-J. Schulze) to the facsimile edition of the autograph fair copy of BWV 541 (Leipzig, 1996), p. 5.
37. Reference in C. P. E. Bach's autobiographical sketch (1773), facsimile ed., ed. William S. Newman (Hilversum, 1967).
38. *NBR*, no. 267. C. P. E. Bach dedicated his Trios, Wq 161 (1751), to Count Wilhelm.
39. *BD* I, p. 124.
40. *NBR*, no. 184, pp. 180f.
41. A description probably from the circle of C. P. E. Bach: Hilgenfeldt 1850, p. 172 (see also Schulze 1984a, p. 19).
42. *NBR*, no. 409; see also *BD* III, commentary to no. 973. Christian Fürchtegott Gellert was from 1745 professor of poetics at Leipzig University. Cramer knew well of the existence of the Bückeburg Johann Christoph Friedrich Bach but did not consider him to be in the same league as the others and omits him from the count of Bach's sons.
43. The St. Thomas School records are missing from 1739, and therefore nothing is known about Christian's progress in school. Johann Christoph Friedrich Bach, however, matriculated at Leipzig University in 1749, which suggests that he had graduated from the Thomana earlier that year. *BD* II, no. 628, p. 504. On the gift of instruments to Christian, see Chapter 12, "Estate and Musical Legacy."
44. Inventories from 1789 and 1823; see Fröde 1983 and Braun 1995. Earlier descriptions (by Richter and Terry, also in *BD* IV, p. 246) are misleading and erroneous.
45. *BD* II, nos. 291, 296, and 308. The school construction project was first discussed in June 1730 and decided on in September of the same year.
46. Wilhelm Friedemann's exercise books were found in a closet of this room when the school was torn down in 1902; see *BD* IV, no. 266.
47. *NBR*, no. 279, p. 253.
48. *BD* II, nos. 602–603.
49. Christoph Daniel Ebeling writing in 1773, based on information provided by C. P. E. Bach (*BD* III, no. 777, p. 250).
50. After Bach's death, Müthel continued his studies with Altnickol in Naumburg. In May 1751, he and Anna Magdalena Bach served as godparents to Altnickol's daughter Augusta Magdalena; *BD* III, no. 640.
51. *NBR*, no. 312b.
52. See *NBR*, p. 315.
53. *NBR*, no. 395, p. 400.
54. *NBR*, no. 359.
55. *NBR*, no. 395, pp. 400, 461.
56. *NBR*, no. 303, p. 290.
57. *NBR*, p. 460.
58. *NBR*, no. 209.
59. *NBR*, no. 279.
60. *Thomana Ordnungen*, pp. 27–32; adapted from the summary in Terry 1928, p. 170.

61. Gesner, in his revised school regulations of 1733, writes that singing after mealtime would contribute to the students' health and well-being (*Thomana Ordnungen,* p. 16).

62. This pattern was by no means unique. When in 1767 C. P. E. Bach was appointed cantor at the Hamburg Johanneum, the school board urged him to "hold the singing lessons according to the school regulations which Telemann, in an irresponsible way, neglected throughout his tenure" (Miesner 1929, p. 118).

63. See Marshall 1972, pp. 63–68.

64. A later version (c. 1746–47) used stationary instruments: 2 litui, 3 oboes, bassoon, strings, and continuo.

65. *NBR,* no. 250.

66. *NBR,* no. 279; *BD* II, no. 628, p. 504. Plausible arguments relate the large harpsichord in the Berlin Instrument Collection, built by Johann Heinrich Harrass, to the Bach estate; see Krickeberg 1996.

67. *NBR,* no. 256.

68. *NBR,* no. 140, pertaining to the first installment of Walther's *Lexicon*, published in 1728.

69. *BD* II, nos. 527–529, 567–568, 363, 373, 492.

70. *BD* III, p. 638.

71. In 1728, Nicolaus Bach delivered two such instruments to a Hungarian nobleman; the instruments must have been small, because together they cost only 8 talers (*BJ* 1989: 214).

72. *NBR,* no. 358e.

73. Unlike other keyboard experts of the time, Bach paid attention not only to mechanical and acoustical details but also to ergonomic aspects of keyboard design. As Agricola relates: "The semitones must anyway be a little narrower at the top than at the bottom. That is how the late Capellmeister Bach required them to be, and he, for the above-mentioned reasons [the player can go from one manual to the other with much more ease], also liked short keys on the organ." *NBR,* no. 358c.

74. *NBR,* no. 358d.

75. *NBR,* p. 429.

76. See Drüner 1987; Smith 1998.

77. *NBR,* no. 364.

78. Johann Sebastian and Anna Magdalena Bach served as godparents to children of Hoffmann's sisters (see *BD* II, nos. 275, 449); in 1743, both Bach and Hoffmann were godfathers to Johann Sebastian Weyrauch, son of the notary public and lutenist Johann Christian Weyrauch of Leipzig.

79. *BD* II, no. 272; see also Kröhner 1988.

80. *BD* II, nos. 573, 613/613a.

81. *NBR,* nos. 37, 75, 110.

82. *NBR,* p. 436.

CHAPTER 12

1. *NBR,* no. 208.

2. See BC D2e. Completing the revision and copying out new performing parts within a time span of ten days would have been extremely difficult. Tying the incomplete revision of BWV 245 to the canceled 1739 performance is, therefore, not without problems.

3. Kobayashi 1988 provides a survey and chronological list of Bach's compositional and performing activities from 1735 through the 1740s.

4. *BD* III, no. 703.

5. *NBR,* no. 306, p. 297.

6. Johann Friedrich Agricola, 1768; see *BD* III, no. 740.

7. *NBR,* no. 236.

8. See Schulze 1967, *NBA* VIII/1, and *NBR,* nos. 162, 230, 236–37.

9. In 1760, Marpurg recalled his "sojourn in Leipzig" when he "discussed with him [Bach] certain materials pertaining to fugue" (*BD* III, no. 701, p. 144); if he heard a performance of cantata BWV 144 (whose fugal texture he describes; see *NBR,* no. 357b) on this occasion, the visit would have taken place around Septuagesimae Sunday, in February 1748 or 1749.

10. G. de Luchesini, Mizler (permanent secretary), G. H. Bümler, C. G. Schöter, H. Bokemeyer, G. P. Telemann, G. H. Stölzel, G. F. Lingke, M. Spiess, G. Venzky, G. F. Handel (honorary member), U. Weiss, C. H. Graun, J. S. Bach, G. A. Sorge, J. P. Kunzen, C. F. Fischer, J. C. Winter, J. G. Kaltenbeck. An invitation to Leopold Mozart as the twentieth and last member to join the society was issued in 1755, but the society disbanded shortly thereafter because of the difficulty of running the business from Mizler's residence in Warsaw.

11. *Tractatus musicus compositorio-practicus* (Augsburg, 1745). See *NBA/KB* VIII/1 (Wolff), pp. 22, 34.

12. *NBR,* no. 247.

13. *NBR,* no. 306, p. 307.

14. *NBR,* no. 268, for this and subsequent quotations.

15. *NBR,* p. 243.

16. *BD* III, no. 703.

17. *NBR,* nos. 222–23.

18. *BD* II, nos. 489, 540, 548. In 1744, Wilhelm Friedemann Bach dedicated his first published sonata to Stahl (*BD* II, no. 528). Cf. also Miesner 1933.

19. *BD* III, Anh. I, no. 3 (p. 623).

20. *NBR,* no. 239.

21. *NBR,* no. 257.

22. *NBR,* pp. 429f; also the subsequent quotations from Forkel's report.

23. *NBR,* no. 394.

24. Schramm 1744, 2: 2248, on the Weimar *turris echonica:* "where two persons who stand at opposite ends from one another and speak softly against the wall can understand each other clearly, without those standing in the middle hearing anything."

25. *NBR,* no. 248.

26. *NBR,* nos. 246, 257.

27. Why and to what end Questenberg approached Bach remains unknown, also how he came to know about Bach in the first place. Questenberg was well acquainted with the Bohemian count Franz Anton von Sporck, whose relationship with Bach dated back to the 1720s; another possibility consists in the manifold Bohemian-Moravian connections of the Dresden court capelle, notably through Jan Dismas Zelenka. Conceivably, too, the Bach-Questenberg connection predates 1749.

28. *NBR,* no. 261.

29. See *NBR,* pp. 337–53.

30. *NBR,* no. 344, p. 343.

31. For a discussion of the genesis of *The Art of Fugue,* see Wolff, *Essays,* Chapter 20.

32. First edition: J. S. Bach, *Die Kunst der Fuge,* BWV 1080, vol 1: Earlier Version (Frankfurt: C. F. Peters, 1986).

33. On this point, see *NBR,* nos. 304–305 (Walther, *Lexicon*).

34. See facsimiles, *NBR,* p. 259.

35. The term "contrapunctus" is used in that very sense in the writings of Fux, Heinichen, and other contemporaries; cf. Wolff, *Essays,* p. 277.

36. *NBR,* no. 280.

37. *NBR,* no. 285.

38. *NBR,* no. 306, p. 304.

39. *NBR,* no. 353.

40. Wollny 1994; see Bach: *Mass in B Minor,* BWV 232, ed. C. Wolff (Frankfurt: C. F. Peters, 1997) pp. 378–83.
41. Cf. Wolff 1968 and Beißwenger 1992.
42. For analytical details, see Wolff 1994.
43. Cf. Wolff, *Essays,* Chapter 26.
44. *NBR,* no. 396, p. 407.
45. *NBR,* no. 306, p. 303.
46. *NBR,* no. 265.
47. *NBR,* no. 266.
48. Composition is not extant.
49. *NBR,* no. 265.
50. *NBR,* no. 306, p. 303.
51. *NBR,* p. 430.
52. Proposed by Kranemann 1990, who also discusses older theories and hypotheses.
53. Surely for reasons of geographic distance, Bach could not travel to Berlin in late September 1748 to attend the christening ceremony for his grandson and godchild, Johann Sebastian, C. P. E. Bach's third child.
54. *NBR,* no. 258.
55. Facsimile: "Wine and Taxes," ed. W. H. Scheide (New York, 1970). For a discussion of Bach's late hand, see Kobayashi 1988.
56. *NBR,* no. 261.
57. *BD* II, no. 582.
58. *NBR,* no. 262.
59. The communion register lists, in a continuing pattern, "Capellmeister Bach and two sons; the last time he partook of the Lord's Supper at St. Thomas's was on December 18, 1749, the 3rd Sunday in Advent" (*BD* II, no. 162).
60. The libretto for this 1749 service has survived; see *NBA/KB* I/40, pp. 225–29.
61. See Ambrose in *WBK* 2: 151. For the textual changes, see *NBA/KB* I/40, p. 136.
62. Bach first wrote "Borilius" which he changed to "Birolius." Spitta does not relate "Birolius" to Brühl; he suggests instead that in mentioning "Hortens," Bach meant to mock Thomasrector Ernesti, who had published a philological edition of the complete works of Cicero (Spitta II, p. 741). Conceivably, Bach intended to do both.
63. Wollny 1993, pp. 306–11.
64. *BD* III, no. 703. C. P. E. Bach's autograph score is dated "Potsdam 25. Aug. 1749." A Leipzig performance is confirmed by Leipzig performance parts; see Wollny 1995.
65. The feast of Visitation (July 2, 1750) cannot be totally excluded from consideration but is much less likely, especially in view of the greater time distance following Friedemann's performance.
66. Wollny 1997, pp. 36–50.
67. *NBR,* no. 263; facsimile: *BJ* 1988: p. 39.
68. *NBR,* no. 264; facsimile: *BJ* 1988: p. 41.
69. *NBR,* no. 267.
70. Cf. Wollny 1997, pp. 36–50, modifying the cut-off date of October 1749 proposed by Kobayashi 1988.
71. *NBR,* no. 306, p. 303.
72. *NBR,* no. 269a. Taylor published what was presumably a translation of his lectures given in Germany under the title *Tractat von Augenkrankheiten* (Frankfurt, 1751).
73. *NBR,* no. 269b.
74. Krahnemann 1990, pp. 57f. I am indebted to Dr. Firmon Hardenbergh (Harvard University) for helping to interpret ophthalmological and pathological details.
75. Probably written by Professor Samuel Theodor Quellmaltz; *BD* II, no. 601.
76. Ibid.
77. *NBR,* no. 270.
78. *NBR,* no. 306, p. 303.

79. For a more detailed discussion of this point, see Wolff, *Essays,* Chapter 21.
80. *NBR,* no. 284.
81. Johann Christoph Altnickol, Johann Nathanael Bammler, and Johann Gottfried Müthel are prime candidates.
82. The manuscript of "Wenn wir in höchsten Nöten sein," BWV 668, has not survived, but its version was published in 1751 as an appendix to *The Art of Fugue.*
83. Known in Bach scholarship as Anonymus Vr. His hand shows up first around 1742 in sources of *The Well-Tempered Clavier* II and later in manuscripts of BWV 195, 232, and 245. After Bach's death, he seems to have worked for C. P. E. Bach in Berlin. See Kobayashi 1988, pp. 29–31.
84. The entry of BWV 668a in the manuscript (*P 271*) is incomplete; the page containing the remainder of the chorale was removed at an early point.
85. Including Bach's two boarding students, Johann Christian Kittel and Johann Gottfried Müthel. The absence of virtually any public reference to Bach's funeral indicates that neither city nor school, in line with precedents, were interested in mounting anything special. As this book was in page proofs, Reinhard Szeskus discovered at the Leipzig University Archives new documents on Bach's funeral and Anna Magdalena Bach's circumstances after her husband's death, to be published in LBB 5 (2001).
86. See Schulze 1984, pp. 178–81, and Wollny 1997, pp. 49f.
87. Paraphrase of the collect "Excita Domine corda nostra" for the second Sunday in Advent, probably by Martin Luther, first published in the so-called *Klugsche Gesangbuch* of 1533; Christoph Bach's motet follows the text version of Henrich Schutz's motet SWV 381 from *Geistliche Chor-Music* (1648).
88. The oaken casket presumably containing Bach's remains (only 12 of 1,400 Leipzigers who died in 1750 were buried in oak caskets) was exhumed on October 22, 1894 (see His 1895). The remains were then reburied in a simple stone sarcophagus and placed in a tomb under the altar of St. John's. The church and the surrounding parts of the cemetery were destroyed in World War II, but the tomb remained intact. In 1950, the two-hundredth anniversary year of Bach's death, his sarcophagus was transferred to the chancel of the St. Thomas Church.
89. *NBR,* no. 272.
90. *NBR,* no. 273.
91. *NBR,* no. 274a.
92. *NBR,* no. 276, and *BD* II, no. 617; *BD* III, no. 634. See also Schulze 1998a, p. 105.
93. *NBR,* nos. 277–288; also *BD* II, no. 628.
94. *NBR,* no. 279.
95. *BD* II, no. 628.
96. *BD* II, no. 503f.
97. *BD* III, no. 650.
98. Spitta II, p. 762; Terry 1993, p. 237.
99. C. P. E. Bach: *Letters,* ed. Clark, p. xxv.
100. *BD* II, no. 573.
101. *BD* II, no. 621.
102. A more detailed analysis of transmission patterns is provided by Kobayashi 1989.
103. The bulk of C. P. E. Bach's estate that remained at the Sing-Akademie, including the Old Bach Archive, had been missing since World War II but was rediscovered in Kyiv, Ukraine, by the present author in June 1999.
104. See Wollny 1995.
105. *NBR,* p. 472.
106. Fortunate circumstances contributed to this fact: virtually all of the Bachiana remained with C. P. E. Bach's family and were acquired, almost completely, by the collector Georg Poelchau before 1800.

107. Major sources in his possession: autograph scores of BWV 541 and of part II of *The Well-Tempered Clavier* as well as A. M. Bach's copy of part I of the *WTC*.

108. About a fourth of the scores had earlier been sold to Johann Georg Nacke, cantor in Oelsnitz. See also Kobayashi 1989, p. 70.

109. *NBR,* no. 391.

110. Kobayashi 1989, pp. 73f.

111. For a comprehensive discussion of the Bach transmission in the eighteenth century, see Schulze 1984a.

112. Some of these questions are pursued by Kobayashi 1989.

113. *NBR,* no. 306, p. 304.

114. *NBR,* no. 389b.

115. *NBR,* no. 385.

116. Performances of BWV 8, 41, 94, 112, 125, and 133 can be ascertained; see *BzBF* 5 (1986): 83.

117. Once again, C. P. E. Bach was among the applicants. While in 1750 Harrer was the candidate imposed on the city council by Count Brühl, in 1755 the city fathers may have been skeptical about considering a court musician for the school post. Doles had previously served as cantor at the gymnasium in Freiberg.

118. *NBR,* p. 488.


EPILOGUE

1. Bach personally distributed the pamphlet among his friends and acquaintances in January 1738; see *BD* II, no. 417, p. 313. Since Birnbaum's second essay of 1739 (responding to Scheibe's reply to the first defense) was published in two hundred copies at Bach's own expense (*BD* II, nos. 437–438), the same may also be true of the first essay.

2. *NBR,* no. 344. Unless noted otherwise, all subsequent Birnbaum quotes stem from this document.

3. "Kleine Schulrede, worin man die von GOTT bestimmte Harmonie in der Musik beurtheilt," *Musikalische Bibliothek* 2.3 (1742): 63f.

4. *NBR,* no. 344, p. 347.

5. Ibid., p. 345.

6. Marpurg, preface to *The Art of Fugue; NBR,* no. 374.

7. *NBR,* no. 344, p. 344.

8. Ibid., p. 342.

9. *NBR,* no. 306, p. 305.

10. *NBR,* no. 366.

11. For a discussion of term and concept, see Schmidt 1985; see also Wolff, *Essays.*

12. C. P. E. Bach to Forkel, 1775; *NBR,* no. 395, p. 399.

13. *NBR,* no. 336.

14. *NBR,* no. 394, p. 397.

15. *NBR,* no. 395, pp. 398f.

16. *NBR,* no. 344, p. 345.

17. *BD* II, no. 441, p. 355.

18. *NBR,* no. 383.

19. *Jenaische Allgemeine Literaturzeitung,* 282 (November 1805).

20. *NBR,* p. 479, slightly revised.

# *Music Examples*

**Ex. 3.1. Toccata in D minor, BWV 565**

**Ex. 3.2. Toccata in D minor, BWV 565**

**Ex. 3.3. Toccata in D minor, BWV 565**

**Ex. 3.4. Toccata in D minor, BWV 565**

### Ex. 3.5. Toccata in D minor, BWV 565

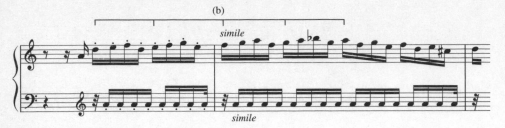

### Ex. 3.6. Toccata in D minor, BWV 565

### Ex. 3.7. Toccata in D minor, BWV 565

### Ex. 4.1. Passacaglia in C minor, BWV 582

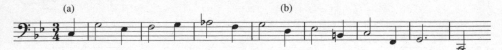

### Ex. 4.2a–b. Passacaglia in C minor, BWV 582

### Ex. 4.2c. Passacaglia in C minor, BWV 582

## Ex. 4.3. Cantata, "Nach dir, Herr, verlanget mich," BWV 150/4

## Ex. 4.4. Organ chorale, "Allein Gott in der Höh sei Ehr," BWV 715

Ex. 5.1. (a) Toccata, BWV 565; (b) Passacaglia, BWV 582

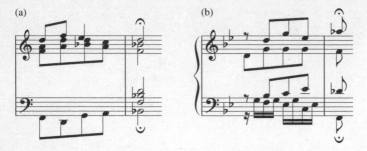

Ex. 6.1. Concerto in F major after Vivaldi, BWV 978/2

Ex. 6.2. Concerto in F major after Vivaldi, BWV 978/1

## Ex. 6.3. Concerto in F major after Vivaldi, BWV 978/1

Bach's
keyboard
version
(a)

Vivaldi's bc
transposed

(b)

(c)                    (d)

## Ex. 6.4. Cantata, "Komm, du süße Todesstunde," BWV 161/3

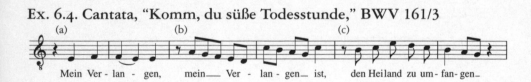

Mein Ver - lan - gen,    mein— Ver - lan - gen— ist,    den Heiland zu um - fan - gen—

## Ex. 6.5. Cantata, "Komm, du süße Todesstunde," BWV 161/3

## Ex. 8.1. Cantata, "Herr, gehe nicht ins Gericht," BWV 105/3

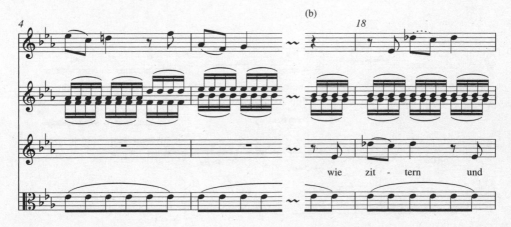

(c)

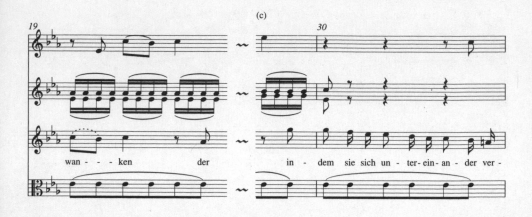

## Ex. 9.1. Canon *trias harmonica,* BWV 1072

## Ex. 10.1. "Confiteor," *Mass in B minor,* BWV 232/20

Con - fi - te - or, con-fi - - - te - or

## Ex. 10.2. Fughetta in E minor, BWV 900/2

**Ex. 10.3a.** Cantata, "Herr, deine Augen sehen nach dem Glauben,"
BWV 102/3

Ex. 10.3b. "Qui tollis," Mass in F major, BWV 233/4

Ex. 10.4. (a) Cantata, "Schau, lieber Gott," BWV 153/5; (b) *Christmas Oratorio*, BWV 248/5

Ex. 10.5a. Cantata, "Gott soll allein mein Herze haben," BWV 169/1, transposed from D major to E major

Ex. 10.5B. Harpsichord Concerto, BWV 1053/1

Ex. 12.1. *The Art of Fugue,* BWV 1080

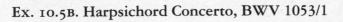

(b) inverted form

(a) principal form

Ex. 12.2. Contrapunctus 4, *The Art of Fugue,* BWV 1080/4

Ex. 12.3. "Et incarnatus est," *Mass in B minor,* BWV 232/16

# *Appendix 1: Chronology*

← March 21 = prior to March 21
March 21 → = after March 21

## EISENACH AND OHRDRUF (1685–1700)

| 1685 | Mar. 21 | Birth of Johann Sebastian, seventh and youngest child of Johann Ambrosius Bach and Maria Elisabeth Bach, née Lämmerhirt |
| --- | --- | --- |
| | Mar. 23 | Baptized at St. George's, Eisenach's main church |
| 1690–93 | | Attends a German school in Eisenach |
| 1693–95 | | Attends the Latin school in Eisenach, *quinta* to *quarta* |
| 1694 | May 3 | Burial of mother, Elisabeth Bach (age 50) |
| | Oct. 23 | Wedding of brother Johann Christoph in Ohrdruf; Ambrosius Bach, Johann Pachelbel, and others perform |
| | Nov. 27 | Ambrosius Bach marries Barbara Margaretha Bartholo-maei, née Keul |
| 1695 | Feb. 20 | Death of father, Johann Ambrosius Bach (age 50); buried Feb. 24 |
| | Spring–summer | Johann Sebastian, orphaned at age 10, and his brother Johann Jacob (13) join the household of their oldest brother, Johann Christoph Bach, in Ohrdruf |
| 1695–1700 | | Attends the Lyceum in Ohrdruf, *tertia* to *prima* |
| 1698–99 | | An autograph copy of a demanding organ piece by Buxtehude attests to the young Bach's remarkable proficiency |
| 1700 | Feb.–Mar. | Calendar reform* |

## LÜNEBURG AND WEIMAR (1700–1703)

| 1700 | Mar. 15 | Leaves Ohrdruf for Lüneburg, St. Midrad's School |
| --- | --- | --- |
| 1700–1702 | | Choral scholar in the *prima* at St. Michael's; contact with Georg Böhm in Lüneburg and frequent visits to Johann Adam Reinken in Hamburg |

*In the year 1700, February 18 (Thursday after Sexagesimae Sunday) was followed immediately by March 1 (Monday before Reminiscere Sunday); Estomihi and Invocavit Sundays were skipped. In this Chronology, all dates through February 1700 are "old style" (Julian calendar); "new style" dates begin in March 1700, when Protestant Germany introduced the Gregorian calendar.

| | | |
|---|---|---|
| 1702 | Apr. (Easter) | Graduation from St. Michael's School and return to Thuringia (probably Ohrdruf) |
| | Jul. 9 → | Successful applicant for the town organist post at St. Jacobi, Sangerhausen; by ducal interference, the post is given to someone else |
| 1703 | Jan.–Jun. | Lackey and musician at the court of Duke Johann Ernst of Saxe-Weimar |
| | ← Jul. 13 | Examines the new organ at the New (also St. Boniface's) Church in Arnstadt |

### ARNSTADT (1703–1707)

| | | |
|---|---|---|
| | Aug. 14 | Acceptance of appointment (dated Aug. 9) as organist at Arnstadt's New Church |
| 1705 | Aug. | Dispute with Johann Heinrich Geyersbach |
| | Nov. → | Visit with Dieterich Buxtehude in Lübeck, stays for 3–4 months |
| | Dec. 2–3 | Buxtehude's oratorios *Castrum doloris* and *Templum honoris* performed in Lübeck |
| 1706 | Feb. 21 → | Disciplinary problems discussed with Arnstadt Consistory |
| | Nov. 28 | Organ examination in Langewiesen, near Gehren |
| 1707 | Apr. 24 | Easter Sunday: audition for the organist position at St. Blasius's Church in Mühlhausen; performance of a cantata (BWV 4 ?) |
| | Jun. 14–22 | Negotiations with the Mühlhausen Town Council; accepts appointment |
| | Jun. 29 | Returns organ keys to Arnstadt authorities |

### MÜHLHAUSEN (1707–1708)

| | | |
|---|---|---|
| 1707 | Jul. 1 | Begins as organist at St. Blasius's in Mühlhausen |
| | Sep. 18 → | Receives 50 florins from the estate of uncle Tobias Lämmerhirt of Erfurt |
| | Oct. 17 | Marriage with Maria Barbara, daughter of Johann Michael Bach (1648–1694) of Gehren, in Dornheim, near Arnstadt |
| 1708 | Feb. 4 | Mühlhausen Town Council election: performance of BWV 71 |
| | Feb. | Submits plans for organ renovation at St. Blasius's |
| | c. Feb. 25 | Cantata BWV 71 published |
| | Jun. | Performs on renovated organ at the ducal palace church in Weimar. Appointed organist and chamber musician at the court of the co-reigning Dukes Wilhelm Ernst and Ernst August of Saxe-Weimar (Jun. 20: ducal salary decree); requests and receives dismissal from Mühlhausen |

### WEIMAR (1708–1717)

| | | |
|---|---|---|
| 1708 | ← Jul. 14 | Moves to Weimar |
| | Dec. 29 | Daughter Catharina Dorothea baptized (d. 1774) |
| 1709 | Feb. 4 | Mühlhausen Town Council election: guest performance of a (lost) cantata (work published) |

|      | Mar.            | Visit of the violinist Johann Georg Pisendel |
|------|-----------------|---------------------------------------------|
| 1710 | Feb. 4          | Mühlhausen Town Council election: guest performance of a (lost) cantata (work published) |
|      | Oct. 26         | Organ examination and dedication in Traubach, near Weimar |
|      | Nov. 22         | Son Wilhelm Friedemann born |
| 1711 | Jun. 3          | The Weimar duke orders a salary increase for Bach |
| 1713 | Feb. 21–22      | In Weissenfels: performance of the *Hunt Cantata,* BWV 208, in conjunction with the birthday of Duke Christian of Saxe-Weissenfels |
|      | Feb. 23         | Twins, Maria Sophia and Johann Christoph, born; Johann Christoph dies shortly after birth. Mar. 15: burial of Maria Sophia |
|      | Jul. 8          | Prince Johann Ernst returns from study trip, bringing with him new musical repertoires |
|      | Sep. 7          | In Ohrdruf: baptism of Johann Sebastian, son of brother Johann Christoph Bach |
|      | Oct.            | Composes birthday aria for Duke Wilhelm Ernst |
|      | Nov. 6          | Participates in festive dedication of the newly built St. Jacobi Church in Weimar |
|      | Nov. 28–Dec. 15 | In Halle: invited to audition for organist post at Our Lady's (Market) Church (successor to F. W. Zachow); Bach elected on Dec. 13 |
| 1714 | ← Jan. 14       | Receives appointment for post in Halle |
|      | ← Feb. 19       | Withdraws candidacy |
|      | Mar. 2          | Appointed concertmaster at the Weimar court; receives salary increase |
|      | Mar. 8          | Son Carl Philipp Emanuel born |
|      | Mar. 25         | Palm Sunday/Annunciation: performance of BWV 182, first cantata after concertmaster appointment |
| 1715 | May 11          | Son Johann Gottfried Bernhard born |
|      | Aug. 1–Nov. 3   | Official mourning period after the death of Prince Wilhelm Ernst |
| 1716 | Apr. 29–May 2   | Organ examination and dedication in Halle, Market Church |
|      | Jul. 31         | Organ examination in Erfurt, St. Augustine's Church |
|      | Dec. 1          | Death of Weimar capellmeister Johann Samuel Drese |
| 1717 | Mar. 26         | Good Friday: guest performance of a (lost) Passion at the palace church of Gotha |
|      | Aug. 5          | Signs contractual agreement to accept capellmeistership in Cöthen |
|      | Fall (Oct.–Nov.) | In Dresden: keyboard contest with Louis Marchand at the royal-electoral court |
|      | Nov. 6–Dec. 2   | Detention in conjunction with his dismissal from Weimar court service |
|      | Dec. 16–18      | Organ examination in Leipzig, St. Paul's (University) Church |

## CÖTHEN (1717–1723)

|      | Dec. 29              | Arrival in Cöthen |
|------|----------------------|-------------------|
| 1718 | c. May 9–Jul. 15     | With Prince Leopold in Carlsbad |
|      | Nov. 15              | Son Leopold Augustus born; baptized Nov. 17 |

|            | Dec. 10                | Birthday of Prince Leopold: performance of BWV 66a, Anh.5 |
| 1719       | Mar. 1 →               | Trip to Berlin; purchase of a harpsichord for the princely court |
|            | ~Jun.                  | Failed attempt at meeting George Frideric Handel in Halle |
|            | Sep. 28                | Son Leopold Augustus dies |
| 1720       | Jan. 22                | Title page of *Clavier-Büchlein* for Wilhelm Friedemann |
|            | Late May–Jul. 7 →      | With Prince Leopold in Carlsbad |
|            | Jul. 7                 | Burial of Bach's wife, Maria Barbara |
|            | mid-Nov.–Nov. 23       | In Hamburg: recital at St. Catharine's Church in the presence of Reinken; performance of cantata(s), incl. BWV 21; candidate for organist post at St. Jacobi Church |
|            | ← Dec. 19              | Withdraws candidacy for St. Jacobi |
| 1721       | Feb. 22                | Death of brother Johann Christoph (age 49), organist in Ohrdruf |
|            | Mar. 24                | Dedication of Concertos "avec plusieurs instruments" to Margrave Christian of Brandenburg |
|            | ← Aug. 7               | Guest performance in Schleiz at the court of Count Reuss |
|            | Dec. 3                 | Marriage to Anna Magdalena Wilcke, princely court singer at Cöthen |
|            | Dec. 11                | Marriage of Prince Leopold to Princess Henrietta of Anhalt-Bernburg |
| 1722       | Apr. 16                | Death of brother Johann Jacob (age 40), royal court musician in Stockholm |
|            | Aug. 9                 | Guest performance in Zerbst: birthday of Prince Johann August of Anhalt-Zerbst |
|            | ← Dec. 15              | Inheritance from the Lämmerhirt estate, Erfurt |
|            | ← Dec. 21              | Application for the cantorate at St. Thomas's in Leipzig |
| 1723       | Feb. 7                 | Audition for the cantorate at St. Thomas's |
|            | Spring                 | Daughter Christiana Sophia Henrietta born |
|            | Apr. 13                | Requests dismissal from Cöthen, which he receives; continues as nonresident princely Anhalt-Cöthen capellmeister |

LEIPZIG (1723–1730)

| 1723       | Apr. 19                | Signs provisional contract with the Leipzig Town Council |
|            | May 5                  | Signs final contract with the Leipzig Town Council |
|            | May 8                  | Theological examination by professors Schmid and Deyling |
|            | May 13                 | Signs visitation article |
|            | May 15                 | First Leipzig salary payment |
|            | May 16                 | Whitsunday: first performance at St. Paul's (University) Church (BWV 59) |
|            | May 22                 | Bach's family relocates to Leipzig and moves into a spacious apartment in the St. Thomas School |

|  | May 30 | First Sunday after Trinity: performance of BWV 75 and beginning of first annual cantata cycle (*Jahrgang* I) |
|  | Jun. 1 | Formal installation at the St. Thomas School |
|  | Jun. 14 | Sons Wilhelm Friedemann and Carl Philipp Emanuel enroll in the St. Thomas School |
|  | Aug. | Performs Latin Ode BWV Anh. 20 at the University |
|  | Nov. 2 | Organ examination and dedication in Störmthal, near Leipzig: performance of BWV 194 |
|  | Dec. 25 | Performance of Magnificat, BWV 243a |
| 1724 | Feb. 26 | Son Gottfried Heinrich born; baptized Feb. 27 |
|  | Apr. 7 | Good Friday: performance of the *St. John Passion,* BWV 245 (1st version) |
|  | Jun. 11 | First Sunday after Trinity: beginning of second (chorale) cantata cycle (*Jahrgang* II), with BWV 20 |
|  | ← Jul. 18 | Guest performance in Cöthen, with Anna Magdalena |
| 1725 | Feb. 23 | Guest performance in Weissenfels (birthday of Duke Christian): BWV 249a |
|  | Mar. 30 | Good Friday: performance of the *St. John Passion,* BWV 245 (2nd version) |
|  | Apr. 14 | Son Christian Gottlieb baptized |
|  | May 30–Jun. 6 | Visit to Gera with Anna Magdalena and Wilhelm Friedemann; organ dedication at St. John's |
|  | Sep. 14 | Petition to the elector of Saxony, King Friedrich August I (re: university service) |
|  | Sep. 19–20 | Organ recitals at St. Sophia's Church in Dresden |
|  | Nov. 3 | Petition to the elector of Saxony, King Friedrich August I |
|  | Nov. 30–Dec. 15 | Guest performances in Cöthen, with Anna Magdalena (birthdays of Princess Charlotte Friederike Wilhelmine and Prince Leopold) |
|  | Dec. 31 | Second petition to King Friedrich August I |
| 1726 | Apr. 5 | Daughter Elisabeth Juliana Friederica baptized |
|  | Apr. 19 | Good Friday: performance of F. N. Brauns's (?) *St. Mark Passion,* with additions by Bach |
|  | Jun. 29 | Daughter Christiana Sophia Henrietta (age 3) dies; buried July 1 |
|  | Nov. 1 | Announcement of the *Clavier-Übung* series (BWV 825) |
|  | Fall | Michaelmas Fair: single edition of BWV 825 published (BWV 826–830 published separately, 1727–30) |
| 1727 | Mar.–Apr. | Renovations of Bach's apartment in the St. Thomas School completed |
|  | Apr. 11 | Good Friday: *St. Matthew Passion,* BWV 244 (1st version) |
|  | Sep. 7–Jan. 6, 1728 | Official state mourning period after death of Electoress and Queen Christiane Eberhardine |
|  | Oct. 17 | Academic memorial service for the electoress of Saxony and queen of Poland (BWV 198) |
|  | Oct. 30 | Son Ernestus Andreas baptized; dies Nov. 1, buried Nov. 2 |

| | | |
|---|---|---|
| 1728 | ← Jan. 5 | Guest performance in Cöthen (for New Year's Day festivities) |
| | Sep. 21 | Son Christian Gottlieb dies (age 3); buried Sep. 22 |
| | Oct. 10 | Daughter Regina Johanna baptized |
| | Nov. 19 | Death of Prince Leopold of Anhalt-Cöthen |
| 1729 | Jan. 12 | Visit in Leipzig of Duke Christian of Weissenfels: performance of BWV 210a |
| | c. Feb. 23 | Several days: guest performances in Weissenfels (birthday of Duke Christian); appointment as titular capellmeister of the ducal Saxon-Weissenfels court |
| | Mar. 5 | Matriculation of son Wilhelm Friedemann at Leipzig University |
| | ← Mar. 20 | Bach absent from Leipzig for 3 weeks (no details known) |
| | Mar. 20 → | Assumes directorship of Collegium Musicum |
| | Mar. 23–24 | Funeral services for Prince Leopold in Cöthen (BWV 244a) |
| | Apr. 15 | Good Friday: performance of the *St. Matthew Passion,* BWV 244 |
| | Jun. 29 | Invites George Frideric Handel (visiting with his mother in Halle) to come to Leipzig, in vain; Bach himself ill, sends son Wilhelm Friedemann to Halle |
| | Jul. 30 | Friedelena Margaretha Bach, sister of Bach's first wife Maria Barbara (age 53), buried (lived in Bach's household since c. 1708) |
| | Oct. 20 | Funeral of Johann Heinrich Ernesti, rector of St. Thomas's (BWV 229) |
| | ← Dec. 24 | Auditions organists for post at St. Nicholas's (Bach's student Johann Schneider appointed) |
| 1730 | Jan. 1 | Daughter Christiana Benedicta baptized; dies Jan. 4, buried Jan. 5 |
| | Apr. 7 | Good Friday: performance of anonymous *St. Luke's Passion,* BWV 246, with additions by Bach |
| | Jun. 25–27 | Jubilee of Augsburg Confession: BWV 190a, 120b, and Anh. 4a |
| | Aug. 23 | Memorandum for a "Well-Appointed Church Music" |

LEIPZIG (1731–1740)

| | | |
|---|---|---|
| 1731 | Mar. 18 | Daughter Christiana Dorothea baptized |
| | Mar. 23 | Good Friday: performance of *St. Mark Passion,* BWV 247 |
| | Spring | Publication of Opus 1: part I of the *Clavier-Übung* |
| | May → | Major renovations of the St. Thomas School building; Bach family moves into temporary quarters |
| | c. Sept. 14 | In Dresden for several days: attends premiere of Johann Adolf Hasse's opera *Cleofide* (Sep. 13); organ recital at St. Sophia's (Sep. 14) and other performances at the court |
| | Oct. 1 | Son Carl Philipp Emanuel matriculates at Leipzig University |

| | | |
|---|---|---|
| | Nov. 12 | Organ examination in Stöntzsch; reexamination Feb. 4, 1732 |
| 1732 | ← Apr. 24 | St. Thomas School building renovations nearly completed; Bach and his family return to their residence |
| | Jun. 5 | Dedication of the renovated St. Thomas School (BWV Anh. 18) |
| | Jun. 21 | Son Johann Christoph Friedrich born; baptized Jun. 23 |
| | Aug. 31 | Daughter Christiana Dorothea dies (age 1); buried the same day |
| | Sep. 21 → | Trip to Kassel with Anna Magdalena; organ examination at St. Martin's Church and dedication recital (Sep. 28) |
| 1733 | Feb. 15–Jul. 2 | Official state mourning period after death on Feb. 1 of Elector and King Friedrich August I |
| | Apr. 21 | St. Nicholas's Church: fealty celebration for August II, elector of Saxony |
| | Apr. 25 | Daughter Regina Johanna (age 4) dies; buried Apr. 26 |
| | Jun. 7 | Son Wilhelm Friedemann applies for organist post at St. Sophia's in Dresden; appointed on Jun. 23 |
| | c. Jul. 27 | In Dresden for several days: dedication of the *Missa* (Kyrie and Gloria), BWV 232, to the new elector, Friedrich August II (Jul. 27) |
| | Nov. 5 | Son Johann August Abraham baptized; dies Nov. 6, buried Nov. 7 |
| 1734 | Jan. 17–19 | Celebration in Leipzig of the coronation of Friedrich August II as king of Poland (BWV 214a) |
| | ← Mar. 13 | Visit of Franz Benda in Leipzig |
| | Sep. 9 | Matriculation of son Carl Philipp Emanuel at the University of Frankfurt-on-the-Oder, where he directs the Collegium Musicum |
| | Oct. 4 | St. Thomas School bids farewell to rector Johann Matthias Gesner, who becomes founding dean of the Arts and Sciences Faculty of newly established Göttingen University |
| | Nov. 21 | Installation of Professor Johann August Ernesti as rector of the St. Thomas School (BWV Anh. 19) |
| | Dec. 25 | Christmas Day: performance of first part of *Christmas Oratorio,* BWV 248[1] (subsequent parts performed on Dec. 26, Dec. 27, Jan. 1, 1735, Jan. 2, and Jan. 6) |
| 1735 | Spring | Publication of part II of the *Clavier-Übung* |
| | Jun. | Trip to Mühlhausen for more than a week: audition of son Johann Gottfried Bernhard for organist post at St. Mary's (← Jun. 9), organ examination at St. Mary's (← Jun. 16) |
| | Sep. 5 | Son Johann Christian born; baptized Sep. 7 |
| 1736 | Mar. 30 | Good Friday, at St. Thomas's: *St. Matthew Passion,* BWV 244 (revised version, using "swallow's nest" organ for first and last movements of part I) |
| | Jul. 17 → | Plans to be absent from Leipzig for two weeks (no details known) |

|      | Nov. 19 | Appointed Royal-Polish and Electoral-Saxon Court Composer |
|------|---------|----------------------------------------------------------|
|      | c. Dec. 1 | In Dresden for several days: organ recital at St. Mary's (Dec. 1) |
| 1737 | Jan. 14 | Son Johann Gottfried Bernhard appointed organist at St. Jacobi's in Sangerhausen |
|      | Mar. 4 → | Resigns temporarily as director of the Collegium Musicum |
|      | Apr. 10 | Town council decision regarding appointment of prefects |
|      | c. May | Trip to Sangerhausen (no details known) |
|      | May 14 → | Learns about Johann Adolph Scheibe's critique |
|      | Sep. 28 | In Wiederau: performance of BWV 30a |
|      | ← Oct. 18 | Cousin Johann Elias Bach begins service as private secretary to Bach and tutor of his children |
|      | Oct. 30 | Daughter Johanna Carolina baptized |
|      | Dec. 12 | The king's decree in the dispute between Bach and Ernesti |
|      | Dec. 16 | Organ examination in Weissensee |
| 1738 | Jan. 8 | Publication of Johann Abraham Birnbaum's defense against Scheibe's attack |
|      | Spring | C. P. E. Bach appointed harpsichordist of the crown prince, later King Friedrich II of Prussia |
|      | ← May 22 | In Dresden for several days |
| 1739 | Jan. 28 | Son Johann Gottfried Bernhard registers at the University of Jena |
|      | Mar. 27 | Good Friday: cancellation of Passion performance |
|      | May 27 | Death of son Johann Gottfried Bernhard (age 24) |
|      | ← Aug. 11 | Son Wilhelm Friedemann back home for 4 weeks; concerts with lutenists Silvius Leopold Weiss and Johann Kropffgans of Dresden |
|      | ← Sep. 7 | In Altenburg: dedication of organ at the Castle Church |
|      | Fall | Michaelmas Fair: publication of part III of the *Clavier-Übung* |
|      | Oct. 2 | Resumes directorship of the Collegium Musicum |
|      | Nov. 7–14 | Trip to Weissenfels with Anna Magdalena (no details known) |
| 1740 | Apr. 17 | Trip to Halle (no details known) |

LEIPZIG (1741–1750)

|      | | |
|------|---------|----------------------------------------------------------|
| 1741 | ← Aug. 5 | Trip to Berlin, for at least one week (no details known) |
|      | Fall | Michaelmas Fair(?): publication of part IV of the *Clavier-Übung* |
|      | ← Nov. 17 | Extended trip to Dresden (return on Nov. 17); visit with Count Keyserlingk |
| 1742 | Feb. 22 | Daughter Regina Susanna baptized |
|      | May 13–20 | Official state mourning period after the death of Empress Maria Amalia |
|      | Aug. 30 | In Kleinzschocher: performance of BWV 212 |

|      |                  |                                                                                                                                                                                                 |
|------|------------------|-------------------------------------------------------------------------------------------------------------------------------------------------------------------------------------------------|
|      | Oct. 31          | Johann Elias Bach leaves Leipzig and his post as private secretary to Bach and tutor of his children                                                                                             |
| 1743 | ← Dec. 13        | Organ examination at St. John's in Leipzig                                                                                                                                                       |
| 1745 | Nov. 30–Dec. 25  | Occupation of Leipzig by Prussian troops                                                                                                                                                         |
| 1746 | Apr. 16          | Son Wilhelm Friedemann appointed organist and music director of Our Lady's (Market) Church in Halle                                                                                              |
|      | Aug. 7           | Organ examination in Zschortau, near Leipzig                                                                                                                                                     |
|      | Sep. 24–28       | Organ examination in Naumburg, St. Wenceslas's Church                                                                                                                                            |
| 1747 | c. May 7–8       | Trip to Potsdam and Berlin: visit with King Friedrich II of Prussia in Potsdam (May 7); organ recital in the Church of the Holy Spirit (May 8); visits new opera house in Berlin                 |
|      | Jun.             | Accepts membership in the Society of Musical Science (L. C. Mizler, secretary, present in Leipzig); contributes publication of *Canonic Variations,* BWV 769                                      |
|      | Jul. 7           | Dedication of *Musical Offering,* BWV 1079                                                                                                                                                       |
|      | Jul. 28          | Start of major organ repairs at St. Thomas's                                                                                                                                                     |
|      | Sep.             | Michaelmas Fair: publication of *Musical Offering,* BWV 1079                                                                                                                                     |
|      | Nov.             | Examination of renovated organ at St. Thomas's                                                                                                                                                   |
| 1748 | Sep. 26          | Grandson Johann Sebastian Bach, son of C. P. E. Bach, baptized in Berlin (Bach not present)                                                                                                      |
|      | ← Dec. 21        | Audition of town musicians                                                                                                                                                                       |
| 1749 | Jan. 20          | Daughter Elisabeth Juliana Friederica marries Bach's former student Johann Christoph Altnickol                                                                                                   |
|      | Apr. 2           | Corresponds with Count Questenberg of Moravia                                                                                                                                                    |
|      | Apr. 4           | Last performance of the *St. John Passion*                                                                                                                                                       |
|      | Apr.             | Conference with organ builder Heinrich Andreas Cuntzius                                                                                                                                          |
|      | May 6            | Sale of a fortepiano to Count Branitzky of Poland                                                                                                                                                |
|      | May 12 →         | Gets involved in the Bidermann affair                                                                                                                                                            |
|      | mid-May          | Hit by sudden critical illness                                                                                                                                                                   |
|      | Jun. 8           | Premature audition of Gottlob Harrer (capellmeister to Count Brühl in Dresden) for the cantorate at St. Thomas's, at the special request of the Saxon prime minister, takes place in the concert hall "Three Swans" |
|      | Oct. 6           | Grandson Johann Sebastian Altnickol baptized in Naumburg (Bach not present); buried Dec. 21                                                                                                      |
|      | Nov. 30          | First Sunday in Advent: W. F. Bach performs his cantata Fk 80 in Leipzig                                                                                                                         |
| 1750 | Jan.             | Appointment of son Johann Christoph Friedrich as court musician of Count Wilhelm of Schaumburg-Lippe in Bückeburg                                                                                |
|      | Feb. 2           | Purification (or Mar. 25, Visitation): C. P. E. Bach performs his Magnificat, Wq 215, in Leipzig                                                                                                 |
|      | Mar. 28–31       | First operation by the London eye surgeon Dr. John Taylor                                                                                                                                        |
|      | Apr. 5–8         | Second operation by Dr. Taylor                                                                                                                                                                   |

|              |          |                                                                                                      |
|--------------|----------|------------------------------------------------------------------------------------------------------|
|              | May 4 →  | Arrival of Bach's last pupil, Johann Gottfried Müthel, in Leipzig                                     |
|              | May 17   | Whitsunday: Bach's assistant Johann Adam Franck appointed substitute and eventually interim cantor, through Sept. 1751 |
|              | Jul. 22  | After a stroke, receives last communion at home                                                      |
|              | Jul. 28  | Death (age 65) at "a little after" 8:15 P.M.                                                          |
|              | Jul. 31  | Burial at St. John's Cemetery                                                                         |

POSTHUMOUS YEARS (1750–1809)

|          |          |                                                                                                      |
|----------|----------|------------------------------------------------------------------------------------------------------|
| 1750     | Fall     | Johann Christian (age 15) joins the household of his stepbrother C. P. E. Bach in Berlin; Gottfried Heinrich joins the household of his brother-in-law Johann Christoph Altnickol in Naumburg |
|          | Aug. 7   | Election of Gottlob Harrer as Thomascantor (other applicants for the position: C. P. E. Bach, A. F. Graun, J. L. Krebs, J. G. Görner, and J. Trier) |
|          | Aug. 29 →| The Leipzig Town Council acquires performing parts of chorale cantata cycle from Anna Magdalena Bach for the use of the St. Thomas cantor |
|          | Oct. 2   | Installation of Gottlob Harrer as Thomascantor                                                       |
|          | Nov. 11  | Settlement of Bach's estate at the probate court of Leipzig University                                |
| 1750–51  | Winter   | Carl Philipp Emanuel Bach and Johann Friedrich Agricola write Obituary (published 1754)              |
| 1751     | May      | *Jubilate* (Spring) Fair: publication of *The Art of Fugue,* BWV 1080                                |
|          | Jun. 1   | Subscription announcement for *The Art of Fugue*                                                     |
| 1752     | May      | Second edition of *The Art of Fugue*                                                                 |
| 1755     | Jul. 9   | Death of Thomascantor Gottlob Harrer                                                                 |
|          | Sep. 29  | Commemoration of the 200th anniversary of the Augsburg Religious Peace: performance of BWV 126, conducted by the prefect (probably C. F. Penzel) |
|          | Oct. 8   | Appointment of Johann Friedrich Doles, cantor at the cathedral in Freiberg (a pupil of Bach's, 1739–43), as Thomascantor |
| 1760     | Feb. 27  | Death of Anna Magdalena Bach (age 59); buried Feb 29                                                  |
| 1763     | Feb. 12  | Death of son Gottfried Heinrich (age 39) in Naumburg                                                  |
| 1774     | Jan. 14  | Death of daughter Catharina Dorothea Bach (age 65) in Leipzig                                         |
| 1781     | Aug. 18  | Death of daughter Johanna Carolina Bach (age 43) in Leipzig                                           |
|          | Aug. 24  | Death of daughter Elisabeth Juliane Friederica Altnickol (age 55) in Leipzig                          |
| 1782     | Jan. 1   | Death of son Johann Christian (age 46) in London                                                     |
| 1784     | Jul. 1   | Death of son Wilhelm Friedemann (age 73) in Berlin                                                   |
| 1788     | Dec. 14  | Death of son Carl Philipp Emanuel (age 74) in Hamburg                                                 |
| 1795     | Jan. 26  | Death of son Johann Christoph Friedrich (age 63) in Bückeburg                                         |
| 1809     | Dec. 14  | Death of daughter Regina Susanna Bach (age 67) in Leipzig                                             |

# Appendix 2: Places of Bach's Activities

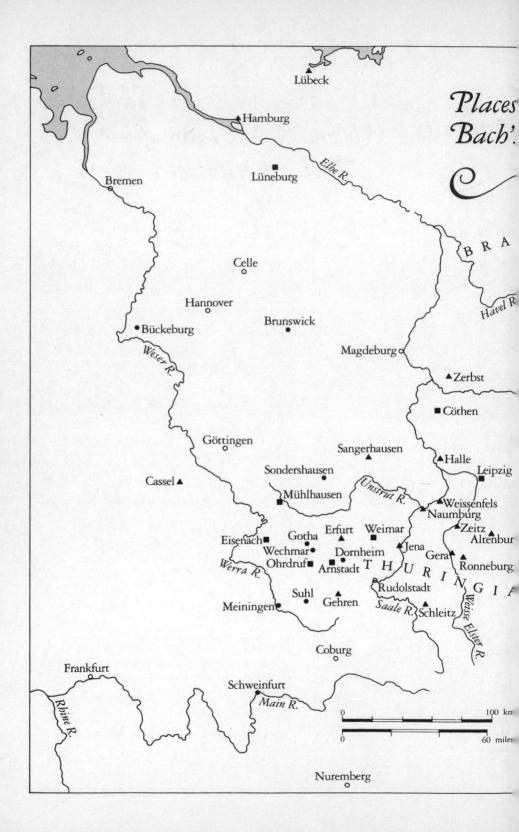

Places
Bach'

BRA

Lübeck

Hamburg

Elbe R.

Bremen

Lüneburg

Havel R.

Celle

Hannover

Brunswick

Bückeburg

Magdeburg

Zerbst

Weser R.

Cöthen

Göttingen

Sangerhausen

Halle

Leipzig

Sondershausen

Cassel

Mühlhausen

Unstrut R.

Weissenfels

Naumburg

Erfurt

Weimar

Zeitz

Eisenach

Gotha

Altenbur

Wechmar

Dornheim

Jena

Gera

Ohrdruf

Arnstadt

T H U R I N G I A

Ronneburg

Werra R.

Rudolstadt

Weisse Elster R.

Suhl

Gehren

Meiningen

Saale R.

Schleitz

Coburg

Frankfurt

Schweinfurt

Main R.

0                    100 km

Rhine R.

0              60 miles

Nuremberg

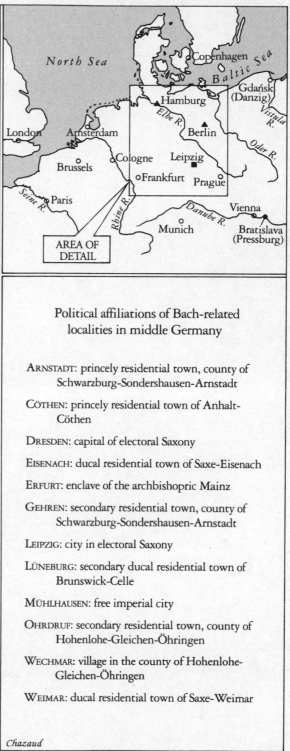

*Activities*

ENBURG

Oder R.

▲ Berlin

Frankfurt/
Oder

Potsdam

Elbe R.

AXONY

Dresden ▲

Carlsbad    BOHEMIA

Prague

Vltava R.

Places J. S. Bach lived in
Places Bach visited
Bach family places
Places for references

---

North Sea

Copenhagen    Baltic Sea

Hamburg    Gdańsk
(Danzig)

Elbe R.    Vistula R.

London    Amsterdam    ▲ Berlin

Oder R.

Brussels    Cologne    Leipzig

Frankfurt    Prague

Seine R.    Paris

Rhine R.    Danube R.    Vienna

Munich    Bratislava
(Pressburg)

AREA OF
DETAIL

Political affiliations of Bach-related
localities in middle Germany

ARNSTADT: princely residential town, county of
Schwarzburg-Sondershausen-Arnstadt

CÖTHEN: princely residential town of Anhalt-
Cöthen

DRESDEN: capital of electoral Saxony

EISENACH: ducal residential town of Saxe-Eisenach

ERFURT: enclave of the archbishopric Mainz

GEHREN: secondary residential town, county of
Schwarzburg-Sondershausen-Arnstadt

LEIPZIG: city in electoral Saxony

LÜNEBURG: secondary ducal residential town of
Brunswick-Celle

MÜHLHAUSEN: free imperial city

OHRDRUF: secondary residential town, county of
Hohenlohe-Gleichen-Öhringen

WECHMAR: village in the county of Hohenlohe-
Gleichen-Öhringen

WEIMAR: ducal residential town of Saxe-Weimar

*Chazaud*

# Appendix 3: Money and Living Costs in Bach's Time

## MONETARY UNITS

| | |
|---|---|
| 1 pf. (pfennig—copper coin) | =smallest unit |
| 1 gr. (groschen—silver coin) | =12 pf. |
| 1 fl. (gulden, florin, *or* guilder—silver coin) | =21 gr. |
| 1 thlr. *or* rthl. (taler *or* reichstaler—silver coin) | =24 gr. (1 fl. 3 gr.) |
| 1 dukat (gold coin) | =66 gr. (2 rthl. 18 gr.) |
| 1 dukat (adjusted parity) | =72 gr. (3 rthl.) |
| 1 louis d'or (gold coin) | =5 rthl. |

## COST OF LIVING

Fundamental socioeconomic changes and inflation make it very difficult to compare the value and purchasing power of eighteenth-century currency with that of today's money. The conversion into a modern decimal currency system is meant to provide merely a general sense of proportions:

| | | | | |
|---|---|---|---|---|
| 1 pfennig | =$    .25 | 1 taler | =$ 72.00 |
| 1 groschen | =$   3.00 | 1 dukat | =$198.00 |
| 1 gulden | =$  63.00 | 1 dukat (adj.) | =$216.00 |
| 1 dukat | =$198.00 | 1 louis d'or | =$360.00 |

1. Selected cost-of-living figures for early eighteenth-century Leipzig* (in 1721, the taler replaced the guilder as the standard currency denomination in Electoral Saxony):

### Household goods

| | | |
|---|---|---|
| 5 pf. | [$  1.25] | 1 quart [Kanne] of milk (1725) |
| 6 pf. | [$  1.50] | 1 quart of beer (1699) |
| 3 gr. 2 pf. | [$  9.50] | 1 quart of ordinary wine |
| 6 gr. | [$18.00] | 1 quart of better wine |
| 3 gr. 3 pf. | [$  9.75] | 1 set of 15 [Mandel] eggs (1762) |
| | | [1 egg =$.65] |

*SOURCE: M.J. Elias, *Umriss einer Geschichte der Preise und Löhne in Deutschland vom ausgehenden Mittelalter bis zum Beginn des neunzehnten Jahrhunderts*, vol. 2 (Leiden: Sijthoff, 1940).

| | | |
|---|---|---|
| 4 gr. 9 pf. | [$14.25] | 1 tub [4 quarts = Fass] of butter (1710) |
| 1 gr. 2 pf | [$3.50] | 1 pound of veal (1699) |
| 1 gr. 3 pf. | [$3.75] | 1 pound of beef (1699) or ham (1697) |
| 21 gr. 6 pf. | [$64.50] | 1 bushel [Saxon Scheffel =c. 103 liters] of grain (rye) |
| 10 gr. | [$2.50] | 1 pound of wax candles (1726) |
| 20 gr. 8 pf. | [$62.00] | 1 ream [Ries = 480 sheets] of ordinary paper (1725) |
| 1 tlr. 2 gr. 5 pf. | [$79.25] | 1 ream of fine paper (1717) |

## Wages

| | | |
|---|---|---|
| 6 pf. | [$1.50] | a maid's (female child) daily pay (1700) |
| 1 gr. 6 pf. | [$4.50] | a maid's (female adult) daily pay (1699) |
| 6 gr. | [$18.00] | a gravedigger's pay per grave (1700–8) |
| 7 gr.; 8 gr. | [$21.00; 24.00] | a carpenter's daily pay: 7 gr. / winter; 8 gr. / summer (1725) |
| 50 rtl. | [$3,600.00] | annual income of a barber (1722–29) |
| 175 rtl. | [$12,600.00] | annual salary of a pastor (1722–29) |

2. Selected examples drawn from Bach documents (references are to *NBR* numbers):

## Salaries, honoraria, fees

| | | |
|---|---|---|
| 400 rtl. | [$28,000] | Bach's annual salary—without benefits—as capellmeister in Cöthen, 1717 (No. 70) |
| 300 rtl. | [$21,600] | Anna Magdalena Bach's annual salary as Cöthen court singer, 1722 (No. 87) |
| 100 rtl. | [$7,200] | Bach's annual fee for private study with him, including room and board, 1712 (No. 312) |
| 50 rtl. | [$3,600] | Bach's honorarium for a congratulatory cantata, 1736, 1738 (Nos. 172, 201) |
| 22 rtl. | [$1,584] | Bach's (variable) organ examination fee, 1746 (*BD* II, no. 548; see also Nos. 73 and 158) |
| 12 rtl. | [$864] | Bach's (variable) honorarium for a guest performance (church music), 1713, 1717 (Nos. 47, 63; see also No. 116) |
| 6 rtl. | [$432] | Bach's fee for a keyboard lesson to a nobleman (No. 250) |
| 1 rtl. | [$72] | cantor's fee for weddings and funerals in Leipzig (*Ordnung der Schule zu St. Thomae*, Leipzig 1723) |
| 16 gr. | [$48] | travel expenses; per diem for meals [*Kostgeld*], 1713 (No. 44) |

## Publications

| | | |
|---|---|---|
| 1 rtl. | [$72] | *Musical Offering*, 1747 = 3 typeset, 26 engraved pages (No. 248) |
| 2 rtl. | [$144] | *Clavier-Übung*, Part I, 1731 = 37 engraved pages (BD II, no., 506); J. D. Heinichen, *Der General-Baß in der Composition,* 1728 = 994 typeset pages (No. 140) |

| | | |
|---|---|---|
| 3 rtl. | [$216] | *Clavier-Übung*, Part III, 1739 = 78 engraved pages (No. 333); *The Art of Fugue*, 1751 = 2 typeset, 67 engraved pages (No. 282) |

*Musical Instruments*

| | | |
|---|---|---|
| 115 rtl. | [$8,280] | fortepiano (No. 262) |
| 50 / 80 rtl. | [$3,600/5,760] | harpsichord (No. 279) |
| 21 rtl. | [$1,512] | lute (No. 279) |
| 8 rtl. | [$576] | violin, made by Jacobus Stainer (No. 279) |
| 3 rtl. | [$216] | spinet (No. 279) |
| 2 rtl. | [$144] | ordinary violin (No. 279) |
| 1 rtl. 8 gr. | [$96] | harpsichord rental (Bach's fee), 1 month (No. 249) |
| 8 rtl. 3 gr. 6 pf. | [$586.50] | Bach's (variable) semi-annual fee for maintenance of instruments belonging to St. Nicholas Church, 1728 (*BD* II, no. 161; see also Nos. 37 and 110) |

# Appendix 4: The Lutheran Church Calendar

| Sunday or Feast | How Determined | Possible Dates[a] |
|---|---|---|
| 1st Sunday in Advent | 4th Sunday before Christmas | Nov. 27 ~ Dec. 3 |
| 2nd–4th Sunday in Advent | 3rd–1st Sunday before Christmas | Dec. 4 ~ Dec. 24 |
| Christmas Day | Fixed according to Gregorian calendar | Dec. 25 |
| 2nd & 3rd day of Christmas | Fixed | Dec. 26–27 |
| Sunday after Christmas[b] | — | Dec. 28 ~ 31 |
| New Year's Day (Circumcision) | Fixed | Jan. 1 |
| Sunday after New Year's Day[b] | — | Jan. 2 ~ 5 |
| Epiphany | Fixed | Jan. 6 |
| 1st Sunday after Epiphany | — | Jan. 7 ~ Jan. 13 |
| Purification | Fixed | Feb. 2 |
| 2nd–6th Sunday after Epiphany[b] | — | Jan. 14 ~ Feb. 21 |
| Septuagesimae | 9th Sunday before Easter | Jan. 18 ~ Feb. 22 |
| Sexagesimae | 8th Sunday before Easter | Jan. 25 ~ Feb. 29 |
| Estomihi (Quinquagesimae) | 7th Sunday before Easter | Feb. 1 ~ Mar. 7 |
| Invocavit | 6th Sunday before Easter | Feb. 8 ~ Mar. 14 |
| Reminiscere | 5th Sunday before Easter | Feb. 15 ~ Mar. 21 |
| Oculi | 4th Sunday before Easter | Feb. 22 ~ Mar. 28 |
| Laetare | 3rd Sunday before Easter | Mar. 1 ~ Apr. 4 |
| Judica | 2nd Sunday before Easter | Mar. 8 ~ Apr. 11 |
| Annunciation[c] | Fixed | Mar. 25 |
| Palm Sunday | Sunday before Easter | Mar. 15 ~ Apr. 18 |
| Good Friday | Friday before Easter | Mar. 20 ~ Apr. 23 |
| Easter Sunday | Varies according to lunar calendar | Mar. 22 ~ Apr. 25 |
| 2nd & 3rd days of Easter | — | Mar. 23 ~ Apr. 27 |

| | | |
|---|---|---|
| Quasimodogeniti | 1st Sunday after Easter | Mar. 29 ~ May 2 |
| Misericordias Domini | 2nd Sunday after Easter | Apr. 5 ~ May 9 |
| Jubilate | 3rd Sunday after Easter | Apr. 12 ~ May 16 |
| Cantate | 4th Sunday after Easter | Apr. 19 ~ May 23 |
| Rogate | 5th Sunday after Easter | Apr. 26 ~ May 30 |
| Ascension Day | 40th day after Easter | Apr. 30 ~ Jun. 3 |
| Exaudi | 6th Sunday after Easter | May 3 ~ Jun. 6 |
| Whitsunday (Pentecost) | 7th Sunday after Easter | May 10 ~ Jun. 13 |
| 2nd & 3rd day of Pentecost | — | May 11 ~ Jun. 15 |
| Trinity Sunday | 1st Sunday after Pentecost | May 17 ~ Jun. 20 |
| 1st–22nd Sunday after Trinity | — | May 24 ~ Nov. 21 |
| St. John's Day | Fixed | June 24 |
| Visitation | Fixed | July 2 |
| St. Bartholomew's Day | Fixed | August 24 |
| St. Michael's Day | Fixed | September 29 |
| Reformation Festival | Fixed | October 31 |
| 23rd–27th Sunday after Trinity[b] | — | Oct. 25 ~ Dec. 2 |
| 1st Sunday in Advent | 4th Sunday before Christmas | Nov. 27 ~ Dec. 3 |

[a]Calendar dates for most feasts can vary, although their sequence remains constant. A few feasts, however, whose dates are fixed, can fall in different places in that sequence, depending on the year. For example, St. John's Day can fall as early as four days after Trinity Sunday or as late as three days following the 5th Sunday after Trinity.

[b]In any given year, the church calendar may omit some or all of these Sundays.

[c]Annunciation may be celebrated on Palm Sunday in certain years to avoid conflicting with Holy Week and Easter.

# Bibliography

## A. Literature Cited in Abbreviated Form

BC     Hans-Joachim Schulze and Christoph Wolff. *Bach Compendium. Analytisch-bibliographisches Repertorium der Werke Johann Sebastian Bachs.* Leipzig and Frankfurt, 1986– .

BD     *Bach-Dokumente.* Lcipzig and Kassel, 1963–72.

BD I     Werner Neumann and Hans-Joachim Schulze, eds. *Schriftstücke von der Hand Johann Sebastian Bachs. Bach-Dokumente,* I. 1963.

BD II     Werner Neumann and Hans-Joachim Schulze, eds. *Fremdschriftliche und gedruckte Dokumente zur Lebensgeschichte Johann Sebastian Bachs, 1685–1750. Bach-Dokumente,* II. 1969.

BD III     Hans-Joachim Schulze, ed. *Dokumente zum Nachwirken Johann Sebastian Bachs 1750–1800. Bach-Dokumente,* III. 1972.

BJ     *Bach-Jahrbuch.* Leipzig and Berlin, 1904– . Ed. Arnold Schering (1904–39), Max Schneider (1940–52), Alfred Dürr and Werner Neumann (1953–74), Hans-Joachim Schulze and Christoph Wolff (1975– ).

BWV     Wolfgang Schmieder. *Thematisch-systematisches Verzeichnis der musikalischen Werke Johann Sebastian Bachs [Bach-Werke-Verzeichnis].* Leipzig, 1950. Rev. and enl. ed., Wiesbaden, 1990.

$BWV^{2a}$     *Bach-Werke-Verzeichnis: Kleine Ausgabe.* Ed. Alfred Dürr and Yoshitake Kobayashi. Wiesbaden, 1998.

BzBf     *Beiträge zur Bachforschung.* Leipzig, 1982–91.

CBH     *Cöthener Bach-Hefte.* Köthen, 1983– .

Forkel     Johann Nicolaus Forkel. *Über Johann Sebastian Bachs Leben, Kunst, und Kunstwerke.* Leipzig, 1802. [Trans. in *NBR,* Part VI.]

Genealogy     Johann Sebastian Bach. "Ursprung der musicalisch-Bachischen Familie (c. 1735)." [Trans. in *NBR,* no. 303.]

LBB     *Leipziger Beiträge zur Bach-Forschung.* 1993– .

MGG     *Die Musik in Geschichte und Gegenwart: Allgemeine Enzyklopädie der Musik.* Ed. Friedrich Blume. Kassel, 1949–79.

NBA     Johann Sebastian Bach. *Neue Ausgabe sämtlicher Werke.* Edited under the auspices of the Johann-Sebastian-Bach-Institut Göttingen and the Bach-Archiv Leipzig. Kassel and Leipzig, 1954– . [*Neue Bach-Ausgabe.*]

NBA/KB      Neue Bach-Ausgabe: Kritischer Bericht.

NBR         Hans T. David and Arthur Mendel, eds. The New Bach Reader: A Life of Johann
            Sebastian Bach in Letters and Documents. Rev. and expanded by Christoph Wolff.
            New York, 1998.

Neumann,    Sämtliche von Johann Sebastian Bach vertonte Texte. Ed. Werner Neumann. Leipzig,
Texte       1974.

New Grove   The New Grove Dictionary of Music and Musicians. Ed. Stanley Sadie. London, 1980.

Obituary    Carl Philipp Emanuel Bach and Johann Friedrich Agricola. "Nekrolog auf Johann
            Sebastian Bach." 1750, published 1754. [Trans. in NBR, no. 306.]

Spitta I–III   Philipp Spitta. Johann Sebastian Bach. 2 vols. Leipzig, 1873 and 1880. [English
            trans., 3 vols. London, 1884–85.]

Thomana     Hans-Joachim Schulze, ed. Die Thomasschule Leipzig zur Zeit Johann Sebastian Bachs:
Ordnungen   Ordnungen und Gesetze, 1634, 1723, 1733. Leipzig, 1985.

Walther,    Johann Gottfried Walther. Musicalisches Lexicon. Leipzig, 1732. [Facsimile. ed.,
Lexicon     Kassel, 1953.]

WBK         Christoph Wolff, ed. Die Welt der Bach-Kantaten. 3 vols. Stuttgart, 1996–99.
            [Contributions by Z. Philip Ambrose, Alberto Basso, Stephen A. Crist, Andreas
            Glöckner, Günter Hoppe, Ton Koopman, Ulrich Leisinger, Daniel R. Melamed,
            Claus Oefner, Martin Petzoldt, Hans-Joachim Schulze, George B. Stauffer,
            Michael Talbot, and Peter Wollny.]

WBK 1       Vol. 1: Johann Sebastian Bachs Kirchenkantaten: Von Arnstadt bis in die Köthener Zeit.
            Stuttgart, 1996. [English trans., New York, 1997.]

WBK 2       Vol. 2: Johann Sebastian Bachs weltliche Kantaten. Stuttgart, 1997.

WBK 3       Vol 3. Johann Sebastian Bachs Leipziger Kirchenkantaten. Stuttgart, 1999.

Wolff, Essays   Christoph Wolff. Bach: Essays on His Life and Music. Cambridge, Mass., and Lon-
            don, 1991; 3d ed., 1996.

## B. GENERAL AND BACH LITERATURE

Note: The bibliographic items listed below are limited to those used for and cited in this book.
For further bibliographic references, see Christoph Wolff, ed., Bach-Bibliographie (Kassel, 1985),
and the subsequent cumulative bibliographies in BJ 1989, 1994, and 1999, as well as Yo
Tomita's Bach Bibliography On-Line, <www.music.qub.ac.uk/~tomita/bachbib>.

Behrendt, Wolfram. "Stimmphysiologische Untersuchungen zur Leistungsfähigkeit und zum
            vermutlichen Klangcharakter des Knabenchores zur Amtszeit Bachs." BzBf 2 (1983):
            19–26.

Beißwenger, Kirsten. Johann Sebastian Bachs Notenbibliothek. Kassel, 1992.

Birke, Joachim. Christian Wolffs Metaphysik und die zeitgenössische Literatur- und Musiktheorie:
            Gottsched, Scheibe, Mizler. Berlin, 1966.

Bojanowsky, Paul von. Das Weimar Johann Sebastian Bachs. Weimar, 1903.

Braun, Brigitte. Der Maurermeister George Werner (1682–1758) und seine Bauten in Leipzig.
            Diploma thesis: Halle-Wittenberg University, 1995.

Braun, Werner. "Ein unbekanntes Orgelbau–Attestat von Bach." BJ 1999: 19–34.

Breig, Werner. "Bach und Marchand in Dresden. Eine überlieferungskritische Studie." BJ 1998:
            7–18.

Brück, Helga. "Die Brüder Johann, Christoph, und Heinrich Bach und die 'Erffurthische musicalische Compagnie.' " *BJ* 1990: 71–77.

———. "Die Erfurter Bach-Familien von 1635 bis 1805." *BJ* 1996: 101–31.

Bunge, Rudolf. "Johann Sebastian Bachs Kapelle zu Cöthen und deren nachgelassene Instrumente." *BJ* 1905: 14–47.

Bunners, Christian. *Kirchenmusik und Seelenmusik: Studien zu Frömmigkeit und Musik im Luthertum des 17. Jahrhunderts.* Göttingen, 1966.

Busch, Hermann J. " 'Für den deutschen soliden Sinn—zu wenig konsistente Nahrung': Johann Sebastian Bach, Louis Marchand, und die französische Tastenkunst." In *Französische Einflüsse auf deutsche Musiker im 18. Jahrhundert.* Ed. Friedhelm Brusniak and Annemarie Clostermann. Arolser Beiträge zur Musikforschung, 4. Arolsen, 1996, pp. 171–83.

Butt, John. *Music Education and the Art of Performance in the German Baroque.* Cambridge, 1994.

Cammarota, Robert M. *The Repertoire of Magnificats in Leipzig at the Time of J. S. Bach: A Study of the Manuscript Sources.* Ph.D. diss., New York University, 1986.

Cohen, I. Bernard. *Revolution in Science.* Cambridge, Mass., 1985.

———. *Benjamin Franklin's Science.* Cambridge, Mass., 1990.

Czok, Karl. "Sächsischer Landesstaat zur Bachzeit." *BzBf* 1 (1982): 25–31.

———. *Das Alte Leipzig.* Leipzig, 1985.

Dadelsen, Georg von. *Bemerkungen zur Handschrift Johann Sebastian Bachs, seiner Familie und seines Kreises.* Tübinger Bach-Studien, 1. Trossingen, 1957.

———. *Beiträge zur Chronologie der Werke Johann Sebastian Bachs.* Tübinger Bach-Studien, 4/5. Trossingen, 1958.

Dahlhaus, Carl. "Zur Entstehung der romantischen Bach-Deutung." *BJ* 1978: 192–210.

Dähnert, Ulrich. *Historische Orgeln in Sachsen: Ein Orgelinventar.* Leipzig, 1980.

Dammann, Rolf. *Der Musikbegriff im deutschen Barock.* Cologne, 1967; 2d ed., 1985.

Dirksen, Pieter. "The Background to Bach's Fifth Brandenburg Concerto." In *The Harpsichord and Its Repertoire: Proceedings of the International Harpsichord Symposium Utrecht 1990.* Ed. Pieter Dirksen. Utrecht, 1992, pp. 157–85.

Dobbs, Betty Jo Teeter, and Margaret C. Jacob. *Newton and the Culture of Newtonianism.* Atlantic Highlands, N.J., 1995.

Dreyfus, Laurence. *Bach's Continuo Group: Players and Practices in His Vocal Works.* Cambridge, Mass., 1987.

Drüner, Ulrich. "Violoncello piccolo und Viola pomposa bei Johann Sebastian Bach: Zu Fragen von Identität und Spielweise dieser Instrumente." *BJ* 1987: 85–112.

Dürr, Alfred. "Wieviel Kantatenjahrgänge hat Bach komponiert? Eine Entgegnung." *Die Musikforschung* 14 (1961): 192–95.

———. "Beobachtungen am Autograph der Matthäus-Passion." *BJ* 1963/64: 47–52.

———. *Zur Chronologie der Leipziger Vokalwerke J. S. Bachs.* 2d ed., mit Anmerkungen und Nachträgen versehener Nachdruck aus *Bach-Jahrbuch* 1957. Kassel, 1976.

———. *Studien über die frühen Kantaten Johann Sebastian Bachs.* Leipzig, 1951; 2d ed., Wiesbaden, 1977.

———. "Heinrich Nicolaus Gerber als Schüler Bachs." *BJ* 1978: 7–18.

———. *Die Kantaten von Johann Sebastian Bach.* 2 vols. Kassel, 1971; 5th ed.,1985.

Ernst, H. Peter. "Joh. Seb. Bachs Wirken am ehemaligen Mühlhäuser Augustinerinnenkloster und das Schicksal seiner Wender-Orgel." *BJ* 1987: 75–83.

Fabian, Bernhard. "Der Naturwissenschaftler als Originalgenie." In *Europäische Aufklärung: Herbert Dieckmann zum 60. Geburtstag.* Ed. Hugo Friedrich and F. Schalk. Munich, 1967, pp. 47–68.

Fock, Gustav. *Der junge Bach in Lüneburg, 1700–1702.* Hamburg, 1950.

————. *Arp Schnitger und seine Schule: Ein Beitrag zur Geschichte des Orgelbaues im Nord- und Ost-seeküstengebiet.* Kassel, 1974.

Freyse, Conrad. "Wieviel Geschwister hatte Johann Sebastian Bach?" *BJ* 1955: 103–7.

————. "Johann Christoph Bach (1642–1703)." *BJ* 1956: 36–51.

————, ed. *Eisenacher Dokumente um Sebastian Bach.* Veröffentlichungen der Neuen Bach-gesellschaft, XXXIII/2. Leipzig, 1933.

Fröde, Christine. "Die Wohnung Johann Sebastian Bachs in der Thomasschule in Leipzig." Beiträge zur Bachpflege der DDR, vol. 10. Leipzig, 1983, pp. 5–22.

Fuhrmann, Hartmut. "Arnstadt zur Bachzeit." In *Der junge Bach in Arnstadt.* Arnstadt, 1993, pp. 22–34.

Fürstenau, Moritz. *Zur Geschichte der Musik und des Theaters am Hofe zu Dresden.* 2 vols. Dresden, 1861–62; reprint, Leipzig, 1971.

Glöckner, Andreas. "Johann Sebastian Bachs Aufführungen zeitgenössischer Passionsmusiken." *BJ* 1977: 75–119.

————. "Neuerkenntnisse zu Johann Sebastian Bachs Aufführungskalender zwischen 1729 und 1735." *BJ* 1981: 43–75.

————. "Zur Chronologie der Weimarer Kantaten Johann Sebastian Bachs." *BJ* 1985: 159–64.

————. "Anmerkungen zu Johann Sebastian Bachs Köthener Kantatenschaffen." *CBH* 4 (1986): 89–95.

————. "Gründe für Johann Sebastian Bachs Weggang von Weimar." In Hoffmann 1988, pp. 137–43.

————. "Die Musikpflege an der Leipziger Neukirche zur Zeit Johann Sebastian Bachs." *BzBf,* 8 (1990).

————. "Die Teilung des Bachschen Musikaliennachlasses und die Thomas-Stimmen." *BJ* 1994: 41–58.

————. "Neue Spuren zu Bachs "Weimarer' Passion." *LBB* 1 (1995):33–46.

————. " 'Von seinem moralischen Character mögen diejenigen reden, die seines Umgangs und seiner Freundschaft genossen haben': Gedanken über einige Wesenszüge Johann Se-bastian Bachs." In *Über Leben, Kunst und Kunstwerke: Aspekte musikalischer Biographie.* Ed. Christoph Wolff. Leipzig, 1999, pp. 121–32.

Göllner, Theodor. "Et incarnatus est in Bachs h-Moll-Messe und Beethovens Missa solemnis." *Sitzungsberichte der Bayerischen Akademie der Wisseuschaften,* vol. 4. Munich, 1996.

Heller, Karl, and Hans-Joachim Schulze, eds. *Das Frühwerk Johann Sebastian Bachs: Kolloquium veranstaltet vom Institut fur Musikwissenschaft der Universität Rostock 11.–13. September 1990.* Cologne, 1995.

Helmbold, Hermann. "Die Söhne von Johann Christoph und Johann Ambrosius Bach auf der Eisenacher Schule." *BJ* 1930: 49–55.

————. "Junge Bache auf dem Eisenacher Gymnasium." In *Johann Sebastian Bach in Thüringen.* Weimar, 1950, pp. 19–24.

Henkel, Hubert. "Die Orgeln der Köthener Kirchen zur Zeit Johann Sebastian Bachs und ihre Geschichte (Teil 1)." *CBH* 3 (1985): 5–28.

Hilgenfeldt, Carl Ludwig. *Johann Sebastian Bachs Leben, Wirken, und Werke: ein Beitrag zur Kunstgeschichte des 18. Jahrhunderts.* Leipzig, 1850.

Hill, Robert. " 'Der Himmel weiß, wo diese Sachen hingekommen sind': Reconstructing the Lost Clavier Books of the Young Bach and Handel." In *Bach, Handel, Scarlatti: Ter-centenary Essays.* Ed. Peter Williams. Cambridge, 1985, pp. 30–56.

His, Wilhelm. *J. S. Bach. Forschungen über dessen Grabstätte, Gebeine, und Antlitz.* Leipzig, 1895.

Hobohm, Wolf. "Neue 'Texte zur Leipziger Kirchen-Music.' " *BJ* 1973: 5–32.

Hoffmann, Winfried, and Armin Schneiderheinze, eds. *Bach-Konferenz Leipzig 1985*. Leipzig, 1988.

Hofmann, Klaus. "Neue Überlegungen zu Bachs Weimarer Kantaten-Kalender." *BJ* 1993: 9–30.

Hoppe, Günther. "Köthener politische, ökonomische, und höfische Verhältnisse als Schaffensbedingungen Bachs." *CBH* 4 (1986): 12–62.

———. "Köthener Kammerrechungen—Köthener Hofparteien: Zum Hintergrund der Hofkapellmeisterzeit Johann Sebastian Bachs." In Hoffmann 1988, pp. 145–54.

———. "Fürst Leopold von Anhalt-Köthen und die 'Rathische Partei': Vom harmvollen Regiment eines 'Music sowohl liebenden als kennenden *Serenissimi.*' " *CBH* 4 (1994): 95–125.

———. Zu musikalisch-kulturellen Befindlichkeiten des anhalt-köthnischen Hofes zwischen 1710 und 1730." *CBH* 8 (1998): 9–51.

Horn, Victoria. "French Influence in Bach's Organ Works." In *J. S. Bach as Organist*. Ed. George Stauffer and Ernest May. Bloomington, Ind., 1986, pp. 256–73.

Horn, Wolfgang. *Die Dresdner Hofkirchenmusik, 1720 bis 1745: Studien zu ihren Voraussetzungen und ihrem Repertoire*. Kassel, 1987.

Hübner, Maria. "Der Zeichner Johann Sebastian Bach d. J. (1748–1778): Zu seinem 250. Geburtstag." *BJ* 1998: 187–200.

Jauernig, Reinhold. "Bach in Weimar." In *Johann Sebastian Bach in Thüringen*. Weimar, 1950, pp. 49–105.

Jöcher, Johann Gottlieb. *Allgemeines Gelehrten-Lexicon*. 4 vols. Leipzig, 1750–51; reprint, Hildesheim, 1960–61.

Jung, Hans-Rudolf. *Johann Sebastian Bach in Weimar, 1708–1717*. Tradition und Gegenwart. Weimarer Schriften, vol. 16. Weimar, 1985.

Junghans, W. *Programm des Johanneums zu Lüneburg, Ostern 1870*. Lüneburg, 1870.

Kaiser, Rainer. "Johann Sebastian Bach als Schüler einer 'deutschen Schule' in Eisenach?" *BJ* 1994: 177–84.

Kobayashi, Yoshitake. "Zur Chronologie der Spätwerke Johann Sebastian Bachs: Kompositionsund Aufführungstätigkeit von 1736 bis 1750." *BJ* 1988: 7–72.

———. "Zur Teilung des Bachsehen Erbes." *In Acht kleine Präludien und Studien über Bach*. Ed. Kirsten Beißwänger. Wiesbaden, 1989, pp. 66–76.

———. "Quellenkundliche Überlegungen zur Chronologie der Weimarer Vokalwerke Bachs." In *Das Frühwerk Johann Sebastian Bachs: Bach-Kolloquium Rostock 1990*. Ed. Karl Heller and Hans-Joachim Schulze. Cologne, 1995, pp. 290–308.

Kock, Hermann. *Genealogisches Lexikon der Familie Bach*. Ed. Ragnhild Siegel. Wechmar, 1995.

König, Ernst. "Die Hofkapelle des Fürsten Leopold zu Anhalt-Köthen." *BJ* 1959: 160–67.

Kranemann, Detlef. "Johann Sebastian Bachs Krankheit und Todesursache—Versuch einer Deutung." *BJ* 1990: 53–64.

Kremer, Joachim. "Die Organistenstelle an St. Jakobi in Hamburg: Eine 'convenable station' für Johann Sebastian Bach?" *BJ* 1993: 217–22.

Krickeberg, Dieter. "Über die Herkunft des Berlin 'Bach-Cembalos.' " In *Jahrbuch des Staatlichen Instituts für Musikforschung 1996*. Stuttgart, 1996, pp. 86–91.

Kröhner, Christine. "Die Streichinstrumente der Leipziger Thomaskirche aus Bachs Amtszeit." In Hoffmann 1988, pp. 155–66.

———. "Johann Sebastian Bach und Johann Friedrich Bach als Orgelexaminatoren im Gebiet der freien Reichsstadt Mühlhausen nach 1708." *BJ* 1995: 83–91.

Krummacher, Friedhelm. *Bachs Zyklus der Choralkantaten: Aufgaben und Lösungen.* Göttingen, 1995.

Küster, Konrad. "Bach als Mitarbeiter am 'Walther-Lexikon'?" *BJ* 1991: 187–92.

———. *Der junge Bach.* Stuttgart, 1996.

Lämmerhirt, Hugo. "Bachs Mutter und ihre Sippe." *BJ* 1925: 101–37.

Leaver, Robin A. *Bach's Theological Library: A Critical Bibliography.* Neuhausen-Stuttgart, 1983.

Leisinger, Ulrich. *Leibniz-Reflexe in der deutschen Musiktheorie des 18. Jahrhunderts.* Würzburg, 1994.

Lester, Joel. *Compositional Theory in the Eighteenth Century.* Cambridge, Mass., and London, 1992.

Lux, Eduard. "Das Orgelwerk in St. Michaelis zu Ohrdruf." *BJ* 1926: 145–55.

Marshall, Robert L. *The Compositional Process of J. S. Bach: A Study of the Autograph Scores of the Vocal Works.* 2 vols. Princeton, 1972.

———. *The Music of Johann Sebastian Bach: The Sources, the Style, the Significance.* New York, 1989.

Melamed, Daniel R. "Mehr zur Chronologie von Bachs Weimarer Kantaten." *BJ* 1993: 213–16.

Melamed, Daniel R., and Reginald Sanders. "Zum Text und Kontext der 'Keiser'-Markuspassion." *BJ* 1999: 35–50.

Miesner, Heinrich. *Philipp Emanuel Bach in Hamburg: Beiträge zu seiner Biographie und zur Musikgeschichte seiner Zeit.* Leipzig, 1929.

———. "Beziehungen zwischen den Familien Stahl und Bach." *BJ* 1933: 71–76.

Müller, Karl, and Fritz Wiegand, eds. *Arnstädter Bachbuch: Johann Sebastian Bach und seine Verwandten in Arnstadt.* Arnstadt, 1950; 2d ed., 1957.

Müller, Rainer A. *Geschichte der Universität: Von der mittelalterlichen Universitas zur deutschen Hochschule.* Munich, 1990.

Neumann, Werner. "Das 'Bachische Collegium Musicum.' " *BJ* 1960: 5–27.

———. "Eine Leipziger Bach-Gedenkstätte. Über die Beziehungen der Familien Bach und Bose." *BJ* 1970: 19–31.

Odrich, Evelin, and Peter Wollny, eds. *Die Briefkonzepte des Johann Elias Bach, LBB* 3 (1999).

Oefner, Claus. *Die Musikerfamilie Bach in Eisenach.* Eisenach, 1984; 2d ed., 1996.

———. "Eisenach zur Zeit des jungen Bach." *BJ* 1985: 45–54.

Petry, Michael J., ed. *Hegel and Newtonianism.* International Archives of the History of Ideas, 136. Dordrecht, Boston, and London, 1993.

Petzoldt, Martin. "Ut probus & doctus reddar. Zum Anteil der Theologie bei der Schulausbildung Johann Sebastian Bachs in Eisenach, Ohrdruf, und Lüneburg." *BJ* 1985: 7–44.

———. "Christian Weise d. Ä. und Christoph Wolle—zwei Leipziger Beichtväter Bachs, Vertreter zweier auslegungsgeschichtlicher Abschnitte der ausgehenden lutherischen Orthodoxie." In *Bach als Ausleger der Bibel.* Ed. Martin Petzoldt. Göttingen, 1985a, pp. 109–29

———. *Bachstätten aufsuchen.* Leipzig, 1992.

———. "Bachs Prüfung vor dem kurfürstlichen Konsistorium." *BJ* 1998: 19–30.

———. "Bach in theologischer Interaktion. Persönlichkeiten in seinem beruflichen Umfeld." In *Über leben, Kunst und Kunstwerke: Aspekte Musikalischer Biographie.* Ed. Christoph Wolff. Leipzig, 1999, pp. 133–59.

Pevsner, Nikolaus. *Leipziger Barock: Die Baukunst der Barockzeit in Leipzig.* Dresden, 1928; reprint, Leipzig, 1990.

Plichta, Alois. "Johann Sebastian Bach und Johann Adam Graf von Questenberg." *BJ* 1981: 23–28.

Rampe, Siegbert, and Michael Zapf. "Neues zu Besetzung und Instrumentarium in Joh. Seb. Bachs Brandenburgischen Konzerten Nr. 4 und 5. In *Concerto,* 14/9 (1997), pp. 30–38; 15/1 (1998), pp. 19–22.

Reul, Barbara. " 'O vergnügte Stunden / Da mein Hertzog funden seinen Lebenstag': Ein unbekannter Textdruck zu einer Geburtstagskantate J.S. Bachs für den Fürsten Johann August von Anhalt-Zerbst." *BJ* 1999: 7–18.

Richter, Bernhard Friedrich. "Stadtpfeifer und Alumnen der Thomasschule in Leipzig zu Bachs Zeit." *BJ* 1907: 32–78.

Rollberg, Fritz. "Johann Ambrosius Bach, Stadtpfeifer zu Eisenach von 1671–1695." *BJ* 1927: 133–52.

Scheide, William H. "Ist Mizlers Bericht über Bachs Kantaten korrekt?" *Die Musikforschung,* 14 (1961): 60–63.

———. "Bach vs. Bach—Mühlhausen Dismissal Request vs. Erdmann Letter." In *Bachiana et alia musicologica: Festschrift Alfred Durr zum 65. Geburtstag am 3. März 1983.* Ed. Wolfgang Rehm. Kassel, 1983, pp. 234–42.

Schering, Arnold. "Die alte Chorbibliothek der Thomasschule zu Leipzig." *Archiv für Musikwissenschaft* 1 (1918–19): 275–88.

———. *Musikgeschichte Leipzigs.* Vol. 2: *Von 1650 bis 1723.* Leipzig, 1926.

———. *Johann Sebastian Bach und das Musikleben Leipzigs im 18. Jahrhundert.* Musikgeschichte Leipzigs, 3. Leipzig, 1941.

Schiffner, Markus. "Johann Sebastian Bach in Arnstadt." *BzBf* 4 (1985): 5–22. Reissued as *Der junge Bach in Arnstadt.* Arnstadt, n.d. [c. 1995], pp. 1–20.

Schmidt, Friedrich. *Geschichte der Stadt Sangerhausen.* 2 vols. Sangerhausen, 1906.

Schmidt, Jochen. *Die Geschichte des Genie-Gedankens in der deutschen Literatur, Philosophie, und Politik, 1750–1945.* 2 vols. Darmstadt, 1985.

Schramm, Carl Christian. *Neues Europäisches Historisches Reise-Lexicon.* 2 vols. Leipzig, 1744; reprint, Heidelberg, 1984.

Schrammek, Winfried. "Bach-Orgeln in Thüringen und Sachsen." In *Beiträge zur Bachpflege der DDR,* 11. Leipzig, 1983. [check]

———. "Orgel, Positiv, Clavicymbel, und Glocken der Schloßkirche zu Weimar 1658 bis 1774." In Hoffmann 1988, pp. 99–111.

Schubart, Christoph. "Anna Magdalena Bach: Neue Beiträge zu ihrer Herkunft und ihren Jugendjahren." *BJ* 1953: 29–50.

Schulze, Hans-Joachim. "Johann Sebastian Bachs Kanonwidmungen." *BJ* 1967: 82–92.

———. " '. . . da man nun die besten nicht bekommen könne . . .'—Kontroversen und Kompromisse vor Bachs Leipziger Amtsantritt." In *Bach-Konferenz Leipzig 1975.* Leipzig, 1977, pp. 71–77.

———. "Über die unvermeidlichen Lücken in Bachs Lebensbeschreibung." In *Bach-Symposium Marburg 1978.* Kassel, 1981, pp. 32–42.

———. " '. . . aus einem Capellmeister ein Cantor zu werden . . .'—Fragen an Bachs Köthener Schaffensjahre." *CBH* 1 (1983): 4–16.

———. "Studenten als Helfer bei der Leipziger Kirchenmusik." *BJ* 1984: 45–52.

———. *Studien zur Bach-Überlieferung im 18. Jahrhundert.* Leipzig, 1984a.

———. "Besitzstand und Vermögensverhältnisse von Leipziger Stadtpfeifern zur Zeit Johann Sebastian Bachs." *BzBf* 4 (1985): 33–46.

———. "Johann Christoph Bach (1671–1721), Organist und Schul Collega in Ohrdruf, Johann Sebastian Bachs erster Lehrer." *BJ* 1985a: 55–82.

———, ed. J. S. Bach, "Jesus nahm zu sich die Zwölfe (BWV 22)." Facsimile ed., Leipzig, 1988.

———. "Von der Schwierigkeit, einen Nachfolger zu finden: Die Vakanz im Leipziger Thomaskantorat 1722–1723." In *Bach-Tage Berlin 1990 (Festbuch),* pp. 11–21.

———. "Johann Sebastian Bach—Thomaskantor: Schwierigkeiten mit einem prominenten Amt." In *Bach-Tage Berlin 1991 (Festbuch)*, pp. 103–8.

———. "Anna Magdalena Bachs 'Herzens Freündin'—Neues über die Beziehungen zwischen den Familien Bach und Bose." *BJ* 1997: 151–53.

———. "Circkel Musici versus unbezirkelte Practici. Zu Lorenz Mizlers Societät der musikalischen Wissenschaften in Deutschland, 1738–1755." In *Arbeitsblätter der Kommission für Kunstgeschichte, Literatur- und Musikwissenschaft, Sächsische Akademie der Wissenschaften zu Leipzig*, 2 (1998): 2–24.

———. "Zwischen Kuhnau und Bach: Das folgenreichste Interregnum im Leipziger Thomaskantorat. Anmerkungen zu einer unendlichen Geschichte." In *Bach für Kenner und Liebhaber: Festschrift zum 70. Geburtstag von Diethard Hellmann*. Ed. Martin Petzoldt. Stuttgart, 1998a, pp. 103–7.

Schulze, Johann Daniel. *Abriß einer Geschichte der Leipziger Universität im Laufe des achtzehnten Jahrhunderts*. Leipzig, 1802.

Seiffert, Max. "Die Chorbibliothek der St. Michaelisschule in Lüneburg zu Seb. Bach's Zeit." *Sammelbände der Internationalen Musikgesellschaft*, 9 (1907–8): 593–621.

Serauky, Walter. *Musikgeschichte der Stadt Halle.* Vol. II, part 1. Halle, 1939.

Smend, Friedrich. *Bach in Köthen.* Berlin, 1951. Eng. trans., ed. and rev. Stephen Daw. St. Louis, 1985.

Smith, Mark M. "Joh. Seb. Bachs Violoncello piccolo: Neue Aspekte—offene Fragen." *BJ* 1998: 63–81.

Söhnel, Marion. "Über ein bisher unbekanntes Dokument zum Nachwirken Bachs und seinen Verfasser: Johann Heinrich Winckler." *BzBf* 2 (1983): 16–18.

Stauffer, George B. "Boyvin, Grigny, d'Anglebert, and Bach's Assimilation of French Classical Organ Music." *Early Music* 21 (1993): 83–95.

———. "Leipzig: Cosmopolitan Trade Centre." In *Music & Society: The Late Baroque.* Ed. George J. Buelow. New York, 1994, pp. 254–95.

———. "The Breitkopf Family and Its Role in Eighteenth-Century Music Publishing." In *Bach Perspectives*, 2. Lincoln, Neb., 1996, pp. 1–8.

Stiehl, Herbert. "Taufzettel für Bachs Kinder—ein Dokumentenfund." *BJ* 1979: 7–18.

———. "Das Innere der Thomaskirche zur Amtszeit Johann Sebastian Bachs." *BzBf* 3 (1984): 5–96.

Stiller, Günther. *Johann Sebastian Bach und das Leipziger gottesdienstliche Leben seiner Zeit.* Berlin, 1970.

———. "Johann Sebastian Bach und Johann Christoph Gottsched—eine beachtliche Gemeinsamkeit." *Musik und Kirche* 46 (1976): 166–72.

Stinson, Russell. *Bach: The Orgelbüchlein.* New York, 1996.

Szeskus, Reinhard. "Bach und die Leipziger Universitätsmusik." In *Alte Musik als ästetische Gegenwart: Bach, Händel, Schütz.* Bericht über den internationalen musikwissenschaftlichen Kongreß Stuttgart 1985. Ed. Dietrich Berke und Dorothee Hanemann. Kassel, 1987, pp. 405–12.

Terry, Charles Sanford. *Bach: A Biography.* Oxford, 1928; 2d ed., 1933.

Thomas, Friedrich. "Einige Ergebnisse über Johann Sebastian Bachs Ohrdrufer Schulzeit, aus der Matrikel des Lyceums geschöpft." In *Jahresbericht des Gräflich Gleichenschen Gymnasiums zu Ohrdruf für das Schuljahr 1899/1900*. Ohrdruf, 1900.

Walker, Paul. "Die Entstehung der Permutationsfuge." *BJ* 1989: 21–41.

Wenke, Wolfgang. "Die Orgel Johann Sebastian Bachs in Arnstadt," In *Der junge Bach in Arnstadt.* Arnstadt, 1993, pp. 36–46.

Werner, Arno. *Städtische und fürstliche Musikpflege in Weissenfels bis zum Ende des 18. Jahrhunderts.* Leipzig, 1911.

Westfall, Richard S. "Newton and Christianity." In *Newton: Text, Backgrounds, Commentaries.* Ed. I. Bernard Cohen and Richard S. Westfall. New York, 1995, pp. 356–70.

Wiegand, Fritz. "Die mütterlichen Verwandten Johann Sebastian Bachs in Erfurt: Ergänzungen und Berichtigungen zur Bachforschung." *BJ* 1967: 5–20.

Williams, Peter. "J. S. Bach—Orgelsachverständiger unter dem Einfluß Andreas Werckmeisters?" *BJ* 1982: 131–42.

———. *The Organ Music of J. S. Bach.* Vol. 3: *A Background.* Cambridge, 1984.

———. "Noch einmal: J. S. Bach—Orgelsachverständiger unter dem Einfluß Andreas Werckmeisters?" *BJ* 1986: 123–26.

Wilson, Edward O. *Consilience.* New York, 1998.

Wöhlke, Franz. *Lorenz Christoph Mizler: Ein Beitrag zur musikalischen Gelehrtengeschichte des 18. Jahrhunderts.* Würzburg, 1940.

Wolff, Christoph. *Der stile antico in der Musik Johann Sebastian Bachs.* Studien zu Bach's Spätwerk. Wiesbaden, 1968.

———. "Johann Valentin Eckelts Tabulaturbuch von 1692." In *Festschrift Martin Ruhnke zum 65. Geburtstag.* Ed. Klaus-Jürgen Sachs. Neuhausen-Stuttgart, 1986, pp. 374–86.

———. "Das Hamburger Buxtehude-Bild: Ein Beitrag zur musikalischen Ikonographie und zum Umkreis von Johann Adam Reinken." In *Studien zur Musikgeschichte der Hansestadt Lübeck.* Ed. Arnfried Edler and Heinrich W. Schwab. Kassel, 1989, pp. 44–62.

———. "The Identity of the 'Fratro Dilettissimo' in the Capriccio in B-flat Major and Other Problems of Bach's Early Harpsichord Works." In *The Harpsichord and Its Repertoire: Proceedings of the International Harpsichord Symposium Utrecht 1990.* Ed. Pieter Dirksen. Utrecht, 1992, pp. 145–56.

———. *Die Bach-Familie.* Stuttgart, 1993.

———. " 'Et incarnatus' and 'Crucifixus': The Earliest and the Latest Settings of Bach's B-Minor Mass." In *Eighteenth-Century Music in Theory and Practice: Essays in Honor of Alfred Mann.* Ed. Mary Ann Parker. New York, 1994, pp. 1–17.

———. "J. S. Bach and the Legacy of the Seventeenth Century." In *Bach Studies,* 2. Ed. Daniel R. Melamed. Cambridge, 1995, pp. 192–201.

———. "Pachelbel, Buxtehude, und die weitere Einflußspäre des jungen Bach." In *Das Frühwerk Johann Sebastian Bachs.* Ed. Karl Heller and Hans-Joachim Schulze. Cologne, 1995a, pp. 21–32.

———. "*Die betrübte und wieder getröstete Seele:* Zum Dialog-Charakter der Kantate 'Ich hatte viel Bekümmernis,' BWV 21." *BJ* 1996: 139–45.

———. "Händel—J. S. Bach—C. Ph. E. Bach—Mozart: Anregungen und Herausforderungen." In *Göttinger Händel-Beiträge,* 6. Göttingen, 1996a, pp. 115–26.

———. "Bach und die Idee musikalischer Vollkommenheit." In *Jahrbuch des Staatlichen Instituts für Musikforschung Preußischer Kulturbesitz 1996.* Ed. Günther Wagner. Stuttgart, 1996b, pp. 9–23.

———. "Carl Philipp Emanuel Bachs eigenhändiges Verzeichnis seiner Clavierwerke von 1733 bis 1772." In *Über Leben, Kunst und Kunstwerke: Aspekte musikalischer Biographie. J. S. Bach im Zentrum.* Ed. Christoph Wolff. Leipzig, 1999, pp. 217–35.

Wollny, Peter. "Studies in the Music of Wilhelm Friedemann Bach." Ph.D. diss., Harvard University, 1993.

———. "Ein Quellenfund zur Entstehungsgeschichte der h-Moll-Messe." *BJ* 1994: 163–69.

———. "Wilhelm Friedemann Bach's Performances of Cantatas by His Father." In *Bach Studies,* 2. Ed. Daniel R. Melamed. Cambridge, 1995, pp. 202–28.

———. "Zur Überlieferung der Instrumentalwerke Johann Sebastian Bachs: Der Quellenbesitz Carl Philipp Emanuel Bachs." *BJ* 1996: 7–22.

———. "Neue Bach-Funde." *BJ* 1997: 7–50. [See also Wollny 1998a.]

———. "Materialien zur Schweinfurter Musikpflege im 17. Jahrhundert: Von 1592 bis zum Tod Georg Christoph Bachs (1642–1697)." *Schütz-Jahrbuch* 1997a: 113–63.

———. "Alte Bach-Funde." *BJ* 1998: 137–48.

———. "Nachbemerkung" [to Wollny 1996]. *BJ* 1998a: 167–69.

Wustmann, Gustav. *Quellen zur Geschichte Leipzigs,* vol. 1. Leipzig, 1889.

———. *Bilderbuch aus der Geschichte der Stadt Leipzig.* Leipzig, 1897.

Zedler, Johann Heinrich. *Großes vollständiges Universal Lexicon aller Wissenschaften und Künste.* Leipzig, 1732–52; reprint, Graz, 1961–64.

Zehnder, Jean-Claude. "Georg Böhm und Johann Sebastian Bach: Zur Chronologie der Bachschen Stilentwicklung." *BJ* 1988: 73–110.

Ziller, Ernst. *Johann Heinrich Buttstedt (1666–1727).* Halle, 1934.

Zimpel, Herbert. "Der Streit zwischen Reformierten und Lutheranern in Köthen während Bachs Amtszeit." *BJ* 1979: 97–106.

# Genre Index of Bach's Works

*Italic* page numbers indicate an illustration or a music example.

# Title Index of Bach's Works

*Italic* page numbers indicate an illustration or a music example.

# General Index

*Italic* page numbers indicate an illustration or a music example.